THE MARTYRS OF CÓRDOBA (850-859):
A Study of the Sources

This dissertation was conducted under the direction of Aloysius K. Ziegler as major professor and was approved by Martin R. P. McGuire and Robert J. Trisco as readers.

THE CATHOLIC UNIVERSITY OF AMERICA
STUDIES IN MEDIAEVAL HISTORY
New Series
Volume XVII

The Martyrs of Córdoba (850-859): A Study of the Sources

A DISSERTATION

SUBMITTED TO THE FACULTY OF THE GRADUATE SCHOOL OF ARTS
AND SCIENCES OF THE CATHOLIC UNIVERSITY OF AMERICA
IN PARTIAL FULFILLMENT OF THE REQUIREMENTS
FOR THE DEGREE OF DOCTOR OF PHILOSOPHY

BY

EDWARD P. COLBERT

THE CATHOLIC UNIVERSITY OF AMERICA PRESS
WASHINGTON, D.C.
1962

Printed in the United States of America
by The Abbey Press, St. Meinrad, Indiana

TABLE OF CONTENTS
AND CHRONOLOGY

vii

Part II

Córdoba and Its Martyrs in the Ninth Century:
A Study of the Sources Concerning the Martyrs

Part III

The Christians of Córdoba after the Martyrdoms:

The Sources on Christian Córdoba after the Martyrdoms

INTRODUCTION
SURVEY OF THE LITERATURE ON MOZARABIC SPAIN

This is by no means the first attempt to write the history of this period. The literature on the subject is fairly ample. Since the late sixteenth century Mozarabic Spain and the episode of the Cordoban martyrs have received the attention of many historians. The sources of the time have been edited with comments and studies of a more or less critical nature.[1] On the basis of the rather plentiful source material historical accounts of the period have been written.

Towards the end of the ninth century the Frankish monk Usuard, who had visited Córdoba in 858, included thirty-two of the more than fifty martyrs of the persecution in Córdoba in his martyrology.[2] Throughout the Middle Ages, however, the Latin works written in Córdoba in the ninth century lay in manuscripts almost unnoticed by the writers of Spanish chronicles and historians. Today the manuscripts are in most cases unique. Except for a few poems, only three works of the period appear in more than one manuscript: a treatise on clerical garb by Leovigildus, a letter by Eulogius, and the vita of Eulogius by Albar. Several manuscripts are extant for a work written in Paris in the ninth century (the account of Usuard's journey to Córdoba in 858) and for a

---

[1] M. C. Diaz y Diaz, *Index scriptorum latinorum medii aevi Hispanorum* (Madrid, 1959), 119-164, lists editions and studies of most of the sources of the eighth, ninth, and tenth centuries, including a number of small items not discussed in the present work.

[2] Cf. B. de Gaiffier, "Les notices hispaniques dans le Martyrologe d'Usuard," AB, 55 (1937), 268-283; *id.*, "Les notices hispaniques du Martyrologe romain," AB, 58 (1940), 79-89; and *id.*, " Un calendrier franco-hispanique de la fin du XIIe siècle," AB, 69 (1951), 285. Usuard's Martyrology is published in PL 123, 452-992, and PL 124, 1-860, after the edition of Jean-Baptiste du Sollier, *Martyrologium Usuardi monachi* (Antwerp, 1714).

vita of the prophet Mohammed of unknown origin. Three sections of the most important work written in Córdoba, Eulogius' *Memoriale sanctorum*, occur separately in other manuscripts, all three of them vitae of martyrs.[3] A number of the martyrs are listed in *calendaria* dating from the Middle Ages.[4] Before 1574 the authors of at least six histories of Spain written in the sixteenth century discuss the martyrdoms, although in vague terms.[5]

The first to bring the manuscripts of the period and their content to the attention of the public was Ambrosio de Morales, who in 1574 edited the rather voluminous writings of Eulogius, the most important sources for the history of the martyrs of Córdoba. Morales also described the period of the martyrdoms at length in his *Corónica general*, published twelve years after the edition of Eulogius' works,[6]

[3] The mss are discussed in the text which follows; cf. *Memoriale*, II, vii and x, and III, viii.

[4] Cf. index, "*calendarium.*"

[5] Lucius Marineus Siculus, *Opus de rebus Hispaniae memorabilibus. . .* (Alcalá, 1533), 25, 26, and 32; republished in Spanish translation (Alcalá, 1539); Latin text edited in *Hisp. ill.*, I, 291-517; cf. Bk. V, ibid., 336, 338, and 348. Pero Anton Beuter, *Primera parte de la corónica general de toda España* (Valencia, 1546), 107. Pedro de Medina, *Libro de grandezas y cosas memorables de España* (Seville, 1549); 2d ed. (Alcalá, 1566), 58. Joannes Vaseus, *Rerum Hispanicarum chronicon* (Salamanca, 1551), 539f.; edited in *Hisp. ill.*, I, 572-727; cf. ibid., 719. Franciscus Tarapha, *De origine, ac rebus gestis regum Hispaniae liber . . .* (Antwerp, 1553), 127v-129. Esteban de Garibay y Zamalloa, *Los XL libros del compendio historial de las chronicas y universal historia de todos los reynos de España* (3 vols.; Antwerp, 1571), vol. I, 471, and Bk. 36, x and xi, vol. III, 986-989. The text of Bk. II, chap. x, of the *Memoriale* according to ms Paris BN 13760 was edited by Laurentius Surius, *De probatis sanctorum historiis . . .*, IV (Cologne, 1579).

[6] *Divi Eulogii . . . opera*, ed. Ambrosio de Morales (Alcalá, 1574). The ms of Eulogius' works was discovered by Pedro Ponce de León, bishop of Placencia. Morales annotated the text and, when Ponce de León died in 1573, obtained the rights of publication. It is not certain whether Morales or Ponce de León should receive credit for establishing the text of Eulogius' writings; cf. Appendix V. Morales, *La corónica general de España que continuava Ambrosio de Morales . . .* (3 vols.; Alcalá, 1574 and 1577, and Córdoba, 1586), III, Bk. XIV. For a

practically transcribing the vitae of the martyrs into Spanish with occasional interpretative remarks of his own. In 1753 Henrique Flórez contributed to the study of the period by publishing almost all of the remaining sources in an edition which has not been superseded.[7] His edition of the Latin texts is accompanied by an exhaustive commentary in Spanish which is still of basic importance. The scope of the work by Flórez is monumental. The works of Eulogius, which had been published from Morales' edition several times in the seventeenth century, were edited again from that edition in 1785 by Francisco Cardinal Lorenzana y Butron, the manuscript for Eulogius' works having been lost. Lorenzana's edition was reprinted in Migne's *Patrologia latina*[8] in 1852. The recent edition of Eulogius' works by A. S. Ruiz[9]

discussion of the Chronicle cf. Appendix V. Manuel Ortiz de la Vega, *Las glorias nacionales* ... (6 vols.; Madrid and Barcelona, 1852), I and II, has re-edited the Chronicles of Ocampo and Morales, as has Benito Cano (8 vols.; Madrid, 1791).

[7] H. Flórez, *España sagrada*, Vols. X and XI, 3 eds. (Madrid, 1753, 1775, 1792). The three editions are practically identical; page references for one edition serve for the other two. Flórez discusses the rule of the Moslems (X, 233-245), the status of Christian worship and Christian churches in Córdoba under the Moslems, the part of Christians in the civil government (X, 245-272), the bishops of Córdoba under the Moslems (X, 272-287), the persecution (X, 336-357), the martyrs of the persecution (X, 357-410), the life and martyrdom of Eulogius (X, 411-471), Esperaindeo and other minor authors (XI, 3-10), and the life and writings of Albar (XI, 10-62).

[8] Cf. the editions of Marguerin de la Bigne's *Bibliotheca veterum patrum, Magna* ... , or *Maxima* ... , in 1589, 1609, 1624, and 1677; the *Sacra bibliotheca sanctorum patrum* of 1575 probably does not contain Eulogius' works; the *Maxima bibliotheca* ... (Lyons, 1677), XV, 242-306, does not contain the *Vita Eulogii*. Cf. Andreas Schott, *Hisp. ill.*, IV, 213-372; Lorenzana, *SS PP Toletanorum*, II, 419-508; Migne, PL 115, 731-818. Flórez did not edit the works of Eulogius as such, but he discusses the martyrs of the persecution individually and edits the texts of some of the vitae written by Eulogius, ES, X, 357-410, especially 410.

[9] A. S. Ruiz, *Obras completas de San Eulogio* (Córdoba, 1959). Henri Leclercq, *Les martyrs; recueil de pièces authentiques sur les martyrs depuis les origines du christianisme jusqu'au XXe siècle* (15 vols.; Paris, 1902-1924), translates several vitae in volume V.

is based on Migne's edition, perhaps also on the edition of Lorenzana, rather than on Morales' edition. The edition by Ruiz contains so many errors, typographical and of transcription, that it cannot be used for work on the text. His translation of Eulogius' works, which is based on the edition of Lorenzana or of Migne, is welcome as the only one available. It is somewhat free, especially in difficult passages. In his introduction Ruiz indicates a wide knowledge of the Cordoban martyrs and the works of Eulogius. His documented thesis that Eulogius and the Christians of Córdoba knew and were influenced by the Rule of St. Benedict is noteworthy.

For many years after the appearance of Morales' *Corónica general* most of the accounts of the martyrdoms were either derived from his account or were confirmations of his account based on further study of the Latin texts.[10] But in

---

[10] The works are too numerous to discuss. Several Spanish authors composed a *Flos sanctorum* which included the Cordoban martyrs. A number of historical accounts of Córdoba discuss the martyrs. Cf. Juan de Mariana, *Historiae de rebus Hispaniae libri XXV* (Toledo, 1592-1595), vols. 30 and 31 of *Biblioteca de autores españoles* (Madrid, 1854); cf. Bk. VII. Martin de Roa, *Flos sanctorum* (Seville, 1615); id., *De Cordubae in Hispania Betica principatu...* (Lyons, 1617); id., *Antiguo principado de Cordova en España ulterior...* (Córdoba, 1636). Jaime Bleda, *Corónica de los moros de España* (Valencia, 1618). Martin Carrillo, *Annales y memorias cronológicas...* (Huesca, 1622), 201-204v. Alfonsus Sanctius, *De rebus Hispaniae anacephaleosis libri septem* (Alcalá, 1634), 138f. Francisco de Cepeda, *Resumpta historial de España...* (Madrid, 1654), 60f. Jean-Baptiste Bellegarde, *Histoire générale d'Espagne...* (9 vols.; Paris, 1723), I, 323-330. Juan Gómez Bravo, *Catálogo de los obispos de Cordova...* (Córdoba, 1739). José Lopez de Baena, *Vida y glorioso martyrio del esclarecido doctor y martyr San Eulogio...* (Córdoba, 1747). Jean de Ferreras, *Histoire générale d'Espagne* (10 vols.; Paris, 1751), II, 596-632; the work is translated from Spanish. C. Hénault, *Abrégé chronologique de l'histoire d'Espagne et de Portugal...* (2 vols.; Paris, 1765), I, 88-90; Alphonse Rabbe, *Résumé de l'histoire d'Espagne...* (Paris, 1823), 4th ed., (Paris, 1828), 103f., agrees almost verbatim with Hénault; there is a Spanish translation of Rabbe's work (Madrid, 1824) and a German translation (Dresden, 1826); Hénault and Rabbe probably oppose the martyrs more than they favor them. Bartolomé Sánchez de Feria y

1587, one year after Morales published the Spanish account of the martyrdoms in the *Corónica,* Louis Turquet de Mayerne published his *Histoire générale d'Espangne,*[11] which contains a brief derogatory account of the martyrs, based on his study of Spanish and Latin secondary works available to him. According to Turquet de Mayerne, the Christians of Córdoba lived in liberty under Abd al-Rahman II, who did not persecute them until they rose up in insolence and rebellion against increased taxes. Bishop Reccafred and Count Servandus, he says, were among the moderate Christians who counseled patience, but they were condemned by a council and attacked by writers of the time who regarded as martyrs those whom Turquet de Mayerne calls "rebels."

I. A. Fessler (1810) blames the Christians for the persecution because of their insults against the Moslems. Alex-

Morales, *Palestra sagrada o Memorial de santos de Córdoba...* (4 vols.; Córdoba, 1772), especially I, 80-158. Juan Francisco de Masdeu, *Historia crítica de España y de la cultura española* (20 vols.; Madrid, 1783-1805), XIII (1794), passim. Joseph Aschbach, *Geschichte der Ommaijaden in Spanien...* (2 vols.; Frankfurt am Main, 1829-1830), I, 271-274 and 283. Charles Romey, *Histoire d'Espagne...* (9 vols.; Paris, 1839-1850), III, 480-484, is rather neutral. Antonio Cavanilles, *Historia de España* (5 vols.; Madrid, 1860-1863), I, 399. Dionisio Aldama, *Historia general de España* (12 vols.; Madrid, 1860-1864), II, 67ff. Victor Gebhardt, *Historia general de España y de sus indias* (6 vols. in 4; Madrid, Barcelona, Havana, 1862-1863), II, 477f. and 482f.

[11] The 1587 edition of the *Histoire,* published in Lyons, was withdrawn from circulation to be rewritten and is very rare. Twenty-one years later, in 1608, a second edition was published in Paris. An English translation of this by Edward Grimeson appeared in London in 1612. A posthumous French edition appeared in Paris in 1635. Turquet de Mayerne was not a historian and evidently made use of his *Histoire* to vent some of his anger upon the Spanish for losses he had suffered on St. Bartholomew's Day (23 August 1572). Earlier he had translated several Spanish and Latin works. Cf. "Mayerne, Louis Turquet de," *Grand dictionnaire du XIXe siècle,* X, 1383, and *id.,* ESPASA, 33, 1311. B. Sánchez Alonso, "Mayerne Turquet y los historiadores españols del siglo XVI," *Estudios dedicados a Menéndez Pidal,* I (Madrid, 1950), 589-599, seeks against odds to show that Turquet de Mayerne was not anti-Catholic or anti-Spanish.

ander de Laborde (1812) criticizes the Christians for an unwise and misdirected zeal and praises Abd al-Rahman II for his prudence and sagacity. He explains that the emir assembled in his court a council of Christian bishops who condemned the martyrdoms as infringements of the treaties under which the Christians lived in Córdoba on an equal basis with the Moslems. M. M. Busk (1833) calls the martyrs maniacs and suicidal fanatics. Although she cites no sources in her brief treatment of the martyrs, Mrs. Busk obviously read a detailed account of the martyrdoms. A. Paquis (1844) argues that the Christians attempted to revolt from the Moslem yoke even though there had been no religious persecution or unusual tax burden. Abd al-Rahman, he explains, unable to endure the outrages of the Christian attacks and insults against the prophet Mohammed, was forced to persecute them. Albert de Circourt (1846) attacks the martyrs bitterly. He wrongly calls the first martyr, Perfectus, an apostate from Islam and says that the death of Eulogius left the zealots without a leader. Louis Viardot (1851) defends the Moslems against the charges that they persecuted the Christians and mentions the council of bishops, which, he says, forbade the martyrs to trouble the state with their zeal.[12]

Criticism of the Christian martyrs found its most influential outlet in 1861, when Reinhardt Pietr Dozy, an avid student of Arabic, published in Leyden his famed work, *Histoire des musulmans d'Espagne*.[13] In seeking to "take hold of his subject by the roots and bring the Mohammedans of Spain to life for the first time in history,"[14] Dozy saw fit to dispense with the work of scholars before him and to subordinate the testimony of the Latin sources to that of Arabic

[12] See end of chapter.

[13] R. P. A. Dozy, *Histoire des musulmans d'Espagne...* (Leyden, 1861); republished with additional notes by E. Lévi-Provençal in Leyden in 1932. It has been translated into several languages, including an English translation by Francis Stokes, *Spanish Islam: A History of the Moslems in Spain* (New York, 1913).

[14] Avertissement to the 1st ed., Dozy, *op.cit.*, ed. Lévi-Provençal, I, vii f.

works. He regarded Arabic works written at the end of the tenth century or later as criteria and made use of the ninth-century Latin works by the Cordoban Christians to illustrate his thesis that the Spanish Visigothic tradition of a Christian Latin culture was "extremely decadent" and that the spiritual life of the Christian church was obstinately kept alive and nurtured by a group of fanatical clergy, obsessed with vengeful feelings, all, it would seem to Dozy, against the general inclinations of the Christian community and against the interests of the country. According to Dozy, the Spanish willingly accepted Mohammedanism, and only a few die-hard fanatics persisted in defying the Moslems, thus bringing about their own deserved repression.[15] Dozy countered the inconvenient fact that the only contemporary sources had been written in defense of the martyrs by questioning the credibility of the Christian authors on the basis that they were themselves participants in the events they reported and by accepting instead the viewpoint of the opponents whom they were engaged in refuting. Dozy, who was unprepared to admit any testimony favorable to the Church or to Latin culture, thus presented the Latin works so that they would conform to his own preconceived notions. He offers a dramatized narrative of events, freely interpreting or omitting passages of text in a way that belittles the martyrs and their defenders.

Dozy's foremost disciple, Evariste Lévi-Provençal,[16]

[15] Bk. II, chap. vi, *ibid.*, 317-362, especially 321.

[16] Cf. Dozy, *op.cit.*, ed. Lévi-Provençal, I, 317-323, footnotes. Cf. also Lévi-Provençal, *Histoire de l'Espagne musulmane* (Cairo, 1944), 158-167. A second edition (2 vols.; Paris and Leyden, 1950) contains augmented notes and a few changes of text; cf. I, 225-239. A Spanish translation of the edition of 1944 by Emilio García Gómez appeared as vol. IV of Ramon Menéndez Pidal's *Historia de España musulmana...* (Madrid, 1950); cf. 150-156. In 1952 Lévi-Provençal added a third volume to his edition of 1950 with the subtitle *Le siècle du califat de Cordoue;* cf. 214-226. This volume constitutes a rather complete revision of another work by the same author, *L'Espagne musulmane au Xème siècle. Institutions et vie sociale* (Paris, 1932); cf. 33-37, especially 34. Although both these works describe the social life of the tenth century, they depend a great deal on Latin sources of the

softens the former's attacks and eliminates some of his errors, primarily because he greatly abbreviates the account of the martyrs of Córdoba in his studies of Moslem Spain. Lévi-Provençal's treatment of the Mozarabs, however, does not appear to be based on a study of the Latin texts. He considers the martyrdoms to be of little importance. Whatever persecution existed, he contends, was directed against the Christians because they formed centers of Spanish nationlism, where apostates from Islam, mystics, and malcontents broke the law of the land by insulting Islam and allying with rebels. These uprisings, according to Lévi-Provençal, had their origin in taxation. Asserting that the martyrs were condemned in accordance with Moslem law, Lévi-Provençal accepts their execution as just. In the few pages he devotes to the martyrs he makes several mistakes. Giving credit to Dozy for "reintroducing" the Latin sources in the nineteenth century, he overlooks the numerous editions of the sources as well as the many studies on the martyrs in the seventeenth and eighteenth centuries, in particular the work of Lorenzana and Flórez. His presentation also contains a number of errors in connection with the role played by Eulogius in the martyrdoms and Eulogius' journey to the north.[17]

Carl Brockelmann in general follows the same point of view as Dozy, but he notes that the example of the martyrs

ninth century for material about the Christians. *Le siècle du califat de Cordoue* was translated into Spanish by E. García Gómez and appears as the first part of vol. V of Menéndez Pidal's *Historia de España musulmana...* (Madrid, 1957); cf. especially 118-126. Cf. also Lévi-Provençal, "Abd al-Rahman I, II, III," EI, I, 82f., and *id.*, "Umaiyads," EI, IV, 1004-1012.

[17] Lévi-Provençal, *Histoire de l'Espagne musulmane*, 2d ed., I, 225f., and 235-239. Noting the objection by Isidro de las Cagigas, *Los mozárabes*, I, 195 and 228f., that Dozy failed to give credit to Morales for making the works of Eulogius known, Lévi-Provençal modified the assertion in his 1st ed., p. 158, that Dozy was the first to bring the Latin sources to light, expressing surprise that Dozy had failed to give credit to his essential source, Morales' account of the martyrs in his Chronicle, published in 1574. Dozy, however, seems to have based his study on the Latin texts of the sources and not on Morales' Spanish account in the Chronicle, published in 1586.

continued to have an effect throughout the century.[18]

As early as 1844 E. Rosseeuw-St. Hilaire[19] sought to take a moderate position between the champions of the martyrs and those who condemned them. He speaks of the indiscreet zeal of the martyr movement but makes clear that he does not wish to blame and ridicule the martyrs as did "historians of the last century." Before the persecution, according to Rosseeuw-St. Hilaire, Moslems and Christians were drawing close together through marriage, and in language, dress, customs, even in faith. Although the religious clergy resisted the trend of the secular clergy to draw close to the Moslems, the martyrdoms cannot, he says, be regarded as an act of resistance by them. The martyrdoms were rather a deed of patriotism in protest against the ascent of Arab civilization. They prepared, several centuries beforehand, the later Reconquista, he concludes, and Eulogius was a precursor of Ferdinand III. The analysis and comments of Rosseeuw-St. Hilaire, which are based on a good knowledge of the sources, have been repeated since in several important works.

José Amador de los Rios, a contemporary of Dozy, views the martyrdoms, and the writings of the Cordoban Christians, as the result of a religious and patriotic resistance against the Arabic culture of the Moslems. Some of the remarks of Amador de los Rios, who studies the sources from a literary point of view, offer valuable ideas about the Latin literature of Córdoba in the ninth century.[20]

In 1872 Wolf Wilhelm Graf von Baudissin published a dissertation on the martyrs. He relies on Dozy for the background provided by the Arabic sources but bases his account on his own study of many Latin sources of the eighth and ninth centuries. Baudissin thinks that the tradition of

[18] Carl Brockelmann, *Geschichte der islamischen Völker und Staaten* (Munich and Berlin, 1939), 167f.; the work has been translated into French (Paris, 1949) by M. Tazeront.

[19] E. Rosseeuw-St. Hilaire, *Histoire d'Espagne depuis les premiers temps...* (14 vols.; Paris, 1844-1879), II (1844), 325-338.

[20] José Amador de los Rios, *Historia crítica de la literatura española* (7 vols.; Madrid, 1861-1865), II, 69-126.

religious controversy between Christianity and its opponents, along with resentment on the part of the Christians against discriminating taxation and restrictions in political and religious life, was responsible for what he regards as the fanatical religious movement of the martyrs. He views Eulogius and Albar as the guiding souls of the movement.[21] Baudissin would also credit political relations of the Christians with the north of Spain and France as having an importance in the martyr movement.[22] For the Christians of Spain, he says, the religious controversy was a real war. He believes that the martyrdoms, which were regarded with veneration in both northern and southern Spain, were important because they stirred up a religious movement which led to the eventual expulsion of the Moslems from Spain.[23] Although he tends to regard the motives of the martyrs from a somewhat rationalistic point of view, Baudissin restores to the martyrs the respect and the integrity of which Dozy deprives them. The number of Latin sources studied by Baudissin is exhaustive.

Many authors who present the Christians from a favorable point of view are inclined to follow in the tradition of Morales and Flórez and keep apart from the critics of the martyrs. They edit, comment on, and present expositions of the texts, analyzing them in the light of the Christian tradition. They neither delve into the motives of the martyrs, nor do they argue that the literature of the Christians should be regarded as more important in the general history of Spain and the West than it has been. In 1874 a study of the martyrs and confessors of Córdoba was published by P. B. Gams as a chapter in *Die Kirchengeschichte von Spanien*. Gams' work is a comprehensive study of the situation of the Chris-

[21] W. W. von Baudissin, *Eulogius und Alvar. Ein Abschnitt spanischer Kirchengeschichte aus der Zeit der Maurenherrschaft* (Leipzig, 1872), 3-40, especially 37f., 63-81, 83, and 87. Cf. also *id.*, "Alvar von Corduba," RE, 3d ed., I, 426-428, and *id.*, "Eulogius," *ibid.*, V, 595-597.

[22] *Eulogius und Alvar*, 88-100.

[23] *Ibid.*, 201.

tians in Córdoba under the Moslems, of their bishops, of the councils and heresies described in the sources, and of the Christian authors whose works are extant. Gams considers that the see of Córdoba came to be of paramount importance in Spain under the Moslems. Taking a sound approach, he states that since the Church of God is built by divine as well as by human forces his description will be of what happened rather than how it happened.[24] Although Gams' work is old, it has not since been surpassed for thoroughness and penetration of insight. This is true also of the rest of his volume, which provides an excellent background for the study of the martyrs. Present day authors tend to neglect Gams' work, as they do that of his friend, the catedrático of Arabic at the University of Granada, Francisco Simonet.[25] The monumental *Historia de los mozárabes de España* was published after Simonet's death in 1897 through the care of Manuel Gómez Moreno, although the work was awarded a prize in 1867 by the Real Academia de la Historia. Simonet is one of the few authors to openly espouse the cause of the Mozarabs and to argue the importance of their culture. His work, which is lengthy and prolix, has been criticized by later writers, but it contains a mine of information which can be dug up elsewhere only with great difficulty. Marcelino Menéndez Pelayo, accepting the viewpoint of the sources, sketches the history of the martyrs briefly as a background for his study of the several heterodox controversies of the period, a work first published in Madrid in 1880.[26]

Antonio Ballesteros y Beretta relies upon prominent secondary works rather than upon his own study of the sources.[27] He follows Dozy for events of the martyrdoms

[24] P. B. Gams, *Die Kirchengeschichte von Spanien* (3 vols. in 5; Regensburg, 1862-1879), II, ii, 299-338.

[25] F. J. Simonet, *Historia de los mozárabes de España*, Vol. XIII of *Memorias de la Real Academia de la Historia* (Madrid, 1897-1903), 319-502.

[26] M. Menéndez Pelayo, *Historia de los heterodoxos españoles*, Bk. II, ii; vol. 36 of *Edición nacional de las obras completas de Menéndez Pelayo* (Santander, 1947), 59-66.

[27] A. Ballesteros y Beretta, *Historia de España y su influencia en la*

but without the latter's prejudice. Ballesteros y Beretta also discusses the relationship of the Mozarabs with Moslem power, the Mozarab church, and Mozarabic culture. In addition to the wealth of detail which he provides in his work he offers large bibliographies of general and particular works. In 1936 Zacarías García-Villada treated the history of the martyrs at length in the third volume of his *Historia eclesiástica de España*.[28] He offers an extensive exposition of the sources based on a painstaking research and study. Although the method of García-Villada is to let the sources speak for themselves, he indicates that in the history of the martyrs he sees illustrated the general policy of repression followed by Abd al-Rahman II towards the Christians in his realm, exorbitant taxation and intensive proselytizing for Islam. This policy of Abd al-Rahman, says García-Villada, came into conflict with the religious fervor of the Christians, their ties to the tradition of the Church from Visigothic days, and their opposition to Islam.[29]

In his monograph on Paul Albar,[30] Carleton M. Sage offers a valuable study of Albar's life and works. He discusses Albar's correspondence with John of Seville and the *Confessio* in detail, besides offering a translation of Albar's *Vita Eulogii*. Half of Sage's monograph is devoted to a penetrating study of the *Confessio*, which he shows to be a manual for contrition for sin apart from the sacrament of Penance. Sage discusses the literary tradition of the *Confessio* and studies parallels and sources of works in the tradition. Technical studies such as Sage's offer the greatest hope for bringing to light more information about the Christians of Córdoba in the ninth century. The edition of Albar's correspondence by Madoz in 1947 contains especially good

historia universal (12 vols.; Barcelona and Madrid, 1922-1943); vols. I-VII have 2d eds. (1927-1953); cf. II (1948), 43-47 and 183-209.

[28] Z. García-Villada, *Historia eclesiástica de España* (3 vols. in 5; Madrid, 1929-1936), III, 71-147.

[29] *Ibid.*, 72.

[30] Carleton M. Sage, *Paul Albar of Córdoba: Studies on his Life and Writings* (Washington, 1943).

studies of Albar's correspondence with John of Seville, Esperaindeo, and Bodo.[31] In the valuable footnotes of this edition Madoz studies in detail references to other works by Albar and his correspondents. Madoz also provides a detailed study of the style and characteristics of the correspondence. Although this edition of the text of the letters was intended to supersede that of Flórez, it contains a number of errors made in transcribing the text from the manuscript and cannot be regarded as a definitive edition.

The popular biography of Eulogius by Justo Pérez de Urbel, first published in 1928, contains a good bit of romanticized narrative, but the work is based on a thorough exploitation of all the sources.[32] In a two-volume work published in 1947-1948 Isidro de las Cagigas studies sociological aspects of the Christians of Córdoba from a speculative point of view. He would argue a movement of Spanish nationalism and independence in religion, culture, and politics against Moslem religious intolerance, Arab racial discrimination, and the central authority of Cordoban rule.[33] Although Cagigas' work is important for its recognition of the role of the Christians in the history of Mohammedan Spain, its value is impaired by a number of inaccuracies and misinterpretations, due, as a rule, to the failure of the author to distinguish between the testimony of the sources and the testimony of Dozy. In 1956 F. Pérez discussed the Mozarabs and the martyrdoms somewhat briefly but with originality and thoroughness.[34] He sees the persecution and the martyrdoms as the result of Malekite fanaticism which came to Spain in the reign of Abd al-Rahman I (756-788). In his study of the martyrs, the bishops, and religious polemics in

---

[31] José Madoz, *Epistolario de Alvaro de Córdoba* (Madrid, 1947).

[32] Justo Pérez de Urbel, *San Eulogio de Córdoba* (Madrid, 1928); the 2d ed. (Madrid, 1942) is referred to in the present work. Cf. an adapted translation into English by a Benedictine of Stanbrook Abbey, *A Saint under Moslem Rule* (Milwaukee, 1937).

[33] I. de las Cagigas, *Los mozárabes* (2 vols.; Madrid, 1947-1948), I, 179-233; cf. *ibid.*, 188-201.

[34] F. Pérez, "Cordoue," DHGE, XIII, 837-871; most of the article deals with the period of the martyrdoms.

Córdoba during Moslem rule Pérez deals directly with a number of difficult problems neglected in lengthier studies. He discusses the many churches and monasteries which existed in the neighborhood of Córdoba during the years of Moslem rule.

In a recent work F. R. Franke, on the basis of a study of the conditions of Spanish Christians and a detailed investigation of the apologetical and polemical source material of the controversy between the Spanish Christians and Islam, endeavors to determine the spiritual motives of the martyrs of Córdoba.[35] Franke's main interest is Christian-Moslem polemics, and his study of the polemical writings of the Christians of Córdoba and their relationship with the writings of Christians of the East is most welcome and enlightening, especially his detailed study of the second part of Albar's *Indiculus luminosus*. One regrets only that Franke did not include in his study the *Apologeticus* of the Abbot Samson and more of the polemics in Eulogius' works, although he justifies not doing so.

Franke, after a close and intelligent reading of almost all of the Latin sources from Córdoba, offers a number of new interpretations of textual passages. Many of these interpretations will be considered in the course of this text. The importance of Franke's contribution to the knowledge of events in Córdoba in the days of the martyrdoms will be evident in the frequent references to his study. Some of his interpretations, however, may be challenged, when he derives, it would seem, more meaning from the text than is warranted. One may disagree with him in his dating of a council of Córdoba in the early part of 852 rather than at the end of that year and in his arguments for a council in 856-857.[36] To understand better the additional meaning which Franke seeks to give to the sources the reader who is not

---

[35] Franz Richard Franke, "Die freiwilligen Märtyrer von Cordova und das Verhältnis der Mozaraber zum Islam (nach den Schriften des Speraindeo, Eulogius und Alvar," *Gesammelte Aufsätze zur Kulturgeschichte Spaniens*, XIII (Münster Westfalen, 1958), 4.

[36] Cf. index, "Council of Córdoba, 852."

familiar with the abundant and rather difficult Latin source material should follow closely the ample footnotes in his work. In his introduction Franke relies upon Dozy, Lévi-Provençal, and Cagigas for a background sketch[37] and so carries forward a number of their unsubstantiated conclusions.

Whatever one's reservations about some of Franke's premises and conclusions, what he says about the historical importance of the martyr movement seems valid enough to be repeated here at length. In the north, says Franke, the martyr movement came to be of greater importance, in a symbolic way, than it did in the south, because Christians in the north could openly attack the Moslems more easily than could those in the south. The Spanish reaction against Moslem domination, in both north and south of Spain, differed basically from the reaction of Christians against the Moslems in the Eastern Mediterranean. Unlike the Christians in the East, whose polemics against the Moslems were rather academic in a tradition going back to early Christianity, Spanish Christians asserted themselves with passion and determination against their enemy, either with weapons, as in the north, or in spiritual protests, where this was the only recourse. For Christians of northern and southern Spain, life itself was of less importance than their determined will to struggle to the utmost for their own sphere of freedom. And of necessity, says Franke, this will overflowed in an attack.

One should not reproach Spanish Christians, he continues, if, in spite of their good knowledge of Islam, they eschewed the polemics of Christians in the East and attacked Islam in a way peculiarly their own, as confessors and not as debaters, and so gained no laurels in the field of Christian-Moslem polemics. Although the zealots of the martyr movement had an intensity of faith which caused them to disregard considerations of worldly wisdom, their bond with the Christian community of Córdoba remained a close one. That this

[37] Franke, *op.cit.*, 4-10.

community survived the attack which threatened to break it apart, an attack not against the essence of their faith but against the form in which they wished to observe it, was due apparently, says Franke, to the co-operation of all members of the community in authoritative positions. As for the martyrs themselves, their bravery and the scrupulousness of their deeds were unassailable and above debate even in their own time, although others were free not to follow in their path. The martyrs illustrate a heroic side of the Spanish nature, says Franke, and they anticipated broader and more permanent trends, such as arise later in the Reconquista.[38]

A crucial matter in the study of the martyrs of Córdoba is the estimate one makes of the relative strength of the advocates of the martyrs and their opponents. Franke regards all but a small part of the Christian community as either opposed to the martyrdoms or neutral, more interested in preserving the integrity of the Christian community and the *status quo*, which brought them daily into close contact with many parts of the Moslem community, than in jeopardizing their fortunes and the future of the Christian community by supporting the determined acts of a small number of zealots.[39] Franke's conclusion that the sense of common identity and common interests of all parts of the Christian community kept it from disintegrating into factions deserves attention.

[38] *Ibid.*, 168ff.
[39] *Ibid.*, 147ff.

[12] I. A. Fessler, *Versuch einer Geschichte der spanischen Nation* (2 vols.; Berlin, 1810), I, 347 and especially 350-355. Alexander de Laborde, *Voyage pittoresque et historique de l'Espagne* (2 vols. in 4; Paris, 1806-1820), II (1812), xvi and 4. M. M. Busk, *The History of Spain and Portugal* (London, 1833), 16. Amadée Paquis, *Histoire d'Espagne et de Portugal depuis les temps les plus reculés...* (2 vols.; Paris, 1844), I, 359f. and 364. Albert de Circourt, *Histoire des mores, mudejares, et des morisques, ou des arabes d'Espagne sous la domination des chrétiens* (3 vols.; Paris, 1846), I, 41-44. Louis Viardot, *Histoire des arabes et des mores d'Espagne* (2 vols.; Paris, 1851), I, 140; cf. *id.*, *Historia de los árabes y de los moros de España* (Barcelona, 1844), 34.

Part I

Mozarab Spain in the Century Before the Martyrs:
The Latin and Arabic Sources

CHAPTER I

EARLY LATIN WRITINGS IN SPAIN UNDER ARAB RULE

The literature of the Christian Latin culture of Spain during the time of the Visigothic kings of Toledo was predominantly ecclesiastical in nature, written by churchmen about religious subjects. The last works of this literature now extant are the works of Valerius of Bierzo and Julian of Toledo, both of whom flourished about 690; the life of Julian by Felix, his second successor in the see of Toledo; and the acts of several councils held in Toledo and Zaragoza. When Spain in 711-712 experienced the first of the invasions it was to undergo in the first half of the eighth century by Mohammedan forces of Arabs and Syrians from the East and Moors and Berbers from North Africa, the Visigothic kingdom came to a precipitate end, after the death of Rodrigo, its last king. The ecclesiastical Christian Latin culture, with deeper roots in Spain than the Visigothic kings, suffered under the alien conquerors but continued to survive. This Spanish culture became isolated from its contemporary cultures, the Arabic of the Moslems and the Latin of Christian Europe. Moreover, the remains of this culture today appear fragmentary and incomplete. As a result, the culture of the Mozarabs has come to be rather neglected in the study of Western European culture. Such a neglect seems to be unjustified.

The word "Mozarab" or "Mozarabic" usually refers to the Christians who lived under Moslem rule in Spain. As a cultural term it embraces the Christians of northern Spain as well, especially for the first few centuries after the Arab conquest of the peninsula. The early Spanish liturgy, dating from the fourth or fifth century and in use in Spain until

19

the end of the eleventh century, is also called, rather inappropriately, "Mozarabic."[1]

The origin of the word "Mozarab" is obscure. It first appears in Latin texts in *fueros* and *privilegios* issued in Toledo in 1101, 1118, 1137, and 1176 as *Muztarabes*, *Mozarabes*, and *Muzarabes*, referring to Christians who had formerly lived among the Arabs, as distinguished from the *Castellani, Franci,* and *Galleci*. For the most part, however, in documents of the early twelfth century no distinction is made between "Mozarabs" and other Christians, all Christians being distinguished as a group from "Moors" and "Jews." Mozarabs are also mentioned in a number of treaties and *fueros* granted by Alfonso I of Aragon or Alfonso VII of León and Castille: to Moors of Tudela in 1115, to Christians from Andalucía in 1126, to Mallen in 1132, to Guadalajara in 1133, and to Aragonese of Zurita in 1156. The name appears in several other writings of the twelfth and thirteenth centuries. Simonet, presumably because the earliest (twelfth-century) *fueros* mentioning "Mozarabs" were from Toledo, thought that the Moslems of Toledo originated the name for the Christians who lived among them.[2] Rodrigo Jiménez de Rada, archbishop of Toledo (1210-1247), evidently refers to "Mozarabs" without using the word when he speaks of *mixti Arabes*, meaning the Christians of Spain who lived "mixed" with Arabs. Jiménez de Rada says that in his day both the name and the people still existed. Others, including Morales and Flórez,[3] have accepted his explanation.

---

[1] Cf. Pierre David, *Etudes historiques sur la Galice et le Portugal de VIe au XIIe siècle* (Lisbon and Paris, 1947), 83-118 and 391-405; Fernand Cabrol, "Mozarabe (Messe)," DTC, X, ii, 2518-2543, and *id.*, "Mozarabe (La liturgie)," DACL, XII, i, 390-491; Henri Leclercq "Messe," DACL, XI, i, 674-690; Henry Jenner, "Mozarabic Rite," *Catholic Encyclopedia*, X, 611-623.

[2] Tomás Muñoz y Romero, *Colección de fueros municipales y cartas pueblas de los reinos de Castilla, León, Corona de Aragon y Navarra* (Madrid, 1847), 360, 363, 375, 380, 417, 503, and 509; Simonet, *Historia*, vii-xv, discusses the term "Mozarab."

[3] *De rebus Hispaniae*, III, xxii, "Arabes enim, quae vi non poterant subiugare, falso foedere deceperunt, Oppa filio Egicae Hispalensi

The meaning given by Jiménez de Rada, but not his etymological derivation, is that generally accepted today. There is, however, another explanation of the origin of the term, with another meaning. In the thirteenth century the famous scholar Raymond Martin translated "Mozarab" as *Arabicus*. In the early seventeenth century the Arabic historian al-Makkari stated that the Moslems of Andalucía included Arabs and Mozarabs. In 1614 Bernardo Aldrete, referring to Alfonso de Alcalá and to Giovanni Leone, denies that the word comes from the Latin *mixti Arabes*, asserting that it comes from the Arabic *Muztaarabi* instead. According to Giovanni Leone, upon whom Aldrete depends, *Muztaarabi* were the descendants of Ismael, who mixed with the pure Arabs of the Arabian peninsula in antiquity and were Arabs by accident, not by birth.[4] In the eighteenth century Gaspar

episcopo suadente, ut subiecti Arabibus viverent sub tributo, et si forte Dominus patriam visitaret, fierent subvenientibus in succursum. Et sic fraudibus circumventi reddiderunt oppida, et praesidia civitatum, et isti dicti sunt mixti Arabes, eo quod mixti Arabibus convivebant, quorum hodie apud nos nomen perseverat et genus." Cf. *SS PP Toletanorum*, III, 70. Morales, *Corónica general*, III, Bk. XII, lxxi, par. 3; Flórez, ES, III, 190ff.; cf. Simonet, *Historia*, xi f.

4 Raymond Martin, *Vocabulario arábigo-latino y latín-arábigo*, ed. Schiaparelli (Florence, 1871). Al-Makkari, *The History of the Mohammedan Dynasties in Spain*, trans. Pascual de Gayangos (2 vols.; London, 1890-1893), I, 142. Bernardo Aldrete, *Varias antigüedades de España, Africa y otras provincias* (Antwerp, 1614), III, xxv, 433. Alfonso de Alcalá, a Jewish medic and convert to Catholicism in 1492, worked on the *Biblia poliglota* of Cardinal Jiménez and, with Coronel translated the Jewish books of the Old Testament into Latin; v. ESPASA, IV, 612. Giovanni Leone l'Africano, born in Granada about 1485, fled with his parents to Fez when Ferdinand and Isabella captured Granada in 1492. He travelled extensively in the Moslem world, was captured by pirates and brought to Rome in 1517, where he was baptized by Pope Leo X in 1520. Here sometime before 1523 he composed his *Descrizione* of the land and peoples of Africa, a work soon translated into Latin, French, English, and Dutch. Cf. Angelo Codazzi, "Leone Africano," *Enciclopedia italiana*, XX, 899. Called Juan León by Aldrete, he writes (I, xxviii): *"E da saper anchora che gli antichi Arabi, i quali furono prima che nascessero gli Ismaeliti, sono chiamati da gli historici Africani, Arabi Ariba, cio è Arabi Arabici, e quelli che sono della origine d'Ismahel vengono appellati Arabi Mustaharabi, cio è*

Ibañez de Segovia, Marques de Mondéjar, reiterated Aldrete's thesis, introducing the added information from Barthélemy d'Herbelot's dictionary that the *Muztaarabi* of old were not to be confused with *Mostarabes* of the eighteenth century, "who are Arabs who live mixed with other nations outside of Arabia," called *Muzarabes* by the Spanish.[5] Miguel Casiri, in his monumental catalogue of Arabic manuscripts of the Escorial, lists a work in ms 1700 which treats of the origin of the Arabs and distinguishes "pure Arabs" from *Mostarabes*. The work was written by an Abu al-Abbasus Mohammed ibn Iazid, who is otherwise unknown. The manuscript is not dated, but other works in it are dated A.H. 200 (A.D. 815/816), A.H. 450 (A.D. 1058/1059), and Casiri describes one writer as *vetustissimus*. According to Casiri, the manuscript contains many old and unusual items on Arab customs, history, words, sayings, etc.[6]

Today Arabists derive "Mozarab" from *musta'riba* ("arabicised" or "not originally Arab"), as distinguished from *arab'ariba* ("original Arabs of pure stock") and *muta'ariba* ("not pure blooded Arabs"). But they do not agree as to its meaning, some denoting by the term the Christians in Spain who became Moslem and some using the word to denote the Christians who lived in Spain under Moslem rule.[7] The explanations based on an Arabic etymology do not apply to Spanish Christians who lived under Arab rule in Spain. All the explanations, however, except the unusual meaning which d'Herbelot applies to *Mostarabes*

Arabi inarabati. Il che tanto è nella lingua italiana Arabi per accidente, percioche essi non sono natii Arabi."

[5] G. Ibañez de Segovia, *Predicación del apostel Santiago*, xxiv; cf. also id., *Advertencias a la historia del P. Juan de Mariana* (Valencia, 1746), 19. B. d'Herbelot de Molainville, *Bibliothèque orientale* (Paris, 1697).

[6] M. Casiri, *Bibliotheca arabico-hispana Escurialensis* (2 vols.; Madrid, 1760-1770), II, 157, "Opusculum de Arabum origine, ubi de *Cahtano* et *Adnano*, a quibus Arabes *puri*, et *adsititi*, qui et *Mostarabes* vocitantur, originem traxisse dicuntur."

[7] Ilse Lichtenstädter, "Musta'rib(a)," EI, III, 771. Lévi-Provençal, "Mozarabs," EI, III, 611f., avoids tieing the meaning of "Christians under Moslem rule" to an Arabic etymology.

of the eighteenth century, distinguish people who pass as Arabs from genealogically pure Arabs.

Neither the Arabic chroniclers of Spain nor Spanish Christian authors before the twelfth century speak of "Mozarabs," either referring to Christians or speaking of "Arabs." The Moslems referred to Christians under their rule as "barbarians" or "foreigners" (*'adjami*),[8] a term which the Christians themselves used when writing Arabic. The Moslems also referred to the Christians as "Christians," "Romans," "polytheists," and "clients." In Latin texts the Christians refer to themselves as *Christiani, Catholici*, or *Latini*. As a rule, Moslem writers of Spain seem to refer to themselves as "Arabs." Christians writing in Latin refer to the Arabs of Spain as *Arabes, Saraceni, Agareni, Smaelitae*, and *Muzlemiti*, with no apparent distinction between the five terms. Considering the relatively infrequent use of the term "Mozarab" by early writers and the uncertainty about the historical and etymological origins of the word, and considering its different meanings, it would seem prudent to withhold any definition of the word until a more exhaustive study has been made. When used in the present work "Mozarab" denotes the Christians who lived under Moslem rule in Spain.

What remains of the culture of the Mozarabs is rather impressive. They passed on to posterity the rich legacy of early Spanish liturgical works, mostly from Toledo. An important chronicle, composed in 754 shortly after the Arab conquest, has survived. The chronicler of 754 speaks of other works written by Christians in Spain in his time which are no longer extant, historical works of his own and works of an ecclesiastical nature by others. He mentions heresies and unorthodoxy, which beset the church in Spain throughout Moslem rule. Besides the Chronicle of 754, there are sources extant which deal with the Migetian heresy and other errors which appeared in Spain about 780 and survived, in one form or another, into the ninth century. The Adoptionist

---

[8] F. Gabrieli, " 'adjam," EI, I, 206, and Lévi-Provençal, "Aljamía," EI, I, 404f.

controversy, fostered by Elipandus, bishop of Toledo, crossed the Pyrenees and in its contest with the Frankish church became of concern to all the Church in the West. By 800, when the heresy had almost disappeared, an extensive body of literature had collected, written not only by authors of Spain, but by authors of Italy and the Frankish kingdom as well. In the literature of the eighth century, from the Chronicle of 754 through the literature of the Adoptionist heresy, the center of Latin culture in Spain appears to have been Toledo, the primatial see of the church of Spain and formerly the capital of the Visigoths. As Arab rule in the peninsula became permanent, however, the hegemony of Toledo in Latin culture seems to have waned somewhat.

In the ninth century Toledo evidently lost much of its prominence as the center of Christian Latin culture in Spain when Latin letters began to emanate from the Christian kingdom of the Asturias and from Córdoba, the center of Arab rule. A group of writings from Córdoba, beginning in 839 with the acts of an episcopal council and continuing until 864, affords an opportunity to study the intellectual and religious life of the Christians of that city. From these sources one can also form an idea about the relations between Christians and Mohammedans under Moslem rule at the time of the persecution of 850-859, which claimed the lives of fifty or more Christian martyrs and which is the central event of the history of the Christians under Moslem rule in Spain. After this group of writings Latin literature in Moslem Spain seems to have dwindled to the accounts of several Christian martyrs of the tenth century and odds and ends illustrative of a persisting Christian Latin culture. In the middle of the tenth century a visit to Córdoba by an ambassador of Otto I makes possible a welcome view of the Christians there. In 1085, when Toledo was reconquered by the Christians of northern Spain, Mozarabs were practicing the Christian faith in that city. There is evidence that the Christians of Betica continued to practice their religion as a group until the region was reconquered from the Moslems by the Christian forces of León and Castille in the thirteenth century.[9] In 1300 Pedro Pascual, bishop of Jaén, a native of Valencia who had studied and travelled rather extensively in Christian Spain, France, and Italy, died as a martyr in Granada as a result of works he wrote there in dispute with his Moslem captors. There is evidence that Christians lived under Moslem rule in Spain as late as 1492, when Granada was captured by Ferdinand and Isabella.[10]

The group of Latin writings from Córdoba in the middle of the ninth century occupies a position of importance in the early history of Spain. The scope of the writings is wide, including, besides the Acts of the Council of Córdoba in 839: a history of the Moslem persecution of the Christians which includes the vitae of fifty martyrs, polemical attacks against the Moslem persecutors and those Christians who sympathized or collaborated with them, a collection of poetry, a treatise on clerical dress and customs, and an apologia of his Christian faith written in 864 by a churchman in dispute with Christian antagonists who were under the influence of Islamic thought. So many writings within twenty-five years would be a worthy contribution from any mediaeval city. Considering that they were written by members of a persecuted faith, people who had been in daily contact with the alien culture of the Moslem religion and the Arabic language for as much as a hundred and fifty years, the achievement becomes more impressive. These works, which witness to the preservation of the Christian Latin cultural tradition among the Mozarabs, are the nucleus for the history of the Christians in Spain under the Moslems. Moreover, the writings are the only sources from Moslem Spain in this early period, no Arabic sources of the time having survived.

In a thirteenth-century Arabic work, however, appears an Arabic text[11] which purports to be a treaty between the Arab

---

[9] Lévi-Provençal, *Seville musulmane au debut du XIIe siècle. Le traité d'Ibn 'Abdun sur la vie urbaine et les corps de métiers, traduit avec une introduction et des notes* (Paris, 1947), passim (cf. the index).

[10] Cf. index, "Pedro Pascual." Simonet, *Historia*, 771-795, discusses the last traces of the Mozarabs in different parts of Spain.

[11] The text, which comes from a biographical dictionary by al-Dhahabi

Abdelaziz, son of Muza (the conqueror of Spain), and the
Visigoth Theodemirus in the year 713. According to the
treaty, Theodemirus agreed to accept the protection of Allah
and the prophet Mohammed, provided that he and his subjects remained free of Arab domination; that he would not
be seized or despoiled of his realm; that his subjects would
not be slain, taken captive, or separated from each other,
their sons, or their wives; that their religion would not be
attacked by the Arabs or their churches burned; that Theodemirus would not have his rule taken away as long as he
was faithful and honest and fulfilled the terms of the treaty.
He agreed not to give asylum to deserters or enemies of
Abdelaziz, not to threaten those under the protection of
Abdelaziz, nor to conceal information about his enemies.
Theodemirus and his subjects agreed to pay an annual
tribute of gold, grain, syrup, vinegar, honey, and oil. The
treaty applied to seven cities in the East of Spain: Orihuela,
Valencia, Alicante, Mula, Bigastro, Eyyo (Elche or Totana),
and Lorca. Witnessed by four Arabs, the treaty was signed
5 April 713. García-Villada points out that this treaty is
referred to in five other Arabic works and in the Latin
Chronicle of 754.[12] The treaty lasted at least until 754 in
the reign of Theodemirus' son, Athanaildus, but by 814 it
seems to have come to an end as Moslem cadis began to dispense Islamic justice in the area covered by the treaty.[13]

Presumably other treaties were concluded between the
Arabs and the people of other cities in Spain, although no

in the Arabic ms Escorial 1676, has been published by Casiri, *op.cit.*, II,
106; by Francisco Codera and Julian Ribera, *Bibliotheca arabico-
hispana* (10 vols.; Madrid, 1882-1893), III, 258f., and by Simonet,
op.cit., 797f. Casiri, *op.cit.*, 105f., Simonet, *op.cit.*, 798, García-Villada,
Historia eclesiástica, III, 30f., Lévi-Provençal, *Histoire de l'Espagne
musulmane*, I, 32f., and others offer translations of the treaty. E. Lambert, "Athanaild," DHGE, IV, 1305, says that the best translation is
that of Mariano Gaspar Remiro, *Historia de Murcia musulmana* (Zaragoza, 1905), 13-15.

[12] García-Villada, *op.cit.*, 31; cf. index, "Theodemirus."

[13] Lambert, "Athanaild," DHGE, IV, 1304f., and *id.*, "Aurariola,"
DHGE, V, 694.

texts are known. Several Arabic historians give some of the terms of a treaty between Muza and the people of Mérida in June 713. According to this treaty, the people of Mérida retained their liberties and their lands, but the lands of the Christians who had fled to the North were confiscated by the Moslems and the goods and riches of the Church, which amazed the conquerors, became the property of the Arab chief.[14]

Two documents, one purporting to be an agreement between the Moslem governor of Coimbra and a neighboring monastery in 734 and the other purporting to be the record of a grant of land from the Christian count of the Christian community of Coimbra to the same monastery in 760, are discussed at some length by Flórez, Simonet, and Gams.[15] According to Simonet, the texts, which lack a manuscript tradition and contain anachronisms, were forged at the end of the sixteenth century by Bernardo de Brito,[16] who first published them. Flórez and Gams, less critical of the authenticity of the texts, consider them to be based on an oral tradition and to offer a fairly representative description of the life of Christians in Spain under the Moslems. Data from these documents, however, should not be applied generally to Christian communities in Spain under the Moslems.

The early treaties between the Arabs and the cities they conquered in Spain were probably as important in the subsequent relations between the Arabs and their Christian subjects as any other element. In the eighth century the terms of the treaties seem to have varied from one city to another. It is frequently assumed that by the ninth century the relationship between Moslems and Christians was uniform

[14] Simonet, *op.cit.*, 52; García-Villada, *op.cit.*, 30. According to the Chronicle of 754, Muza departed for Damascus in 712.

[15] Flórez, ES, X, 265f., and *ibid.*, XIV, tr. 45, par. 21; Simonet, *op.cit.*, 180-184; Gams, *Kirchengeschichte*, II, ii, 304f.

[16] Bernardo de Brito, *et al.*, *Monarchia Lusytana* (8 vols.; Lisbon, 1597-1727), II (1609), 287v f. and 292v f. (Bk. VII, vii-viii). The authenticity of both documents has been questioned by Portuguese and Spanish historians since the date of publication; cf. Simonet, *op.cit.*, 183.

throughout the conquered area and conformed to the relationship between the two peoples in the East. This assumption should not be accepted too readily. The early treaties were broken or abrogated by Moslem rulers in Spain more than once. Syrian troops who entered the peninsula in 742 took property and rights from the Christians rather than at the expense of the conquerors of 711-713. When Abd al-Rahman I brought Umaiyad rule into Spain in 755, a similar revision of rights must have taken place, although there is no record of new treaties. It is not known what rights Christians and the Christian religion had in Spain in the ninth century, when Malekites apparently undertook to make Spain conform with the Moslem East, but there is no more reason to think that Mozarabs occupied the same position as Christians in the East than there is to think that their position was the same as it had been in 713, when their religious liberty seems to have been unrestricted. One need not believe that the Moslems were being magnanimous when they did not restrict the exercise of the Christian religion in Córdoba in the ninth century as in the East nor enforce there certain Moslem regulations which were enforced in the East. The sources are too sparse to tell what were the conditions of the surrender of the Christians in the eighth century and what were their rights at the time of the martyrdoms in Córdoba in the ninth century. Christian authors of Córdoba discuss their religious rights repeatedly, but from the point of view of justice and religious truth. Likewise, they indicate that treaties of long standing were broken by the Moslems and they challenge any right of the Moslems to determine their religious freedom, but they do not complain about the violation of "constitutional" rights. Moslem laws may have violated the rights which Christians held by treaty as much as Christian martyrs may have violated Moslem laws in their professions of faith.

It is unfortunate that more is not known of the rights of Christians as individuals and as a group in Córdoba in the five centuries of Moslem rule. Such knowledge would permit one to study the executions of the martyrs from a legal point of view. Moreover, the cause of the martyr movement, a matter that has occupied almost everyone who has studied the martyrs, could be fruitfully discussed. Did the Christians suffer a status of inferiority for more than a century and then rise up in protest? Were they prompted by Christian rulers in northern Spain and France? Or was their action spontaneous? Did the emirs permit the free exercise of the Christian religion for more than a century and then decide to repress it? Were they influenced by such people as the apostate to Judaism, Bodo-Eleazar, and the Malekite fakih, Yahya ibn Yahya? Or did they fear the allegiance of a number of their subjects to rulers to the north? Evidence for various causes can be found in the sources. It is very difficult to determine which ones were really significant.

Although Latin and Arabic works mention a number of public officials, not much is known about the role of the Mozarabs in the civil government of Córdoba. The picture of a Mozarab community there with its own officials, separate from the municipal government, seems to go back to Morales' description of the office of *comes* (count).[17] The idea of three officials appointed by, and responsible to, the king—a *comes* (the chief Christian official), an *exceptor* (tax collector), and a *censor* (judge)—which seems to begin with Flórez, has been repeated by several historians.[18] Neither a separate administration nor a triumvirate of Mozarab officials, however, seems to describe the part of the Christians in the government of Córdoba adequately. Eulogius indicates that the Christians expected to participate in the government of

[17] Morales, "Qui status christianae religionis Cordubae sub Arabum imperio divi Eulogii tempore fuit," *Divi Eulogii . . . opera*, 5 unnumbered prefatory pages (PL 115, 917-922, especially 920) ; cf. also *Memoriale*, scholium 1 to II, ii, where Morales says the *exceptor* is a scribe, and scholium 2 to III, xvi, where he says that he does not know what the *censor* is.

[18] ES, X, 263-265. Gams, *op.cit.*, II, ii, 300; Simonet, *op.cit.*, 111f.; García-Villada, *op.cit.*, III, 39; Cagigas, *Los mozárabes*, I, 57 and 66; Franke, "Die freiwilligen Märtyrer," 10; Dozy, *Histoire*, II, ii (ed. Lévi-Provençal, I, 275) ; Lévi-Provençal, *L'Espagne musulmane au Xème siècle*, 37-44.

the realm.[19]   There are several indications that the *comes* had authority over the whole city and not just over the Mozarabs. The *exceptor* seems to have been an official of the chancery rather than a tax collector.   Among themselves Christians and Moslems evidently followed their own codes of law, in the case of the Christians a modified version of the *Forum iudicum* of the Visigoths, and Christians who apostatized to Islam seem to have escaped the jurisdiction of the *Forum iudicum*, even for past deeds.   But it seems that Christian judges, of whom there were more than a single *censor*, were not without a voice in matters of concern to both peoples. A definitive study of Mozarab officialdom is lacking at the present.

Pierre David points out that the administration of parishes, churches, and monasteries in Galicia and Portugal was not basically disturbed by more than a century of Moslem rule.[20]   According to Henrique da Gama Barros, after the conquest of Spain by the Arabs the system of *patrocinium* was more than ever in use in Spain, in the south as well as in the north.   Monasteries and powerful lords both served as protectors.[21]   Da Gama Barros also thinks that the municipal organization of the Romans, manifested in collective administration, persisted under the Moslems.   Since officials of municipal organizations in areas reconquered from the Moslems were known by Arabic titles rather than by Latin ones, he concludes that the municipium survived under the Arabs and was not reintroduced as a result of the Reconquest.   He finds further proof of the Roman municipal organization in allusions to the ancient liberties of the inhabitants in *privilegios* granted by Christian kings to the inhabitants of

[19] *Memoriale*, II, xvi, 2; III, i, and iv.

[20] David, *Etudes*, 254.

[21] Henrique da Gama Barros, *Historia da administração publica em Portugal nos seculos XII a XV*, 2d ed. by Torquato de Sousa Soares (11 vols.; Lisbon, 1945-1954), I, 178ff., 388 (no. xxiv), and IV, 55, 62f.   One may also refer to C. Sánchez-Albornoz, "Las behetrías: la encomendación en Asturias, León y Castilla," AHDE, I (1924), 158-336, and *id.*, "Muchas páginas mas sobre las behetrías," *ibid.*, IV (1927), 5-157.

lands reconquered from the Moslems. Louis the Pious in 826 makes such an allusion in a letter to the people of Mérida. A *privilegio* granted to Toledo in 1101 recognizes that the *Forum iudicum* had been the legal code in that city under Moslem rule, and in 1241 the *Forum iudicum* was part of the charter granted to Córdoba, which had recently been taken from the Moslems.[22]

Under the *Forum iudicum* of the Visigoths the clergy performed many civil acts. The bishop not only was the head of the clergy but he entered into the judicial and administrative systems. Judging from the Latin sources of the ninth century, the bishop was the leader of the Christians of Córdoba and was recognized as such by the emir. Bishop Saul was twice imprisoned in retaliation for martyrdoms and he had to flee to escape death when the martyrdoms broke out under King Mohammed I in 853.[23] Next to the law of the emir the highest authority among the Christians of Córdoba seems to have been the decision of the bishops in council.[24]

The highest secular official among the Visigoths, apart from the king, was the *dux,* who was the chief civil and military official of a province. Although the Latin sources of Córdoba in the ninth century refer to no *dux,* Eulogius reports that on one occasion a councillor persuaded the emir to renounce his intention to slay all the Christians inasmuch as no *personalis dux* had led the confessors forth.[25] *Civitates* (city districts or territories) among the Visigoths had at their head a *comes,* who held judicial, financial, and police powers. A *defensor,* who, as the chief magistrate of the

---

[22] Da Gama Barros, *op.cit.,* I, 77ff.; cf. also A. García Gallo, *Curso de historia del derecho español,* I, 5th ed. (Madrid, 1950), 253; cf. index, "Louis the Pious."

[23] A. K. Ziegler, *Church and State in Visigothic Spain* (Washington, 1930), 123-145; da Gama Barros, *op.cit.,* II, 17ff. *Vita Eulogii,* 4; *Memoriale,* II, xvi, 2, and III, vii, 4.

[24] Acts of the Council of Córdoba in 839; *Memoriale,* II, xv, 3; Samson, *Apologeticus,* preface to Bk. II, 7-8; Letter X of the Albar correspondence.

[25] Ziegler, *op.cit.,* 20; da Gama Barros, *op.cit.,* VII, 393f. *Memoriale,* III, vii, 4.

civitas, was to defend the people against oppression,[26] is not mentioned in the Latin sources of the ninth century.

Four counts of Córdoba are known by name and a fifth person (Romanus Medicus) is thought to have held the office. Two of the four counts, Adulphus and Guifredus, are known from poems of dedication only,[27] but a fair amount is known about the other two counts. Count Rabi held the office from about 817 to 822 and was the chief of the palace guard, which apparently was made up of mercenaries and captives from Christian lands to the north. Rabi was responsible for the collection of taxes beyond those specified in the Koran, presumably due from Christians and Moslems alike.[28] Count Servandus, known in two Latin sources, functioned as a judge and tax collector. In Albar's letter to Romanus Medicus, Servandus appears to have the responsibility of reviewing charges brought against Albar. Samson says that Servandus asked the king to deliver the Christians to him for 100,000 solidi. Although Servandus is not stated to have held military authority, he may have done so. Samson accuses Bishop Hostegesis of Malaga, who was in league with Servandus, of relying on military troops (praesidalis manus) to oppress the clergy in Córdoba. Ibn Haiyan reports that in 890 Servandus fled from Córdoba and began to lead raids in the environs of the city, an action which would seem to require military experience. Rabi's authority extended beyond the Christian community, and Samson, in referring to the office of Servandus as the "comitatus Cordubae urbis patriciae," implies that his authority did also.[29]

The office of *censor* (judge) seems not to be correctly represented by some modern writers. Eulogius calls the

[26] Ziegler, *op.cit.*, 20; da Gama Barros, *op.cit.*, VII, 394-398 and 411-426.

[27] ES, XI, 524 and 525.

[28] Lévi-Provençal, *Histoire de l'Espagne musulmane*, I, 164, 166, and 196.

[29] Letter IX of the Albar correspondence, 6; *Apologeticus*, preface to Bk. II, 2, 5, and 8; cf. José Guarieb, "Al-Muqtabis de Ibn Hayyan," CHE, XXI-XXII, 341, and XXIII-XXIV, 343.

Moslem cadi both *censor* and *iudex* and uses the terms else-where as synonyms. Both he and Albar indicate that among the Christians and in the government of Córdoba there were a number of judges. The king's councillors, before whom some of the martyrs were tried, had judicial authority. No single *censor*, whose function was to settle disputes among the Christians according to the *Forum iudicum* in the time of Moslem rule, is mentioned in the sources. As in the time of the Visigoths, judicial authority seems to have been exercised by a number of officials.[30]

The earliest known work which provides background information for the Christian martyrdoms in Córdoba in the ninth century is the Latin chronicle written in 754 by an unknown author who probably lived in Córdoba. The chronicle, the Spanish Continuation of Isidore of Seville's chronicle up to the year 754, is also known as the Continuation of Isidore of Beja, of Isidore of Badajoz, or of John *Biclarensis;* as the Anonymous Chronicle of Córdoba, or of Toledo; as the Rimed Chronicle of the Last Kings of Toledo; and as the Anonymous Mozarab Chronicle of 754.[31] Very little can

---

[30] Ziegler, *loc.cit.*, n. 38; da Gama Barros, *op.cit.*, VII, 399-402, "Vicarius."

[31] The earliest ms of the Chronicle of 754, dating from the eighth or ninth century, lacks the beginning and end parts of the text as now known. Four folios of this early fragment are in the Biblioteca Nacional of Madrid and two folios are in the British Museum. The best edition of the Chronicle is by Theodore Mommsen, MGH, *Auct. antiq.*, XI, *Chronica minora*, II (Berlin, 1894), 323-369. The elaborate edition by Jules Tailhan, *Anonyme de Cordoue, Chronique rimée des derniers rois de Tolède et de la conquête de l'Espagne par les arabs* (Paris, 1885), contains numerous explanatory notes, indexes, and plates of the texts of the tenth-century ms of the Academia de la Historia in Madrid and the fourteenth-century ms of Arsenal. The Chronicle is also edited by Flórez, ES, VIII, Appendix II, and in *Revista mensual de filosofía, literatura y ciencias de Sevilla*, II (1870), passim. The edition in PL 96, 1245-1280, is based on that of Flórez. The numerous variant readings, lacunae, and interpolations are indicated in Mommsen's edition. Mommsen discusses the mss, *op.cit.*, 330f., the sources used by the author of the Chronicle, 324-326, and his chronology, 326f., criticizing the chronicler for errors of dates and facts. García-Villada,

be determined about the author except that he was a Spanish Christian, probably an ecclesiastic with an intimate knowledge of military and political events of his day.[32]

The Chronicle begins with a rather long account of the reign of the Emperor Heraclius (610-641) and his wars against the Persians and the Arabs. It takes up Spanish history from the reign of Sisebut in 612, repeating some of what Isidore reported at the end of his chronicles, and completes the history of the Visigothic kingdom to the fall of Rodrigo in 712. The chronicler records the history of the caliphate in the East from the prophet Mohammed to the first of the Hashemite Abbasids, Abu'l Abbas al-Saffah (750-754). The most important part of the Chronicle describes events in Córdoba and in several other parts of Spain during the period between the conquest of Spain by the Arabs in 712 and the landing in Spain of the first Umaiyad emir, Abd al-Rahman I, in 755. For the history of Spain under the Visigoths and under the Arabs the chronicler composed his own account from sources not otherwise known. For his account of the Byzantine emperors and the eastern caliphate he seems to have depended in part on another chronicle devoted to those two histories, the Byzantine-Arabic Continua-

op.cit., III, 32-38, discusses the Chronicle in detail. Cf. also Flórez, ES, II, Part I, pars. 71-98.

[32] Cf. Mommsen, *op.cit.*, 354, no. 76, where the chronicler refers to Arabic as "lingua eorum." Mommsen, 327ff., interprets the author's knowledge of Toledo and his interest in that see to preclude an author from Córdoba, which was in the hands of the Arabs. Gams, *op.cit.*, 345ff., holds that the author was a Nestorian from the East who entered Spain about 740 with Syrian forces; cf. also *ibid.*, 324-326. The attention the chronicler pays to the church of Toledo may indicate that he came from that city, but the greater attention he pays to Arab history in Córdoba indicates that he resided there. He seems to have been Spanish in any event, his expression of distress at the entry of the Syrians into Spain negating Gams' arguments. Gams argues at greater length his thesis of a strong influence of Nestorian Syrians on the intellectual life of Córdoba in the wake of the Arab conquest, *op.cit.*, 261-267. Evidences of Syrian influence in Latin works of the Mozarabs appear intermittently as late as 961 in the *calendarium* of Recemundus. Gams' thesis warrants greater consideration than it has received.

tion of Isidore up to 741, which neglects events in Spain.[33]

Theodore Mommsen, who has published both chronicles in parallel texts, regards the Chronicle of 741 as reliable but deals rather harshly with the Chronicle of 754.[34] It should be pointed out, however, that the Chronicle of 741 contains but eight dates (all in the Spanish Era)[35] and, for the rest,

[33] Cf. Mommsen, *op.cit.*, 323-359. Mommsen, *ibid.*, 323f., 329f., and 333, discusses the Chronicle of 741. Flórez published it in ES, VI, Appendix X, as the "Continuación del chronicón del Biclarense." For a comparative study of the Chronicles of 741 and 754, cf. César E. Dubler, "Sobre la crónica arábigo-bizantina de 741 y la influencia bizantina en la peninsula ibérica," *Al-Andalus*, XI (1946), 283-349. Dubler argues for a strong Byzantine influence on early Spanish historiography.

[34] Mommsen, *op.cit.*, 324-327.

[35] The Spanish Era is a system of chronology with its point of origin in the year 38, B.C., e.g., Era 792 being A.D. 754. Although Hydatius, a bishop in Galicia (427-468), may have used the Era for two entries in his chronicle (Mommsen, *op.cit.*, 6), the first historian to use the system extensively was Isidore of Seville. From as early as the third century, however, the term occurs in inscriptions; cf. Joaquín M. de Navascués, *La Era "... AS*," Vol. I of *Scripturae monumenta et studia* (Madrid, 1951)." José Vives, "über Ursprung und Verbreitung der spanischen Ära," *Historisches Jahrbuch*, 58 (1938), 97-108, shows that the term came into use in western Spain before it did in eastern Spain, where Roman dating was followed. Vives associates the official acceptance of the Era with the entry of the Visigoths into the Church, *ibid.*, 107. Cf. also J. Vives, *Inscripciones cristianas de la España romana y visigoda* (Barcelona, 1942), 177-185; T. Mommsen, "Aera," NA, 18 (1893), 271-273; and W. Kubitschek, "Aera," in Pauly-Wissowa, I, i (Stuttgart, 1893), 611-613 and 639f. Flórez, ES, II, Part I, has a fundamental but prolix study of the Era; cf. also Gaspar Ibañez de Segovia, *Obras chronológicas* (Valencia, 1744), who devotes 200 pages to a discussion of the Era. Isidore's explanation of the origin of the Era in his *Etymologiae*, V, xxxvi, 4, (PL 82, 222), that it derived from the institution of the Roman world and the universal tribute levied by Augustus beginning in 38, B.C., has frequently been disregarded in favor of the thesis that the Era originated in the conquest of Spain by the Romans in 38, B.C. Reginald Lane Poole, *Medieval Reckonings of Time* (London, 1918), 36-39, suggests that the origin of the Era was arrived at by computing backward from the Easter cycle used in Rome which began 1 January 298. The same date of origin would have been obtained by computing backward from the Cycle of Cyril of Alexandria

restricts its chronology to reporting the number of the By-zantine emperor in the line of imperial succession and the length of his reign, after the system used by Hydatius.[36] The Chronicle of 754, on the other hand, undertakes to integrate and reconcile dates in several chronological systems: the Spanish Era, the Arabic year of the Hegira, the year of the world,[37] and the year of the Lord—besides reporting the number of the emperor in the line of succession and the length of his reign. In pursuing this ambitious task the chronicler introduces a number of erroneous dates. His chronology, however, is not so bad as is generally assumed.[38]

Almost every date in the Chronicle is recorded in the same way: "Spanish Era, *n*th year of the Byzantine emperor's reign, Arab year of the Hegira, and *n*th year of the caliph's reign." In entries for the coronation date of Byzantine emperors the Arab date is not recorded. The Spanish Era, which the author always records first, appears to be his

and from the Cycle of Theophilus of Alexandria. In all three cases, Poole admits, the computation involves an error of one year. F. K. Ginzel, *Handbuch der mathematischen und technischen Chronologie* (3 vols.; Leipzig, 1906-1914), III, 175-178, discusses the Era, noting that it was used by Arabic writers in Spain, 175, and briefly con-sidering the etymological derivation of the word, 177. Ziegler, *Church and State*, 69, notes that the *capitula* of Visigothic codes were originally called *erae*. The Era continued to be used in Spain even after it was officially abandoned in A.D. 1384. Infrequently the Era has been used erroneously as the equivalent of A.D., as in the case of the martyrs of Cardena, ES, I, 37, where Era 872 is used for A.D. 872. Christian works from Córdoba in the ninth century give dates according to the Era. Albar and Eulogius, however, each use the year of the Lord once.

[36] Hydatius' chronicle is edited by Mommsen, *Chronica minora*, II, 1-36.

[37] The year of the Hegira, A.H., was instituted retroactively in A.D. 638 by the caliph Omar I. It began 16 July 622, the date of Moham-med's flight from Mecca. The year A.H. 136, during which the Chronicle of 754 was concluded, ran from 7 July 753 through 26 June 754. Many historians, from the time of the Jews, have sought to establish a chronology based on an Era beginning with Adam; cf. Louis de Mas-Latrie, *Trésor de chronologie d'histoire et de géographie* (Paris, 1889), 30ff.

[38] Cf. Mommsen, *op.cit.*, 326f.

native system of chronology. In the only place in the chronicle where the day of the month is given Roman chronology is followed, "Sunday, the nones of April."[39] The errors in the chronicler's dates derive from his erroneous computation of the year of the Hegira (which began 16 July 622) as Era 655/656 (A.D. 617/618). He obtained this result by subtracting 136 (A.H. then current) from 792 (Era then current) when he concluded his work sometime during A.D. 754 before 27 June. He used the figure 655/656 as a constant factor of conversion from the Era to the Arab year and vice versa, failing to note that 136 Arab years equal only 132 Julian years.

The chronicler's errors provide information about his sources. He must have used both Spanish and Arab sources. For events in Spanish history his date according to the Era is generally correct and his Arab date is wrong. For events in Arab history the Arab date is correct and the Era is wrong. An example will illustrate his method. He dates the second year of Othman's reign (A.D. 644-656) as Era 680 (A.D. 642) and A.H. 25 (A.D. 645/646). He dates the accession of Chindaswinth in A.D. 642 in the same way (Era 680 and A.H. 25).[40] Beginning with his account of the invasion of Spain in A.D. 711, however, the dates in the two systems begin to agree with each other. Although this agreement may result from the fact that over a short period the error is not noticeable, it is more likely that the agreement derives from the fact that for this period the author was composing his own account and knew both dates.

The year of the Lord appears only once, at the end of the Chronicle. The year of the world is used only to mark the terminal year of Byzantine reigns, and again at the end of the Chronicle. For the number of years from Adam to Christ the chronicler follows Julian of Toledo, whom he quotes twice, and adopts the figure 5200, passing over the figure 5196 arrived at by Eusebius of Caesarea, Isidore (to

[39] *Ibid.*, 366.
[40] *Ibid.*, 341, nos. 25 and 26.

whom he refers), and Jerome.[41] Unable to reconcile Isidore's year of the world, which he took over in the beginning of his Chronicle,[42] with that of Julian, he did violence to Byzantine chronology.

The chronicler had more than a passing interest in history, as is evidenced by his passion for intimate details, his unusual interest in chronology, his references to other historical writers (whom he may have known second-hand from Julian of Toledo), and his collection of material of all sorts for the history of late Visigothic and early Arab rule in Spain. Moreover, in three passages of the Chronicle he mentions another historical work written by him, an *epituma* dealing with the wars among the Arabs and Moors in Spain and Africa.[43] This work is not extant.

The Latin of the Chronicle is erratic with frequent ellipses, but the author follows a rather formalized literary style which appears to be based on parallel constructions. As a result of the parallelism rime frequently occurs at the end of clauses. Dozy, Tailhan, Gams, and Polheim consider the Chronicle to be written in rimed prose.[44] But the rime, although it appears to result from a deliberate literary device and seems not to be just an accident of the Latin language, is not very consistent and there are places where the author could have used it but did not. Polheim, who takes note of the inconsistency of the rime, discusses in the introduction to his work the influence of parallelism and antithesis on rimed prose and a number of irregularities which he would

[41] *Ibid.*, 367f. Cf. Julian of Toledo, *De comprobatione aetatis sextae*, Bk. III, par. 15, in *SS PP Toletanorum*, II, 129f.   (PL 96, 576). Julian quotes several authors, especially Eusebius.

[42] Mommsen, *op.cit.*, 478ff., and 334.

[43] *Ibid.*, 364, no. 120; 365, no. 125; 367, no. 136. Gams, *op.cit.*, 241, Tailhan, *op.cit.*, ix f., and García-Villada, *op.cit.*, 37, interpret these passages to refer to several works.

[44] Dozy, *Recherches*, I, 4; Tailhan, *op.cit.*, xvi f.; Gams, *op.cit.*, 241; Karl Polheim, *Die lateinische Reimprosa* (Berlin, 1925), 304ff. Cf. also Tailhan, "Les espagnols et les wisigoths avant l'invasion arabe," *Revue des questions historiques*, XXX (1881), 5-46, and *id.*, "La ruine de l'Espagne gothique," *ibid.*, XXXI (1882), 341-408.

admit in the rime. Nevertheless, it seems better to agree with Mommsen and deny that the work is written in rimed prose.[45] Much the same phenomenon may be noticed in many of the works written in Córdoba a century later during the period of the Christian martyrs. To a lesser extent it is also found in the narrative parts of chronicles written in the northern kingdom of Oviedo. Gams notes a similarity of style between the Chronicle of 754 and a vita of Ildefonsus by Cixila, metropolitan of Toledo, a similarity which may be ascribed, he notes, to the general style of the times.[46]

According to the Chronicle of 754 Rodrigo seized the rule of the Visigothic kingdom in 711 (Era 749, A.H. 92) upon the urging of the "senate" and ruled for one year. In 712 (Era 750, A.H. 93) he took an army and marched against a force of Arabs and Moors under Tarik which had been sent into Spain by Muza, the emir of Kairouan.[47] This force had been devastating the country for some time. In the battle which took place the army of the Visigoths fled and Rodrigo fell. The chronicler introduces here another instance of flight before the Arabs in the example of Sinderedus, the pious but imprudent bishop of Toledo, who, "a little after the invasion of the Arabs, became frightened, and, not as a shepherd but as a hireling, deserted the sheep of Christ against the decrees of the Fathers, and betook himself to *Romania,* his homeland."[48]

[45] Polheim, *op.cit.*, ix-xx; Mommsen, *op.cit.*, 326.

[46] Polheim, *op.cit.*, 360ff., credits Albar, Eulogius, and Esperaindeo with the use of rimed prose; cf. Traube, MGH, *Poetae latini aevi carolini,* III, i, 123, n. 4. Gams, *op.cit.*, 246f.

[47] Kairouan, the capital of Moslem North Africa and Spain, was built by the Arabs as a fort about a hundred miles south of Carthage shortly after they seized the area in A.D. 670; cf. G. Yver, "Al-Kaira-wan," EI, II, 646-649, and P. W. Ireland, "Qairwan," *Encyclopaedia Britannica,* XVIII, 806f.

[48] Mommsen, *op.cit.*, 352. Sinderedus signed the acts of a council in Rome in 721; cf. J. Mansi, *Sacrorum conciliorum nova et amplissima collectio,* XII (Florence, 1766), 265. The word *Romania* describes the world of the Latin speaking Roman empire, of Rome and Byzantium, contrasted with the world of the non-Latin speaking barbarians;

Following this the author tells of the invasion of the Arabs from Africa under Muza himself. This took place, according to the chronicler, in 711 (Era 749, A.H. 92), before the fall of Rodrigo. When Muza entered Spain the force under Tarik was already devastating the country, which was torn by internal disruption. Muza took Toledo and eventually Zaragoza, destroying and killing as he went. Some of the towns made peace, and some of the people fled to the mountains. The Arabs established their kingdom in the wealthy city of Córdoba. In 712 (Era 750, A.H. 94) after fifteen months in Spain Muza was recalled to Damascus by the caliph. He left his son "Abdelaziz" with certain Spanish lords and, taking with him enormous treasures in gold, silver, and jewels, "returned home and presented himself to King Walid in the last year of his reign."

In a passage marked by lacunae at beginning and end praise is accorded to Theodemirus, who slew many Arabs and who had, in the reigns of Egica and Witiza, defeated "Greeks" who landed on his shores. Theodemirus was famed even in the East among Christians. He was a lover of Holy Scripture, wonderfully eloquent, and staunch in battle. He visited the caliph in Damascus, who honored him for his wisdom and confirmed the treaty which Theodemirus had concluded with Abdelaziz.[49] The treaty was still in force at the time of writing in 754, none of the successors of the

cf. P. de Labriolle, *De la mort de Théodose à l'élection de Grégoire le Grand*, Vol. IV of *Histoire de l'église*, ed. Fliche and Martin (Paris, 1937), 355-367; and H. Leclercq, "Romani, Romania, Romanus," DACL, XIV, ii, 2507-2514. Sinceredus is also mentioned in a list of the metropolitans of Toledo given in ms Escorial d-I-l; cf. Guillermo Antolín, "El códice emilianense de la biblioteca de el Escorial," *La ciudad de Dois*, 74 (1907), 388. E. A. Lowe, *The Beneventan Script. A History of the South Italian Minuscule* (Oxford, 1914), 5, mentions a Spanish priest Diapertus in Monte Cassino about 720. Pérez de Urbel, *Los monjes españoles en la edad media* (2 vols.; Madrid, 1933-1934), I, 527, and II, 255f., discusses a St. Pirminio or Pimenio, an abbot who fled with his belongings from Spain in 711 to the Rhineland. Pirminio, who died in 753, founded several monasteries and left most of his library of fifty codices in Reichenau. Cf. LTK, VIII, 288f.

[49] Cf. index, "Theodemirus."

Arabs daring to break it. Athanaildus, noted for his riches and largess, succeeded Theodemirus. When Abulcathar came to Spain, the passage continues, for some reason he took vengeance upon Athanaildus and levied a fine of 27,000 solidi on him. But the army which had come to Spain with Baldj about 744 heard of this and paid the fine in three days, restoring Athanaildus to Abulcathar's favor with many gifts.[50] The alliance between Athanaildus (of Valencia) and the Syrians seems to appear in the war discussed below between the "Orientals" under Baldj and the "Occidentals" under the son of the slain governor of Córdoba.

Muza's son, Abdelaziz, succeeded his father in Spain. He married Rodrigo's queen, Egilo, and ruled for three years. He was assassinated for reportedly attempting to free himself from the Arab yoke and keep Spain for himself. His successor, Alaor (715-718), restored goods to the Christians so that they might be taxed.[51] He inflicted punishments on Moors wandering about Spain seeking hidden treasures. At the beginning of 720, according to the chronicler, an eclipse of the sun occurred. Under Zama, Alaor's successor, from 718 to 721, the Arabs confiscated for the treasury part of property which had hitherto been left intact. At this time the chronicler singles out Fredoarius, bishop of Guadix, Urbanus, *katedralis veteranus melodicus* of Toledo, and Evantius, archdeacon of Toledo, as pillars of the Church for their learning and sanctity.[52]

Ambiza, who ruled Spain from 721 to 725, doubled the taxes for the Christians to support his wars against the Franks. In what may be an interpolation it is stated that at this time the Jews were seduced by one of their own

[50] Mommsen, *op.cit.*, 354, "quo auditu exercitus, qui cum duce Belgi advenerunt, sub spatio fere trium dierum omnia pariant et citius ad Alozzam cognomento Abulcatar gratia revocant, diversisque munificationibus remunerando sublimunt."

[51] *Ibid.*, 356, "resculas pacificas Christianis ob vectigalia thesauris publicis inferenda instaurat."

[52] *Ibid.*, 358. A treatise by Evantius on ecclesiastical discipline is discussed below. Cf. Rodrigo Jiménez de Rada, *Historia arabum*, xi, in *SS PP Toletanorum*, III, 253.

number, the Antiphrasis[53] Serenus, who proclaimed himself
to be the Messias ready to lead them to the promised land.
On his instructions the Jews disposed of everything they
possessed and were left without anything. When Ambiza
heard of this he confiscated all the possessions they had disposed of and, calling Serenus to appear before him, told him
that if he were the Messias he should seek to do the things
of God.[54]   Ambiza died as he was preparing an expedition
against the Franks, but appointed Hodera "consul of the
country" and leader of the army.[55]

Ambiza was succeeded in 725 by the "Saracen" Iaie, who
took many things away from the Saracens and Moors which
they had stolen and restored many things to the Christians.
Under the year 728 or 729 is found the account of a punishment meted out to an Arab official who was captured after
an overthrow of the government. This punishment is almost
the same as that administered to the rebel Argemirus by
King Reccared (586-601) and to the Christian John in 851
at the beginning of the Christian martyr movement. After
he had been beaten his head was shaved, and, loaded with
chains, with his hands tied behind his back, he was paraded
through the streets seated backward on an ass.[56]

[53] Antiphrasis, employed by several Mozarab writers, is the use of
words ironically in a sense opposite to the proper meaning.

[54] Mommsen, *op.cit.*, 359, n. 1.   Cagigas, *op.cit.*, I, 84, interprets
Ambiza's action as a dispossession of the Jews. Salo Wittmayer Baron,
A Social and Religious History of the Jews (3 vols.; New York, 1937),
II, 81, says that the messianic movement of Serenus reflected the dis-
appointment of Spanish Jewry in their hopes of relief at the hands of
the Moslem invaders from the desperate lives they led under the last
Visigothic kings. Tailhan, *Chronique rimée*, 34, n. 4, would identify
Serenus with a Syrus mentioned by the Byzantine historian Theophanes as a false Messias in the year 713; cf. *Theophanis chrono-
graphia*, ed. C. de Boor (2 vols.; Leipzig, 1883-1885), I, 401, and II,
260.

[55] "Consul patriae et princeps exercitus." R. Aigrain, "L'Espagne
chrétienne," *Gregoire le grand*, Vol. V of *Histoire de l'Eglise*, 269, says
that Ambiza (Anbasa) was killed in a raid along the Rhone.

[56] *Chronica* of John *Biclarensis*, Mommsen, *op.cit.*, 219f., and Eulogius, *Memoriale sanctorum*, I, 9.

The author gives an account of a rebellion of the Moors in Spain against their Arab ruler Abdarrahman in 731 or 732 because of the oppression of their fellow Moors in Africa under the Arabs. The leader of the Moors in Spain, Munnuz, a formidable warrior, made peace with the Franks, receiving in marriage the daughter of Odo (king, or duke, of Aquitaine), and then prepared to overthrow the Saracens in Spain. Abdarrahman, however, marched against Munnuz and besieged him in Cerdagne, where Munnuz slaughtered many Christians, including the bishop, Anambadi, by fire and the sword.[57] Munnuz fled from the besieged city, but, delaying in order to save his Frankish princess from the Arabs, he allowed his own escape to be cut off and was trapped among rocks, from which he threw himself to his death. The daughter of Odo was captured and sent across the seas *honorifice* to the caliph. Finding himself master of the country, Abdarrahman entered Aquitaine and defeated Odo north of the Garonne and the Dordogne. The Arabs then penetrated to Tours, where they fought the "consulem Francie interioris Austrie nomine Carrullum," i.e., Charles Martel, in a fierce battle, which, according to the chronicler, lasted for seven days. At last, the Franks, holding as solid as a wall and as firm as a cordon of ice, slew the Arabs and succeeded in killing their king, Abdarrahman. The Arabs fled silently and in close order during the night. In the morning the "Europeans" to their surprise found the Saracen camp abandoned, but, fearing an ambush, did not pursue the enemy. After taking and dividing the spoils of the camp, they returned to their homes. The battle of Tours is described in the Chronicle of 754 with a freshness of detail not found in other accounts of that battle.

Under Abdelmelec, "of a noble family," who came to rule in 734, Spain fell into a miserable and hopeless state, chiefly because of the corruption of judges. Upon orders from the emir of Kairouan, Abdelmelec attempted to conquer the

---

[57] *Cerritania* is not found in any of the early lists of Spanish sees. Aigrain, *op.cit.*, 271, thinks that Anambadi may have been bishop of Gerona.

bands of Christians in the Pyrenees, but met with defeat. He was replaced in 737 by the powerful Aucupa, who put him in bonds and condemned the judges appointed by him. Aucupa initiated a legal reform, expanding the processes of the law, ordering a census of the people, and exacting taxes strictly. He exiled the corrupt and the undesirable and ordered that no one was to be condemned except under his own law. He set out on an expedition against the Franks and had proceeded as far as Zaragoza when a rebellion of Moors broke out in Africa. Abandoning his campaign, he hastened to the assistance of the Arabs in Africa, where, it appears, he succeeded in putting down the rebellion of *contradictores, vifarii, mali macinatores,* and *heretici* "which they call *Arures.*"[58] Shortly after this, in 742, Aucupa restored the rule of Córdoba to Abdelmelec. At this point the author again pauses to praise Urbanus and Evantius of the cathedral of Toledo and to commemorate their deaths.

In the same year another great rebellion of the Moors broke out in Africa, and an Arab army sent from Syria to repress them met with a crushing defeat. The Moors in Spain rose up to subject Abdelmelec to themselves and to prevent the remnants of the defeated Syrian Arabs from crossing over to Spain from Africa. Abdelmelec defeated the Spanish Moors but afterwards lost his kingdom to the Syrian Arabs under Baldj,[59] after he had belatedly and reluctantly admitted them to Spain. Baldj and the Syrians resented the hardships they had undergone in Africa while waiting for Abdelmelec to transport them to Spain. In a rare injection of his personal feelings into his account, the chronicler expresses distress at the entry of Baldj and the Syrians into Spain. The seizure of power by Baldj was accompanied by a general war, between the "Orientals" under him and the "Occidentals" under Humeia, the son of Abdelmelec. The

---

[58] Haruriya is an early name for the Kharidjites, q.v., index.

[59] For Baldj cf. M. Schmitz-(A. Huici-Miranda), "Baldj b. Bishr," EI, I, 990f.; A. Lambert, "Balech ben Baxir el Coxairi," DHGE, VI, 379; *id.,* "Assamah ben Malik," DHGE, IV, 1081-1083; *id.,* "Astorga," *ibid.,* 1209f.

"Orientals," it would appear, came from the eastern part of Spain (Valencia) and the "Occidentals," from Betica (Córdoba). This is the war about which the author of the Chronicle wrote another work, or *epituma*. The war was brought to an end with the arrival of Abulcathar in 744 on orders from the emir of Kairouan. But within two years he, too, was overthrown by Toaba, who ruled for a year, until he died a natural death.

At this point a note which may be an interpolation is introduced in memory of Cixila, metropolitan of Toledo, famed for his holiness and the restoration of churches, "most firm in faith, hope, and charity." On one occasion Cixila delivered a man seduced by the Sabellian heresy from possession by the devil before the whole congregation of the church. After nine years in the performance of his apostolic duties Cixila died in grace. Complete information about Cixila and the man possessed by the devil cannot be had due to lacunae in the text, but it appears that Cixila had devoted himself to the service of God from early youth, had been in the church of Toledo from the time of the Arab invasion, and was consecrated metropolitan between 744 and 746. This would place the death of Cixila about 754, when the Chronicle was being completed. According to the list of metropolitans of Toledo in ms Escorial d-I-1, Sinderedus was succeeded in the see of Toledo by Sunieredus, Concordius, Cixila, Elipandus, Gumersindus, Wistremirus, Boniti, and John.[60]

After the rule of the usurper Toaba the "senate" of the palace acclaimed Iuzzif, an aged elder, as ruler of the country. It appears that Iuzzif held a position of greater power, with greater independence of the emir of Kairouan, than did any of the previous governors of Spain. This appears also to have been true of Abdelaziz, Muza's son, who was assassinated because of his independence of the caliph of Damascus.[61]

---

[60] Mommsen, *op.cit.*, 365, n. 1; cf. Antolín, *op.cit.*, 388.

[61] For a discussion of the authority of the governors of Spain at this time, cf. Salvador Vila, "El nombramiento de los walies de al-Andalus," *Al-Andalus*, IV (1936), 215-220. Vila concludes that for the most part

It is noteworthy that Iuzzif was acclaimed king by the "senate" of Córdoba. The last of the Visigothic rulers, Rodrigo, had been urged to take power by the "senate".[62] Eulogius, whom Albar says was born of senatorial nobility, frequently mentions the *consules* of the government. Three centuries later, after the end of the Umaiyad caliphate in Córdoba, the "senate" appears to have assumed responsibility for the executive authority.[63] Iuzzif ordered a new census because of the increase in population. He also ordered that the names of many Christians who had been slain be removed from the public list, even though they were still delinquent in taxes. During his reign, on Sunday, 5 April 750, from six o'clock until almost nine o'clock in the morning, all the citizens of Córdoba witnessed the appearance of three suns in the heavens, "preceded by a fiery emerald sickle."[64] This phenomenon was followed by an intolerable drought over all of Spain, which the author looks upon as a punishment of God. The author mentions a Peter, deacon of Toledo, famous throughout Spain at this time for his musical talent and knowledge of Scripture. Peter compiled a book from the Fathers and other writers for the people of Seville, who were celebrating Easter at the wrong time.[65]

After telling of the end of Marwan II, the last Umaiyad ruler in Damascus, the author concludes his chronicle in 754 in the reign of Iuzzif with a discussion of the date of the birth of Christ, which he places in the year 5200 of the world. Others would date the Nativity in the year 5196, he states, quoting from Julian of Toledo and referring to Eusebius of Caesarea and Isidore directly, and indirectly to Tertullian and Jerome. Four years is not an error of great consequence, he points out, when it is so easy to err in going

the emir of Kairouan confirmed as governors leaders chosen and supported by local groups in Spain.

[62] Mommsen, *op.cit.*, 366 and 352.

[63] Dozy, *Histoire*, III, 4f.

[64] Mommsen, *op.cit.*, 366.

[65] Peter may have been the person who wrote a letter discussed below to Felix, bishop of Córdoba, regarding an improper observance of Jewish fasts by Christians.

from the regnal years of one ruler to those of the next. There is no apparent reason why the chronicler concluded his Chronicle in 754, except that he was bringing it up to date.

Although Eulogius and Albar seem to have known works which were related to the Chronicle of 754 in some way, and although later Arabic chroniclers of Spain and Latin chroniclers of the Asturias may have known the Chronicle, it does not seem to have been used as the basis for an historical account before the *Historia arabum* of Rodrigo Jiménez de Rada,[66] archbishop of Toledo (1210-1247). Lucas of Tuy did not know it. In 1586 Ambrosio de Morales, referring to the Chronicle as that of Isidore of Beja, speaks as if he had studied the work directly.[67] But it seems unlikely that he did. Morales takes information from Jiménez de Rada which derives from the Chronicle of 754, without noting its early origin. He does not report much information from the Chronicle which would have been of interest to him with his passion for amassing data. Since Morales' time the Chronicle has been condemned by a number of historians because of its difficult language and its chronological errors. Others have defended it because of its unique value as a contemporary source from the early eighth century in Spain, the Chronicle of 741 containing only two brief entries concerning Spanish history during this time. The impartiality of the chronicler as an observer has been noted.[68] He praises Arabs and Christians alike, and rarely voices disapproval of people or events. A fair share of the Chronicle deals with Christians under Arab rule in Spain, most of the information about them being concerned with additional taxes levied upon them by certain rulers and the restitution of their goods by other rulers. There are a number of reports about illustrious churchmen of the times, especially of the see of

---

[66] The *Historia Arabum* has been edited in *SS PP Toletanorum*, III, 243-282.

[67] Morales, *Corónica general*, III, Bk. XII, xl, 11, and chaps. ff.; also Bk. XIII, vii.

[68] H. Leclercq, *L'Espagne chrétienne* (Paris, 1906), 21f., and Tailhan, *Chronique rimée*, x.

Toledo. Dozy, in using the work to supplement Arabic
accounts, neglected much of the information about Christians.[69]

In spite of inaccuracies, interpolations, and faulty Latin
the Chronicle is of great importance for the history of Spain
during the first fifty years of the eighth century. For these
years, during which the author appears to have lived, the
Chronicle contains much information for which it is the only
contemporary source. The chronicler says nothing of persecution of the Christians by the Moslems. Neither does he
speak of apostasy by Christians or proselytizing by the Moslems. The distresses he describes resulted from war and
invasion. In addition to civil war and maraudings, the
chronicler indicates that the Spanish at this time suffered
from excessive and arbitrary taxation and, intermittently,
from the maladministration of justice. Whether or not the
Moslems discouraged conversions to Islam so that they would
obtain a maximum income from discriminating taxation, as
is sometimes said,[70] cannot be determined from the Chronicle. In the ninth century they did seek conversions to
Islam.

Dozy's description of the allotment of land in Spain after
the conquest,[71] which has been repeated by a number of
writers since, derives from the general practice in Moslem
conquests rather than from Spanish sources during this time.
According to Dozy, the land of districts which were conquered, plus the lands of the Church and of those nobles who
had fled to the North, were divided among the conquerors.
The serfs remained on the land and paid four-fifths of the
harvest to the Mohammedan lords. The serfs on state lands,
which consisted of one-fifth of the conquered lands, paid only
one-third of their harvests. Taxes on state lands at first
went to the treasury but later to Arabs and Syrians who

[69] Dozy, *Histoire*, Bk. I, x-xii; *id.*, *Recherches*, I, 2-14.

[70] Dozy, *Histoire*, Bk. I, x (p. 140f.), and Bk. II, ii (p. 277);
Cagigas, *Los mozárabes*, I, 55; F. R. Franke, "Die freiwilligen Märtyrer," 4; E. Amann, *L'époque carolingienne*, Vol. VI of *Histoire de
l'église*, 130.

[71] Dozy, *Histoire*, Bk. II, ii (275-277).

received the lands as fiefs. Other Christians, says Dozy, depended on treaties. According to Isidro de las Cagigas,[72] Moslem authority in Spain was rooted in these contractual treaties, the terms of most of which are not known. He points out that the only such treaty which is extant, that beween Theodemirus and Abdelaziz, is very moderate in its terms and provides for the protection of individuals and the continuation of the administrative system, Christians coming under the protection of Moslem law. Two kinds of tribute (also described by Dozy) were paid: a personal head tax in specie at the end of each lunar month (except for women, children, men devoted to prayer if poor, the useless, the blind and the sick if poor, beggars, and slaves); and a land tax on the products of the fields. Usually the latter tax was about twenty per cent, depending on the fertility of the soil. In Spain, Cagigas thinks, this tax was about ten per cent, less than was paid to the Visigothic kings. The Moslems also levied extraordinary taxes, such as those for their armies. In the ninth century Eulogius and Leovigildus, both members of the clergy, complain of the head tax. A land tax as such is not mentioned in the Latin sources, but a complaint is made for having to pay for the use of space in the public market.[73]

Another work from this time is the vita of St. Ildefonsus, metropolitan of Toledo (657-667), written by Cixila, bishop of the same see.[74] According to the Chronicle of 754, Cixila was metropolitan of Toledo for nine years and died about 754. The vita of Ildefonsus is important because it bears testimony to the status of the Christian cult and the devotion to Ildefonsus in Toledo during Moslem rule. Cixila heard the account of Ildefonsus from Urbanus and Evantius, who died in 742, according to the Chronicle of 754. The vita begins with the early life of Ildefonsus and tells how he

---

[72] Cagigas, *op.cit.*, I, 61-66.

[73] *Indiculus luminosus*, 25.

[74] The chief ms for Cixila's work is the tenth-century *Codex Aemilianensis*, ms Escorial d-I-1, but the vita is a later insertion at the end of the codex. The text has been edited by Flórez, ES, V, Appendix VIII, and in *SS PP Toletanorum*, I, 96-99.

became bishop of Toledo when Eugene died, but it does not account for Ildefonsus' death. Most of the work is devoted to the narration of miraculous appearances of the Blessed Virgin and St. Leocadia to Ildefonsus, whose life was one of exemplary chastity and devotion to the Blessed Virgin. The author apologizes for not writing everything that Urbanus and Evantius told about Ildefonsus, but, he explains, it would be too long.   He makes several other parenthetical remarks about his own day: that the church of SS Cosmas and Damian, over which Ildefonsus once presided, is situated in a suburb of Toledo; that several *missae* composed by Ildefonsus are to follow the text of the vita;[75] that the teachings of Ildefonsus still flourish in the church; and a note that the only bishop to dare to sit in the cathedra of the bishop of Toledo after the Blessed Virgin appeared seated there to Ildefonsus was Sisebert, who immediately lost his see and was exiled.[76]

[75] These *missae* are not in the mss. *Missae* are prayers in the Mozarabic liturgy which initiate the Mass of the faithful after the Mass of the catechumens has been completed. A *missa* is ordinarily a supplication to the Father or the Son, a series of pious exclamations, or a lyric chant in honor of the mystery or martyr of the feast. Cf. Férotin, *Le liber mozarabicus sacramentorum et les manuscrits mozarabes*, Vol. VI of *Monumenta ecclesiae liturgica* (Paris, 1912), xx and xxxviii f. Cf. also F. Cabrol, "Mozarabe (Messe)," DTC, X, ii, 2528, and H. Leclercq, "Messe," DACL, XI, i, 679. The *missae* of Ildefonsus in honor of the Blessed Virgin Mary are believed to be his treatise *De virginitate perpetua sanctae Mariae* (SS PP *Toletanorum*, I, 107-161 and 386-389; PL 96, 53-110 and 280-283). Cf. J. F. Rivera, "San Ildefonso de Toledo, autor de un sermón de filiación dudosa," *Revista española de teología*, VI (1946), 573-588; Cabrol, "Mozarabe (La liturgie)," DACL, XII, i, 400 and 440f.; Férotin, *op.cit.*, xvi and 754ff.; Sister Athanasius Braegelmann, *The Life and Writings of St. Ildefonsus of Toledo* (Washington, 1942), 154-156; Charles Lynch, *Saint Braulio, Bishop of Saragossa (631-651). His Life and Writings* (Washington, 1938), 117ff. In 794 the bishops of Germany, Gaul, and Aquitaine in a letter to the bishops of Spain charged Ildefonsus with having written Mass prayers tainted with the heresy of Adoptionism; cf. index, "Council of Frankfort."

[76] Rodrigo Jiménez de Rada, *De rebus Hispaniae*, III, xix, says that Urbanus succeeded Sinderedus, despite the intervention of Oppas. Cf. Aigrain, *op.cit.*, 270, and Antolín, *op.cit.*, 388.

CHAPTER II
EARLY PROBLEMS OF DISCIPLINE AND HERESY

The history of Spain in the latter half of the eighth century is known, in Latin works, almost exclusively from letters and treatises describing religious controversies about ecclesiastical discipline and dogma. The continual concern with doctrinal matters and the consuming interest in Holy Scripture follow in the Visigothic tradition. Even the Chronicle of 754, devoted principally to non-Christian secular history, interrupts its account periodically to commemorate men and events of religious significance. Besides several exemplary churchmen it mentions three instances of religious heterodoxy in Spain: the Jew Serenus who claimed to be the Messias in 721, the Sabellian heretic delivered from a devil by Cixila of Toledo, and the celebration of Easter at the wrong time by the people of Seville in 750. The second half of the century is marked by religious controversies which are in general of a more serious nature: Migetianism, disciplinary errors condemned by Pope Adrian I, and Adoptionism. Since the dates of most of these sources are not known, the chronological sequence of events has to be established by conjecture.

The Latin literature of Spain in the late eighth century is more closely connected to the martyrs of Córdoba in the ninth century than might be thought. Although written in Toledo and in the Asturias, it formed part of the tradition of the Christians of Córdoba, who seem to have maintained ties with the rest of Spain throughout the eighth and ninth centuries—even during the time of persecution when King Mohammed I (852-886) sought to exclude Christians from his realm. The intellectual milieu seen in the dispute between Elipandus of Toledo and Beatus of Liébana reappears in the works of Albar and Samson. A study of Mozarab culture should include a survey of the sources of the late eighth century.

The earliest known text dealing with a disciplinary matter was written before the middle of the century. Cardinal Sáenz de Aguirre without identifying the manuscript of origin edited the text of a letter[1] which he shows to have been written by Evantius, archdeacon of Toledo, about 730. Evantius wrote the letter against certain Christians of Zaragoza who were maintaining that anyone who consumed the blood of animals was unclean. Such people, charges Evantius, follow the letter of the law which kills and disregard the spirit which quickens. Why do they not follow other customs of the Jews? he asks, enumerating several. Quoting a number of passages from Holy Scripture, Evantius criticizes the Christians for abstaining from strangled animals and blood but failing to follow the words of St. Paul and observe penances. Some years later Pope Adrian I (776-795) criticized certain Christians in Spain for the same belief.

Two passages of text from a letter (or two letters) taken from an eleventh-century manuscript of the monastery of Silos[2] describe a disciplinary matter in Córdoba in 764 concerning the observance of a fast according to the Jewish custom. In that year, says one of the texts, Holy Thursday and the Pasch of the Hebrews fell on 22 March, "the beginning of the year according to the Egyptians, who are renowned above everyone in computations." Moreover, the proclamation of the jubilee year and the observance of the new moon according to the Jews fell on the Kalends of September.[3] As a result, some Christians wished to celebrate a fast jointly with the Jews on Monday, 10 September 764, the Day of the Atonement, against the Christian regulations, which called for "litanies" on Wednesday, Thursday, and Fri-

---

[1] José Sáenz de Aguirre, *Collectio maxima conciliorum omnium Hispaniae et novi orbis...* (4 vols.; Rome, 1693-1694), III, 87; 2d ed. (6 vols.; Rome, 1753-1755), IV, 88ff.; and PL 88, 717-722. Flórez mentions the text, ES, V, Tr. 5, v, 35, but says nothing about the ms.

[2] G. Morin, "Un évêque de Cordoue inconnu et deux opuscules inédits de l'an 764," *Revue bénédictine*, XV (1898), 289-295.

[3] According to Louis de Mas-Latrie, *Trésor de chronologie d'histoire et de géographie* (Paris, 1889), 119 and 171, the new moon began on 2 September 764.

day.[4] What was more important, these Christians looked down upon Christians who would not go along with them in the extraordinary fast. Apropos of the matter, Bishop Felix of Córdoba wrote to a certain Peter asking for his opinion. Peter replied expressing surprise that bishops should have any doubts about the matter and condemning those who sought to follow the Judaic law. Peter may have been the deacon of Toledo mentioned in the Chronicle of 754 as the compiler of a work, no longer extant, for the people of Seville, who were celebrating Easter at the wrong time.

Peter says that Christians under threat of canonical sentence cannot participate in the Jewish synagogue nor observe any of the Jewish feasts or fasts. How can they observe one of their ceremonies and not all? he asks. Moses did not keep the forty-day fast at the same time as do Christians. For, says Peter, Moses made Pentecost (*quinquagesimarum dies*), which is a day of rejoicing for Christians, a day of fasting to commemorate his speaking with God. But Christians terminate their penance at Easter. The Jews had another day of fast after Pentecost, but Christians, participating in the sorrow of the apostles because the Lord was taken away from them at His Ascension, "make a common plaint of longing" before Pentecost.[5] The Jews fast on the Day of the Atonement before the Feast of the Tabernacles (15-21 September 764), but Christians observe a three-day devotion after this feast,[6] venerating neither the seventh day nor the

---

[4] Cf. F. Cabrol, "Litanies," DACL, IX, ii, 1540-1571.

[5] Cf. H. Leclercq, "Pentecôte," DACL, XIV, i, 260-274, and Charles L. Souvay, "Pentecost," *Catholic Encyclopedia*, XI, 661. In early times some Christians sought to terminate the Pentecostal period on Ascension Thursday, forty days after Easter, rather than fifty days after Easter to correspond with the forty-day Lent before Easter. According to a tradition of the Jews, Pentecost commemorates Moses speaking with the Lord on Mount Sinai, but it was a day of festivity, not of fasting.

[6] The three days are probably the Ember Days, celebrated after Pentecost, after 14 September, after 13 December, and during Lent. They were not fixed until the time of Gregory VII (1073-1085) and are supposed to have been adopted in Spain in the eleventh century. Cf. H. Leclercq, "Quatre-temps," DACL, XIV, ii, 2014-2017; A. Molien,

seventh month (Tishri). Finally, Peter says, the Jews fast on the Kalends of November.[7] But Christians will not commemorate the pagan Kalends, observing instead three days of prayer afterwards if there is no feast day.

Germain Morin, the editor of the texts, suggests that the shorter text is a fragment of the letter of Bishop Felix. This fragment, however, has no signs of being an inquiry and is as decided in its denunciation of the Judaizing Christians as is Peter. It seems that it can as easily be part of Peter's letter. Both texts are of interest because of bad Latin and many unusual words. A good bit of the vocabulary in the two texts appears again in the literature written in Córdoba in the middle of the ninth century.

The little known exchange of letters between Ascaricus and Tusaredus exists almost in a vacuum.[8] Ascaricus, according to his own letter, was a bishop residing in the Asturias. He is probably the same person whom Pope Adrian criticized as being, together with Elipandus of Toledo, an Adoptionist, and whom Elipandus in a letter to an Abbot Fidelis mentions with favor. Ascaricus also composed for Tusaredus an acrostic epitaph formed with excerpts of the last verses of the *Hamartigenia* of Prudentius.[9] Tusaredus is known only from this exchange of letters and his epitaph. Although he appears here as the mentor of Bishop Ascaricus, he has no title other than "servant of God." The minor errors described in the two letters do not seem to derive from other

"Quatre-temps," DTC, XIII, ii, 1447-1455; Francis Mershman, "Ember-days," *Catholic Encyclopedia*, V, 399.

[7] Elipandus of Toledo mentions a fast on the Kalends of November; cf. infra, 81.

[8] These two letters were discovered by G. Heine in ms Escorial J-I-3, a codex dated in 1047 which formerly belonged to the church of Zaragoza. They are published after Heine's edition in PL 99, 1231-1240. For Ascaricus cf. A. Ferrua, "Ascarico," *Enciclopedia cattolica*, II, 82; A. Lambert, "Ascaric," DHGE, IV, 881-884; R. Ceillier, *Histoire générale des auteurs sacrés et ecclésiastiques*, new ed. (Paris, 1858-1869), XII, 151f.

[9] The acrostic is in De Rossi, *Inscriptiones Christianae urbis Romae*, II, ii (Rome, 1888), 295, and in the article by H. Leclercq, "Acrostiche," DACL, I, i, 361.

known errors of this time, nor do they seem to have precipitated events of historical importance. For themselves, however, they are of interest because they illustrate the unusual interest in Holy Scripture and spiritual affairs characteristic of the literature of Spain at this time. The letters, which are not dated, provide little information about the surroundings of Ascaricus and Tusaredus. The Latin of Ascaricus is particularly bad, full of errors and ellipses, but that of Tusaredus is about normal for the times.

First Ascaricus offers sympathy to Tusaredus for the tribulations suffered by him as a result of the schismatic errors which have sprung up "from here in the Asturias to the coast." One of the errors of concern to Ascaricus was the contention that the bodies of the sleeping saints which arose after the death of Christ were corrupted and not glorified. The other error was the contention that the Blessed Virgin died on earth and that her body is still in the sepulcher. Admitting that Tusaredus is beset with difficulties of his own, Ascaricus entreats him nevertheless to come to his assistance against the "barking dogs" and "the infidels who are in Judaea."

Tusaredus in his reply states that he has had to restrict his research to Holy Scripture and Gregory the Great because of a shortage of codices. He arranges his answer systematically in eleven points supported with quotations from Scripture, liturgical prayers, and several Fathers, including a long passage from the *Etymologiae* of Isidore. Most of his quotations come from Gregory. The sketchiness of his whole treatment of the questions may indicate that many of his quotations from the Fathers are second-hand. The bodies of the saints which Christ raised from limbo were glorious, i.e., spiritual, he says, and they went to the heavenly Jerusalem not the earthly one. With regard to the Assumption of the Blessed Virgin, Tusaredus holds the less usual opinion that there is no tradition that she suffered passion or death of any kind.[10] The Scriptural reference to the

---

[10] Cf. Martin Jugie, *La mort et l'assomption de la sainte Vierge*, Vol. 114 of *Studi e Teste* (Vatican, 1944), 274f. and 510; Charles Balić,

sword which pierced her heart, he notes, should not be taken literally.

Except for a passing reference to Migetius in a letter of Pope Adrian to the bishops of Spain, all that is known of that heretical figure is learned from two letters of Elipandus, bishop of Toledo and the foremost representative of Adoptionism. Elipandus wrote one of the letters[11] against Migetius during the period when the influence of the latter was still strong. Its date is not known. In the other letter,[12] written in the name of the bishops of Spain to the bishops of Gaul shortly before 794, Elipandus compares Migetius with Beatus of Liébana, whom he regards as his archenemy. Since the letter of Elipandus against Migetius does not contain an explicit statement of Adoptionism but only the germs of the heresy, it is likely that Elipandus wrote this letter before Pope Adrian wrote his letter to the bishops of Spain openly charging Elipandus and Ascaricus with Adoptionism. Migetius flourished in the province of Seville, where it seems he was proclaimed anathema in a council presided over by Elipandus. In both his letters Elipandus colors his description of Migetius with a language of unseemly vituperation characteristic of all his writings, a language which Paul Albar and the Abbot Samson of Córdoba use in their writings a few generations later.

The main error for which Elipandus attacks Migetius is his heretical teaching about the Trinity. According to Elipandus, Migetius maintained that there were three corporeal persons in the Divinity, that the person of the Father is *specialiter* David, that the person of the Son of God is the second person in the Trinity, which was assumed from the Virgin *(Et iterum [de] persona Filii Dei asseris, quod ea sit*

Testimonia de assumptione Beatae Virginis Mariae ex omnibus saeculis (2 vols.; Rome, 1948-1950), I, 178-180.

[11] The letter against Migetius was discovered in 1727 in a ms of Toledo. Flórez edited the text from a copy furnished him, ES, V, Appendix X.

[12] This letter, from the same ms of Toledo, has been edited by Werminghoff in the MGH, *Concilia*, II, *Concilia aevi carolini*, I, i (Hanover, 1906), 111-119.

secunda in Trinitatis persona, quae assumpta est de Virgine), and that the third person, the Holy Spirit, is the Apostle Paul.[13] Elipandus condemns Migetius for teaching that if priests are holy they cannot call themselves sinners, and if they are sinners they cannot perform their ministry.[14] At the same time he denies Migetius' claim to be holy and free from sin himself. He condemns Migetius' assertion that the food of infidels pollutes the minds of the faithful and his practice of not eating with those whom Migetius calls "sinners." He denies Migetius' contention that "the power of God is in Rome alone, where Christ dwells," and that Rome is the new Jerusalem coming down from heaven. Each of these teachings Elipandus refutes at some length with quotations from Scripture and the Fathers.[15]

In the very beginning of his letter against Migetius, Elipandus applies invective. "We have received your letter to be read, written like a treatise, sprung from the horrid tomb of your heart, given forth from the ashes of the sepulcher of your breast, written not in the tone of an inquirer but with the authority of a teacher. We have seen, I say, we have seen and laughed at the fatuousness and vapid madness of your heart. We have seen the ignorance of your mind and regard it as ridiculous." He continues with invective, abandoning it only to attack the teachings of Migetius.

Elipandus attacks Migetius with a quotation from Ephraem of Syria which Samson uses later in his *Apologeticus*: "Behold, he who came to be instructed wishes to teach before he learns. Before he has learned fundamentals he wishes to promulgate the law, and before he learns the order of syllables he begins to philosophize."[16] Gams regards this quotation, which he notes is the first reference to Ephraem in the literature of Spain, as an indication that Nestorian Syri-

---

[13] Elipandus' Letter against Migetius, par. 3.

[14] It was presumably this teaching of Migetius that caused Albar to refer to Bishop Saul as a Migetian; cf. Letter XII of the Albar correspondence, 2.

[15] *Ibid.*, pars. 10-13.

[16] *Ibid.*, par. 2; cf. Samson's *Apologeticus*, II, vii, 2.

ans exerted a strong influence on Spanish intellectual life after the Arab conquest.[17] Although Samson's quotation differs from that of Elipandus in the Latin text, the difference can be ascribed to translation. Ephraem, however, was known and quoted by Jerome, an author widely read in Spain.

The other letter, ascribed to Elipandus, from the bishops of Spain to the bishops of Gaul, provides additional information about Migetius. Elipandus says that Migetius had himself stigmatized on the head by a medical doctor and thought himself to be like Christ, choosing for himself twelve apostles. Reportedly Migetius said to a certain woman standing before him and weeping over him, "Amen, Amen, I say to thee: this day thou shalt be with me in paradise" (Lk. 23:43). Once when Migetius was intoxicated, Elipandus charges, he ordained a certain Rufinus as abbot for animals, saying to him three times, "Simon Peter, lovest thou me? Feed my sheep" (Jn. 21:17). Elipandus also says that Migetius when he was about to die predicted that he would arise on the third day.[18] In a letter to the Abbot Fidelis, discussed below, Elipandus adds that Migetius was condemned in Seville for, among other errors, the celebration of Easter at the wrong time.

In the period 853-859 Bishop Saul of Córdoba wrote a letter to Paul Albar in which he asks Albar who it is that Albar calls *Migentiani*. Associated with the Albar-Saul correspondence perhaps is a letter of vague meaning written by an unknown bishop. The letter (Letter X) discusses at length the validity of sacraments administered by priests

[17] Gams, *Kirchengeschichte*, II, ii, 265. Gams also points out that Ephraem is one of the Fathers quoted in the *Liber scintillarum*, a work which has been attributed to Paul Albar of Córdoba without good reason; cf. ES, XI, 48; Sage, *Paul Albar*, 227-230. The text of the *Liber scintillarum* has been edited by H. Rochais, *Defensoris Liber scintillarum*, Vol. 117 of *Corpus Christianorum, series latina* (Turnhout, 1957), vii-xxxv and 1-308.

[18] Werminghoff, *op.cit.*, 118f. The prophet Mohammed, according to a text quoted by Eulogius, is said to have made the same prediction about himself; V. infra, 338.

who are not holy and briefly refers to the authority of metropolitans, with regard it seems to the authority of the see of Rome. Although the letter is generally thought to have been written by a bishop of Betica in the ninth century, it may have been written by a bishop involved in the Migetian controversy of the eighth century.

It is sometimes assumed that the irregularities and errors listed by Pope Adrian I (772-795) in a letter to all the bishops of Spain are also to be attributed to Migetius. But such would not seem to be the case. Adrian attributes the errors to certain bishops, and his references to Migetius do not identify Migetius as the representative of all the errors.

Adrian's letter to the bishops of Spain is probably the original and master epistle of three letters by him which are appended to the end of the *Codex Carolinus*.[19] The other two letters are addressed to Egila, who was a bishop on a mission in Spain rather than a bishop of Spain, and appear to be supplementary to the first letter. Adrian wrote to the bishops after receiving reports by letter and word of mouth that certain bishops in Spain were contemning the teaching of the Church and seeking to introduce heresies into Spain. He had also heard that Bishop Egila after his arrival in Spain had succumbed to certain errors of "his teacher" Migetius. The Pope explains that Wilcharius, archbishop of Sens (769-778),[20] in seeking permission and authority to consecrate Egila and send him to Spain to preach, had praised Egila

[19] The principal ms for the *Codex Carolinus* dates from the end of the ninth century. The best edition of the letters is that by Wilhelm Gundlach in MGH, *Epistolarum* III, *Epistolae Merowingici et Karolini aevi* I (Berlin, 1892), 636-648. For a discussion of mss, editions, and the chronology of the letters cf. *ibid.*, 469-475. Gundlach dates all three letters between 785 and 791. The edition of the letters by Flórez, ES, V, Appendix X, is not so definitive as that of Gundlach. The edition by Gaetano Cenni, *Monumenta dominationis pontificiae...* (2 vols.; Rome, 1760-1761), I, 389-404 and 442-458, reprinted in PL 98, 333-346 and 373-386, offers several informative footnotes. Cenni dates the two letters to Egila in 782 and the letter to the bishops of Spain in 785.

[20] Cenni, PL 98, 337f., indicates that Wilcharius "bishop of the province of Gaul," referred to by Adrian, and Wilcharius, archbishop of Sens, were two different persons.

warmly. Adrian had consented on the condition that Egila first be examined for orthodoxy. Egila was not, states Adrian, to usurp any see in Spain, "but only to be offered the reward of souls for God." A third matter Adrian brings up is the report he has heard that Elipandus and Ascaricus are preaching that Christ was the adoptive Son of God. After this summary description of reports reaching him from Spain, Adrian begins the body of his letter, a lengthy condemnation of the errors themselves.

The first error condemned by Adrian is the celebration of Easter at the wrong time, an irregularity which the Chronicle of 754 reported in the year 750. Adrian also condemns as unreasonable and anathematizes the eating of strangled cattle and swine or their blood.[21] He refutes at length with quotations from Scripture the heretical belief that predestination to heaven or hell is in the hands of God and it is therefore pointless for men to be good or bad. At the end of the letter Adrian condemns in summary other errors reported to him. They call themselves Catholics, he says, but they live in common with Jews and unbaptized pagans and say that they are not polluted by their food or drink. Adrian cannot be referring here to Migetius, who was criticized by Elipandus for maintaining, as Adrian seems to, that the food of infidels pollutes the minds of the faithful. Despite the fact that it is forbidden, Adrian continues, they give their daughters in marriage to infidels and thus deliver them to pagans.[22] Certain priests mentioned are ordained without examination so that they may preside over the church (as bishops). The pernicious error has grown so monstrous that pseudo-priests choose women in marriage, even when their husbands are alive. Adrian finally mentions their error concerning free will and leaves others unmentioned. Anyone guilty of these offenses is to be excommunicated, he instructs. If, however, he wishes to mend his ways he should purge himself and show himself obedient to the

---

[21] Cf. Férotin, *Le liber ordinum,* 172, the Mozarabic *"Oratio super his qui morticinum comedunt vel suffocatum."*
[22] "Pagans" apparently are the Moslems and Jews.

Church. Elsewhere, in a separate letter, Adrian informs Egila that the Church does observe a fast on both Fridays and Saturdays.[23] The errors listed by Adrian, one may note, differ from those attributed to Migetius by Elipandus, except for the error in the celebration of Easter.

Adrian's second letter is addressed to Bishop Egila and his associate, the priest John, in Spain.[24] The letter is almost the same as that sent to all the bishops of Spain, except for its introduction, which acknowledges receipt of a letter from Egila and John and lacks any criticism of the two missionaries for succumbing to the teachings of Migetius. Adrian states that on the recommendation of Archbishop Wilcharius he has allowed the two to be ordained and sent to Spain to preach the orthodox faith and the Holy Catholic Church. The Pope expresses joy at the success achieved by the two and exhorts them to remain unsullied by heresy. Thereafter Adrian continues with the long refutation of the errors in a text almost identical to that in his letter to all the bishops.

The third letter of Adrian is addressed to Egila alone[25] and appears to have been written in conjunction with the letter just discussed. After asserting appreciation for the expressions of love and respect for the apostolic see received from Egila, Adrian explains that he has already given in a previous letter the Church's teaching on the points of heresy about which Egila inquires. But, taking Egila's word that he did not receive the previous letter and prompted by Bishop Peter of Pavia,[26] the legate of Charlemagne sent to endorse Egila's request, the Pope has had the letter copied from his register and sent again to Egila. He then exhorts Egila to resist the temptations of the heretics and to regard as *ethnici* and *publicani*[27] those who will not accept the teachings of the

---

[23] Gundlach, *op.cit.*, 648.

[24] *Ibid.*, 644-647. Apparently Adrian had this letter sent to Egila and John after they protested to him that they had not received the letter just discussed, which was sent to the bishops of Spain.

[25] *Ibid.*, 647f.

[26] Cenni, PL 98, 334, states that Peter died in 783.

[27] *Publicanus* is used here with the meaning of "public sinner" rather than "public official" or "tax-collector." Cf. E. Habel, *Mittellateinisches*

true faith. The only matter of ecclesiastical discipline discussed by Adrian in his letter is his confirmation that the
Church observes a fast on both Fridays and Saturdays, a
point not brought up in his other two letters. It would appear that Egila's letter to Adrian, supported by the intercession of Charlemagne's legate, was a diplomatic request to
have Adrian retract criticism of Egila contained in the first
letter.

Unless Letter X of the Albar correspondence, by an anonymous bishop, is part of the correspondence concerning
Egila, all that is known about Egila and his mission to Spain
is what Adrian tells about him. Gams is willing to identify
Egila with the bishop of that name in a list of the bishops
of Elvira (Granada), the only other place a bishop of the
name is encountered.[28] The initiation of Egila's mission by
Wilcharius, whom the Pope had sent to Gaul to preside over
the church there, and the intervention by Charlemagne on
Egila's behalf indicate that the Franks had more than a rou-
tine interest in his mission. Adrian's careful explanation
of the conditions under which he agreed to let Egila be sent
into Spain, that he was to be examined beforehand for orthodoxy and that he had no authority to obtain any see in
Spain, leads one to think that Egila stirred up resentment
among some of the bishops of Spain for intruding into their
jurisdiction. The only evidence for this resentment, however,
apart from the inference from Adrian's letters, comes from
Elipandus, who in correspondence of the Adoptionist controversy shows a certain amount of antagonism towards the
Franks and an exaggerated jealousy of the authority of the
see of Toledo with regard to that of Rome.

In all three letters Adrian frequently asserts that the see
of Rome is the head of the whole Church. Such reiteration

Glossar (Paderborn, 1931), and L. Diefenbach, *Glossarium latino-
germanicum mediae et infimae aetatis e codicibus, mss, et libris
imprimis* (Frankfurt, 1857). The same use of the word occurs, it
appears, in the *Indiculus*, 18.

[28] Gams, *op.cit.*, 254; cf. the list of the bishops of Granada, Antolín,
"El códice emilianense," *La ciudad de Dios*, 74 (1907), 389.

implies that schismatic trends were appearing in Spain, as a result it would seem of contact with the teachings of Islam. Adrian also mentions the "great interval of distance" which separates Spain from Rome,[29] but it should be noted that his letters themselves attest to a freedom of communication. He received letters and oral reports from Spain, and couriers travelled between him and Egila. There must have been communications between Egila and Charlemagne, probably at a time when Egila was in Betica. All the letters and treatises of this period testify to normal communications between different parts of Spain. Elipandus of Toledo communicated with Seville, Córdoba, the Asturias, and even France. One of his letters received such widespread publication in the Asturias that Beatus and Eterius wrote a long treatise against him to counteract the damage it could cause them and the Church. The usual couriers for correspondence seem to have been trusted clerics.

[29] Gundlach, *op.cit.*, 637.

CHAPTER III
THE WEAKENING OF CHRISTIAN UNITY DURING THE ADOPTIONIST CONTROVERSY

Even more than the religious irregularities discussed in the previous chapter the heresy of Adoptionism tended to weaken Christian dogma with respect to the divinity of Christ and to divide the Christian community in Spain in the late eighth century, thus setting the stage for Moslem attacks against Christianity in Córdoba some years before the martyrdoms of the ninth century.[1] By denying that the Incarnate Son of God is the true Son of God and maintaining instead that Christ as man was only the adoptive son of God, Adoptionism necessarily implies two persons in Christ even though it may not so state. It would make Christ similar to Mohammed and would make of Christianity a religion similar to Islam. In the beginning a philological or semantic error seems to have served as a basis for the Adoptionists' teachings. They maintained that the word *adoptio*, as used in the Mozarabic liturgy and in passages they quoted from earlier authors, referred to the adoption of Christ or His human nature by God the Father, and not, as was the case, to the adoption of human nature by Christ or the adoption of believers as children of God because of the grace of Christ.

[1] Amann, *L'époque carolingienne*, Vol. VI of *Histoire de l'Eglise*, 129-152, inclines to meliorate the position of the Adoptionists; Gams, *Kirchengeschichte*, II, ii, 261-298, provides a good historical account of the heresy; for a discussion of the doctrine cf. H. Quilliet, "Adoptionisme au VIIIe siècle," DTC, I, i, 403-413; García-Villada, *Historia eclesiástica*, III, 58-70; Amann, "L'adoptionisme espagnol de VIIIe siècle," *Revue des sciences religieuses*, XVI (1936), 281-317; M. Menéndez Pelayo, *Historia de los heterodoxos españoles*, Bk. II, i; A. Grillmeier, "Adoptionismus," LTK, I, 153-155. García-Villada, *op.cit.*, 58, and J. Madoz, "La literatura en la epoca mozárabe," *Historia general de las literaturas hispánicas*, ed. G. Diaz-Plaja (5 vols.; Barcelona, 1949-1958), I, 260, point out that Adoptionism is an attempt to reconcile Christianity with the Koran.

For many years doctrinal disputes gave rise to ill feelings among the hierarchy of the Church in Toledo and the Asturias. Adoptionism, however, may have originated in Córdoba, the Moslem capital, which was also, it seems, the birthplace of the chief exponent of the heresy, Elipandus, bishop of Toledo. Felix, bishop of Urgel, was another prominent exponent of Adoptionism. According to the ninth-century Mozarab author Paul Albar of Córdoba, Betica was devastated by the heresy. Albar says that Teudula, the metropolitan of Seville, attacked the heresy, but his work is no longer extant. Albar quotes from the treatise of Beatus and Eterius and adduces a long quotation from an otherwise unknown work by a Basiliscus, who may have been a legate from Alfonso II of the Asturias to Charlemagne in 798.[2] Teudula may be possibly the anonymous bishop who wrote Letter X of the Albar correspondence. Although that letter does not discuss any Adoptionist belief, it speaks of heretics and the devastation of the province.

Elipandus wrote several letters attacking a number of people and was himself attacked, but not much is known about him before he became metropolitan of Toledo or about his associates in the heresy. J. F. Rivera has reconstructed an account of the early years of Elipandus based on references to a hypothetical heretic made by Beatus of Liébana and Eterius of Osma in their treatise against Elipandus. Many of the passages probably are oblique references to the bishop of Toledo, but others, even though they may refer to Elipandus, appear intended rather to typify him than to attack him with innuendo about his past. According to Rivera's deductions,[3] Elipandus was originally a monk from Córdoba, born 25 July 717. As a student he was deceived by the vain eloquence and perverse doctrine of "philosophers." He neglected the study of Holy Scripture and would not participate in discussions with his brothers, and thus could not have his

---

[2] Albar correspondence, Letters I, 5 and 7; III, 6; IV, 24, 27, and 28; V, 4. A. Lambert, "Basiliscus," DHGE, VI, 1240.

[3] J. F. Rivera, *Elipando de Toledo, nueva aportación a los estudios mozárabes* (Toledo, 1940), 18-20.

errors corrected. As priest and bishop he deceived many with his errors, especially the laity, and as bishop of Toledo, which he seems to have become by improper means, he exiled those of his clergy who would not agree with him, making use of the secular authority to enforce his will.

A fertile soil for the growth of the Adoptionist heresy existed in the conditions surrounding the episodes of Ascaricus, Migetius, and Egila, discussed in the previous chapter. Elipandus' extraordinary pride in his authority as metropolitan of Toledo and primate of Spain, manifested in attacks against Beatus of Liébana and Alcuin, seems to have been a major factor in the persistence of the error. Charlemagne undertook to have the heresy condemned in ecclesiastical councils because Urgel formed part of his Spanish March and because Elipandus, in the name of the bishops of Spain, had ventured to expound the heretical doctrine in letters addressed to Charlemagne, to Alcuin, and to the bishops of the Frankish realm. Adoptionism is discussed in chronicles, pronouncements of councils, and epistolary debates originating in France, Italy, and Spain. Much of this literature falls outside the scope of the present study, which will survey only what is peculiar to Spain and Mozarab life and culture.

In his letter condemning the teaching of Migetius that there were three persons in the Divinity, Elipandus put great stress on the spiritual nature of God.[4] He does not in this letter explicitly profess Adoptionism. But the seeds of the heresy may be seen in his words, and the letter illustrates his jealousy of the authority of Toledo and his intent to play down the authority of Rome. Elipandus complains that Migetius presumed to speak to him with the authority of a teacher rather than in the tone of an inquirer. He makes the same complaint against Beatus of Liébana in a letter to the Abbot Fidelis and at the same time praises Ascaricus for addressing him in the tone of an inquirer. Charlemagne turns the same words against Elipandus in a letter written

---

[4] ES, V, Appendix X, ii, especially par. 7.

after the Council of Frankfurt, reminding Elipandus of his own arrogance.

By 785 Elipandus' doctrine of Adoptionism had been definitely stated and propagated, and he himself was confronted with a comprehensive attack against his teachings. The treatise of Beatus of Liébana and Bishop Eterius of Osma, written to defend themselves against the accusations of Elipandus and to refute his errors, is a solid work exhibiting wide learning and accomplished apologetics. It is perhaps the most important text composed in Spain at this time.[5] Not much is known of the two authors of the work. Beatus of Liébana was probably a monk,[6] and Eterius was bishop of Osma. At the time they composed their work (A.D. 785) they were both living in the Asturias. Besides his part of the treatise against Elipandus, Beatus compiled a Commentary on the Apocalypse, which he dedicated to Eterius. The Commentary comprises excerpts from previous commentaries with but little original composition by Beatus. In letters in 794 and 799 Elipandus implies that Beatus, who continued even then to be his greatest enemy in Spain, had a special relationship with Charlemagne. So little being known about Beatus and Eterius apart from this treatise, there is no basis to determine the part of either of them in its composition.

The treatise (or letter) is addressed to "Our most eminent and the beloved of God, Elipandus, archbishop of the see of Toledo." On 26 November 785 Beatus and Eterius had read a letter which Elipandus had sent secretly under seal in October 785 to the Abbot Fidelis, of whom nothing more is known. Although they had heard of the letter they had not seen its contents until the occasion of the entry of Adosinda,

[5] The treatise occupies the first half of the ninth-century ms Madrid BN 10018. It is edited in PL 96, 893-1030, after the edition of A. Galland, *Bibliotheca graeco-latina veterum Patrum antiquorumque Scriptorum ecclesiasticorum* (14 vols.; Venice, 1765-1781).

[6] A vita of Beatus, regarded as a saint in the Asturias, introduces the information that he was a Mozarab (*ex Muzarabibus Gothis*), but Mabillon has shown that this vita is unreliable and probably of recent date; cf. PL 96, 887-894.

widow of King Silo of Oviedo, into the cloister.[7] Fidelis, who appears to have sided with Beatus and Eterius in the dispute, informed the two that the letter, attacking them and their faith, had been made public in all the Asturias. Feeling that Elipandus' letter jeopardized the unity of the Faith in the Asturias, they undertook to answer it.

Much, if not all, of Elipandus' letter to Fidelis is incorporated in the treatise of Beatus and Eterius. Elipandus speaks as follows:

> Whoever does not confess Jesus Christ to be adoptive in humanity but by no means adoptive in divinity is a heretic and is to be exterminated. "Put away the evil one from your land" (1 Cor. 5:13). They do not inquire of me, but seek to teach me, for they are servants of Antichrist. This letter of Lord Bishop Ascaricus[8] I have therefore sent to Your Fraternity, dearest Fidelis, that you may know how much humility reigns in the servants of Christ and how much pride reigns in the disciples of Antichrist.
>
> Lord Ascaricus was willing to write those things to me not with the command of a teacher but with the devotion of an inquirer, as true humility taught him. But they contradict me and act as if I were ignorant; they are not willing to ask what is right but teach instead. God knows, even though they have written insolently, I would have obeyed willingly if they had spoken truth, mindful of that which is written, "If it has been revealed to a junior, the elder is silent." And again, "He is near to God who knows how to be silent with reason."[9] For it is unheard of that people from Liébana teach those of Toledo. Everyone knows that this see has

[7] Rodrigo Jiménez de Rada, *Appendix prima, Series regum hispaniae*, says that Adosinda entered the monastery in accordance with the decrees of the thirteenth council of Toledo and the third council of Zaragoza, lest she remain in the world *ignobilis et inhonora* after the death of Silo (*SS PP Toletanorum*, III, 295).

[8] The letter is not extant.

[9] The source of the first adage is unknown; the second, from the *Disticha Catonis*, I, 3, 2, is cited in Elipandus' letter to Alcuin, par. 19 (ES, V, Appendix X, v). Both are cited again in a letter from Elipandus to Charlemagne.

from its beginnings been outstanding in the holy doctrine of faith, and never has anything schismatic emanated from it. And now, a sick sheep, you seek to be a doctor to us. Still, I was unwilling for our other brothers to learn of this before such an evil can be cut off at the roots in the place where it sprang up. For it would be ignominy for me to have this heard about[10] Toledo, so that what I and my other brothers for so long condemned in Seville, with God's help correcting the heresy of the Migetians, both with regard to the feast of Easter and other errors, they now, on the other hand, find wherewith to accuse us. Even if it has been done halfheartedly and you let it go uncorrected, I shall bring it to the attention of the brothers, and it will be ignominy for you if they find wherewith to reprehend you.[11]

Elipandus urges Fidelis to undertake to instruct the young Eterius (bishop of Osma), who has not yet reached full intelligence and has been handicapped by associating with the ignorant and schismatic Felix and the Antiphrasis Beatus. It is not known who Felix is. He may be the Felix of Córdoba mentioned above, but he would not seem to be Felix of Urgel, who Elipandus says elsewhere was an associate with him since his youth. Beatus is no different, continues Elipandus, from the heretic Bonosus. "To whom shall I liken him if not to Faustus the Manichaean?"[12] Faustus condemned patriarchs and prophets, he condemns doctors early and modern. I beseech you that, kindled with the fire of faith, heated with great desire and thirst, you put away the error

[10] *intraditionem.*

[11] PL 96, 918f.

[12] Bonosus, bishop of Naïssa in Dacia, heretic and schismatic at the end of the fourth century, denied the virginity of the Blessed Mother, attributing to her other children. The heresy taught that Christ was human only and the adoptive Son of God. This Arian Adoptionism was current in Gaul and Spain in the sixth and seventh centuries. Cf. H. Rahner, "Bonosus," LTK, II, 602f., and X. Le Bachelet, "Bonose," DTC, II, i, 1027-1031. Faustus was a Manichaean bishop in Carthage at the end of the fourth century, against whom Augustine wrote a treatise; cf. H. Rahner, "Faustus von Mileve," LTK, IV, 43, and PL 42, 207-518.

mentioned from your midst. As the Lord eradicated the Migetian heresy from the bounds of Betica by his servants, so may He by you pluck out completely the Beatian heresy from the bounds of the Asturias. I have heard that the precursor of Antichrist has appeared in the midst of you and announces that he is born, and so I would ask that you inquire of him where, how, and when was born that lying spirit of the prophets which speaks in him. We anxiously await your reply."[13]

This is one of the most interesting letters of Elipandus. Appearing as it does in the body of a definitive refutation of his teachings after having been shown to his opponents by the person to whom it was addressed, the letter shows that seven years before the first council called by Charlemagne to condemn Felix of Urgel, Adoptionism had received a major setback in Spain itself. In the letter Elipandus refers to a previous attack against him by Beatus and Eterius which is not extant.

After explaining how they came to know the contents of Elipandus' letter to Fidelis, Beatus and Eterius proceed to refute Adoptionism. "Let both the metropolitan bishop," they say, "and the prince of the land be put away completely from your land, for they work the vengeance of schism and heresy with equal might, one with the sword of the word and the other with the rod of authority." The "prince of the land" would seem to be either the emir of Córdoba or the ruler of Toledo. By attacking him Beatus and Eterius may be attesting to the general antagonism between the kings of the Asturias and the Moslems to the south besides implying that the Moslem ruler was acting to the ruin of the Church.[14] Already the report has spread, Beatus and Eterius continue, through all the Asturias, through all Spain, and even to France, that the church in the Asturias is divided, and the division is not among ordinary people but among bishops. We are prepared to suffer exile and death for our faith, they

---

[13] PL 96, 919. Elipandus may be alluding to Beatus' *Commentary on the Apocalypse.*

[14] Cf. Letter X of the Albar correspondence, 1 and 4.

assert. Though an angel come from heaven and go about inculcating your alien (*peregrina*) faith, we will regard it as *anathemata maranatha*.[15] In criticizing Elipandus for comparing himself with Christ, the authors introduce a note of historical interest. "Witiza was a king. But today many take from him the name *Witizani*, even poor people, so that by the name it may be known that they are of royal stock and could have been king, if the name made one a king."[16]

Although Beatus and Eterius indicate that the secular authority assisted Elipandus in the oppression of his opponents, there was no real persecution in connection with the heresy. The Church can be persecuted in two ways, they say, by words and by the sword. Now is a time of persecution by words, although the heretics feign humility. But in time to come there will be persecutions of the sword. "Then all the heavenly ones who have been caught in that tribulation will remember the just time in which now the Church has peace of faith and bends the proud necks of heretics, not with the power of might but with the yoke of reason."[17] They give information about the frequency of receiving the Eucharist. "A Christian should communicate often. If no sins prevent him, he should receive the body of the Lord daily."[18] Christians suffer insults from the pagans and Jews on account of the humanity of Christ. "What kind of God do you worship,"

[15] PL 96, 901f. In the prologue to Bk. II of the *Commentary on the Apocalypse* Beatus explains *maranatha* thus: Et qui supra evangelizaverit quam isti, non Christianus sed anathema in perpetuum erit, maranatha, id est, perditio in adventum Domini," *Beati in Apocalypsin libri duodecim*, ed. Henry A. Sanders (Rome, 1930), 117. The quotation from Gal. 1:8-9 is widely used by Eulogius and Albar in their writings later.

[16] PL 96, 930. Pérez de Urbel, *San Eulogio*, 149, and Cagigas, *Los mozárabes*, I, 195f., say that a party of *Witizani*, descended from Visigothic magnates, sought to preserve peace with the Moslems in order to preserve privileges and offices they held under them. Another party of Mozarabs, they say, defended the cause of Rodrigo and was hostile to the Moslems. Neither author gives the source of his information.

[17] PL 96, 933.

[18] *Ibid.*, 941.

the pagans cry out to the Christians, "who was born of woman?" "What kind of God do you worship, who was seized by men, crucified, died, and was buried?" ask the Jews.[19] The Jews deride the Christians for their God who hung naked on the cross, the authors say later. "We withdraw from each other, so that they do not receive us nor do we receive them. We flee the Jews as one enemy, but we find many enemies within the house, heretics worse than the Jews."[20]

Many times the two apologists interpret the meaning of a word, such as *basilica* or *symbolum*, through its Greek components. To an extent they seem to do this to show that they are as learned as Elipandus. Their interest in semantics is illustrated also by a passage in which they explain allegory. "Four kinds of allegory are to be found in Holy Scripture. First, according to *translatio*, as in, 'The Lord was angry' and 'He came down.' Here the reasons and the motions of men are transferred to God. Second, according to *imaginatio*, or *hypotyposis*, as in, 'A certain man went down from Jerusalem to Jericho' (Lk. 10:30) and in the parable of the workers in the vineyard. Here Christ tells those things which He did in the image of another person occupied with something of another nature. Third, according to *comparatio*, or *similitudo*, as in, 'The kingdom of heaven is like to a grain of mustard seed, etc.' (Mt. 13:31). Here what is important is not the story, such as in the example above, but only the effect of the causes. Fourth, according to *modus proverbialis*, as in the saying of Solomon, 'Drink water out of thy own vessels and thy own wells' (Prov. 5:15). Here Scripture seeks to warn that carnal concupiscence is to be restrained even within the rights of marriage. The Jews do not admit these allegories of ours. Carnal Christians do not understand them and so do not confess the man Christ to be God."[21]

[19] *Ibid.*, 944.
[20] *Ibid.*, 1003.
[21] *Ibid.*, 955f. Except for the last two sentences, this passage is an almost verbatim quotation from Junilius Afer, *Instituta regularia divinae legis*, Bk. I, v (PL 68, 18f.). Junilius, a Byzantine official who flourished about A.D. 550, wrote his work, which is based on the teach-

The ideas of Beatus and Eterius in the field of psychology are of interest. Man is composed of soul, body, and spirit, they say. This teaching, encountered frequently in Spanish literature of the early Middle Ages, was condemned by the Council of Frankfurt in 794. They continue: "The soul itself (*anima*) has many names for the actions it performs, although it is one substance. When it contemplates God it is *spiritus*. When it feels it is *sensus*. When it knows it is *animus*. When it understands it is *mens*. When it discerns it is *ratio*. When it consents it is *voluntas*. When it remembers it is *memoria*. When it causes its members to grow it is *anima*."[22] And later: "As man is formed of three, so our *bibliotheca* [Bible] is one book but is formed of three, that is, *littera*, *tropologia*, and *mistica intelligentia*. *Littera* is according to the body of man. This *littera* is *historia*. *Tropologia* is according to the soul of man. *Mistica intelligentia* is according to the spirit of man."[23]

In Book II of the treatise, which is on "Christ and His body, which is the Church, and the devil and his body, which is Antichrist," Beatus and Eterius seek to show that evil attributes, such as lying and pride, belong to heretics and Antichrist, while good qualities belong to the Church of Christ. Having exposed the wrongdoings of Elipandus, whereby he called them heretics and disciples of Antichrist, the authors proceed in this book to an *apologeticus*, which they define as an exposition in which one defends oneself against accusations. Your charges against us, they tell Elipandus, have been made known throughout the lands, and anyone who reads them will take you for the Catholic doctor of the see of Toledo, one of the new archbishops,[24] and us

ing of Paul of Nisibis, in Syriac and in Greek before composing it in Latin; H. Hurter, *Nomenclator literarius theologiae catholicae,* I (Innsbruck, 1903), 530f.

[22] PL 96, 957; the quotation is from Isidore, *Differentiarum sive de proprietate sermonum libri duo*, II, xxix, 97 (PL 83, 84).

[23] PL 96, 958. In general this quotation follows Jerome, *Epistola 120*, xii (PL 22, 1005), who enumerates *historia*, *tropologia*, and *intelligentia spiritualis;* cf. also Sanders, *Beati in Apocalypsin*, 200.

[24] "novellus archiepiscopus"; P. David, *Etudes*, 119f., says that the

for unlearned Liébanenses, heretics, and disciples of Antichrist. You charge us with ignominy and evil fame and wish to appear the only one with good fame in the Church. You mislead people, they charge. "For many who read your nebulous words which are written allegorically understand that the dispute is over interpretation, and they explain that you, as a new prophet, speak in enigmas (*aenigmatice*)."[25]

More information about the times is given. Some Christians are sent to school and offered to Christ by their parents that they may be priests, while others, in preparation for the married life, are taught only to read and to know Christ.[26] The discussion by Beatus and Eterius of vestments worn by the pontifex may be compared with the treatise on clerical garb by Leovigildus of Córdoba in the ninth century. Of the eight vestments listed and explained in the treatise—the *ephod*, the *tunica*, the *zona*, the *catenulae*, the *femoralia*, the *fimbriae*, the *socci*, and the *tintinnabula*—only the *tunica* is mentioned by Leovigildus.[27]

As the authors bring their treatise to a close they accuse Elipandus of arrogance. St. Peter, they say, did not venture to compose a creed himself but collaborated with the other apostles. Elipandus, however, believes that he has the grace of all the apostles and has composed the doctrine of a new faith alone without conferring with his brothers. He has elevated himself above the whole church and regards every-

term "archbishop" was not used in Spain before the end of the eleventh century except occasionally as a courtesy, the term "metropolitan" being used instead. In England and the Frankish empire in the eighth century, he says, the term came to mean more specifically a bishop who had received the pallium and was invested with a large amount of pontifical authority. Evidently Elipandus had not been "recently" elected "archbishop" in 785; cf. the list of bishops of Toledo in ms Escorial d-I-1, published by Antolín, "El códice emilianense," *La ciudad de Dios*, 74 (1907), 388; Sanders, *op.cit.*, 123, "Neofitus Graece, Latine novellus, et rudis fidelis, vel nuper renatus interpretari potest."

[25] PL 96, 978ff. In a gloss attributed to Isidore of Seville *aenigma* is explained as "figura, sive typus, vel species" and *enigma* as "obscuriloquium" (PL 83, 1333 and 1348).

[26] PL 96, 998.

[27] PL 96, 1005f.; Leovigildus, *De habitu clericorum*, v-vii.

one else as a brute animal. The text of his faith is not only contrary to the apostolic faith, they charge, but is inconsistent in itself.[28]

The treatise of Beatus and Eterius resembles Augustine's *City of God*, which devotes its first part to an apologia and its second part to an exposition of the contrast between the societies of good and evil. The treatise also bears a resemblance to another Mozarabic work, the *Indiculus luminosus* written in 854 by Paul Albar of Córdoba. Albar, who knew both Augustine's work and the treatise of Beatus and Eterius, first defends his position and then, after arguing that the prophet Mohammed is a type of Antichrist, delineates the contrast between Christ and Mohammed and between Christianity and Islam. The use of parallelism and antithesis, examples of which are seen here, appears to have been very popular among Mozarab authors, especially in the case of Albar. Albar's *Indiculus* ends with a discussion of the days of Antichrist described in the Apocalypse, as Albar sees them in Córdoba in his own day.

Antichrist figures prominently in another work by Beatus, his Commentary on the Apocalypse,[29] a long work which was transmitted through the Middle Ages in many manuscripts. The Commentary consists of two long prologues and twelve books of commentary on the Apocalypse. The whole is a collection of excerpts from earlier commentators on the Apocalypse arranged by Beatus with a few passages on collateral

---

[28] PL 96, 1026ff.

[29] Beatus' Commentary on the Apocalypse was edited by Flórez, *Sancti Beati presbyteri Hispani Liebanensis in Apocalypsin, ac plurimas utriusque foederis paginas commentaria, ex veteribus nonnullisque desideratis Patribus mille retro annis collecta, nunc primum edita* (Madrid, 1770) ; copies of this edition are rare. The text has also been edited by Henry A. Sanders in Vol. VII of *Papers and Monographs of the American Academy in Rome, Beati in Apocalipsin libri duodecim* (Rome, 1930) ; Sanders, *ibid.*, xi, notes that the work was completed in 786. A painstaking study of the mss of Beatus' work has been made by Wilhelm Neuss, *Die Apokalypse des hl. Johannes in der altspanischen und altchristlichen Bibel-Illustration. (Das Problem der Beatus-Handschriften)* (2 vols., text and plates; Münster Westfalen; 1931).

topics taken from Isidore, Augustine, or of uncertain origin. Of particular interest is the prologue to Book II, a lengthy treatise dealing with the terms *ecclesia* and *synagoga*, the former defining the members of the Church and the latter the forces of evil, or Antichrist. This prologue, which discusses in a technical way the same general subject as Book II of the treatise against Elipandus, abounds with philological explanations of terms, referring back to Greek, Hebrew, and Syrian origins. More important than the text of the Commentary itself are the excellent illustrations in the many manuscripts of the work. The illustrations, according to Wilhelm Neuss, provide a unique opportunity to study the transition of Christian art from the days of the Fathers to the early Middle Ages.[30]

Adoptionism might have been contained in the Spanish peninsula were it not that one of its main protagonists, Felix, bishop of Urgel, occupied a see that had come under the rule of the Franks. Felix moreover appears to have propagated the heresy with zeal in Septimania, Gaul, and Germany.[31] In 792 he abjured his error before a council in Regensburg and again in Rome. But when he returned to his see in Spain he relapsed into his error.

The major event in the history of Adoptionism in the Western Church was the Council of Frankfurt in 794, which neither Felix nor Elipandus attended. This council was a general council of the West, attended by bishops from France, Germany, Italy, and England, but not Spain. It dealt primarily with Byzantine unorthodoxy. What gave Charlemagne occasion to take up in the council a heresy originating outside his empire, albeit threatening it, was the receipt of two letters addressed to him and to the Frankish episcopate from the bishops of Spain, both evidently written by Elipandus of Toledo and both asking for a reply. After receipt of the letters Charlemagne began communications with Rome about the matter and convoked the Council of Frankfurt. Following the council he sent his reply to Eli-

---

[30] Neuss, *op.cit.*, 3.
[31] Cf. Jonas of Orleans, *De cultu imaginum*, I (PL 106, 307ff.).

pandus and the bishops of Spain: a condemnation of Adoptionism by Pope Adrian, two separate condemnations by the bishops who attended the council, and a letter from Charlemagne himself.[32]

The letter from the bishops of Spain to the bishops of Gaul consists primarily of an attack on Beatus of Liébana and an exposition of Adoptionism. Elipandus first attacks Beatus with abusive invective and then compares him to Migetius, who is charged with the preposterous actions already listed. He accuses Beatus further. "And Beatus on the vigil of Easter prophesied to Ordoño of Liébana in the presence of the people that it was the end of the world. And so the people became terrified and out of their mind, and are said to have fasted that night without any food and on Sunday until three o'clock in the afternoon. When Ordoño realized that he was suffering from hunger he said to the people, 'Let us eat and drink, and if we are to die, at least let us be filled.' But the same Beatus, feigning illness, arose on the third day, alive in his body but dead in his soul. But we anathematize Bonosus . . . we anathematize Sabellius[33] . . . we anathematize Arius . . . we anathematize Manicheus . . . we anathematize the Antiphrasis Beatus, given over to lascivity of the flesh, and the ass Eterius, teacher of beasts. . . ."[34] At the end of the letter the bishops of Gaul are asked to scrutinize what has been said and make it known to Charlemagne. If they find anything amiss in the letter they should reply and enlighten their Spanish brethren.

The letter to Charlemagne is a strange mixture of obsequiousness and insult. The king is not mentioned by name, though there is praise for *domino inclito adque glorioso*

---

[32] The two letters of Elipandus are found in the eleventh-century ms Toledo 14,23. The four letters sent by Charlemagne are found in ms Munich Latin 14468, dated 821. All six letters, plus the Acts of the Council of Frankfurt, are edited by Werminghoff, MGH, *Concilia*, II, *Concilia aevi carolini*, I, i, 110-171.

[33] Sabellius advocated an antitrinitarian heresy of the third and fourth centuries; cf. A. Stohr "Sabellianismus," LTK, IX, 52f., and G. Bardy, "Monarchianisme," DTC, X, ii, 2204ff.

[34] Werminghoff, *op.cit.*, 118f.

diversarum gentium principi m.[35] The burden of the letter is a criticism of "the Antiphrasis Beatus" and his influence. Elipandus asks Charlemagne to judge between "Bishop Felix, whom we have known from his youth to stand firm beside us in the service of God, and those who defend sacrilege and the Antiphrasis Beatus already mentioned, obese with the vices of the flesh." Elipandus would inform Charlemagne of other important matters but elects to communicate to him orally by messenger what he feels he cannot write. He beseeches Charlemagne to restore Felix to his see, calling to mind the fate of the Emperor Constantine, who, he explains, became a Christian after having been an idolator but ended his life as an Arian and went to hell. He urges Charlemagne to eradicate the influence of Beatus in his realm. It would be fearful, he continues, if the devil through the Antiphrasis Beatus should invisibly invade a place where the visible power of the pagans has not entered. Towards the end of the letter Elipandus confronts Charlemagne with the statement, "It is said that you conquer many by the terror of power, not by justice." He informs Charlemagne that Beatus, whom he accuses of impurity, boasts in writing that he has converted the Frankish king from error.[36] Finally he quotes three adages, two which were cited in Elipandus' letter to the Abbot Fidelis discussed above, one from the *Disticha Catonis*, to induce Charlemagne to be guided by the right counsel of the many.

In his letter of reply,[37] which is a rebuke of Elipandus and his followers, Charlemagne provides some general information about the subjection of the Christians to the Moslems in Spain. Elipandus had sent two letters, Charlemagne begins, one general to the bishops and one special to the king. He could not tell in these letters, Charlemagne says in words reminiscent of Elipandus' complaint against Migetius and Beatus, if Elipandus was seeking to teach the Franks with

[35] *m.* may stand for *meo* or *magno.* Charlemagne's reply definitely identifies him as the recipient.
[36] Werminghoff, *op.cit.*, 120f.
[37] *Ibid.*, 157-164.

pedagogical authority or to learn from their humble learning. But whichever it was, he continues, Christian charity would not let him spurn an answer to Elipandus. He grieves at the oppression the Spanish suffer among the pagans, but he would grieve more to see them suffer diabolical oppression through lack of the Faith and schismatic error. He is happy therefore to correct their error. This has been done in a council. Four embassies have been sent to Rome to find out the Pope's mind on the matter. Now four letters are sent to Elipandus, one from the Pope, one from the bishops of Italy, one from the bishops of Gaul, and one from Charlemagne himself. As urged by Elipandus, Charlemagne remarks, he has taken the advice of many rather than that of a few. Elipandus warned him to beware the fate of Constantine, lest the same befall him through Beatus, whom Elipandus calls the Antiphrasis. Charlemagne promises to take precautions against this happening not only through Beatus but through anyone preaching contrary to the Faith. He cautions Elipandus to take care not to let that which he warns Charlemagne against happen to him, for the interior servitude of the devil is worse, he says, than the external servitude of an enemy people. Until now he has wept over the corporeal servitude of the Spanish and rejoiced at their rectitude of faith. Now he weeps over the diabolical deception of their hearts and the enemy oppression of their bodies. He urges Elipandus to return to the unity of Holy Mother Church, so that Christ, who freed him from original sin by Baptism, may save him from the servitude of this world. Charlemagne concludes his letter with a long credo of the correct faith. Repeatedly through the letter he ironically makes it clear that he has scrupulously followed the line of conduct recommended to him by Elipandus and the bishops and a clear denunciation of their error has resulted.

Pope Adrian in his letter[38] urges the bishops of Spain to return to the true faith or suffer perpetual anathema.

As Charlemagne's letter was a point by point reply to the letter he had received from Spain, so is the letter of the bish-

[38] *Ibid.*, 122-130.

ops of Germany, Gaul, and Aquitaine a point by point refutation of the exposition of Adoptionism sent to them. "You did not mention the names of books and the number of chapters," they charge Elipandus and his brothers, "so that your error is investigated with great difficulty." Furthermore, they continue, you have falsified texts. In some of their criticism the Frankish bishops show a lack of familiarity with certain authors of Visigothic Spain. "It is better to believe the testimony of God the Father about His Son than that of your Ildefonsus, who has composed Mass prayers for you such as the universal and holy church of God does not have. Nor do we think you are heard [by God] in them. And if your Ildefonsus called Christ adoptive in his prayers, our Gregory, on the other hand, bishop of the see of Rome and most famous doctor throughout the world, in his prayers did not hesitate to call him always the Only-begotten."[39]

The fourth enclosure of Charlemagne's letter to the bishops of Spain is the *Sacrosyllabus*[40] composed by Paulinus of Aquilea and sent in the name of the bishops of Italy, who had not been addressed by the bishops of Spain. It refutes Adoptionism at length, using many quotations from Holy Scripture.

Adoptionism was also condemned in the first of the sixty-six articles of the Acts of the Council of Frankfurt in 794.[41] This condemnation of Elipandus, Felix, and their followers, coming from many sides and on all levels, did not suffice to end the dispute. Felix and Elipandus continued to defend their views, and they were answered in voluminous treatises by Paulinus of Aquilea and, especially, by Alcuin. Felix was persuaded to appear before a council in Aachen in 799, where he debated for six days with Alcuin. In the end Felix acknowledged his error and wrote a letter to the clergy and laity of the diocese of Urgel condemning his old error and professing the true faith. He was not permitted to return to Urgel, however, but spent the rest of his life in the custody

---

[39] *Ibid.*, 143ff.; cf. index, "*missae.*"
[40] Werminghoff, *op.cit.*, 130-142.
[41] *Ibid.*, 165-171.

of the bishop of Lyons. After his death a composition was discovered which caused Agobard, bishop of Lyons at the time, to believe that Felix had relapsed into the heresy. Agobard then composed a treatise against Felix and sent it to Louis the Pious.

Flórez edits a letter of Elipandus written to Felix after the latter's conversion, without giving any notice of the manuscript from which it comes. Elipandus is believed to have written the letter in 799, shortly after Felix left Spain to appear before the Council of Aachen. The information in the letter about the mind of Elipandus and the conditions in which he lived at this time is of unusual interest. In the last paragraph of the letter Elipandus apparently seeks to ingratiate himself with Charlemagne. "Know that on 25 July I entered my eighty-second year, decrepit old age, and pray for us as we do zealously for you, so that God may join us also to the region of the living.[42] I have asked all the brothers to offer sacrifice to God for you. May I deserve to be made happy as soon as possible by your answer. I commend this letter and our priest Venerius to you, if God grant that he reach you."

Elipandus begins his letter stating that he had written a reply to a letter from Felix but that it had been burned in a recent fire. Forty days after the fire he was able to return to his work and write a letter to "that pitch-black heretic *Albinus*" which he asked Felix to forward to Alcuin.[43]

> I have sent you a short work received from brother Milito, who has a correct belief of God. He also sent me four gatherings, which I sent against that pseudo-prophet, the most foul Un-Beatus. Let me know who has been placed in Rome.[44] I received

[42] ES, V, Appendix X, vi, par. 4, "ut nos Deus in regione vivorum pariter iungat."

[43] Elipandus' communication to Felix was despatched 31 October. The text should read, it appears, "Modo tamen egressus est de me ieiunio (*not* de mele Junio) Kalendarium Novembrium. Direxi vobis...," par. 1. The letter to Alcuin is edited in ES, V, Appendix X, v. On the fast of the Kalends of November cf. index, "Felix of Córdoba."

[44] "Certifica me qui est positus in Roma."

your letter which got through to me with the help
of God at the end of July, and I gave great thanks
to my God with arms outstretched for gladdening
me with your words in the midst of these daily
tribulations in which we endure rather than live.

I sent your letter to Córdoba for the brothers who
have a correct belief of God, and they have written
me many things which I ought to have sent to you
for your assistance. But I sent them to that heresiarch the Antiphrasis Beatus, teacher of Alcuin,
to be read. But you, send that writing I have sent
you to your faithful and glorious king before it
comes to that child of death, Alcuin. . . . Concerning
our brother who died, I understand that he ordered something sent to us, and so I ask that you
send your servant Ermedeus to inquire of the Jews
who have wives and sons there and to take the trouble to send us whatever God has granted. And do
this so that the other Jews who live here do not find
out, or, if possible, send it by one of your humble
ones who come here as merchants. Let us know
what you decide to do.[45] And especially inform me
about the two books Ermedeus has that I sent to
the brother who died, that is, the epistles of St.
Jerome and the works of St. Isidore, which he bor-
rowed from me because he had found others like
them.[46] Therefore receive Ermedeus and teach him
the true doctrine of faith in your words, as I have
told him you would.[47]

Elipandus' description of his distress and comparative
isolation indicates that he had experienced a siege and a sack
in Toledo and was still in danger at the time he wrote the
letter. He seems to fear betrayal at the hands of the Jews
where he is if they learn from their fellow Jews where Felix
is that correspondence is passing between the two men. He
cautions Felix therefore to deal only with Jews who have
wives and children (and would be less likely to betray him)
or, better still, with humble Christian merchants. The con-

---

[45] "Et quid egeritis de vestra intentione nobis certificate."
[46] "Unde et mihi demandaverat quos alios similes repererat."
[47] ES, V, Appendix X, vi, pars. 1 and 3.

nection between the brother who died and the Jews is not clear; perhaps he had left money to be sent to Elipandus. Elipandus' willingness to loan two volumes of Jerome and Isidore to compare with copies of their works that had been discovered attests to continued authoritative scholarship in the see of Toledo. The priest Venerius, who acted as courier for Elipandus, may have been bishop of Alcalá when Eulogius passed through that city between 848 and 850 after a trip to the north of Spain. Elipandus tries to build up further his case against Alcuin and Beatus, for whom his hate endures. His letter to Alcuin is an attack on them and an *apologeticus* for Adoptionism. It is remarkable that he could have composed such an intense and lengthy tract in the straits he describes. He blames the oppression of the infidels for preventing him from writing more.[48]

Little is known of Milito and the "brothers" in Córdoba mentioned by Elipandus. Ordinarily "brother" is a term of address between bishops, but Elipandus seems to use it loosely in his letters, including abbots as well. It seems unusual that Elipandus should transmit a letter from Felix to the "brothers" in Córdoba and later transmit a short work to Felix from the "brother" Milito, who seems to have been able to speak in the name of the "brothers" in Córdoba. There may have been a council in Córdoba, which Elipandus could not attend because of his eighty-two years or the distress he suffered. It is interesting to observe the waning of Elipandus' authority, which, before 785, was felt in the province of Seville. In 799 he seems to defer to Córdoba, but apparently he never relinquished his claim to authority in the Asturias. In the midst of the controversy Elipandus does not seem to have appealed to the king of the Asturias or to the emir of Córdoba. Instead he addressed himself to the king of the Franks.

The troubles of which Elipandus speaks in his letter of 799 to Felix can be surmised from Arabic histories. In 797, after a rebellion was put down in its environs, Toledo experienced the "Day of the Ditch," when many of its nobility were

[48] *Ibid.*, X, v, par. 7.

slaughtered treacherously by the future Abd al-Rahman II. From 798 to 800 al-Hakam I of Córdoba (796-822) was engaged in civil war with his uncle, Soleyman, who disputed the succession to the throne.[49] Elipandus probably experienced the ruthless repression for which al-Hakam I was famed.

Elipandus' doleful letter to Felix, unyielding as it is in his own theological position and filled with hatred for those who resisted him, is probably the last source of information about Christians in Spain under the Moslems before the country came to be fairly isolated from the rest of Christendom. The next sources of information about Christians under the Mohammedans in Spain are a letter of Louis the Pious in 826 offering succor to the people of Mérida against the common enemy in Córdoba and the acts of a council held in Córdoba in 839 condemning a group of heretics with strange practices. These two works will serve to introduce the story of the Cordoban martyrs of the ninth century.

As an introduction to his account of Adoptionism, Gams presents an elaborate and well-argued hypothesis about the source of the error. According to Gams, Nestorian Syrians followed the Arabs to Spain and occupied the same privileged position as intellectual leaders in Córdoba which they held in other Moslem capitals. These Nestorians fashioned and elaborated the doctrine of Adoptionism, and Elipandus was their willing disciple and propagandist. Gams cites a statement by Alcuin that Córdoba was the real origin of the heresy and Elipandus' references to the "brothers" in Córdoba and to texts received from the "brother" Milito, in addition to other cogent arguments, to substantiate his thesis. Amann, while admitting a Nestorian renaissance in the East, denies them any influence on religion in Spain and asserts that the error in Spain developed in isolation.[50]

Whatever were the elements of Spanish culture at this time, intellectual life was in ferment and intercommuni-

[49] Cf. Ibn Idhari, *Al-Bayan al-mughrib,* trans. Fagnan (2 vols.; Algiers, 1901-1904), II, 112.
[50] Gams, *op.cit.,* 261-267; Amann, *op.cit.,* 132, n. 2.

cation was rather free. Opposing schools of thought disputed about theology and the merits of literary expression. Treatises were written, communicated, and preserved. Various languages were studied.[51] As in the first half of the century, the Latin works in the second half of the eighth century say nothing of apostasy to Islam or of proselytizing and persecution by the Moslems. The influence of Islam on Christianity in Spain at this time seems to have consisted of attempts to modify traditional Christian discipline and doctrine in order to lessen the differences between it and Islam. These attempts found both support and opposition among Spanish Christians.

[51] Gams, *op.cit.*, 271, in explication of his thesis that Nestorian Syrians fathered the doctrine of Adoptionism argues that the misinterpretation of the word *adoptio* may be attributed to the activity of men of an alien tongue and culture searching Spanish literature for confirmation of their own heretical views.

CHAPTER IV
CHRONICLES OF THE KINGDOM OF OVIEDO

It is doubtful that any claims to kingship were successfully asserted in the Iberian peninsula from the time of the Arab conquest to the reign of Alfonso I (739-757). One can view the establishment of an emirate in Córdoba after 756 as related to Alfonso's success in establishing a kingdom in the Asturias, just as one can regard the proclamation of the caliphate of Córdoba in 929 as a reaction to the consolidation of a strong kingdom in León between 911 and 929 by Alfonso's successors, or just as one can accept the entry of the Almoravides of Morocco into Spain as the result of the capture of Toledo in 1085. The traditions of separatism and of a central monarchy, both of which existed in the time of the Visigoths, survived the Arab conquest. Opposition to the kings of Oviedo came not only from Córdoba but from Galicia and Navarre, where Christians were as anxious to preserve their autonomy as the kings of Oviedo were to restore a monarchical hegemony in Spain.

Both Oviedo and Córdoba had political traditions of a close bond or union between church and state. In the case of Oviedo the Christian religion served as a basis of union with the Galicians and Basques, although ecclesiastical claims for traditional representation in the government of the kingdom seem to have conflicted with the kings' ideas of rule. The Moslem emirs of Córdoba were in the position of having to rely on the provincial or municipal loyalty of Christian subjects and on a religious bond with the Moslem rulers of cities in their realm. The emirs either did not wish to or could not, by expelling Christians from their dominions, pursue a policy similar to the Repopulation which was being carried out in the north in the wake of the Reconquest. Probably more than anyone else in Spain, the Mozarabs were personally aware of the political situation in the peninsula.

Some of them went north to take part in the Repopulation and some of them remained in their homes.

The history of the origins and the expansion of the Christian kingdoms in the north of Spain is very complicated and involves too many difficult and technical problems to be discussed here in any detail, but a general study of the sources pertaining to the kingdom of the Asturias will be of assistance in the study of the martyrs of Córdoba. Many of the royal and private documents of the period are forgeries, and others contain interpolations or are dated earlier than they should be. The explanation of this seems to be the reluctance of some bishops in the north to relinquish rights and privileges to the kings or to concede territory and rights to old sees which were being restored to Christian rule in the Reconquest.[1] A body of Latin chronicles composed after the middle of the ninth century but containing in some instances later interpolations is the basis for the history of the kings of the Asturias. The dominant theme in the chronicles seems to concern the position of the kings of the Asturias with regard to the tradition of the Visigothic kings of Toledo. Intimately associated with this theme it seems is an underlying dispute about the role to be played by the church in the expansion of the new kingdom. The ecclesiastical point of view seems to have been that the Reconquest depended on the will of God; and certain bishops were unwilling to relinquish rights held in reconquered areas to a king who would not recognize the bond of church and state and the authority of councils after the tradition of the Visigothic kingdom of Toledo. The royal point of view seems to have been that it was the force of arms that was bringing about the Reconquest and the authority of the king did not depend on the wishes of nobles and the church in council. In the

---

[1] Pierre David, *Etudes historiques sur la Galice et le Portugal de VIe au XIIe siècle* (Lisbon and Paris, 1947), 119-184, especially 143-168. L. Barrau-Dihigo, "Etude sur les actes des rois asturiens (718-910)," *Revue hispanique*, 46 (1919), 1-191, and *id.*, "Recherches sur l'histoire politique du royaume asturien (718-910)," *ibid.*, 52 (1921), 1-360, edits and discusses the documents.

study of textual problems associated with the chronicles this dispute seems to emerge as a fundamental element. Two more or less distinct chronicles, the Chronicle of Roda and the Chronicle of Albelda, which may derive from a common source, offer an account of the kingdom of the Asturias.[2] The Chronicle of Roda formerly was regarded as a later variant text of the Chronicle of Alfonso III (also called the Chronicle of Sebastian) but now has been advanced as the earlier of these two texts. In addition, a "Prophetic Chronicle" which can be dated in April 883 is found, rearranged and revised, at the end of the Chronicle of Albelda, which comes to an end in November 883.

The Chronicle of Roda was so called by its editor, Manuel Gómez Moreno, because its text comes from a tenth-century codex of the monastery of Roda rediscovered in 1927. Previous editions of the chronicle were based on twelfth-, sixteenth-, and eighteenth-century copies of the text of Roda. The Chronicle of Alfonso III (or of Sebastian) is so named because of a vague letter from Alfonso III to "our Sebastian" at the beginning of the chronicle. Editions of the chronicle depend on sixteenth- or seventeenth-century copies of the codices *Soriensis* and *Ovetensis*, which are no longer extant.[3] The dispute about the authorship and the priority

---

[2] Jaime Villanueva, *Viaje literario a las iglesias de España* (22 vols.; Madrid, 1803-1852), VIII, 47f., speaks of a Prince Quintila (Chintila) in Catalonia (?) in 736, about whom little is known. No dynasty descended from Quintila. Cf. R. Aigrain, "L'Espagne chrétienne," *Gregoire le grand*, Vol. V of *Histoire de l'église*, 270f.

[3] The Chronicle of Roda has been edited by Manuel Gómez Moreno, "Las primeras crónicas de la Reconquista. El ciclo de Alfonso III," BRAH, 100 (1932), 609-621; García-Villada, *Crónica de Alfonso III* (Madrid, 1918), 99-131; and L. Barrau-Dihigo, "Une rédaction inédite du pseudo-Sébastien de Salamanque," *Revue hispanique*, 23 (1910), 235-264. Cf. García-Villada, "El códice de Roda recuperado," *Revista de filología española*, XV (1928), 113-130. The Chronicle of Alfonso III is edited and discussed by García-Villada, *Crónica de Alfonso III*, and by Flórez in ES, XIII, Appendix VII (PL 129, 1111-1124). Cf. also Gómez Moreno's book review in BRAH, 73 (1918), 54-58; García-Villada, "Notas sobre la Crónica de Alfonso III," *Revista de filología española*, VIII (1921), 252-270; Claudio Sánchez-Albornoz, "La

of the two texts of the chronicle, which vary significantly from each other, probably should not be regarded as definitely settled. To judge from the titles, both texts were composed in the early tenth century: the Chronicle of Roda after the death of Alfonso III and perhaps while Ordoño II was reigning in Galicia, i.e., in 913 or 914; and the Chronicle of Alfonso III while García was reigning in León and perhaps before the death of Alfonso III, i.e., in 911 or 912. But both chronicles terminate in 866 at the end of the reign of Ordoño I, and the basic text of the Chronicle of Roda appears to have been completed in the beginning of Ordoño's reign shortly after 850. Apart from the question of revisions and interpolations, which probably have been made in the case of both texts, Gómez Moreno seems to be correct in considering the Chronicle of Roda earlier than the Chronicle of Alfonso III.

In the light of ideas presented in 1947 by Pierre David in his *Etudes*[4] it seems reasonable to propose that a bishop of Galicia rather than the king of the Asturias must have been the author of the Chronicle of Roda. A comparison of the texts of the Chronicle of Roda and the Chronicle of Alfonso III, which cannot be presented here, shows that the many variations form a consistent and meaningful pattern. Both texts deal with Galicia almost as much as with the Asturias and list the cities of Galicia first among those captured by Alfonso I, but the Chronicle of Roda seems to have an ecclesiastical point of view oriented towards Galicia and the Chronicle of Alfonso III seems to have a royal point of view readjusted towards the Asturias. In the Chronicle of Alfonso III the elective aspect of the kingship and the role of ecclesiastics and councils in the affairs of state are played down. Its author devotes more attention to details of a military nature and exhibits considerable literary ability, which seems to be no more indicative of ecclesiastical training than

redacción original de la Crónica de Alfonso III," *Gesammelte Aufsätze zur Kulturgeschichte Spaniens*, II (Münster Westfalen, 1930), 47-66; and David, *Etudes*, 317-319.

[4] David, *Etudes*, 119-184.

it is of courtly learning. He shows, or seeks to show, a better knowledge of the environs of Oviedo, especially with regard to churches and other edifices built there by the kings. The two texts seem to show different attitudes towards Witiza, Rodrigo, and Pelagius, the Chronicle of Roda favoring Rodrigo somewhat and that of Alfonso III appearing to be more favorably inclined towards Witiza and Pelagius. Quite a few statements in the Chronicle of Roda which tend to derogate the regal status of the the kings of Oviedo are corrected or rephrased in the Chronicle of Alfonso III, which also omits two slurs on the reputation of Toledo as a see and as the capital of all Spain. The Chronicle of Roda says that the Northmen landed on "our" shores in the reign of Ramiro I, who came to defeat them at La Coruña. The chronicler's knowledge of the activities of the Northmen after their attack on his region suggests that he was familiar with the Atlantic littoral. The use of the word *patria* in the Chronicle of Roda seems to refer to Galicia. Braga is called a metropolitan see in the Chronicle of Roda but not in the Chronicle of Alfonso III.

A statement in the Chronicle of Roda that "in our early days" Viseu was repopulated "at our command" ("by us" in the Chronicle of Alfonso III) has been interpreted as evidence that the king (Alfonso III) is the author of the Chronicle of Roda. David, however, argues that the Repopulation was carried out initially by bishops, who gradually re-assimilated under their jurisdiction areas which the warrior kings of Oviedo had rendered a "desert," i.e., a no man's land without any organized administration, but where the organization of parishes, churches, and monasteries of former days had not been basically disturbed by the Arab occupation.[5] Credit for the repopulation of Viseu may belong to the metropolitan of Braga rather than to the king of the Asturias. Viseu, according to the Chronicle of Albelda, was repopulated in the beginning of the reign of Alfonso III (866-910). The remark that it was repopulated "in our early days" could have been made by either Alfonso III or Flavius, the metro-

[5] *Ibid.*, and 254.

politan of Braga, resident in Lugo, from about 867 to after 923.[6] Whether the words "at our command" preclude anyone but a king may not be a critical point. The main part of the Chronicle of Roda seems to have been completed shortly after Ordoño I began to rule in 850, perhaps when Gladila was metropolitan of Braga. The last part of the chronicle, which deals with military events on the eastern border of the Asturias, a region not discussed in the rest of the chronicle, may be the work of another author. Unlike the main part of the chronicle, it agrees almost word for word with the text of the Chronicle of Alfonso III. It also bears a similarity to the last part of the Chronicle of Albelda. Unless the Chronicle of Roda and the Chronicle of Alfonso III were composed in the beginning of the tenth century, it would seem that the remark about the repopulation of Viseu is in both cases an interpolation, probably made in the early tenth century.

The Chronicle of Alfonso III gives the appearance of being a more unified work than the Chronicle of Roda. It is introduced by a letter, part of which seems to be missing, in which Alfonso tells "our Sebastian" that the work is a true account based on reports of his predecessors and those before them. The chronicle ends with a liturgical flourish, "... per numquam finienda semper saecula saeculorum. Amen." The importance of the Chronicle of Alfonso III should not be underestimated. It may yet prove to be an earlier text than the Chronicle of Roda. Moreover, the variations between it and the Chronicle of Roda indicate that both texts are of great value as sources for the period when the earlier of them was revised.

The second chronicle of the kings of the Asturias, the Chronicle of Albelda, named after the monastery from which a codex containing the text came, was evidently intended as a universal chronicle.[7] It appears at first to be a hetero-

---

[6] *Ibid.*, 125-142.

[7] The Chronicle of Albelda is found in several mss, including the codex of Roda, the *codex Aemilianensis* (ms Escorial d-I-1), and the *codex Vigilanus* (ms Escorial d-I-2). The best edition of the chronicle

geneous collection of different items, but it is really a coherent work which focuses all the previous history of the world on the years 881 and 883 in the reign of Alfonso III. After being terminated in 881, the chronicle was resumed and continued to November 883. Except for the reign of Alfonso III, especially the years 877 to 883, the entries in the chronicle are rather terse. Flórez dated the Chronicle of Albelda earlier than the Chronicle of Alfonso III because it does not contain the reference to the repopulation of Viseu, but, inasmuch as the remark may be an interpolation, the reason is not very strong. No one seems to have seriously disputed Flórez, although David would date the Chronicle of Roda first, followed in turn by the Albelda text of 881, the Chronicle of Alfonso III, the Prophetic Chronicle, and finally the Albelda text of 883.[8] The basic text of the Chronicle of Albelda, which corresponds to the texts of the Chronicles of Roda and Alfonso III, may be a summary of those texts as easily as they may be an elaboration of it. Variations seem to point both ways. Unlike the Chronicle of Roda, the Chronicle of Albelda is oriented towards the Asturias rather than towards Galicia, and unlike the Chronicle of Alfonso III, it seems to be rather favorably inclined towards ecclesiastics. Since a number of entries in the Chronicle of Albelda do not appear in the Chronicles of Roda or Alfonso III, some writers think that all three texts derive from a chronicle no longer extant.

Of interest for the present study is a list of the six provinces of Spain and the province of Gaul with their suffragan sees.[9] The list confirms the organization of sees as given

is that of Gómez Moreno, "Las primeras crónicas," BRAH, 100 (1932), 600-609 (cf. *ibid.*, 593ff.), but this edition has to be supplemented with the fuller edition of Flórez in ES, XIII, Appendix VI (PL 129, 1123-1146). Theodore Mommsen, in MGH, *Auct. antiq.*, XI, *Chronica minora*, II, 370-375, without editing the text, provides an excellent summary of the mss, published editions, and contents of the chronicle. Cf. also David, *Etudes*, 125f., for a discussion of the editions.

[8] ES, XIII, 421; David, *Etudes*, 322.

[9] The list is published apart from the chronicle with two similar lists in ES, IV, Tr. 3, par. 346. Cf. David, *Etudes*, 1-6, for a discussion of

in the Acts of the Council of Córdoba in 839, and mentions all of the thirteen bishoprics mentioned by Samson in his *Apologeticus* except Martos. To the metropolitans of Spain (Toledo, Seville, Mérida, Braga, Tarracona, and Tangiers) is added that of Narbonne, which "was under the rule of the Goths." Seventeen sees are listed under Toledo and thirteen under Mérida. The nine sees under Seville are: Italica, Medina Sidonia, Arepla, Ecija, Córdoba, Cabra, Malaga, Granada, and Guadix. No sees are listed under Tangiers. Another list of twelve bishops and their sees, in riming verse, is of historical interest more for the kingdom of the Asturias than for the Cordoban martyrs. The list shows that, although the capital of the northern kingdom was in the Asturias, most of the sees were in Galicia. The list is also of interest in that it shows that the metropolitan of Braga had precedence over the bishop of Oviedo.[10] This list is followed by nine lines of riming hemistiches in praise of Alfonso III.

The Chronicle of Albelda and the two texts of the other chronicle all mention churches built by the kings. Alfonso II (792-842) built four churches besides palaces and other royal edifices. According to the Chronicle of Albelda, he established the whole order of the Visigoths in Oviedo as it had been in Toledo, in the church as well as in the palace.[11] For the most part, however, the chronicles report the victorious battles of the kings, especially against the Saracens. Alfonso I (739-757) seems to have been the first to regain territory from Arab rule. He also brought Christians back

the ecclesiastical organization of Spain. For other lists cf. ES, IV, Tr. 3, pars. 349 and 355, and Simonet, *Historia*, 808-812.

[10] David, *Etudes*, 125-130, would move the first verse to the end, but it seems better to make it the second verse and let it determine the rime of the first verse. The first two lines probably should read: Flaianus Bracarae Luco episcopus arcet, / Regiamque sedem Hermenegildus tenet.

[11] Alfonso's actions would have posed a challenge to the ecclesiastical authority of Toledo, where Elipandus had already entrenched himself in the heresy of Adoptionism, and to the royal authority of the emir of Córdoba, where the persecution of Christians broke out about eight years after Alfonso's death.

to his own realm. Ordoño I (850-866), according to the
Chronicle of Roda, built walls around León, Astorga, Túy,
and Amaya and filled the cities with people from his own
land and from "Spain." The Chronicle of Alfonso III reports
that the immigration of Christians to the north began in the
days of the Arab conquest. Of those who fled before the invaders, it says, some went to *Francia* but most came to the
Asturias. The chronicles also report that a *mollites* of
Mérida named Mahamuth rebelled against Abd al-Rahman
II in the beginning of his reign and fled to Alfonso II. For
seven years Mahamuth lived in Galicia with his followers
but then rebelled against the king and began to raid the land.
Alfonso slew him and his followers in a siege of the castle
in which they had taken refuge. In accounts which seem to
have a common point of view the chronicles report military
campaigns against the Banu Kasi of Zaragoza by Ordoño I
and Alfonso III. The Banu Kasi were seeking to set themselves up as the third kingdom in Spain, but Mohammed I
dealt with them in a way that caused them to seek an alliance
with Alfonso III. The miltary successes of Alfonso III appear to have been so outstanding that they aroused a hope
that he would drive the Saracens out of Spain. He repopulated Coimbra, and in 881 he led an expedition which crossed
the Guadiana in the region of Mérida. In 882 and 883 the
emir of Córdoba retaliated with expeditions to the region
around León but then made overtures of peace. In September 883 Alfonso sent Dulcidius, a priest of Toledo, with
letters to Mohammed I. In November, the Chronicle of Albelda concludes, Dulcidius had not yet returned. A Breviary
of Oviedo records that Dulcidius returned to Oviedo in January 884, bringing with him the relics of the Cordoban
martyrs Eulogius and Leocritia. In the opinion of Bishop
Pedro Ponce de Léon, who brought to light the works of
Eulogius in Oviedo in the sixteenth century, Dulcidius also
brought back with him the manuscript of Eulogius' works.[12]

---

[12] Cf. ES, X, 457. Gil González de Avila, *Historia de las antigüedades
de la ciudad de Salamanca* (Salamanca, 1606), 57-59, says that Dulcidius obtained the relics in Córdoba through the help of a Christian

Following the Chronicle of Albelda in the codex of Roda are several notices pertaining to the Saracens, their conquest of Spain, and a prophecy of their expulsion from Spain, compiled in April 883. The notices, which show what the Christians of the North knew of the Saracens and what their attitude towards them was, evidence the spirit of a crusade or a holy war. Gómez Moreno edits them as the "Prophetic Chronicle." As edited by Flórez at the end of the Chronicle of Albelda, the notices appear to have been rearranged and revised about 976.[13]

The Prophetic Chronicle begins with a quotation allegedly from Ezechiel, found in a *liber Pariticinus*. "O son of man, set thy face against Ismael, and speak to them, saying, I have given thee most strong to the peoples. I have multiplied thee. I have strengthened thee. And I have placed in thy right hand a sword and in thy left hand arrows, that thou mayest strike down peoples, and that they may be prostrate before thy face, as straw before the face of fire, and that thou wilt enter the land of Gog on an even footing, and wilt slay Gog with thy sword, and wilt place thy foot upon his neck, and make them tributary slaves. Indeed, because thou hast abandoned the Lord thy God I shall lead thee in circles and abandon thee and deliver thee into the hand of Gog, and thou and thy whole troop will perish by his sword in the bounds of Libya. As thou hast done to Gog so will he do to thee. After thou hast possessed them in servitude 170 times he will render to thee in turn what thou hast done to him."[14]

Gog represents the Gothic people; from him they come and after him they are named, says the chronicler, quoting

named Samuel. Not only Breviaries tell of this, he says, but also "councils" in the Escorial which Ambrosio de Morales used. Ponce de León's remark is in his letter of dedication of the edition of Eulogius' works to Philip II; cf. PL 115, 913.

[13] Gómez Moreno, *op.cit.*, 622-628. In the edition of Flórez the prophecy seems to be associated with interpolations of 976 concerning the kings of Pamplona.

[14] David, *Etudes*, 313-328, discusses the prophecy and offers several valuable notes about the Prophetic Chronicle and the other chronicles of Oviedo.

Isidore of Seville to support his claim. Now the time of the prophecy of Ezechiel is come, he continues, for Spain is the land of Gog, which the Ismaelites invaded because of the sins of the Gothic people and still possess. The Saracens entered Spain 11 November 714 in the third year of Rodrigo's reign. Now in 883, in the seventeenth year of Alfonso of Oviedo and the thirty-second year of Mohammed I of Córdoba, the 170 years are accomplished. Our hope is Christ, the chronicler states. When the 170 years are soon completed, He will reduce the effrontery of His enemies to nothing and restore His peace to Holy Church. Even the Saracens, in the light of their own signs, predict the end of their reign, and they say that Alfonso will restore the rule of the Goths.[15] And it has been revealed to many Christians that our prince will soon rule over all Spain. The fortune of God's enemies declines daily as that of His Church rises. As the dignity of Christ's name increases so the calamity of His enemies become more ignoble.[16]

There follows a genealogy of the Saracens, who wrongly, the chronicler states, claim to be descended from Sarah. The genealogy traces the descent of the Saracens from Abraham, Ismael, through the prophet Mohammed and Abd al-Rahman I, to the sons of Mohammed, Almundar and Abd Allah. The vita of the prophet Mohammed included by Eulogius in the *Apologeticus martyrum*[17] follows the genealogy in the codex of Roda. An account according to the Saracens of the invasion of Spain is then given. When Spain was rent by dissension caused by the sons of Witiza and a faction wished to overthrow the kingdom, Abuzubra invaded the peninsula, followed by Tarik the next year. In the third year, when Tarik was battling Rodrigo, Muza entered and brought to an end the reign of Goths. Nothing is known of the death of Rodrigo to this day, the notice states. The Arabs possessed

---

[15] Albar, *Indiculus luminosus*, 21, discusses a prophecy of the Jews that the end of the reign of the Arabs in the world was to come after 245 years, a terminus due in 870.

[16] This statement occurs also in the Chronicle of Roda.

[17] Cf. index, "Mohammed, vita."

the land and the kingdom. All the honor of the Gothic people perished through fear and the sword, for they did no fitting penance for their sins. And because they abandoned the laws of God and the institutes of sacred canons the Lord abandoned them. By the hand of God a few Arabs reduced the Goths to nothing, and many still are subject to them. Toledo, the victrix of all peoples, was subjugated by the Saracens.[16]

The Prophetic Chronicle continues with an account of the Goths who remained in the cities of Betica (*Ispaniensis*). After a messenger announced the fall of Rodrigo to all the cities and castles held by the Goths, the war with the Saracens continued for seven years. Then the Goths agreed to surrender, withdrawing from the cities to castles and towns. They elected counts to conclude treaties with the Arab king. The Arabs drove them out of every city they had conquered and hunted them down as slaves. A list of Arab rulers from Muza to Toaba is given next. They ruled briefly, states the chronicler, because they were appointed by the *amir al-mauminin*. He then gives a list of the kings of "Spain" from Yusuf to the thirty-second year of Mohammed I. Altogether the Arabs have been in Spain 168 years and five months, he notes. Seven months remain till 11 November when 169 years will be completed and the 170th year will begin,[18] in which according to the prophecy of Ezechiel vengeance will come to the Saracens and salvation to the Christians. May the Lord redeem His Church from the yoke of the Ismaelites. The last item in the Prophetic Chronicle is a list of the Catholic kings of León. From Pelagius, who began to rule in 718, to today in 928 are 211 years, the list begins. The last king listed in the codex of Roda is Ramiro II (931-935 to 950); the last listed in the edition of Flórez is Ramiro III (965-984).

The Prophetic Chronicle is closely associated with the

---

[18] Like the author of the Chronicle of 754, the author of the Prophetic Chronicle seems to have treated the Christian year and the Arab year as of equal length. A.H. 270 ran from 11 July 883 to 28 June 884, but A.H. 100 ran from 3 August 718 to 23 July 719.

basic theme of the other chronicles, i.e., the relationship of
the kings of Oviedo with the former Visigothic kings of
Toledo. Apart from interpolations which serve to bring notices up to date in the tenth century, it seems to be the work
of an author writing in April 883, based, however, on earlier
material. Like the author of the Chronicle of Roda, the author of the Prophetic Chronicle has an ecclesiastical point of
view. Several phrases and sentences occur in both works.
The two chronicles speak of a persecution of the Church and
of a yoke of the Saracens on the Church. The references,
which probably reflect the ecclesiastical interests of the authors, may pertain to events in Córdoba rather than to a
general opposition of Islam to Christianity. Unlike the
Chronicle of Roda, the Prophetic Chronicle shows no partial-
ity to Galicia, and it openly expresses a loyalty to "our
prince" Alfonso III.

CHAPTER V

CHRISTIANS IN ARABIC ACCOUNTS OF MOSLEM RULE IN CÓRDOBA

Almost from the beginning of the Arab conquest of Spain the invaders and the Spanish Christians learned to live together on amicable terms it seems. Intermarriages were fairly common and took place mostly between Christian women and Moslem men, although there were some marriages between Christian men and Moslem women. The mixed marriages occurred in all classes of society and continued as long as the Moslems ruled in Spain. When the marriages resulted in the conversion of spouses to Christianity or in the rearing of children as Christians, as they did during the period of the Cordoban martyrs, they gave rise to conflict between the two peoples. There seems to be no basis for the assumption that Christians lived outside the walls of the city of Córdoba. A good number of them were citizens of Córdoba, and their churches were within the walls. It seems unlikely that Mohammed I, who in 858 ordered the inhabitants outside the *civitas* when he marched against Toledo,[1] would have done so had Moslems only been in the city. According to the Latin sources, Christians used a market in common with the Moslems and entered into legal affairs with them. Christians held offices in the government, especially it seems in the chancery and in the military forces. There was some exchange of intellectual and religious ideas, but the exchange proved dangerous in the ninth century, and by the tenth century each group seems to have kept its religious and cultural tradition apart from the other group. Christians are hard to identify in Arabic works, but a general idea of the conditions in which they lived in Córdoba, as well as some information about an occasional Christian, can be obtained from the Arabic histories.

[1] Aimoin's *Translatio*, 10.

In general the picture described in Arabic works[2] agrees with what Christian authors say in Latin works, although the Arabic histories which deal with Córdoba in the eighth and ninth centuries are all of late date and have nothing at all to say about the Christian martyrs of the ninth century. Two of the earliest of the Arabic histories are Ibn al-Kutiya's *History of the Conquest of Spain* and the anonymous *Akhbar madjmua (Collected Stories)*,[3] both written about A.D. 1000 and both found in a unique manuscript (Paris BN 706). Neither work concerns itself with the Christians living in Córdoba, but Ibn al-Kutiya, "the son of the Gothic woman," i.e., descended from Sarah the Goth, in describing persons of Spanish descent treats of several Christians.

The *History of the Conquest of Spain* begins with the invasion of Spain under Tarik and Muza. Its detailed account of the descendants of Witiza does not agree with other sources. According to Ibn al-Kutiya, Witiza's sons, Alamundo, Romulo, and Artobas, remained in Toledo with their mother as regent after their father's death. When Tarik in-

[2] A cursory survey of Arabic historiography is given by B. Sánchez Alonso, *Historia de la historiografía española* (2 vols.; Madrid, 1941-1944), I (2d ed.; 1947), 162-202. Arabic names in this chapter, as in the rest of the present work, are spelled as much as possible according to the *Encyclopaedia of Islam* (EI). When it appears, however, that this policy serves no purpose, the name is left as it appears in the text cited.

[3] *Colección de obras arábigas de historia y geografía que publica la Real Academia de la Historia*: vol. I, *Ajbar Machmua (Colleción de Tradiciones) Crónica anónima de siglo XI...*, ed., trans., and annotated by E. Lafuente y Alcántara (Madrid, 1867); vol. II, *Historia de la conquista de España de Albenalcotía el cordobés, seguida de fragmentos históricos de Abencotaiba, etc.*, trans. Julián Ribera (Madrid, 1926). Lafuente y Alcántara does not study the authorship and date of composition of the *Akhbar*, but Ribera in vol. II of the *Colección* discusses these matters for both works. C. Sánchez-Albornoz has published a lengthy monograph based on his study of translations of the *Akhbar* and other Arabic works with which he compared it, *El "Ajbar Maymua'a" Cuestiones historiográficas que suscita* (Buenos Aires, 1944). Although the *History of the Conquest of Spain* is attributed to Ibn al-Kutiya, it was probably written by one of his disciples after his death; Ribera, *op.cit.*, xx f., and Sánchez Alonso, *op.cit.*, 168f.

vaded the peninsula, Rodrigo, a general who had established himself with his troops in Córdoba, called upon the sons of Witiza to aid him. Though they mistrusted him they came to his assistance with troops. But in the battle which took place they betrayed him to the Arabs, with whom they signed a pact securing land and privileges for themselves. Alamundo, who lived in Seville, died leaving a daughter, Sarah the Goth, and two sons, one the metropolitan of Seville and the other, Opas,[4] "who died in Galicia." From Witiza's second son, Romulo, in Toledo, was descended Hafs ibn Albar, *cadi adjami* (judge of the Christians).[5] Why Ibn al-Kutiya mentions Hafs ibn Albar is not clear. He may have been a member of Ibn al-Kutiya's family who was well known in the history of Córdoba. As judge of the Christians, he would seem to have been a Christian. He may have been the Christian father of Omar ibn Hafsun (d. 918)[6] and possibly too a relative of another person who boasted of his Gothic ancestry, Paul Albar of Córdoba. When Witiza's third son, Artobas, who lived in Córdoba, attempted to seize part of the possessions of Sarah the Goth, she appealed in person to the caliph in Damascus, where she met the future founder of the Umaiyad dynasty in Spain, Abd al-Rahman I, when he was a youth. Later she visited Abd al-Rahman in Córdoba, and he decided which of two Arab lords seeking her hand should have her in marriage.[7]

Ibn al-Kutiya describes the civil war of 742 in Spain between the Syrian refugees from North Africa and the original Arab conquerors of Spain. This war was temporarily resolved when a governor sent from Kairouan, Abulcathar, sent the leader of the Syrians to Tangiers and allocated the lands outside Córdoba to the Syrian troops. The Syrians were thus settled in Spain at the expense of the Christians, who had surrendered to the Arabs by treaty, and the original

---

[4] Opas is mentioned in the Chronicle of 754 and in the Latin chronicles of the North.

[5] Ibn al-Kutiya, page 5 of the Arabic text; cf. index, "cadi."

[6] Cf. Lévi-Provençal, "Omar b. Hafsun," EI, III, 981f.

[7] Ibn al-Kutiya, 1-4 of the Spanish translation.

Arab and Berber invaders of the peninsula kept what they had got by conquest.[8]

The conquest of Spain by the Umaiyad Abd al-Rahman I (756-788) is treated in detail. He faced many insurrections in his reign, "for most of Spain wanted to get rid of Abd al-Rahman."[9] In 797, a year after al-Hakam I began to rule, the baleful "Day of the Ditch" took place in Toledo, as al-Hakam's son, the future Abd al-Rahman II, slew "exactly 5300" of the nobles in the rebellious city under the guise of receiving them for a banquet in the Alcazar.[10] Al-Hakam executed a heretical sect of Moslems called Kharidjites in Algeciras, and in 817 with his palace guard of "mutes" he put down in Córdoba a serious uprising of a group associated with the Malekite sect.[11] Those who had taken part in the uprising he exiled, some of them journeying to the East and later seizing the island of Crete. There was no opposition to al-Hakam, states Ibn al-Kutiya, except on the part of the Banu Kasi of Zaragoza,[12] a family of Visigoths who, according to the Chronicles of Roda and Alfonso III, left Christianity and became Moslems.

Ibn al-Kutiya describes at length and with many notes of

[8] *Ibid.*, 15; cf. index, "Abulcathar."

[9] Ibn al-Kutiya, 25 of the Spanish translation.

[10] *Ibid.*, 39. According to data used by Lévi-Provençal, *Histoire de l'Espagne musulmane*, I, 157 and 195, Abd al-Rahman was only five years old at this time.

[11] The Kharidjites, also called the Haruriya, formed the earliest religious sect of Islam. In general, they advocated a strict code of conduct and tolerance towards non-Arabs and non-Moslems. They maintained that any irreproachable Moslem could become caliph and that a caliph who had deviated from the right path was *ipso facto* deposed. They rejected the doctrine of justification by faith without works. Their rebellions, especially in Mesopotamia and Arabia, were instrumental in the rise of the Umaiyad and Abbasid dynasties. G. Levi della Vida, "Kharidjites," EI, II, 904-908. The usual explanation for the palace guard being called "mutes" is that they did not speak Arabic, but cf. the Byzantine *silentiarii*. Malekites were the followers of Malik ibn Anas (d. A.D. 795), a Moslem jurist of Medina. He was important among those who established Islamic law on religious and moral ideas. J. Schacht, "Malik ben Anas," EI, III, 205-209.

[12] Ibn al-Kutiya, 41f.

interest the incursions of the Northmen who raided Seville in 844 and 858. The Latin chronicles of the North also report the raids of these Northmen. Abd al-Rahman II had to deal with more serious threats than that of the Northmen, one from the Christian kings of the Asturias and another from rebellions within his realm, particularly in Mérida. Ibn al-Kutiya mentions a rebel of Mérida named Mahmud, probably the same person who, according to the chronicles of the North, fled to Alfonso II and died later in rebellion against Alfonso. Ibn al-Kutiya, however, reports that Mahmud died and the rebellion in Mérida came to an end.[13]

The ruler during most of the Christian martyr movement in Córdoba was Mohammed I (852-886). Like his father, he faced revolts at home and wars with the Christians of the North. In his reign a rebel of Mérida named Ibn Meruan captured Haxim, whom Ibn al-Kutiya portrays as the most important person after the king in the court of Córdoba, and delivered him to Alfonso III of Oviedo, from whom he was ransomed for 100,000 gold solidi.[14] Rebels like Omar ibn Hafsun set themselves up in fortified positions as independent rulers and even threatened the trade routes and supply lines to Córdoba. Another enemy with whom Mohammed had to contend was Muza ibn Muza of Zaragoza, who was encroaching upon Mohammed's realm. This same Muza built the fort of Albelda which was destroyed by Ordoño I, as described in the chronicles of the North. Ibn al-Kutiya says that Muza's family continued in power until 924.[15]

Ibn al-Kutiya provides much information about the cadis and ministers of Abd al-Rahman II and Mohammed I. He notes that Abd al-Rahman held Yahya ibn Yahya, a powerful Malekite fakih who refused to hold office, in high respect and honored him as a good son would his loving father.[16] The

---

[13] *Ibid.*, 50-53.

[14] *Ibid.*, 74; the event is confirmed in the Chronicle of Albelda, no. 62. Cf. index, "solidus."

[15] Ibn al-Kutiya, 74-85.

[16] *Ibid.*, 46. "Fakih" was used to translate the *(juris)prudens* of Roman law. Its meaning of one who possessed knowledge and understanding of a thing became successively restricted to religious knowl-

picture of Mohammed I in Ibn al-Kutiya's work, as one would expect, is somewhat different from that in the Latin sources of Córdoba. Ibn al-Kutiya records that Mohammed I was calm and composed, not addicted to severity in punishments, and a good ruler until he came under the influence of Haxim and began to rely on younger men rather than his older and more judicious subjects.[17] The change in Mohammed's reign which can be discerned in the Latin sources is only that he left off the bloody persecution of the martyrs and the destruction of churches and took up instead a course of taxation and corruption of the Christian clergy. Ibn al-Kutiya's statement that Mohammed kept the ministers of his father on coming to the throne is modified but not contradicted by Eulogius' statement that one of his first acts after coming to the throne was to expel all the Christians from the court.[18] Three officials discussed by Ibn al-Kutiya are of interest in the present study: Nasr, a prime minister whose father spoke only "Romance,"[19] mentioned by Eulogius; Comes (Gómez) ibn Antonián, a fallen away Christian, secretary to King Mo-

edge (theologian), religious law (canon lawyer), and finally derivative details of religious law (casuist). D. B. Macdonald, "Fakih," EI, II, 46.

[17] Ibn al-Kutiya, 56.

[18] *Memoriale sanctorum*, III, i.

[19] According to Lévi-Provençal, *Histoire*, I, 266, Ibn Hazm says that Nasr's father was a Christian of Carmona who apostatized to Islam. Dag Norberg, *Syntaktische Forschungen auf dem Gebiete des Spätlateins und des frühen Mittellateins* (Leipzig, 1943), 21-24, permits a distinction between the spoken language, "Romance," and written Latin in Gaul as early as 800 but finds no basis for a distinction in Italy before the tenth century. Spain is practically excluded from his study, there being only one reference to a Latin work written there after 711 (the Chronicle of 754), *ibid.*, 161. Norberg notes that the lack of definitive editions of the Latin texts of Spanish writers is a serious handicap in the investigation of syntactical changes in their Latin usage. The hegemony of the Arabic language and the absence of the Carolingian renaissance differentiate Moslem Spain from Gaul, which is the basis of Norberg's study. The most irregular Latin written in Moslem Spain appears to be that in the Chronicle of 754; cf. also the letters of Ascaricus and Tusaredus, and Felix of Córdoba and Peter. In 864 Samson ridicules Hostegesis for syntactical variations in his Latin which are more irregular than the rather good Latin of Eulogius and

hammed; and Amer ibn Abd Allah, a cadi[20] of Spanish descent. According to Ibn al-Kutiya, Haxim was responsible for the downfall of two of these native Spaniards, Comes and Amer.

Ibn al-Kutiya's account of the minister Nasr agrees with that given by Eulogius. According to Ibn al-Kutiya, a favorite wife of Abd al-Rahman II, named Tarub, sought by gifts to ingratiate her son Abd Allah with the palace servants so that they would favor him rather than Mohammed to succeed Abd al-Rahman. Nasr hated Mohammed and willingly sided with Tarub. When Abd al-Rahman in his last years showed a predilection for Mohammed, Nasr decided to kill the emir and Mohammed so that Abd Allah might become king and Nasr's position might be saved. Nasr obtained a poison from a physician, "el-Harraní," who sent a warning to Abd al-Rahman. As a result, when Nasr offered the drink to the king he was forced to drink it himself and died quickly thereafter.[21] Eulogius relates that in 850 Perfectus, the first martyr, prophesied to Nasr, who was prime minister (clavicularius proconsul) "and managed the administration of the whole government in Spain," that within a year after his death Nasr would die.[22]

Comes ibn Antonián, the fallen away Christian who was secretary[23] to King Mohammed, may be the person referred

Albar. The pompous verbosity which appears here and there in all Mozarab authors may reflect the influence of Arabic letters, although it was characteristic of Latin in the Visigothic period. The "Romance" spoken in ninth-century Córdoba was presumably Latin. Ramon Menéndez Pidal, *Orígenes del español, estado lingüístico de la península ibérica hasta el siglo XI*, Vol. III of *Obras completas de R. Menéndez Pidal*, 3d ed. (Madrid, 1950), 431, says there is no text for Romance before the eleventh century.

[20] The cadi, the judge in the Moslem juridicial system, a religious authority, and the leader of prayer in the mosque, is discussed below. Cf. T. W. Juynboll, "Kadi," EI, II, 606f., and Lévi-Provençal, *L'Espagne musulmane au Xème siècle*, 82ff.

[21] Ibn al-Kutiya, 61f.

[22] *Memoriale*, II, i.

[23] The *katib* (writer or scribe) who was private secretary to an Arab

to in the *Indiculus luminosus* as a "mad dog *publicanus* persecutor of the Church" who attacked his own faith, or the person referred to in the *Memoriale* as the fallen away Christian *exceptor* (secretary or public official) who first caused the martyrs to be anathematized.[24] Ibn al-Kutiya's account of him may be supplemented with al-Khushani's in the *History of the Cadis of Córdoba*.[25] Comes' ability in the performance of his duties, his elegant correctness of speech, and his lively intelligence so impressed Mohammed that when the king's secretary died after an incapacitating illness Mohammed expressed the wish that Comes, who had been in fact filling the office, were a Moslem so that he could be appointed to the office. Comes thereupon proclaimed himself a Moslem and received the appointment. Comes and Haxim, who also held great influence with Mohammed, were rivals for the king's favor. Haxim envied the rise of Comes, who frequently countermanded Haxim's orders. According to al-Khushani, Comes so feared for his life at the hands of Haxim that he would not open his door to anyone calling on him at night.[26] After some time Haxim and a group of Arabs complained to Mohammed of the shame of having the son and grandson of Christians hold such a high position when there were Arabs available for the office. As a result of their complaints, Comes was deposed and replaced by an Arab. Thereupon he withdrew to the mosque and prayed in such a way as to convince the Moslems that his conversion to Islam had been sincere and was not the result of opportunism.

ruler was the *wazir* or prime minister; F. Krenkow, "Katib," EI, II, 819. Lévi-Provençal, *op.cit.*, 69ff., describes a *katib* in charge of the chancery and another in charge of the treasury. Ibn Khaldun, *The Muqaddimah*, trans. F. Rosenthal, II, 12f., describes the *wazir* as a *katib* and says that the *wazir* who held the title of doorkeeper *(hajib)* and served as liaison between the *wazirs* and the caliph came to be the prime minister.

[24] *Indiculus*, 18; *Memoriale*, II, xv, and III, iii. Coupled with the identification of Comes is the determination of the meaning of *publicanus* and *exceptor*, q.v. index.

[25] Ibn al-Kutiya, 67-69, and al-Khushani, *Historia de los jueces de Córdoba*, ed. and trans. Julián Ribera (Madrid, 1914), 159-164.

[26] Al-Khushani, 160f.

When Comes died and his estate was being divided among his heirs, Haxim protested that he had died as a Christian, and "a multitude of most important witnesses belonging to the principal families of Córdoba appeared before the cadi and declared that Comes had died as a Christian."[27] Had this accusation been sustained, the state would have confiscated the estate from the heirs. But the cadi advised Mohammed that he did not regard the testimony of the men as true, since nothing of reproach had been proven against Comes and none of the witnesses had taken the name of God in their oaths. Mohammed then decided that Comes had not returned to Christianity and decreed that the property be divided among the heirs.

Comes, the *exceptor* mentioned by Eulogius, and the *publicanus* persecutor mentioned in the *Indiculus luminosus* may be the same person. He may be too Romanus Medicus, whom Albar indicates to have held the office of count of Córdoba and whom Samson describes as an octogenarian imbued with anthropomorphist notions of God in 864.[28] It is not known when Comes lost his post as secretary to the king, but the question of his estate arose when Soleiman ibn Asuad was cadi, from approximately 870 to 873.[29] Although "Comes" probably stands for the Latin title *comes* (count), Comes could not have been Servandus, count of Córdoba and enemy of Samson in 864. Servandus died in 890 when Abd Allah was king. Accordingly it would appear either that there were a number of "counts" among the Christians in Córdoba at the same time or that Servandus succeeded Comes during the latter's lifetime. Eulogius says that the *exceptor* accused him in a council with having instigated the martyrs. In 852 the *exceptor*, who chose earthly honors before heavenly things, decreed that the martyrs and their supporters be

[27] Al-Khushani, 162. The account of the death of Comes is not given by Ibn al-Kutiya.

[28] Cf. Letter IX of the Albar correspondence, greeting and 6; *Apologeticus*, preface to Bk. II, 6.

[29] According to Ibn al-Kutiya, 58, Amer ibn Abd Allah was out of office as cadi and in Zaragoza for only a few years. According to al-Khushani, 175, he began his second term in 873.

anathematized. Later he himself, the only one of the Christians left in the government, lost his position. After he joined the Moslem sect he was restored to his earlier honor, and proceeded apace with the persecution of the Christians.[30] Eulogius says nothing more about him. Comes cannot definitely be identified with any of the persons mentioned by Eulogius, Albar, and Samson. Such an identification would be of interest, but it is of less importance than the fact that three contemporary Christian sources and two later Arabic sources agree in portraying certain Christians as denying their faith for political preferment and gain.

The third person of interest in Ibn al-Kutiya's account, Amer ibn Abd Allah Abu Abd Allah, was the first person of Spanish descent to be cadi of Córdoba, and the first cadi to have the title "Cadi al-djamâ'a [of the Community]" rather than that of "Cadi of the Military," as the cadi of Córdoba had been called up to then.[31] Amer had been cadi in Ecija and secretary to his predecessor in Córdoba before becoming cadi of Córdoba in 864, the year in which Samson wrote his *Apologeticus*. Al-Khushani says that when Amer was appointed the Arabs protested against having a non-Arab to lead them in prayer in the mosque, one of the functions of the cadi. Mohammed then appointed an Arab as leader of prayer but kept Amer as cadi, saying that he found qualities in him which he did not find in the Arabs. Al-Khushani praises Amer for sound judgment and excellent conduct, noting too that when his son died there was a funeral procession such as Córdoba had never seen before. There may be no special significance in the appointment of a person of Spanish descent to the office of cadi so soon after the martyrdoms of Córdoba (850-859), but it is natural that in the course of that long struggle certain problems concerning the juridicial system in Córdoba should arise. The change in the cadi's title and the appointment of a cadi of Spanish descent

[30] *Memoriale*, II, xv, and III, iii.
[31] Ibn al-Kutiya, 57-59; al-Khushani, 144; *"al-djamâ'a"* is a loosely used term which could apply to any group.

both point to some kind of integration of Moslem and Mozarabic law in Córdoba.

Mohammed deposed Amer, according to al-Khushani, on the advice of Haxim in an attempt to bring to an end the trial of Baki ibn Mohallad for heresy. According to Ibn Idhari, Baki, who was a sage from the East, with Haxim's help defeated his opponents, who are not named, in debate before King Mohammed and thus established himself as a juridicial authority in Córdoba.[32] Ibn al-Kutiya has yet another account. According to him, Amer's deposition followed charges against him of peculation. Abd al-Rahman II (822-852) had sent a certain Cosbí as ambassador to King Charles of France and to Byzantium. Cosbí died on the embassy and Amer, about A.D. 870, became the guardian of his wealth and his orphaned children. When the money entrusted to him disappeared Amer was accused of theft by his own secretary and one of the sons of Cosbí. Mohammed was greatly upset about the loss because Cosbí had received the money from Abd al-Rahman, who had held him in high esteem. Mohammed called a council, which advised him to exact a solemn oath from Amer, but Baki ibn Mohallad argued that the Moslems would be scorned by Christians and Jews if they were seen to exact a solemn oath from the cadi, a man to whom they committed the honor of their wives and their orphans, and their bequests of piety. He advised that the lost amount be paid from the public treasury. Mohammed followed this advice, but, having deposed Amer, nevertheless secretly sent the eunuch Eidon to exact from him a solemn oath of his innocence on the Koran. This Amer made. Cosbí appears to have been a Moslem, but it is possible that his orphans and his wealth would have been entrusted to the cadi even if he was a Christian, as long as he was in the king's pay.

Shortly afterwards Amer was appointed cadi of Zaragoza, where he remained for several years. When he wrote from there to Córdoba requesting the return of property and other

[32] Al-Khushani, 154f.; Ibn Idhari, *Al-Bayan al-mughrib*, trans. Fagnan, II, 181.

things due his family and his sons, he was recalled to Córdoba by King Mohammed to replace Soleiman ibn Asuad, who had succeeded him. Amer resumed his position in 873 with the new title of "Cadi al-djamâ'a" and continued in office until 876.[33]

Ibn al-Kutiya's *History*, as he approaches his own day, becomes thinner and more devoted to military expeditions and idle anecdotes, to the neglect of political life.

The other early Arabic history, the *Akhbar Madjmua*, is a collection of anecdotes associated with the history of Spain under the Arabs up to the end of the reign of Abd al-Rahman III (912-961). About a third of the work describes the military campaigns of Abd al-Rahman I (756-788). For the most part the *Akhbar* repeats Ibn al-Kutiya's history. It states that al-Hakam I (796-822), "extinguished the fire of discord in Spain, put an end to the crowds of rebels, and humbled the infidels [Christians] throughout the realm," and notes that Abd al-Rahman II (822-852) "began to rule when the state was tranquil and firm."[34] The *Akhbar* reports nothing except a series of anecdotes about Mohammed I (852-886). Towards the end of the work poems appear in the text, the last two pages being devoted entirely to poems by and about Abd al-Rahman III.[35]

In both Ibn al-Kutiya's work and the *Akhbar* it is difficult to identify Christians, perhaps because they are not mentioned, perhaps because their identity as Christians is concealed when they are mentioned. It would seem, however, that Christians played fairly important roles in Moslem Spain. Louis the Pious seems to have appealed to a Christian element in Mérida in 826, Ibn Meruan of Mérida turned over a captive Moslem lord to a Christian king, and Ibn Hafsun, the rebel master of Bobastro at the end of the ninth century, became a Christian, as his father evidently had been. An-

[33] Ibn al-Kutiya, 59; al-Khushani, 175-177.
[34] *Akhbar*, 112f., and 120.
[35] The *Antapodosis* of Liutprand of Cremona, composed at about the same time as the *Akhbar*, and Ibn Haiyan's *Muktabis* also contain poetry inserted in the narrative.

other Arabic history, the *Muktabis,* attributes more prominence to Christians in the affairs of Andalucía than they are generally thought to have had.[36]

The *Muktabis,*[37] a work by Ibn Haiyan of Córdoba (988-1076), appears to be the most detailed and best written account of Moslem rule in Spain. Only parts of this work are extant. One part deals with the reign of al-Hakam I (796-822) and most of the reign of Abd al-Rahman II (the years 822-846). Unfortunately the manuscript for this part of the *Muktabis* comes to an end just before the period of the Cordoban martyrs. A second part of the *Muktabis* deals with the reign of Abd Allah (888-912) and a third part covers the years 971-974 of the reign of al-Hakam II. Ibn Haiyan

---

[36] Cagigas, *Los mozárabes,* I, 163f., says that many of the rebels were Christians.

[37] For a discussion of the life and works of Ibn Haiyan cf. García Gómez, "A propósito de Ibn Hayyan," *Al-Andalus,* XI (1946), 395-423. The text of the *Muktabis* dealing with the reigns of al-Hakam I and Abd al-Rahman II comes from 203 folios of a ms of Fez which has not been edited. The contents of this part of the *Muktabis* have been discussed by Lévi-Provençal in his *Histoire de l'Espagne musulmane,* 2d ed. (Paris and Leyden, 1950), I, 150-225. The part dealing with the reign of Abd Allah comes from 107 folios of ms Bodleian 509, which has been dated as earlier than A.D. 1249. It has been edited by Melchor M. Antuña, *Ibn Haiyan, Al-Muktabis, tome troisième: Chronique du regne du calife umaiyad Abd Allah à Cordoue* (Paris, 1937), with an introduction based on an earlier study by Antuña, "Abenhayán de Córdoba y su obra historica," *La ciudad de Dios,* 139-140 (1924-1925), passim. Cf. the corrections by C. Brockelmann in *Orientalische Literaturzeitung,* 44 (1941), 168-171. This part of the *Muktabis* has been translated into Spanish by José E. Guarieb, "Al-Muqtabis de Ibn Hayyan," CHE, 13-32 (1950-1960), passim. Cf. Lévi-Provençal, *op.cit.,* 329-396. The part dealing with the few years of the reign of al-Hakam II came from ms 339 of the library of the heirs of Sidi Hammuda in Constantine, dated A.D. 1249. Lévi-Provençal, *ibid.,* II, 165, believes this ms to be lost. A copy of it exists in the Real Academia de la Historia in Madrid. Its content is discussed by Lévi-Provençal, *ibid.,* 171f., and a list of the chapters has been published by F. Codera, "Manuscrito de Aben Hayán en la Biblioteca de los herederos de Çidi Hammouda en Constantine," BRAH, XIII (1888), 53-61. Cf. also M. Antuña, "Ibn Hayyan de Córdoba y su historia de la España musulmana," CHE, IV (1946), 5-72.

quotes extensively from earlier writers, especially an Isa ibn Ahmad al-Razi, who died towards the end of the tenth century and whose works are known only through quotations by other authors.[38] These quotations show that al-Razi was an accomplished historical writer. Only that part of the *Muktabis* dealing with the reign of Abd Allah has been edited and translated. The other two parts, available in manuscripts, have been discussed in secondary works.

To judge from Lévi-Provençal's account of the reigns of al-Hakam I and Abd al-Rahman II, which is based on the *Muktabis*, Ibn Haiyan's history of these reigns devotes most attention to military campaigns against the Christian rulers in the north of Spain and to constant rebellions against Córdoba, especially on the part of the rulers of Zaragoza, Toledo, and Mérida. The *Muktabis* describes the loss of Barcelona to the Franks in 801.[39] Evidently Lévi-Provençal's account of the uprisings in Córdoba against al-Hakam in 805, 806, and 818 are based on the *Muktabis*. In 805 al-Hakam executed seventy-two conspirators. In 806 he executed a number of Cordobans for demonstrating against him. The *Muktabis* dates the well-known uprising in Secunda, a suburb of Córdoba, in 818, rather than in 817 as does Ibn al-Kutiya. The inhabitants of Secunda, Malekites for the most part it would seem, rose up against al-Hakam and besieged him in his palace. He succeeded in massacring them and laying waste their homes, finally expelling the survivors from his realm. For some reason he pardoned the Malekite fakihs who led the disturbance. Lévi-Provençal infers that Moslem resentment against a Christian official of al-Hakam occasioned the uprising.[40] This Christian official was Count Rabi, son of

---

[38] García Gómez, *op.cit.*, 414-418, points out that the *Muktabis* is little more than a cento of earlier chronicles, mostly that of Isa ibn Ahmad al-Razi, collected by Ibn Haiyan into an edition. Isa ibn Ahmad was the son and grandson of Arabic historians of Moslem Spain. The grandfather came to Córdoba from Persia in A.D. 864. The father is believed to be the author of a part of the *Fath 'l-Andalus*, discussed below; cf. Lévi-Provençal, "al-Razi," EI, III, 1136f.

[39] Lévi-Provençal, *Histoire*, I, 175-185.

[40] *Ibid.*, 162-173.

Theodulphus, whom al-Hakam put in charge of his palace guard of foreign mercenaries and entrusted with the collection of taxes. When Abd al-Rahman II succeeded al-Hakam he had Rabi executed, apparently in an effort to court favor with the Malekites and others who had chafed at the rule of al-Hakam.[41]

The *Muktabis* depicts the reign of Abd al-Rahman II as felicitous for both the king and his subjects, a period of intellectual renaissance.[42] Under Abd al-Rahman the annual revenue almost doubled that obtained in the reign of his predecessor. He reorganized the administration of the government. The monarch became the center of the administration and retained control over all authority, even that which he delegated. He was regarded as infallible, even in religion, and could be corrected only in secret by the cadi or the grand mufti.[43] He established a hierarchy of governmental offices and determined the position of social classes in the protocol of his court. He divided the administration of the government into a chancery and a treasury, with secretaries and *wazirs* belonging to the first and inspectors and accountants to the second. Financial records were kept and treasury funds were administered constantly. A "prime minister" presided over the chancery, which occupied an office at the entry of the palace. Details about the organization of Abd al-Rahman's government may be gleaned from the works of Albar, Samson, and especially Eulogius, who mentions a number of officials, calling them by classical Latin titles.

Abd al-Rahman also reorganized the municipal administration of Córdoba. To the lone official, the master of the market, he added others, all with definite jurisdictions. The municipal police were divided into two groups and everything was placed in the hands of a master of the city. He increased his palace guard with troops from both sides of

[41] *Ibid.*, 164, 166, 196.
[42] *Ibid.*, 195.
[43] For mufti cf. D. B. Macdonald, "Fatwa," EI, II, 92f. A *fatwa* is a formal legal opinion given by a mufti or canon lawyer.

the Pyrenees. He built up the army and the navy. He brought water from the sierra to the palace in conduits, and in 850 he provided a public fountain in front of the palace fed from this source. He completed additions to the mosque of Córdoba in 833, and in 848 inaugurated further additions under the supervision of the eunuch Nasr which apparently had not been completed at the time of his death in 852.[44]

Lévi-Provençal says, apparently on the authority of the *Muktabis,* that Abd al-Rahman II was the most cultivated of all Umaiyad rulers of Córdoba, excepting al-Hakam II. He promoted the study of *hadiths*[45] in the Malekite tradition and cultivated the study of medicine, philosophy, occult sciences, augury, and the interpretation of dreams. In pursuit of these studies he sent, before he became king, emissaries to Baghdad to obtain books for him. They brought back books containing Hindu lore on astronomy and astrology, which thereafter were widely studied in Córdoba. Abd al-Rahman surrounded himself with a number of men proficient in poetry, philosophy, and astrology. This picture does not agree very well with the intellectual intolerance which Miguel Asín Palacios says existed under the emirs of this time, but it is confirmed by what Paul Albar in 854 says of Arabic letters and their influence on Christian youths.[46] Albar's polemics against Islam in the *Indiculus* point to a body of Moslem teachings which may have come from the East. A less obvious but more important consequence of contact between Córdoba and the Moslem East may be seen in a number of passages where Eulogius and Albar reveal in their spiritual background a mystic or quasi-mystic discipline. Neither writer mentions mysticism or sufism as an element of the Moslem culture in Córdoba, but a number of the Christian writings, especially Albar's *Confessio,* may represent

[44] Lévi-Provençal, *Histoire,* I, 255-262.

[45] *Hadiths* are the traditions on which, next to the Koran, the authority of Islam is based. The first part of the *hadith* consists of an enumeration of the people who have transmitted the second part, which is the textual content. T. W. Juynboll, "Hadith," EI, II, 189-194.

[46] Lévi-Provençal, *Histoire,* I, 272f.; *Indiculus,* 35; Asín Palacios, "Ibn Masarra y su escuela," *Obras escogidas,* I (Madrid, 1946), 23.

the Christian side of a vital spiritual debate in Córdoba, a debate in which ascetics and martyrs rendered starker testimony.

According to the *Muktabis*, one of the concubines of Abd al-Rahman II, named Kalam, was the captive daughter of a noble of Navarre. Ibn Haiyan also says that the sister of Mahmud, the rebel of Mérida who fled to Alfonso II, became a Christian after her brother's death, and her son became bishop of Santiago de Campostella. The *Muktabis* provides detailed accounts of the landings on the Spanish coast in 844 by the Northmen and of the beginnings of the kingdom of Navarre.[47]

The constant uprisings and civil wars which took place in the reign of Abd Allah monopolize the third part of the *Muktabis*, which also contains numerous poems by Arab chiefs noted for their chivalric traits. More than any other Arabic work the *Muktabis* takes note of Christians in the affairs of Andalucía, among the Cordoban "royalists" as well as among the "seditious" rebels. The chief figure of rebellion is Omar ibn Hafsun of Bobastro, "the champion of the independence of al-Andalus," who sought openly to destroy the Moslem government.[48] Ibn Hafsun fostered a racial and religious antagonism between Arabs and *mollites* (offspring of Moslem-Christian marriages)[49] through all of Andalucía. Although Ibn Hafsun did not openly declare himself a Christian until 899, thereby turning Moslems against him in a war without quarter,[50] he had had close ties with Christian elements previously. There seems little doubt that his father was a Christian, to judge from an account which Ibn Haiyan quotes from al-Razi. In 893, when the army of Córdoba raided the outskirts of Bobastro, Ibn Hafsun left his stronghold to prevent them from doing damage to a church "which his accursed father Hafs had built." Since the army

---

[47] Lévi-Provençal, *Histoire*, I, 268, 210, and 213-225.

[48] Guarieb, CHE, XVII, 156, and XXV-XXVI, 336.

[49] On *mollites* cf. Simonet, *Historia*, xv ff. Moslem law required such children to become Mohammedans, but not all did so.

[50] Guarieb, CHE, XXVIII, 172.

of Córdoba would hardly have sought to damage a mosque and a Moslem would hardly have built a Christian church, a Christian Hafs evidently built a Christian church. The fact that Ibn Hafsun with the support of non-Moslems was able to resist Córdoba until the reign of Abd al-Rahman III (912-961) argues that a considerable number of Christians lived in the area of Bobastro. Al-Razi also narrates that in 893 Alfonso III (called Ordoño) rebuilt Zamora with the aid of a Christian architect and workers from Toledo.[51]

Of particular interest are a number of dates according to the Christian calendar in one part of the *Muktabis*. Some of the dates are entered as the equivalents of Arab dates but others appear without any Arab equivalent. The dates occur in a part of the *Muktabis* which seems to be an extended quotation from a chronicle of military expeditions in 896 and 897.[52] So attentive is the chronicler to details of a military nature (the dates and lengths of marches and encampments, the number of men and horses lost in battle or because of thirst, numerous entries about the rain and bad weather which hindered operations), that one concludes that he accompanied the expeditions. In addition to dates of the Christian calendar he twice refers to the feast of Pentecost celebrated by Christians.[53] This chronicler seems to have begun his account after King Abd Allah on 2 January 896 executed his own son and a general, following their return from an expedition against Seville.[54] Abd Allah then appointed a new general, Abu al-Abbas Ahmad ibn Mohammed ibn Abu Abda. The new general, says the chronicler with praise, commanded an elite troop of cavalry selected from the army of Córdoba.[55] The Christian date entered for the execution of Abd Allah's son and the general in 896 may also be the hand of this chronicler. Another instance of a Christian date in the *Muktabis* is connected with a military record.

[51] *Ibid.*, XXV-XXVI, 336.
[52] *Ibid.*, XXVII, 164-172.
[53] *Ibid.*, 169 and 171.
[54] *Ibid.*, XXV-XXVI, 342.
[55] *Ibid.*, XXVIII, 173.

Abd Allah's army is said to have camped near Poley on "Thursday, 15 April 891, Era of the Christians," previous to an important battle against Ibn Hafsun.[56] The appearance of these dates in a military chronicle suggests that the Christian element in the army of Córdoba at this time was fairly strong, not only in the rank and file but in the command and organization of that force.

In the course of the *Muktabis* the *mollites* are identified rather ambiguously, comprising Christians and apparently apostates from Islam. Although Jews are mentioned in the *Muktabis* they took no part in the uprisings on either side, as far as one can tell.

Several people met in the Latin sources of the ninth century are mentioned in the *Muktabis*. The prime minister of Abd al-Rahman II, Nasr, who, according to Eulogius, died in 851, owned a plot of land on the banks of the Guadalquivir just outside Córdoba, "near the old cemetery." After Nasr's death the land came into the hands of Abd Allah, who at that time was seven years old.[57] In 889/890 "Sarband ibn Hayyay al-Comes" fled from Córdoba because of excesses he had committed there and took refuge in Poley, a fortress not far to the south of Córdoba held by Ibn Hafsun. "Sarband" seems to have been Count Servandus, the antagonist of the Abbot Samson (who died in 890) and the subject of discussion in a letter by Albar. From Poley, Servandus raided the territory around Córdoba until on one of his excursions he was slain. His father Hayyay was then crucified in Córdoba with his son's head hung above him. Later the *Muktabis* says that the son of Servandus also conducted raids around Córdoba.[58] The Servandus who was count in 864, born from among "the slaves of the Church," could have been either the father or son in 890.

In an account which he apparently took from al-Razi, Ibn Haiyan records an event which may be the martyrdom of a

---

[56] *Ibid.*, XXIII-XXIV, 334. The date is A.D. and not the Spanish Era, perhaps indicating a Frankish author.

[57] *Ibid.*, XV, 169.

[58] *Ibid.*, XXI-XXII, 341, and XXIII-XXIV, 343.

Christian. "In A.H. 287 [A.D. 900] was crucified the per-
fidious one known as Isaac, friend of the enemy of God, Omar
ibn Hafsun. In the company of Isaac was crucified a friend
of his who said when they lifted him up on the cross, 'You
have deceived me, O Isaac,' words which remained as a popular saying in all Córdoba. His day is very famous in this
city."⁵⁹ The death of a traitor would hardly have been
"famous" in Córdoba unless the person was also regarded
by some as a martyr. Although there is a difference of fifty
years between the date given here, A.H. 287, and the date
of the Christian martyr Isaac (one month before A.H. 237),
this strange account may pertain to that martyr.

One of the more reliable Arabic sources for this period
of the history of Spain is Ibn Idhari's *Al-Bayan al-mughrib*
(*The Conquest of the Moghreb*).⁶⁰ Nothing is known about
the author except that he lived in North Africa in the thirteenth century. The work is divided into two parts, the first
dealing with the rule of the Arabs in North Africa and the
second with that in Spain. Throughout the *Bayan* Ibn Idhari
refers to earlier works, many of which are no longer extant,
and he frequently gives more than one account of an event,
indicating which he believes to be correct. His work differs
from many Arabic compilations in that it is orderly and
manifests critical evaluation on the part of the author. In
the volume on Spain he refers often to a history of Rasis and
several times to "foreign" works, by which he probably
means Christian works. The *Bayan* mentions no events
connected with the persecution of the Christians. More than
anything else the part of the work devoted to Spain consists
of the annals of the military expeditions of the different

⁵⁹ *Ibid.*, XXVIII, 173.
⁶⁰ Ibn Idhari's work is found in several mss. Dozy's edition (2
vols.; Leyden, 1848-1851) has been re-edited by G. S. Colin and Lévi-
Provençal (2 vols.; Leyden, 1948-1951). The chronicle has been translated into Spanish by Francisco Fernández y González, *Historia de al-
Andalus por Aben-Adharí de Marruecos* (Granada, 1860), and into
French by E. Fagnan, *Histoire de l'Afrique et de l'Espagne intitulée
al-Bayano-l-Mogrib* (2 vols.; Algiers, 1901-1904); Fagnan's translation is referred to in the present study.

rulers of Córdoba, with occasional anecdotes and accounts of important men.

Ibn Idhari agrees with the other Arabic chroniclers and the Latin chroniclers of the North in portraying Rodrigo in a bad light. "According to the books of foreigners," he says, "Rodrigo was not a prince of royal blood but a bastard, who was governor of Córdoba and who killed the king after revolting against him. He changed the rules of the government and corrupted the traditional customs of royalty."[61] Ibn Idhari describes the campaign of Tarik and Muza with considerable detail. According to one of the accounts he gives, Muza's son, Abdelaziz, ruled in Seville and married the widow of Rodrigo, who persuaded him to wear a crown in the privacy of their home. When the Arabs saw him thus arrayed they slew him, believing that he had become a Christian. Another account says that Abdelaziz was slain because he made the Arabs approach him through a low door which forced them to bow before him. A third account says that he was slain on the orders of the caliph of Damascus.[62] Ibn Idhari confirms other Arabic writers in his history of the first governors of Spain and the war between the original conquerors of Spain and the Syrian troops who fled from the Berbers of North Africa. Like Ibn al-Kutiya, he notes that the Syrian troops received "the lands and livestock of non-Arabs" as a settlement.[63] In the wake of this war, however, Ibn Idhari introduces a new personality, al-Sumayl (Eç-Çomeyl), a leader of great valor, reputed to have been the real power behind the last governor, Yusuf. Al-Sumayl continued the war against the Syrians until Abd al-Rahman I seized power in 756 and captured him. When Yusuf went into rebellion against Abd al-Rahman and was assassinated by one of his own men, al-Sumayl was executed in prison.[64]

Ibn Idhari says that the Moslems regarded the expeditions against the Christians in the north as a holy war.[65] He praises Abd al-Rahman II as a man of letters, a man of

---

[61] Ibn Idhari, II, 4.
[62] *Ibid.*, 30ff.
[63] *Ibid.*, 49.

[64] *Ibid.*, 77.
[65] *Ibid.*, 118 and 140.

great plans, a great warrior, and adds: "The Mohammedans never experienced evil under him nor saw adversity. It was he who first adopted the traditional usages of the caliphs in matters of pomp, exterior formality, organization of service, the use of the most sumptuous dress. He beautified the palaces and brought in water. He built the promenade and repaired the streets, alongside which he had water flowing. He built mosques for the community all over Spain, had fine embroidery thread made (for clothing) and cultivated the manufacture of such thread. He established a mint in Córdoba,[66] and in a word, let his royalty be felt. It was during his reign that rich tapestries and all kinds of precious things came to Spain from Baghdad and elsewhere. After the murder of al-Amin [809-813], the son of Harun al-Raschid, and the pillage of his goods, many precious and rare objects came into Spain, as well as gems."[67] Abd al-Rahman himself lavished money and jewels on a favorite wife named Tarub. Ibn Idhari says nothing of the first Christian martyrs put to death during the last two years of Abd al-Rahman's reign, but he notes that in 851 the leader of a Moslem heresy was crucified. The standard method of execution, to judge from Ibn Idhari's work, was crucifixion. In 804 al-Hakam I crucified seventy-two Cordobans for plotting against him.[68] Most of the Christian martyrs of the ninth century were beheaded and then hung up on the *eculeus*.

The military levy owed to Mohammed I, according to Ibn

[66] Important details concerning coinage and mints in Córdoba remain unsettled. Robert S. Lopez, "Mohammed and Charlemagne: A Revision," *Speculum*, XVIII (1943), 29f., says that after Abd al-Rahman I (756-788) Spain was on a silver standard and Abd al-Rahman III (912-961) was the first Moslem ruler in Spain to mint gold coins regularly. The Chronicle of Albelda, no. 62, says the Mohammed I (852-886) paid a ransom in gold solidi to Alfonso III for the release of Haxim. Albar says that Saul paid 400 solidi to assume his episcopacy, and Samson says that 100,000 solidi were offered to Mohammed I for the right to tax the Christians of Córdoba. The solidus is supposed to be a gold coin, but the term is also used as a means of indicating the total amount of money, a measure of counting.

[67] Ibn Idhari, II, 148f.

[68] *Ibid.*, 146f. and 114.

Idhari, was about 22,000 troops, including 6790 from Medina Sidonia, 2900 from Granada, 2600 from Malaga, 2200 from Jaén, 1800 from Cabra, and 1400 from Morón. In Mohammed's reign the levy on Córdoba became voluntary rather than obligatory.[69] Like other Arabic chroniclers, Ibn Idhari mentions Mohammed's expeditions on his northern frontier and against the Northmen and local rebels. He includes several anecdotes to illustrate the care which the astute Mohammed gave to ruling matters. In February 854 Abd al-Malik ibn Habib, one of the wisest men in Spain, died. Ibn Idhari praises him as a grammarian, a poet, one who knew the Koran by heart, and one versed in story telling and genealogies. Abd al-Malik composed a number of chronicles and works of law and literature.[70] Later Ibn Idhari notes that the mother of Hisham II (976-1009) was from Navarre.[71]

The anonymous *Fath 'l-Andalus* (*The Conquest of Spain*) is another Arabic chronicle written in North Africa. The editor of the chronicle, Joaquín de González, attributes the work to an author of Kairouan of the twelfth century, but the late seventeenth- or early eighteenth-century manuscript contains a notation which would date the work in A.D. 1375.[72] Although shorter than the *Bayan* of Ibn Idhari, the *Fath 'l-Andalus* has a similar orderly presentation and its text runs closely parallel to Ibn Idhari's work, at times even agreeing with it in the phraseology of unusual statements. The *Fath* is divided about evenly between accounts of the

[69] *Ibid.*, 178f.

[70] *Ibid.*, 181f.

[71] Ibn Idhari, II, 389 and 418. The origin of the mother of al-Hakam II (961-976), son of Abd al-Rahman III (912-961), is unknown; cf. Lévi-Provençal, *Histoire*, II, 121, 173. One of the wives of Almanzor, actual ruler of Córdoba from 981 to 1002, was a princess from León; another wife, the mother of one of his heirs, was a princess from Navarre; *ibid.*, 241-244. Cf. also Dozy, *Recherches*, II, 201-210.

[72] Ms 1143 of the Bibliothèque Nationale of Algiers is the unique ms for this work. The only edition is that of the Arabic text and a Spanish translation by J. de González, *Fatho-l-Andaluci. Historia de la conquista de España. Códice arábigo del siglo XII* (Algiers, 1889); cf. pp. v and 106.

original conquest of Spain by the Arabs, the rule of the early governors, and the first Umaiyad emir, Abd al-Rahman I. Only a few pages at the end are devoted to the emirs after Abd al-Rahman I. The last item in the work is a catalogue of uprisings of different cities in Spain after the year A.D. 1009.

Under the rule of Anbaça, governor of Spain from 721 to 725, there is an unusual entry to the effect that the "infidel" Balaya (Pelagius), son of Fafala, rose up against the Arabs in Galicia and expelled them, ruling himself for two years. He was succeeded by his son Fafala (Favila) until in 750 he lost the kingdom to Adfanx (Alfonso), son of Bitra (Peter), father of the Banu Adfanx, "a race which still exists." [73] The close agreement between the texts of the *Bayan* and the *Fath* seems to indicate a relationship between them, either directly or through a third work.

The chronicle attributed to the Moor Rasis is little more than an item of historiographical curiosity.[74] The Spanish text which exists begins with a statement that a Portuguese translation of the work was made from the Arabic for a King John of Portugal. The first part of the work is a geographical description of a large part of Spain reportedly under Arab rule.[75] Most of the geographical descriptions consist of a statement that there are many castles in an area with a list of the products for which the area is famous. Gayangos did not publish the second part of the work, which covers the history of Spain from antiquity through the fall of Rodrigo, because he considered it to be a later interpolation. The third

[73] *Ibid.*, 29.

[74] The mss for this chronicle are defective and of late date, none earlier than the fourteenth century. Most of the text of the chronicle has been edited by P. de Gayangos, "Memoria sobre la autenticidad de la Crónica denominada del moro Rasis," Vol. VIII of *Memorias de la Real Academia de la Historia* (Madrid, 1852), in 100 pages numbered separately. Gayangos also discusses the mss and authenticity of the work. It is unlikely that this is the work referred to by Ibn Idhari above.

[75] Lévi-Provençal, "al-Razi," EI, III, 1136f., would attribute this part of this work to the father of Isa ibn Ahmad al-Razi, who is widely quoted by Ibn Haiyan.

part of the chronicle describes the rule of the Arabs from Muza to the end of the reign of al-Hakam II (961-976). It is replete with errors and fanciful tales. Of this part, over a third is devoted to Muza, a third to the governors of Spain up to the arrival of Abd al-Rahman I in the year 138 "of the Moors," which is erroneously equated with Era 763 (A.D. 725), and the remainder to the Umaiyad emirs and caliphs, the later rulers receiving very scant notice.

An account of the early conquest of Spain attributed to an Ibn Abi Riqa, a disciple of the Abd al-Malik ibn Habib mentioned above, contains legendary tales about Muza, but the last part of the text, written about A.D. 888, prophesies the downfall of the Umaiyads in Córdoba, the removal of the kingdom to Seville, and the eventual extinction of Christians who live in and around Córdoba.[76] An account of the Arabs in Spain by the Egyptian al-Nuguairi (1278-1332) seems to be based a good deal on Ibn Idhari's *Bayan*.[77] The North African Ibn Khaldun (1332-1406) in a summary account of the wars of the emirs of Córdoba, says nothing of the Christians of Córdoba, but his account of the reigns of Abd al-Rahman II and Mohammed I is of interest.[78]

A work of special significance in the study of the martyrs of Córdoba is the *History of the Cadis of Córdoba*, written by al-Khushani, a native of Kairouan, at the request of al-Hakam II (961-976). Al-Khushani, who had access to a number of sources,[79] gives an account of each cadi in office, with a brief summary of their backgrounds. Like other public

[76] Cf. "Notas de Ibn Abi Riqa de las lecciones de Ibn Habib acerca de la conquista de España por los arabes," trans. Melchor M. Antuña, CHE, I-II (1944), 253-268; the translation was edited postumously by C. Sánchez-Albornoz, who provides a foreword, *ibid.*, 248-253.

[77] *Historia de los musulmanes de España y Africa por En-Nuguairí*, ed. and trans. M. GGaspar Remiro (2 vols.; Granada, 1917-1919), I, 37-50.

[78] Cf. "Historia de los arabes de España por Ibn Jaldun," trans. Osvaldo A. Machado, CHE, IV-VIII (1946-1948), passim, especially VIII, 148-158; cf. also *id.*, "La historia de los godos segun Ibn Jaldun," *ibid.*, I-II, 139-155.

[79] *Historia de los jueces de Córdoba por Aljoxaní*, ed. and trans. by Julián Ribera (Madrid, 1914), viii f.

officials in Córdoba, the cadi (or judge) derived his authority from the emir, the highest religious and secular authority. The emir held for conservative Moslem orthodoxy and persecuted deviating Moslem sects. He could recall the authority of the cadi or exercise it in person when he wished. Besides functioning as the religious and legal arbiter, the cadi led prayer in the mosque. He was the chief Moslem official with whom the Christian martyrs came into contact. According to al-Khushani, the cadis held court in the mosque, but occasionally they would hold it elsewhere.[80] Eulogius reports that most of the martyrs went to the forum to proclaim their belief in Christ and to denounce the prophet Mohammed before the cadi and other officials. Both the royal palace and the mosque, it seems, fronted on the forum. Since Christians were forbidden to enter the mosque itself, they probably appeared before the cadi and his court in an antichamber or vestibule of the mosque.

Al-Khushani speaks of Christians several times in his work. Three instances are of some interest. During the reign of al-Hakam I (796-822) the Christian count Rabi fell out of favor with the king, who ordered those who were holding money of Rabi to make the fact known within three days, presumably with a view of confiscation. Yahya ibn Yahya, the Malekite zealot who wielded great influence over the cadis of his time, advised a Said ibn Mohammed who was holding money of Rabi that the tradition of the prophet Mohammed required one to honor contracts involving money received from anyone, whether he was honorable or dishonorable. Said maintained this position towards the king when he later demanded why Said had not obeyed his order. On the basis of his reply, al-Khushani reports, Said was appointed cadi.[81]

In the reign of Abd al-Rahman III (912-961) a Spanish rebel who had surrendered to the caliph under treaty and who spoke only Romance was married to a noble Moslem woman in Córdoba. When his wife appealed to the cadi for protection from her husband, the chancellor sent word to the cadi that

<hr>

[80] *Ibid.,* xxxii.   [81] *Ibid.,* 86f.

the rights of those Spanish who spoke Romance and who had surrendered under treaty must be respected, and that the cadi should not intervene between the Latin Spaniard and the "slave" who was in his power. The cadi maintained that he was bound by religious law to disregard the doings of the court in favor of the "free" Moslem woman. The chancellor replied that he did not wish to oppose the law but asked only that justice be rendered to the allies of the caliph, and the cadi well knew what was required in such a situation.[82]

The Christian martyrs of 850-859 are not referred to by al-Khushani, but during the term of office of the cadi just mentioned, Aslam ibn Abd al-Aziz, a Christian came before the cadi "seeking death." The cadi asked why the man was seeking his death when he had done nothing wrong. With the usual Moslem misunderstanding al-Khushani explains that the Christians, out of wickedness or ignorance, regard it as a great good to offer themselves for death, although their "prophet" left them no such example. The Christian affirmed, according to al-Khushani, that not he but a semblance of him in his body would die and he would go to heaven. The cadi had the Christian whipped and, when the man acknowledged that it was he who was being whipped, the cadi said that the same would be true if the sword were to fall on his neck.[83]

The Latin sources say little about the cadi except to describe him as expostulating pompously or offering blandishments to some martyrs. Al-Khushani in his work rarely gives dates, but, since he evidently deals with the cadis in chronological order, those in office during the persecution of the Christians can be identified. According to al-Khushani, there were ten appointments as cadi in the reign of Abd al-Rahman II (822-852), nine before the death of the Malekite fakih Yahya ibn Yahya in 848. In the thirty-four-year reign of Mohammed I (852-886) there were five appointments, two being second terms of office.[84] The instability of

[82] *Ibid.*, 227f.
[83] *Ibid.*, 231ff.
[84] *Ibid.*, 97-139 and 139-191; Ibn Idhari, *Bayan*, II, 131, reports

the office when Yahya was the power behind the scenes attests also perhaps to a deterioration of the authority of the Moslem judiciary in the years before the persecution and the Cordoban martyrs. Said ibn Soleiman, the last cadi under Abd al-Rahman II, probably held office from 848, the year of Yahya's death, to 854, continuing in office for two years under Mohammed I. Most of the martyrs died during his term of office. Said's immediate predecessor, Mohammed ibn Ziad, was deposed because he failed to order the execution of a Moslem who had blasphemed in a moment of anger. When Abd al-Rahman learned of the case he deposed Mohammed ibn Ziad and had the blasphemer executed.[85] This example provided the next cadi, Said, with a precedent for his decisions on the fate of the Christians who came before him proclaiming the divinity of Christ and the wickedness of the prophet Mohammed. Even so, Said referred the case of Isaac, the first voluntary martyr, to Abd al-Rahman for judgment.[86]

Said ibn Soleiman came from Gáfec in the vicinity of Seville. Before becoming cadi of Córdoba he had been cadi in Mérida and other places. In Arab tradition, says al-Khushani, Said was one of four cadis in the Moslem world noted for his justice, the other three being cadis of Syria, Egypt, and Kairouan. Al-Khushani's first anecdote about Said tells how the emir's messenger found him plowing with a yoke of oxen when he arrived to notify him of his appointment as cadi. When he came to take office dressed in a white garment, a white cape, and a high white conical hat,[87] Said

eleven cadis for Abd al-Rahman's reign, noting that Ibn al-Kutiya names twelve; cf. also *ibid.*, 152.

[85] Al-Khushani, 127ff.

[86] *Memoriale*, preface to Bk. I, 3.

[87] In 719 the wearing of the "suf," or cloak of white wool, was considered by Moslems a foreign and reprehensible fashion of Christian origin, but by 1050 it had become an eminently orthodox Moslem fashion; cf. L. Massignon, "Tasawwuf," EI, IV, 682. "Tasawwuf" denotes the practice of wearing the woolen robe and hence the act of devoting oneself to the mystic life on becoming what is called in Islam a "sufi," *ibid.*

incurred the contempt of the lawyers and procurators of his court, which was in the mosque. They spread acorn shells under his prayer rug, mocking him for coming from the "Plain of the Acorns." For their joke, Said banned them from their professions for a year. Another anecdote tells how Said himself furnished the indemnity payment enabling a wife to divorce her husband, who would not allow her to leave him for want of it. Said was then holding court in his own house. On another occasion the father of Nasr the prime minister, "surrounded by the guard which usually accompanied him," approached Said and wished to speak with him. He called out to Said to wait for him in Romance,[88] which was the only language he spoke. Said had him answered in Romance that he should return that evening to the mosque where Said would hold public court. Said usually walked between his home and the mosque and was known to stop off en route to obtain his own bread from the oven of the baker. He died in office, without progeny, as far as al-Khushani knew. Although the anecdotes about Said show him to have been a person of simple ways they do not illustrate any judicial acumen.

The rest of the martyrs perished while Ahmed ibn Ziad was cadi (854-864).[89] Ahmed was the brother of Mohammed ibn Ziad, Said's predecessor. Mohammed brought Ahmed to Córdoba from Medina Sidonia. He was a religious man, noted for irreproachable conduct, a very harsh and severe cadi, says al-Khushani. He was particularly noted for not permitting anyone to approach him about court affairs except in the proper time and place, not even on the street as he went with his retinue to and from his court in the mosque. He was quick to imprison those who criticized him or persisted in what he regarded as error. There were at least thirteen martyrdoms during his period of office, among them that of Eulogius. It can be deduced that Ahmed was a relative of Aurea, the last martyr described by Eulogius in

[88] Al-Khushani, 136. Ribera, *ibid.*, xx-xxii, discusses the continued use of "Romance" speech in Córdoba; cf. also *ibid.*, 118.
[89] *Ibid.*, 139-143.

the *Memoriale sanctorum.*[90] Ahmed had to resign because of a scandal involving his son in Medina Sidonia. He was succeeded by his secretary Amer ibn Abd Allah, the first cadi of Spanish descent, who has already been discussed.

Ribera gives a critique of the cadis of Córdoba in which he points out that al-Khushani's account of them would seem more appropriate for the cadis of a small town than for those of the capital of the realm. It is difficult to understand, he says, how they obtained such great prestige. But he points out their many virtues, especially as compared with cadis in other parts of the Moslem world. The area of their jurisdiction was limited. Moreover, they did not handle cases between Christians or Jews, who had their own systems in Córdoba. They did not occupy themselves with minor cases, leaving these to minor officials. They had no other offices at the time they were cadi, except that of leading the Mohammedans in prayer. They personally performed their duties in a small and simple court. The office was in general a stable one, and the rulers heeded the wishes of the people in selecting the cadi. No persons of immoral reputation occupied the office, nor did the cadis enter into politics or religion to any extent. Ribera concludes that there are sufficient points of similarity between the actions of the cadis as told by al-Khushani and the *Forum iudicum* to warrant a study of the possible influence of the Visigothic code on the application of law by the Mohammedans in Spain.[91]

The History of the Mohammedan Dynasties of Spain by al-Makkari[92] is frequently used as a source for the history of Moslem Spain. The work is actually a secondary history written in the early seventeenth century. By this time Ambrosio de Morales had published his *Corónica general* and had been dead for almost twenty years. The English trans-

---

[90] *Memoriale,* III, xvii.

[91] Al-Khushani, xxxiv-xliii.

[92] Al-Makkari, *The History of the Mohammedan Dynasties in Spain,* trans. Pascual de Gayangos (2 vols.; London, 1890-1893). Al-Makkari began to write his work sometime after 1618; cf. *ibid.,* I, 2. He died in 1632.

lation of al-Makkari's work by Gayangos, although lengthy and supplemented with an abundance of notes and appendices, does not include the whole of the text.

Al-Makkari depends upon and agrees with most of the Arabic histories of Moslem Spain, quoting at length from many of the earlier chronicles. He refers to three earlier authors in particular: Ibn Haiyan (twelfth century), Ibn Said (thirteenth century), and Ibn Khaldun (1332-1406). As published by Gayangos his history is composed of eight books: two describing the people and the land of Andalucía (about two hundred pages), one describing Córdoba (fifty pages), one devoted to the early conquest of Spain by the Arabs (fifty pages), one to the rule of the governors (fifty pages), one to the rule of the Umaiyads (one hundred and fifty pages), and two on the decline and fall of Córdoba and the history of Moslems in Spain up to 1610 (two hundred pages). It is only for the last part of his work that al-Makkari can be considered a source. He includes much of the legend and anecdote from earlier Arabic chronicles, saying nothing about the martyrs of the ninth century and little about Córdoba in those days.

In Book III, chapter iv, of his work al-Makkari introduces an account of interest by Ibn Said, believed by Gayangos to be a poet who lived in the middle of the eleventh century and identified by García-Villada as a councillor of Abd al-Rahman V (1023-1024). Ibn Said gives a description of the churches of the Christians and an account of a Mass he attended. The main church of the Christians in Córdoba, he says, was called Santa Maria, and it was visited by pilgrims from distant lands. The Christians had other churches and chapels too, within and without Córdoba, and monasteries in the recesses of neighboring mountains. The Mass took place at night in a church bedecked with branches of myrtle and lit with candles. Bells rang. The Moslem was astonished at the jubilation. He observed that the Christians banished mirth from their faces and rid their minds of amusement. The priest was dressed in rich vestments and altar boys assisted him at the altar. The wine in the chalice attracted

the attention of Ibn Said, who noted that it was forbidden
to Moslems. After the ceremony the Christians made gracious overtures to their Moslem guest, but he left them.[93]

Al-Makkari mentions that Omar ibn Hafsun, the rebel of
Bobastro, was of Christian origin, and he identifies the
Christian bishop whom Abd al-Rahman III first sent as ambassador to Otto I as a Bishop Rabi. He attests to the presence of Christians after 1121 in the area of Granada, from
where they were expelled to Africa for collaborating with
the armies of Alfonso VII, which were invading the country.[94]

[93] *Ibid.*, I, 246f. García-Villada, *Historia eclesiástica*, III, 170.
[94] Al-Makkari, *op.cit.*, II, 130, 139, and 306f.

Part II

Córdoba and Its Martyrs in the Ninth Century:
A Study of the Sources Concerning the Martyrs

CHAPTER VI

MINOR LATIN WORKS

The Latin sources which describe the history of the Christians of Córdoba in the middle of the ninth century are, as were the sources of the eighth century, ecclesiastical in nature. Like most of the writings of the previous century and of the days of the Visigoths, they were written by ecclesiastical authors on ecclesiastical subjects. Some lyrical poems by Paul Albar of Córdoba, which will be discussed later, are an exception, as is a letter of Louis the Pious to the people of Mérida in 826 seeking an alliance with them against their king, Abd al-Rahman II, a work not of Mozarabic origin.

The *Chronicon Moissiacense* regularly reports the incursions north of the Pyrenees made by the "Saracen" forces of the governors of Córdoba after 714. The chronicle records that in 752 a "Goth" Ansemundus turned over to the Franks several cities held by him, and in 759 the "Goths" of Narbonne turned the city over to the Franks after slaying the "Saracen" garrison. An entry in the chronicle which should be dated about 793 describes Hischam I (788-796) as the cruelest of the kings of Córdoba. He so oppressed Christians and Jews with taxes, says the chronicle, that they had to sell their children, and all Spain was depopulated because of his oppression. Beginning in April 812 a series of charters and diplomas were issued by Charlemagne, Louis the Pious, and Charles the Bald confirming the right of refugees from Spain to live in Septimania and Gothia for the most part under their own law and free of certain local taxes on their lands (*aprisiones*). The Spanish were given unpopulated areas which they cultivated under their own counts. In 812 forty-three Spanish refugees appealed to Charlemagne about local injustices. In July 854 Charles the Bald ordered that two Spaniards, Sumnoldus and Riculfus, should

133

retain their *aprisiones* with the same rights as had their father and grandfather. It may be pointed out that a document of June 844 does not say, as is sometimes reported, that Charles the Bald recommended or suggested that the Spanish refugees commend themselves to a local count, but merely notes, as does a document of Louis the Pious in 816, that the Spanish have a choice of living under their own counts or becoming the vassals of Frankish counts and holding benefices with the same rights as Frankish vassals.[1]

Louis' letter of 826 is addressed to the magistrates and people of Mérida (omnibus primatibus et cuncto populo Emeritano).[2] Because they thought that Frankish interest could not extend so far into the Moslem region as Mérida on the Guadiana, the editors of the letter in Bouquet's *Recueil* arbitrarily changed Mérida to Zaragoza. Karl Hampe in the MGH, however, notes that the city is Mérida on the Guadiana; Philipp Jaffé in *Monumenta Carolina* also leaves the address Mérida.[3] Louis may well have been seeking an alliance with Mérida, which was almost continually in rebellion against the rule of Moslem Córdoba. Apparently his plan was not to send an army into Lusitania but to divide the military strength of Córdoba between the forces of Mérida and his own forces in the Spanish March, where Louis was having troubles of his own. In 826 an Aïzon and a Willemund organized a rebellion against Louis in the March and in 826 or 827 they allied with Abd al-Rahman II of Córdoba, who in 827 sent an army to besiege Barcelona.[4]

[1] *Chronicon Moissiacense*, ed. George Pertz, MGH, *Scriptores*, I (Hanover, 1826), 294 and 300; Claude Devic, Joseph Vaissete, *et al.*, *Histoire générale de Languedoc avec des notes et les pièces justificatives* (16 vols. in 17; Toulouse, 1872-1892), II, cols. 73ff., 97ff., 109ff., 194ff., 228ff., 243ff., and 294f.

[2] The best edition of the letter, which is found among Einhard's letters, is that by Karl Hampe, MGH, *Epistolarum* t. V, i (Berlin, 1898), 115f. Hampe lists previous editions.

[3] Martin Bouquet, *Recueil des historiens des Gaules et de la France*, VI (Paris, 1870), 379; Philipp Jaffé, *Monumenta Carolina*, Vol. IV of *Bibliotheca rerum Germanicarum* (Berlin, 1867), 443f.

[4] Léonce Auzias, *L'Aquitaine carolingienne (778-987)* (Toulouse and Paris, 1937), 91-93.

Louis' letter is the first Latin source of the ninth century to offer information about conditions under the rule of Córdoba. In the letter Louis offers sympathy to the people for the unjust taxes and tribute levied upon them by Abd al-Rahman II (822-852) and by his father al-Hakam I (796-822). He encourages them to continue to resist the king and to defend their liberty. Proposing a plan against their common enemy, Louis promises to send an army to encamp in the Spanish March in the coming summer which can be called into action if Abd al-Rahman should attack Mérida. In conclusion, Louis offers the people of Mérida their full liberty of old without diminution, exemption from taxation, and the right to live under their own law, if they will turn away from Abd al-Rahman and become his friends and associates.

It is somewhat surprising that Louis seems to consider the authorities in Mérida to be Christian and not Moslem. Evidently by their "rights of old" he was recalling to mind their rights in Visigothic days and asking them to question the basic authority of the rule of Córdoba. But he may have been referring only to violations by the Arabs of existing treaty arrangements between Mérida and the Arab rulers of Córdoba. Unfortunately the results achieved by the letter in Mérida are not known, nor is an answer extant. Whatever one can infer from the letter about conditions in Mérida should not be applied to Córdoba and other cities under Arab rule in Spain. Louis appears to be speaking of the tribute levied upon the city of Mérida by the emirs of Córdoba rather than any discriminating taxation of the Christians of the city, such as later sources of Córdoba say existed there.

Most of the ecclesiastical sources from Córdoba at this time, even the letters of Albar, are rather informal treatises of a polemical or apologetical nature written by a single author. The next known source, however, the Acts of the Council of Córdoba in 839, is a formal document dealing with the heresy of the Acephali, which had become of concern to the Church in all of southern Spain. Besides describing the heresy, the Acts show how the Church was organized under Arab rule in Spain.[5] The council condemned the heresy of the Acephali or Cassiani.[6] They came from outside Spain, from Rome they claimed, and landed on the seacoast in the vicinity of Seville at a place called Epagrus, which cannot be identified. This could not be the Ipagrus identified by Flórez as Aguilar, nor Poley, as Pérez de Urbel says, which are not on the coast.[7] From the coast the heretics moved inland to infect Córdoba also. Two of their churches are mentioned, one in Epagrus, which was under Seville, and the other in Córdoba; and the complaint against them in the council was made by Bishop Reccafred of Córdoba and Cabra and Bishop Quiricus of Guadix. A Cassian is mentioned as the author of the sect and an Antiphrasis Quuniericus is associated with it. The council looked upon their doctrine as a mixture of several heresies, the bishops mentioning the Cassians, the Jovinians, the *Simoniaci*, the Manichaeans, and the Vigilantians. Evidently adhering to the Jewish food law, the heretics abstained from "the foods of the Gentiles," considering them unclean. Like the Manichaeans they fasted on Christmas if it fell on a Friday. Like the Vigilantians they would not venerate the relics of saints. They baptized with saliva. They called themselves "saints," not eating food with others and communicating from different sacramental chalices. According to their practice, men and women acting as deacons give the Eucha-

---

[5] The unique ms of the text is ms 22 of the Cathedral of León. The text was published by Flórez in ES, XV (1759), in eight unnumbered pages at the beginning of the volume; the second edition of ES, XV (1787), contains a slightly better text. For the organization of the church in Spain in this period cf. García-Villada, *Historia eclesiástica*, III, 47-53, and his discourse upon his reception into the Academia de la Historia, *Organización y fisionomia de la iglesia española desde la caida del imperio visigótico en 711 hasta la toma de Toledo en 1085* (Madrid, 1935). Cf. David, *Etudes*, 1-6. Cf. Hefele, *Histoire des conciles*, trans. H. Leclercq (8 vols. in 16; Paris, 1907-1921), VI, i, 104f.

[6] In 619 Isidore of Seville was responsible for the condemnation of an acephalous bishop, Sirus; cf. Chronicle of 754, no. 16, Mommsen, *Auct. antiq.*, XI, *Chronica minora*, II, 339f.

[7] ES, XII, 2; Pérez de Urbel, *San Eulogio*, 85.

rist into the hand. The people, however, only pretend to put it in their mouth and later throw it away. To prevent this abuse, according to the acts of the council, the Fathers had decreed that the faithful receive the Eucharist in their mouth from the hand of a priest. The heretics excommunicated those who left them and warned them not to receive penance at the hand of Catholics, even at the end of their lives.[8] The marriages of the Acephali were incestuous; and they practiced bigamy and divorce. Contrary to what one would expect of people who regarded the food of the Gentiles as unclean, they gave their daughters in marriage to infidels. Their priests practiced worldly pursuits, such as surgery and tavern keeping, and dwelt with women servants other than those permitted by the sacred canons. There are apparently some further details about the heresy, probably about the origin, which cannot be determined because of the lacunae at the beginning of the manuscript.

The council of 839 condemned the heresy in very severe terms and decreed stringent ecclesiastical penalties against its followers, but there was no invoking of the Moslem secular authority. Catholics were forbidden to permit the heretics to participate in any way in their religious services or to allow the members of their clergy, whose ordination was not according to the canons, to minister in Catholic churches. The bishops of the council accused the heretics of having bishops who were not nominated by the clergy or the people and of having a clergy who assumed orders of their own accord. The heretics claimed that their episcopal consecration was conferred by a single bishop: *"ut aiunt Abafilanem Ementiae solus solum ordinare episcopum."*[9] The bishops warned all Catholics of Spain, including those not at the council, to extirpate the heretics. The council formally condemned and anathematized both the heresy and its authors and exhorted the heretics to return to the Catholic faith.

---

[8] The sacrament of Penance is discussed at length below; cf. index, "Penance."

[9] ES, XV, 2d ed., reads, "ut aiunt ab Agilanem Ementiae, etc." A similarity of these names to "Fulano" and "Egila" can be noted.

Their church was declared not to be a church; and as for their church in Córdoba, "it has pleased us that that cave, and not a church, should lie broken and destroyed in subjection and affliction, until it comes to the true Catholic faith, and until through the hands of their bishop, Reccafred, they have a church erected and consecrated which is established by the Metropolitan John of Seville, and they receive the ointment of chrism for anointing neophytes."[10]

The Acephali, or Cassiani, seem to be related to earlier heretics in Spain, such as the Migetians and those described by Pope Adrian I. Echoes of some of their tenets, especially with regard to the validity of sacraments administered by heretical clergy, occur later in the midst of the persecution, when a number of Christians apparently objected to the administration of the sacraments by clergy they considered unqualified.[11] The more serious problems of heresy after the middle of the ninth century, the denial of the Trinity and the divinity of Christ, referred to in Albar's letter to Esperaindeo and Samson's *Apologeticus,* have no connection with the Acephali. The council repeats Pope Adrian's condemnation against Christians who gave their daughters in marriage to "infidels," but the practice continued, as is evident in the number of mixed marriages mentioned by Eulogius.

Besides describing the heresy and illustrating the exercise of episcopal authority in council, the Acts show that the ecclesiastical organization of part of Spain during this period was the same as it had been at the time of the Visigoths. The metropolitans of the three provinces were Wistremirus of Toledo, John of Seville, and Aliulfus of Mérida. The suffragans were Quiricus of Guadix, Leovigildus of Ecija, Reccafred of Córdoba and Cabra, Amalsuindus of Malaga, and

---

[10] ES, XV, 7th unnumbered page of the text of the Acts. José Orlandis, "Los monasterios familiares en España durante la alta edad media," AHDE, XXVI (1956), 10-13, points out that from early times in Spain churches and monasteries could not be erected without the consent of the bishop. After the seventh century private churches called monasteries were frequently erected in an effort to be free of economic ties with the bishop.

[11] Cf. Letter X of the Albar correspondence, 3.

Nifridius of Granada. After signing the Acts the bishops provided that they be sent out to their priests for signature. The Acts are dated in the same way as are events in the works of Eulogius: day of the week, date according to the Roman calendar, and year of the Spanish Era, "Friday, 10 Kalends March [20 February], Era 877 [A.D. 839]." In addition to the names of the eight bishops the Acts give that of the clerk, a priest named Flavius.

The list of bishops of Seville, Toledo, and Granada given in ms Escorial d-I-1 does not include John as a metropolitan of Seville. Nifridius of Granada and Wistremirus of Toledo are mentioned. Three lists of bishoprics from manuscripts of the ninth, tenth, and a later century published by Flórez and three lists from manuscripts of the eighth, ninth, and eleventh centuries published by Simonet offer more information about the organization of the church in Spain at this time.[12]

The Acts of the Council of 839 show that bishops continued to occupy the dioceses of Visigothic times, to intercommunicate freely, and to function as they had before under Christian kings. The composition of the council, the metropolitan and a number of suffragan bishops of Betica, joined by other metropolitans, is presumably that of a council which met in Córdoba in 852. In 839 the bishops issued their decree without any hesitancy of language and showed no deference to or dependence upon the civil authority. Their words evidence none of the indecision and fear which Eulogius and Samson criticize in councils held ten or twenty years later.

Latin sources of the ninth century do not provide a clear picture of the procedure followed in ecclesiastical councils, but isolated details indicate that the rules for conciliar procedure determined at the Fourth Council of Toledo (633) in Visigothic Spain were followed. A review of this conciliar

---

[12] Cf. Antolín, "El códice emilianense," *La ciudad de Dios*, 74, 388f.; ES, IV, Tr. 3, vi; Simonet, *Historia*, 808-812. Simonet also edits the Arabic texts from which two of his lists were translated. Cf. also a list of sees in the tenth-century ms 1279 Archivo Historico Nacional in Madrid, ed. J. Leclercq, "Textes et manuscrits de quelques bibliothèques d'Espagne," *Hispania sacra*, II (1949), 93.

procedure, drawn up by Isidore of Seville,[13] may be of interest here. "Before sunrise on the day the council convened the church in which it was to be held was cleared of people, and the doors were locked, with the exception of one, which was guarded. Through this the bishops entered, taking places according to seniority in the episcopate; next came the priests who were privileged to attend and then the deacons. The former were seated in a circle immediately back of the bishops, the latter remained standing before them. Lastly, the laity who were to attend entered with the necessary notaries. At a word from the archdeacon (of the metropolitan see, in the case of a provincial council) all prostrated themselves in prayer. A senior bishop rose to recite a prayer aloud, to which the others answered 'amen,' and then were bidden to rise from their knees. After a deacon clad in an alb had read from the 'Book of the Canons' the rules for holding councils the bishops were free to bring up matters for legislation, each point being settled before a new one was introduced. When the bishops' wishes were taken care of any cleric or layman desiring to bring a case before the council could secure its introduction through the archdeacon of the metropolitan. The bishops were required to stay until the conclusion of the council, and adjournment could take place only when all business had been disposed of."[14]

In ecclesiastical councils of Visigothic Spain the king played an important role. He informed the council of the matters he wished it to deal with, at first in person and later by means of a document wherein he presented his wishes to them. Royal approval applied to conciliar legislation made it the equivalent of civil law.[15] It seems certain that the Moslem king of Córdoba did not attend ecclesiastical councils in person, but he may have been represented at the councils by an official of his court who served as a secretary or a no-

---

[13] Canon 4; Mansi, *Sacrorum conciliorum...*, X, 617f. Cf. Jacques Fontaine, *Isidore de Séville et la culture classique dans l'Espagne wisigothique* (Paris, 1959), II, 808f., and Paul Séjourné, *Le dernier père de l'Eglise. Saint Isidore de Séville...* (Paris, 1929), 133-137.

[14] A. K. Ziegler, *Church and State in Visigothic Spain*, 41f.

[15] *Ibid.*, 42f.

tary. Such a person, a Christian *exceptor*, appears to have taken part in a council in Córdoba in 852. The power of the king also seems manifested in a council held in Córdoba in 862 and in a travesty of a council held in 864. Somehow too he seems to have been able to demand and prevent the convocation of councils. He probably supported only that legislation which suited him, but he was not indifferent, as far as one can tell, to the business of the councils.

According to Arabic sources, in A.H. 225 (839/840) the emperor of Byzantium sent an embassy to Córdoba offering a treaty of friendship. Abd al-Rahman II returned the embassy in the same year with a discourteous reply.[16]

Another source as ecclesiastical in content as the Acts of the Council of Córdoba in 839 is the undated *De habitu clericorum* of Leovigildus,[17] a treatise on clerical discipline and

[16]Lévi-Provençal, "Un échange d'ambassades entre Cordoue et Byzance au IXe siècle," *Byzantion*, XII (1937), 17-24, edits and translates the text of the reply into French.

[17] Morales knew Leovigildus' work; cf. Chronicle, XIV, iii. The work at present is known in two mss, the sixteenth-century ms Escorial b-III-14 and a tenth-century ms of the Biblioteca de Heredia-Spínola in Madrid, the texts of which are identical except for minor variations. Two other mss have disappeared, a Visigothic codex of homilies delivered to the Escorial in 1576 from which the two above-mentioned mss probably were copied, and a copy of the text of b-III-14 made in 1753 by the Escorial for Flórez. Until Luciano Serrano published the complete work, "*De habitu clericorum*, obra inédita del presbítero cordobés Leovigildo (siglo IX), publicada según un manuscrito visigodo, único que se conserva," BRAH, 54 (1909), 496-517, the text was not generally known. Flórez, ES, XI, 522f., published only the preface to the work in 1753. Serrano's edition was made from a ms in private hands which had come from San Millan; although he does not identify the owner, Serrano almost certainly used the Heredia-Spínola ms. In the following issue of the *Boletín*, Guillermo Antolín, "*De habitu clericorum* (siglo IX)," BRAH, 55 (1909), 102-120, presents a list of variants between Serrano's text and ms Escorial b-III-14. In addition, Antolín gives an interesting history of ms b-III-14, which was used by Flórez and his collaborator Francisco Ravago. According to his own correspondence, Flórez had, along with Ravago, cut two folios out of ms b-III-14 and burned them together with the copy which had been sent to him from the Escorial in 1753. Antolín also indicates his belief that they were responsible for cutting out the same passages from the

dress written for the clergy by an ecclesiastic. As the Acts of the Council of 839 show the general and official organization of the Church, so this treatise offers a glimpse of matters of concern to clerics in the performance of their ecclesiastical duties.

Not much is known about the author of the work. A Leovigildus is mentioned in five other writings of this time. In 839 a bishop of Ecija of that name signed the Acts of the Council of Córdoba. In the *Memoriale sanctorum* Eulogius describes the martyrdom in 852 of a monk from Granada named Leovigildus. Albar wrote a long poem of uncertain date in praise of a Bible made for a Leovigildus. A more extensive account about a Leovigildus is contained in Aimoin's history of the translation of the relics of George and Aurelius from Córdoba to Paris in 858. According to Aimoin, Sunifridus, second only to the count in Barcelona, recommended the pilgrims Usuard and Odilard to his friend Leovigildus in Córdoba, "a man learned in Christian laws and sacred customs." When the two monks arrived in Córdoba, "Leovigildus Abadsolomes" received them and with the help of the Abbot Samson obtained for them the relics of the martyrs George and Aurelius. Aimoin again praises the kindness of Leovigildus when he remarks that the cleric joined them in the train of King Mohammed en route from Córdoba to Toledo, noting that Leovigildus had not been in the train when it left Córdoba because he had been occupied by business with the king. Samson in the *Apologeticus* states

ms which Serrano used, the Heredia-Spínola ms. Flórez and Ravago had destroyed the passages "in defense of the honor of the nation," because they contained an opinion of Leovigildus "unfavorable to the honor of the nation" (Antolín, *op.cit.*, 109ff.). It should be pointed out that the text published by Serrano and the table of variant readings published by Antolín both contain errors, and close work on the text should be based on the microfilm copy of the Heredia-Spínola ms available through Servicio Nacional de Microfilm; cf. Pilar León Tello, "Inventario de códices y fondos documentales fotocopiados," *Servicio Nacional de Microfilm. Boletín num. 2 (año 1954)*, (Madrid: Dirección General de Archivos y Bibliotecas, 1954), no. 170. Variants of the text published by Serrano from the Heredia-Spínola ms are given in Appendix I.

briefly that when Hostegesis came to Córdoba in 864 "Leovigildus, son of Ansefredus," reprehended him for having introduced a wicked heresy.[18] Neither the bishop of Ecija in 839 nor the martyr of 852 would seem to be the author of the treatise on clerical garb. Albar, Aimoin, and Samson, however, may be speaking of the same person, a learned and influential cleric who may be the author of the *De habitu clericorum*. In the course of the work Leovigildus shows himself to be a mild and modest man, pious and devout, with a zealous solicitude for ecclesiastical propriety and an uncommon knowledge of the meaning of clerical dress and discipline.

The date of the treatise is not known, but it seems to have been written after the persecution broke out in Córdoba in 850. It may have been the basis for Leovigildus' reputation in 858 as "a man learned in Christian laws and sacred customs." As an historical source the work has more value for the light it sheds on clerical life and customs in Córdoba than for any information it contributes about the persecution. Like several other works from Córdoba in this period the treatise appears to have been intended for oral delivery as well as for reading.

From the prologue it appears that Leovigildus was prevailed upon to compose the *De habitu clericorum* by a person of some authority, whom he addresses as "Your Serenity," "Your Clemency," "Your Excellency," and "Your Sanctity," presumably the bishop of Córdoba, Saul. The work as a whole is addressed to clerics in general, and in the initial sentence of the prologue Leovigildus dedicates or addresses the work to the clerics of the Basilica of St. Cyprian. But in the two paragraphs of the prologue he gives the impression that he is addressing a particular person, whom he asks in the epilogue to approve the treatise for reading. Moreover, in the prologue and epilogue Leovigildus uses the second person plural

---

[18] *Memoriale*, II, xi: ES, XI, 281-286; *Translatio*, 13; *Apologeticus*, II, iv. Franke, "Die freiwilligen Märtyrer," 12, calls Leovigildus "Abd as-Salam," "Servant of Peace," one of many Arabic epithets for "Servant of God."

consistently, whereas at only one point does he do so in the main part of the treatise,[19] which as a rule is rather formal and impersonal. Whether it was at the request of a person of authority or of the clerics of St. Cyprian, Leovigildus agreed to compose the treatise in the face of an increasing frivolity (*fatuitas*) and a lack of zeal (*defuere alacritas*) for the clerical dress and discipline among some of the clergy as a result of the persecution.

The two aspects of the persecution which Leovigildus points out as undermining the spirit of the clergy were the abuse they suffered at the hands of the Moslems because of their distinctive attire and a monthly tax they were required to pay. It was for those of the clergy who could not, because of the tax or physical weakness, come to the doctors who were left (*ad remanentes doctores*) that Leovigildus composed the *De habitu clericorum*, in the hope that those of them who thought it necessary would read it within the privacy of ecclesiastical walls. Eulogius mentions the monthly tax in the *Memoriale*. Men devoted to prayer, if poor, along with women, children, and others, were supposed to be exempt from the head tax levied by the Moslems.[20] It is possible that Leovigildus and Eulogius are complaining of a tax which the clergy had not previously paid, a tax intended to handicap the ministry of the Church. The tax may also have contributed to the withdrawal of Christians from Córdoba into monasteries outside the city. Before taking up his subject, Leovigildus, in true mediaeval fashion, protests profusely that he is not worthy of the task.

The body of the treatise comprises ten chapters explaining the symbolic meanings of clerical garb and discipline. The work is replete with quotations from Scripture, but it differs in text and ideas from Isidore and other early mediaeval authors who wrote on liturgical matters, including the passage on clerical garb inserted in the treatise of Beatus and Eterius.[21] In the first chapter Leovigildus explains that the

[19] *De habitu*, x; Serrano, *op.cit.*, 517.
[20] *Memoriale*, I, 21; v. supra, 49.
[21] PL 96, 1005f.

clergy, as the elect, are expected to wear a uniform dress different from other people. He exhorts them not only to hold on to the garb which they have received from the apostles but to be able to explain its meaning to those interrogating them about it. In several places throughout the treatise Leovigildus apparently seeks to provide the clergy with answers to questions directed to them about their dress and discipline, in addition to instilling in them a pride in their dress and a zeal for lives of perfection. In the second and third chapters he explains the meaning of the tonsure. In chapter ii he directs his argument against those who claim that the exercise of good works (almsgiving in particular), and not faith, is of primary importance for salvation, while in chapter iii he emphasizes the role of mortification of the flesh in the fight against sin. The fourth chapter explains why European clergy shave their beards, while those of Asia and Africa do not. Two folios have been cut out of the text in the middle of this discussion, but it appears that Leovigildus presents the European practice as an example of the dissociation of Europe, the capital of which was Rome, the see of Peter, from the practices of the Old Testament followed by the Jews. In the next three chapters Leovigildus discusses the meanings symbolized in the alb (modesty and confession of sins), the amice (cleanness of heart), and the stole (devotion to ecclesiastical duties).

In the eighth and ninth chapters Leovigildus explains why bishops wear on their heads white mitres with hanging fringe on feasts and cover their heads with cowls on other days. The white mitre signifies the honor of old age which the bishop enjoys. Men are chosen to be bishops, says Leovigildus, who can resist opponents with holiness and reason rather than because of "crude holiness," and so they must be "adorned with the light of knowledge and imbued with the manners of old age." The cowl is worn, like a shroud, as a reminder that the clergy are dead to the world. In the last chapter of the work Leovigildus defends the western practice of a celibate clergy against the eastern practice, which permits priests to marry. He does not venture to criticize the custom of the East, not knowing "the councils of their Fathers, because they use Attic characters and the Greek language." He does, however, give the arguments of the "Arians," which he recalls. In a brief epilogue Leovigildus states that he has learned what he has written in part from the Fathers of old and in part from the masters of his own time. The tenth-century ms Heredia-Spínola lacks two folios at this point, but the sixteenth-century ms Escorial b-III-14 contains an additional sentence asking that "Your Clemency" approve the treatise for reading, followed by an *explicit* of the work.[22]

The over-all structure of the *De habitu clericorum* is rather loose, probably because it was not intended to be a comprehensive study of the subject, but rather a series of essays on several matters of ecclesiastical discipline, those about which the clergy were questioned most it would seem. There is, however, some order to the arrangement of topics in chapters: tonsure and shaving of the face, the sacred vestments of the priests, the mitre and cowl of the bishop, and finally clerical celibacy. In style and thought the treatise is labored and diffuse for the most part, rather than brilliant. The exact meaning of many words is difficult to determine and the grammar is inconsistent and erratic. Eulogius and Albar write in simpler and better Latin.

Leovigildus and his work are ascribed to the period of the Cordoban martyrs on the basis of references to a Leovigildus in other works of that time, and on the basis of references in the work itself to the clerics of St. Cyprian, to oppression by the Ismaelites, and to the monthly tax referred to also by Eulogius. Neither Córdoba nor a date is mentioned in the work, but there is no reason to ascribe it to another locale and date.

The autonomy of the Church seen in the Acts of the Council of Córdoba and the ideal of clerical piety portrayed in the *De habitu clericorum* are factors which merit attention in a study of the history of Córdoba at this time. When Eulogius, Albar, and Samson later raise complaints about

---

[22] Serrano, *op.cit.*, 518, and Antolín, *op.cit.*, 120.

compromise of principles and abuses, they speak from a personal experience of integrity and zeal, and not on the basis of an academic knowledge gathered from writings of old.

A work written in 845 by a Bishop Eldefonus *Hispaniensis* ("of Spain," or "of Seville"), who is otherwise unknown, may belong to Mozarabic literature.[23] Eldefonsus calls his work the *Revelatio,* and claims that the Holy Spirit has revealed to him specifications for hosts which are used in the Mass. He describes the size of the hosts, large and small, their weight, and the inscriptions to be made on them. He tells how many hosts are to be consecrated on different feasts and gives the patterns in which they are to be placed on the altar, with accompanying illustrations. From his specifications it appears that the hosts were similar to those used today. The work provides data of interest about weights and measures.

---

[23] Eldefonsus' work is from a Vatican ms, probably of the twelfth century. It is published in PL 106, 881-890, after the edition of Mabillon. Cf. L. C. Guasch, "Mozarabica liturgia," *Enciclopedia cattolica,* VIII, 1500ff.

CHAPTER VII

PAUL ALBAR

In the twenty years from 840 to 860 Latin letters in Córdoba appear to have been ruled by a man of unusual temperament and ability, Paul Albar.[1] He came into contact with almost every known figure of the period and participated in almost every series of events known, but information about him comes almost entirely from his own works. He did not hesitate to discuss theology or to delve into Scripture and the Fathers. He undertook to defend the divinity of Christ against an apostate to Judaism. The major Mozarabic polemical work against Islam, the *Indiculus luminosus*, is attributed to him. The *Indiculus*, which purports to be a beacon of truth, is also a vehement attack against those Christians, including members of the ecclesiastical and civil hierarchy, who condemned or would not support the martyr movement. Albar's *Confessio*, an examination of conscience and an act of contrition, is primarily a prayer intended for devotional use. His *Vita Eulogii* is a hagiographical work, and the passio of Eulogius in the vita appears to have been

---

[1] The works of Albar dealing with Eulogius were first published by Ambrosio de Morales, *Divi Eulogii . . . opera* (Alcalá, 1574). The rest of his works were first published by Flórez, ES, XI, 81-218, together with a biographical account of Albar, *ibid.*, 10-61. Migne's edition (PL 121, 397-566) is after that of Flórez. Carleton M. Sage, *Paul Albar of Córdoba: Studies on His Life and Writings* (Washington, 1943), pursues the study further. José Madoz, *Epistolario de Alvaro de Córdoba* (Madrid, 1947), provides an excellent study of the letters and re-edits the text of them. His edition of the text cannot be used for definitive work on the letters, however. A microfilm copy of the original ms, the Albar codex of Córdoba (probably of the tenth century), can be obtained from Servicio Nacional de Microfilm, Madrid. A copy of this ms made in 1751 is in the cathedral of Córdoba. Ms Madrid BN 7365, 120-216, contains a copy of Albar's works made from the Albar codex for Nicolas Antonio in 1662; ms Madrid BN 7345, 469-532v, contains another copy. Variants between the text of Madoz and the text of the Albar codex are given in Appendix II.

148

intended for liturgical use. Albar is the author of almost all the Latin poetry extant from the period. He prefigures in some ways the universal man of the Renaissance.

The most puzzling question about Albar is that of his authority or position in the Christian community. He was a property owner and apparently belonged to a prominent family,[2] but so far as is known he held no office, civil or ecclesiastical. Despite his description of himself at the beginning of the *Indiculus* as one of the learned (*peritissimi*) Catholics of the church and despite his proclivity to treat of matters generally reserved to the clergy, one can hardly doubt the preponderant evidence that he was a layman. In one place he indicates that he had practiced law,[3] and the forensic quality of his writings confirms his statement. His teacher, the Abbot Esperaindeo, and his friend Eulogius, a priest, deferred to him as a censor and editor of their writings.[4] The fact that one of the martyrs, Aurelius, sought advice from Albar before adopting a course which led to his martyrdom[5] illustrates the eminence of Albar's position. Albar's apparently religio-secular status in life may actually be two periods of his life. At one point in his life he received the sacrament of Penance, which customarily required the recipient to sever his ties with the world and live thereafter as a religious. Esperaindeo's deference to Albar, however, appears to have been expressed before Albar received the sacrament. No explanation for Albar's status has been found which does not leave questions unanswered. Most of the difficulties about Albar's position arise out of the authoritative stand taken by him in ecclesiastical affairs in the *Indiculus luminosus*, a work which, although it lacks a title of author-

---

[2] For the life of Albar cf. Sage, *op.cit.*, 1-42, and Madoz, *op.cit.*, 13-24.

[3] Letter IX of the Albar correspondence, 6.

[4] Letter VIII, 3. Although Esperaindeo says, "Whatever the Paternity of our lord your father (*vestri genitoris*) finds in error," he leaves no doubt that it is Albar who is to do the correcting. In fact, Esperaindeo appears to dignify Albar with the title "The Paternity of our lord Your Father." Cf. also the three letters which Eulogius wrote to Albar, all in 851.

[5] *Memoriale*, II, x, 18.

ship, can hardly be assigned to anyone other than Albar.
Albar could write courteous and gracious Latin, but in the
final analysis he bowed to no one, not even to his bishop.[6] He
was endowed with an impetuous personality, a tough and
tenacious mind, considerable skill in dialectics, and an accomplished literary style. With his tendency to use strong
invective, he may have been less gifted, perhaps, in prudence
and judicial moderation.

Except for his works dealing with Eulogius, all of Albar's
writings are found in a ninth-century codex devoted to his
works. One of the main parts of the codex is that entitled
Liber epistolarum Albari, a series of twenty letters exchanged between Albar and five other men. It appears that
the earliest of these letters are the last seven in the codex,
those between Albar and the apostate to Judaism, Bodo-
Eleazar.[7] In these letters Albar seeks to prove to his antagonist that Christ is the Messias. His argumentation here,
as in his other works, follows the standard pattern of quoting and interpreting passages from Scripture and the Fathers of the Church to prove his own point and show the
inconsistency of a contrary thesis. The method is followed
by Eulogius, by Leovigildus in the *De habitu clericorum,* in
the treatises of the Adoptionist controversy, and in most
mediaeval disputation. The bitter and abusive invective
dispensed by Albar, and later by Samson, with the same
largess as by Elipandus are not, however, characteristic of
all Mozarab authors.

The third of the seven letters between Albar and the
Transgressor, or Eleazar, is dated in 840.[8] There seems to
be no doubt that Eleazar is mentioned in the *Annales Bertiniani*[9] as a deacon named Bodo who in 839 left the Catholic
faith and became a Jew. In the court of Charles the Bald,
Bodo enjoyed some favor, if he is the same Bodo to whom

---

[6] Cf. Letter XIII.
[7] PL 121, 478-512; cf. Sage, *op.cit.,* 11ff.
[8] Letter XVI, 6.
[9] G. Waitz, MGH, *Scriptores ... in usum scholarum* (Hanover, 1883),
17f.

Walafrid Strabo addressed a poem.[10] He was of noble birth, and his apostasy was lamented by Amulo of Lyons, Lupus of Ferrières, and Hincmar,[11] as well as in the *Annales*. What makes Bodo's conversion to Judaism so striking is the vehemence with which he turned against the members of his former faith. To begin with, according to the *Annales*, he celebrated his change of faith in 839 by selling into slavery the members of the pilgrimage with whom he was travelling as a member of the clergy in southern France. He then grew a beard, girded himself with a sword, and took the daughter of a Jew to wife. Changing his name to Eleazar, he went to Zaragoza and later to Córdoba, where he attempted to incite the Moslem rulers to action against their Christian subjects, proposing that Christians become Moslem or Jewish or else suffer death. In 847 the Christians of Córdoba, according to the *Annales*, wrote to Charles the Bald and asked him to recall his subject. This is the last known reference to Bodo. Bodo's stay in Spain extends from the time of the Council of Córdoba in 839 almost up to the death of the first of the martyrs in April 850.

There is not much to the Albar-Bodo correspondence outside of Albar's first three letters. Albar's last letter is brief, and all three of Bodo's letters have suffered losses of text through censorship by erasure and mutilation. Albar begins the correspondence thus: "To my dear Eleazar from Albar. To begin with, my beloved friend, I pay thee the respects of health with as much sweetness as love and at the same time, if your sect and rite permit, I attach thereto salutiferous blessings. Furthermore, I pray that our offering of love may not irritate you, but I hope that it may enrich you in the Lord."[12] Albar goes on to protest his innocent intent and plain words in quite verbose rhetoric, introducing the subject of his letter dextrously by saying that it would be nice

[10] Ernest Duemmler, MGH, *Poetae latini aevi carolini*, II (Berlin, 1884), 386.

[11] Amulo of Lyons, *Liber contra iudaeos*, 42 (PL 116, 171); Lupus of Ferrières, Epistola VI (PL 119, 449); Hincmar of Reims, Epistola XXIII (PL 126, 154).

[12] Letter XIV, 1.

if the nativity of Christ were expected in a number of years so that the dispute between Christians and Jews would come to an end. The time for the coming of the Messias was fulfilled with the coming of Christ, Albar argues, and, as was promised in prophecy, the Jews have not had a leader since then. In this letter Albar depends upon Julian of Toledo's *De comprobatione aetatis sextae* for most of his arguments,[13] which are presented courteously. In his second letter Albar shows some irritation with the disrespect for Christianity manifested by Bodo in his reply. Most of this letter Albar devotes to the chronological argument that Christ is the Messias and to proof that the Jews have not had a leader. He depends upon a number of works by Jerome for his arguments here.[14] Albar's third, and longest, letter claims to take up Bodo's arguments and refute them. Here, in addition to Jerome and Julian, Isidore of Seville provides a source for Albar's arguments.[15] In the third letter Albar abuses Bodo with many offensive epithets and taunts him with the captivity of the Jews and their rejection by Christ. He begins his letter thus, "We have seen your vile letter, composed of lies and reeking with reproach, and it has not taken us long to reply to what we immediately saw to be erroneous." Later Albar attacks Bodo in a lengthier apostrophe. "But because you are polluted and have said many polluted things, and I cannot close my eyes and pass over reproach of the Most High, hear what truth, and not pride, has to say. Hear, O enemy of the Most High God; hear, O profaner of the Divine Law; hear, O violator of holy sanctuaries; hear, O thief of the vessels of the Lord! Who ever drank so much wine from the vineyards of Sodom and imbibed so much of the wine of malice, of dragons and asps, as you, who have dared to stand up in pride against the Most High and to devise with the devil calumny against the Son of God? Who was ever struck with such blindness as to say that purity is overcome

[13] For Julian's work cf. *SS PP Toletanorum*, II, 88-139, or PL 96, 537-586; cf. Madoz, *op.cit.*, 211-221.
[14] Madoz, *op.cit.*, 223-238.
[15] *Ibid.*, 241-276.

by pollution? See, O miserable one, that the rays of Phoebus penetrate the sewer, and neither lack their own light nor absorb the filth of the sewer."[16] Albar ends this letter with the hope that God will open the eyes of his opponent. Albar's last letter is a brief note bringing to an end the name-calling between the two men. In this brief letter Albar draws upon Isidore's *Historia Gothorum* and shows the influence of St. Jerome.[17]

Several times in his letters Albar censures Bodo for intemperance, for boasting of sacrilege, and for blasphemy against Christ and His mother. In his second letter he ventures to criticize Hebrew Scriptural scholarship. He also criticizes Bodo for a pretended knowledge of Hebrew and for his obstinate blindness. To judge from the censorship of Bodo's letters and Albar's replies, Bodo must have been crude and indelicate in his arguments, even resorting to what was for Albar outrageous blasphemy. But Albar's approach from the beginning was forensic, trying to prove that Bodo was wrong, and he could hardly have entertained any hope of convincing Bodo to return to Christianity with his subsequent vindictive letters. On a personal level Albar succeeded only in exchanging insults with Bodo. The correspondence, however, aired a matter which must have been of some importance for Christians in Moslem Spain, and it is probably for this reason that it has been preserved in the Albar codex. Even though the theology in the letters is greatly debased by rancor, the letters represent in the Latin literature of Córdoba an example of Jewish-Christian disputation in mediaeval times.[18]

---

[16] Letter XVIII, 11.

[17] Madoz, *op.cit.*, 276-281.

[18] Allen Cabaniss, "Bodo-Eleazar: A Famous Jewish Convert," *The Jewish Quarterly Review*, 43 (1952-1953), 313-328, portrays Bodo as a man disillusioned with what he knew of Catholic culture, who responded to the higher ideals of Judaism. He regards Bodo's anti-Catholic actions and campaigns as the natural consequence of his being a Jewish missionary. Cabaniss refers to many sources, but his attempt "to read through the bigoted accounts and to disclose the man as he actually was" (314) falls outside the discipline of history. Madoz, *op.cit.*,

Besides the bitter debate with Bodo, Albar also engaged in an epistolary debate with John of Seville. Although the six letters between the two men are the first to appear in the manuscript, there is reason to believe that Albar in his letters makes use of material brought back from the north of Spain by Eulogius about 848 or 850.[19] Because the martyrdoms are not mentioned in them, the letters are assumed to have been completed by 851. It seems unlikely that John of Seville was the metropolitan of Seville of that name at the Council of Córdoba in 839, because Albar opens the correspondence with familiarity and engages in cajolery with John. The men address each other as "Aurelius Flavius," a title which should indicate an elevated civil status. If the position of either were known, it could be inferred to be that of the other also. Both men salute the *decorem domui* of the other. This salutation is frequently taken to refer to the mistress or the women of their household,[20] but the relationship between the two men may be based on spiritual ties rather than on ties of blood. The *pater communis Johannes* mentioned by Albar and generally taken to be John's father and Albar's father-in-law could be John, the metropolitan of Seville, although it should be noted that the metropolitan of Seville in 851 appears to have been Reccafred. Albar appears to prevail over John with his arguments, but John was rather obviously reluctant to enter into the discussion.

The subjects of the first four letters, Christian use of secular rhetoric and the two natures in the one Person of Christ, which may seem somewhat academic at first glance, are closely related to actual problems of the times. At the end of the *Indiculus* Albar complains that Christian youths are abandoning the sacred writings of the Church, the Scriptures and the Fathers, in favor of the Arabic rhetoric of the Mos-

56ff., assembles Latin texts dealing with Bodo; cf. also Sage, *op.cit.* 11ff.

[19] Traube, MGH, *Poetae latini aevi carolini*, III, i (Berlin, 1886), 122f.

[20] Cf. Sage, *op.cit.*, 18, and Madoz, *op.cit.*, 17ff. In a *Differentiarum sive de proprietate sermonum liber* attributed to Isidore of Seville *decus* is said to refer to *virtus* and *decorem* to *corpus* (PL 83, 1322).

lems.[21] Latin letters in Córdoba may not have been in such
dire straits as some modern historians think them to have
been, but the situation was serious enough to cause some
Christians to attempt to offset the influence of Arabic letters. Besides literary and historical compositions, the Arabic
works seem to have consisted of Moslem teachings, including
perhaps works of spiritual guidance and sufism. Albar's
insistence in his letters to John on the doctrine of the one
divine person and the two natures in Christ obviously struck
against the denial of the divinity of Christ on the part of
the Mohammedan religion. The immediate importance of
this theological argument in Córdoba at this time can be seen
in the *Memoriale* and the *Indiculus,* where both Eulogius and
Albar base their condemnation of Mohammed on his effrontery in denying the divinity of Christ.[22] John showed
little interest in the discussion of the divine and human natures of Christ. Both authors have orthodox views. Albar
perhaps tended to merge the two natures somewhat, and
John in placing emphasis on the human nature clearly separated them.

In the course of the Christological debate Albar adduces
arguments from authors who combatted the Adoptionist
controversy some years before. Besides the treatise of
Eterius and Beatus, he cites a work by a Teudula, metropolitan of Seville, against Elipandus. He also quotes at
length from a work by a Basiliscus, who may have been a
legate from Alfonso II of the Asturias to Charlemagne in
798.[23] Neither Teudula nor Basiliscus, nor their works, are
known apart from Albar's references. Nor is a doctor mentioned by Albar, a Vincentius, presumably a contemporary
of Albar in Córdoba.[24] Albar also argued with John against

---

[21] *Indiculus,* 35.

[22] *Memoriale,* I, 7; *Apol. mart.,* 19; in the second half of the
Indiculus Mohammed is treated as Antichrist.

[23] Cf. the year 798 in the *Annales regii,* ed. Kurze, MGH, *Scriptores
. . . in usum scholarum* (Hanover, 1895), and ed. Pertz, MGH, *Scriptores,*
I, 184 and 185.

[24] Teudula, or Vincentius, may possibly be the author of Letter X of
the Albar correspondence.

the use of rhetoric in Christian education. The latter championed the cause of rhetoric with some warmth in his answer, but then abandoned the controversy. As far as the literature of the time goes, almost all authors show a tendency to compose in an elaborately rhetorical style, but they quote Scripture and Patristic sources as authorities almost without exception.

At the end of his last letter to John, Albar introduces problems of the origin of the soul and the existence of evil, especially as it concerns children, which he had got from St. Augustine, asking John for an answer on the subject. John replied with quotations arguing that the soul is created directly by God and infused into the body in the womb. He admits that he has no answer on the problem of evil.

Appended to the end of some of their letters are brief messages on current matters between them, several of which pertain to exchanges of books. In John's last letter he includes a biographical note on Mohammed. The chronological data at the beginning and end of the account agree with data in the Chronicles of 741 and 754 and repeat the text of the vita of the prophet Mohammed quoted by Eulogius in the *Apologeticus martyrum*,[25] a vita Eulogius found in a manuscript of Leyre on his journey to the north. Of four items to appear in John's account of Mohammed: that Mohammed took the wife of another in lust, that his corpse was eaten by dogs, that he occupied the mind of a camel (*in camelum cuius intellectum gerebat presideret*), and that the followers of Mohammed claimed miracles for him—the last two do not appear in the account quoted by Eulogius. Sage's argument that John's vita of Mohammed is not based on that quoted by Eulogius, because Albar, being closer to Eulogius than was John, would have had access to the latter is reiterated

---

[25] Letter VI, 9; *Apol. mart.*, 19; Chronicle of 741, 12-17, and Chronicle of 754, 9-12, ed. by Mommsen, MGH, *Auct. antiq.*, XI, 336ff. The dates in John's account as edited by Flórez and Madoz are not accurately transcribed from the ms. All three X's should be XL's, as they are in the ms, and the last figure should be CCCCLXLVIII. When read as they are in the ms, the dates agree: Era 747 and A.H. 91; Era 1143 and A.H. 498.

by Franke, but ignored by Madoz.[26] Immediately after the account of Mohammed in his letter John requests Albar to send him a transcription of what appears to be a lexicon or an alphabetical word list belonging to Eulogius, if he cannot send the volume itself. If, as seems probable, John and Albar were exchanging books for their mutual benefit, John may have sent his account of the prophet Mohammed for Albar to compare with the account belonging to Eulogius, having himself, perhaps, just completed a collation of the two accounts. His account therefore may be telescoped, with the ellipses not apparent. He may be confirming specific data in both accounts and offering two further items about the prophet not in the account from Leyre. In the *Apologeticus martyrum* Eulogius speaks of a project by the "learned" (*peritissimi*) Christians of Córdoba to collect polemical material against Islam. The fruits of Albar's labors appear in the second part of the *Indiculus*.

The letters between Albar and John are long and offer little of immediate interest concerning events in Córdoba at this time. They are, however, a rich source for determining the learning and the curriculum of the Christians of Córdoba. Sage and Madoz have studied them in some detail.[27]

Although little is known of the Abbot Esperaindeo and little of his work is extant, he can be recognized as one of the most important Christians in Córdoba, especially in the generation before Eulogius and Albar. It was in his school that these two as youths obtained their enthusiasm for their studies. Besides his part in the renaissance of Latin letters Esperaindeo has been credited with a part in the development of the monastic and ascetic fervor which characterized Christian culture in Córdoba in the middle of the ninth century.[28] His vita of the earliest martyrs known from the period, the brothers Adulfus and John, who died shortly

---

[26] Sage, *op.cit.*, 20, n. 98; Franke, "Die freiwilligen Märtyrer," 38, n. 273; Madoz, *op.cit.*, 170, n. 21.

[27] Sage, *op. cit.*, 43-81, and Madoz, *op.cit.*, 34-46.

[28] Franke, *op.cit.*, 18.

after Abd al-Rahman II came to the throne in 822, is no longer extant. He wrote a treatise against Islam, from which Eulogius quotes an excerpt condemning the Mohammedan idea of paradise.[29] His letter to Albar is his most extensive work extant. There is reason to believe that he died in late 851 or early 852. It is unlikely that he died as a martyr, as one may gather from the *calendarium* of Recemundus,[30] for Eulogius would hardly have failed to mention such an event in the *Memoriale*.

The exchange of letters between Albar and Esperaindeo is not an epistolary debate, but it shows something of the heretical influence of Islam on the Christians of Córdoba. Madoz and others have fixed the date of the two letters as previous to 840, partly because Albar, protesting that he is not an accomplished apologist, yields the floor to his master Esperaindeo. This argument fails to consider Esperaindeo's protestations in the beginning of his letter that Albar himself could easily have answered the questions had he wished, nor does it take into account Esperaindeo's deference to Albar as one to whom the censorship of letters was deputed. It would seem better to agree with Franke in dating the letter about 851, near the end of Esperaindeo's life.[31]

In Albar's letter to Esperaindeo he acknowledges that the abbot is suffering from tribulation and oppression but asks him to lend his assistance to refute a heresy which is doing injury to the Church. From among the charges of the heretics which he has made known to Esperaindeo previously Albar cites their basic errors. They do not believe in the Trinity, they deny the words of the prophets, they reject the teachings of the doctors, they say that they have received the Gospel. They misinterpret, "I ascend to my Father and

---

[29] Cf. *Memoriale*, II, viii, 9, and I, 7.

[30] Franke, *op.cit.*, 48, notes that Eulogius speaks of the abbot as if alive in the *Memoriale*, I, 7, which was probably written at the end of 851, and speaks of him as if deceased in the *Memoriale*, II, viii, 9, which was written in early 852, perhaps later; cf. Sage, *op.cit.*, 13f.; cf. index, "Recemundus."

[31] Madoz, *op. cit.*, 30; Franke, *op.cit.*, 59f. These two letters are also edited in PL 115, 959-966.

to your Father, to my God and to your God'" (Jn. 20:17), and they say that Christ our Lord and God is man only because of what they read of Him in the Gospel, "But of that day and hour no one knoweth: no, not the angels of heaven, nor the Son,[32] but the Father alone" (Mt. 24:36). Albar asks Esperaindeo to treat these two errors in his usual custom, with excerpts from the Scriptures, and to reply to the charges of an *assertor* which Albar had sent to him.

F. R. Franke argues that the heresy described by Albar is actually Islam.[33] He compares Albar's description of the heresy with a similar description of Islam by Eulogius: "Mohammed rejects the prophecies of the prophets and defames the doctrine of the apostles, abuses even the truth of the Holy Gospel, and denies the teachings of the pious doctors. . . . He taught that Christ is the Word of God and indeed a great prophet, though sustained by no power of Divinity, like other men but not equal to God the Father."[34] Moreover, as Franke points out, the two quotations from Holy Scripture (Jn. 20:17 and Mt. 24:36) are presented by the Moslem participant in the Religious Controversy of Jerusalem,[35] a dispute which took place in the East between A.D. 830 and 850. The errors brought up for discussion by Albar seem clearly Islamic in origin, but from Esperaindeo's letter it seems that they were being expressed by Christians whom the abbot was unwilling to condemn too quickly.

Esperaindeo's letter is composed of three parts. The first part, like Albar's letter, to which it replies, comes from the Albar codex of Córdoba. The last two parts come from ms 22 of the Cathedral of León and are a credo on the Trinity and a refutation of the *assertor*'s attempt to show that Christ was human only. Esperaindeo begins by stating his surprise to hear from Albar in the midst of his tribulations, when, "penetrated by the javelins of envious people, my mind and spirit seethed."[36] He goes on to remind Albar that one should

[32] The Clementine Vulgate lacks "nor the Son."
[33] Franke, *op.cit.*, 49-59; also 29f. and 40.
[34] *Memoriale*, I, 7.
[35] Franke, *op.cit.*, 35-37, and 50f.
[36] Letter VIII, 1.

show compassion for "the fall of a brother" and not hasten to condemn him on hearsay. Esperaindeo then excuses himself from discussing the mystery of the nativity of Christ by noting that not Jerome, not the Evangelists, not an unidentified doctor whom he quotes would discuss it. Albar himself, who never suffered any tribulation or worldly adversity,[37] says Esperaindeo, could have refuted the charges noted in his letter with testimonies from the Gospels and "the apostles" better than could Esperaindeo. But since he evidently seeks only a credo of faith from Esperaindeo, the abbot will comply with his command. He asks Albar to emend any errors he might make, for to Albar "has been designated the emending, the pruning, and the adding." "But those charges which are written out in your letter I shall introduce writing them under the name of the *assertor*, and I shall produce testimonies from the true text of the Holy Scriptures, and when I add, to the best of my ability, what the doctors say I shall make my reply."[38] This is the end of the first part of Esperaindeo's letter.

Practically none of the second part of the letter, a long credo on the Trinity taken, as Madoz shows,[39] almost verbatim from the *De Trinitate* of pseudo-Vigilius, can be attributed to Esperaindeo. Those who make one person of God, says the text echoing that of pseudo-Vigilius, make Jews of themselves, and those who say three Gods are like the pagans, who adore that which is made by hand.

The third and last part of the letter, in which two charges by the *assertor* are answered, is in dialogue form. The *assertor*'s first charge is that Jn. 20:17, where Christ says that He ascends to His Father and His God, shows that Christ is not God. Esperaindeo's reply is an extended excerpt taken directly from Canon thirteen of the Second Council of Seville (A.D. 613), to which are added other quotations from

[37] *Ibid.*, 3. This statement dates the letter before Albar's illness and probably before the *Indiculus*, completed in 854.

[38] *Ibid.*, "et cum doctorum dicta ut quivero conectam que respondendo conscribam." In these words Esperaindeo does not necessarily promise to write words of his own in reply.

[39] Madoz, *op.cit.*, 177, n. 14.

Scripture to prove that Christ is God. The second charge is that Mt. 24:36 shows that Christ did not know the day and hour of the Last Judgment and so cannot be God. F. R. Franke shows a close resemblance between Esperaindeo's reply to the charge and the text of the Religious Controversy of Jerusalem, in refutation of the same Moslem argument, concluding that Esperaindeo knew of the text of the Controversy through one of a number of Christians who came to Spain from the East.[40] It may be noted that in this passage of Esperaindeo's letter both the *assertor* and the defender address each other in direct discourse rather than in the impersonal presentation of the previous charge and reply.

One may agree with Franke that Albar in his letter describes the theological errors of Islam and that the last part of Esperaindeo's letter corresponds closely with the text of the Religious Controversy of Jerusalem, but one need not therefore conclude that Albar and Esperaindeo in their letters were speaking of Islam. In the beginning of his letter Esperaindeo apparently seeks to alleviate Albar's anxiety about the heresy and is careful not to criticize or exaggerate "the fall of a brother." The circumspection of Esperaindeo, if he was dealing with Islam, is difficult to understand. A person who had earlier written the vita of two martyrs of the Moslems' persecution and a treatise against the Moslems' beliefs would have been, it seems, more forthright when dealing with Islam before one of his former pupils. Moreover, as Franke notes,[41] Esperaindeo seems to refer to a Christian heresy when he follows pseudo-Vigilius in his credo on the Trinity, comparing the doctrine of one person in God with Judaism and polytheism with pagan idolatry, making no reference whatsoever to Islam. For some reason Esperaindeo seems to be avoiding an attack on Islam.

As part of his argument that the heresy mentioned in the

[40] Franke, *op.cit.*, 52-59; the fact that neither of two Syrian monks mentioned by Franke arrived in Córdoba until after the date which Franke would set for the death of Esperaindeo does not affect the validity of his argument; cf. Gams, *Kirchengeschichte*, II, ii, 261-267.
[41] Franke, *op.cit.*, 51.

letters is Islam Franke shows that Albar and Eulogius called Mohammed the author of heresy and a heresiarch. Although Franke notes that Christian authors frequently called the Moslems "pagans" (*gentiles*), and even cites a use of the word by Albar to show that the errors under discussion were errors of the Moslems, he also says that for Eulogius and Albar there was no doubt that Islam was a Christian heresy.[42] This argument implies that the Christians regarded Moslems as fellow Christians. It seems more likely that Eulogius and Albar used the term "heresy" loosely when speaking of Islam. Eulogius devotes a large part of the *Apologeticus martyrum* to the argument that the Moslems did not worship God and His law, and Albar through most of the *Indiculus* argues that, as Mohammed is a type of Antichrist, so Islam is the contrary of Christianity and is to be attacked as such. Mohammed is usually referred to as *vates* or as *maledictus,* and his religion as a sect or cult, whose members were unbaptized. Throughout Latin letters of the eighth and ninth centuries in Spain the Moslems were frequently spoken of as pagans. Pope Adrian I in the late eighth century and the Council of Córdoba in 839 both condemned the marriage of Christians and "infidels." Eulogius' own statement indicates that from the term "heretics" he excluded apparently only orthodox Christians, Jews, and idolators: "For that same author of perverted teaching and pernicious destroyer of many souls, alone among the other institutors of heresies after the Ascension of the Lord, founding a sect of new superstition at the instigation of the devil is separated far from union with the holy Church."[43]

It may be that the Christians of Córdoba should be credited with more originality in their polemics than Franke admits. Although he finds no precedent for the designation of the Moslem paradise as a brothel in Esperaindeo's treatise against Islam, Franke would assign it an eastern origin on the basis that Esperaindeo took most of his other extant work

---

[42] *Ibid.,* 50.
[43] *Memoriale,* I, 7; cf. also *Apol. mart.,* 19.

from other authors.[44] One should note, however, that Eulogius praises Esperaindeo as if for an original contribution to ecclesiastical literature and describes his method thus, "as if deriving his argument from the words of that cult and then setting forth his own judgment."[45] The activities of the "learned" cannot be overlooked in this respect. Eulogius says of them, "Some of our wisest men, armed with the zeal of God, have pounded with the rams of justice against the folly of his [Mohammed's] error, his delirious preachings, and his commands of impious novelty."[46] Franke doubts that many of these "wisest men" came from Spain,[47] but the *peritissimi* to whom Eulogius and Albar refer seem to have been for the most part Spanish. Eulogius' own vehement denunciation of Mohammed's gross blasphemy against the Blessed Virgin,[48] which Franke does not discuss, seems to be original. Despite reservations about some of Franke's arguments, however, he appears to be basically correct in considering the Albar-Esperaindeo correspondence in a study of Christian-Moslem polemics in Spain and in emphasizing the indebtedness of Spanish Christian polemicists to the Christian polemicists of the East.

The remaining five letters of the Albar correspondence deal with Albar's later life. Since they also contain information about Bishop Saul of Córdoba and perhaps about a council which took place during the persecution of the martyrs they will be discussed later.

Albar is the author of five hundred and forty of the six hundred and thirteen lines of verse extant from the literature of Córdoba at this time. Eleven of Albar's poems are from the codex of Córdoba.[49] The date of their composition is unknown. They may not have been written until Eulogius returned in 848 or 850 from his journey to the north with

---

[44] Franke, *op.cit.*, 59.

[45] *Memoriale*, I, 7.

[46] *Ibid.*, 8; cf. also *Apol. mart.*, 13 and 20.

[47] Franke, *op.cit.*, 47.

[48] *Memoriale*, I, 7.

[49] The edition of the poems by Traube, *op. cit.*, 126-139, is superior to that of Flórez in ES, XI, 275-290.

Latin classics or until he mastered previously unknown Latin metrics while imprisoned in 851.[50] The meter of Albar's poems is hexameter, except for forty-four lines of elegiac couplets. Three other poems by Albar,[51] in honor of Eulogius, who died in 859, include eighty lines of asclepiadeans. They come from the Azagra codex and were in the manuscript of Eulogius' works, which is no longer extant. The consensus of opinion is that the meter of all the verse is rather bad. The first two poems by Albar are devoted to praise of the nightingale and are modelled after a similar poem by Eugene of Toledo.[52] The next four poems are devoted to praise of other creatures of God. The seventh poem, of about thirty lines, beseeches God to cure the author of his spiritual ills, and the eighth is a *memento mori* applied to Albar himself. The next poem, of one hundred and sixty-eight lines and the longest in the collection, is devoted to the Bible and appears to be, as Traube and Manitius point out,[53] modelled after a similar poem by Theodulfus of Orleans. Manitius speculates that Eulogius brought back the work of Theodulfus with him in 848. The first part of Albar's poem catalogues the different books of the Bible. The second part discusses the Bible as a panacea for all ills. The last twenty-seven lines praise a wonderful Bible of Leovigildus and remind the reader that the pleasures of life are but transitory. Of two poems of about fifty lines each, one is devoted to praise of the Cross, which is the symbol of Christ, and the other to praise of St. Jerome, Albar's favorite author after Holy Scripture. Appended to the second of these poems

[50] Traube, *op.cit.*, 124, dates them after 851, on the basis of Albar's statement about Eulogius in prison in 851, "ibi metricos quos adhuc nesciebant sapientes Hispaniae pedes perfectissime docuit nobisque post egressionem suam hostendit," *Vita Eulogii*, 4. The meters which Eulogius explained to Albar may, however, have been others than those Albar uses in the poems of the codex of Córdoba.

[51] The poems are edited by Traube, *op.cit.*, 139-142, and in ES, X, 560-563.

[52] For Eugene's poems cf. *SS PP Toletanorum*, I, 57-79; cf. also Traube, *op.cit.*, 126f.

[53] Traube, *op.cit.*, 132-136, and Max Manitius, *Geschichte der lateinischen Literatur des Mittelalters*, I (Munich, 1911), 422.

is a ten-line coda which describes the brilliance of Lucifer and his fall. The first of the last three poems by Albar, all in memory of Eulogius, consists of the eighty lines of asclepiadean quatrains and forms an acrostic, "Albarus te rogat salves." It praises Eulogius and recounts his arrest, trial, and death. The second is a ten-line epitaph for Eulogius, and the last is an eight-line prayer of Albar asking Eulogius to remember him.

The remaining seventy-three lines of verse are divided among eleven poems,[54] mostly epitaphs, eight by the Archpriest Cyprian and three by the Abbot Samson. All come from the Azagra codex. The first of Cyprian's is a twenty-seven-line poem describing a Bible owned by a Count Adulfus, which he gave to his son Fredenandus. The poem also tells how Adulfus offered a memorial of St. Acisclus in Córdoba for his own soul. Another poem was appended to a Bible which Cyprian had "written" for the Archdeacon Saturninus. Two poems are short pieces in connection with fans given to Guisinda, the wife of Count Guifridus. Unusual in the collection is a three-line piece by Cyprian expressing a *carpe diem* philosophy: "Cease your weeping, you see the green fields, birds sing sweet songs, and let wine flow into the mouth of the fearful." Cyprian composed three epitaphs: for the Abbot Samson, who died 21 June 890; for a Hermildis; and for John, who suffered prison and dire iron bonds for the love of Christ. Samson composed three epitaphs: for an Abbot Athanagildus;[55] for a priest Valentinian; and for an Offilo. The last is an acrostic.

Traube adds six other poems,[56] comprising one hundred and twenty-one lines, from the Azagra codex. These poems, one by a Vincentius, one by a Receswinth, and one an epitaph for a Servus Dei, cannot be assigned to Córdoba with certainty nor can their date be determined.

A deep religious consciousness emphasizing the coming

---

[54] The poems are edited by Traube, *op.cit.*, 144-147, and in ES, XI, 524-528.

[55] For Samson, John, and Athanagildus cf. index.

[56] Traube, *op.cit.*, 147-150.

loss of present pleasures and glories characterizes this Mozarabic poetry. The poets also take delight in describing the beauties and grandeurs of nature in extended enumeration. Both these themes are associated with the theme of the power of God. In spite of appearing academic and labored, the poems have a certain rustic simplicity which compensates for their metric deficiencies.

CHAPTER VIII

OUTLINE SURVEY OF THE APOLOGETICAL WORKS DEALING WITH THE MARTYRS OF CÓRDOBA

The major event in the history of Córdoba at this time, and perhaps the most critical event in the history of Moslem rule in Spain, is the persecution of the Christians of Córdoba which was in force by 850 under Abd al-Rahman II and continued through the early part of the reign of Mohammed I. It is possible that this persecution signaled the end of Arab Mohammedan rule in Spain by bringing into the open a fundamentally irreconcilable incompatibility between Moslem rule and Spanish Christian subjects. The Arab empire of Córdoba did not become firmly established until after the reign of al-Hakam I (796-822).[1] The persecution began about 850, and the revolts that sprang up through the realm immediately thereafter were superseded only by continual warfare against the Christian forces of León and Navarre in the tenth century. Despite exploits of military prowess and works of culture produced in eras of strength or peace after the ninth century, the empire of the caliphate of Córdoba was disintegrating for many years before it came to an end. In such a light, the persecution in which Mohammedan rulers shed the blood of their Christian subjects before the eyes of their Christian brothers living in religious freedom in the north deserves attentive investigation.

Several writers (Eulogius, Albar, Samson, Leovigildus, Aimoin, probably Bishop Saul, and perhaps the anonymous author-bishop of a letter in the Albar codex) speak of the persecution, but only Eulogius and Albar actively defend the martyrs in their works. The *Memoriale* and the *Apologeticus martyrum* of Eulogius and the *Indiculus* of Albar are essentially apologetical and polemical works, addressed to the whole Christian community, or, as Eulogius says, to

---

[1] Lévi-Provençal, *Histoire des musulmans d'Espagne*, I, 185-191.

the whole Church. Perhaps because the purpose of each of these works was to defend the martyrs, in their first parts the rhetorical structure and content are similar. The *Memoriale* encompasses more in its scope than either of the other works. It is longer than the *Apologeticus martyrum*, which is a sequel to it, and it concerns itself with the justification of the martyrs as genuine rather than with the placing of blame for the persecution on the Moslems and those who will not support the martyrs, as does the *Indiculus*.

All three works divide readily into two parts. The first part in each instance is an apologia for the martyrs; but, whereas Eulogius' two works continue thereafter with an account of the martyrs, the *Indiculus* goes on to an elaborate exposé of the Moslem religion and a discussion of Mohammed as a type of Antichrist. In the second part of the *Indiculus* the same technique of argumentation is used as in theological sections in Albar's correspondence and in a later work, Samson's *Apologeticus*. Holy Scripture is quoted and explained. The second part of the *Indiculus* can be regarded as part of the theological literature of the Christians of Córdoba if its subject matter, Mohammed as Antichrist, is accepted as theological.

In the first part of all three works the authors undertake a defense of the martyrs. In the *Memoriale* and the *Indiculus* the defense assumes two tasks, to justify the zealous preaching of the confessors against the Moslems and to refute detractors of the martyrs. The *Memoriale* refutes both Moslem and Christian detractors, whereas the *Indiculus* concerns itself with Christians only. In the *Apologeticus martyrum* there is no defense of the martyrs' preaching and only Christian detractors are refuted, even though half of the refutation is a treatise against Mohammed and his followers. In defending the martyrs against detraction by the Moslems the *Memoriale* seeks to justify the corruption of the martyrs' bodies and the absence of miracles in connection with their relics. Neither subject comes up in the *Indiculus*. The *Apologeticus martyrum* considers the lack of miracles but not the corruption of the bodies.

The prefaces to the three works are dissimilar. That of the *Memoriale* is unusual in that most of it is devoted to a lengthy historical account of the martyr Isaac. In the preface to the *Apologeticus martyrum* Eulogius explains that he has combined apologetics with an account of the martyrs and so does not call the work *Gesta martyrum*. In the preface to the *Indiculus* Albar prays God to grant him the ability to edify the faithful and destroy his opponents.

In the discussion to follow what are referred to as the first parts of the works are the preface and Book I of the *Memoriale*, paragraphs one to twenty (1-20) of the *Apologeticus martyrum*, and paragraphs one to twenty (1-20) of the *Indiculus*. It may be helpful to begin with a very brief sketch of the contents of these first parts. The *Memoriale* first explains why Eulogius ventures to speak forth (pars. 1-4), tells what the martyrs did (5-11), and then answers the charge regarding the absence of miracles (12-17); it next defends the preaching of the martyrs (18-25) and answers the charge regarding the corruption of the bodies (26); after answering the Christian detractors (27-33), it ends with an appeal for veneration of the martyrs as saints (33-38). The *Apologeticus martyrum* begins with the standard deference of a "sinful" author who presumes to discuss the deeds of saints (1-2) and then answers the objections of those who feel that the Cordoban martyrs, because of their quick and easy death, cannot be compared with the martyrs of the early Church (3-6); it then justifies the absence of miracles (7-10), and goes into a long treatise showing that, contrary to what some Christians think, the Mohammedans who slew the martyrs do not worship God and His law, introducing evidence of their villany and the villany of their prophet (11-20). The first part of the *Indiculus* falls into two parts, one (2-11) in defense of the martyrs' right to preach and one (12-20) in defense of the martyrs themselves. Albar first explains that he is defending the martyrs, not attacking the Church (1). He then defends the preaching of the confessors (2-3) and refutes those who say that there was no persecution (3-7); he defends the cursing of the

Mohammedans (7-8) and, criticizing Christians who are lukewarm in their fervor (9-10), argues for a policy of firmness and harshness towards the enemies of the Church (11). Then he defends the voluntary martyrs (12-13) and argues that the persecution derives not from the actions of the martyrs but from the failings of the Christians (14-19), inserting two paragraphs against those who advocate feigned concurrence with the Mohammedans (16-17). After calling for praise of the martyrs (19-20), he ends with a justification of the work he has written (20).

Eulogius uses more Scriptural quotations in his works than does Albar in the *Indiculus*. He relies a great deal on historical tradition as an argument, whereas Albar uses quotations for the rational value of their arguments. Book I of the *Memoriale* contains about a hundred Scriptural quotations or close references to Scripture and twelve quotations from other sources; the pertinent paragraphs of the *Apologeticus martyrum* contain thirty-five Scriptural quotations and three from other sources; and the pertinent paragraphs of the *Indiculus* contain twenty-six Scriptural quotations or references and five from other sources. Only one quotation is common to all three works, "If anyone preach to you a gospel, besides that which you have received, let him be anathema" (Gal. 1:9). Five quotations occur in both the *Memoriale* and the *Indiculus*, (Tob. 13:16; Gal. 1:9; Is. 56:10; Ps. 138:22; and Wisd. 1:11). Only one quotation is in both the *Indiculus* and the *Apologeticus martyrum*, (Gal. 1:9). There are seven quotations which occur in the *Memoriale* and in the *Apologeticus martyrum*, (Mt. 10:40; Ps. 138:17, twice in the *Memoriale;* Ps. 115:15; Mt. 10:22, twice in the *Apologeticus martyrum;* Mk. 16:15, twice in the *Memoriale;* Ex. 8:7, and Gal. 1:9). Of the last five quotations to occur in the *Memoriale*, three, (Ps. 138:17, twice in the *Memoriale;* Ps. 115:15; and Mt. 10:40), occur within the first four quotations of the *Apologeticus martyrum*. This may be explained by the fact that the general idea of this part of the *Memoriale* (34-38) is repeated in brief in the beginning of the *Apologeticus martyrum* (2): Eulogius hopes for a heavenly reward for writing of the deeds of the martyrs. None of the quotations from sources outside Scripture occur in more than one text.

The general lack of coincidence of Scriptural and other quotation in the three works confirms the conclusion one derives from a study of the arguments of the three works in their first parts; that is, that the argumentation in each work supplements rather than repeats that in the others.

In the *Apologeticus martyrum* and the *Memoriale*, however, appear two extensive passages that are almost identical. One of these passages occurs in the justification of the absence of miracles, and the other in an attack against Mohammed.[2] The passages in the *Apologeticus martyrum* seem to be later modifications of those in the *Memoriale*. Apart from these two passages, the arguments concerning the absence of miracles and Mohammed in the *Apologeticus martyrum* are supplementary to those in the *Memoriale* rather than based on them. The bulk of the discussion of the absence of miracles in the *Apologeticus martyrum* (7-10) consists of Scriptural quotations, none of which occur in the corresponding part of the *Memoriale* (12-17). The ideas in paragraphs fifteen and sixteen of the *Memoriale*, that one should be impressed by the virtues of miracle workers rather than their deeds and that Eulogius is not attempting to belittle the gift of miracles but to defend the martyrs, do not occur in the *Apologeticus martyrum*. Both discussions of the absence of miracles come to an end with the same short statement that "The root and foundation of all virtues is faith."[3]

The almost identical passage against Mohammed in the *Memoriale* occurs at the beginning of a discussion of the Moslem prophet and his teaching (7); in the *Apologeticus*

---

[2] *Memoriale*, I, 14, and *Apol. mart.*, 7, "Miraculorum . . . populorum." *Memoriale*, I, 7 and 8, has a continuous resemblance to *Apol. mart.*, 19 and 20; in both places a basic verbatim text is punctuated by lengthy parenthetical annotation.

[3] *Memoriale*, I, 17, and *Apol. mart.*, 9; cf. the same statement in Samson's *Apologeticus*, I, i, 5.

martyrum it occurs at the end of such a discussion (19).
The part of the *Apologeticus martyrum* that discusses Mohammed (11-20) consists of a large number of Scriptural
quotations warning Christians against false prophets and
of a history of Mohammed which Eulogius obtained in the
monastery of Leyre in the north of Spain. In the *Memoriale*
Eulogius introduces an attack on Mohammed for blasphemy
against the Blessed Virgin and a quotation from a lost work
of Esperaindeo refuting the sensual idea of paradise held by
the Moslems. In the *Indiculus* Albar discusses Moslem sensual beliefs at length.[4] Eulogius' arguments against Mohammed in the *Apologeticus martyrum*, based on the New
Testament, supplement Albar's in the *Indiculus,* based on
the Old Testament. The first part of the *Apologeticus martyrum* seems intended to supplement argumentation previously advanced in the *Memoriale* and the *Indiculus* and to
answer a new objection that the Cordoban martyrs had not
died at the hands of pagans.

In some ways the first part of the *Indiculus* and the first
part of the *Memoriale* are very much alike. The incipit of
both works is the same, *Peritissimorum.*[5] Both works seek
to justify the preaching of the confessors and to defend the
voluntary martyrs against those who would detract from
the genuineness of their sacrifice. The two works also corroborate each other in their accounts of the first martyrdoms.
They both describe the provocations of the Moslems which
caused the outbreak and the means used to repress the martyr movement.

The *Documentum martyriale* is not of the same pattern
as the three works just discussed, but it may be surveyed
here briefly. In the *Documentum* Eulogius praises the actions of the virgins Flora and Maria and urges them to per-
severe in the truth, enumerating the deeds of saints before

[4] Cf. *Apol. mart.,* 16, *Memoriale,* I, 7, and *Indiculus,* 23-24.

[5] The incipit of Julian of Toledo's *De comprobatione aetatis sextae,* an
apologetical work written against the Jewish denial that the age of the
Messias had arrived, is *Peritorum.* In the Cordoban sources the word
"peritissimi" may denote a quasi-official group devoted to the defense
of the Faith, the "learned."

them (1-7). Regardless of what happens to the church of Spain, he says, they should continue to maintain the truth publicly and not, as the church does, in secret (8-18). He urges them not to abandon merits already earned in heaven and pictures for them their future glory, asking for their intercession for him after their martyrdom (19-25). Being written to edify the virgins and for their contemplation while awaiting martyrdom, the *Documentum* is, as one would expect, rather full of quotations from Scripture, thirty-four in the comparatively short work.

In the *Vita Eulogii*, written after the persecution it seems,[6] Albar devotes himself to praise of Eulogius and omits any arguments he may have against the Moslems.

[6] Cf. *Vita*, the beginning of par. 12.

CHAPTER IX

EULOGIUS AND THE BEGINNING
OF THE MARTYR MOVEMENT

The most important sources for the history of the persecution of the Christians in Córdoba are the works of Eulogius, all of which deal with the martyrs. Eulogius, a priest of Córdoba, championed the martyrs from the beginning, and after eight years of devotion to them was himself martyred in 859. His vita and passio were written by his friend Paul Albar.[1] Eulogius himself gives the names of his immediate family: a grandfather Eulogius; his mother Elizabeth; three brothers, Isidore, Albar, and Joseph; and two sisters, Anulo and Niola.[2] Neither Eulogius nor Albar mention the father of Eulogius, who apparently died before 848 or 850 when Eulogius visited Navarre.

Albar's biography of Eulogius divides conveniently into two parts, the vita proper (1-11) and the passion (12-20). The vita may be used here to introduce Eulogius to the reader and the passio later to conclude the discussion of Eulogius and the martyrs. In the preface Albar indicates that he himself was a layman. Eulogius, a priest, flew higher on the wings of virtue, he says, while he, tainted by the flesh, crept on the earth. What he writes about Eulogius is the truth as he himself has seen and experienced it, he continues. His rather strong protestations that he will not introduce

---

[1] The *Vita Eulogii* (PL 115, 705-720) was first published by Morales in 1574 with the works of Eulogius. It is extant in the Azagra codex (ms BN Madrid 10029) and was in the ms of Eulogius' works which was lost after the edition of 1574. It appears in almost all editions of Eulogius' works and in ES, X, Appendix VI. Morales translated it into Spanish in the *Corónica general*, XIV, xxvii, in 1586, and it has been translated again by A. S. Ruiz, *Obras completas de San Eulogio* (Córdoba, 1959), 1-41. Carleton M. Sage translated it into English, *Paul Albar of Córdoba* (Washington, 1943), 190-214.

[2] Letter of Eulogius to Wiliesindus, 1 and 5 (PL 115, 845 and 847).

information of a dubious nature about Eulogius cause one to think that already then legends were arising about the saint.[3] Eulogius, Albar begins, was born of the senatorial[4] nobility of Córdoba and lived in the college of clerics of the Basilica of St. Zoilus. Imbued with high ideals of ecclesiastical life, he was zealous in the study of Holy Scripture and the law of God and overlooked no teacher in his pursuit of learning. Although younger than those about him, Eulogius was eminent in erudition and doctrine, "a doctor of masters." Albar and Eulogius met as pupils in the school of Esperaindeo, "who at that time was enriching all Betica with the streams of his wisdom." The two youths engaged in epistolary disputation about Scripture as a game and wrote verses in praise of each other. Later Albar put this training in epistolary disputation to use when he debated with Bodo and John of Seville in letters. All the sources of the time point to the study of Holy Scripture as the basis of intellectual life among the Christians of Córdoba. Although Albar calls the verses he and Eulogius wrote "rithmici versus," it is unlikely that he speaks of rhythmic verse. All of the Latin poetry extant from Córdoba in the ninth century is metrical.[5] Later, Albar says, he and Eulogius destroyed these works of their youth.

Eulogius became a deacon and a priest in turn, Albar continues, and soon was one of the masters of the Christian community. He practiced ascetic austerities and, though a secular cleric, was greatly interested in monastic life, which then seems to have been attracting large numbers of Christians in and around Córdoba. Eulogius spent much time in monasteries[6] and even composed rules for the monks. Out

---

[3] There is a fair resemblance between par. 1 of the *Vita Eulogii* and par. 1 of the vita of Flora and Maria, *Memoriale*, II, viii.

[4] *Vita*, 2; Morales in a scholium here interprets the reference to the senate to mean that Eulogius was descended from Roman ancestors, but there are indications in the sources that a senate may actually have existed in Córdoba in the time of Eulogius.

[5] Cf. Manitius, *Geschichte der lateinischen Literatur des Mittelalters*, I, 422; Traube, MGH, *Poetae latini aevi carolini*, III, i, 122-124.

[6] *Vita*, 3; "monasteria frequentare, coenobia invisere"; Albar may in

of religious fervor he sought to undertake a pilgrimage to Rome in order to purge himself of the faults of his youth, Albar reports, but his friends dissuaded him, apparently because of the dangers of the journey. Albar uses the terms "doctor" and "master" in this part of the *Vita* as if they were recognized titles or degrees in an organized educational system: "magistrorum doctor est factus" (Eulogius), "nec contentus magisterio doctorum suorum," "auditorioque more," "Eram . . . auditorium," "auditores viri," and especially "magistris ordine et vitae moribus sociatur" (Eulogius). In the *Indiculus* too Albar speaks of doctors of the church of Córdoba then alive as if their title was official.

Meanwhile, says Albar, "Bishop Reccafred fell upon churches and clergy like a violent whirlwind and threw as many priests as he could into jail, among whom he [Eulogius] was included as an 'elect ram' and was imprisoned along with his own bishop and other priests."[7] Although Bishop Reccafred here is generally assumed to have been metropolitan of Seville and the same person who signed the Acts of the Council of Córdoba in 839 as bishop of Córdoba and Cabra, it is possible that he was neither. The power he seems to have exercised in Córdoba at this time may have derived from the support of the Moslem government as much as from any metropolitan rank. Hostegesis of Malaga, the enemy of Samson, was neither bishop of Córdoba nor metropolitan of Seville, but he held exceptional authority in Córdoba with Moslem support. If Reccafred is the bishop of Córdoba and Cabra who signed the Acts of the Council in 839, he may have relinquished the see of Córdoba to Saul and remained simply bishop of Cabra shortly before the actions Albar ascribes to him in the *Vita*. If one accepts the date of 849-851 for Letters I-VI of the Albar correspond-

this paragraph intend a distinction between "monasterium" and "coenobium."

[7] *Vita*, 4; Albar refers to a "pontifex suus" of Eulogius distinct from "episcopus" Reccafred here and in par. 7. Eulogius, Letter to Albar, *Semper, mi frater*, says that the "cruel tyrant" was responsible for his imprisonment; in Letter to Albar *Olim, mi frater*, Letter to Wiliesindus, 12, and *Doc. mart.*, 11, he speaks as if the king were responsible.

ence, which is probable, and identifies Albar's correspondent John of Seville as the metropolitan of Seville, which is less probable, Reccafred likewise would have become metropolitan of Seville only a short while before he "fell upon the churches" of Córdoba. Neither Reccafred nor John is listed as a metropolitan of Seville in the list of bishops in ms Escorial d-I-1. There are, however, indications in the *Indiculus luminosus* and in Letter X of the Albar correspondence that the metropolitan of Seville was such a person as Albar describes Reccafred to be in the *Vita*.[8] In the present work Reccafred is referred to as the metropolitan of Seville, but the strong arguments against his having held the office should be kept in mind.

After 852 the metropolitan of Seville all but disappears from the sources. He may be the anonymous author of Letter X to another bishop who seems to be Wistremirus of Toledo, or he may be the target of oblique remarks by Albar in the *Indiculus*. In the *Apologeticus* Samson mentions briefly that the metropolitan, left anonymous, was ordered by Hostegesis and Count Servandus, in collusion with the Moslems, to come to Córdoba in 864. After 852 Reccafred (or a metropolitan) may, on the one hand, have led those Christians in Córdoba who were opposed to the martyrdoms and Bishop Saul, and so was ignored by Eulogius and Albar. On the other hand, he may have meliorated his attitude towards the martyrs in later years and thus have lost the favor of the Moslems, the basis of his power in Córdoba.

During his imprisonment by Reccafred in 851 Eulogius composed the *Documentum martyriale* for the virgins Flora and Maria and also, Albar reports, fortified them for martyrdom by word of mouth. While he was in prison Eulogius learned metrics "which until then Spanish scholars did not know"[9] and later showed them to Albar. Albar adds that

---

[8] Cf. Madoz, *Epistolario*, 28f.; Antolín, "El códice emilianense," *La ciudad de Dios*, 74, 388; *Indiculus*, especially 19; Letter X, 2 and 5.

[9] *Vita*, 4; "ibi metricos quos adhuc nesciebant sapientes Hispaniae pedes perfectissime docuit." Albar may be saying here that Eulogius learned metrics unknown then in Spain rather than that Spanish

he received two letters from Eulogius in prison, one recounting the passion of the virgins and the release of the priests from prison and the other telling about the *Memoriale sanctorum*.[10] Albar neglects to mention that Eulogius also sent him the first part of the *Memoriale* for his inspection at this time.

It is worthwhile, Albar continues, to tell how Eulogius conducted himself later in the persecution. For while bishops, priests, clerics, and the scholars of Córdoba trod a devious path in regard to the marytrdoms recently taken place and almost denied the faith of Christ out of fear, tacitly if not in words, Eulogius was adamant and was never seen to waver in the least. He went to meet all those going to their death, encouraged them all, venerated their remains and prepared their bodies for burial. Because of his zeal for righteousness he was attacked with insults and threats, Albar states. Prominent among his enemies was a magnate whom Eulogius mentions in the *Memoriale* (II, xv, 2, and III, ii), says Albar. The magnate was the *exceptor*, a secretary or official in the Moslem government, who denounced Eulogius in a council of bishops in 852. This man, Albar says, lost his faith, stupidly fighting against it while he still had it. Albar interpolates this paragraph (5) about the *exceptor* into his discussion of Bishop Reccafred (paragraphs 4 and 6-7), thus separating (paulo altius incedentes) the time of the council of 852 from Reccafred's activities in late November of 851. The interpolation would seem to be an argument that the council was held in December of 852 rather than in January of 852.[11]

But let us go back to the days of Bishop Reccafred, says Albar. In those days everyone was bound to Reccafred, to the king, and to the devil, and those who had stood up against Reccafred "in the earlier uprising" were now bound

scholars did not know metrics. Elsewhere too he uses the indicative in restrictive relative clauses.

[10] *Magnificavit Dominus* and *Olim, mi frater*, PL 115, 841-844 and 731-734.

[11] Cf. index, "Council of Córdoba, 852."

to him in terror lest he do them further harm. The king too was raging against the Christians with constraining laws, Albar says, and did away with their freedom, giving them over to the devil. But this, he says, is discussed in another work.[12]

Eulogius was overwhelmed by sorrow to see the plottings of Reccafred spreading successfully all around him while he himself, since he had given sureties,[13] was not free to move elsewhere. One day Albar had a deacon read before the bishop, presumably Reccafred, a letter of Bishop Epiphanius of Salamis written to Bishop John of Jerusalem, in which St. Jerome and another priest, Vincent, are praised because they refrained from saying Mass, evidently in protest against Bishop John's refusal to condemn Origen. As Albar expected, Eulogius perceived that in the same way he could separate himself from the error of Reccafred. Glancing at Albar and turning to the bishop, Eulogius said that if the lights of the Church refrained from saying Mass, so too would be, covered as he was with sins. But his own bishop, Saul, forced him to resume his priestly function under threat of anathema.[14] Albar's authority to determine what a deacon read before Bishop Reccafred must have been associated with an authority as censor and clerk for certain Mozarabic writings which seems to be alluded to in correspondence he had with Eulogius and Esperaindeo. The assembly before which the letter of Bishop Epiphanius was read was hardly a council, but it may have comprised the group which Albar refers to as the *peritissimi* or the "fra-

---

[12] *Vita*, 6; "disseretur" (future) may be a mistake for "disseritur" (present), and the work referred to may be the *Memoriale* or the *Indiculus*. Albar calls the devil "hostis iniquus et trux."

[13] Franke, "Die freiwilligen Märtyrer," 96, interprets "fideiussoribus datis" as surety against further provocative acts with regard to the martyrdoms rather than as surety given by a priest that he will not leave his clerical duties without permission, as seems more likely.

[14] *Vita*, 7. Cf. also Letter XIII of the Albar correspondence, 4. Sage, *op.cit.*, 197, says that Albar misinterprets the episode, that Jerome and Vincent did not refrain from saying Mass in protest against Bishop John and that Epiphanius did not praise them for their action. For Jerome's Latin translation of Epiphanius' letter v. CSEL 54, 295-412.

ternal college." Most of the Latin treatises from Córdoba at this time seem to have been written for delivery before audiences.

Albar seems to identify the "days of Reccafred" to which he "goes back" with the troubled times of late 851 when Eulogius was imprisoned and, it would seem, early 852. But whether it can be inferred that Reccafred lost the basis of his power in Córdoba after these days is not clear. F. R. Franke interprets the words to mean that Reccafred was dead by the time of Albar's writing, which he would put in 860.[15] Eulogius' unusual decision not to celebrate the Mass probably was made some time after his release from prison. When he was in prison he complained that practically all ecclesiastical functions in Córdoba had ceased,[16] and it is unlikely that he would have been moved to this expedient until further difficulties with Reccafred developed. The "earlier uprising" against Reccafred may have been about June 850, after the death of Perfectus, the first martyr, or in June 851, when the first voluntary martyrs appeared. Reccafred's second move against the martyrdoms, during which Eulogius was imprisoned, may have begun as early as 16 July 851, on the arrest of Sisenandus, or as late as November 851, on the arrest of Flora and Maria.

The genius of Eulogius was universal, says Albar. Although he was more learned than anyone, he seemed the humblest of all. Distinguished and honored, eloquent, exemplary, champion of the martyrs, skilled in discourse, he knew the writings of Catholics, philosophers, heretics, and heathens, works of poetry and prose and works of history, musical verses and hymns, and exotic works (peregrina opuscula). "Daily he brought to light new and unusually wonderful things as if digging up hidden treasures from ruins and ditches."[17] His energy was endless. He gave everything to others and kept nothing for himself. He corrected what was at fault and restored what had fallen into

[15] Franke, *op.cit.*, 93.
[16] *Doc. mart.*, 11 and 16; Letter to Wiliesindus, 10.
[17] *Vita*, 8.

disuse, fulfilling in his own life what he learned from the deeds of men of old. He was severe as Jerome, modest as Augustine, mild as Ambrose, and patient as Gregory.

Albar bestows special praise on Eulogius for his scholarly pursuits. As a result of his devotion to learning, Eulogius was able to reap an unexpected reward from a journey on which he failed to fulfill his main purpose. In seeking to visit two of his brothers in exile in Bavaria, Eulogius was unable to travel beyond the Pyrenees. He then visited monasteries in the area of Pamplona, where he found many rare works to peruse and bring back for the students of Córdoba. The works included Augustine's *City of God,* Virgil's *Aeneid,* Juvenal's metrical works, the satires of Horace, the treatises of Porphyrius,[18] Aldhelm's epigrams, the fables of Avienus in meter, "glorious verses of Catholic hymns," and many items on fine points of religious questions compiled by different men. All but the last of these items enumerated by Albar are of value in the study of belles-lettres. Eulogius in his selection appears to have been primarily interested in obtaining models for the study of secular Latin letters in Córdoba, probably to revive interest in Latin culture among the laity. Albar in the *Indiculus* complains of a lack of interest among the laity for the Latin language, and Albar and John of Seville debated the matter of secular letters against ecclesiastical writings, evidently after Eulogius' return. "These he brought back not for himself alone but to share with those engaged in most studious research," Albar remarks. This remark, made in 860 or later, modifies the well-known complaint of Albar in the *Indiculus* (854), which has served as the basis for a bleak picture of Christian scholarship in Córdoba at this time.

Morales dated Eulogius' journey to Navarre in 839 or 840. Pérez de Urbel has dated it in 845. Carleton Sage and F.

---

[18] *Vita,* 9, "Porphyrii depicta opuscula"; Morales' scholium says Porphyrius of Tyre, the disciple of Plotinus, but Elsa Kluge, *P. Optatiani Porfyrii carmina* (Leipzig, 1926), xxix, correctly it seems identifies the "depicta opuscula" with the architectonic verse of the Latin poet of the fourth century. Cf. Martin Schanz, *Geschichte der römischen Litteratur. . .*, II, i, 2d ed. (Munich, 1914), 11-14.

R. Franke accept the date of Flórez (848) for the journey. The argument of Flórez and Sage is based on entries from two Frankish chronicles describing insurrections which would have prevented Eulogius from crossing the Pyrenees.[19] It will be shown below, however, that 850 is at least as reasonable a date for the journey as is 848.

Albar is the only source for the information that Eulogius was elected to the see of Toledo as the successor of Wistremirus. Unfortunately, Albar does not provide details on two aspects of the election that are of great interest: the date, and the reasons which prevented Eulogius from being consecrated and occupying the see. When obtacles which Albar does not specify prevented Eulogius from assuming the position, the bishops of the province of Toledo refused to elect another in his stead. Albar gives several hints as to why Eulogius could not occupy the see. Divine Providence placed the obstacles in his way, he says, and he was cleverly debarred from his rank (argute frustraretur ab ordine). In what may be innuendo Albar adds that Eulogius nonetheless did attain episcopal honor by martyrdom, "for all saints are bishops but not all bishops are saints." Bishop Saul of Córdoba in a letter to Albar refers to a "pseudobishop" with whom Albar was on friendly terms.[20] It is unlikely that Saul had Eulogius in mind, for all that is known of Eulogius indicates that he was obedient and devoted to his bishop. The sureties which prevented Eulogius from escaping the influence of Reccafred may also have prevented him from going to Toledo. Franke's thesis that elements of the Christian community of Córdoba would not go along with the clergy of Toledo in their defiance of the emir of Córdoba[21] seems valid, but the emir may still have influenced the decision of these Christians. Another condition which would have prevented Eulogius from occupying the see is the long

[19] Morales, *Corónica*, X, ix, 54, and XIV, xxix, 2-5; cf. also scholia by Morales: 14 of *Vita Eulogii*, 2 of Letter to Wiliesindus, and 2 of *Memoriale*, II, vii. Pérez de Urbel, *San Eulogio*, 90; Flórez, ES, X, 443-445; Sage, *op.cit.*, 16-18; Franke, *op.cit.*, 38.

[20] Letter XII, 2.

[21] Franke, *op.cit.*, 165f.

and serious revolt of Toledo against King Mohammed of Córdoba from 853 to the year of Eulogius' death (859).[22] Albar concludes his account of Eulogius' life with a summary of his virtues. Eulogius was outstanding in virtues and teachings, Albar says, and like a lamp placed on a pedestal or a city set on a mountain top (Mt. 5:14f.) he gave light to all far and wide (*procul altius*), and like a learned scribe (*doctus scriba*) he provided from his master's treasure things new and old for all the household (Mt. 13:52) — being first among the priests, highest (*summus*) of the confessors, and not the least among the judges (in *judicibus*). Albar's fondness for parallelism makes one think that his *judices* refers back to the *scriba* of Mt. 5:20 and Mt. 13:52, just as his *summus* refers back to the *procul altius*. The implication of the statement that there were a number of Christians of judicial status in Córdoba is confirmed elsewhere in the sources, and conflicts with the attribution of some historians that there was one judge, a *censor*, for the Mozarab community of Córdoba.[23] To make it more convenient for the reader and for the annual celebration of Eulogius' feast, Albar notes that he has composed the passio of Eulogius separately.

In mid-November 851, three years after Eulogius' journey to Navarre if the trip was made in 848 but only about a year afterwards if the trip took place in 850, Eulogius wrote a letter to Wiliesindus, bishop of Pamplona, thanking him for his hospitality and informing him of the recent persecution and martyrdoms in Córdoba. The letter, which is mentioned by Albar in the *Vita*,[24] offers much information of interest about Spain in general and about Eulogius and his family

---

[22] Cf. Ibn Idhari, *Bayan*, II, 152-157.

[23] *Vita*, 11. Cf. Lévi-Provençal, *L'Espagne musulmane au Xème siècle* (Paris, 1932), 37, and *id.*, *Histoire de l'Espagne musulmane*, III (Paris, 1953), 218-220, a description accepted by Cagigas, *Los mozárabes*, I, 57, and Franke, *op.cit.*, 10. Cf. index, "Mozarab officials."

[24] *Vita*, 9; the letter, from the ms of Eulogius' works no longer extant, is in all editions of Eulogius' works (PL 115, 845-852). Flórez, ES, X, 448, says that in Toledo there were parchment copies of the letter which antedated Morales' edition of 1574.

in Córdoba. Being a note of thanks sent with relics promised by Eulogius to Wiliesindus, the letter is somewhat elaborately written and recounts details which Wiliesindus already knew from the time of Eulogius' stay in Pamplona. F. R. Franke says that the letter shows that Eulogius expected to find more sympathy and support outside Córdoba than in his native city.[25]

Information about William and Sancho, whose rebellions prevented Eulogius from crossing the Pyrenees, contributes to an understanding not only of the letter of Eulogius to Wiliesindus, but of the general history of Córdoba during these years. Two Frankish chronicles, the *Annales Bertiniani* and the *Fragmentum chronici Fontanellensis*, describe the insurrection of William. The rebellion of Sancho seems to be known only from Eulogius' letter. William's father, Bernard, duke of Septimania, was executed for rebellion against Charles the Bald in 844. His mother, Dhuoda, composed a delightful manual for William when he was sent to the court of Charles as a hostage.[26] In 848 William, whose lands appear to have been in Autun, perhaps in Toulouse, moved against territory of Charles south of the Pyrenees. In 849 with the support of Abd al-Rahman II of Córdoba he took Barcelona. Pepin of Aquitaine then joined the rebellion against his father Charles. In 850 William captured governors Charles had left in the Spanish March but later in the same year, after more fighting, was himself captured and executed in Barcelona. In June 850, a month or so after the first martyrdom in Córdoba, two dukes of Navarre sent ambassadors of peace to Charles. Galindo Iñiguez, who took Eulogius' letter to Wiliesindus in Navarre, may have been in Córdoba on a diplomatic mission in late 851. In 852 Sancho Sanchez captured Pepin and delivered him to Charles, bringing the troubles of the Frankish monarch in

---

[25] Franke, *op.cit.*, 104f.

[26] The manual has been edited and translated into French by E. Bondurand, *Le manuel de Dhuoda (843)* (Paris, 1887); cf. H. Leclercq, "Manuel de Dhuoda," DACL, X, ii, 1586-1603, Manitius, *op.cit.*, I, 442-444, and PL 106, 109-118.

the Spanish March to an end.[27] On 22 September 852 Abd al-Rahman II died in Córdoba.

The *Annales Bertiniani* date William's capture of Barcelona in 848, the *Fragmentum* in 849. Both date his action against the governors of Charles and his own subsequent capture and death in 850. On the basis of disturbances in the Spanish March there is as much reason to date Eulogius' journey in 850 as in 848. Moreover, in his account of the martyr Perfectus, who died in Córdoba in June 850, Eulogius stipulates twice that he depended on the reports of others, Christians and Moslems, for his information.[28] A number of consequences follow the acceptance of 850 as the date of the journey. Eulogius would not have been in Córdoba at the time of the outbreak of the martyrdoms and probably took no part in the first "uprising" against Bishop Reccafred or the disturbances after the death of Perfectus. The persecution would have begun before Eulogius returned with the treasure of Latin works with which he evidently hoped to revivify secular Latin studies in Córdoba. The derogatory biography of the prophet Mohammed may not have been generally known in Córdoba until late 850, after the persecution began. Eulogius' brother Joseph would have been removed from the principate, probably, in the disturbances which followed the martyrdom of Perfectus. Eulogius would have been in Córdoba only about six months before the first voluntary martyr, Isaac, came forward and about a year before he himself was imprisoned. Having associated with those allied against the allies of Abd al-Rahman, he would have been regarded by the Moslems with

---

[27] Léonce Auzias, *L'Aquitaine carolingienne (778-987)* (Toulouse and Paris, 1937), 259-270. *Annales Bertiniani,* ed. Waitz, MGH, *Scriptores ... in usum scholarum* (Hanover, 1883); *Fragmentum chronici Fontanellensis,* ed. Pertz, MGH, *Scriptores,* II (Hanover, 1829), 301-304.

[28] *Memoriale,* II, i, 5, "sicut plurimorum fideli relatione comperimus," and "quae viris catholicis referentibus, qui eius contuberniis a principio in vinculis adhaeserunt: sed et ipsorum ethnicorum relatione vera esse cognovimus, dum nos tempore compeditionis nostrae omnes cum quibus ille martyr futurus morabatur vix paucos solutos reperimus."

distrust and disfavor on his return to Córdoba. It was in the reign of Ordoño I (850-866) that Astorga was reconquered and repopulated with Christians, and perhaps in 847 that a council of "bishops, religious, and well-born men" met in Astorga and established the southern boundary of the new diocese near Zamora.[29]

In the salutation of his letter "Eulogius the priest" greets "my lord and father Wiliesindus, bishop of Pamplona." The same misfortunes which forced his brothers Albar and Isidore away from their native land into exile in the realm of King Louis of Bavaria, Eulogius says, caused him to undertake extensive and troublesome trips because of them. Around Pamplona his way through the Pyrenees was barred because of the "unfortunate invasion" of William, with the support of "Abd al-Rahman, king of the Arabs," against "Charles, king of the Franks." Another insurrection against Charles by Sancho Sanchez blocked passage through the Pyrenees completely. In these straits Eulogius, who says that he and his family were destitute at this time, was received with hospitality by Wiliesindus. Although it seems that Eulogius would have said so if the death of his father was connected with his journey to the north, one is tempted to associate the economic distress of his family, the exile of his brothers, and his silence about his father when he speaks of the members of his family with the eve of the persecution in Córdoba.

While delayed in Pamplona Eulogius made a pilgrimage to neighboring shrines and monasteries, accompanied by a deacon, Theodemundus, whom evidently Wiliesindus had assigned to him as a guide. After visiting the monastery of Leyre, Eulogius and his guide arrived at the *acysterium* of St. Zachary in Serasa (or Siresa), a monastery of almost a hundred monks famous throughout the West.[30] Eulogius

[29] A. Lambert, "Astorga," DHGE, IV, 1210 and 1212f.

[30] Letter to Wiliesindus, 2; for *acysterium* cf. index. Albar, *Vita*, 9, says that the monastery had one hundred and fifty monks. For the dispute as to whether the monastery of St. Zachary was the monastery of Serasa or whether they were two monasteries cf. J. Mabillon, *Annales O S B ...* (Paris, 1703-1739), Bk. XXXIV, no. 26. E. Lambert,

praises the monks of St. Zachary for their zeal in the exercise of a rule of discipline, as well as for their humility, their obedience, their care for pilgrims, and their nocturnal vigils and prayers. "What can mortal tongue tell of the virtues of saints," he asks, "who, placed on earth, live like angels? who, although they live among men, bear a heavenly ideal?" Resisting the pleas of the monks to remain longer at the monastery of St. Zachary, Eulogius returned with his guide to Pamplona, accompanied by the Abbot Odoarius and the prior John, who rode with them till nightfall "speaking of Holy Scripture all the way." Wiliesindus also failed to persuade his visitor to stay longer in Pamplona, for the absence of his brothers and the desolation of those he had left at home was of constant concern to Eulogius. Upon his departure from Pamplona Eulogius promised Wiliesindus to send back relics of St. Zoilus, the patron of the basilica in which Eulogius served in Córdoba, so that a basilica might be built in his honor in Pamplona.[31]

Eulogius' detailed review of the hospitality he received on his journey reflects his conscientious nature. It also, inasmuch as it describes the universal bond of Christian brotherhood in the north, provides an ideal background for the remainder of his letter, which deals with the persecution in Córdoba. From his praises of monastic life in the north one may obtain an insight into the ideals of monasticism around Córdoba, especially since in the vitae of a number of the martyrs recorded in the *Memoriale* he praises the same virtues. Even before he visited Pamplona he had practiced asceticism and composed rules for the monasteries then thriving in the environs of Córdoba. Not much is known about the origins and the basis of this Mozarab monasticism. It may have been eclectic, derived from monastic rules and ideals of the East, from earlier Spanish

"Le voyage de Saint Euloge dans les Pyrénées en 848," *Estudios dedicados a Menéndez Pidal*, IV (Madrid, 1953), 557-567, discusses the monasteries visited by Eulogius and identifies that of St. Zachary as San Pedro de Siresa.

[31] Letter, 5 and 9.

monastic customs, and from the monasticism of northern
Spain, where, among others, the Benedictine rule was followed. A. S. Ruiz has selected passages from this letter to
Wiliesindus and from the *Memoriale* to argue a fairly strong
influence of the Benedictine rule on the monastic life around
Córdoba at this time. One should, however, give attention
to the cogent theses of Aimé Lambert that it was Mozarab
monasticism in the person of refugee monks and laity from
the south which expanded to the north, as far as Astorga at
least, by the beginning of the tenth century, and that Mozarabic culture, especially the liturgy, successfully resisted the
Frankish influence in northern Spain in the tenth century.[32]

The close relationship between monasticism and asceticism
in Córdoba in the middle of the ninth century has been
pointed out by F. R. Franke, who notes that an ascetic could
regard martyrdom as but a final stage of asceticism whereby
he could bring to an end the temptations and afflictions of
the world, which had prompted his ascetic life in the first
place. In the time of Eulogius not only did most of the martyrs come from the monasteries, but the monasteries supported the martyrdoms with more constancy than did any
other group. Some Christians, Franke says, turned to asceticism for additional strength in the bad times the Church
was suffering, bad times which they believed had been
brought on by their sins, while other Christians, who practiced their faith in secret because of stringent Moslem laws,
required penance because of their feeling of guilt. According to Franke, who agrees with Asín Palacios against Pérez
de Urbel, the asceticism which became popular about this
time among Moslems derived from the Moslems of the East

---

[32] Ruiz, *Obras completas de San Eulogio*, xviii-xxiv; A. Lambert,
"Astorga," DHGE, IV, 1210-1219. Cf. Pérez de Urbel, *Los monjes españoles en la edad media* (2 vols.; Madrid, 1933-1934), II, 263-276,
especially 275f.; C. J. Bishko, "The Date and Nature of the Spanish
Consensoria Monachorum," *American Journal of Philology*, 69 (1948),
377-395; *id.*, "Salvus of Albelda and Frontier Monasticism in Tenth-
Century Navarre," *Speculum*, 23 (1948), 559-590; and *id.*, "Gallegan
Pactual Monasticism in the Repopulation of Castille," *Estudios dedicados a Menéndez Pidal*, II (Madrid, 1951), 513-531.

rather than from the Christians of Spain. Decades of war and unrest in Spain, says Franke, had set the stage for ascetic movements among both Christians and Moslems.[33] Christian monasticism and asceticism, and the martyrdoms, may be viewed as more than a reaction to and a retreat from the culture of the Moslems. It would seem profitable to study some of the Latin sources of Córdoba for elements of mysticism and to relate these elements to the teachings of sufism in the Moslem East. Whether Christianity or Islam exerted the greater influence in Córdoba in this respect probably cannot be demonstrated, but to show that there were separate and perhaps rival mystic or quasi-mystic movements in Córdoba at the time of the martyrdoms would cast a great deal of light on the literature and events of the time.

Eulogius went directly from Pamplona to Zaragoza, expecting to find his brothers there among a group of merchants recently arrived from France. How these merchants came from France to Spain when Eulogius could not travel in the opposite direction is not clear. He was told in Zaragoza that his brothers were in Mainz, a report his brothers confirmed when they returned to Córdoba. In Zaragoza Eulogius stayed for a while with Bishop Senior. From here he passed quickly through Segovia, where Sisemundus was bishop, and came to Alcalá, where he stayed five days and was received by Bishop Venerius. From Alcalá he went to Toledo, "where I found still alive our most holy old man, the torch of the Holy Spirit and the lamp of all Spain, Bishop Wistremirus, the sanctity of whose life, illuminating the whole world, still keeps kindled the flock of Catholics by probity of ways and high merits."[34] He stayed with him many days, says Eulogius, and kept his angelic company.

Eulogius' words "adhuc vigentem" raise difficulties. If he meant "still living," he would seem to imply that Wistre-

---

[33] Franke, *op.cit.*, 19-25; Miguel Asín Palacios, "Ibn Masarra y su escuela," *Obras escogidas*, I (Madrid, 1946), 27ff., and Pérez de Urbel, *San Eulogio*, 67.

[34] Letter to Wiliesindus, 7.

mirus had died in the interval between the time he passed through Toledo, possibly in the latter half of 850, and the time he was writing, in November 851. This interpretation is supported by the great praise Eulogius bestows upon Wistremirus, more than he has for any other bishop he names, even Wiliesindus, the recipient of his letter. If Wistremirus were no longer alive in November 851, then Eulogius was probably elected to the see of Toledo about the time he was in prison writing the letter to Wiliesindus. The sources give no clue to the date of Eulogius' election as archbishop of Toledo, unless one understands Albar's remark that Eulogius could not move elsewhere to escape the influence of Reccafred[35] as a reference to his occupation of the see. There is reason, however, to believe that the metropolitan of Toledo is the recipient of a letter written by an anonymous bishop[36] somewhat later, it appears, than November 851. Albar says that the see of Toledo was vacant between Wistremirus' death and the martyrdom of Eulogius, in March 859. It seems better to interpret "adhuc vigentem" as "still flourishing" or as a later interpolation.[37]

When he returned to Córdoba, Eulogius found his mother, brother, and sisters all well and glad to see their pilgrim after so long a time. But Abd al-Rahman, in a bad humor, had removed Joseph, the youngest of Eulogius' family from "the principate."[38] Now, says Eulogius, more than long distances of hard travel separate him from Wiliesindus. He in Córdoba suffers under the "evil rule of the Arabs" while Wiliesindus enjoys the rule of a Catholic prince, and the two

---

[35] *Vita*, 7.

[36] Letter X of the Albar correspondence.

[37] Flórez, ES, X, 441-448, refutes weak arguments against the authenticity of the letter by José Pellicer de Ossau y Tovar, *Annales de la monarquia de España, despues de su perdida* (Madrid, 1681), V, 52 (p. 233). Gaspar Ibañez de Segovia, Marqués de Mondejar, *Examen chronológico del año en que entraron los moros en España* (Madrid, 1687), par. 8, among a few others, repeats Pellicer's error.

[38] Letter to Wiliesindus, 8, "saeva tyranni indignatio . . . a principatu deicerat."

rulers, constantly fighting each other, cut off communications between them. For this reason Eulogius was unable to send Wiliesindus the relics of St. Zoilus, being unwilling to entrust them to just anyone. Now that Galindo Iñiguez (*Enniconis*) is returning home from Córdoba, Eulogius sends in his care not only the promised relics of St. Zoilus but relics of St. Acisclus as well, so that Wiliesindus may build a basilica in their memory as promised and the saints may come to the assistance of the Christians of Córdoba.

Eulogius concludes his letter with a review of the persecution Christians were suffering in Córdoba "because of the shackle of our sins." In the year 851, he says, with savage fury the tyrant rages against the Church, overturning, laying waste, and scattering everything, imprisoning bishops, priests, abbots, deacons, and all the clergy, binding them in irons and plunging them in underground caverns, where Eulogius is at the time he writes the letter. "He has bereaved the Church of her sacred ministry, deprived her of speech, separated her from her office. And at this time we have no offering or sacrifice, no incense or place to offer gifts to God."[39] The sound of hymns and psalms has been transferred from the churches to the prisons. But Galindo can narrate to Wiliesindus further details which cannot fit into the scope of the letter.

Eulogius then quotes for Wiliesindus a typical denunciation of the Moslem prophet made by the martyrs. "This man you venerate so exceedingly and whose charlatan sect inspired by the devil you have accepted with so great honor we know for a magician, an adulterer, and a liar, and those who believe in him we say will be delivered to the chains of eternal perdition. Why then do you, who are most prudent men, communicate in such sacrileges and not rather heed the truth of the Gospel?"[40] For these words the martyrs are slain, Eulogius says, and their bodies are hung up on stakes, burned, and cast into the river. Some are left unburied before the gates of the palace to be devoured by birds and dogs, with guards to prevent Christians from burying them. This

[39] Letter, 10.   [40] Letter, 11.

is why he is bound in jail, "for they think whatever they have done inspired from on high is at our instigation and they ascribe it to our tutelage." Please pray for us and make our imprisonment known to all the monasteries so that they too many pray for us. Eulogius asks Wiliesindus to convey his salutations to the abbots of monasteries he had visited on his pilgrimage, especially Fortunius in Leyre, Athilius in Cillas, Odoarius in Serasa, Scemenus in Igal, and Dadilo in Urdaspal. Finally he chronicles briefly the first twelve martyrdoms and tells of Flora and Maria in prison awaiting death, making a rare use of the year of the Lord, 850, to date the martyrdom of Perfectus. The letter concludes with the date, 15 November Era 889 (A.D. 851), and the notation that it is committed to Galindo Iñiguez.

Eulogius probably wrote other works which have been lost. The codex of his works, no longer extant, was evidently a monument to one man, as is the Albar codex. But, whereas the works of the Albar codex cover several phases of Albar's life, the extant works of Eulogius pertain only to the persecution and the dispute over the martyrs. No other treatise and no poetry by him are extant. But his chief work, the *Memoriale sanctorum,* is the most important work from Córdoba at this time.

Although at first glance the division of the *Memoriale sanctorum*[41] into three books appears orderly, its over-all pattern is somewhat fragmentary. Book I is a disputation supported by rather vague and general references to events and marked by several passages which appear to have been inserted after the original composition. Book II is a chronicle of events of the persecution up to the death of Abd al-Rahman II and the accession of Mohammed I in September 852. Accounts of twenty-nine martyrs appear here. Book III is a chronicle of the persecution during the reign of Mo-

---

[41] The ms of the *Memoriale* is not extant. Morales' edition of 1574 from the ms was re-edited very accurately by Lorenzana in 1785, *SS PP Toletanorum,* II, 419-508 (PL 115, 735-818), and does not appear in the contemporary volumes (X and XI) of the *España sagrada.* For other editions cf. the Introduction or Bibliography of this volume.

hammed I up to July 856, accounting for seventeen martyrs. Books II and III are divided into chapters, almost all of which are separate units dealing with martyrs. All three books have prefaces. In addition, Book II, chapter vii, and Book III, chapter x, begin with prefatory paragraphs. An examination of these prefaces and the material before and after them reveals that Eulogius wrote the *Memoriale* over a period of six years at irregular intervals. After completing his work he apparently did not go over it thoroughly, and it lacks a certain amount of coherence and unity.

The preface to Book I can serve as the preface for the whole work, but it seems to have been intended as the preface for the original composition only, which was Book I and the first six chapters of Book II. The preface to Book II is little more than a note that the remaining part of the work will be divided into chapters rather than written as a unit as was Book I. Book II, chapter vii, begins with a paragraph stating that additional events have necessitated the continuation of the work beyond the scope originally planned. Book III begins with a preface longer than any but the one at the beginning of Book I. The events related in the first chapters of Book III are a sequence of those related at the end of Book II, but there was a lull of nine months between the last martyrdoms of Book II and the first martyrdoms of Book III. Meanwhile too it seems, a council had met and issued a decree which, without condemning the martyrs, discouraged further martyrdoms. In addition, Abd al-Rahman II had been succeeded by his son in the interval. The two persecutions, an earlier and a later, spoken of by Eulogius and Albar seem to be the persecutions under the two rulers. Eulogius expected the end of Book II therefore to be the end of the *Memoriale*. When five martyrdoms occurred within three days, however, he resumed the work in a third book. After a brief treatment of the five martyrs, he introduced chapter x three months later with a prefatory paragraph, saying that new martyrdoms required the continuation of the work. He then treats two virgin martyrs at some length. The last six chapters of the *Memoriale*, dealing with martyrs who died at intervals between July 854 and July 856, begin without any prefatory remarks. From appearances Eulogius composed much, if not all, of Book III while absent from Córdoba.

The only formal conclusion in the *Memoriale* comes at the end of Book II in the form of a long prayer. Book III comes to an end with its final chapter ending in much the same fashion as do all the other chapters before it.

The *Memoriale* does not begin with the beginning of the martyr movement. The first martyr treated in the *Memoriale*, in the preface to Book I, is Isaac, but Isaac died more than a year after the first martyr, Perfectus. Moreover, Book I itself is an apologetical treatise written in the midst of a crisis which took place more than eighteen months after the death of Perfectus, whom Eulogius does not discuss until Book II. The history of the martyrs becomes more intelligible if the martyrs are considered in chronological order and if the martyrs who died before Eulogius composed Book I are discussed before the contents of that book.

As an introductory paragraph to the chapter devoted to Perfectus, who was slain in April 850, Eulogius offers a brief sketch of Umaiyad wealth and power in Córdoba on the eve of the martyrdoms. "In the name of the Lord. Our Lord Jesus Christ reigning in perpetuum, in the year of His Incarnation 850, Era 888, in the twenty-ninth year of the reign of Abd al-Rahman, in whose days the Arab people, having increased their possessions and authority in Spain, have occupied almost all Iberia with dire right. Córdoba, however, once called Patricia, now called the Royal City, because of his residence, has been exalted by him above all, elevated with honors, expanded in glory, piled full of riches, and with great energy filled with an abundance of all the delights of the world, more than one can believe or express. So much so that in every worldly pomp he exceeds, surpasses, and excels the preceding kings of his race. And meanwhile the church of the orthodox groans beneath his most grievous yoke and is beaten to destruction."[42] This

[42] *Memoriale,* II, i, 1; the clause "dumque sub eius gravissimo iugo

description by Eulogius of the flourishing status of Córdoba contrasts with his picture at the beginning of Book III of the disintegration of Umaiyad glory under the rule of King Mohammed I of Córdoba.[43]

Eulogius then treats of the first martyr. The priest Perfectus was born in Córdoba and educated at the Basilica of St. Acisclus, where he spent most of his manhood. His rather good education, consisting of ecclesiastical training, letters, and some Arabic, deserves as much attention as Albar's complaint about the indifference of the laity towards ecclesiastical Latin culture,[44] a complaint cited frequently in illustration of the Christian Latin learning in Córdoba at this time. Most of the early martyrs were ecclesiastical scholars, and their deaths deprived Mozarabic culture of much of its finest flowering.

Perfectus was stopped one day on the streets of Córdoba by Moslems and asked to explain the Catholic faith and what he thought about Christ and Mohammed. Immediately, says Eulogius, he proclaimed that Christ was divine but said that he dared not say what Catholics thought of Mohammed out of fear of Moslem vengeance. If the Moslems would make a pact of peace and friendship with him, however, he would speak freely. The Moslems fraudulently promised faith. Perfectus then in Arabic said that Mohammed was a false prophet and a false teacher who had seduced many. In fact, he was the greatest of false prophets, filled with the trickeries of the devil, seduced by demons, given over to sacrileges, corrupting the hearts of many with venom and committing them to hell, whither he too went. How can Mohammed be a prophet and how can he avoid the curse of heaven, Perfectus asked, when he committed adultery with Zeinab, the wife of his slave Zaid? And the author of impurity has dedicated all Moslems to eternal impurity,

---

ecclesia orthodoxorum gemens usque ad interitum vapularet" seems to belong to the previous sentence and to bring to an end par. 1.

[43] *Ibid.*, III, i, iv, and v.

[44] *Indiculus*, 35; Eulogius calls the Basilica of St. Acisclus a *coenobium*. Cf. also *Memoriale*, I, 9.

Perfectus concluded. Perfectus also denounced other things in the law of Mohammed, says Eulogius, which he does not report. The Moslems were infuriated but let Perfectus go in peace then. Somewhat later, when he again passed their way, they set up a cry against him for having cursed their prophet and carried him off to the cadi.

Perfectus at first denied their charges out of fear of death, but when he was sentenced to imprisonment and death anyway he confirmed his statements and willingly went to prison. Before he was executed he prophesied the death within a year of the eunuch Nasr, the prime minister (clavicularius proconsul), "who then managed the administration of the whole government in Spain."[45] The prophecy was inspired from heaven, Eulogius says, as Perfectus revealed to his confessor, who was in prison at the same time. The confessor probably was not Eulogius, who gives the impression that he was not even in Córdoba at this time.

After a few months in prison Perfectus was brought forth for execution in the forum the day after the thirty-day fast of Ramadan, when, Eulogius says, the Moslems "are more prone than usual to orgies of gormandizing and the floods of passion."[46] They thought, says Eulogius, that they did a service to their God in slaying Perfectus, who, on being led forth to execution repeated his confession. "I have cursed and do curse your prophet, a man of demons, a magician, an adulterer, and a liar. As I have testified, I now testify. I proclaim the profanations of your sect to be the inventions of the devil. And I bear witness that you too will suffer punishment in the eternal torments of darkness with your leader."[47] The Moslems were holding their festivities in the large plain south of the Guadalquivir rather than in the mosque next to the palace and the forum in Córdoba, but they came back to the forum to witness the execution of

[45] *Memoriale,* II, i, 3.

[46] *Ibid,* 4; Eulogius adds "as is stated in Book I." Bk. I, 7, speaks of banquets and the flesh but not of Ramadan. Gormandizing and the flesh during Ramadan are mentioned in the *Indiculus,* 3 and 33.

[47] *Memoriale,* II, i, 4.

Perfectus. Happy that they had participated in the martyr's death, they then returned to their festivities across the river. Later when they were returning to their homes in Córdoba, a number of them crossed the river by boat rather than use the bridge. One such boat capsized and two of the eight occupants were drowned. Eulogius regards these drownings, which he learned of by the report of many people, and the subsequent death by poisoning of the prime minister Nasr in less than a year as vindications of Perfectus by the Lord. Thus were the faithful solaced with hope, he says, and the Moslems upset in astonishment.

Perfectus died on Friday, 18 April 850, twelve days after Easter. He was buried with pious rites by the bishop and priests in his own church, the Basilica of St. Acisclus. Eulogius depended on the word of Catholics who were imprisoned from the beginning with Perfectus for his account of the martyr, he says, but Moslems too confirmed the story. "At the time when we were in prison we found but a few freed of all those with whom the future martyr dwelt there," he says. These Christians had been in prison when Eulogius met them for almost two years, from a date several months before Perfectus' death in April 850 until November 851, when Eulogius was imprisoned. Their fate is not known. They were not martyrs, for in Book III Eulogius says that he made it a point to record all the martyrs[48] and he does not again mention these companions of Perfectus in prison. The imprisonments show that the Moslems meted out punishments other than death to some Christians. They show too that relations between Christians and Moslems in Córdoba were deteriorating for a year before Isaac gave his voluntary profession of faith.

Eulogius describes the Christian reaction to the death of the first martyr and the resulting Moslem fear of the martyr movement which they had provoked. "But such a shameful deed committed against a priest compelled many who enjoyed a quiet and peaceful profession of faith, contemplating God in desert mountains and wild forests, to go forth to

[48] *Ibid.*, III, x, 1.

show their hatred for the wicked prophet and curse him freely and publicly. And it kindled in everyone a greater ardor of dying for justice. What the treacherous procedure of the persecutors at first wrung by force from that one man, and what they vengefully work against this one with persuasion and cunning guile, afterwards raged against many who offered themselves of their own accord for such a trial. For the whole group of pagans was shaken with exceeding terror at the step taken by the confessors, so that they believed the ruin of the state and the downfall of their dynasty was imminent, and they pleaded suppliantly that our athletes refrain from such pursuits."[49]

"This one (*hunc*)," against whom the Moslems worked vengefully with persuasion and guile, would seem to be Eulogius himself. It may, however, refer to the merchant John. There is an over-all similarity between this paragraph (II, i, 7) and the paragraph (10) following Eulogius' discussion of Perfectus and John in Book I. The sentence seems to be an elaborate statement that the persecution later erupted with more deaths and more insidiousness. Eulogius implies that soon after the death of Perfectus Christians came forth to curse the prophet Mohammed publicly and the Moslems pleaded with them to stop doing so. There would have been, accordingly, voluntary public confessions of faith before that of Isaac in June 851, and Isaac's confession would have been striking only because it was delivered before the cadi, the highest official of the Moslem judicial system. Eulogius, however, regards it as Isaac's great merit that he gave his confession voluntarily. It seems more likely therefore that, as has been intimated above, this paragraph was interpolated by Eulogius afterwards without sufficient regard for chronology. In this chapter Eulogius gives a transliteration of phonetic interest and a translation of an Arabic phrase into Latin, "Zalla Allah Halla Anabi Va Zallen," "Psallet Deus super eum, et salvet eum," or "May God bless him and save him."[50]

---

[49] *Ibid.*, II, i, 7.
[50] *Memoriale*, II, i, 3; cf. Albar's translation of Arabic in the *Indicu-*

Albar in his account of the martyrdom of Perfectus makes use of his literary talent and fashions a dramatic and picturesque narrative, but he tells less about the martyr than does Eulogius. Albar indicates that Perfectus was aware of laws forbidding denunciations of Islam. As reported by Albar, Perfectus' initial denunciation of the prophet Mohammed and Islam was concerned with fleshly indulgence only and condemned Moslem marriages as adulterous. Once imprisoned, however, Perfectus made "other stronger charges." "They brought him forth," Albar says, "on that horrible paschal day of theirs, on which they are wont to eat grazing animals and to minister abundant food to their belly and their lust, and they slew him with their avenging sword."[51]

Albar then discusses the persecution of the merchant John, whom Eulogius treats rather briefly.

> Let us go on then to treat the case of the second one. One year later, or somewhat longer, the livid eye of the Gentiles did not rest; but, as it is their wont to mock Christianity and insult all us Christians, the sellers of merchandise tried to tell lies against and to vex this John whom the walls of prison have held a long time; and burning with envy because of their love of goods they brought many charges reprehending him saying, "Thinking little of our prophet, you always use his name in derision and to ears that do not know that you are a Christian you often confirm your lies with oaths of our religion, false as they seem to you." Since, in good faith and not suspecting anything of the trap set for him, he wanted to show himself guiltless of those things which were charged against him, with crackling fury and blind anger he emphatically repeated the same things which he had often said, pounding them in, and saying them over and over. Then, not bearing any longer the threats of such a group, becoming angry, and

lus, 23, "*alkaufeit*," and 25, "*Cobar*" and "*Almozen*"; and Samson's "Hemmor Pater Sicem, quod in latinum sonat asinus pater aegritudinis," *Apologeticus*, preface to Bk. II, 3.

[51] *Indiculus*, 3.

adopting a rather smooth urbanity, he answered with pride and disdain, "May the curse of God fall upon anyone who wants to call upon the name of your prophet." At once a great clamor arose, and the close mob of damned ones, the throng full of hateful iniquity, like bees collected in one treacherous swarm,[52] in one heaped up mass, covered over with malice, they led him half dead to the cadi, and when witnesses of questionable suitability[53] had been presented from among that crowd of infidels, they made stronger and graver charges against him from his own testimony. All this he denied, and he recounted the consuming envy which they showed in their speech against him. But the iniquitous cadi beat him with four hundred blows of the scourge and he made him go through the churches of all the saints while a herald's voice cried out, "So must he suffer who insults God's prophet." And then he committed him to prison under strict guard, threatening to inflict worse things on him.[54]

Eulogius says that John was beaten with five hundred lashes rather than four hundred, as Albar reports. When John collapsed in the hands of the floggers, according to Eulogius, he was placed backwards on an ass and loaded with chains so that he collapsed on the animal's back. He was then paraded through the whole city with a crier going before him proclaiming, "To this shall the detractor of our prophet and the mocker of our religion deserve to come." This punishment resembles punishments administered under the Visigoth King Reccared (586-601) and under an Arab

---

[52] Eulogius also, *Memoriale*, II, i, 3, likens the crowd of Moslems who attacked Perfectus to a swarm of bees.

[53] "Testibus minus idoneis"; Leo Wiener, *Commentary to the Germanic Laws and Medieval Documents* (Cambridge, Mass., 1915), 165ff., says that "testes idonei" are witnesses not of an inferior class. The term is used a number of times by Eulogius and Albar; cf. also Julian of Toledo, *De comprobatione aetatis sextae*, I, 1 (*SS PP Toletanorum*, II, 92).

[54] *Indiculus*, 5; John was in prison from about April 850 until the first part of the *Indiculus* was composed in 853 or 854.

governor in the early days of the conquest of Spain.[55] After the contumelious treatment John, loaded with chains, was put in prison, where Eulogius found him later in 851 at the time of his own imprisonment. The persecution of John, which followed the martyrdom of Perfectus by about a year, inspired many to martyrdom, Eulogius says.

A few months after John's ordeal the monk Isaac came before the cadi and voluntarily confessed what the Moslems by trickery had succeeded in getting Perfectus and John to say. Isaac was born of noble and wealthy citizens of Córdoba. After a privileged youth he became an *exceptor* (secretary or official) of the state, being skilled in Arabic. He gave up this position, however, and withdrew to the town of Tabanos, in the wilds seven miles from Córdoba. Here a cousin on his father's side, Jeremias, along with his wife, Elizabeth, their family, and kin, had established a double monastery (for both sexes), so that they might live without interruption under the law of God. For three years Isaac lived in Tabanos under the Abbot Martin, Elizabeth's brother, before he went down to Córdoba and voluntarily gave a confession before the cadi.[56]

The double monastery was not unusual among Mozarabs. From what Eulogius says,[57] the one at Tabanos appears to have served as a refuge built around a family permitting those living there to practice their faith in complete liberty, and probably free of the head tax imposed by the Moslems on their subjects. The position of Elizabeth is worthy of note. Mozarab women apparently controlled their own wealth and enjoyed much independence of action. The vitae of later martyrs emphasize their importance in Mozarab life. It should be noted too that Eulogius calls Mozarabs citizens and describes them as wealthy and noble.

Eulogius describes Isaac's confession in the preface to Book I of the *Memoriale*. Isaac presented himself before the cadi in the forum with these words.

---

[55] *Memoriale*, I, 9, and II, x, 5; cf. supra, 42.
[56] *Memoriale*, II, ii.
[57] *Ibid.*, III, x, passim, especially 6.

"I would like, O cadi, to become an ardent follower of your faith if you will at once explain to me its system and reasonableness." Gladly then, as if to a young tyro of his faith ready to believe ... his lying tongue gave forth to him the words of instruction. First he said that Mohammed was the author of this sect, and that, enlightened through the teaching of the angel Gabriel, he received the voice of prophecy from the Most High to pass on to the Gentiles, founded the law, discoursed on paradise, and taught a kingdom of heaven full of banquets and throngs of women. And too long to be set forth here, many other things from a religion made to conform to an empty belief. Suddenly the youthful and venerable monk, who had been well instructed in Arabic letters, answered him in Arabic: "He lied to you," he says, "(and may he waste away under the divine curse) who, entangled in such sin, seizes upon whole troops of lost souls and enslaves them with himself in the depths of hell. Filled with the devil and relying on diabolical tricks, offering the cup of death to the sick, he shall be destroyed by eternal damnation. Why do you who are endowed with learning not renounce such dangers? And why do you not denounce the ulcerous and pestiferous tenets and choose the perennial and salutary Gospel of the Christian faith?"

These and words similar spoken by Blessed Isaac modestly but sharply ... cause the excited cadi quite struck out of his senses and as if driven crazy, to burst out in abundant tears, and, seized by a sort of mental stupidity he can hardly come to answer the monk's reproaches. And so, reaching out he struck the face of the monk, who said quickly, "Do you dare to strike the visage made like the image of God? See what account you will have to render for this." He was checked by the wise men sitting with him and censured because he forgot his dignity as cadi and lightly took it on himself to strike the martyr: especially because, according to a teaching of their law, anyone worthy of death for a crime must not suffer the insults of anyone at all.[58] Then the cadi turned

[58] This article of the Moslem penal code was broken more than once with regard to the martyrs.

and spoke to Blessed Isaac, "Perhaps you are drunk with wine or seized with madness and you cannot easily heed what you say. For the mind of him our prophet, whom you rashly attack with insults, remains inexorable and we must punish those who do not fear to say such things about him." The venerable Isaac stoutly made answer to him, "Indeed, O cadi, I am not drunk with wine nor afflicted with any sickness, but, burning with the zeal of justice, with which your prophet and yourselves I am sure are unfamiliar, I have shown you the truth; if for this raging death is to be the result, willingly shall I accept it, calmly undergo it, and not move my head from its stroke. For I know that the Lord has said, 'Blessed are those who suffer persecution for justice' sake; for theirs is the kingdom of heaven' (Mt. 5:10)." After the cadi delivered him to prison, straightway his case became known to the king, who was exceedingly frightened that such a charge should be made, and then and there fiercely issues an edict to souls more fierce, saying that anyone bringing such insults against the author of their faith shall become liable in every instance to death. So the servant of God, condemned, submits to death; thus is he raised up on a stake head down and placed across the river in sight of the city, it being Wednesday, 3 June 851. After a few days his body together with those of the others who were put to death for imitating him was cremated, reduced to ashes, and then thrown into the river.[59]

Before concluding his account of Isaac in the preface Eulogius recounts two marvelous events about him as a child and one from the time after his death to show that he was chosen by heaven to be a martyr. Perfectus, he points out, had consummated his passion manfully earlier, but he had not come forth to it voluntarily as did Isaac. Albar in discussing the martyrs of Córdoba points out that a number of martyrs of the early Church came to their passions voluntarily.[60]

[59] *Memoriale*, preface to Bk. I, 2-3. Usuard adds in his martyrology that Isaac was twenty-seven years old.
[60] *Indiculus*, 3.

Eulogius does not seem to distinguish between the *stipes* and the *eculeus,* saying here that Isaac was hung up on the one and later (II, ii) that he was hung up on the other. Likewise he says in one place (I, 11) that the six martyrs of 7 June 851 were hung up on the *eculeus* and in another (II, iv, 3) on the *stipes.* The form of death for all the martyrs seems to have been the same, decapitation by the sword, as in the case of Perfectus. It was believed that Jeremias was first beaten to death. Flora was beaten when she was accused of being a Christian, six years before she was condemned to death. Rogellius and Servius-Dei had their hands and feet cut off before decapitation because they had dared to enter the mosque. Eulogius was condemned to be beaten to death with rods until he attacked the prophet Mohammed, whereupon his sentence was changed to decapitation.[61]

Eulogius thought that Perfectus and Isaac were justified in their denunciations of the prophet Mohammed and Islam and overlooks the rashness of Isaac in baiting the cadi. The Moslems, on the other hand, in their reactions to Perfectus and Isaac and in the reply of the cadi to Isaac show that they were by no means used to hearing such things said of their prophet. It is significant that the denunciations were a novel event, and the nature of the denunciations should be noted. What the Mozarabs said about Islam is of importance because, unlike the Christians of the East, they attacked the prophet and his religion freely.[62] They did not depend on visiting monks and imported works from the East for their knowledge of Mohammed and Islam. The cadi's exposition of Islam to Isaac illustrates Eulogius' statement that the Moslems taught their doctrine openly in Córdoba so that

[61] *Memoriale,* II, iv, 3; II, viii, 7; II, xiii, 3; and *Vita Eulogii,* 15. Cf. Hitzig, "Eculeus," Pauly-Wissowa, V, ii, 1931f.; and Joseph Vergote, "Eculeus, Rad- und Pressefolter in den ägyptischen Märtyrerakten," *Zeitschrift für die neutestamentliche Wissenschaft,* 37 (1938), 239-250 (reviewed by R. Devos, AB, 60, 225). The *eculeus* was so commonly used by the Romans that Latin writers did not describe the instrument. In Eulogius' time many of the martyrs were suspended from it after decapitation, some upside down.

[62] Franke, *op.cit.,* 44f., 61-67, 117f., 131, 142, and 169f.

anyone would learn it.[63] Derogatory information about the Moslem prophet, such as the vita which Eulogius brought to Córdoba from Navarre,[64] may have come from any part of the Christian world or from Christians living in the Moslem East. It may even have come into Spain with the invaders of 711. Not only Perfectus and Isaac, both of whom knew Arabic well, but also Esperaindeo and Eulogius[65] attacked Mohammed with a wide variety of charges before Albar in 854 introduced a whole catalogue of charges against Mohammed and Islam in the *Indiculus.*

Two days after Isaac, Sanctius died for the same profession. A captive from the fort of Alba in *Gallia Comata,* he was at the time of his death a freeman serving as a soldier in the pay of the king.[66] The fact that he was a pupil of Eulogius would seem to indicate that basilica schools in Córdoba were not restricted to clerics.

The next group of martyrs is the group of ascetic monks whom Eulogius says were inspired by God to come forth and publicly defy the Moslems with confessions of Christ and denunciations of Mohammed. They reflect the general indignation of the Christians at the measures the Moslems had taken against the confessors. Six monks, almost all in the prime of life, as had been the earlier martyrs, came into Córdoba from three different neighboring monasteries to repeat the profession of Isaac and Sanctius. They died on the fourth Sunday after Pentecost,[67] 7 June 851, four days after Isaac. The priest Peter from Ecija and the deacon Walabonsus from Elche, the latter the brother of Maria, one of the first women martyrs, had come to Córdoba for "meditation"[68] but had turned to more liberal studies. They became so outstanding in knowledge of Holy Scripture that they were placed over the monastery of the Virgin Mary, a

[63] *Apol. mart.,* 20.

[64] *Ibid.,* 16.

[65] Cf. especially *Memoriale,* I, 7.

[66] *Memoriale,* II, iii.

[67] Cf. the Mozarabic liturgy for this Sunday, especially the Gospel (Mt. 12:30-50); PL 85, 634-637.

[68] Meditation may be associated with the *acysterium.*

convent of sisters in the town of Cuteclara, not far to the west of Córdoba. Both men were under the Abbot Frugellus. Two monks, Sabinianus from the town of Fronianus in the mountains north of Córdoba and Wistremundus from Ecija, came from the monastery of St. Zoilus, thirty miles north of Córdoba in the middle of the mountain wilderness on the stream Armilata, which supplied the monks with fish. Sabinianus had been a monk for many years but Wistremundus had only recently entered the monastery, where both submitted to an abbot and a rule. The monk Habentius was a citizen of Córdoba,[69] from the monastery of St. Christopher, located within sight of Córdoba downstream on the Guadalquivir, which Eulogius calls the Betis. Habentius, an old man, lived under a very strict rule and had undertaken public penance shut in a small enclosure. With him stayed another old man, Jeremias, who with his wife Elizabeth had founded the monastery of Tabanos, also practicing harsh penances. All six men came before the cadi on Sunday and made professions like those of Isaac and Sanctius, calling Mohammed a precursor of Antichrist and the author of a profane teaching, who had poisoned his followers and delivered them to the devil. "We weep very much over your blindness and ignorance," they said to the Moslems. For some reason unknown to Eulogius the Moslems first beat the old man Jeremias, to death as some believed, contrary to their penal code, which forbade other punishments to those doomed to death, and then dragged him to the place of execution, where he was beheaded with the others. The bodies were hung up on stakes and later burned. The ashes were thrown into the river to prevent the Christians from obtaining relics, as they had those of Perfectus.[70] After this there were no more martyrdoms for a month.

The Mohammedans left the bodies of the next three martyrs lying unburied for several days before the gates of the palace, presumably to show that they would not be miraculously preserved from corruption. The Christians retrieved

---

[69] Apparently he did not lose his citizenship when he became a monk.
[70] *Memoriale*, II, iv.

them, however, and buried them with reverence in the Basilicas of St. Acisclus and St. Zoilus. All three of these martyrs were imprisoned for some time before their execution. Sisenandus had come from Beja to Córdoba to study. He was educated at the Basilica of St. Acisclus, to which Perfectus had belonged, and became a deacon there. He ventured forth to martyrdom, he said, called by SS Peter and Walabonsus, who probably had been educated at the same basilica. When the executioners came for him in prison, he was writing a reply to questions received from a friend, possibly Eulogius. Prophetically knowing that his hour was at hand, he gave the unfinished letter to the boy who was acting as courier just before "lictors" led him away with slaps and blows to the place of his execution. Here before the cadi he made the same profession of faith he had made previously. He was slain on Thursday, 16 July 851. His body was left unburied and then thrown into the river, from which it was retrieved by certain Christian women to be buried in the Basilica of St. Acisclus.[71]

The next martyr, Paul, was a kinsman of Eulogius and a deacon in the Basilica of St. Zoilus, where Eulogius was a priest. Like Sisenandus, Paul was a youth. While in prison he promised a priest from Beja named Tiberinus to intercede in heaven for his release, which later was accomplished. Tiberinus had been imprisoned for twenty years for some charge made against him by his enemies before the king. He had entered prison in the prime of life and left a decrepit old man. As did several other martyrs afterwards, Paul made his profession before the princes and consuls of Córdoba rather than before the cadi. Eulogius himself, when his moment came, was condemned by the king's councillors. It thus appears that the cadi did not have the authority to try and condemn to death people of a certain rank. Paul died on Monday, 20 July. On the Saturday following, 25 July, the monk Theodemirus of Carmona, about whom nothing else seems to have been known, was slain. Their bodies were left unburied before the gates of the pal-

[71] *Ibid.*, v.

ace and after several days were removed in stealth by Christians to be buried in the Basilica of St. Zoilus. In this chapter Eulogius describes the place of imprisonment of the martyrs as being underground and full of parricides, other murderers, thieves, and perverts. But the martyrs could receive visitors.[72] Only in these first six chapters of Book II does Eulogius give the day of the week on which the martyrdoms occurred. For some reason none of the other dates in the *Memoriale* or in the *Apologeticus martyrum* include the day of the week. Nor does the date of his letter to Wiliesindus.

Between the death of these martyrs and the death of the next martyrs in late November 851 a strong reaction against voluntary martyrdom took place in Córdoba. Many Christians who had at first supported the martyrs now turned against them, and those who were regarded as responsible for the martyr movement were imprisoned. Although the reaction may have followed in the wake of the martyrdoms of July, it would seem that the imprisonments took place in November, after Flora and Maria, both of whom the law of Islam claimed as Moslems, appeared before the cadi to denounce Islam and its prophet. A new aspect of the martyrdoms, which the Moslems could attribute to proselytizing on the part of the Christians, was then introduced. To this time belong two of Eulogius' three apologetical treatises and all five of his letters. He was working on the *Memoriale* when he was cast into prison. Besides completing Book I of that work there, he composed the *Documentum martyriale* for the virgin martyrs Flora and Maria. A number of historians would also date about this time the council of bishops which banned confessions of faith and discouraged further martyrdoms.[73]

Although the *Documentum martyriale* and Book I of the *Memoriale* were written about the same time, their subjects are separate. In the *Documentum* Eulogius is concerned almost exclusively with the virgins Flora and Maria, whom he encourages to remain steadfast in their confessions of

---

[72] *Ibid.*, vi.   [73] Cf. index, "Council of Córdoba, 852."

faith. In Book I of the *Memoriale* he is concerned almost exclusively with the martyrs who died before Flora and Maria, whom he defends as genuine martyrs.

The *Memoriale* is introduced by two letters between Eulogius and Albar.[74] Eulogius in his letter tells how the martyrdom of Isaac upset the peace of the whole city. Everyone, he says, lay and cleric, at first praised what Isaac had done, but when crowds of Christians followed Isaac and went down to the forum to profess their faith and denounce the enemy of the Church, many other Christians took fright at the anger of the cruel tyrant and changed their minds. They began to curse the martyrs, says Eulogius, declaring that both those who made confessions such as they made and those who encouraged them were guilty of sin.[75] A few Christians, Eulogius admits, did remain loyal to the martyrs. In hopes then of settling the dispute about the martyrs Eulogius undertook to write the *Memoriale,* intending it to be also a testimony of the martyrs for future generations. Hardly had he collected it together in notes, he says, when soldiers broke into his house and arrested him. Fortunately the notes were not lost in the disturbance and Eulogius was able to complete the work in prison and have it transcribed elsewhere. From prison he sent it to Albar on cheap parchment with a letter asking Albar, whom he calls "frater," "vestra serenitas," and "serenissime frater," to emend and polish the work, or else suppress it entirely if it did not merit to be made public. In this letter Eulogius is speaking of the first part of the *Memoriale* only, that covering the persecution up to November 851.

Albar's answer glows with praise for Eulogius' work. You have brought to life again the endeavors of our forefathers, he says. For He who out of compassion for the ignorance of our age has brought about the inscrutable contest of His athletes has inspired you, the greatest doctor of

---

[74] *Olim, mi frater,* and *Repriorasti,* PL 115, 731-736.

[75] Cf. also Letter to Albar, *Semper, mi frater,* Letter to Wiliesindus, 12, and *Doc. mart.,* 11. Albar, *Vita,* 4, blames the imprisonments at this time on Bishop Reccafred.

all. You are the first soldier of the Church to rally to the defense of martyrdom and the Church, says Albar. He who prepared the martyrs for their battle has enlightened you to defend them in one little volume. You have surpassed Livy, Cato, Demosthenes, Cicero, and Quintilian. Writers on transitory and worldly matters who not long ago were outstanding in style, and every carefully devised doctrine though presented in the most opulent dress, are now obsolete and tarnished. You have adorned our age and given a most valuable gift to future ages. There is no need for you, Albar says, to submit such a precious work to me, whom more than once you have found to be lowly and ignorant. But, since you ask, my judgment is that you have written a work of genius, which exorcises the fear of death, warms long hardened souls, and drives the cold away. The warmth of life and the divine fire which Christ came to bring to us burns in your work. By its breath dead coals and lifeless bodies are brought to life and receive the light which Arab guile has extinguished. So much the more wonderful is it that not even the fetters and sufferings of prison could keep you from writing it. Albar calls Eulogius, "pater," "domine," "doctor," "vestra prudentia," and "mi sanctissime."

Eulogius' preface to Book I consists essentially of the account of the martyr Isaac. At first he composed the *Memoriale*, Eulogius says, for those *ascisteria* from which the first group (*globus*) of monks had come forth to attack "the most mendacious of prophets,"[76] but when men and women from all parts came forth to defy death before the tribunal in defense of their faith he dedicated the work to all the churches. After narrating the story of Isaac at length, Eulogius explains that he has devoted the preface to Isaac and the other voluntary martyrs rather than to Perfectus, because, although Perfectus died before them, he did not come forth voluntarily with his confession of faith. And he has placed the preface before his work, he says, so that it may

---

[76] In his letter to Albar, *Semper, mi frater*, presumably written about the same time as the preface to Bk. I, Eulogius speaks as if he had written a work in defense of the martyrs some time earlier.

contradict a certain profane author, perhaps the *exceptor* discussed later.[77] It remains for his readers, Eulogius says, to make up their own minds about him and the martyrs.

Except for one other use of the word *ascisterium* in his letter to Bishop Wiliesindus of Pamplona, Eulogius always refers to a monastery as a *coenobium* or a *monasterium*. He seems to use the three words as synonyms. According to Morales, *ascisterium* is a word of Greek origin denoting a monastery or a place intended for the exercise and development of virtue. Henrique da Gama Barros offers certain data about monasteries and *asceterios* which may apply to those institutions among the Christians of Córdoba. Some monasteries were chapels or hermitages, he says, churches which lords founded on their estates for devout life and converted to *asceterios*. Albar in his letter to Romanus Medicus speaks of a monastery on his estate as a church. Apparently from the sixth century not all monks, according to da Gama Barros, took vows, some living solitary lives in the wilds. Those in the monasteries lived under the personal law of an abbot, under a tradition, or under a written rule. In the seventh century people banded together in families, making monasteries of their homes, but the custom was condemned by Fructuosus of Braga. From these family monasteries developed double monasteries, where both sexes lived separately, which the Council of Nicaea forbade in 787. Double monasteries founded by families, under the personal rule of an abbot or abbess, existed in the environs of Córdoba in the middle of the ninth century. Women, says da Gama Barros, devoted their lives to piety in monasteries, hermitages, and in their homes. In the time of Eulogius women dedicated themselves to lives of devotion and piety in monasteries and in their homes, but no women hermits are known. One of the virgin martyrs of Córdoba, however, was permitted to live a life apart from the community in a monastery. The statement of José Orlandis, that churches and monasteries from early times could not be erected with-

---

[77] *Memoriale*, preface to Bk. I, 6; II, xv, 2; and III, ii.

out the consent of the bishop, may be repeated here.[78]

In beginning the *Memoriale* Eulogius takes longer than Albar in the *Indiculus* to tell why he, though unworthy, presumes to write of holy things. In a time of peril, says Eulogius, when the Church is weakened and its adversary grows bolder, no one has raised his voice in protest. He, however, prompted by love of God and concerned over the indecision among Catholics about the martyrs, will oppose those who attack the martyrs, poor though his talent may be. He speaks first to the "brothers and sisters" of the "colleges" from which the first martyrs came forth, i.e., the Basilicas of St. Acisclus and St. Zoilus and the monasteries of Tabanos, Cuteclara, Armilata, and St. Christopher. At some length Eulogius points out that, as it is his office to preach, so are the faithful obliged to listen to him. They must not despise his words because he lives in confusion and is cast down in a shameful way of life. Later Eulogius refers to imprisonment and loss of goods suffered by him because of the professions of faith.[79] As does an anonymous bishop in a later letter, Eulogius emphasizes that the faults of an official of the Church do not entitle the faithful to ignore his words or to presume to judge him.[80] Eulogius here seems to be speaking of himself rather than of another, who would be Bishop Reccafred if anyone. From what he says, Eulogius gives the impression that he had a particular office to preach to those he addresses, that his way of life had been demeaned, and that he was being adversely judged by the laity at this time. It is possible that his unusual interest in the monasteries was linked with an official responsibility for them, and that the wealth of his family, as he indicates

[78] Letter to Wiliesindus, 2; Morales' scholium to *"ascisterium"* in preface to Bk. I; *"asceterium,"* Du Cange, *Glossarium,* and TLL; H. da Gama Barros, *Historia da administração publica em Portugal,* II, 83-88, and 108, and IV, 229; Letter IX of the Albar correspondence, 4; Columba in *Memoriale,* III, x, 7-8; J. Orlandis, "Los monasterios familiares en España durante la alta edad media," AHDE, XXVI (1956), 11.

[79] *Memoriale,* I, 19.

[80] *Ibid.,* 4; Letter X of the Albar correspondence, 4.

also in his letter to Bishop Wiliesindus of Pamplona, suffered ruin at this time.

They are worthy of praise, he says, who have carried through their love of God and their renunciation of this world to victory under the sword. If they are to follow the words of the Gospel they must preach the truth openly, regardless of peril. His defense of the martyrs begins with an apologia for those monks who left their ascetic lives in the wilderness to come forth and denounce the prophet Mohammed in public, caring nothing for the danger of death. Although the fearful have the right to escape the fury of the persecution, he says, the perfect (*perfecti*) are not obliged to do the same. God has selected them from numberless legions to fight His battles. The loss of their bodies matters little to them. If they die for truth they are sure to gain eternal life for their souls. They follow the way pointed out by Christ (Mt. 16:25) and devote their lives to Him completely, i.e., judging the way of holy confession (via sanctae confessionis) to the only fulfillment of His words. They leave the city and the things of the world and burn with an avid desire for the kingdom of God. "They wandered about in sheepskins, in goatskins, being in want, distressed, afflicted; of whom the world was not worthy: wandering in deserts, in mountains and in dens and in caves of the earth" (Hb. 11:37-38), "waiting for the Lord who saved them from pusillanimity of spirit and a storm" (Ps. 54:9). Not satisfied with lives of such penitence and recognizing that their daily struggle with the devil is a dubious one, by the grace of God they yearn for a quick consummation of this life,[81] and, as St. Paul says, they "desire to be dissolved and to be with Christ" (Ph. 1:23). They seek the "nearer way" (2 Kgs. 18:23), whereby, delivered from this life, they may arrive quickly in their heavenly home and grasp the kingdom of God by pious force.

Eulogius describes the lives of "holy confession" led by these "perfect" as one approved by the Church. Most of the

---

[81] *Memoriale*, I, 6, "nutu Dei mortificatione subita temporalis vitae accenduntur."

"confessors" recorded in the *Memoriale* were associated with monasteries. Elsewhere Eulogius takes pains to note this fact, but here he speaks of them as if their ascetic lives were independent of the rule of a monastery. These confessors, or some of them, may have voluntarily received the sacrament of Penance in order to lead more perfect lives. In Córdoba at this time the sacrament of Penance could be received only once in life and bound the person who received it to a strict penitential discipline thereafter. A part of the penitential discipline, such as exclusion from Holy Communion, was dispensed after a period of time, but the penitent was bound by his new state for the rest of his life. Such penitents were expected to change their place of abode and live according to the discipline which their bishop had prescribed. In the time of the martyrs they probably availed themselves of the monasteries outside Córdoba, and some of their number may have bound themselves further to the rule of an abbot or abbess. At times Eulogius uses the word "confessor" in the broader meaning of confessors of the faith. But it should be kept in mind that many of these "confessors" may have been living under a penitential discipline similar to that from which Albar wished to be released by Bishop Saul.[82] The rule of their lives may have been a *Confessio*, such as that composed by Albar. Eulogius in the *Memoriale* reports that tearful compunction and bodily austerities figured rather prominently in the penitential lives of a number of the martyrs before their death. The *via sanctae confessionis* of the ascetics may be nothing less than a mystic way of life under the direction of the bishop following the reception of the sacrament of Penance.

Thus, continues Eulogius, armored with the breastplate of justice, the confessors march into the forum preaching the Gospel of God to the princes and the Gentiles. From the words of the Psalmist they know that the justice of God should be declared in a great church (Ps. 39:10). And so, with a perfect hatred against the adversaries who have risen up against the Church, they charge the Moslems with the

---

[82] Letters XI-XIII of the Albar correspondence; cf. index, "Penance."

deceitful doctrine of their iniquitous prophet, full of trickeries, sacrileges, and the vanities of the world. They attack
the author of such perversity with curses and they condemn
with perpetual anathema the Moslems themselves, who follow such a cult. Thus they fearlessly raise the unfurled
standard of truth against the public enemy, says Eulogius,
and bear testimony against the leader of perdition, confusion, and ignominy all the way up to the gates of the guard
and in the very entrance of the palace.[83] They are not afraid
to suffer torment or risk danger for the truth. Indeed, an
ardent desire to enter into heaven urges them on, eager to
see His face whom they have served.

The Moslems, eager for revenge, take swift reprisal
against those detracting their sect, "not knowing that they
would receive this sudden death."[84] Coming forth of their
own free will, the confessors resist the enemy of justice and
the adversary of the Church with uninhibited speech,
"speaking of the testimonies of the Lord in the presence of
kings" (Ps. 118:46). For them death is nothing else than
life eternal, and they freely choose the death of the flesh,
offering to God the willing sacrifice of their souls. Of them
justly is it sung by the prophetic voice, "O you of Israel,
that have willingly offered your lives to danger, bless the
Lord" (Jg. 5:2). And by this, Eulogius remarks, they seem
to be true imitators of the apostle Paul, who says, "If anyone preach to you a gospel, besides that which you have received, let him be anathema" (Gal. 1:9). Guided by the
words of St. Paul, they march forth against "the messenger
of Satan and the herald of Antichrist, confessing openly

[83] The offices of the governmental administration, which employed a
number of Christians, were located at the entrance of the palace.

[84] The text here is vague and it is not clear whether Eulogius says
that the martyrs did not know that they would be slain or that the
Moslems did not know that the martyrs would be willing to accept
death: "Stimulatur zelo ultionis cohors iniqua gentilium, celerisque
animadversionis emergit vindicium in obtrectatores sectae suae. Nes-
cientes quia illi, ut hunc praecocem obitum exciperent, liberis vocibus
inimico iustitiae et adversario ecclesiae Dei progressu ultroneo resti-
terunt."

those things which are holy, which even now the whole church of Spain preaches, although in clandestine voices, being oppressed."

Eulogius goes on to show why the confessors condemned the prophet Mohammed: for rejecting the prophets of the Old Testament, the doctrine of the apostles, the truth of the Gospel, and the teaching of the doctors; for teaching that Christ is not divine; for promising sensual pleasures in paradise; and for blaspheming against the Virgin Mary. In connection with Mohammed's sensual paradise Eulogius quotes a passage from a lost work of Esperaindeo against the Moslems which calls the Moslem paradise of houris a brothel and denies that there will be marriage in heaven.[85] In reply to Mohammed's blashemy against the Mother of God, Eulogius denounces the Moslem prophet in bitter invective and defends the Blessed Virgin in what seems to be his own composition.[86] Except for the quotation from Esperaindeo and the condemnation of Mohammed's blasphemy, this passage of the *Memoriale* corresponds almost verbatim with a passage in Eulogius' *Apologeticus martyrum*.[87] Mohammed, according to Eulogius, also fashioned other vanities at the instigation of the devil, who appeared to him in the guise of the angel Gabriel. And in Moslem sanctuaries the worst teachings are taught. "Some of our wisest men, armed with the zeal of God, have pounded with the rams of justice against the folly of his error, his delirious preachings, and his commands of impious novelty."[88]

After a brief account of Perfectus and John, in which he remarks that Perfectus turned a necessity he could not avoid, his persecution, into martyrdom, Eulogius sketches the gen-

---

[85] Franke, *op.cit.*, 59, says that Esperaindeo is the first known polemicist to call the Moslem paradise a brothel, but that he probably got the idea from the East.

[86] Lorenzana, *SS PP Toletanorum*, II, 433, punctuates this composition as Esperaindeo's. Morales, *Divi Eulogii ... opera*, 18, uses no quotation marks at all. Franke, *op. cit.*, does not discuss the passage as part of Christian-Moslem polemics in Spain.

[87] *Memoriale*, I, 7-8, and *Apol. mart.*, 19-20.

[88] *Memoriale*, I, 8; cf. *Apol. mart.*, 20.

eral indignation among the Christians after the punishment
of these first victims of the persecution. This indignation
culminated in the martyrdoms of six monks whose bodies
were hung up on the *eculeus* and then cremated in order to
prevent the Christians from having their relics. The date
Eulogius gives for the cremation, "the twelfth of June, five
days after they died," identifies the martyrs as those who
died on 7 June 851.[89]

Next Eulogius takes up the argument of the Moslems that
the martyrs showed no signs and miracles to justify themselves. The matter of miracles was of special importance
with regard to the martyrs because Christian polemicists
against Islam, at least in the East, based much of their repudiation of Mohammed as a prophet on the fact that he
showed no miracles to justify himself.[90] The *Memoriale* at
this point contains the grammatical monstrosity of a parenthetical remark several sentences long inserted in the middle of another sentence. The Moslems claimed, according to
the remark, that Mohammed received his law from the angel
Gabriel and that the Creator in paradise spoke to Adam
praising Mohammed above all other men.[91] Eulogius' repeated assertions that the martyrs of Córdoba were predestined to martyrdom from the beginning of the world may
have been intended to oppose the Moslem claim that Mohammed was predestined as a prophet from the time of Adam.
For those Christians who demand miracles of the martyrs
Eulogius quotes Gregory the Great to the effect that miracles
will be withdrawn in the later days of the Church,[92] and
himself points out that miracles depend on the faith of those
seeking them. In the discussion of the latter point the

[89] *Memoriale*, I, 10-11, and II, iv, 3.

[90] Franke, *op.cit.*, 138.

[91] *Memoriale*, I, 12. Franke, *op.cit.*, 140, says that the Moslem claim
that Adam saw the name of Mohammed written in the heavens in
paradise appears, apart from Eulogius' work, only in the *Apologia* of
al-Kindi, who notes a Moslem claim that the prophet's name was written before all time on the throne of God. The claim was debated among
the Moslems themselves.

[92] Gregory, *Liber moralium*, XXXIV, 7 (PL 76, 721).

Memoriale again agrees verbatim with a passage in the *Apologeticus martyrum*.[93] Eulogius also ventures to assert here that the Holy Spirit prevented the Apostles from preaching the Gospel in Asia because He knew that there was in Asia no one worthy to receive the truth of the Gospel. The statement may show a certain amount of caprice on the part of Eulogius. Leovigildus in explaining why European clergy shave their beards while those of Asia and Africa do not and why western clergy are celibate and those of the East are not suggests that there may have been a debate of sorts in Córdoba about whether the East or the West was culturally superior. Albar in the *Indiculus* refers to the East in a way that may be equivocally good or bad (tenebras aevi corusco sidere eoi climatis inlustrare).[94]

It is the virtue of miracle workers that we should admire, says Eulogius, not their deeds. He concludes his justification of the lack of miracles asserting that his object is to defend the martyrs against an unjust criticism and not to belittle miracles. Again he describes how the Mohammedans slew the martyrs, "priests, deacons, confessors, and holy virgins," and how they left some of the truncated bodies in front of the palace exposed to dogs, refusing them burial. The first virgins to be martyred in Córdoba were Flora and Maria. Although they were in prison while Eulogius was completing this part of the *Memoriale*, they did not die until after he completed it. Eulogius probably inserted the phrase "holy virgins" later. At one time he did not contemplate himself writing the passions of Flora and Maria, to judge from a request he made of Albar to compose their passion.[95] This minor inconsistency illustrates an erratic quality of Eulogius' composition and makes clear the difficulty of determining when he composed the several parts of the *Memoriale* and which martyrs he has in mind in any particular passage of the work. The martyrs, Eulogius says, made their profes-

[93] *Memoriale*, I, 14, and *Apol. mart.*, 7.

[94] Leovigildus, *De habitu clericorum*, iv and x, and *Indiculus*, 3.

[95] Letter to Albar, *Magnificavit Dominus* (PL 115, 841-844).

sions of faith before a "council of princes," which he also calls a "pack of Gentiles."[96]

Some Christians and even priests, he continues, charge that the martyrs offered themselves up for their passion out of pride, the beginning of all sin. These critics loudly quote Holy Scripture in a twisted way and pervert the hearts of many, calling evil good and good evil. He has shared the passion of the martyrs himself, Eulogius believes, because he has suffered prison and damage to property for defending them. And he and the martyrs do follow the commandments, he maintains, for they show their love for their enemies by preaching the truth to them. By prayers and by the shedding of their blood, they bring about the salvation of many. The setting of a good example and the avoiding of scandal in the persecution, which both Eulogius and Albar considered important, is probably the basic justification for the voluntary confessions of the martyrs.

Eulogius denounces Mohammed again as a false prophet. Quoting Zacharias 13:2-3, he says that if Mohammed still lived it would be better to destroy him than to let him destroy so many peoples. The destruction of Mohammed which Eulogius speaks of is the ruin of his doctrine by means of the "sword of faith," more than his personal death. When it is wrong not to attack the enemies of the faith, he asks quoting Arnobius, how much worse is it to attack those who are attacking evil?[97]

To those who claim that the martyrs were unprovoked he answers much as does Albar in the *Indiculus*: destroying basilicas, dishonoring priests, levying monthly taxes do constitute molestation.[98] If it is right to curse the works of the

[96] *Memoriale*, I, 17; the martyrs made confessions also before the cadi, "judges," and before the king's councillors.

[97] *Memoriale*, I, 20; cf. Arnobius the Younger, *Commentarium in Psalmos*, CXXXIX (PL 53, 549).

[98] Franke, *op.cit.*, 86, attaches importance to the fact that Eulogius uses the word *molestia* and not *persecutio* to describe the actions of the Moslems. Franke's point, *ibid.*, 87, that it is not certain that the "molestations" occurred before the voluntary martyrdoms does not take into consideration the fact that Eulogius must have known that

devil, how can it be wrong to curse the prophet Mohammed? Who has raised a worse persecution against the Church than this unmentionable one? We are not safe among them, he says, they attack priests with vile abuse. "As soon as they notice the marks of holy orders on us when we have to leave the corner of our hut to go to the forum or out in public for any household necessity, with a cry of derision as if they were attacking mad men and fools, they attack us from behind continuously with stones, not satisfied with verbal invective and indecent gestures—to say nothing of those daily mockeries by the children. What shall I say about how they cry out insults at the revered sign, when the time of psalms and the time of prayer have to be announced to the faithful according to custom? As soon as they hear the sound of ringing metal in their ears, as if seduced by a false cult, they begin to exercise their tongues in all kinds of cursing and foulness."[99] Many of them regard us as not fit to come into contact with their garments and curse us if we come too near them. We are well advised to be astute in the face of their malice and to reserve our humility for ourselves. Eulogius quotes Eusebius of Caesarea and, again, Arnobius, who says that the enemies of the Lord are to be slain with "the spiritual sword."[100]

After showing that there is a persecution, Eulogius marshalls a large number of saints, in addition to Our Lord, as exemplars who voluntarily offered themselves to danger: Emetherius and Celedonius, John the Baptist, the seven brothers in the acts of Julian, Paul, Felix, Sebastian, Thyrsus, Adrian, Justus and Pastor, Eulalia, and Babilas. In brief but detailed accounts he shows how each of these saints professed his faith openly in the face of persecution when he knew that his martyrdom would result.[101]

Against those who object to the corruption of the martyrs'

---

his readers in 851 would have been aware of such a fact. Moreover, Eulogius and Albar both speak elsewhere of "persecutors" and a "persecution."

[99] *Memoriale*, I, 21.
[100] Arnobius, *op.cit.*, (PL 53, 549).
[101] *Memoriale*, I, 22-24.

bodies he points out that all men come to dust, partriarchs, prophets, apostles, and martyrs. He exhorts the Christians to ignore the critics of the martyrs, who are wanting in piety and faith. They call the martyrs heretics, he says, and have even ordered those who would follow them to be condemned in notices of anathema in various places.[102] Later in almost the same words Eulogius speaks of a ban, rather than an anathema, on confessions leading to martyrdom but says nothing of the charge of heresy when he describes the council of 852. Albar in 853 or 854 in the *Indiculus* complains of the charge of heresy, an ecclesiastical ban on confessions, and an oath not to seek martyrdom.[103] The text of Book I of the *Memoriale* was complete in the main by the end of 851. If this statement is not a later interpolation, it seems that Bishop Reccafred of Seville may have issued a decree of anathema against the confessors in 851. Such a decree would have been more stringent than the decision arrived at in the council of 852. It may also be noted that one can regard the letter of the anonymous bishop (Letter X of the Albar correspondence) as a statement by Bishop Saul of Córdoba to Reccafred that he had undertaken to absolve certain Christians from Reccafred's anathema.[104]

Let each of us conduct himself according to the talent which has been given him, Eulogius continues. It is not everyone's lot to be a martyr, but if we cannot resist the enemy ourselves, at least let us not oppose the martyrs. Who can believe, he asks, that those who attack the author of their crime [the prophet Mohammed] are not martyrs because they are not forced into Mohammedan wickedness? Eulogius rejects the notion that Christians are permitted to practice their religion by leave of the Moslems rather than by Divine Judgment, and thus have no right to reprove the errors of the Moslems. "It is not by the favor of this impious people, in whose sway the sceptre of Spain has been transferred by dint of our sins after the destruction and expulsion of the

[102] *Ibid.*, 28.
[103] *Ibid.*, II, xv, 2-3, and *Indiculus*, 15.
[104] V. infra, 327.

kingdom of the Goths, which long ago was outstanding in
the most blessed practice of the Christian faith and blos-
somed forth with worthy and venerable priests, and was
radiant in wonderfully constructed basilicas."[105] What will
we do on Judgment Day when we see the martyrs justified,
he asks, if we attack them now?

After pointing out that it was love of heaven and fear of
hell, not love of death, which motivated the martyrs, Eulogius concludes Book I with an exhortation to the Christians
(viri fratres) to venerate the martyrs and thus participate
with them in their reward. The martyrs belong to the whole
Church, he says, and not just to those from whose midst
they came, the "brothers and sisters," to whom he again
speaks. He himself has a kinsman, Paul, and a pupil, Sanctius, among the martyrs,[106] and although he has not come
forth in person to do battle he has fortified many who have.
What does it matter what kind of death they suffer who gain
heaven? he asks. He ends his lengthy peroration with a
paragraph addressed to the sainted martyrs in which he
beseeches their intercession for himself, noting that he is
constrained by difficult times and overwhelmed with threatening dangers.

Book I of the *Memoriale* parallels the first part of Albar's
Indiculus, a number of themes being treated in both works
in similar fashion. Albar's work seems to have served for
a particular occasion whereas Eulogius seems to have written more generally. As a result, Eulogius provides fewer
details about his times than does Albar. Eulogius' thoughts
too, unlike those of the layman Albar, are bound more closely
to the spiritual world in the tradition of Holy Scripture and
the Fathers.

---

[105] *Memoriale,* I, 30; cf. *ibid.,* III, iii, where Eulogius says that King
Mohammed ordered destroyed all "crudely fashioned additions," even
roofs, on basilicas which dated back to the days of the Visigoths. Other
writers too blamed the fall of Spain to the Moslems on the sins of
Christians.

[106] *Memoriale,* II, ii, and II, vi.

CHAPTER X

THE CONTINUATION OF THE
MARTYRDOMS UNDER ABD AL-RAHMAN II

It is difficult to determine when Eulogius resumed writing the *Memoriale*. In an introductory paragraph to the first chapter of the continuation he says that, contrary to his expectations and despite all the trials the churches have undergone and the imprisonments Christians have suffered, others, men, women, and youths, have been inspired to march forth to battle.[1] By youths he probably refers to Christopher, who died in August 852, and Emila and Hieremias, who were martyred in September 852, rather than to Flora and Maria. September 852 is near the end of events narrated in Book II. Eulogius may have composed chapters vii-xvi of Book II after all the events had taken place. Judging from a letter he wrote, presumably at the end of 851, urging Albar to compose the vitae of Flora and Maria,[2] he evidently did not regard himself as the chronicler of the martyrdoms at this time. In chapter x of Book II he says that he was asked to write the vitae of the saints recorded there nine months after they died,[3] showing that as late as April 853 he had not written the chapter. In chapter viii, devoted to Flora and Maria, and in chapter x Eulogius provides more details about the lives of the saints before their passion than he does in the case of other martyrs of Córdoba. He may have done so because, unlike the previous martyrs, Flora and Maria and four of the saints of chapter x were slain because the Moslems learned that they were secret Christians. Being regarded as apostates from Islam, they were liable to death. Eulogius probably wished to make sure that everyone learned of the Christian lives of these martyrs. Inasmuch as

---

[1] *Memoriale*, II, vii, 1.
[2] *Magnificavit Dominus*, 3.
[3] *Memoriale*, II, x, 17.

the voluntary profession of faith was of secondary importance in their case, he may have felt too that the apologia of Book I, written primarily for the ascetic monks, did not do justice to these martyrs. He may also have felt that it was significant that Flora and Maria were the first women martyrs of Córdoba, and Aurelius, Felix, and their wives were the only married couples to die as martyrs in the persecution.

The first chapter of the continuation of the *Memoriale* is devoted to the virgin martyrs Nunilo and Alodia, who died outside Córdoba before Flora and Maria. Eulogius dates their deaths 22 October 851, but Morales believed the date should be eleven years earlier. Morales' basis for believing Eulogius mistaken is a notice from another manuscript that the relics of the two martyrs were translated to the monastery of Leyre in 842.[4] Their translation to Leyre must have taken place after Eulogius visited there in 848 or 850, because Eulogius says in the vita that their tomb was still in the neighborhood of the town where they died, Bosca. Morales, however, seems to have held that Eulogius' journey to the North took place in 839 or 840.[5] It would seem that Eulogius is correct and the notice of translation is in error.

Eulogius received the account of Nunilo and Alodia from Bishop Venerius of Alcalá. His account is somewhat briefer than that of these two martyrs in *Passionales* and *Sanctorales* of mediaeval Spain.[6] Eulogius introduces their passion before that of Flora and Maria because "reason and the course of months" require it. The fact that their names

[4] Morales publishes the notice of translation in a scholium. This notice, which comes from a ms thought to date from before the eleventh century, and a longer notice, which reports that the translation took place twenty-nine years after the martyrdoms, were published by José Pellizer de Salas in Madrid in 1668 and appear in AASS, October, IX, 645-646.

[5] Cf. scholia 2 and 8 of *Memoriale*, II, vii, and 2 of Letter to Wiliesindus. García-Villada, *Historia*, III, 95, accepts the readings in the *Passionales* of Huesca for Bosca, a reading Morales, scholium 3, did not accept. Morales, scholium 14 of the *Vita Eulogii*, seems to date Eulogius' trip to the North about 850.

[6] V. scholium 6.

have been entered in the heavenly codex, he says, is reason to include them in his work, even though they suffered in another part of Spain.

Nunilo and Alodia were two sisters in the town of Bosca, born of a prominent Moslem father and a Christian mother. They grew up as Christians, but when their father died and their mother remarried a Moslem, their stepfather refused to permit them to live as Christians. Thereupon the sisters left their mother's home and went to live with a Christian aunt. Their case became known to the prefect of the city, who summoned them before him and attempted to persuade them with promises of wealth and marriage to adopt the Mohammedan religion. They replied to him in a rather lengthy statement which has characteristics of a credo and a prayer, rejecting his offer. He thereupon delivered them to Moslem women to be instructed in the doctrines of Islam. The sisters continued steadfast in their faith and were beheaded in the forum on 22 October "the year mentioned above" [851]. Their bodies were left lying where they fell and Christians were prevented from burying them. The Moslems finally tried to hide their bodies among rocks, but signs and miracles made their whereabouts known.[7]

The chapter about Flora and Maria begins with a brief prefatory paragraph in which Eulogius indicates that the vita and passion are intended for the edification of the faithful in connection with the feast of the two saints. He also states, in words similar to those Albar uses to begin the *Vita Eulogii,* that he will speak only the plain truth, not adding things that did not happen.[8] He treats of the two virgins in turn.

Flora was the daughter of a noble Christian mother from Ausianos, a town eight miles west of Córdoba, and a Moslem father from Seville. For some reason, Eulogius says, the parents came to Córdoba to live. When the father died the

[7] *Memoriale,* II, vii.

[8] *Ibid.,* viii, 1, and *Vita,* 1; this chapter appears separate from the *Memoriale* in PL 115, 835-842.

mother raised Flora, then seven years old,[9] in the Christian religion until the girl was far advanced in piety and holy practices. On an occasion when Eulogius visited their home the mother told him of the rigorous Lenten fast which the young girl insisted on observing.[10] Because of a brother who adhered to the Mohammedan religion Flora could not practice her religion publicly. She and her sister therefore without consulting their mother fled from their home to freedom among the Christians. Their brother sought after them furiously, venting his wrath on clerics and the convents of sisters. Flora, learning of his actions, returned home and declared herself to be a Christian. After failing with either force or blandishments to make her give up her faith, the brother brought her before the cadi and accused her of lapsing from Islam. Formerly, he charged, Flora had venerated "the ceremonies of the law" and had performed "the service owed to the cult" of Islam, but Christians had enticed her into their faith.[11] The cadi then asked Flora for her reply. She denied that she had ever been a Moslem, asserting that she had been a Christian from infancy and had vowed her life to Christ. The cadi, in a rage, had her held between two of his servants and beat her until the bone in the nape of her neck was laid bare. When Flora continued firm in her faith, the cadi returned her half dead to her brother so that he might cure her of her wounds and again strive to convert her. But if she persisted in the Christian faith, she was to be brought before him again. Flora recovered from her wounds and one night climbed over the wall of her home to flee to Christian friends, later going to stay with her sister in a town near Martos, where the Abbot Samson took refuge in 864. Eulogius saw her at this time and even touched the scar of her wound. These events occurred in 845, six years before the martyrdom of Flora.[12]

Maria, on the other hand, was born of an humble Christian father from Elche and an Arab mother converted to Christianity by her spouse. The father, not being able to

[9] Cf. *Magnificavit Dominus*, 2.   [10] *Memoriale*, II, viii, 3.
[11] *Ibid.*, 7.   [12] Cf. *Documentum martyriale*, 21.

live on his own land with his wife because of her conversion, wandered about with her and their two children, Walabonsus and Maria, until they came to the town of Fronianus, twelve miles from Córdoba. After a while the mother died here, and the father entered the religious life, placing his son in the monastery of St. Felix under the priest, Salvator, to be raised under ecclesiastical rule. Maria, the older of the two children, he placed in the convent of the Blessed Virgin at Cuteclara under the renowned and pious Artemia, the mother of the martyrs Adulphus and John, who had died at the beginning of the reign of Abd al-Rahman II.[13] Walabonsus became a deacon and was one of the martyrs to die a few days after Isaac. Maria mourned his death deeply until the saint appeared to one of her co-religious and advised her that Maria should leave off grieving, since she herself was destined to become a martyr. This news filled Maria with an ardent desire for martyrdom.

One day Maria left the convent to go down to the forum, stopping on the way at the Basilica of St. Acisclus, where she found Flora praying to the martyrs. When the two found out that they both desired martyrdom, they went together, firmly resolved in their purpose, down to "the judges" and, proclaiming themselves Christians, denounced Mohammed as a false prophet, adulterer, magician, and evil-doer, and his religion as the invention of devils. The cadi, furious, threw them into prison, where they continued to fast and pray, singing hymns. When Eulogius was subsequently thrown into prison, he says, he composed the *Documentum martyriale* to fortify them against the efforts of "certain people" who were seeking to persuade them to abjure their faith.[14] After the third warning by the cadi Flora and Maria were beheaded in the forum on 24 November 851, and their corpses were left for dogs and birds to devour. The next day they were thrown into the river. The body of Maria was recovered and buried in the convent of Cuteclara, where she had lived. Flora's body was not recovered. The heads of both virgins were preserved in the Basilica of St. Acis-

---

[13] *Memoriale*, II, viii, 9.   [14] *Ibid.*, 14.

clus. Five days after their death Eulogius was released from prison in accordance with a promise they had made to him before their deaths.

Eulogius also describes his release from prison in a letter he wrote exhorting Albar to write the passion of Flora and Maria.[15] In this letter he records Flora's description of an interrogation of her by the cadi and her brother more than ten days before her death. When the Christians in prison received news of the martyrdoms they all, says Eulogius, praised God in prayer, from three o'clock in the afternoon, through vespers and matins, and in the Mass the following day. They committed themselves to the protection of the two martyrs and regarded their release from prison, which occurred within a few days, as due to the intercession of Flora and Maria. In another letter[16] Eulogius very briefly informs Flora's sister Baldegotho, perhaps the sister with whom Flora stayed while living near Martos, of Flora's martyrdom. At the same time he sends her the sash worn by Flora in prison. Baldegotho, whom Eulogius calls "domina soror," also had dedicated her life to virginity.

The fact that Eulogius composed such a treatise as the *Documentum martyriale* in Latin for two maidens, one with a Moslem background, shows that Latin culture in Córdoba was neither on the point of extinction nor restricted to an intellectual elite. The *Documentum* is introduced by an exchange of letters between Eulogius and Albar.[17] Burdened by his sins and cast down in prison, says Eulogius, trouble has beset him ever since that day when Albar, whom he calls "serenitas vestra," advised him not to abandon his defense of the martyrs lest he nullify the effect of his first statement about them. Eulogius' earlier defense of the martyrs probably was made in June 851, when Isaac and other monks became martyrs. It is to the earlier defense of the

[15] *Magnificavit Dominus*, PL 115, 841-844.
[16] PL 115, 844f.
[17] *Semper, mi frater*, and *Luminosum vestri*, PL 115, 819-820. In the *Vita Eulogii*, 8, Albar calls Eulogius *"luminosus,"* and in the *Vita*, 9, he speaks of Eulogius' *luminosa vestigia;* cf. *Indiculus luminosus*.

martyrs, evidently, that he refers in his first words in the preface to Book I of the *Memoriale,* "I had dedicated this volume. . . ." Because the martyrs resisted the enemy of justice the cruel tryant, presumably the king, has imprisoned him, charging that it was because of his instigation that confessors came forth. As if, Eulogius exclaims, imprisonment could make him attack them now! He has composed the *Documentum* as a testimony of his belief in the martyrs and to aid the virgins, Flora and Maria, in their struggle. It is for Albar to give the work authority and to expunge from it any chance error against the Catholic faith before Flora and Maria read it. It seems strange that Eulogius, a priest, should submit his work for approval to a layman who could give it authority (auctoritatem donare).

Albar answers with lavish praise for the work "written with scholastic erudition" and says it is only humility that causes Eulogius to send the work to him. He has not transcribed[18] it, however, "lest I offend your friendship." He asks Eulogius to transcribe it in another manuscript[19] in a "more open hand" for the "sisters," presumably Flora and Maria, and then to send it back to him to be transcribed. The reference to a "more open hand" seems to mean that Eulogius first wrote in a kind of shorthand or in a very abbreviated script. Bishop Saul in a letter to Albar also indicates that Albar used an abbreviated script or a shorthand in writing to him.[20] Albar's role in the transcription of the *Documentum,* into a permanent record probably, seems to have been that of an official clerk. Why he did not transcribe it immediately is not clear.

In the preface to the *Documentum* Eulogius philosophizes, "The rich man thinks and does, but the poor man in thinking in undone." Poor though his talent may be, however, he has undertaken to compose this work for the instruction of Flora and Maria and for those to come after them. Let readers approach the work with open minds and excuse its poor style in view of its plain thought.

---

[18] "rescribere."   [19] "quaternio."
[20] Letter XII of the Albar correspondence, 2.

Eulogius praises Flora and Maria for their courage and exhorts them to remain constant in their faith in the trial of prison and in the face of threats of public shame to their virtue. The Lord has care for them and will not let them be tried beyond their endurance. Purity of mind is more important than an unsullied body, he says, quoting Jerome and Augustine and pointing out that whatever happens to them is in accordance with the plan of God. He gives the examples of Jonas, Malchus, and Paulinus of Nola as saints who suffered affliction for the Lord's sake. Harsh punishments are quickly undergone, he reminds Flora and Maria, and lighter ones are easily borne. Your sufferings will purge you of the corruption of this life, all of which is vanity. Each of us must pursue his own path to heaven through divers trials, he says, introducing next a description of the general plight of the Christians of Córdoba.

"And to be sure, we do not believe that we shall be outcasts from Divine favor and we hope that we shall not be deprived of, or ungrateful for, the heavenly reward. For, even though against our will, still we have been bound and tied in deep prison dungeons for the sake of His name. The insides of the prison are filled with crowds of the clergy. The Church has been emptied of consecrated bishops and priests. The divine tabernacles lie deserted in squalid solitude. The spider spins its web in the church. Silence grips everything. Priests and ministers of the altar are in confusion, because 'the stones of the sanctuary are scattered in the top of every street' (Lament. 4:1), and the hymns and heavenly canticles have ceased in the churches and the recesses of the prison resound with the holy murmur of Psalms. The cantor does not sing his divine song in public. The sound of Psalms is not heard in the choir. The lector does not preach in the pulpit. The deacon does not preach the Gospel among the people. The priest does not bear incense to the altars. For when the pastor has been struck, the adversary brings about the dispersion of the Catholic flock, and the Church is deprived forthwith of all sacred service. And although we bear all this unwillingly, we trust

that our detention will not be without return before the
Lord."[21] The situation described by Eulogius here is that
in Córdoba when Bishop Saul and many of his clergy were
thrown into prison. Albar ascribes the imprisonment to
Bishop Reccafred.[22] Eulogius here seems to blame the Moslems.

Do not give up the good struggle you have begun, he urges
the two maidens, for the prize is awarded not to those who
begin a contest, but to those who finish it. Fear not the persecutors, for the Lord is with you. Certain people [appar-
ently Christians] think that the virgins should be prevented
from their purpose, he says, and they have ordered them to
deny that they ever cursed the prophet Mohammed, arguing
that as a result of their act desolation and tribulation have
come upon the Church. Eulogius forbids the virgins this
course and urges them not to retract the profession they
have made. He points out that the course offered them is
nothing more than a lie and exhorts them to speak out in
public what is only the truth and what the whole Church
believes. For is not Mohammed, he asks, a man of demons,
the minister of Satan, full of lies, the son of death and eternal perdition? Heed not those who blame you for the desolation of the Church. God, he says, will take care of His
Church. The church in Spain, he regrets, is too prudent and
fears to speak out against the Mohammedans. He recalls
ruefully that the Visigothic government, under which "the
happiness of the churches was in full bloom and the high
dignity of priests shone brightly," has been supplanted by
"the rule of the worshippers of that nefarious seer." He
views all this as God's punishment for the sins of the Christians. "They burden the necks of the faithful with a most
grievous yoke, and . . . attempt to exclude Christians from
the bounds of their kingdom, now permitting us to practice
Christianity only by their pleasure, now, like Pharaoh, making us pour out our sweat in cruel servitude, now extorting
from us an intolerable tax bill, now imposing on our wretch-
ed necks a public service, now making us give up our goods

[21] *Documentum*, 11.   [22] *Vita Eulogii*, 4.

and suffer a cruel loss of property."[23] They oppress the
Church with all manner of persecutions, thinking that thereby they render a pleasing service to their god. "How much
greater glory would be given us by the Lord, if, aroused
by your example, we throw off our lethargy, hasten to do
such things as you, and do not permit ourselves to suffer
under the divine goad of an evil people!" Quite the contrary,
he says, the Christians mingle with the Moslems and accept
their rule gladly. "And from daily habit we adopt their
sacrilegious customs and choose their company rather than
to seek safety in the mountain after the example of the patri-
arch Lot, who left the land of Sodom.

Flora and Maria, it appears, were not condemned to death
until after a formal profession of faith in the forum. Such
a second, formal statement seems to have been required of
several other martyrs following the initial statement which
brought about their arrest. A denial, or retraction, when
making the formal statement, of the initial profession of
faith and denunciation of the prophet Mohammed, such as
"certain people" were urging upon Flora and Maria, was
probably the "prevarication" and "dissimulation" which both
Eulogius and Albar condemn as a renunciation of Christianity.[24]

After once more exhorting the two maidens not to repudi-
ate the profession they had made, Eulogius reminds Flora
that her vocation is not like that of the other martyrs, since
her ties to Islam are closer than theirs and her case is widely known among Christians and Moslems. He recalls the
sympathy he has had for her since the beginning of her
trials, six years ago, when he saw the wound on her neck.[25]
Do not forfeit now the merits of your long exile, he begs
her. He urges them both to follow in the path of the previous martyrs, whom he names.

In conclusion he asks the two to intercede for him in heav-
en. He has written the meager work, he says, in spiritual

---

[23] *Documentum*, 18.
[24] Cf. *Indiculus*, 16-17; *Memoriale*, II, xv, 2.
[25] *Documentum*, 21.

love for them and in solicitude for their salvation. Through it he has instructed them, incited them to wage the battle of the Lord, and armed them to preach in the struggle. He has shown them what to flee and what their reward will be, and has written their praises as best he could. He asks their intercession that he may be rid of vices and faults and not know how to fail, that he may enjoy their company and that of others of whom he has written in the *Memoriale*. As yet, the persecution has prevented him from completing that work, he says. At the end of the *Documentum* Eulogius adds a short prayer composed for the maidens. The prayer is an admirable one and illustrates well the spirit of Eulogius and that which he sought to inculcate in the martyrs.

Lord God Almighty, who art the true solace for those who hope in thee, the unflagging remedy for those who fear thee, the perpetual joy for those who love thee, light the fire of love in our heart and put the flame of thy charity in the recesses of our breast, so that we may be able to consummate the martyrdom already begun; so that, the fire of thy love growing in us, the temptation to sin may fall away from us and the wicked pleasures of vices may flee far away; so that by the gift of thy illuminating grace, we may be able to despise all the delights of the world and love thee at all times in purity of mind and simplicity of devotion; so that we may learn to fear thee, desire thee, and seek thee. Aid us, O Lord, in tribulation, for the safety of men is vain. Give us the strength to fight in this battle and look down from Sion with the intent to free us; so that, following thy footsteps, we may drink the chalice of passion with happiness.[26] For thou, O Lord, not only liberated with powerful arm thy Israelites once suffering under the dire yoke of the Egyptians, but even consumed completely Pharaoh and his army sunk in the middle of the sea for the honor and glory of thy name. In our fragility in this battle give us an unconquerable fortress for resisting the enemy. In the midst of the ranks of the demons and of men

---

[26] "iucundo ore." Eulogius also combines "mente," "ritu," and "iure" with adjectives to form adverbs.

rising up against us lend us the irresistible help of thy right hand. Raise up in our defense the shield of thy divinity and grant us leave to fight manfully for thy sake unto death, so that by shedding our blood, we may be able to pay our debt for thy passion. Just as thou didst deign to die for our sake, so make us also die for thy sake by the appropriate and fitting death of a martyr; so that, avoiding the torments of eternal sufferings by means of the temporal sword and putting aside the baggage of the flesh, we may deserve to reach thee in happiness. May thy most loving power also assist, O Lord, the Catholic people without hindrance and defend thy Church from the evils of the devastator, and mayest thou command the crown of all thy priests, blessed with the wealth of sanctity and chastity, to enter the heavenly fatherland after the unblemished ministry of their holy office. Among whom place thy servant Eulogius, by whose teachings, following thy grace, we are instructed, by whose writings we are taught, by whose solace we are encouraged, and by whose preachings we are animated—make him cleansed of all sin and washed clean of all crime, a faithful servant to thee, bound forever to thy service, in which, giving pleasing service to thee in this life and held worthy of the gifts of thy graces in the future, let him obtain at least the lowest place of rest in the land of the living. Through Christ our Lord, who lives and reigns with thee forever. Amen.[27]

Eulogius' reference to the "sanctity and chastity" and the "unblemished ministry" of priests, somewhat unexpected in the prayer, may be related to the reluctance of certain Christians to accept the ministry of priests who seem to have compromised with the forces of the persecution, a reluctance referred to in the letter of an anonymous bishop, discussed later.[28]

Flora and Maria died 24 November 851. Two months later there were two more martyrs, Gumesindus and Servus Dei. The priest Gumesindus had come to Córdoba from Tole-

[27] PL 115, 834.
[28] Letter X of the Albar correspondence, especially 3-4.

do as a boy with his parents. He was educated and became a deacon at the Basilica of SS. Faustus, Januarius, and Martial. As a priest he was assigned to a certain church in the environs of Córdoba. He and the monk Servus Dei confessed their faith before "the princes and judges" and died on 13 January 852. Their bodies were taken away in stealth by Christians and buried in the Basilica of St. Christopher martyr, across the river to the south of Cordoba.[29]

A number of those who have studied the martyrdoms date the council of 852 before the deaths of the next martyrs, who, accordingly, would be responsible for disregarding to an extent the decision of that council discouraging martyrdom.

The chapter devoted to the five martyrs, Aurelius, Felix, George, Sabigotho, and Liliosa shows the effect that the martyrdoms had on Christians practicing their faith in secret. It is the longest chapter in the *Memoriale*.[30] Aurelius, born of a Christian mother and a pagan father, was endowed with nobility and riches. Up to his adolescence he was raised in the Christian faith by a paternal aunt. Then, upon the insistence of his relatives, he was instructed in Arabic learning,[31] which appears to have consisted of religious studies. He was unaffected by the Moslem doctrine and continued to practice his faith in secret. Although his marriage seems to have been arranged by his Arab relatives, he had the good fortune to secure the hand of the virtuous Sabigotho, a secret Christian. Their marriage was celebrated in a Christian manner. Banns were announced, earnest money was exchanged, and finally the marriage was celebrated by the ministry of priests,[32] presumably in se-

---

[29] *Memoriale*, II, ix.

[30] A text of the passion of these five martyrs, varying slightly from the text of the *Memoriale*, appears in ms Paris BN Lat. 13760, 59-82v, together with Aimoin's account of the translation of relics of three of the martyrs from Córdoba to Paris in 858, *ibid.*, 90v-147v.

[31] "Arabica erudiendus literatura traderetur cogentibus affinibus."

[32] *Memoriale*, II, x, 3, "completis sponsalium titulis, arrarumque pignore alternanti in invicem exhibitione contradita legitima, ad ul-

cret. Sabigotho had been born of pagan parents with the name Nathalia, by which she is known in the tradition of the monk Aimoin. When her father died her mother married a Christian who brought about the conversion of mother and daughter to Christianity. The child was then baptized Sabigotho, by which name she is called in the *Memoriale*.[33] The family practiced their religion in secret.

A relative of Aurelius named Felix had once apostatized to Islam and when he returned to the Christian faith he too had to practice it in secret. His wife Liliosa was the daughter of secret Christians and had to practice her faith in secret also. The only Christian in this whole family relationship not stated to have practiced her faith in secret was the paternal aunt of Aurelius, and since she was the sister of his Moslem father she probably also had to conceal her faith.

Some years after his marriage Aurelius one day witnessed the punishment of the merchant John, who was beaten and paraded through the streets as an example for those who showed disrespect for the prophet Mohammed. Aurelius, greatly moved by the strength and courage of John and shocked by the cries of those who said that death was a more fitting punishment for anyone who attacked the prophet Mohammed, returned home resolved to lead a more perfect life, as his wife Sabigotho had been urging him. The couple thereupon began to live celibately, fasted, prayed, meditated on the Psalms, and kept vigils. They also practiced many works of mercy, ministering to the poor and needy and, from the time of the first voluntary martyrs, visiting Christians in prison.[34] It was on such a visit that Aurelius met Eulogius and asked him what he should do to

timum ministerio sacerdotum ex more sacrantur." For the Mozarabic *ordo* of marriage cf. Férotin, *Le liber ordinum*, 433-443.

[33] The instance of someone apparently not of Visigothic ancestry adopting a Visigothic name shows that one cannot conclude to the ancestry of Mozarabs from the evidence of a name.

[34] The life led by Aurelius and Sabigotho is similar to that which one would lead after receiving the sacrament of Penance, q.v. index, but Eulogius makes no reference to the sacrament.

prevent his property from going to the Moslem treasury and his two children from falling into the Moslem religion in the event of his death. Eulogius advised him to place his children in a safe place and to sell all his property and give the proceeds to the poor. He pointed out to Aurelius, however, that one must put one's trust in the providence of God, for in some cases Christians raised with the greatest care lost their faith while heathens from the worst backgrounds came to Christ.

Meanwhile Sabigotho was visiting the virgins Flora and Maria in prison. Later, after their death, the two saints appeared to her and promised her a crown of martyrdom, prepared for her from the beginning of the world. As a sign of her martyrdom they promised to send a monk who would be martyred with her. The justification for the martyrdom of Sabigotho, it may be noted, is supported by the argument of predestined martyrdom, the vision of the martyrs Flora and Maria, and the sign of the monk who would be sent to her. After this event the couple sold all their belongings and began to renounce the things of the world. They visited monasteries, especially that of Tabanos, where they placed their daughters, one eight and the other five years old.[35] At this point Eulogius inserts a statement that nine months after the death of the parents their younger daughter asked him to write the account of their passion.[36] This dates the composition of this chapter as no earlier than the end of April 853, six months after the last recorded events of Book II (the reign of Abd al-Rahman II) and about six weeks before the first martyr of Book III (the reign of Mohammed I). In remarking at this point that his work is afflicted by mundane troubles and that he is the object of undeserved reprehension from his brethren Eulo-

---

[35] J. Mabillon, *Acta SS OSB* . . . , *saeculum quartum*, ii, in his preliminary remarks to the Translation of SS George, Aurelius, and Nathalia, and in *Annales*, XXXV, 41; and Laurentius Surius, *Historiae seu vitae sanctorum* (first published in Cologne, 1579), 27 August, par. 10, both base their accounts on ms Paris BN Lat. 13760 and note that the daughters were named Felicitas and Maria.

[36] *Memoriale*, II, x, 17.

gius refers apparently to the condemnation of the defenders of the martyrs by some Christians following the council of 852. It is probably of these same days that Albar complains in the *Indiculus*, the first part of which may have been written about this time.

Eulogius mentions that during these days, before the end of July 852, he went to the home of Albar to confer with him about problems in the interpreting of Holy Scripture and there met Aurelius seeking advice from Albar about martyrdom. Albar, whom Eulogius calls teacher and doctor, advised Aurelius to weigh his power to remain steadfast; to withdraw in secret and scrutinize his own soul; to decide whether he was strong enough to bear torments when they were at hand and receive the sword on his neck or whether he would evade them; to determine if he was more interested in obtaining the merits of a martyr or in being called a martyr, if he sought more to have his name inscribed in the list of the elect with flowering merit in heaven and be unknown on earth or to have less of a reward in heaven and have a famous name as a martyr of the times. When Aurelius decided that he was prepared to die as a martyr, he again conferred with Eulogius.

Albar's advice shows that he and Eulogius were not fanatics urging their brethren on to their deaths. Although he confesses earlier in the *Memoriale* to have been the champion of the martyrs, Eulogius mentions only a few martyrs with whom he came into contact before they professed their faith publicly; first Flora and Maria, now Aurelius and his companions, and in the following month Leovigildus. Four of the martyrs (Sanctius, Paul, Christopher, and Louis) were either relatives or pupils of Eulogius, but there is nothing to indicate that he advised them before their martyrdoms.[37] As for Leocritia, the Arab girl martyred at the same time as Eulogius, the priest was endeavoring to conceal her from the Moslems rather than encouraging her to make a public confession.[38] So far as is known, Albar gave advice to none of the martyrs besides Aurelius.

---

[37] *Ibid.*, II, iii, vi, xi, and III, xiii. [38] *Vita Eulogii*, 13-16.

Sabigotho, several days before her martyrdom, had another heavenly vision, in which a child who had died announced that the hour of martyrdom was at hand. A week before the arrest of Aurelius and Sabigotho the monk who had been promised as a sign to them appeared in the person of George, a monk from the East.

George was born in Bethlehem and lived for twenty-seven years in the monastery of St. Sabas outside Jerusalem, a monastery of five hundred monks. His superior there, the Abbot David, sent him to Africa to obtain a stipend for the monastery, but when George found the church there laboring under dire persecution[39] he proceeded to Spain and came to Córdoba, where he impressed everyone with his abstemiousness and holiness. He was skilled in various languages, Greek, Latin, and Arabic, yet, Eulogius says, he showed no pride because of this accomplishment. Eulogius thus indicates that in Córdoba it was unusual to know all three of these languages. George had not bathed since he had entered the monastery, twenty-seven years before. Before he went to martyrdom he prepared a commentary on his last days for those he had left in Jerusalem. He sent this commentary, written in Latin, to Eulogius for correction. Eulogius includes it verbatim in the chapter. The fact that George left an account with the Christians of Córdoba to be forwarded to Jerusalem argues that communications between Christians in the two areas were fairly dependable.

George writes that when he came from Africa to Spain and found that land also under persecution he stopped to deliberate whether to return to his native land or to go on to "the kingdom of the Christians, that is, *Francia*." The abbot Martin and the abbess Elizabeth prevailed on him to remain at the monastery of Tabanos outside Córdoba, where

---

[39] The existence of a persecution in North Africa would indicate that the persecution in Córdoba involved more than a local reaction against the confessions of faith by the Christians. Cf. Heinrich Goussen, *Die christlich-arabische Literatur der Mozaraber*, Vol. IV of *Beiträge zur christlich-arabischen Literaturgeschichte* (Leipzig, 1909), 11ff., on the alms paid to eastern churches by those in the West after the Moslem conquest.

Sabigotho recognized him as the monk who had been promised as a sign to her. That night she appeared to him in a vision, and the following day they went down to the city, where George met Aurelius, Felix, and Liliosa, who had sold their property and were preparing for martyrdom. George took leave of the group for a while, as he says, to dispose of the affairs with which he was charged.[40] The group decided that the best way for them to come to the crown of martyrdom was for Sabigotho and Liliosa to go to church with unveiled faces.[41] When the two were coming back from church, a Moslem official (quidam praepositus) recognized them as Christians because of their unveiled faces and asked their husbands what was the meaning of their wives going to the church of the Christians. The husbands replied that they were all Christians. For this they were denounced to the cadi. After this Aurelius went to bid his daughters farewell. This is as far as the commentary of the monk George goes.

Aurelius came to ask Eulogius for his prayers before going to martyrdom. Soldiers took Aurelius and Felix and their wives to the cadi, who was grieved to learn that Aurelius was responsible for the affair. When George saw that he was not to be arrested he cried out condemning the Mohammedans, whereupon they beat him and arrested him. The cadi asked Aurelius why the two couples had fallen away from the Mohammedan rite, offering them enticements to return. Aurelius replied that for them eternal wealth and the faith of Christ were of more value than a cult which denied the divinity of Christ and the essence of the Holy Trinity, which rejected Baptism and insulted Christians. The cadi had them imprisoned for four days, after which

[40] *Memoriale,* II, x, 26, "eadem hora exivi ab eis, et causas, quibus praepediebar, in omni festinatione composui." "Francia" is used also by Eulogius in his letter to Wiliesindus, 6, and by Aimoin in his *Translatio,* 7.

[41] Franke, "Die freiwilligen Märtyrer," 110, says that the device of going publicly to a Christian church was decided on as a means of evading the ban against martyrdom issued by the council of 852, which he would date in the early part of the year.

they were taken to the forum and brought into the palace before "the consuls," where again an attempt was made to bring them back to Islam. George was told to go away since they, the magnates of the palace, had not heard him speak ill of the prophet Mohammed. George then cursed Mohammed as a disciple of Satan, a believer in the devil, a minister of Antichrist, a labyrinth of all vices, who was committing himself and his followers to hell. He added that the angel that appeared to Mohammed was really a devil. George's words, as reported by Eulogius, are of some interest in the light of Franke's suggestion that he may have brought to Spain material which Mozarab polemicists used against Islam.[42] Although George does not repeat the charges spoken by most of the confessors, as Eulogius reports their words (false prophet, magician, adulterer, and liar), he introduces no new charges against Mohammed. Eulogius mentions the report of the angel appearing to Mohammed in Book I of the *Memoriale*,[43] although in a way that suggests it might be an interpolation.

Following George's denunciation the magnates ordered them all executed. The five martyrs died on 27 July 852. The Christians stole their bodies at night[44] and buried them in churches and monasteries. George and Aurelius were buried in the monastery of Pinna Mellaris (*Pilemelaria*), Felix in the Basilica of St. Christopher across the river, Sabigotho in the Basilica of SS. Faustus, Januarius, and Martial, Liliosa in the Church of St. Genesius martyr. Because of a lacuna of a line and a half in the manuscript Morales could not determine where the heads of the martyrs had been buried.

There is evidence of a cult of these martyrs. Six years after their death, in 858, relics of them were brought from Córdoba to Paris. The account of this translation, written

---

[42] Franke, *op.cit.*, 58.

[43] *Memoriale*, I, 21.

[44] *Ibid.*, II, x, 34. Ms Paris BN Lat. 13760, "noctu Christiani furantes," seems better than Morales, "nostri Christiani furantes." Cf. also Aimoin's *Translatio*, 12, "Christiani . . . nocte venerunt."

by the French monk Aimoin, will be discussed immediately before the martyrdom of Eulogius. From Aimoin's account it is learned that the complete body of George and the body of Aurelius with the head of Sabigotho were buried in Pinna Mellaris.[45]

After the account of the martyrdoms of Aurelius, Felix, George, Sabigotho, and Liliosa, Eulogius tells of six men martyrs who came forth in pairs to denounce Mohammed and his religion. The first two were Christopher and Leovigildus. Christopher was a monk, born in Córdoba, who in his youth had studied under his kinsman Eulogius and then had entered the monastery of St. Martin in a place called Rojana in the mountains outside Córdoba. After he learned of the slaying of the preceding martyrs he went down into the city with determined step and did not fear to present himself before the cadi, where he preached the holy things of the Lord and condemned those believing the evils of Islam. The cadi ordered him bound and cast into prison. Leovigildus likewise was a monk, from Granada but staying then outside Córdoba in the mountains in the monastery of SS. Justus and Pastor in a place called Fraga, near the *viculus Leiulensis*, which was twenty-five miles from Córdoba. Before his martyrdom he came to Eulogius to ask his blessing and the help of his prayers, promising his own intercession in return after his death. Confirmed in his resolution and at peace, he left Eulogius and went before the cadi to give his testimony of faith. He was insulted and beaten and then cast into prison. When they were executed 20 August 852, Christopher begged Leovigildus to precede him because of his precedence in age. Their bodies were rescued by the Christians before they had been completely burned and were buried in the Basilica of St. Zoilus.[46]

Following them, Emila and Hieremias, two youths born

---

[45] Neither Eulogius nor Aimoin gives the resting place of the head of Aurelius.

[46] *Memoriale*, II, xi. Chaps. xi-xvi have been misnumbered as chaps. x-xv by Lorenzana and Ruiz. References here follow Morales and Migne (xi-xvi).

of noble citizens of Córdoba, were martyred. They had received their training in letters at the Basilica of St. Cyprian, the one of them a deacon and the other a layman. They made their denunciation of the Mohammedans in Arabic, and so bitter was it, says Eulogius, that the Arabs forgot the words of the previous martyrs and began to think not only of killing those who opposed them but of destroying the whole church. For they began to fear that their reign was at an end when even youths showed so great courage. After imprisonment the two youths were put to death. At the moment of the beheading the clear day was rent by a violent clap of thunder, hail fell, and the day was darkened. Their bodies were hung on the *eculeus* across the river on 15 September 852.[47]

Two more martyrs, Rogellius and Servius-Dei, came forth and made their professions while Emila and Hieremias were still in prison. Rogellius was born in Granada and came into Córdoba an old man, a monk, and a eunuch. Servius-Dei was a youth, also a eunuch, who had come as a pilgrim from the East across the seas. They made a pact with each other to remain constant and then entered the mosque (*fanum*), preaching the Gospel and condemning the "iniquitous sect," proclaiming the kingdom of heaven to be at hand for the faithful and the punishment of hell for the infidel. The Mohammedans raged at them, striking them and trying to kill them, for, says Eulogius, they considered it a great crime for others to enter their mosques. The cadi succeeded in keeping the people from killing them on the spot and cast them into prison, where they continued to preach to the end, saying that the death of "the tyrant"[48] was imminent. The "tyrants" and the consuls decreed that their hands and feet be cut off first for entering the mosque and then they were to be beheaded. The two rejoiced at the sentence. "Impatiently the fierce and bloodthirsty execu-

---

[47] *Memoriale,* II, xii. Hieremias may be added to Sanctius (II, iii) and Albar as an example of a layman educated at a basilica school.

[48] The "tyrant" is probably Abd al-Rahman II, but the word is used immediately following in the plural with another meaning.

tioner cries out, gnashes his teeth, threatens; those whom he sees have a greater love of going to death than he has of inflicting it he orders to hasten to their punishment. Who can describe the cruelty of that moment, O brothers most dear? Who can tell of the slaughter? Who can describe the racks? And who can narrate the admirable steadfastness of the saints? The pagans themselves were amazed at such a sight, and I am not sure but that they felt more indulgent to Christianity."[49] In turn the hands, legs, and heads of the two were cut off and their bodies were fixed to racks[50] across the river on 16 September 852.

Rogellius and Servius-Dei, the last martyrs to die in the reign of Abd al-Rahman II, are the last martyrs recorded in Book II of the *Memoriale*. Eulogius concludes Book II with three short chapters concerning: the intensification of the persecution after the eleven martyrdoms of July, August, and September; the resulting perturbation among the Christians and the ambiguous decision arrived at by a council of bishops in Córdoba; and the death of Abd al-Rahman II and the succession of Mohammed I. To the end of Book II he attaches a long prayer upon what he thought was the completion of his work. The first six chapters of Book III, also narrative, describe the measures against the Christians taken by Mohammed I. Together, these nine chapters account for events in Córdoba during the interlude of nine months between what the sources call the first and the later persecutions, when both sides hoped that the martyrdoms had come to an end.

As the martyrdoms continued in the late summer of 852, says Eulogius, the anger of the king increased. He consulted with his advisors ("the sages," "the philosophers," and "the consuls of his kingdom") for a way to put an end to the martyrdoms. Their decision was to imprison the Christians and do away with all obstacles to the execution of any Chris-

---

[49] *Memoriale*, II, xiii, 2.

[50] "Quorum cadavera, ut erant truncata, patibulis affigentibus, ultra fluvium crucibus ceterorum adsciscunt." This is the only use of "crux" by Eulogius for the structure on which the martyrs' bodies were hung.

tian who in the future should denounce the prophet Mohammed. The Christians learned of the decision and scattered into hiding, going about surreptitiously at night and in disguise, fearful at every movement, changing their dwelling places often, "fearing to die by the sword and about to die anyway by the law." Among these was Eulogius himself, who says that they did not believe themselves worthy of martyrdom, which was predestined only to certain ones from the beginning of the world.[51]

Some Christians, however, succumbed to the threats of the king and abjured their faith rather than flee. They joined the ranks of the Moslems and conspired against their erstwhile brethren. Others, both clergy and laity, who had sided with the martyrs at first, now changed their attitude and began to criticize the martyrs for "being unwilling to suffer with those weaker than they," for seeking to purchase their own peace of soul by martyrdom rather than consider the welfare of the persecuted Church. Such critics are rationalizing their own inconstancy, says Eulogius, and they should remember that in the hour of trial saints cannot be torn away from love of Christ by life, cruel perils, or death itself. Still other Christians had without success opposed and maligned the martyrs from the beginning. They now turned against him, says Eulogius, and accused him of instigating the movement. Such a one was an *exceptor* of the government then, "eminent in vices and riches," who attacked Eulogius during a council of bishops. "He decrees the saints be anathematized, he orders those meditating such things be cursed, he commands the elect be persecuted by the pen. Most unhappy of all, he fears that he himself will suffer a loss of honor. He not only set out to show no reverence to the saints, but even declared that their preaching among the people is wrong."[52] This *exceptor* may have been a Comes (Gómez) ibn Antonián known in Arabic chronicles and perhaps the Romanus Medicus to whom Albar wrote a letter and whom Samson mentions. He held his office be-

---

[51] *Memoriale*, II, xiv; cf. also *ibid.*, xvi, 1.
[52] *Ibid.*, xv, 2.

cause of his skill in Arabic, according to Eulogius, and he persecuted the confessors with the pen. From what Eulogius says of him the *exceptor* was an official of the chancery, probably the chancellor, rather than a tax-collector, as is frequently assumed.[53] He was later discharged from the ministry and the palace, where both the chancery and the treasury were located, but after he became a Moslem he was restored to his post. His presence at the council of bishops in 852 can be explained better as a secretary or chancellor than as a tax-collector. He may have been the official representative of the king and told the council what the king wished it to do. Inasmuch as the decisions of the council seem to have been enforced by threats of physical punishment, it would appear that vestiges of the relationship between the Visigothic state and the church in Spain may have continued in Córdoba under Moslem rule.[54]

The Christians, says Eulogius, moved about and hid to escape the relentless persecution of the Moslems. Bishop Saul was again imprisoned, and none of the Christian nobles would dare to enter the gates of the palace (where the governmental offices were located) in fear of imprisonment.[55] During this time Abd al-Rahman II went up to the highest roof of his palace to inspect his forts and, beholding the bodies of the martyrs across the river hanging on stakes, ordered them to be burned. These were the last words uttered by Abd al-Rahman, says Eulogius, for the Lord struck him dumb immediately. His attendants carried him to bed

[53] *Ibid.* and III, ii. Morales, *Memoriale*, II, ii, scholium i, regards the *exceptor* as a scribe; Flórez, ES, X, 264f., as a tax-collector. Most later historians follow Flórez; cf. supra, 29, n. 18. Fiebiger, "Exceptor," in Pauly-Wissowa, VI, ii, 1565f., describes the *exceptor* of the Roman empire as a stenographer, scribe, or secretary; cf. F. Krenkow, "Katib," EI, II, 819.

[54] Cf. *Indiculus*, 15; Ziegler, *Church and State in Visigothic Spain*, 32-43.

[55] *Memoriale*, II, xvi, 2; Saul was imprisoned also in November 851 at the time of Reccafred's attack on the clergy of Córdoba; cf. *Vita Eulogii*, 4. In June 853 he would flee arrest and a sentence of death following the martyrdom of Fandila, *Memoriale*, III, vii, 4.

and he died the same night, before the funeral pyre of the martyrs was extinguished. Arabic sources date the death of Abd al-Rahman II on 22 September 852.[56] The bodies which the king saw across the river were presumably those of the four martyrs who died on 15 and 16 September (whose ashes were later preserved by Christians and buried in sacred places), and perhaps too those of Christopher and Leovigildus, who died on 20 August (whose bodies were rescued by Christians before they were completely burned). The first-born of Abd al-Rahman, Mohammed, an enemy of the Church and persecutor of Christians, succeeded to the throne the day after his father's death.[57]

It was King Mohammed I apparently who summoned the metropolitans, of Seville and Mérida it would seem, to Córdoba, and the council of bishops of 852 probably met in Córdoba in the first months of his reign, when he received homage from the lords and magnates of his realm.[58] The council decided upon a course of dissimulation, letting the king and the people think that they had condemned the martyrdoms without really doing so. Eulogius devotes a paragraph to the council. "And although compelled by fear and the judgment of the metropolitans, who had been brought together by the king from divers provinces then for the same matter, we might have said something, that it may reach the ears of the tyrant himself and the people that

---

[56] Ibn Idhari, *Bayan*, II, 132 and 147.

[57] *Ibid.*, 152, and *Memoriale*, II, xvi, 2.

[58] Cf. Ibn Idhari, *Bayan*, II, 97, for oaths of fidelity given to Hischam I in 788; *ibid.*, 98, for oaths received by Soleyman from Toledans at the same time; *ibid.*, 125, for oaths al-Hakam had sworn to his two sons before he died; *ibid.*, 147, for oaths Abd al-Rahman II obtained from his brothers, family, viziers, and the people on his succession; and *ibid.*, 200, for an oath of fidelity Ibn Hafsun gave to Abd Allah. As a rule, Ibn Idhari says only that the emirs were "enthroned." Cf. Lévi-Provençal, *L'Espagne musulmane au Xème siècle* (Paris, 1932), 57f. Ibn Khaldun, *The Muqaddimah*, trans. F. Rosenthal, I, 380, says that when Almanzor tried to take the caliphate in addition to the executive power which he already held the Umaiyads and other Qurashites took the oath of allegiance to a cousin of Hisham II. Cf. Hefele, *Histoire des conciles*, trans. H. Leclercq, IV, i, 189f.

martyrdom was forbidden and no one was permitted from then on to seek to make a public contest of the profession of faith, still in a preceding episcopal decree the very words say, and from the document itself, which does not at all impugn the struggle of those who have died, it appears that future martyrs should be praised. But it was phrased allegorically so that only the prudent could notice. We, however, do not think that that decision of dissimulation was without blame, that did one thing but sounded different, and seemed as it were to restrain the people from the course of the martyrs. Nay more, unless there is some proper satisfaction, at least for the sake of the people, we maintain that it should in no wise be forgiven."[59]

This passage is of basic importance in the study of the martyrdoms. The metropolitans, who, according to Eulogius, were responsible for the decision of dissimulation in the first place, may be those who, in a later letter,[60] are said to have sanctioned "dispensations" defended by an anonymous bishop. One of the metropolitans who attended the council in Córdoba was probably Reccafred of Seville, who may be the author of the anonymous letter. The other metropolitan was probably Ariulfus of Mérida. The third metropolitan in Moslem Spain, Wistremirus of Toledo, the primate of all Spain, to whom the anonymous letter seems to be ad-

---

[59] *Memoriale*, II, xv, 2; Eulogius' Latin is probably as difficult to understand as that of the decision he speaks of. "Et quamquam metu compulsi seu metropolitanorum iudicio, qui ob eamdem causam tunc e diversis provinciis a rege fuerant adunati, aliquid commentaremur, quod ipsius tyranni ac populorum serperet aures inhibitum esse martyrium nec licere cuiquam deinceps ad palaestram professionis discurrere, praemisso pontificali decreto ipsae litterae nuntiarunt eademque scheda, minime decedentium agonem impugnans, quod futuros laudabiliter extolleret milites percipitur, verumtamen allegorice edita nisi a prudentibus adverti non poterat. Non tamen inculpabile illud fuisse putamus simulationis consultum, quod aliud gestans et aliud sonans, quasi a discursu martyriali plebem compescere videbatur. Quinimmo nisi legitima satisfactione, saltem pro plebe, nullatenus remittendum esse confitemur." The punctuation in the text given here varies slightly from that in *SS PP Toletanorum*, II, 485.

[60] Albar correspondence, Letter X, 2 and 5.

dressed, probably did not attend the council. Eulogius includes himself among those who let it be understood that martyrdom was forbidden, attesting to the role of priests in the council. Albar may have been one of those who misunderstood what was actually done. In the *Indiculus* he blames the "fraternal college" of bishops, abbots, priests, nobles, and magnates for acting against the confessors and martyrs,[61] indicating perhaps that laymen other than the *exceptor* attended the council. Although Eulogius dissociates the "something which might have been said" from the episcopal decree issued before it, he seems to include them both under the decision of dissimulation, which did one thing (the decree) and "said" something else.

Some who have studied the martydoms date the council at the beginning of 852 rather than at the end of that year. Their basis for doing so are statements by Eulogius that the *exceptor* lost his office after the twelfth month (post biseno mense), when he had decreed that the saints should be anathematized at the council, and a few months after Mohammed I began to reign.[62] Understanding "post biseno mense" as "a year," one would arrive at a date in late 851 or preferably early 852, a year before January of 853, which was a few months after Mohammed I came to the throne on 23 September 852. But "bisenus mensis" can be a synonym for December (the twelfth month), and there is no need to account for a year's lapse. There are other reasons for dating the council in December 852, one of which is that Eulogius treats of it in the interval between the martyrs in the reign of Abd al-Rahman II and those in the reign of Mohammed I. The council of 852 will be considered again later, in connection with the first part of the *Indiculus* and the letter of the anonymous bishop, both of which may refer to the council. Before these works are taken up, however, the remaining martyrdoms will be discussed.

Although the persecution continued to threaten under the new emir of Córdoba and although Eulogius did not approve

---

[61] *Indiculus,* 14.
[62] *Memoriale,* III, ii.

of the decision of the council, he showed his faith in the modus vivendi by bringing the *Memoriale* to what he believed was its conclusion. The only *explicit* found in the work occurs at the end of Book II and is followed by a long prayer. In the prayer Eulogius states that he has done the best he could despite his faults and that the peace of the Church, the glory of the martyrs, his own fate, and the fate of his work are in the hands of God.

CHAPTER XI

THE MARTYRS UNDER MOHAMMED I

The course of evasion adopted by the council failed to halt the persecution or to settle the dispute among the Christians about the martyrs. Eulogius concluded Book II of the *Memoriale* in early 853, but as the persecution continued and new martyrs came forth he resumed the work sometime after June 853. The first part of the *Indiculus*, which appears to have been written in 853, testifies that the dispute about the martyrdoms also continued.

The preface to Book III is fairly long. Eulogius, who never seems to tire of writing prefatory material, notes that his work may seem to be going on endlessly. He protests that he is neither trying to squeeze every drop out of his subject, which is indeed more like a flood, nor is he taking every opportunity to interrupt it. It is just that the persecution keeps going on after he believes it to have come to an end. He continues from the ascent of Mohammed I to the throne and the expulsion of Christians from the palace and government.

After expelling the Christians from the government King Mohammed levied a tax of tribute on Christians. He took away the royal awards from many who had been living on military pensions for a long time. He turned over the administration of the city of Córdoba to officials who were as eager as he for the destruction of the Christians. With these officials he sought to prevent attacks against the Moslem prophet and to force Christians into Islam. Many Christians, says Eulogius, did apostatize in the course of such a persecution.[1] Eulogius, Albar, and Samson all seem to imply that the Moslems as a whole, especially under Abd al-Rahman, were not anti-Christian and that the provocation of the martyrs was the work of a group of Moslem zealots,

[1] *Memoriale*, III, i.

251

apparently Malekite and associated with Mohammed I. The sources indicate too that a good number of Christians were amenable to a life under Moslem rule, adopting many Moslem ways and regarding Islam as not very different from Christianity.

Some Christians, Eulogius points out, joined the ranks of the Moslems voluntarily. Such a one was the *exceptor* spoken of in Book II. "After the twelfth month" (December), when he had condemned Eulogius and the martyrs before the council of bishops he too lost his office and was expelled from the palace, having succeeded in keeping his post for several months under Mohammed because of his skill in Arabic. He thereupon "spurned the faith of the Holy Trinity," became a Moslem, and was restored to his office, where he became the "gyves and hook" for binding some Christians and a scandalous example of apostasy for others. He was expelled from the churches of the Christians. Even when he was a Christian, says Eulogius, he had been negligent in the practice of his faith.[2]

Although King Mohammed persecuted Christians everywhere with much energy, he failed to destroy the Church in his realm. Seeing this, he ordered the destruction of churches which had been recently constructed and any additions which had been made to the basilicas during the years of Arab rule. His agents even pulled down roofs of churches which had been built more than three hundred years earlier "in the time of peace."[3] The recent construction of churches in Córdoba would seem to contradict the thesis that the number of Christians there was diminishing.

Wars of rebellion began to break out against him and Mohammed's armies were beaten and put to flight. He saw the realm which he had received from his father Abd al-Rahman begin to disintegrate under his rule. In the face of these difficulties he put off the destruction of the Christians which he was planning and worked instead intermittently at the ruin of their churches. He permitted no Christians to remain with him unless they apostatized. Why then,

[2] *Ibid.*, ii.   [3] *Ibid.*, iii.

if he were free to reign as he pleases, asks Eulogius, does he not expel the Jews also from around him and rule over his own folk only, whom he is leading to hell? And then the unity of the damnable cult will not be split by another religion.[4] It grieved Mohammed sorely to see many leave Islam for Christianity[5] and die for Christ, says Eulogius, while others, suffering in their hearts, were secretly confessing Christ the King. The last two statements are of much interest, the one implying that Mohammed had the right to rule only over those who were represented in his government and the other indicating that the conversion of Moslems, or the return of apostate Christians, to Christianity was a matter of concern to the king.

As a result of his policies Mohammed became hateful to everyone, even his own family and his concubines. "He reduces the pay of the soldiers, forces offerings from the tribunes, and diminishes the monthly course of prizes."[6] When the provinces reacted against him by not paying the full amount of their taxes, he farmed out an intolerable tax burden on the Christians of Córdoba to certain of their number who seized the opportunity to profit at the expense of their brethren. Eulogius describes these Christians in a series of bitter epithets. "Always envious, always iniquitous, everywhere malicious, angry with each other, allied in the overthrowing of others, unfaithful in alliances, prone to conspiracies, cunning in circumvention, most adroit in devising wickedness; disunited among themselves, united in destroying others, eager to deceive, slow to show mercy; pompous in their carriage, proud in their statements, untrustworthy in their promises; giving with avarice, being generous with parsimony, receiving with greed; promising that which

---

[4] *Ibid.*, iv, "Quinimmo, ut iam alibi praemissum est (II, xvi, 2), si commodam regnandi haberet licentiam, Iudaeos etiam a se repelli compelleret, quo solius gentis suae comitatu vallatus, his praeesse solummodo mereretur, cum quibus inextricabilia aeterni barathri lueret tormenta, nec alterius diversitate religionis unitas damnabilis culturae scinderetur."

[5] *Ibid.*, "plures admodum recedentes et pietati adhaerentes."

[6] Arab chroniclers too note the stinginess and avarice of Mohammed I.

they cannot give, giving that which is not theirs to dispose of, they never sleep without having done evil, and they rise in haste to do evil. They are glad when they have done wicked deeds and they rejoice in the greatest evils."[7] Like Judas, they crucify Christ in His members for money, forcing Christians whom they ought to have protected to deny Christ. With regard to the taxes refused by the provinces Eulogius makes a statement of political significance. "If he has been brought to the scepter by the fault of the crowd (culpa vulgi), God willing, nevertheless, cities and tribes, induced by the wickedness of his deserts to retaliate with recalcitrance, do not let him have the full amount of the tribute of the provinces."[8]

Meanwhile the king began to boast of what he would do to the Christians once he was free to attack them. Several of the nobles too began to mock the Christians, asking them where their courage had gone. Where are your martyrs, they asked, have they lost their taste for battle?[9]

Even as the king and the nobles were mocking the Christians for the disappearance of their martyrs and heroes, five martyrs came forth within three days, 13, 14, and 15 June 853. Book III continues from this point and accounts for all seventeen martyrs between 13 June 853 and 19 July 856, which is the last date recorded in the *Memoriale*.

The first martyr of Book III is the priest Fandila, who receives a moderately long account. He was a young priest from Guadix who came to Córdoba to study. After his studies he became a monk and joined the monastery of Tabanos, living there under the rule of the abbot Martin. Against his will he was prevailed upon by his abbot to minister as priest for the monks of the monastery of the Holy Savior, not far from Córdoba at the foot of *Pinna Mellaria*. The fame of his holy life became widespread. One day he appeared before the cadi to preach the Gospel and condemn Mohammed, say-

[7] *Memoriale*, III, v; cf. *Indiculus*, end of 31, where Albar denounces the Moslems in a similar passage.

[8] *Memoriale*, III, v.

[9] *Ibid.*, vi.

ing that the Moslems would all be damned if they did not come to their senses and accept the faith. He was bound and cast into prison with thieves, and the cadi reported the case to the king immediately. "He was incensed with a great and furious fire, and numbed with horror he dazedly wonders what is that conquering audacity which does not fear a king of such great glory, and in such sublime vanity and pride was resisting a chief, as he thought himself, excellent above all with such bold lack of respect." In his fury the king commanded that the bishop be seized, but he was saved by flight. Besides decreeing immediate punishment for the bishop, Mohammed ordered that all Christians be slain in a general sentence and their women be publicly sold into slavery and dispersed, unless they give up Christianity and become Mohammedans. "And if this edict had not been stopped by the advice of his subordinates, who asserted that, since none of the wise or the cultured, none of the leaders of the Christians had perpetrated a deed of this kind, he should not kill everyone, for no personal leader (personalis dux) had led them to battle, then I believe that he would have eradicated our Christianity completely by now, partly by the sword and partly by forswearing."[10] Fandila was beheaded by royal decree and hung up across the river. His martyrdom is the only one in the *Memoriale* which is undated, but from the next chapter the date can be determined as 13 June 853. Bishop Saul, who fled at this time, was evidently under sentence of death. It may be he who is called *Biothenatus* (doomed to death) in the *Indiculus*.[11] It is not known how long he stayed in hiding.

The next chapter, about Anastasius, Felix, and Digna, illustrates how Eulogius accords women martyrs longer treatment than men in the latter books of the *Memoriale*. It may be quoted here at length.

The next day the priest Anastasius followed him [Fandila]. From his earliest days he had been instructed in disciplines and letters at the Basilica

---

[10] *Ibid.*, vii, 4.   [11] *Indiculus*, 19.

of St. Acisclus of Córdoba, where he had remained up to the prime of his life feeding the hungry in the office of deacon. Afterwards he lived a monastic life, which had long delighted him in spite of his ministry, among old men, and was finally made a priest. Going to the palace with quick step, he stood before the consuls, and, striking the enemy of the faith with the sting of true assertions, he was immediately laid low with the sword and hung up.

With him the monk Felix who came from the town of Alcalá, of the tribe of Gaetulus,[12] who went into the Asturias on a certain occasion, where he learned the Catholic faith and the monastic religion, was on the same day and for the same profession slain and strung up.

And when that day, fulfilling the maximum extent of its course, had hardly come to the ninth hour, a certain young virgin, Digna in name and in merit, from the convent of venerable Elizabeth, an account of whom was given in Book II,[13] went to her crown, the Lord inspiring and comforting her. For a little before her martyrdom she saw a maid stand before her in a dream, arrayed in the garb and beauty of an angel and holding roses and lilies in her hand. When she inquired about her name and the reason of her coming, she was answered, "I am Agatha, who once suffered dire torments because of Christ, and now I have come to give you a part of this crimson gift. Accept the gift willingly and act bravely in the Lord. For after you I shall give the remains of the roses and lilies which I have in my hands to travellers in this place." Then the sacred virgin, radiant with such a vision and gift, took a rose from the hand of the one speaking, who was caught up in heavenly breezes and lifted up from the eyes of the beholder.

But this maid in her deep humility and obedi-

---

[12] Dessau, "Gaetuli," in Pauly-Wissowa, VII, i, 464f., describes the *Gaetuli* as nomads in northwest Africa south of Mauretania and Numidia, the ancestors of the modern Tuaregs, a Berber tribe.

[13] *Memoriale*, II, ii; cf. also *ibid.*, III, x, 4-9. The monastery of Tabanos evidently was not destroyed and the sisters did not move to the premises of the Basilica of St. Cyprian in Córdoba until after the martyrdom of Digna.

ence regarded herself as the least among her sister virgins, and she was a servant of incomparable accomplishments. Still she never suffered herself to be called Digna, but would say with tears, "Do not call me Digna, but rather Indigna, for I ought to be called by a name that befits my merit." And from the day of the revelation to her she was filled with the love of martyrdom and she began to mull over in her mind in secret very often by what reasons she could aspire to it. Enlightened by the martyrdom of these [Anastasius and Felix], she became much happier, and she could gain her crown by walking more confidently in their footsteps. And so when she learned that the blessed martyrs were hung up, she went out through the opened gates of the monastery and quickly sought the cadi. In a brave assertion she told him why he had killed her brothers, the heralds of justice. "Is it not because," she said, "we are worshippers of God and in our faith we worship the Holy Trinity, the Father, the Son, and the Holy Ghost, confessing one true God, and we not only deny all that disagrees with this belief, but indeed hate, curse, and confound it? Is that not why we are killed?"

When the maid spoke this and things similar from her holy and immaculate mouth, the cadi did not delay but committed her to the lictors for beheading. And they soon put the sword to her delicate neck. Immediately her stricken body fell to the ground, and it is hung up on the *eculeus* upside down and added to the others across the river. In this order then these three were called, Anastasius the priest, Felix the monk, and the holy virgin Digna. They were killed on the same day separately, 14 June 853.[14]

The next chapter on Benildis is very brief and gives an

---

[14] *Memoriale*, III, viii; much of this account appears almost verbatim in Lucius Marineus' *Opus de rebus Hispaniae* ... (Alcalá, 1533) more than forty years before Morales' edition of Eulogius' works. Morales, *Corónica general*, Bk. XIV, xx (Cano ed. VII, 335), notes that these three martyrs were known in martyrologies and venerated in some churches. Most of what Eulogius wrote about them, Morales says, had been copied in the martyrologies.

idea of what the succinct notices are like. "Then Benildis, a woman already advanced in age and, as they say, not mildly fearing God, followed them. For the profession of the others she died 15 June 853. After some days their bodies were cremated in a giant fire and thrown into the depths of the river and scattered."[15]

Of the remaining twelve martyrs only the virgins Columba, Pomposa, and Aurea (the last martyr) are dealt with at length, more than half of Book III being devoted to them. Book III, chapter x, begins with a prefatory paragraph explaining that, contrary to what had been expected, more martyrdoms have occurred. Eulogius' statement of his intention to record the passion of every martyr testifies that up to this point at least he has accounted for all of them. He then tells the story of Columba.

Columba, born in Córdoba, was the sister of Martin and Elizabeth, the abbot and abbess of the double monastery of Tabanos. When she had been quite young she had visited Elizabeth, who was then, with her husband Jeremias, living a religious life dedicated to Christ in the world. Years later the couple went to the monastery and Jeremias became a martyr.[16] During the course of her visits to Elizabeth, Columba grew attached to the spiritual life, but her mother objected and remonstrated with Elizabeth for seeking to persuade Columba to leave the world after her example. An attempt by the mother to secure a marriage for Columba was without success. After her mother's death Columba joined Elizabeth in paying for the construction of the monastery of Tabanos, where she later went to live. These actions show that Christian women of Córdoba could own, bequeath, and inherit property.

Eulogius praises at length the virtuous life of Columba in the monastery of Tabanos. The details of her virtue are of interest because they seem to exemplify the monastic life in Córdoba. One may compare Eulogius' praises of Columba here with the praises he bestows on the monks of Navarre

---

[15] *Memoriale*, III, ix.
[16] Cf. *ibid.*, II, ii and iv.

in his letter to Wiliesindus.[17] Columba lived under the rule of Martin and Elizabeth. She studied Holy Scripture, seeking the meaning of difficult passages. Eulogius praises her for her way of life, her humility, chastity, charity, her devotion to prayer, her obedience, mercy, tolerance, her skill in preaching, and her willingness to instruct. Frequently she prayed with weeping. She overcame temptations of depression, of disgust, of the flesh, of boredom, and of divers fancies. She never criticized other sinners, never judged the acts of others, never despaired of the salvation of others, never despised anyone no matter how ill-famed. She was never moved by anger without cause except to upbraid negligent children or fellow sisters with a glance. She never slandered anyone, never indulged in or listened to idle chatter or silly stories. Christ was always in her mind and on her lips. She sought to converse only with those who were virtuous and ascetic. Columba asked her sisters to let her live in a cell within the cloister apart from the bustle of the *coenobium.* They agreed, anxious to encourage Columba in her sanctity. "For holy works are a common enterprise," says Eulogius. In her cell Columba meditated and prayed, at times coming out to instruct her sisters in the community. She prayed prostrate in her cell for three or four hours at once, at times as long as half a day, and her tears wet the ground beneath the mat on which she lay. Later Eulogius adds that Columba fasted and kept vigils.[18]

Eulogius describes the double monastery of Tabanos as divided by a high wall with the nuns living in the utmost seclusion in one part. Only the abbess Elizabeth in case of necessity would communicate with the outside world through a window.[19] When the king decreed the destruction of recently constructed churches,[20] the women from this monastery moved to the premises of the Basilica of St. Cyprian in Córdoba and continued their devout way of life.

---

[17] Cf. Ruiz, *Obras completas de San Eulogio,* xviii-xxiv.
[18] *Memoriale,* III, x, 4-8 and 10.
[19] *Ibid.,* 6.
[20] *Ibid.,* iii.

One day Columba left the basilica and went to the home of the cadi to confess her faith and denounce the Mohammedan religion. The cadi had her taken to the palace, where she repeated her assertions before a "council of satraps." When "the consuls" saw that they could not sway her from her purpose, they ordered her slain immediately in the forum before the gates of the palace. After her execution on 17 September 853 her body was wrapped in cloth and thrown into the river and not left neglected before the gates of the palace or hung up on the *eculeus*, as had been the case with the other martyrs' bodies. Five days later, says Eulogius, monks recovered her body intact and brought it to "us" for burial in the Basilica of St. Eulalia in Fragellas, a town outside Córdoba.[21] Eulogius concludes his account of Columba with the statement, "This (*hoc*) has been told to us about her on faith." Since Eulogius uses *"hoc"* instead of *"haec,"* it would seem that he has in mind the notice of Columba's burial rather than the account of her passion. But his indication that he was in Fragellas at the time her relics were buried would mean the contrary. It is possible that Eulogius learned of Columba's martyrdom while he was in Fragellas, perhaps in hiding with Bishop Saul. At the end of Columba's passion Eulogius addresses a prayer to her asking her to save him from the snares and troubles of the world and to secure heaven for him after death. A long passage in this chapter, devoted to criticism of those who criticize others unjustly, appears to have a personal interest for Eulogius.[22]

The next chapter deals with the virgin martyr Pomposa. After Pomposa heard of the martyrdom of Columba, she came down from the monastery of the Holy Savior at *Pinna Mellaria*, which her parents had built and where she had been dwelling with them and other relatives in piety and sanctity. Eulogius learned many things about her piety from Felix, the abbot of the monastery. Unlike Tabanos, *Pinna Mellaria* was not destroyed by Mohammed's edict. Five years later, in 858, Samson, who wrote the *Apologeti-*

[21] *Ibid.*, x, 12.   [22] *Ibid.*, 5.

cus in 864, became abbot of the monastery.[23] Pomposa, one of the youngest of those in the monastery, yearned to go to martyrdom but was prevented by certain safeguards used in the monastery because of the persecution. One night the latch on the monastery gate was left ajar, however, and she slipped out of the walls and through the night to Córdoba. Early in the morning she appeared before the cadi and affirmed her faith, denouncing the prophet Mohammed. The cadi ordered her executed immediately before the gates of the palace and her body thrown into the river on 19 September 853. Certain "mercenaries" then buried it in a ditch, from which monks recovered it twenty days later. Pomposa was buried in the Basilica of St. Eulalia at the feet of Columba.[24]

At some time during this same year (853) Albar seems to have composed the first part of the *Indiculus,* a vehement attack against the opponents of the martyrs. In the work he censures Christians of all ranks for opposing the martyrdoms during and after the council of 852.

The next five chapters deal briefly with nine martyrs: three priests, four monks, one layman, and one whose state of life is not indicated. The priest Abundius came from the town of Analellos outside Córdoba. Finding himself trapped by plan of the Mohammedans, he professed his faith and denounced the prophet Mohammed before the cadi. He was slain on 11 July 854, ten months after Pomposa, and his body was left for animals to devour.[25] Amator had come to Córdoba from Martos with his father and brothers to study. On 30 April 855 he was slain with the monk Peter and Louis, both born of citizens of Córdoba and the latter a kinsman of Eulogius and the brother of the martyr Paul. Their bodies were thrown into the river. The body of Amator was not recovered, but the body of Peter was buried in the monastery of *Pinna Mellaria* and that of Louis was buried in the town of Palma in the province of *Italica,* watered by the river *Singilium.*[26] Also slain in 855 was Witesindus, an old

---

23 Aimoin's *Translatio,* 9.
24 *Memoriale,* III, xi.

25 *Ibid.,* xii.
26 *Ibid.,* xiii.

man from Cabra, who had lapsed from Christianity into Mohammedanism but returned to his faith. Eulogius gives neither the day or the month of his martyrdom.[27] The priest Helias was an old man from Lusitania. Together with the monks Paul and Isidore he was martyred on 17 April 856, and their bodies were thrown into the river.[28]

Argemirus, a "confessor," was an elderly nobleman and a monk, with relatives in Cabra. He had once been appointed *Censor* of Córdoba by the king. After he retired from the administration of justice, he withdrew to a monastery. Some of the Moslems (*ethnici*) accused him before the cadi of derision of the prophet Mohammed and profession of the divinity of Christ. Argemirus admitted their charges. After several days in prison he was again brought before the cadi, who unsuccessfully attempted to entice him into Islam. Argemirus was hung up on the *eculeus* still alive and slain by the sword on 28 June 856. After many days the cadi ordered his body taken down, and a certain religious took it to the Basilica of St. Acisclus where it was buried by priests near the body of Perfectus. What Eulogius says of Argemirus is of some interest. He is one of seven martyrs whom Eulogius calls noble: Isaac, Flora, Emila, Hieremias, Columba, Argemirus, and Aurea. It seems that the office of *censor* which he held was a unique office in Córdoba[29] and that he was expected to approve of Moslem religious doctrine after having held the office. Eulogius calls the Moslem cadi *censor*, but his more usual term for the cadi is *iudex*. A number of modern historians think that the *censor* presided over the administration of justice for the Mozarab community only, but there is reason to think that the judiciary of the Mozarabs was more complicated. There is also reason to believe that Moslem and Christian judges presided together over certain matters pertaining to both peoples. Unfortunately, too little is known of the juridicial system of

[27] *Ibid.*, xiv.
[28] *Ibid.*, xv.
[29] *Ibid.*, xvi, "Cordubae Patriciae Censor a rege praefectus extiterat." Cf. index, "Mozarab officials."

Córdoba at this time to determine what the specific nature of Argemirus' authority was.

The *Memoriale* concludes with the rather long account of the virgin martyr Aurea. She was the sister of Adulphus and John, who had been martyred soon after Abd al-Rahman II came to the throne in 822. Esperaindeo wrote the Acts of these two martyrs, but his work has been lost.[30] Aurea lived with her mother Artemia in the monastery of Cuteclara, where for more than thirty years after the death of her brothers she practiced her religion. Since she was born of Arab nobility, no one would attack her faith. But some of her relatives came from Seville to investigate rumors they had heard of her religion, and when they saw that she was not only a Christian but a religious they reported her to the cadi, who was related to her. He entreated her to return to Islam or die after great torment. Aurea acceded to his demands, and Eulogius states that he does not presume to decide why she did this. Perhaps, he says, it was to take care of some personal matter, or out of fear of death. When she was released by the cadi she returned to her home and continued to practice her Christian faith in the Christian community as before, regretting her lapse before the cadi and making amends with compunction and penances. Ordinarily an apostate would have been excommunicated. Perhaps Eulogius glosses over an excommunication of Aurea and devotes himself instead to a rather long exculpation of her.[31] Perhaps he seeks to explain why she was not excommunicated. Her case seems to illustrate the policy of "dissimulation" which both he and Albar decried.

The devil, says Eulogius, was very much irritated at Aurea for breaking her word to him and set about to persecute her anew. The pagans noticed that she was continuing in the practice of her faith and again brought her before the cadi, who threatened her for breaking her promise. Aurea replied that never had she been separated from Christ or His religion, even though her tongue had lapsed. She

[30] Cf. index, "Adulphus and John."
[31] *Memoriale*, III, xvii, 3-4.

was thrown into prison and her case was made known to the king. By his decree she was executed the following day, 19 July 856. Her body was hung on the rack with that of a murderer executed several days before and then thrown into the river along with the bodies of thieves executed with her. It was not recovered. With this account Book III of the *Memoriale* and the work itself come to a rather abrupt end.

This third book of the *Memoriale* spans a period of three years. During twenty months of this period, for ten months before and after July 854, only one martyrdom is recorded, but the *Indiculus* testifies that during these months the persecution and the dispute about the martyrdoms continued. Although one might argue that the decline in the number of martyrdoms indicates a decline in enthusiasm for the martyrs on the part of the Christians, it may be pointed out that Albar in the *Indiculus* argues that, were the Christians to join ranks behind the martyrs, the persecution would abate.[32]

The burial place is given for only five of the martyrs of Book III: two in the town of Fragellas, one in the monastery of *Pinna Mellaria*, one in the town of Palma, and one in Córdoba. Some of the bodies were not found, but Eulogius may not have known what became of others. He may have been in Fragellas, where Columba and Pomposa were buried, in September 853 with Bishop Saul, who may have been there after his flight in June 853. No bishop seems to have attended the burial of Argemirus in the Basilica of St. Acisclus in Córdoba in June 856, Eulogius saying only that priests were there. In 857 a bishop, presumably Saul, was in the town of Tertios for the burial of the martyr Rudericus.[33] In 858 Saul presided over the translation of relics from the monastery of *Pinna Mellaria* and was accessible to at least certain ones of his flock.[34] But he may have been in hiding from the Moslem government all this time. Neither the length of Saul's hiding nor his place of refuge is

[32] *Indiculus,* 14 and 18.
[33] *Apol. mart.,* 34.
[34] *Translatio,* 10-11.

known with any certainty. It is possible that he continued in hiding for the rest of his life. Eulogius' account for these years is rather sparse, so much so that one may wonder how much of the time he was in Córdoba and whether he recorded all the martyrdoms for the period. There are no indications elsewhere, however, that he was absent from Córdoba or that he omitted any of the martyrdoms.

CHAPTER XII

THE *INDICULUS LUMINOSUS*

The major work of Albar is the *Indiculus luminosus*.[1] Apart from the works of Eulogius, it offers more information about the persecution than does any other work from ninth-century Córdoba. The *Indiculus* is found in the Albar codex with almost all of Albar's other works but with no indication of authorship. Its title is given inconspicuously at the end of the preface in a sentence which begins with a small illuminated capital. There is no reason to think that a more elaborate title mentioning the author is missing from the codex, because the *Indiculus* begins on the recto side of the sixth folio of an eight-folio gathering, immediately after Albar's last letter to Bodo. The author's name was omitted probably to prevent the Moslems from discovering who he was, and the title was concealed in hope that the work would not be noticed in a cursory examination of the codex. It is possible too that Albar in his later years was not so proud of the treatise, which attacks important people in the Mozarab community. That Albar is the author seems rather likely, judging from internal evidence.

The stand taken by the author in a matter of ecclesiastical importance would seem to exclude a layman as author. The word *Indiculus* itself denotes an authoritative tract of official character.[2] In the first words of the treatise the author, as

---

[1] The unique ms for the *Indiculus* is the Albar codex of the cathedral of Córdoba, folios 122 to 164v; Nicolas Antonio notes (ms Madrid BN 7365, 142v) that a ms of Barcelona contained a fragment of the *Indiculus*. The edition of Flórez, ES, XI, 219-275, is reprinted in PL 121, 513-556. The footnotes in this chapter refer to paragraph and (page number of ES, XI). Variations of Flórez' edition from the ms and the identification of a number of quotations by Albar are given in Appendix IV.

[2] A. Giry, *Manuel de diplomatique* (Paris, 1894), 713; DuCange, *Glossarium;* and TLL.

one of the learned (*peritissimi*) Catholics of the Church, feels that he must rise up against the enemies of the Lord with spiritual vigor and exterminate error with the sword of the Gospel. He has fulfilled this service (in writing the work) out of zeal for God and religion. On the other hand, it was not unusual for Albar, layman though he was, to treat of ecclesiastical matters, and several passages in the *Indiculus* seem to point to a layman as author. In the prayer which serves as a preface to the work the author asks that he not be condemned as rash and iniquitous or as a usurper. He beseeches the Lord for His help, referring to himself as one "who walks daily through ways devious and broken, vain and unstable, pompous and stupid, shameful and arrogant, frivolous and pretentious, serving the works of evil, but speaking of those things which I believe to be acceptable to Thee."[3] Such humility seems exaggerated, for Albar at least, and the statement may be a partly ironical reference to an accusation in a letter by an anonymous bishop which Albar seems to have interpreted as directed against himself.[4] The words seem to describe the lay world better than the ecclesiastical. "Purify, O Lord, my tongue infected with worldly filth," Albar also says, and later adds, "We have become, O fellows (if you deserve the title) of our faith, dumb dogs, unable to bark."[5] Albar's complaint at the end of the *Indiculus* against the laity for their ignorance of Holy Scripture and the Fathers[6] also seems a layman's criticism of the laity rather than criticism by an ecclesiastic. Another passage which points to Albar as the author appears near the end of the first part of the *Indiculus*. I am not so stupid, says the author, as to expect glory from a work which unfortunately displeases powerful men. Neither in the discipline of liberal arts nor in the study of religious matters (cultus proprius) am I ignorant, he states. And I know my own ignorance, he adds. I can only

---

[3] *Indiculus*, preface (220).
[4] Cf. Appendix III, 10.
[5] *Indiculus*, preface (220) and 10 (235).
[6] *Ibid.*, 35 (274).

impart to others what I have learned from human teachers myself. My crudeness of style, he says with some irony it would seem, should have caused me to keep silent and not come into conflict with the learned (*peritissimi*) and those of outstanding eloquence.[7] Taken together with Albar's opening words associating the author with the *peritissimi*, who appear to have been a recognized group, this passage shows that this learned group was itself divided about the course of action to be followed with regard to the martyrs. As far as the literary style of the *Indiculus* goes, the argumentativeness and vehemence are characteristic of Albar. Elsewhere Albar calls Eulogius' *Documentum martyriale* a *luminosum documentum*, he calls Eulogius *luminosus*, and he speaks of the *luminosa vestigia* of Eulogius.[8]

The matter of address is probably more difficult to resolve than that of the authorship of the *Indiculus*. F. R. Franke says that the work is addressed to the clergy, citing a passage in which Albar addresses "renowned preachers and exemplary elect of the flock, good and solicitous pastors."[9] In another passage, however, Albar addresses a "fraternal college" and enumerates as the "pillars the Church" pastors, doctors, bishops, abbots, priests, nobles, and magnates,[10] evidently including laymen. Moreover, the continued use of the second person singular through one paragraph[11] would seem to indicate that this paragraph is addressed to a particular person. Several references to a "someone" (*aliquis*)[12] may also have been obliquely intended for a particular person. The person addressed in the second person singular and the "someone" referred to appear to be Reccafred, the metropolitan of Seville, or perhaps Bishop Saul of Córdoba. Albar's remarks about this person in these passages and elsewhere in the *Indiculus* are so abusive, however, that it is unlikely that they were spoken in the presence of that

---

[7] *Ibid.*, 20 (246).
[8] Albar's letter to Eulogius, *Luminosum vestri; Vita Eulogii*, 8 and 9.
[9] Franke, "Die freiwilligen Märtyrer," 117, and *Indiculus*, 9 (233).
[10] *Indiculus*, 14 (239f.).
[11] *Indiculus*, 13 (238f.).
[12] *Ibid.*, 2 (228), 7 (230), 15 (240) twice, 16 (241), and 20 (246).

person, who, according to Albar, at that time still exercised authority over the Christians of Córdoba.

On the other hand, the *Indiculus*, especially the first part, like Book I of the *Memoriale*, has signs that it was delivered orally before a group of people. In the *Vita Eulogii* Albar mentions that he attended what seems to have been an assembly which included the metropolitan of Seville, the bishop of Córdoba, Eulogius, and other clerics where a public reading took place.[13] Not only the treatises of Eulogius and Albar, but those of Leovigildus and Samson may have been delivered before such a forum. A number of transitions in the *Indiculus* indicate that, if the work was not intended as a speech, it was intended to have a colloquial style.[14] There is so much confusion in the work, in particular as regards the address, that it seems to contain insertions from previous writings or addresses by Albar. Inconsistent as the address is, most of the work is directed to an important group of Christians, most of whom were clerics.

The second part of the *Indiculus* was evidently intended for the same general audience as was the first part, but Albar's presentation, particularly in the exposition of the prophet Mohammed as a type of Antichrist, is more academic and impersonal than in the first part of the work. In fact, it seems at times in the second part as if Albar were addressing an audience from which not even Moslems were excluded. An academic exposition such as that in the second part of the work does not lend itself to oral delivery, however, and one would expect Albar in writing it to address himself to a larger more general audience.

In the second part of the *Indiculus* Albar, by way of illustration, dates a passage in A.D. 854 and A.H. 240[15] (in 854 after 1 June). The date applies only to the passage in which it occurs and probably to the second part of the *Indiculus*. The first part of the work seems to have been com-

---

[13] *Vita Eulogii*, 7.

[14] Cf. the beginnings or endings of paragraphs 5, 8, 9, 11, 17, 18, 20, 21, and 25.

[15] *Indiculus*, 21 (250).

pleted as much as a year earlier, not long after a council held in December of 852 it would seem, perhaps shortly after the letter of the anonymous bishop, to whom Albar seems to reply in a number of passages in the *Indiculus*.[16] Eulogius, writing after April of 853, introduces into the *Memoriale* the information that before 27 July 852 he went to Albar's home to confer with him about certain problems in the interpretation of Holy Scripture,[17] but he may not be referring to the composition of the *Indiculus*. When referring to the *Indiculus* as a whole, one should use the date 854.

The basic structure of the *Indiculus* resembles that of Augustine's *City of God* and that of the treatise written by Beatus and Eterius, both of which Albar knew. All three works consist of two parts, an apologia in reply to an accusation and a discussion of the societies of good and evil. Albar's *Indiculus* concludes with a reference to the Apocalypse, a subject to which Beatus devoted a lengthy work. F. R. Franke has shown that the second part of the *Indiculus*, directed against the prophet Mohammed and his work, has a relationship with a polemical work of the Eastern Mediterranean region which is attributed to an al-Kindi. Both Albar and al-Kindi are, in Franke's opinion, probably indebted to a third work which is no longer extant.[18]

In the preface before the *Indiculus* Albar beseeches the Lord at length to enlighten him so that he may attack His enemies in a worthy manner. His work is called the *Indiculus luminosus*, he says, because it teaches that those things which are to be followed have been made clear (*luminasse*) and it exposes with evident signs (*indicia*) the enemy of the Church, who is to be avoided.

The learned (*peritissimi*)[19] Catholics of the Church have been enjoined from the beginning to rise up against the

---

[16] A list of peculiarly similar phrases from the two works is given in Appendix III.

[17] *Memoriale*, II, x, 18.

[18] Franke, *op.cit.*, 139ff.

[19] The *incipit* "Peritissimorum" is the same as that of Eulogius' *Memoriale* and similar to that of Julian of Toledo's *De comprobatione aetatis sextae*.

enemies of the Lord with spiritual strength and to cut down all errors with the sword of the Gospel, the text begins. We, from their number, Albar says, although unworthy, seeking to prepare ourselves for the next world and wishing to bark like dogs for the Lord, moved by zeal for God and religion, act out of love for this our service, relying on the Lord and presuming nothing of ourselves. We do not rise up against the community of the faithful (communes fidei) but we attack the worldly learning of the "Chaldeans." This we wish to state at the beginning, he says, so that critics may not accuse us of fighting against the Church. We, like the Church, have a high regard for martyrs, he continues. And we do not, with the fickleness of time, lessen the glory of a past deed.[20] Book II will show that what we believe is confirmed by the authority of our elders (*majores*).

Without much ado Albar takes up the subject of the *Indiculus,* the defense of the martyrs, and moves rather quickly to attack their opponents. He maintains his attack relentlessly to the end of the work. His first words echo the text of the letter of the anonymous bishop, discussed below, "But because there are some, unworthy of spiritual fervor, frozen in love of the faith...."[21] Let those who have attacked the martyrs give ear to our reply, Albar cries. Those he attacks appear to include those he addresses throughout the *Indiculus.* How can they speak of the truth when they deem it error to die for Christ and the truth? he goes on. Let the weak flee and leave the fight to the strong. The only reason for which one may flee persecution is to spread the Gospel elsewhere, he points out, quoting Jerome in his support. Christians cannot hide the truth in their hearts even though to do so means that they will be safe from persecution, he adds, quoting Gregory the Great to the effect that Christians must defend the cause of justice.

All preachers and doctors, as well as the apostles, says Albar, have been commanded to attack the errors of the

---

[20] *Indiculus*, 1 (222); "unius operis gestum" would seem to mean the martyrdoms rather than a previous document or treatise.

[21] Cf. Appendix III, 3.

Jews, the Gentiles, and all heresies. For Albar these three groups seem to have embraced all non-Christians. Samson says that the term "Gentiles" was reserved for those who worshipped idols,[22] but both Eulogius and Albar call the Moslems Gentiles as well as heretics. They use both terms loosely it seems. Later in the *Indiculus* Albar compares Islam with heresies and other "errors" in a way that shows that he regarded Islam as worse than a Christian heresy.[23] On two occasions also it appears that Albar did not regard the deity of the Moslems as the true God.[24] He never mentions Allah in the *Indiculus* nor does he call the prophet Mohammed by name. Eulogius and Albar, it may be pointed out, were combatting Christians who evidently looked upon Islam as deviating but little from Christianity.

Everyone knows that the Gentiles did not persecute the Church until Christians began to preach, Albar continues, referring to the persecution of the early Church. Read the lives of those martyrs, he urges his readers, and you will find that many of them came forth to martyrdom voluntarily. "And what you are more wont to blame, they wearied the governors and princes with many insults."[25] Uninhibited courage and not meticulous fancies had hold of their hearts. Many of them were attacked by the persecution, he states, but countless others came to battle voluntarily. Although this rather long passage describes the martyrs of the early Church rather than those of Córdoba, Albar obviously wished to compare the martyrs of his day with those of the early Church. Eulogius in the *Memoriale* discusses briefly several martyrs of the early Church who came to martyrdom voluntarily.[26]

The next point argued by Albar is that there is a perse-

[22]*Apologeticus*, II, vii, 5; cf. Letter VIII of the Albar correspondence and Jerome, *Dialogus adversus Luciferianos*, 2-3 (PL 23, 155ff.), which Albar may have known.

[23] *Indiculus*, 31 (269) and 33 (271).

[24] *Ibid.*, 16 (242), "Nec ad idola . . . conversi," and 25 (254f.), the discussion of *Maozim*.

[25] *Ibid.*, 3 (224).

[26] *Memoriale*, I, 22-24.

cution going on in spite of what some Christians say. In support of his thesis he introduces data in agreement with Eulogius' account of the persecution. You say, he begins, that it is not a time of persecution. But I say that it is not a time of apostles. For apostolic zeal is diminished, and it was supposed to move our spirits agaisnt adversaries until the end of the world and to light up the darkness of time with the bright star of the East.[27] I am afraid, he remarks, that those who look on the persecution of Antichrist in our time without a word will say with annoyance that what I have to say is not the truth but, as they think, temerity. Whoever says that there is not a persecution in our land today is either asleep under the yoke of servitude or is collaborating with the Moslems against the Christians. "For are we not given into the yoke of servitude, burdened with an unbearable tax, stripped of our goods, beaten with rods, mocked in slogan and song, made a spectacle for all the Gentiles? They say (illi dicunt) it is not a time of persecution; I say against their claim on the other hand that deadly times have come upon us. They assert that the Moslems have proceeded without hostile intent; I shall prove by their own statement that the martyrs have been crushed out of hatred by the Gentiles."[28] The tax which Albar calls unbearable may be the monthly tax which Eulogius and Leovigildus complain about. Eulogius says too that when the provinces refused to pay King Mohammed tribute in full after he came to the throne (23 September 852), the king levied an intolerable tax burden on the Christians of Córdoba.[29] The unusual change from the second person (*adicitis*) to the third person (*dicunt, asserunt*) by Albar should be noted. The change seems suited for an address before an assembly, parts of

[27] "tenebras aevi corusco sidere eoi climatis inlustrare." In view of indications by Eulogius and Leovigildus that the Christians of Córdoba were engaged in a debate with the Moslems as to the relative superiority of the East or the West, Albar can be interpreted as saying here that the bright star of apostolic zeal was supposed to light up the darkness of the eastern clime.

[28] *Indiculus,* 3 (225).

[29] *Memoriale,* I, 21, and III, v.

which Albar could address alternately. It would also suit the presentation of a legal case.

The extended accounts of Perfectus and John provided next by Albar have been discussed previously.[30] Be now just judges, Albar pleads, and render a true sentence of reason, one based on justice. Who started the persecution? Is it not clear that the Moslems are the instigators of evil, the champions of error, the inflicters of pain? Did they not in their anger and fury and out of zeal for their belief fraudulently break the pact they had made with Perfectus? Perfectus was not the bold person you blame him for being. Rather was he timid. And he was martyred not by worshippers of God but by disciples of Antichrist. Who can deny that the Moslems began the persecution?[31]

> Now would not one who still denies that this is a time of persecution be wrapped in a cloud of error, and splattered with the dregs of iniquity? And what persecution could be greater, what more severe kind of suppression can be expected when one cannot speak by mouth in public what with right reason he believes in his heart? Behold the public law hangs over our heads and a legal order courses through their whole kingdom to the effect that *qui blasphemaverit flagelletur, et qui percusserit occidatur.*[32] Behold, every day, day and night,

[30] *Indiculus*, 3 (225ff.) and 5 (227f.).

[31] *Indiculus*, 4 (227).

[32] Part of the text seems to have been omitted in this vague passage. Just previously Albar was speaking of Perfectus and John, one of whom was slain and the other whipped. The Moslems whipped John, according to Albar, for swearing falsely, as they claimed, on the name of Mohammed. John also declared before the cadi that anyone who swore by the prophet Mohammed should be accursed. The Moslems proclaimed later that his punishment had befallen him for defaming *(derogare)* their prophet. Perfectus was executed because he denounced the prophet Mohammed for evil deeds. *Percusserit* would seem therefore to denote the "denunciation" on the part of Perfectus as distinguished from the "blasphemy" of John. According to Eulogius, some Moslems thought that John should have been condemned to death for attacking *(impetere)* their prophet. And to judge from the account of Eulogius, the Moslems charged John with hardly less than a denun-

in their towers and foggy heights they curse the Lord, when, raising their voice in testimony, they extol their shameless prophet, perjuror, mad and iniquitous, together with the Lord. And alas and woe to this our time, wanting in the wisdom of Christ, full of diabolic envy, in which no one can be found who according to the command of the thundering Lord of the heavens carries the banner of the cross of the faith atop the mountains of Babylon and the foggy towers of pride, offering the evening sacrifice to God. And not only happily, with calm acceptance and modest bearing, do we receive the poisons, drink the potions, savor the deadly germs, but what is more pernicious, we oppose those who fight back and are filled with the zeal of God like Elias, and with a deaf ear bind ourselves in friendship with the enemies of the highest God and discredit our faith to be pleasing to them. And certainly it is more, in my opinion,[33] to do battle with the sword like Elias than to offer resistance like our heroes with the tongue. Daily covered with dishonor and beaten with a thousand contumelious rods, we say that we do not have a persecution. For, not to speak of other things, certainly when they see the bodies of the dead carried by priests, as the ecclesiastical custom is, for burial, do they not with open mouths and shameless faces say, "God, have no mercy on them," and

---

ciation. Eulogius says that the Moslems accused John of "insistere in subsannationem doctoris nostri eumque maledicis verbis irreverenter impetere" (*Memoriale*, I, 9) and of being "exprobrator vatis nostri cultusque irrisor" (*ibid.*, II, x, 5). Another explanation of Albar's words may lie in the events of Eulogius' trial. The Moslems probably regarded professions of Christ and of the Trinity as blasphemy. Eulogius was condemned to be whipped (to death) after discoursing on the divinity of Christ. He called upon the Moslems to sharpen the sword, however, and began to denounce the prophet Mohammed. Thereupon his sentence was changed to decapitation (*Vita Eulogii*, 15). The possibility that Albar is offering here a Latin translation of the text of an Arabic law may also be considered.

[33] "plus est iuxta nos ut Elias gladio decertare"; Franke, "Die freiwilligen Märtyrer," 27, n. 187, interprets this as a reference to violent action by the Mozarabs. But cf. later "plus est ut reor capulo tempora perforari.... Ampliorque merces est ... pugnas spirituales praeliare," *Indiculus*, 8 (231).

throwing rocks at the priests of the Lord, calling the people of the Lord by ignominious names, in their unspeakable nastiness shower the passing Christians with the slime of their insults? And woe again and a third time, innumerable times woe to us, who bear this derision of their mockery, and doubt of the time of the persecution of Antichrist. Thus in the same way when by chance in the streets they come upon the priests of God, they roll stones before their labored steps and insult them with an outrageous and infamous name, defaming them with vulgar sayings and disreputable songs, and making fun of the sign of the faith with shameful expression. But when they hear the sign of the basilica, that is, the sound of ringing bronze, which is struck to bring together the assembly of the church at all the canonical hours, mouthing their derision and contempt, moving their heads, they wail out repeatedly unspeakable things; and they attack and deride with curses both sexes, all ages, and the whole flock of Christ the Lord, not with one mockery but with a thousand insulting infamies.[34]

As further proof of the persecution of the Christians Albar points out that daily their churches are destroyed and their sacred buildings are levelled to the ground.

How can anyone say that the Moslems should not be cursed, he asks, when every year the Church openly and not in secret calls down a curse upon people such as these who hate her?[35] Moreover, he notes, the angel of the Lord commands that people who do not come to the assistance of soldiers of God should be cursed. But Christians who attack the champions of the Lord and the holy things of God claim that it is not right, and even wicked, to curse the Moslems, he complains. To them Albar replies with arguments from Holy Scripture. The physical attacks against the enemies of the Lord described in the Old Testament were more violent than the preaching of the truth, he points out. And the Church today, he says, maintains that it is better to fight spiritual battles for the holy of holies than to fight for

[34] *Ibid.,* 6 (228ff.).   [35] Cf. Eulogius, *Memoriale,* I, 21.

things of this world. Whoever says that those who curse the Moslems are accursed, himself hates religion, Albar says turning the attack against his opponents. After such a person has attacked the deeds of the saints of today he will turn against the deeds of the saints of earlier days. Let him curse Jahel and Judith, and numberless Fathers who fought with the sword as well as with words, and even the Church herself if he is her enemy. If they cannot learn from strong men to fight for the faith, then let them learn from women, Albar exclaims. How can one curse the martyrs and not curse the Church herself? Did not St. Paul say that if anyone, even an angel from heaven, preach a Gospel other than that which we have received, he should be anathema? How then, Albar asks after some rather abstruse argument, can Mohammed, who was under the influence of a deceiving angel and who more than anyone else had preached a false gospel, be regarded as less than anathema?[36]

Albar berates Christians for their lukewarmness, attributing it especially to the tendency they have to curry favor at and serve the Mohammedan court. They seek to conceal their religion from the Moslems. "For they do not say their prayers openly before the pagans," Albar complains. "They do not fortify themselves with the Sign of the Cross when they yawn. They do not profess Christ as God openly before them but in surreptitious words. They profess a Word of God and a Spirit, as the Moslems say, and make their own confession of faith in their heart, as it were to God who sees all things."[37] They are half-hearted Christians, Albar charges, changeable as leopards. And we, he complains, prohibit and attack things which are good and not those which should be condemned. We do not curse those Christians who fight on the side of the Moslems against their fellow Christians, but we anathematize fervent religious out of fear of the king and seduced by the transient glamor of the court. And those who attack the Moslem errors we adjudge heretics and fools, he adds. Our arms fight against ourselves and our iniquity falls upon our own necks.

[36] *Indiculus*, 8 (230ff.).   [37] *Ibid.*, 9 (232).

O you outstanding preachers and exemplary elect of the flock, good and solicitous pastors, has Christ taught us thus? have all the apostles and doctors taught us thus? and all those who struggled through divers trials to lay down their lives for truth?

In this passage Albar may be speaking of the decision of the council of Córdoba at the end of 852, although his term "anathematize" seems too strong for what Eulogius says of the council's decision. Elsewhere in the *Memoriale*, however, Eulogius speaks of an anathema against the confessors and he notes that the *exceptor* "decreed" an anathema against them in the council.[38] Albar specifies that the fear mentioned by Eulogius in connection with the council was a fear of the king, and later Albar seems to indicate that it was a fear of death.[39] The Christians evidently were anxious to please the king and regain their positions in the palace, from which they had been expelled when Mohammed I came to the throne. Albar here, especially in the phrase "heretics and fools," may be attacking the words of the anonymous bishop.[40]

There is no precedent for this clemency towards error, Albar continues. Which apostle ordered us to be mild? Did Christ come down from heaven to enlighten blind people who were unconcerned about their salvation? Christ commanded that the Gospel be preached, and not only in apostolic times but for all time. And one preaches even at the risk of his life to those who do not know or believe. I doubt[41] that there has not been a preacher among these Ishmaelite people to make them debtors to the faith, he says, but it seems to me that the confessors and martyrs have fulfilled the apostolate and preached to them and made them debtors to the faith. Christians should recognize that the confessors are evangelists of justice, Albar asserts, and not call them

[38] *Memoriale*, I, 28, and II, xv, 2.
[39] *Indiculus*, 16 (242).
[40] Cf. Appendix III, 6.
[41] "*Puto*"; Albar seems to use the word with the meaning of *dubito* ascribed to it in a work attributed to Isidore of Seville, *Differentiarum sive de proprietate sermonum liber* (PL 83, 1330).

madmen. The Moslems boast that they are more philosophical than any other people, but they are deservedly despised by humble ones who know Christ only, and Him crucified.

Albar then gives a number of examples of harshness from Holy Scripture (Elias, Moses, Samuel, Phinees, Peter and Paul) for those who argue that Christians should be mild in the face of persecution. Let them regard these examples of harshness, Albar says, and desist from their talk of humility when holy things are involved. Let those who are stern and inflexible towards their own but meek and humble towards the enemies of God learn from Christ, from the Prophets, the Apostles, and all the Fathers to suffer their own opprobrium in meekness but to avenge contempt of God with severity.

Having argued his point of view about zealous preaching and the origin of the persecution, Albar turns to the voluntary martyrs. He praises Isaac for going before the cadi and freely professing his faith, unlike others of his time, such as a "weak boaster" whose courage failed when he was being beaten.[42] Isaac showed that the Lord could produce victorious martyrs in their day too, Albar points out. He goes on to censure someone, probably Bishop Reccafred, for condemning the martyrs. The Moslems have tried to deprive them of the life of this world. You seek to separate them from life eternal, he charges, implying it would seem that it is a bishop he addresses.

Evidently some of the Christians complained that because of the martyrs the churches were without priests and as the persecution grew more intense the Mass was forbidden. Albar counters their argument with his own charge that the persecution was a divine punishment upon the Christians for rising up against the martyrs. He accuses a "fraternal college" of the elect, comprising "pastors of Christ, doctors of the Church, bishops, abbots, priests, nobles, and magnates," of having gone before (heard?) the cadi of their

---

[42] *Indiculus*, 12 (237); Albar's vague words may refer to two people, Perfectus and John; cf. also *Memoriale*, I, 9.

own free will and defamed the martyrs, calling them heretics.[43] In 854 a new cadi, Ahmed ibn Ziad, was appointed
in Córdoba.[44] The appearance of the "fraternal college"
before the cadi (or vice versa) may have been associated
with his taking office. The "fraternal college" seems to have
formed a council, perhaps at the time Albar was addressing
it in the text of the *Indiculus*. It is possible too that the council referred to in the letter of the anonymus bishop,[45] if it
is not the council of 852, may be the assembly addressed by
Albar in the *Indiculus*.

Albar goes on to elaborate his rather obscure account of
the defamations of the martyrs by some Christians in a way
which does not agree with what Eulogius says about the decision of dissimulation in regard to the martyrdoms arrived at
by the council of 852. Eulogius says that it was intended that
the king and the people misunderstand the words of the decision, which really was not a condemnation of the martyrs
but only apparently such. Albar says twice that denunciations of the martyrs were made in public before Moslem
authorities. Where Eulogius says that no one was allowed
to seek to make a contest of his faith, Albar says that an
ecclesiastical interdict was involved, that certain Christians
were forbidden to attack the errors of the Moslems and were
compelled to swear never to go to martyrdom nor to attack
with curses the "false prophet." These oaths and prohibitions were associated with threats of physical torture.

It is almost inconceivable that Albar misunderstood the
true attitude of the council of 852. Although he and Eulogius for all practical purposes contradict each other in this
matter, they do discuss the same things: a condemnation of
past martyrs and a prohibition of future confessions that
could lead to martyrdom. The difference may reflect a difference in their points of view towards the council of 852.
Eulogius, who seems to have taken part in that council, may

----

[43] *Indiculus*, 14 (239f.); cf. Appendix III, 6. Flórez' conjecture,
"*adierunt*" for ms "*audierunt*," seems good.

[44] V. supra, 127f.

[45] Letter X of the Albar correspondence.

not have wished to attack it too strongly before the results of its decision could be determined. Albar may have exaggerated his picture in utterly refusing to countenance the dissimulation decided upon by the council. A third point of view defending the decision of the council of 852 is perhaps to be seen in the letter of the anonymous bishop. Albar, however, speaks of things which happened, and it may be that the defamation of the martyrs before the cadi and the oaths extorted from certain Christians took place after the council of 852, just as it may be that the council referred to in the anonymous bishop's letter may be another than the council of 852 or another than the group addressed in the *Indiculus*.

Not only did certain Christians call the martyrs heretics in a public lie and wrongly restrict the confessors with prohibitions and oaths, Albar continues, but they sought to dispense themselves for their "officious lie" of dissimulation by citing examples from Holy Scripture. Jehu simulated in order to destroy the worshippers of Baal and thus assure a greater good, Albar points out. David feigned madness in fear of death but not to the danger of his soul. And St. Paul in participating in Jewish ceremonies was still worshipping the living God,[46] says Albar indicating that he did not regard the deity of the Moslems as the true God. Albar cites Eleazar as an example from Scripture of one who would not dissimulate in a matter of religious importance.

In arguing that the examples of Jehu and David did not

---

[46] *Indiculus*, 16 (241f.). Eulogius (*Memoriale*, II, xv, 3) and Albar both use the word *simulatio*. Eulogius' meaning seems to be "dissimulation"; Albar seems to use the word to mean "simulation" as well as "dissimulation," although the difference in the case of the Christians of Córdoba would seem to be technical rather than real. Cf. Isidore, *Differentiarum* (PL 83, 62, 64, and 1322), "We dissimulate what we know, when we say we do not know what we know and when we do not wish to seem to do what we do; we simulate what we do not know, when we act as if we know what we do not know and when we wish to seem to do what we do not do." Cf. also H. Sander's edition of *Beati in Apocalipsin*, 130f., "Hypocrita Graeco sermone Latine vero simulator dicitur."

justify the actions of those who condemned the martyrs, Albar may be explaining Eulogius' vague phrase "compelled by fear and the judgment of the metropolitans." Previously Albar indicated that it was fear of the king that acted upon those he condemns, and here he seems to indicate that it was a fear of death. In the letter of the anonymous bishop a fear of death and a pragmatic concern for what was regarded as a higher good seem to have motivated metropolitans and the council.

From Eulogius' account of the council of 852 the "dissimulation" seems to have been in the decision of the council, the meaning of which was other than it seemed. From what Albar says the "dissimulation" was in the actions of certain Christians, those who took part in the council perhaps. By dissimulation Albar may have meant too a dispensation for certain Christians to conceal their faith because of the rigor of the Mohammedan law. The Moslems of Córdoba, just as the pagan persecutors in the early days of the Church, preferred to have examples of apostasy and scandal rather than to make martyrs of the Christians. Some of the martyrs were required to make a formal profession of faith about Christ and Mohammed on which the fate of their life depended. Invoking a dispensation, they would have been able to deny or retract the previous profession of Christian belief which had brought about their arrest. The cadi, it may be recalled, asked Isaac if he were not mad or drunk when he made his profession. Eulogius in the *Documentum martyriale* urges Flora and Maria not to retract their profession, as certain people were asking them to do.[47] The dispensations defended by the anonymous bishop are vaguely enough described to include both the decision of the council and individual Christians in fear of their lives.

The traditional doctrine of the Church on dissimulation or lying is based on St. Augustine's eight categories of lies. The most serious kind of lie, according to Augustine, is that *in doctrina religionis*, which is the occasion of error for one's neighbor. Whether spoken formally by an official of the

[47] *Memoriale*, preface to Bk. I, 3; *Documentum*, 14.

Church or uttered in the affairs of everyday life, such a lie is never excusable. Even lying which seeks to prevent harm to the Faith or one's neighbor or applies to frivolous situations is not viewed by Augustine as without guilt.[48]

In punishment for their sins against the memory of the martyrs and for their evil ways of life which endanger the salvation of their souls, the Lord has justly delivered the Christians to the beast (the devil or Antichrist). He has delivered them to persecution at the hands of King Mohammed (*maledictus*) as a punishment for their daring to defend the prophet Mohammed (*maledictus*), even in their churches. Moreover, certain Christians, public sinners (*publicani*) rather, have risen up against their fellows. One such public sinner (Reccafred, or perhaps the *exceptor* mentioned by Eulogius), whom Albar calls a mad dog persecutor of the Church, has lent the Moslems the sword with which to slay Christians. The Lord has sent him as a trial for the Church, Albar says, but in time he will be punished, as will the Moslems. Disturbances in nature, insurrections of peoples, and invasions seem to Albar to be a punishment for the Moslems because of their persecution of the Christians, but for the faithful they offer an opportunity to gain reward.[49]

Eulogius, in the *Documentum martyriale,* also puts the blame for the downfall of the Christians on their sins. Both he and Albar speak of the "hidden and just judgment of God." Later Samson blames the oppression of the Christians by Count Servandus on the sins of the people, and the chronicles of the North lay the blame for the fall of Spain to the Arabs on the sins of Rodrigo and the priests of Spain.[50] The argument appears prominently in Augustine's *City of God* with regard to the sack of Rome. It is probable that all the Mozarab authors used this argument to induce their fellow Christians to amend their lives. The same argument explained for them the tyrannical rule of the Moslems. Nei-

---

[48] L. Godefroy, "Mensonge," DTC, X, i, 555-559, especially 557.
[49] *Indiculus,* 18 (243f.).
[50] *Documentum,* 18; *Apologeticus,* preface to Bk. II, 5.

ther Eulogius nor Albar makes an issue of the justice of the Moslem authority, both apparently accepting it.

In blaming the persecution under King Mohammed on the condemnation of the martyrs by certain Christians Albar dates the condemnations, it would seem, in the first part of 853, before the martyrdom of Fandila. The condemnations appear to have followed the council of 852, which seems to have been in December, and with Fandila's death in June 853 the persecution broke out anew.

Albar goes on to say that some Christians condemn both the *Praesul* and the martyrdoms. In quite vague terms he says, it seems, that they venerate the sentences of men against the bishop and at the same time venerate a decree which they wrongly think condemns the martyrs. Justly are they delivered to the *Praesul* when they refuse to bless the martyrs. But how they can reject the accursed (*biothenatus*) *Praesul* and at the same time agree to a condemnation of the martyrs Albar does not understand.[51] Flórez' identification of the *Praesul* as Bishop Saul[52] seems open to debate. Albar calls him the *Praesul episcoporum* it seems, i.e., the metropolitan of Seville, Reccafred. Moreover, Albar's account of Reccafred in the *Vita Eulogii*[53] seems to tie in with the *Praesul* here. The *Praesul* may be the anonymous bishop, who indicates that members of his flock had turned against him and who seems to be Reccafred rather than Saul. Not only did some of his flock oppose the anonymous bishop, but they evidently complained of him to another metropolitan (of Toledo). Reccafred too may be the "pseudobishop" who, Saul seems to imply in a letter to Albar, usurped Saul's authority as bishop of Córdoba.[54]

Albar brings to a close the first half of the *Indiculus* with an exhortation to Christians who cannot themselves preach the truth to aid those who do preach, at least with their prayers. Our words, Albar says, have been addressed

---

[51] *Indiculus*, 19 (245); cf. Appendix III, 5.
[52] ES, X, 276.
[53] *Vita Eulogii*, 4 and 6.
[54] Letter XII of the Albar correspondence, 2.

to our brethren not with ill feeling but in peace. To our adversaries, however, we have spoken with constancy and pride, as Catholics. Unpolished writing bores readers, Albar notes, but they will accept sincere and not uncultivated devotion. I am not so stupid as to think, he says, that I will obtain glory for a work which I am afraid offends powerful men. He then attests to his training in liberal arts and ecclesiastical studies in the passage which has been noted at the beginning of the discussion of the *Indiculus*. I should have taken care, he says, as someone probably thinks, not to have rashly come into conflict with the learned (*peritissimi*) and those renowned for eloquence. But I have foregone the praise of philosophers for the sake of truth, and my tongue could not keep my lips from the defense of justice. Albar ends the first part of the *Indiculus* with a rhetorical flourish, asking his readers to forgive his rustic ineptitude of style in the light of his purity of intention. He prides himself on doing without the language of philosophers and grammarians (*Donatistae*), whom he affects to despise. And in a cloud of rhetorical verbiage he lays claim to evangelical simplicity.

> Et ideo si qua forte adversantia catholico docmate negligenter disserui, non voto sed cecitate mentis urgente, ea rogo lectores mei fletibus diluant, precibus tergant, orationibus mundent, sermonum vero vitia tota oro intemerata relinquant. Judex enim ille cui hanc intentionem devotionis libavi, non verborum folia sed radicem cordis discernit, nec ad curationem coruscam prose sed operis finem intendit. Agant eructuosas questiones philosophi et Donatiste, genis impuri, latratu canum, grunnitu porcorum, fauce rasa, et dentibus stridente, saliva spumosi grammatici ructent. Nos vero evangelici servi, Christi discipuli, rusticanorum sequipedi, quibus injungitur plena, quibus percipitur fortia, et non cava, levia, et inflata, sed holocaustomata injuncta sunt medullata; sectemur solida, et sententiarum vivacitate prespicua, non quod absit, vacua et letali peste turgentia, atque laudis humane ultro citroque fumosa, que magis mentem auctoris et tractantium macerat, quam textum aperiendo

lectionis animos fece conturna infectos inlustrat. . . .
Hec contra Donatistas dixisse sufficiat.[55]

The second part of the *Indiculus* is an attack on the prophet Mohammed as a precursor of Antichrist. It is composed
of what Albar himself calls a packet of testimonies (*testimoniorum fascis*). He models his portrayal of Antichrist
after Jerome on the book of Daniel and Gregory the Great's
Moralia in Job. But his dependence on them is limited to
their method of commenting on the Scriptural passages
phrase by phrase and to an intermittent reliance on their
words or their train of thought. Albar is much briefer than
either Jerome or Gregory, and he interprets Scripture independently of them, accommodating his interpretation to his
own rather extensive knowledge of the prophet Mohammed
and Islam. It has generally been thought that the *Indiculus*
is incomplete and that its second book is wanting, but actually Albar accomplishes everything that he promises in the
work. In paragraph 21, which seems to be the beginning
of the second book, Albar says that after he treats the prophecies of Daniel and Job in the tradition of SS. Jerome and
Gregory and says a few words with reference to the Apocalypse he will conclude his work, leaving it to doctors and
famous men of the future to complete the discussion. In the
second book he wishes to confirm his own laborious little
work, he says, with the distilled wisdom of men who speak
the truth.[56]

Albar's knowledge of the prophet Mohammed and the customs of the Moslems of his day is discussed at some length
by F. R. Franke, who shows that Albar was original in his
polemics and did not depend on the more sophisticated and
moderate Christian polemicists of the East.[57] Franke points
out, however, that a number of points in Albar's denunciation of the prophet agree with a work of eastern origin,
the *Apologia of the Christian Faith* attributed to al-Kindi

[55] *Indiculus,* 20 (247); some variations from the text of Flórez can
be noted.
[56] *Ibid.,* 21 (248).
[57] Franke, "Die freiwilligen Märtyrer," 117-142, especially 117f.

(ca. A.D. 830), which, though more or less contemporary
with the *Indiculus,* is known in a text at the earliest from
the tenth century.[58] The *Indiculus* and the *Apologia,* Franke
says, represent the earliest efforts in Christian-Moslem
polemics to attack the prophet Mohammed and the Moslems
for their immoral lives.[59] Since information about Mohammed and Islam is relatively scarce even in works as late
as the ninth century, what Albar has to say in the second
part of the *Indiculus* is of interest and importance, and may
be surveyed in some detail. It may be noted that Albar cites
Latin authors on whom he depends but mentions no source
for his rather extensive knowledge of Islam.

Because earlier doctors regarded Nero, Antiochus, and
other enemies of the Church as Antichrist or types of Antichrist, Albar fears that his enemies will attack his attempt
to picture the prophet Mohammed as a type of Antichrist.
The fourth beast and the fourth kingdom mentioned in
Daniel 7:23 is Rome, he says. And the eleventh horn of this
beast fits Mohammed. For he conquered three kingdoms,
that of the Greeks, that of the Franks (who ruled in the
name of the Romans, says Albar), and that of the West
Goths. Mohammed also tried to do away with the Decalogue
and rose up in pride against the Trinity. "He fashioned
words against the Most High God in petulant obstinacy,
pondered grandiose things, and wove together those nebulous
things which indeed precede Antichrist and are very much
opposed to our humble religion. He thought to enshroud in
a hazy mist the law of God shining bright with miracles.
He made up ridiculous and frivolous stories for his partisans
as if on the command of the Most High Lord, with ridiculous
boldness, with a lying pen, impure effrontery, and theatrical
applause. He made up fables and lies lacking the force of
both reason and manliness. He broke up the saints of God
and trod with his scurrilous foot on the honor of the stars of
heaven, i.e., the sons of the Church. This you can see more
plainly with your eyes than I can explain with words. But
now the 'time and times and half a time' (Dn. 7:25) is to

[58] *Ibid.,* 135-141 and 29.   [59] *Ibid.,* 118 and 126f.

be applied to his head specifically as Antichrist."⁶⁰ These
three and a half times, according to the calculations of the
Hebrews, who count seventy years as a time, amount to a
reign of 245 years for the Mohammedans, says Albar. In the
year A.D. 854, Era 892, or A.H. 240 (which Albar erroneously equates with 229 solar years), there were, according
to Albar, but sixteen years left to this term. The rule of
the Moslems thus was to come to an end in A.D. 870. This
computation of the year A.D. 625 as the beginning of the
Moslem era does not agree with fact, nor with the chronology
of the Chronicle of 754, which Albar seems to have known,
nor with Eulogius' account of the prophet Mohammed in
the *Apologeticus martyrum*, which agrees with the chronology of the Chronicle of 754. Albar should have equated 232
rather than 229 solar years with 240 lunar years. Since the
Arab year 240 began on 2 June 854, this part of the *Indiculus* was written, it may be assumed, in the latter part of
854.

Professing to know little of prophecy, Albar explains that
there may be several legitimate interpretations of one prophecy, that one prophecy may refer to several times or several
prophecies to one time. His ideas, which are based on Daniel
12:4, do not follow Jerome. His view of prophecy, Albar
says, if regarded with respect and friendliness, will prove
valid and cannot be attacked by those who are spiteful towards him. Having sought to justify his method, Albar
proceeds with his analysis of the prophet Mohammed as a
type of Antichrist. What was said about Nabuchodonosor
in Habacuc applied to the Chaldeans as a whole, Albar argues, and what is said about Antichrist in Daniel applies
to the prophet Mohammed. Mohammed paid no respect to

⁶⁰ *Indiculus*, 21 (249); for the three and one-half years of the
prophecy cf. *Beati in Apocalipsin*, ed. H. Sanders, 16f. Beatus, *ibid.*,
608, gives the three kingdoms conquered by Antichrist as Egypt, Ethi-
opia, and Libya. An *Indiculum de adventum Enoc et Elie adque Antichristi* which appears at the end of the Albar codex of Córdoba gives
the three kingdoms as Egypt, Africa, and Mauretania; cf. A. C. Vega's
edition of a variant text from ms Escorial R-II-18, *La ciudad de Dios*,
171 (1958), 265.

the idols of the Ishmaelites, which were still worshipped in his day, says Albar, and he added his own false law [the Koran] to the Old and New Testaments. Thereafter, apropos of "And he shall follow the lust of women" (Dn. 11:37), Albar introduces two paragraphs of his own describing the gross boasting of the Moslems about their sensuality and the sensual delights awaiting them in paradise. One of the claims which Albar attributes to the Moslems, that their prophet had, as a gift from heaven, the potency of forty men, occurs, according to Franke, only in the *Indiculus* and in al-Kindi's *Apologia*.[61] Such a gift, says Albar, comes not from above but from Venus, also known as Aphrodite, or *alkaufeit*[62] as Mohammed called her. Comparing the lust of the Moslems with the description of the Egyptians in Ezechiel and Jeremias, Albar refers to Mohammed's adultery with Zeinab, the wife of his neighbor Zaid. Mohammed sought to justify this act, Albar states, as having been commanded him by the angel Gabriel. They are all fornicators and adulterers, he adds, divorcing and remarrying, keeping concubines and three or four wives. In their search for new ways of lust they violate the natural law, he charges, declining out of shame to say more. In a later paragraph (33) Albar accuses the Moslems of incest, and he may have that in mind here. But none of them was more debauched than their prophet, he says, who promised his believers as a reward in paradise a never-ending life with the houris (*scorta*). Other things too, more gross, Mohammed promised his followers, says Albar, but these things he will discuss in a later work, if God grants him life.[63]

In these paragraphs, says Franke, Albar was not exaggerating, for the morals of the Mohammedans were known to all his readers.[64] A connection between the goddess Venus and the sensual powers of Mohammed had been indicated earlier by John of Damascus (ca. 650 to ca. 750), who re-

---

[61] Franke, *op.cit.*, 127f.
[62] "'lKfyt" in Arabic script is written in the ms above *alkaufeit*.
[63] *Indiculus*, 23-24 (252ff.).
[64] Franke, *op.cit.*, 120f. and 128.

lated the black stone of the Kaa'ba to Venus.[65] In the *Apologia* of al-Kindi, Venus is said to have bestowed her gifts on Mohammed in return for his allowing worship of the Kaa'ba as her sanctuary to continue. Franke links Albar's data to the East and al-Kindi's work through Albar's use of the word *alkaufeit* for Venus, which Franke says should read *al-kaukaba*, the Arabic form of *kawkabta*, Syriac for the female (or morning) star, which the pagan Arabs had worshipped. Franke notes that there were a number of possible contacts between Syria-Palestine and Córdoba.[66]

Striking at Mohammed's worship of God, Albar uses Daniel 11:38, "But he shall worship the god Maozim in his place." Though *Maozim* means "great" and "greatest," or "strong" and "strongest,"[67] Mohammed merely appears to adore the strongest god. Albar quotes Theodotion to show that actually Mohammed introduced a strange god among his people in order to increase his own power and domination.[68] "This they cry out daily in their smoky towers with proud and monstrous trumpeting, and like savages, with lips and throats open wide like people with sick stomachs, and yelling like madmen, they cry out in order 'to fortify *Maozim* with a strange god, whom he hath acknowledged' (Dn. 11:39), i.e., in order to fortify in one venerated name *Maozim*, whom they call *Cobar*,[69] i.e., the greatest, with a strange god, i.e., the demon who appeared to him in the person of Gabriel, so that thus he may cover over his error in the hearts of his believers, while he extols a ritual of

[65] *Ibid.*, 122.

[66] *Ibid.*, 128f.

[67] F. Buhl, "al'Uzza," EI, IV, ii, 1069f.; *al'Uzza* means "strong powerful" and was an old Arabian goddess; the name is rarely found among the Syrians, who use instead *kawkabta*, the female star. Franke, *op.cit.*, 128f., discusses al'Uzza.

[68] Only half of Albar's quotation of Theodotion, as punctuated in ES, XI, 254 and 255, is from Jerome (PL 25, 572A). The second sentence, "Ideo ... dominatum," although repeated by Albar, is not in Jerome. For Theodotion cf. R. Ceillier, *Histoire générale des auteurs sacrés et ecclésiastiques*, II, 143f.

[69] Franke, *op.cit.*, 123f., says that Albar refers to the eulogy *allahu Akbar*.

yelling in the name of the greatest God and infects the souls of noble people with superstitious doings and a wicked spirit. But lest I appear to say these things enigmatically (*enigmatice*) and not specifically and lest I be thought to speak things my human ingenuity has sought out rather than things which the divine spirit has made clear, more evident proofs must be introduced. For behold, given over to the same ritual, they still call by the same word those days on which they consecrate madness in the house of the idol, and because of the difference of the Arabic language, which in many words differs from the Hebrew to an extent, those feast days are called *Almozem*. And at the same time of the year when the same people, or Gentiles, of old flocked together from all over to the idol mentioned, nowadays the same lost throng comes together every year, and they continue to serve the same demon whom they think had been extirpated from that place by the magnitude of their faith. Even today they worship *Maozim* 'in his place,' as the prophet, by the divine spirit, says."[70] Albar speaks with accuracy of the Moslem holy months of the pilgrimage (the last month of the Arab year) and *al-Muharram* (the first month). As he points out, the annual Moslem pilgrimage to Mecca in the holy month *Hadjdj* had a relationship with the *Mawsim*, annual markets or festivals of pre-Islamic Arabia. Under the Moslems the name *Mawsim* came to designate a religious festival.[71] As far as one can tell, Albar's plans to write a book setting forth Moslem beliefs and practices, mentioned here for the second time, never materialized. Albar's knowledge of Hebrew is probably secondhand from Jerome. He says elsewhere that he did not know Hebrew.[72]

Albar continues with other statements of interest. "All these things that eleventh horn, speaking great things, in-

[70] *Indiculus*, 25 (254f.).

[71] A. J. Wensinck, "Hadjdj," EI, II, 196-201; *id.*, "Mawsim," *ibid.*, III, 422; and M. Plessner, "al-Muharram," *ibid.*, III, 698f.

[72] Albar correspondence, Letter XVI, 4; cf. Madoz, *Epistolario*, 231, n. 33.

stituted. For rising up a little out of his tribe and growing to greater strength not by power but by guile, and as if in envy of the law, he invaded the kingdom a little at a time and in certain places conquered the arms of the Romans, i.e., the forts of the Emperor Heraclius. So, in the part in which the beast is said to come from a small people this whole prophecy conforms to him. So in the horn of the beast 'eyes like a man's' (Dn. 7:8) are said to have been seen. For what is signified by eyes, through which vision is directed, except that law which at the instigation of demons he brought to those lost people by the hidden judgment of God? 'The commandment of the Lord is lightsome, enlightening the eyes' (Ps. 18:9). But because they have been revealed not in the tenth number but in the eleventh, and have been denoted not as 'eyes' but 'like eyes,' so, properly speaking, it is not to be called a law, but it should be regarded as a usurped law. And are those things opposed to the divine testaments actually to be approved thus? This is that speaking of great things against God. This is the strength raised up against the Most High. This is the presumptuous treading down of the honor of the stars of heaven by the foot of victory. I skip many things because I rush much."[73]

Albar's brief mention of the invasion of the Byzantine empire by the Moslems is in close enough accord with both the Chronicle of 741 and the Chronicle of 754 to warrant belief that he knew one or both works. Both chronicles say that the Byzantine empire was invaded by stealth rather than by force.[74] Moreover, the Chronicle of 741 says that Heraclius ordered whatever Roman legions were in forts in divers places to come to Damascus (ut quantaecumque Romanae legiones praesidiis patriarum diversis locis inerant).[75] These forces failed to drive out the Moslems. Al-

[73] *Indiculus*, 25 (256).

[74] Chronicle of 741, 12, "furtim magis quam publicis obreptionibus"; Chronicle of 754, 9; "furtim magis quam virtute ... atque non tantum publicis irruptionibus quantum clanculis incursationibus"; Mommsen in MGH, *Auct. antiq.*, XI, 336 and 337.

[75] Mommsen, *op.cit.*, 337, par. 15.

bar, who previously called the Byzantines "Greeks,"[76] says that the Moslems conquered the arms of the Romans, i.e., the forts of Heraclius in certain places (brachiaque Romanorum, id est praesidia Eraclii Imperatoris, in quibusdam locis perdomuit). It would seem that Albar relied on the Chronicle of 741 rather than on the Chronicle of 754, except that he says that Mohammed came from a small people, whereas the Chronicle of 741 says that he came from a very noble tribe.[77] Eulogius' vita of the prophet Mohammed also seems to have a relationship with the two chronicles.[78]

Albar then turns to the treatment of Behemoth in the book of Job. Antichrist is shown to be like the evening star, he says, with a hazy light, coming before the darkness, enshrouding the hearts of men. *Behemoth,* Hebrew for the Latin *animal,* well describes Mohammed, who did not know how to read or write. Mohammed consumed the Gentiles as grass, Albar states, and bound them to himself in his law of licentiousness. "He setteth up his tail like a cedar" (Job 40:12). "We have had experience of that tail when, living in recent days, we undergo the very fearful persecution of the same beast."[79] Mohammed's ministers show a face of piety to the Moslems, but they have no fruits of piety. They imitate hypocrites and not saints. They emulate the crafty and not the humble. Mohammed had such great gifts of evil because he was inspired by the devil, who was a first substance (prior substantia) of creation, Albar says, following Gregory. Demons, princes, and philosophers offer Mohammed an assortment of lies, and he has sucked his venom from many sects. Heretics, philosophers, and Jews have contributed to his doctrine. Albar goes on to denounce the debilitation of Moslem morals, the falsity of their teaching, Mohammed's commerce with demons, and the sterility of the Mohammedan religion.

His followers pray for him frequently according to the foolish rite he fashioned, says Albar. Just as Christians frequently pray "Christ save us," Albar notes, so Moslems

---

[76] *Indiculus,* 21 (249).
[77] Mommsen, *op.cit.,* 337, par. 13.
[78] *Apol. mart.,* 16.
[79] *Indiculus,* 26 (257).

constantly repeat the phrase "May God bless him and save him" in daily speech in their homes and in cries from their minarets. So is he blessed by those he has ruined. But he will not be saved by the prayers of those whom he has deceived with the soft words of his teaching, fashioned while he was dreaming, Albar asserts. As the law of God speaks to angels and men, so his law speaks to demons and damned men, Albar argues further. In it Mohammed frequently says, "O multitudo demonum et omnium," which in Arabic is "Jemahascar algen" (ja ma'schara 'l-dschinn).[80] He is called *Behemoth* or *animal*, Albar goes on, because his origins were crude and unlettered. He is called a serpent or dragon because of his guile. He is also called a bird because, proud and haughty and vagrant, he flies in the air, where the princes of darkness have power, with no rein of temperance. Those who expose his deceits and show him to be an enemy of the Church, Albar points out, are friends of the Lord. "He is cut to pieces as often as he is branded with anathema," Albar says in a paraphrase of Gregory's words. Continuing to rely on Gregory, Albar explains that Mohammed seduces the lowly and the weak and afterwards conquers the prudent and the strong. It is said to the Church, Albar asserts, "Remember the battle; and speak no more" (Job 40:27), especially when the battle has been offered and accepted in a consecrated way. Albar turns to the persecution of his own day and addresses the church of Córdoba, retaining the voice and address of the quotation from Job. "Call to mind his intestine battle against you and do not accuse the Lord of the mighty exterior power, which you can see. And to be sure, remember that this battle is given to you so that those who fight for my [the Lord's] law may be crowned."[81] Mohammed, Albar concludes, would have been prefigured in the Leviathan even

[80] *Ibid.*, 28 (261); ms *"Jemahascar,"* as Franke, *op.cit.*, 126, n. 817, notes it should be. Franke says that the Latin should read "O multitudo daemonum et hominum" for a corrected Arabic reading of "ja ma 'schara 'l-dschinn wa 'l-ins."

[81] *Indiculus*, 28 (262).

had he not sought in his pride to rise above the law of God, for "his faith shall fail him" (Job 40:28) to avoid eternal punishment at the hand of the Creator and to obtain the sensuous paradise he expects.

After pointing out that the Lord, who governs all things, has raised Mohammed up as a punishment for sinners, Albar discusses Moslem proselytizing in Córdoba. The Christians of Córdoba, he says, read Mohammed's words and the eloquent prayers for him in the volumes of his followers. But what the Moslems do is idle, he states. By the yoke and the "multiple oppression of the head" which they relentlessly impose on the land with boasting, they will come to eternal punishment, Albar predicts, his reference being evidently to both a head tax and a land tax. Anything that is not based on the faith of Christ will prove vain and even harmful at the time of judgment, he says. There is no virtue apart from Christ. Who can fathom the craftiness of Mohammed's iniquitous law? he asks, employing Gregory's words. And who can examine in sharp discussions the complicated error and the mass of words which he has woven into certain places of his law of fables? His teaching will spread unless I make clear to "my elect and the little flock" that it is deceitful, says Albar. The text here, which gives the impression that Albar is a bishop, is a rephrasing of a sentence of Gregory. Although it would seem that Albar in elaborating on Gregory's sentence would have eliminated such an impression, he may have intended that the sentence be spoken in the name of the Lord. Mohammed has armed his lie, Albar continues, with a severe and vengeful law, and his preachers, united in their iniquity, are as hard as metal shields in the obstinacy of their minds. Miserable and fallen in their way of life, they arrogantly contradict the Church and slay themselves with the vices of the flesh. Their fierce law, which attacks Christianity, has been called splendor, he remarks, but it is not even a little gleam of light, only the black fire of incineration. It is the dark fire of hell which does not illuminate but burns.

In the next paragraph (30) Albar ceases to follow Gregory

and deals more with the situation in Córdoba. The law of God corrects the manners of men and provides for their salvation in peace, he argues, but the law of Mohammed fosters carnal desire, worldly love, and endless ambition contrary to the peace of the Lord. Power and royal authority are on their side, Albar states, but they lack a promise of truth, a true doctrine, and signs of miracles and spiritual power. As the Moslems cling to one another in their iniquity in this world, so will they be joined together in their future damnation, he asserts. "His heart shall be as hard as stone" (Job 41:15), because no one, or certainly few, return to the true faith from him. He has condemned patient Christians and cruelly killed those preaching the truth to him. He terrifies bishops (*praesules*), whose office it is to preach, and the brave ones of the Church collapse and come to terms with him. He chafes the strong, mocks the nobles, and ignores ecclesiastical preaching. The stones of the sanctuary [the elect] are like stubble to him because they are either reduced to nothing by the sword, or, consenting to his error, they become as soft as grass in the snare of seduction. But why wonder that he despises stones when he contemns the hammer beating him, i.e., the Lord Jesus Christ, the King of all the worlds, Whom he imagines as equal or similar to Adam!

Mohammed scorns as mad the words of those who foretell the destruction of himself and his followers, Albar continues. He attacks Christians, profanes holy things, and derides the law of God. He stirs up wars and cupidity for worldly things. He breeds lust and legalistic instincts. He boasts that all that he does against those opposing him he does in zeal for rectitude and faith. This has happened in the present time, says Albar. The Moslems offer the blood of Christians to the Lord as if in defense of His law, and they burn the bodies of the martyrs. What is worse, Albar laments, many Christian doctors anathematize Christians who suffer such things. Mohammed lacks neither an exposition of his doctrine nor doctors to expound it, Albar says. For after the death of Mohammed there were so many teachings and superstitions (*suppetitiones*) that, but for the grace of God, his worldly splendor would have deceived the faithful. Everyone knows the countless trivia he taught about cleanliness and bathing, and the ablutions for public prayer— minutiae of discipline, says Albar, for bodily members only. Every "shining path" (Job 41:23) of theirs shines in what ministers to lusts and the debilitating of the flesh, he adds, not to what by strict morals prevents the soul from being deceived and debilitated. Explaining that at this point he does not follow Gregory, who was speaking of Origen, Albar points out that Mohammed regarded the law of God as outmoded and introduced a new testament contrary to it. Mohammed, Albar charges, was inspired by an apostate angel, who, not content with the honor given him in heaven, aspired for more and finally fell into the depths below other creatures. Like Lucifer, Mohammed was proud. All precious worldly goods are subject to the Moslems and are given to them, Albar notes. Their prophet was the proudest of the proud and ruled over all heretics and iniquitous authors of error. He comes out into the open where others lurked concealed, Albar explains, and where they interpreted the law of God evilly he has composed a new law. Albar here and again somewhat later avoids calling Mohammed a heretic, describing him instead as an enemy of the Church greater than a heretic.[82] Rightly is he called the king of the sons of pride, Albar comments, to judge from his followers. Albar then attacks the Moslems in a series of epithets somewhat similar to those with which Eulogius attacked Christians who collaborated with the Moslems. "They [the Moslems] are swollen in pride, haughty with swollen hearts, languid in the enjoyment of carnal acts, gourmands in eating, usurpers in the seizing of things and greedy in the pillage of the poor, grasping without any feelings, liars without shame, false without any discrimination, impudent with no modesty of mind, cruel without mercy, usurping without justice, without honor or truth, knowing neither benignant affection nor the feeling for godliness, following modes and

[82] *Indiculus*, 31 (269) and 33 (271).

fads, foppish, sly, crafty, and besmirched with the dregs of all evils, not moderately so but mainly so, deriding humility as madness, spurning chastity as something dirty, detracting virginity as rust or mildew, treading upon the virtues of the soul with the vice of the body, showing their own morals in their dress and actions."[83]

In his exposition, Albar says, he has tried to apply in brief to Mohammed what Gregory enumerated at length about Antichrist, with no deviation from the rules for expositors. Not daring on his own to give new meanings to things, he has kept the meanings and prefigurations learned in his studies. He has transplanted the complete image of Antichrist to Mohammed. Albar goes on to consider the machinations of Mohammed from another angle.

Taking up the doctrine of Mohammed, Albar contrasts it with that of Christ. Mohammed spurned the celebration of the Lord's Resurrection on Sunday and chose instead to dedicate Friday to gourmandizing and lust, a day which Christians commemorate with sorrow and fasting because of the Lord's passion. Where Christ taught peace and patience Mohammed taught war and violence. Christ purified his followers with virginity and chastity, Mohammed besmirched his with lust and incest. Christ taught marriage, Mohammed divorce. Christ taught self-denial and fasting, Mohammed gourmandizing. Christ taught continence and temperance, Mohammed license and debauchery. Christ commands abstinence from one's own wife in time of fasting, Mohammed consecrates such days to Venus in excess.[84] Christ promises an angelic and spiritual heaven, Mohammed a carnal and bestial paradise. All previous heresies and errors, says Albar, came from Judea or the Church. Only Mohammed opposed a reign against that of Christ, making

---

[83] *Indiculus*, 31 (269f.) ; cf. *Memoriale*, III, v.

[84] Franke, *op.cit.*, 134f., points out that the Christians of Córdoba were not impressed by the penitential observance of Ramadan when the Moslems compensated for the abstinence of the day with excesses at night. Dozy, *Histoire*, II, vi (ed. Lévi-Provençal, I, 320), seems to interpret Albar's criticism as evidence of a lack of knowledge about Islam.

use of rebellion and the sword. With good reason is he called Antichrist who is the most open defamer and the most subtle destroyer of Christianity. Christ had precursors who foretold His coming. So, too, Mohammed has precursors of his wickedness who prefigured him completely in his guile. "If my readers wish to reprehend these words," Albar says in his defense, "let them first go through the volumes of the doctors and by meditating on what they read learn more, and not malign what has been openly expounded."[85] This statement indicates that a number of Christians did not regard Mohammed or Islam as really serious evils. Again Albar speaks of Mohammed and Islam in comparison with other "heresies and errors" in a way that implies that he regarded them as more dangerous than a heresy.

It is better, Albar goes on, to discuss what is evident than what is obscured with difficulties. He prefers, he says, to treat of present evils than of what to expect in the future, that is to say, he prefers to treat of the yoke of servitude prophesied of old which was in his time oppressing the Christians of Córdoba. Earlier doctors who called Antiochus, Nero, and others precursors of Antichrist would today call Mohammed the organ for Antichrist, says Albar. Jerome says that all heresiarchs are Antichrist and that Antiochus and Nero represented Antichrist only in part, and St. John's assertion that there are many Antichrists is corroborated by others, Albar argues. Lest he be accused of relying on Jerome only, he quotes from Hilary's *Contra Arianos*.

Many doctors have pointed out, Albar notes, that Antichrist attempts to re-establish the Mosaic law with the "evil" of circumcision. Mohammed not only has restored circumcision but prohibits the flesh of swine to his followers. Albar then begins his interpretation of the Apocalypse as applied to his own surroundings in Córdoba. The passage contains a great deal of information about the Christians of Córdoba and has been quoted frequently by those who have studied the martyrs. Everyone, Albar says, opens his

[85] *Indiculus*, 33 (271).

mind to Antichrist (Mohammed) almost continuously. Christians have his mark on them when they neglect their own ways, proven by the Fathers, and follow those of the Gentiles. They have his name on their foreheads, Albar says, when they forget the Sign of the Cross for the expression of the Moslems. This statement probably refers to the blessing which Moslems regularly invoked upon the prophet Mohammed, "May God bless him and save him." When Christians undergo circumcision to avoid Moslem scorn and despise the circumcision of the heart which the Lord has commanded, what else do they do, asks Albar, but bear his mark in their minds and on their bodies? "And when we delight in their verses and in their thousand fables and even pay a price to serve them and to go along with them in their most evil deeds, and when we hereby lead a life in the world and gorge our bodies, gathering together from the unlawful service and execrable ministry abundant riches, jewels, perfumes, and a wealth of clothes and different things, making provision far into the future for ourselves, our sons, and our grandsons, and writing with our hands rather than theirs the name of the infamous beast with the honor and reverence which they are wont to pay to it; do we not openly bear the name of the beast in our right hand when our feelings are such? And when we sinfully accuse the brethren to the impious kings because of worldly honors, and when we hand the sword of betrayal to the enemies of the Most High God for the slaying of the Lord's flock, and buy with money authority and office for the sake of carrying out the same villainy, what else do we do but traffic with the name of the beast, wearing his most cruel mark ourselves and sin by exposing the sheep of God to the teeth of wolves by our evil commerce?"[86]

Thus too, says Albar, when Christians inquire concerning Mohammedan rites (*sacramenta*), and when they gather

[86] *Ibid.*, 35 (273f.). The "sword of betrayal" (gladium revelationis) probably refers also to a betrayal of Christian beliefs by those who advised the Moslems of quotations from Holy Scripture to use against their fellow Christians.

together the teachings of Mohammedan philosophers, not to refute them but to study their style, meanwhile neglecting holy reading, they place the number [666] of the name of the beast in the Christian temple as an idol. At this point Albar begins his oft-quoted complaint. "What trained person, I ask, can be found today among our laity who with a knowledge of Holy Scripture looks into the Latin volumes of any of the doctors? Who is there on fire with evangelical love, with love like that of the prophets, like that of the apostles? Do not all the Christian youths, handsome in appearance, fluent of tongue, conspicuous in their dress and action, distinguished for their knowledge of Gentile lore, highly regarded for their ability to speak Arabic, do they not all eagerly use the volumes of the Chaldeans, read them with the greatest interest, discuss them ardently, and, collecting them with great trouble, make them known with every praise of their tongue, the while they are ignorant of the beauty of the Church and look with disgust upon the Church's rivers of paradise as something vile. Alas! Christians do not know their own law, and Latins do not use their own tongue, so that in all the college of Christ there will hardly be found one man in a thousand who can send correct letters of greeting to a brother. And a manifold crowd without number will be found who give out learnedly long sentences of Chaldean rhetoric. So that from the more sophisticated song of those people they embellish their final clauses metrically and in more polished beauty with the bond of a single letter, according to the demands of that tongue, which closes all phrases and clauses with riming vowels and even, as is possible for them, the various expressions containing the letters of the whole alphabet are all metrically reduced to one ending or to a similar letter. There are many other things which would have shown the reliability of this explanation of ours; that is, which would have brought out into the light the things we are exposing."[87]

Albar's complaint may be compared with the surprise which the abbot Esperaindeo expressed in a letter to Albar

[87] *Ibid.*, (274f.).

that someone should come to him with difficult problems concerning Holy Scripture when so many people were occupying themselves with popular writings.[88] A few comments may be made about the passage quoted above. Albar speaks of a laity untrained in Scripture and the Fathers, unlike himself, and his complaint does not include the clergy. His references to "one man in a thousand" and to a "manifold crowd" may be stereotyped phrases, but they suggest a numerous Christian community of Córdoba. The "Chaldean" works mentioned may indicate that Arabic learning in Córdoba was oriented toward Syria and Mesopotamia rather than toward Egypt and Arabia. Albar's description of Arabic poetry, it may be noted, is also an approximate description of rimed Latin prose, which was used frequently by Mozarab writers.[89]

The *Indiculus* ends rather abruptly. There was probably more to the text, for the manuscript comes to an end at the end of a gathering, which gives the catchwords for the following page: "quam exponimus."[90] Although the sense of the sentence is complete, it is unlikely that these two words represent the end of the text. They are placed at the bottom of the page where the manuscript regularly places the catchword. When the copyist wishes to crowd in final words of a text he places them immediately below the last line. Probably, however, the author did not add more than the express statement that he was not going to write about the "many other things" which he knew.

The last quarter of the Albar codex contains assorted writings, some of which seem to pertain indirectly to the *Indiculus*. In the thirteen folios immediately after the *Indiculus* appears an *Interrogatio* in which are discussed terms which can be used in reference to God: *natura, substantia, persona, nomina appellativa, nomen principale aut consequentiale, nomina essentialia que ad unitatem nature perti-*

---

[88] Albar correspondence, Letter VIII, 1.
[89] Wilhelm Meyer, *Gesammelte Abhandlungen zur mittellateinischen Rythmik* (2 vols.; Berlin, 1905), II, 13.
[90] Albar codex, folio 164v.

nent, and especially *nomina que solum in Christo filio Dei diquntur que ad unitatem pertinent, et ipsa nomina non conveniunt patri nec spiritui sancto, sed solum in ipso filio incarnatum.*[91] The next seventeen folios contain an *Indicium penitentie* based mainly on the Irish penitential of Cumian (590-622). The penitential of the Albar codex also derives in part from the *Collectio hispana* of councils, from a penitential of Egbert of York (d. 766), and from an *Excerptum de diversis criminibus et remediis eorum* attributed to Pope Gregory III (731-741). Penitentials of Silos and Albelda also seem to have an indirect relationship with the penitential of Córdoba.[92] The Albar codex contains too a brief *De genealogiis* which distinguishes Biblical persons of the same name. A brief treatise attributed to Augustine, On Adam and the Forbidden Tree, follows. The next seven folios are devoted to an *Indiculum de adventum Enoc et Elie adque Antichristi libris duobus id est Daniellis et Abocalissin Ioannis a beato Iheronimo expositum,* which has textual relationships with Jerome's Commentary on Daniel, Isidore's Etymologies, and the commentaries on the Apocalypse by Apringius of Beja (531 to 548) and Beatus of Liébana (ca. 786). The text of the *Indiculum,* which seems also to have a relationship with Albar's treatment of Antichrist in the *Indiculus luminosus,* contains many ellipses and errors of grammar and orthography which seem to be the fault of the scribe.[93] A brief Apostles' Creed is followed by a one-

[91] Jean Leclercq, "Un tratado sobre los nombres divinos en un manuscrito de Córdoba," *Hispania sacra,* II (1949), 327-338, discusses briefly the last folios of the codex and edits the text of the *Interrogatio.*

[92] The text is edited and discussed by J. Pérez de Urbel and Luis Vázquez de Parga, "Un nuevo penitencial español," AHDE, XIV (1942-1943), 5-32. Cumian, PL 87, 979-998; Egbert, PL 89, 401-436; Gregory III, PL 89, 587-698.

[93] The text has been edited from ms Escorial R-II-18 by A. C. Vega as part of his article, "El 'Liber de haeresibus' de San Isidro de Sevilla y el 'Códice Ovetense,'" *La ciudad de Dios,* 171 (1958), 262-268, with a brief introduction. Vega suggests the work may be the work of a Spanish author as early as the fifth century. Cf. Jerome, Commentary on Daniel, PL 25, 531A and especially 566D-567A; Isidore, *Etymologiae,* VIII, xi, 20-22 (PL 82, 316); *Apringii Pacensis episcopi tractatus*

page liturgical text with musical notes and a thirteen-folio *Lectio de assumptio sancte Marie* which has been identified as the work of Paschasius Radbertus (785-860).[94]

in Apocalysin, ed. A. C. Vega (Escorial, 1940), 46 and especially 47f.; *Beati in Apocalypsin*, ed. H. Sanders, 82f., 128, 397, 462, 474f., 496f., 500-505, and 608.

[94] C. Lambot, "L'homélie du pseudo-Jerome sur l'assomption et l'évangile de la nativité de Marie d'après une lettre inédite d'Hincmar," *Revue bénédictine*, 46 (1934), 265-282; cf. also PL 30, 126-147.

CHAPTER XIII

LATER LETTERS OF THE ALBAR CORRESPONDENCE

Only one martyr died in the year the *Indiculus* was written, the priest Abundius on 11 July 854. No other year recorded in the *Memoriale* lists so few martyrs. It had been ten months since the death of the previous martyr, the virgin Pomposa, on 19 September 853, and it would be almost ten months before the next martyrdoms on 30 April 855. These years were not uneventful in the history of the martyr movement, however. Besides the *Indiculus* there are five letters (IX-XIII) of the Albar correspondence which indicate that for the Christians of Córdoba the years 853-855 were filled with controversy about the martyrdoms. The additional information which the letters provide about the controversy complicates considerably the general picture of the martyrdoms presented by Eulogius and in the *Indiculus*. The letters raise more questions than they settle, but they offer much information about aspects of life not discussed in the other sources and they serve to warn the reader that important episodes having to do with the martyrdoms may be unrecorded or so vaguely alluded to in the major sources as to escape notice. Recently the long-accepted date of 860-861 for the letters has come to be questioned and earlier dates of 854 or 857 have been suggested. The earlier date seems more likely, and the letters will be discussed before the *Apologeticus martyrum* of Eulogius, written in 857.

Letters IX-XIII[1] of the Albar correspondence seem to constitute a unit, although it is not easy to account for the role of Letter X in the group. In Letter IX, to Romanus Medicus, Albar defends himself against charges of defrauding a monastery in connection with legal arrangements he made to safeguard his property while he was suffering from

---

[1] Madoz, *Epistolario*, 185-210; ES, XI, 151-171; PL 121, 464-478.

a serious illness. In Letter X, from one anonymous bishop to another, the author defends dispensations he had granted, perhaps to Christians who had compromised their faith in some way with the Moslem persecutors. In Letters XI-XIII Albar asks Bishop Saul to dispense him from the effects of the sacrament of Penance which he had received when near death from clergy not in communion with Saul, and, after being refused by Saul, reproaches his bishop with an account of irregularities of Saul's own life. Madoz follows Flórez in dating the letters in 860-861. Pérez de Urbel dates them between 854 and 857. Franke dates them about 857.[2] The dates are hypothetical, however, and all that can be stated definitely is that the last three letters should be dated sometime between June 853 and March 859. Since Albar in Letter XIII refers to the first stage of the persecution, the lines would seem to have been written after the second stage of the persecution began in June 853. In the same passage Albar mentions Eulogius without any epithet of praise, a fact which inclines one to believe that the lines were written before Eulogius' martyrdom in March 859.[3] Letter IX seems to have been written shortly before Letter XI, and Letter X can be dated almost any time between early 853 and 860-861 (or even a hundred years earlier), according as one interprets it. The contents of Letters IX and XI-XIII will be surveyed here before Letter X and the problems associated with it are taken up.

Since Albar does not mention the persecution in Letter IX, one can argue that it was written before the second stage of the persecution began. The argument is weak, however, because Albar may have had no reason to bring up the persecution. The illness of Albar should not be related with advanced age. He blames his troubles in part on "the ignorance of youth," and Letters XI and XIII, which he wrote after recovering from the illness, show that his intellectual vigor did not suffer from it. Romanus Medicus, "most

<hr />

[2] Madoz, *op.cit.*, 30-32; Flórez, ES, XI, 39f.; Pérez de Urbel, *San Eulogio*, 214; Franke, "Die freiwilligen Märtyrer," 157f.

[3] Letter XIII, 4.

serene and highest lord of all Catholics," to whom Letter IX is addressed was a Christian of high position and influence, closely associated with Count Servandus of Córdoba. He appears as an octogenarian imbued with anthropomorphist notions of God and as the enemy of Samson in 862-864. He may also be the Comes ibn Antonián mentioned in Arabic works.[4]

Albar's letter to Romanus is a reply to charges that he had defrauded a monastery of land it held from his father. Albar begins by recalling the friendship between his family and that of Romanus. In a passage that provides information of interest about Mozarab judicial processes he asks Romanus, "trained in solemn law and adorned as a prince with the powers of moderation," at least to hear what he has to say. Although a prosecuting attorney (*assertor*) may make his charges convincingly and at length, says Albar, honest judges will never be moved by a one-sided presentation of a case. After the defense has been heard, everything is weighed without haste and a final judgment is given. This is all I ask, says Albar.

You who have known me from the cradle know well enough that I am not guilty of pride, thievery, and insolence. It is clear for all to see that I am besieged by troubles which would upset the most patient soul. But I have succeeded in keeping the friendship even of my adversaries.[5] True, my iniquity and the ignorance of youth rise up against me, so that whatever I do turns out to my disadvantage. But, God is my witness, that whatever Felix the Manichean and Julian the Confessor falsely and importunately charge me with before you was a matter of accident and not of plan. And well does that "religious" know this, but he treads on his conscience, disregarding what is known, concocting and defending something else. Apart from this letter, Felix and Julian are not mentioned in the sources. F. R. Franke indicates that Julian may be the enemy whom Albar in Letter XIII, to Saul, decries as neither a confessor nor a religious

---

[4] *Apologeticus*, preface to Bk. II, 6.
[5] Letter IX, 2; ms "omnes *adversantes* mihi."

if the truth be told,[6] but Albar's words there seem rather to be an indirect reference to Saul himself.

Permit me to explain what took place, Albar requests. Before my illness and the "remedy of penance" which I received, I endowed the site of that monastery with many gifts and other things. The accuser cannot deny that I did this freely and on my own, as neither my father of blessed memory nor any of my ancestors did, and the whole neighborhood can testify to the truth of what I say. Why should I lie about this matter when I am on the threshold of death and under the law of penance? he asks, indicating that the letter was written before his correspondence with Saul. For the benefit of those who are now accusing me, Albar says, I shall make clear what the agreement was and how it came to cause trouble. I wanted to buy back the whole place for myself and, in an effort to avoid the disturbance of the *Romani,* I sought out that prince whom you know. It seems that Albar here is not referring to Romanus himself as the "prince," as he later seems to refer to Saul as an anonymous "mean little man." The prince may have been Moslem or Christian. For, Albar continues, as the Confessor had said correctly, those people wished to sell what they had bought from my father or me. The prince and I agreed that I should collect my goods through him, relying on his honor and position and trusting that no one could prevent him from accomplishing what I wanted done. When he came to see me during my illness, I explained what I wanted and he promised to do everything without causing any difficulty. Not at all suspecting what would later take place, I made the sale signed by witnesses. By bringing him in I hoped to keep the others off and gather together the whole estate for myself using him as an agent.[7] But he, having other things to do and not being very enthusiastic about our agreement, neglected my property and affairs, in which he had

---

[6] Franke, *op.cit.*, 155; Letter XIII, 2.

[7] Letter IX, 4 "ut ingressione ipsius alios seduceremus, et nobis per eum totum terminum adplicaremus"; ms "inpeditus *et* de *quod* fuerat *gestum* non satis."

no investment. Robberies and the licenses of the *Romani* increased, and they threatened to take over the whole estate, as if I had no rights there. And the prince was unwilling[8] to take action against them. What could I do in such a situation, sick as I was? Six months later the prince came to see me in person and asked me to sell him in fact what he was holding under our agreement. God is my witness that I refused to turn over my inheritance to him at first. But he argued that he had done so many favors for me that he deserved to have it as a gift. When I reconsidered my contract with him and compared his power with my weakness, I saw that I had no choice. But I outlined the rights of the church (terminum ecclesiae indicavi), which I, and not my father, had granted, and I signed a separate agreement about it with witnesses. I commended the confessors to him many times, and I made ceaseless appeals about their place. Unfortunately our agreement was not what I wanted. He gave what he wanted, when he wanted, and how he wanted.

What can I do now, most serene lord? I cannot resist him, I cannot turn it over to anyone else, I cannot buy it back. I am ashamed, but I cannot repair what has been done. I have tried to buy it back from him many times for much more than what he paid for it, but without success. Everyone reproaches me, but no one more than myself. I make my appeal to that sentence of our doctors which says that the motive is more important than the deed. I have recounted for you in detail what took place because I have heard that Confessor boast of many things as if you said them. But I did not believe them because I have experienced too often your feelings for me. Please treat me as if I were in your presence, pleads Albar, although poverty and weakness keep me away from you. Destroy the malevolent complaints against me with paternal judgment and turn a deaf ear to their contentions. I ask you to eradicate anything that Felix, the son of the judge Gratiosus, and that Confessor have planted in the ears of Count Servandus. In your time we could argue the cases of others. How much more then are

---

[8] Ms "invasiones *n*olebat."

we entitled to look after our own affairs? Recall the friendship of our families and receive me as a son. I would like to say more but I do not wish to impose on you with more than a letter. Please do not scrutinize too closely my words which I have written down in haste. May the increased happiness of Your Paternity continue to flourish for many years. Amen.

This letter is particularly valuable because of the information it provides about the judicial arrangement among the Christians in Córdoba. Albar indicates that sentences were issued only after both sides of a case had been presented by attorneys. He also indicates that he himself had previously served as an attorney. From what he says of Romanus and Servandus, they appear to have been of quasi-judicial rank if not judges. A judge Gratiosus is also mentioned. The rather respectable court procedure described by Albar seems to resemble somewhat the court of the Moslem cadi, where attorneys also argued cases before the cadi and those who sat with him.

Letters XI-XIII deal with Albar's dispute with Saul. In Letter XII Saul indicates that both he and Albar wrote other letters to each other in their dispute besides the three which appear in the Albar codex, but Letter X is not one of these. Albar's attitude in Letters XI and XIII seems a change from his uncompromising defense of right and truth in the *Indiculus*. In the letters he argues the cause of leniency in ecclesiastical matters, much as the anonymous bishop does in Letter X. Bishop Saul's position in his letter to Albar seems rather uncompromising for some reason towards the clergy who had admitted Albar to the sacrament of Penance.

The administration of the sacrament of Penance in ninth-century Córdoba differed from what was followed in later centuries. It could be received only once in life and entailed a very rigorous discipline. Most Christians postponed the reception of it until the moment of death because of the difficult life it demanded and in order to insure that they would not lapse into sin again with no hope of receiving the sacrament. When the sacrament was received on one's death bed from a priest or a bishop, reconciliation to the Church could follow immediately, but in case of recovery the penitent was bound by all the obligations of public penance. The obligations were assigned by the bishop. The penitent was excluded for a time from Holy Communion. He was required to devote himself to prayer, almsgiving, and fasting, to wear a distinctive garb, and to refrain from social life and the conduct of business. These effects of the sacrament as a rule were carried out in the season of Lent. On Good Friday the bishop in a solemn ceremony with prayer and the imposing of hands reconciled the penitent to the Church and restored him to Holy Communion. Thereafter the penitent was obliged to live like a monk in the world. He was not permitted to marry, become a cleric, or hold public office. As a rule, if the penitent again lapsed into sin he had to rely on compunction or perfect sorrow for forgiveness from his sin.[9]

If the sins of the penitent did not deserve excommunication, he was not obliged to present himself regularly before the bishop for the imposition of hands, as public penitents did, nor was he ineligible to become a cleric. Those who voluntarily received the penance from a desire to expiate their sins by a more perfect life, as a number of the Christians of Córdoba seem to have done, were not barred from Holy Communion even temporarily, nor do they seem to have been barred from the clerical state.[10] Albar's major complaint to Saul is that he is barred from the reception of the Eucharist, but he seems to think that he is entitled to consideration different from that given to public penitents.

Recovering from his illness, Albar seems to have performed his penitential discipline for an unusually long time. As Good Friday approached, he sought reconciliation from Bishop Saul, even though the "pseudobishop," as Saul calls the person who administered the sacrament to Albar, was

[9] Sister Patrick Jerome Mullins, *The Spiritual Life according to Saint Isidore of Seville* (Washington, 1940), 89-104; Sage, *Paul Albar*, 104ff.

[10] Mullins, *op.cit.*, 93f.

still at hand. Saul, however, would not appoint a priest to dispense Albar from the effects of the sacrament when Albar would not come to him in person. The eventual resolution of the situation is not known. Albar must have come back into the good graces of Saul to have been able to compose the vita and passio of the martyr Eulogius, but it may be noted that he does not refer to Saul by name in the *Vita Eulogii*. In their letters both Albar and Saul speak of "absolution" (*absolutio, solvere*) from the discipline of the penance, although Albar seems to prefer the terms *reconciliatio* and *remedium*. In the following discussion "absolution" is translated as "dispensation" from the effects of the sacrament in order to avoid the misunderstanding that it is absolution from sin.

Albar's first letter appears somewhat peremptory. He would have written much more to Saul, he says, had not the "storm of the world" and the "calamity of our time" shackled his tongue. He has even omitted salutations in the letter "because bitter difficulties and cruel scourges have closed the font of eloquence."[11] He points out that he has been subject to penitential discipline since the time of his illness, presumably longer than the usual period. Although he could have obtained his "reconciliation" elsewhere,[12] he prefers to receive it from Saul (*permissum vestrum inquirere*) as the Fathers have ordained. He asks Saul therefore to send a letter authorizing the one of his priests whom he regards as 'first, best, and most suitable" (spoken in irony perhaps) to grant him "reconciliation." He is willing to comply wholeheartedly with Saul's "saving precepts," to perform any fast, almsgiving, or good work required of him, as long as he may return to Holy Communion. In nothing will he deviate from the "rules of truth and possibility," and he is prepared "with the brake of temperance" to force his mind which has

[11] Letter XI, 1; ms "propiamque *miseriee mee* suggessionem."
[12] Madoz, *op.cit.*, 201, contains an omission. Ms reads, "exclusus *mansi remedio. Et licet reconciliationem aliunde valerem frui* si vellem." Ms also reads in this paragraph "sententia*m* formidavi," "illis reconciliationem," and "operis bon*i*."

thus far wandered through devious things to keep away from everything declared illicit and prohibited by paternal command, as much as possible. To an extent Albar's words here seem to echo the words of the anonymous bishop in Letter X.[13] If, Albar continues, he does not receive an answer within the week [Holy Week], he will seek the reconciliation "from your brothers and bishops," for he does not intend to pass "this feast" [Easter] bound with the other penitents.

Saul begins his letter (XII) with practically the same statement as did Albar, saying that afflictions prevent him too from writing. He finds it strange that Albar, recovered from his illness, cannot come to seek the dispensation in person, yet expects Saul to send a letter to a priest in Córdoba to dispense him.[14] Saul notes that Albar has said that many were forced to make a statement (*enarrare*) against their will. There is, however, no statement to this effect in Albar's letter. Saul's words are vague. *Enarrare* seems to be used instead of *confiteri*. It could mean a public confession of sin in connection with the sacrament of Penance, and mean that Albar had not received the sacrament voluntarily, or it could mean a public statement of faith before the persecutors which did not "confess" the religion of Christ, and mean that Albar had been forced to make such a statement of dissimulation.[15]

What shall I say to you, Saul continues, when I am committed to silence in these days? I prejudge no one. I neither condemn or justify nor punish what I do not know. Saul tells Albar that if he cannot come to Saul he should seek the dispensation from those from whom he received the penance, for if their imposition of hands was worthy then, their dispensation is no doubt acceptable now. As he has told Albar before, he says, it is not in his competence to judge concerning such things unless the question of them

---

[13] Letter XI, 2; cf. Appendix III, 10.
[14] Letter XII, 1; ms "sed velle ut."
[15] Cf. *Indiculus*, 9, 14, and especially 15-16.

and him is taken up in a legitimate council.[16] But, as he has said before, this thing (*negotium*) is not permitted to any member of the clergy when the bishop is present and able to do it. Since Saul is available in person, why does Albar seek to communicate with him in letters rather than come to see him? And who might they be, he asks, whom Albar calls *Salsuginosae*, identifying them practically with Migetians, Donatists, and Luciferians? Although Albar says nothing about these rigorist heretics in Letter XI, he does refer to *Salsuginosae* in Letter XIII and in the *Indiculus* he condemns his enemies as Donatists.[17] Consequently, Saul continues, I wonder why you, a prudent man, condemn those who still abide by the censure of the council, who do not follow the example of the indolent crowd bent on ruin, but instead are guided by the authority of the Fathers until the sentence of a majority of the bishops is either confirmed as an edict or is modified as law in a decree. Albar's extant letters to Saul contain no such condemnation. It would seem that Albar condemned those who refused to recognize the "pseudobishop" connected with his penance, who was apparently the object of the council's censure. The sentence of the majority of bishops may be the sentence of bishops referred to in the *Indiculus*,[18] apparently against the *Praesul episcoporum*, who would be Reccafred. The "authority of the Fathers," which was probably a guide for all councils, figures prominently in the anonymous bishop's defense of the council mentioned in Letter X. The "crowd bent on ruin" would seem to be Christians who failed to live up to the demands of their faith in the persecution rather than the zealots of the martyr movement.

---

[16] "non est mensure mee iudicandum de talibus, nisi fuerit inspirante Deo concilio legitimo eorum et nostra questio ventilata." Ms "aut imbe*cill*itatis corporis."

[17] Letter XIII, 4; *Indiculus*, 20. Cf. E. Amann, "Migetius," DTC, X, ii, 1720ff.; G. Bareille, "Donatisme," DTC, IV, ii, 1701-1728; E. Amann, "Lucifer de Cagliari," DTC, IX, i, 1032-1044. For Donatists and Luciferians cf. Isidore, *Etymologiae*, VIII, v, 51 and 55 (PL 82, 302 and 303).

[18] *Indiculus*, 19.

As I have said, Saul states, we who are subject to ecclesiastical laws are not to rebel against the churches, and I wrote you previously about this most lovingly but incompletely, because I did not understand your writing. But now that I find proper words and recognize your hand I write to you in amicable love urging you for the remedy of your soul to follow things which are holy and avoid association with evil people, lest you be contaminated by the touch of pitch. What good would a dispensation to receive the sacraments do you, Saul asks, if the next day you bound yourself in some way to a "pseudobishop"? He urges Albar to keep always in his heart the words of Scripture to trust in the Lord and not to fear those who cannot harm the soul, and thus admit himself to the "sacrament of reconciliation,"[19] Holy Communion it would appear. But if something else please you, he adds, do what seems good to you, or what seems prudent. I have said all I can, Saul concludes. Of the many things I have known I have directed a few to Your Charity. The saints of God are mindful of you, as am I in all things. We greet with a holy kiss all those in the walls of your villa.

Saul indicates, as does Albar in a letter to Eulogius,[20] that the Christians of Córdoba in the ninth century used a type of abbreviated writing or shorthand in writing to each other. Albar evidently was included, as a result of his penance if not for any other reason, among those subject to ecclesiastical laws, who Saul says were not to rebel against the churches. Saul's last statement, however, suggests that Albar lived with his family. What Saul remarks in the letter about the "pseudobishop" is about all that is known of him. In the next letter Albar refers, probably with irony, to those who imposed penance on him as *prevaricatores*, a term which describes apostates as well as those who abrogated their penitential discipline without episcopal dispensation.

[19] "Hec et horum similia rogo ut prius tecum semper tractare et sic te sacramentum reconciliationis admittere." Cf. Férotin, *Le liber ordinum*, 92.
[20] *Luminosum vestri*, before the *Documentum martyriale*.

It is possible that an attempt was made to replace Saul as bishop of Córdoba, just as in 863 there was an attempt to replace his successor, Bishop Valentius, with a pseudobishop. Aimoin reports that in 858 Saul was held in veneration as their bishop by the Christians of Córdoba,[21] indicating that any rival bishop (pseudobishop) had disappeared by that time.

It is difficult to tell whether Albar was seeking to play the role of peacemaker between Saul and the "pseudobishop," as Franke suggests,[22] or whether he wanted to return to communion with Saul without incurring the displeasure of the pseudobishop. In his letter to Albar, which seems neither antagonistic nor capricious, Saul seems to have considered both possibilities.

Albar reacted petulantly to Saul's letter. His reply (Letter XIII) is explosive and indignant. The words of your letter, he begins, are not yours but those of that mean little man (*homunculus*), destroyer of the fatherland and sower of heresies. Whereas we have written to you sincerely and simply in our own hand seeking a remedy of the soul, you have written to us with harshness and deceit, not from your heart but from a stomach upset by too much drinking, and you hand us not the cup of life but poison, rejecting a son from your love. And you think, I know not by what counsel, that not only I but your whole flock is sick, and you do not treat it with healing remedies but you tear it to pieces with angry teeth and you destroy your members with your own hands. Oh how vulnerable would that wicked man be if he would come out in the open and fight like a brave man, and not hidden like a turtle, sharpening his sword in the shadows like a woman. He is condemned by his own judgment. He is not properly a confessor nor a priest (*sacerdos*). His dress identifies him as a confessor but his tongue brands him as a derider [of the faith]. He wears the woolen cloth of a religious and the beard of a layman. He acts holy but he is really a proud detractor. No wonder that he criticizes priests (*sacerdotes*) of today when he attempts to attack the

[21] *Translatio*, 10-11.   [22] Franke, *op.cit.*, 156.

doctors! No wonder he seeks to condemn clerics when he is not afraid to lessen the deeds of the martyrs! With how many testimonies could I not destroy that "most stupid" and not "most wise" little man (*homunculus*) and his confused[23] letter, if I were not bound by reverence for your honor.

Apparently not too much bound by reverence for Saul, Albar proceeds to attack "that most stupid little man," seemingly Saul's worser self. There seems to be no distinction between the accusations Albar makes in the letter against his enemy, the *homunculus*, and the criticism he directs against Saul in the second person plural. The person is probably only a rhetorical contrivance to permit Albar to attack Saul indirectly. What Albar says about the dress of the *homunculus* could apply to someone who should have been observing the tonsure and the garb of a public penitent. He may also have been a Mozarabic bishop, who, according to Leovigildus, would have been without a beard and whose cowled dress probably resembled that of a "religious."[24] It is possible too that Saul was a penitent.

The end of Saul's letter contradicts the beginning, charges Albar. In avoiding holiness and wisdom the author fell into stupidity, and he spends time making accusations against people who have been condemned when he is dispensing one who is bound by penance. Anyone whom he dispenses with his invective will find out that he is not really dispensed. When I described my affliction, my lord, I requested a remedy. But this letter, in an inimical tone, quibbles about words, and you seek to change my feelings for you from sympathy to enmity. You advise me to trust in the Lord and not to fear those who cannot harm the soul, but you yourself have ignored this advice for a long time. Before becoming our bishop,[25] he says, you communicated with a certain anathematized person many times against the insti-

[23] "*Incondita,*" which may mean "fetid" also.

[24] *De habitu clericorum,* iv and ix.

[25] Letter XIII, 3, "ante nostrum episcopum honorem . . . post honorem."

tutes of the Fathers and the decrees of our predecessors, and after becoming bishop you have communicated with priests (*sacerdotes*) in communion with him, not out of fear but of your own free will. Remember how strongly I advised you not to give him a chasuble for saying Mass, in those days when I was motivated by love for you.

The anathematized cleric could be almost anyone of authority and power in ecclesiastical circles in Córdoba. Albar brings him in as a reply to Saul's remark about the "pseudo-bishop." The cleric may have been someone like Bishops Samuel of Granada or Hostegesis of Malaga. He may be the "pseudobishop" even, or the *Praesul maledictus seu bio-thenatus* (anathematized?) of the *Indiculus*,[26] or Reccafred of Seville. Earlier Saul was in communion with Reccafred, even, apparently, after Reccafred had him imprisoned, but Reccafred is not known to have been anathematized. Had Reccafred sought to replace Saul as bishop of Córdoba, a see he himself probably occupied once,[27] Saul could have called him a "pseudobishop."

Albar continues: How many people anathematized by the Fathers have not been absolved at your command irregularly outside a council?[28] It is difficult to tell whom Albar has in mind here. Bishops were not allowed to absolve those excommunicated by other bishops without a council,[29] but Albar says that those Saul absolved were anathematized by the Fathers. Everyone admits, Albar asserts, that your beginnings would have been praiseworthy if 400 solidi had not been openly paid to the eunuchs and others, not secretly but through documents written in Arabic. These solidi were taken from the income of the church, which even debtors cannot claim. It is not permitted to the laity, even the faithful, to receive any of these funds, gathered from the ministry itself, for the pittance of the church is distributed to

---

[26] Cf. *Apologeticus*, preface to Bk. II, 2-4; *Indiculus*, 19.

[27] Cf. Acts of the Council of Córdoba in 839 and *Vita Eulogii*, 4 and 6-7.

[28] Ms "impulsus suggesser*int*. Quant*i* a patribus."

[29] I Council of Nicaea, canon 5, part of the *Collectio hispana*.

priests alone. How many priests have been ordained without testimonials? How many bishops have been consecrated without the approval of the clergy and the faithful? How many churches have been divided, with two pastors, against the institutes of the Fathers? How many have been placed in divers offices by you in all the basilicas contrary to the canons? I ask you, see for yourself. With the double clergy Albar accuses Saul of having appointed, the clergy whom the anonymous bishop seems to have reinstated, and whatever clergy were associated with the "pseudobishop," there must have been a great deal of confusion about clerical orders in Córdoba at this time. Such confusion would have been much to the liking of the Moslems. It is striking, however, that even in the midst of the persecution there was no want of candidates for clerical office in Córdoba.

But you disregard all this, Albar complains to Saul, and only in our case do you look with disfavor upon these priests of our time, and you do not do this at any other time except when we appeal to you. For face to face you saw the honorable abbot Athanagildus and you willingly said (granted?) this to him in person, and you ordered Eulogius to offer the sacrifice of the Mass in the first stage of the persecution. And now when my case arises you go against yourself. Athanagildus and Eulogius were clergy in whose cases Saul evidently did not insist on rules he would not overlook in the case of Albar. The case of Athanagildus is not known, but Eulogius suspended himself from saying Mass in order to dissociate himself from the errors of Reccafred of Seville until Saul made him return to his priestly duties.[30]

Happy will he be, Albar continues, who lives to see the day of the council you await! Would that peace would return! Then would your voice and many others be stilled. How can you speak bravely about putting trust in the Lord and not fearing those who cannot harm the soul and meanwhile hide and move about separated from your own through

---

[30] *Vita Eulogii*, 6-7. There is extant an epitaph of an abbot Athanagildus attributed to the abbot Samson. The date, Era 998 (A.D. 960), may be erroneous; cf. ES, XI, 319 and 527.

fear of men? In the beginning you ordered me ironically to get dispensation from those who bound me, and you added, "If their imposition of hands was worthy then, their dispensation is no doubt acceptable now." That simpleton cannot see that he speaks against himself in this and *Sardorum salsedinem devitans, quomodo salsuginem incurrerit nescit.* Albar mocks Saul here, it seems, for his query in Letter XII about the *Salsuginosae.* The meaning is not clear, but the gist seems to be that Saul, in seeking to avoid the errors of the Luciferians of Sardinia, who refused to recognize the orders of bishops who had associated with Arians, has unknowingly come to the same end by another way in his attitude towards Albar's penance and the "pseudobishop."

If he says this in earnest, Albar argues, then why does he in the end forbid me to associate with "evil people" and refer to them as tainted with pitch? But if he is mocking us in his beginning words, as is probably the case, then let that rough and earthy *assertor,* who prides himself on being without any courtly refinement, answer this: why does your own pastor bother about the dispensing in person of someone bound by those *prevaricatores*[31] who have no power to bind? How can he be dispensed who has not been bound in the first place? Let this be an answer to you then: we have another judge of our conscience, the Lord of all, who can, without delay, cure an invalid. Albar, after referring to the parable of the Good Samaritan, who assisted the man beaten by robbers after the priest and levite had passed him by, concludes by telling Saul that he will not seek a judgment from anyone else, for he is sick of being subject to judgments other than those of his own bishop.

In seeking his dispensation directly from God, Albar could have turned to his *Confessio,* which is a long general accusation of faults and an act of sorrow. The work has been studied in detail by Carleton M. Sage. The *Confessio* is of interest for the theology and cosmology of Albar and offers

---

[31] Albar uses the word, referring to those from whom he received Penance, with irony. Whether he accurately represents Saul's attitude towards them, however, is uncertain.

an extraordinary insight into his mind. Albar's theology and cosmology may be compared with the elaborate presentation of Samson in the *Apologeticus*. In several passages Albar's attitude towards man's salvation seems to reflect an almost fatalistic idea of predestination. The literary images used by Albar are also of interest. Although certain passages in the *Confessio* suggest that the work was written while his correspondence with Saul was still fresh in Albar's mind, the fact that Albar reveals so little about himself argues that the work is a manual of prayer and does not pertain to any particular situation of Albar's life. The *Confessio* could have been written and used by Albar in the days before he received his penance as well as afterwards. It may have served as a vade mecum for other "confessors." In the *Confessio* Albar prays that he may overcome sin and the devil and be restored to what God created him originally, evidencing a very heavy reliance upon the Lord for the purgation of his soul. He shows no tendency to identify himself with God in love as he does with Eulogius in the *Vita Eulogii*, but there seems to be a number of other similarities between the *Confessio* and the thought of Hallaj (d. 922). Such similarity in spiritual works of similar nature is not unexpected. In several points the *Confessio* is similar to the "Ri'ayah" of the sufi Muhasibi of Baghdad (781-857). Sage discusses earlier Latin works in the tradition of the *Confessio*.[32]

Letter X is perhaps the most difficult Cordoban source to interpret. It is undated, and neither author nor addressee is named. In the Albar codex the letter has neither title nor greeting. Letter XVII, from Bodo to Albar, the beginning of which has been mutilated in the codex, is the only other letter in the codex without a title. Six of the twenty letters

---

[32] Sage, *Paul Albar*, 83-183; *Vita Eulogii*, 18; Louis Massignon, *La passion d'al-Hasayn-ibn-Mansour al-Hallaj, martyr mystique de l'Islam exécuté à Bagdad le 26 mars 922* (2 vols.; Paris, 1922); id., *Akhbar al-Hallaj, recueil d'oraisons et d'exhortations du martyr mystique de l'Islam, Husayn ibn Mansur Hallaj...*, 3d ed. (Paris, 1957), 103-165; id., *Essai sur les origines du lexique technique de la mystique musulmane* (Paris, 1954), 245f. and 314.

have no greeting.[33] Saul's indication in Letter XII that he and Albar had exchanged anonymous letters may mean that the Christians of Córdoba occasionally protected themselves by leaving their writings anonymous. The compiler of the Albar codex may not have known who the author of Letter X was, but he may too have left the letter, like the *Indiculus*, anonymous to protect its author from reprisals at the hands of the Moslems because of derogatory remarks in the letter which can be interpreted as directed against the prophet Mohammed, King Mohammed of Córdoba, and the Moslems. It is possible also that the author may have been regarded as quasi-heretical or infamous and his name was omitted to deprive him of any historical fame. Albar, it is rather certain, neither wrote nor received the letter. The best reason to come to mind for its appearing in the codex where it does, immediately before the Albar-Saul correspondence, would seem to be that it offers an introduction to that correspondence. García-Villada and Franke regard the letter rather as an epilogue to the Albar-Saul letters.[34] It may be pointed out that, while the groups of letters in the Albar codex are not arranged in chronological order, individual letters within the groups are so arranged. It would seem therefore that, were Letter X intended as the epilogue to the Albar-Saul correspondence, it would follow rather than precede Letters XI-XIII in the codex. Letter X (and Letter IX) may be erratic single entries in the codex, however.

There seems to be no doubt that both author and addressee of the letter are bishops. The addressee, "most sublime lord, vicar of the apostles," "most holy lord," whose office was enjoined on him for the whole church, and who was at a distance from the afflictions besetting the author of the letter, appears to be not only a metropolitan but the primate of Spain, the archbishop of Toledo. The problem arises whether the addressee is Wistremirus or his successor in

---

[33] Letters XII, XIII, and XVII-XX.

[34] García-Villada, *Historia eclesiástica*, III, 106f.; Franke, *op.cit.*, 158ff.

the see of Toledo. When Eulogius was prevented from occupying the see of Toledo, to which he had been elected, the see remained vacant until after Eulogius' martyrdom in March 859.[35] It is not known when Wistremirus died. The hypothetical date of 858, which has been advanced by several authors, is intended evidently to accommodate as late a date as possible for Letter X in Eulogius' lifetime. The death of Wistremirus is one of several variable factors which have to be considered in dealing with Letter X.

The problem of the authorship of the letter seems at present insoluble. The study offered here seems to indicate that the author was Reccafred (the metropolitan of Seville) who practically took over affairs in the church of Córdoba at one time, or perhaps the person Saul in Letter XII calls a "pseudobishop," who evidently took the place of Saul when the latter was in hiding. This so-called "pseudobishop" could have been Reccafred. There are signs that the author of the letter is a metropolitan. He refers to the afflictions of "this our province." In vague terms he says: "Especially because Our Fraternity in a most firm decree bearing our personal signature affirms once and for all that the flock entrusted to us is guiltless and free from the infamy of all whisperings. And this decree is to be observed at all times with the same force as any other decree which has been confirmed by metropolitan sanction in the past and in the present."[36] If he is a metropolitan, the author is probably Reccafred of Seville. Ariulfus of Mérida, the only other metropolitan see known in Mozarabic Spain at this time apart from Toledo, would seem to be neither author nor addressee. According to the canons of the *Collectio hispana,* the acts of which appear to have been generally followed by the Christians of Córdoba, the only person who could summon a council of bishops, which the author of Letter X appears to have done, was the metropolitan of the province.[37]

---

[35] *Vita Eulogii,* 10.

[36] Letter X, 5.

[37] II Council of Arles, canon 18 (PL 84, 243f.); Council of Milevum, canon 10 (PL 84, 231); Martin of Braga's Excerpts from Eastern

In the *Apologeticus* some concern for this prerogative is shown in the summoning to Córdoba of the metropolitan, whom Samson leaves anonymous, for the "council" of Stephen, who was seeking to replace Bishop Valentius in the see of Córdoba, and two other bishops.[38] The metropolitan of Seville, as easily as any other bishop, could have regarded the persecution spoken of in Letter X as an affliction. And if he were Reccafred, who actually had assumed an independent authority in Córdoba in 851, he could have had as much occasion to grant dispensations as did the author of Letter X. An argument against Reccafred's being the author of the letter is that he had, as far as is known, held the attitude of the author of the letter from the beginning of the persecution, and the author says that he had changed to an attitude of leniency only shortly before writing the letter. Reccafred could, of course, have professed that his attitude was a changed one when in reality it was not.

The general consensus of opinion that Bishop Saul is the author of the letter is not without reason. One would expect the bishop of Córdoba to be the author of such a letter which seems to deal with the persecution in Córdoba. Saul's position is known to have been such that he would have had to change it to hold that of the author of the letter. Saul as well as Reccafred could have defended metropolitan authority and could have spoken of "this our province." Albar's accusation in Letter XIII that Saul absolved Christians from anathema on his own authority irregularly without a council[39] seems the best argument for Saul's authorship of Letter X. The anonymous bishop appears to defend himself against just such a charge. It seems somewhat unusual, however, that the metropolitan of Toledo and the bishop of Córdoba should communicate about matters which should have been taken up between the metropolitans of Toledo and Seville.

Fathers, canon 18 (Laodicea, 40) in PL 84, 577. Cf. A. M. Stickler, "Hispana collectio," LTK, V, 390.

[38] *Apologeticus*, preface to Bk. II, 8.

[39] Letter XIII, 3.

One may point out too that Reccafred as well as Saul could have absolved Christians from anathema too freely to suit Albar. In order to accommodate a change in Saul's attitude towards the martyrdoms one should date the letter as late as possible, towards the end of the martyrdoms, as one of the last recorded acts of Saul, and Saul is known to have venerated the martyrs as late as 858, when Odilard and Usuard visited Córdoba.[40] Saul's attitude in Letters XI-XIII is quite different from that of the author of Letter X. Moreover, it says little for the integrity of Saul that, after venerating the martyrs for so long and even suffering imprisonment because of them, he should, as the author of Letter X, turn against them and yield to their opponents because of arguments he must have heard in the first days of the martyr movement—that the martyrdoms were hurting not only the zealots but the whole Christian community.[41] Since both Saul's reputation and the repute of the martyrdoms among the Christians of Córdoba during the later days of the persecution are at stake in the matter of the authorship of Letter X, one should not conclude that Saul is the author without some care.

A possibility which has not heretofore been considered is that the "pseudobishop" mentioned by Saul in Letter XII,[42] someone who evidently was seeking to replace Saul as bishop of Córdoba, is the author of Letter X. He would have had such an attitude towards the martyrdoms as has the anonymous bishop. The existence of such a "pseudobishop" could explain Albar's letter (XI) to Saul asking for a dispensation from the effects of the sacrament of Penance. Such a "pseudobishop" could have been the one who admitted Albar to Penance at the time of his illness. The name of the "pseudobishop" could have been deleted from the codex because of his subsequent ill-fame. One of the

---

[40] *Translatio,* 10-11.

[41] Eulogius, *Memoriale,* II, xv, 1, *Documentum martyriale,* 11 and 16f., in 851 and Albar, *Indiculus,* 14, in 853-854 note that the opponents of the martyrs were using the argument that the martyrdoms were hurting the welfare of the church.

[42] Letter XII, 2.

vaguest passages in the letter[43] can be interpreted as a defense by a "pseudobishop" of his orders and his convoking of a council whose actions had been questioned. The personality of a "pseudobishop," better than either Reccafred or Saul, fits the author of Letter X. But almost nothing is known of him, and it is almost too simple a solution to regard him as the author of Letter X. Moreover, one may wonder why the metropolitan of Toledo would correspond with someone who was seeking to replace Saul as bishop of Córdoba while Saul was still alive. If the "pseudobishop" is the author of Letter X, he obviously felt obliged to defend himself against an important group of Christians in agreement with Saul at the time the letter was written, perhaps as early as 853. And contrary to the usual opinion that Saul yielded to the forces of compromise, Saul, who seems to have had undisputed episcopal authority in 858, would seem to have triumphed over the "pseudobishop" in the end.

Another possibility simpler than it is satisfying is that the letter was written in the eighth century, perhaps in one of the controversies involving Migetius or Elipandus, and is quoted by Albar to support his request to Bishop Saul in Letter XI. Inasmuch as Letter X cannot be reconciled satisfactorily with what is known of either Reccafred or Saul, it is possible that it pertains to another situation entirely.

F. R. Franke thinks that the letter was written by Bishop Saul to the metropolitan of Seville, Reccafred or his successor, and that it shows that Saul eventually yielded to the opponents of the martyrs.[44] The letter, however, appears to be a rebuttal of criticism which the addressee had previously made of the author. Since the attitude of Reccafred as given by Albar[45] is much like that of the author of the letter, Reccafred would not seem to be the critic-addressee. Nor would it seem that in the letter Saul, after a long struggle with Reccafred, is acceding to the metropolitan's point of view, because the letter repudiates rather than accedes

[43] Letter X, 2.
[44] Franke, *op.cit.*, 158ff.
[45] *Vita Eulogii*, 4 and 6-7.

to the point of view of the addressee. The addressee could be, of course, Reccafred's successor in the see of Seville if his attitude towards the martyrdoms were entirely different from that of Reccafred, but this solution, just as the solution of the "pseudobishop" as the author, seems too simple, because no successor of Reccafred is mentioned in the sources and nothing is known about him.

The letter can lend itself to a quite different interpretation, that Saul is telling Reccafred that he will no longer go along with him in his opposition to the martyrdoms and is dispensing from excommunication those anathematized by "our unwarranted sentence." Some parts of the letter confirm this interpretation rather strongly, but other parts lend themselves to it with difficulty. The metropolitans of Mérida and Toledo would have had to be in agreement with Saul in his defiance of Reccafred. And Saul, while usurping Reccafred's prerogative to convoke a council, would at the same time be acknowledging Reccafred's privileges as metropolitan. It is ironical that the letter should lend itself to two such different interpretations. According to one interpretation, those Saul, as the author of the letter, calls "heretics"[46] are the defenders of the martyrs; according to the other, they are the opponents of the martyrs.

One last possibility may be presented. The letter may have been addressed to the metropolitan of Braga, who, according to Pierre David, resided in Lugo in the mid-ninth century[47] and who may easily have been informed about events in Córdoba at this time. The author of the Chronicle of Roda, who may have been a bishop of Galicia, knew a good deal about the attack on Seville by Northmen in 848, and about this time Christians were immigrating to the north to take part in the repopulation of areas reconquered from Moslem rule. If the letter is addressed to the metropolitan of Braga, the author could be the metropolitan of Toledo, the metropolitan of Seville, or the bishop of Córdoba. The tendency of the author to quote Julian of Toledo

[46] Letter X, 2.
[47] David, *Etudes*, 119-184.

suggests that he may have been the metropolitan of Toledo. In view of the extensive defense of the validity of sacraments and the right to grant dispensations presented in the letter, the hypothesis that the letter was written to the metropolitan of Braga poses questions of considerable importance with regard to any ecclesiastical reform which may have been associated with the Reconquest.

The problem of dating Letter X is related closely to most of the other problems associated with the letter. A similarity in phraseology and ideas between the letter and the first part of the *Indiculus*[48] argues for an early date of 853 or 854. If the reference in the letter to a respite in the persecution is interpreted to refer to the end of the persecution, the letter can be dated in 860-861. Indeed, one could probably make a case for the letter's having been written in 864 by the pseudobishop, Stephen of Córdoba,[49] were it not that the letter then would have less than ever to do with other letters in the Albar codex. The actual date of the letter is of less importance than are two relative aspects of the date. How much does the letter have to do with the council of 852? And was the letter written before or after the Albar-Saul correspondence? In the present study neither of these questions is settled, but it seems that both the letter and the *Indiculus* are in some way related to the council of 852 and that the letter precedes rather than follows the situation seen in the Albar-Saul letters.

Those who date the letter in 857 or 860-861 interpret it and the Albar-Saul correspondence to show that a deep split developed between the Christians of Córdoba over the martyrdoms and that a rival group of clergy opposed to Saul arose after he went into hiding in 853. By 857 or 860, they conclude, the majority of Mozarab officialdom, ecclesiastical and civil, had combined to bring about a reunification of the Christian community of Córdoba more or less to the liking of the opponents of the martyrs. The letter of the anony-

---

[48] Cf. Appendix III.
[49] *Apologeticus,* preface to Bk. II, 8.

mous bishop, they say, attests to this conclusion.[50] If, on the other hand, one dates the letter in 853 and interprets it to refer to the council of 852, or to another council soon after that of 852, the decision against the martyrdoms appears to have been unpopular among the Christians of Córdoba from the beginning. It may be pointed out that, apart from what one may conclude from Letter X, there is no evidence that the devotion to the martyrs waned in later years. Eulogius' position in the *Apologeticus martyrum* in 857 seems no weaker than in the *Memoriale* in 851. The fact that he undertakes to refute new arguments against the martyrdoms rather than to repeat old ones indicates, if anything, that his previous arguments had prevailed.

By report and by actual presence, the bishop begins his letter, you know of the afflictions which I suffer. And so I ask for your fraternal aid, so that the Lord, who justly punishes me for my offenses, may be moved to clemency by your prayers. You know too, he continues, of the misfortunes of our province, torn by the bestial and savage tooth of barbarity to the point of death. The Lord has now given us a respite from our afflictions, removing that plague which in His anger He imposed. These words seem to be a reference to a lull in the persecution, specifically perhaps to the death of Abd al-Rahman II in September of 852, after which the persecution abated for nine months. The bishop took advantage of the situation, he goes on, to promote harmony and root out discord among the Christians. Accordingly, he presented himself before his fellow bishops,[51] priests, and the laity, who argued so convincingly from Holy Scripture and the Fathers on behalf of compassion for the people that the bishop changed for the better his own sentence about the matter discussed, which is not clearly identified any-

[50] Cf. especially Franke, *op.cit.*, 158-163.

[51] Letter X, 2, "presentiam nostram fratribus nostris et consacerdotibus sive filii[s] peculiarem exhibere protinus nancti." Franke, *op.cit.*, 158, thinks the assembly was a diocesan synod, but he does not, *ibid.*, 160, reconcile the apparent presence there of other bishops and at least one metropolitan (Letter X, 2, "Certe in horum . . . pre manibus exhibentur").

where in the letter. He did not wish to be the cause of discord himself, he says, nor did he wish to condemn the innocent or please heretics and ignorant little men (*homunculi*), "cutting off the member from the head" with "our undeserved sentence" and a "cruel edict."[52] García-Villada interprets these words to refer to a sentence of excommunication previously issued by Saul.[53] When the canons of the Church command that the sins of a people be passed over unpunished, how, he asks, can one blame those who, terrified by the inhuman times, have taken refuge in honorable dispensations? He cites the apostles and St. Jerome to support his position.

Although the dispensations (apparently in favor of Christians who had compromised their faith in the persecution) which are the main concern of the bishop's letter are not mentioned by Eulogius in his brief account of the council of 852, it seems from what the bishop says that they did have a relationship with a council. If they were a result of the council of 852, they appear to have been of equally great, if not greater, importance than the statement forbidding martyrdom. The bishop continues in one of his most difficult passages. When the metropolitan of Seville in person, he seems to say, and the metropolitan of Mérida by letter, together with the bishops of Betica, whose orders are as valid as those of the bishops of Toledo, have arrived at an equitable sentence supported by Holy Scripture and the Fathers, they have no one to answer to but the see of Rome.[54]

[52] Letter X, 2; ms "crudelitate ed*i*ctu."

[53] García-Villada, *op.cit.*, 106f.

[54] "Certe in horum consensionis sententia non inferiores nostri ordini habentur episcopi: et non solum episcopi sed metropolitanorum partim epistolari decreto partim presentiali participationis communio manifestis probationis pre manibus exhibentur: et insolentie vel levitati adscribitur inminuto metropolitanorum primatu contra terminos equitatis libra compositos superbie elevare calcaneum: cum inretrectabilis illa iugiter habeatur omni mundo sententia qua iubetur non confinitimis sed apostolice sedis metropolitanorum privelegia ventilare." If the letter is addressed to the metropolitan of Braga, the metropolitans of Mérida and Seville may have attended the council in person and the metropolitan of Toledo may have concurred in the decision by letter.

One may read the passage too, it seems, as a defense by a "pseudobishop" of his orders and the council's actions. Bishop Saul in Letter XII may be referring to the "pseudobishop" and the council mentioned here when he states, "It is not my competence to judge concerning such things unless the question of them and us is taken up in a legitimate council."[55] Whether the council mentioned by the anonymous bishop was that of 852, the assembly addressed by Albar in the *Indiculus*, or yet another assembly is difficult to say.

There are some, the author-bishop says, who claim that sacraments are valid (*sancta*) only when they are administered by holy men. Eulogius' voluntary suspension from his priestly duties in an attempt to dissociate himself from the error of Reccafred may have been an act such as the bishop protests against, although Albar seems to indicate that Eulogius' action took place before the death of Abd al-Rahman II in September 852,[56] i.e., probably before the council of 852. The importance of the discussion of the validity of sacraments in the letter is one reason for associating it with the controversies of the eighth century. The author quotes several earlier sources[57] to prove that the validity of sacraments does not depend on the holiness of the minister.

Pope Celestine I says that the people are to be taught and not followed,[58] he continues, and so the bishop has approved temporary ecclesiastical dispensations when necessary, not wishing to be "over just" (Eccl. 7:17). He quotes Pope Innocent I to the effect that bishops are to concern themselves with the peace and well being of their churches and not rise up against their head, even if he does something reprehensible. If bishops are thus forbidden to judge their head, what right have the people to arrogate to themselves the right to judge the faults of priests? The author defends his position of not excommunicating, or of freeing from excommunication, those it seems who out of fear made some

---

[55] Letter XII, 2.
[56] *Vita Eulogii*, 6-7.
[57] Augustine, Isidore, and Pope Anastasius II.
[58] Letter X, 3; ms "Et quia *ut* canonica."

concessions to the religious persecutors.[59] We, the bishop adds, should remember our own shortcomings when dealing with those subject to us. How many things would not every pontifex among us have done beyond the letter of the law, out of compassion for his flock, for a time, out of necessity, and in terror of those in power!

In conclusion the bishop asks the metropolitan he addresses to recognize any of his clergy who may visit him and asserts, in the passage which has been quoted above, that he personally in a decree has declared his flock to be blameless and orthodox and that his decree has the same authority as any other with metropolitan sanction in the past or in the present. Finally, the author asks his addressee to ignore the complaints of malcontents who may appeal to him.

Except for resemblances in thought and language with the first part of the *Indiculus* and a general relevancy of the dispensations to the situation Albar decries in the *Indiculus*, there is no particular reason to connect Letter X with the council of 852. If one dates Letter X, and the other four letters, more than a year or so after 853, it appears that a council was held in Córdoba after 852, one which Saul, and the metropolitan of Toledo (or the metropolitan of Braga), may not have recognized as legitimate. Insofar as Letter X has a relationship with the *Indiculus* it would seem that it was written before the three letters of the Albar-Saul correspondence. If the letter is assigned a late date, there is about as much reason to argue that it was written before the Albar-Saul letters as that it was written afterwards. It is difficult, on the basis of all evidence, to argue that Saul, Reccafred, or the "pseudobishop" is the author of the letter, but there seems to be good reason to think that the letter was written to the metropolitan of Toledo (if not to the metropolitan of Braga).

[59] *Ibid.*, 4, "Nec ignoro. . . .cur improvida insequuntur *a minus* ordine vel aliorum de vita plectantur sententia omnino non video." The last statement could refer to someone not a bishop who is making the accusations against the author of the letter. Conceivably, it could be Albar, the author of the *Indiculus*, who is not the addressee.

CHAPTER XIV

LAST YEARS OF THE MARTYRDOMS

The remaining historical work of Eulogius, the *Apologeticus martyrum*,[1] tells in the same style as the *Memoriale*, of which it is a sequel, the acts of two martyrs, Rudericus and Salomon, who died 13 March 857. Most of this work is devoted to argumentation as to the genuineness of the martyrs and has been discussed previously in the comparison of the argumentation used in the *Memoriale*, the *Indiculus*, and the *Apologeticus martyrum*.

In the prologue Eulogius says that he has called the work *Apologeticus sanctorum* rather than *Gesta martyrum* so that readers may better understand the nature of the work. Morales evidently obtained the title of the work, *Apologeticus martyrum*, from the manuscript, which is no longer extant. Eulogius begins his text by carefully explaining once more that it is the exemplary goodness of the saints which is to be regarded in his work, and not his sinfulness. Although this self-deprecation is standard in mediaeval literature, Eulogius recurs to it so often that one concludes that in his day critics charged him with being presumptuous in his deeds and writings. He argues in the *Apologeticus martyrum* that the martyrs of Córdoba were as genuine as those of the early Church, who were slain by the worshippers of all sorts of idols and who showed signs and miracles.[2] Their critics claim that the martyrs of Córdoba have died swiftly

---

[1] The *Apol. mart.* is in all editions of the works of Eulogius; PL 115, 851-870. In an introductory note to the *Apol. mart.* Morales comments on the bad state of the ms and the great task of emending the text of the *Apol. mart.* The author of the *Indiculus*, he says, wrote that work with the same general ideas in defense of the martyrs.

[2] *Apol. mart.*, prologue, 3, 4, and 12. F. R. Franke, "Die freiwilligen Märtyrer," 149, interprets Eulogius as comparing the earlier martyrs of the persecution in Córdoba (Perfectus, Isaac, *et al.*) with Rudericus and Salomon.

at the hands of worshippers of God, and, Eulogius adds with irony, as if in punishment for crimes. The critics fail to take into account what the martyrs have suffered in chains and irons, in prison, and in other punishments. What difference does it make whether a martyr dies swiftly or slowly, he asks, as long as his motive is zeal of God and love of heaven? as long as he dies for the faith and for Christ? For the end crowns the work. As for those who question the lack of miracles by the martyrs, let them look rather to the faith of the martyrs, which is above miracles.

Eulogius then turns to refute the argument that the Moslems were worshippers of God. They say that the martyrs were slain after having been invited not to the sacrifice of idols, but to the worship of the true God, he says. By no means do they possess God and the law, he replies, when they attack the Gospel, Christ, and His Church. Their prophet was possessed by the devil and was a precursor of Antichrist, he says, quoting at length from SS. Peter and Paul to show the Mohammedans to be an ungodly and deluded folk with a false doctrine. Many of the learned (*peritissimi*) agree with him in this, states Eulogius, and they note that not in vain have the Christians of Córdoba collected together from Holy Scripture so many quotations against Mohammed and his followers.[3] This statement seems to corroborate the impression gained from other references by Eulogius and Albar that the *peritissimi* were a specific group of Mozarabs, especially devoted to the study of faith and dogma.

Eulogius then inserts the text of a history of Mohammed which he found while perusing manuscripts in the monastery of Leyre in Pamplona in 848 or 850. Although he did not know who was the author of the life of Mohammed, which has no close parallel or precedent, Eulogius seems to have thought that the work was written before the conquest of 711. He says that he will offer testimony of the Moslem prophet from earlier doctors so that Christians may know how ecclesiastical men judged him "then (*tunc*)." How the

---

[3] *Apol. mart.*, 13.

Moslems regard him and how he is known in Córdoba in Eulogius' time can be learned from those who say that Mohammed was the author of a law and truly worshipped God, Eulogius adds.[4] The first few sentences of the vita, which report events in Spain contemporary with the rise of Mohammed, were evidently written by a Spanish author, but data about the prophet Mohammed in the vita itself would seem to have come originally from the East. The vita apparently was one of several texts the Christians of Córdoba collected for their polemics against Islam. The text appears also in two tenth-century codices of Councils now in the Escorial, the *Codex Aemilianensis* and the *Codex Vigilanus*,[5] and in the codex of Roda.

F. R. Franke associates the vita, of which he has a low opinion, with the Chronicles of 741 and 754 on the basis of similarity of details. He suggests that Eulogius discovered the vita in a manuscript which contained those chronicles also. Being an attack on the person of Mohammed, the vita was not, in Franke's opinion, the work of eastern polemicists but rather based on popular rumors. Franke states that Eulogius did not use it until he was in bad straits.[6] The vita repeats an erroneous dating found also in the Chronicles of 741 and 754: the year of the Hegira (A.D. 622/623) as the seventh year of the reign of Heraclius (610-641) and Era 656 (A.D. 618).[7] The invasion of Byzantine dominions by the Arabs, which the Chronicle of 754 equates with the year of the Hegira, did not occur until 634, and the Byzantines were not decisively defeated until 636. Moreover, the invasion of Byzantine territory took place under the caliph Omar and not under the prophet Mohammed.[8] The error of equating the year of the Hegira with Era 656 was made by

---

[4] *Ibid.*, 14.

[5] Mss Escorial d-I-1, 314v, and d-I-2, 247v. Morales was familiar with both mss and Ponce de León, the discoverer of the ms of Eulogius' works, owned d-I-1.

[6] Franke, *op.cit.*, 38-47, especially 44ff.

[7] *Apol. mart.*, 16; cf. Mommsen, MGH, *Auct. antiq.*, XI, 337.

[8] George Ostrogorsky, *History of the Byzantine State*, trans. Joan Hussey (New Brunswick, New Jersey, 1957), 99.

the Chronicle of 754, an error which derives from the fact that the Arab year is shorter than the Julian year. This error of computation would have been made about A.D. 754, when A.H. 136 equated with Era 792. The error could, of course, have been copied later, just as the first few lines of the vita, pertaining to Spain, may have been added later or may be the work of Eulogius. In one detail the dating at the beginning of the vita differs from that in the Chronicle of 754. The chronicler always gives the Spanish Era first in dates. The vita gives the year of Heraclius' reign before it gives the Era.

To show Eulogius' attitude towards Islam and Mohammed the full text is given here in translation.

> The heresiarch Mohammed arose in the time of the Emperor Heraclius in the seventh year of his reign, Era 656 [A.D. 618]. At this time Isidore, Bishop of Seville, was outstanding in Catholic doctrine, and Sisebut held the royal throne in Toledo. In the city of Iliturgi the church of St. Euphrasius was built on his tomb. In Toledo also the church of St. Leocadia, a wondrous work, came to completion under the orders of the king mentioned.[9] The nefarious prophet Mohammed mentioned above held power for ten years, after which he died and was buried in hell. And his beginnings were as follows. Being an orphan, he became the servant of a certain widow. While he was in business as an avaricious money lender he began to commit to memory some of the discussions he had heard among the Christians, and he became the wisest of all among his stupid Arabs. But, the tinder of his lust was enkindled and he lived with his patroness in lawless passion.[10] Soon the spirit of error appeared to him in the guise of a vulture, showing him a golden mouth. It said it was the Angel Gabriel and ordered him to go forth as a prophet. And filled with swollen pride, he began

[9] These lines, which reflect a nostalgia for Visigothic days, resemble closely the opening lines of John of Seville's account of Mohammed in Letter VI, 9, of the Albar correspondence.

[10] "iure barbarico in ira congressus est"; Eulogius also uses *mente, ritu,* and *ori* to form adverbs of adjectives.

to preach things unheard of to brute animals and with a certain pseudo-reasoning he convinced them that they should leave off the worship of idols and adore the incorporeal God in the heavens. He orders those who believe in him to take arms and, as if with a new zeal of faith, instructs them to kill the adversaries with the sword. And God, by a hidden judgment, permitted them to do harm, as He once had spoken through the prophet, "For behold, I will raise up over you the Chaldeans, a bitter and swift nation, marching upon the breadth of the earth, to possess the places that are not their own.... Their horses are swifter than evening wolves, and their face is like a burning wind, for an accusation of the faithful and for rendering the land into desert" (Hab. 1:6, 8-9). First they killed the brother of the Emperor, who ruled over that land. And, exultant in the glory of their victorious triumph, they founded in Damascus in Syria the capital city of the kingdom.[11] The false prophet himself then composed psalms in the mouth of insensible creatures, that is, commemorating a red calf. He also contrived a history like the trap of a spider web for catching flies. Then he composed certain songs of the upupa and the frog, so that while the foul odor of the one should spew from his mouth the garrulity of the other should be always on his lips. Others too he fashioned himself in honor of Joseph, Zachary, and even Mary,[12] the Mother of the Lord, to season his error. Perduring in the great error of his prophecy, he lusted for the wife of his neighbor, named Zeid, and subjected her to his passion. When her husband found out about the crime he was horrified, and surrendered her to his prophet, whom he could not contradict. But he, as if by the word of the Lord, made note of it in his law, saying, "The wife of Zeid was displeasing in his eyes and he repudiated her. And we associated her to our prophet (*prophetae*

---

[11] Franke, *op.cit.*, 46, regards the failure of the author to note the transfer of the Moslem capital from Damascus to Baghdad after 750 as reason to think that the vita was written in the last decades of the eighth century. The author would not seem to have been obliged to make this observation, however.

[12] Koran, suras 2, 29, 27 (20ff.), 7 (130), 12, and 19.

nostro) in marriage, as an example for others,
and so that it may not be a sin for the faithful
after us who wish to do it."[13] After a deed of such
great sin, the death of his soul and his body approached together. But, feeling his death imminent
and knowing that he could by no means rise again
of his own power, he predicted that on the third day
he would be resurrected by the Angel Gabriel, who,
as he used to say, was wont to appear to him in
the form of a vulture. When he had committed
his soul to hell they commanded his body to be
guarded with a strict watch, for they were concerned about the miracle which he had promised
them. When they saw it fetid on the third day
and by no means rising again, they said angels
had not come because they were afraid of their
presence. On salubrious counsel, as they thought,
they left his body without a guard, and immediately, instead of angels, dogs came in attracted by
his stench and devoured his body. When they discovered this deed, they committed the rest of his
body to the earth. And to revenge the injury done
to him, every year they order dogs killed, so
that they may rightly have part with him who
have merited to suffer a fitting martyrdom for
his sake (*ut merito cum eo habeant illic par-
ticipium qui pro eo dignum meruerunt subire
martyrium*).[14] And it was fitting that such a great
prophet like this, who had committed to hell not
only his own soul but those of many, should fill
the belly of dogs. He did many other crimes that
are not written in this book. This much has been
written so that readers may know what kind of
a man he was.[15]

"Behold," says Eulogius, "many fear not to regard a people given to such illusions and a leader of such impiety in
the name of pious religion." In their assertions that the

---

[13] Sura 33, 37; Franke, *op.cit.*, 40, notes that this is the first translation of a passage from the Koran into Latin in polemical literature.

[14] Franke, *ibid.*, 44, says that the account of the dogs is not found
elsewhere than in this vita. The words, which are spoken in scorn, may
be a parody of a liturgical prayer and may too be a gloss to the text
of the vita.

[15] *Apol. mart.*, 16.

martyrs of Córdoba have been slain by men worshipping God and in possession of the law critics of the martyrs show themselves unwise and fail to notice that "if the cult or the law of such people is to be called true, then the strength of the Christian religion will inevitably be weakened."[16]

The true Gospel has been preached throughout the whole world, and their doctrine is anathema, says Eulogius. He then repeats verbatim a long passage enumerating Mohammed's errors found also in the *Memoriale*[17] and tells how his grandfather Eulogius would bless himself and cover his ears at their sacrilegious cries from the minarets. Any Catholic who wishes to know what madness they preach has only to watch them, for they make their dogma public. Also, says Eulogius, Catholics will find many things written against them in the works of certain of "our writers," in his own *Memoriale* for one.[18] The two paragraphs in the *Memoriale* (7-8) contain attacks on the Moslem paradise and on statements of Mohammed about the Blessed Virgin which are not repeated in the *Apologeticus martyrum*. The almost verbatim repetition of the two paragraphs may mean that they represent a summary indictment of the teachings of Mohammed prepared, perhaps, by some authority in Córdoba.

Eulogius then takes up the vita of Rudericus and Salomon. Rudericus was a priest in Cabra who had two brothers, one a Christian and the other an apostate to Islam. The two brothers fought frequently over various matters, and one night when Rudericus sought to intervene as peacemaker they both turned on him and beat him into unconsciousness. In this state the Mohammedan brother had him put on a stretcher and brought through all the area, proclaiming that Rudericus had chosen the Mohammedan religion and did not wish to leave the world without making this known. Rudericus recovered in a few days and, discovering what his brother had done, had to leave Cabra. At this time, says

---

[16] *Ibid.*, 17.
[17] *Ibid.*, 19-20, and *Memoriale*, I, 7-8.
[18] *Apol. mart.*, 20; *Memoriale*, I, 8, reads "our philosophers."

Eulogius, the persecution raged violently against the Christians in Córdoba. Basilica towers were overthrown, church vaults and even bell towers were pulled down. Mohammed had at last obtained the longed for peace of reign enjoyed by his father, which enabled him to attack the Church as he pleased. Rudericus hid in the mountains around Córdoba, but one day when he went into Córdoba his brother recognized him and brought him before the cadi, accusing him of apostasy from Islam. Rudericus denied this, saying that he had never been a Mohammedan and that furthermore he was a priest. When the cadi sought to entice him to profess that Mohammed was the prophet of the Almighty and that Christ was not God, Rudericus answered that he would not leave the source of life for the filth of lies and vices. The cadi committed him to prison.

There Rudericus found Salomon, "of a different order and nation,"[19] who had been imprisoned for returning to Christianity after lapsing into Islam. They provided each other mutual consolation and help, and devoted themselves to prayer and rigorous penance. The cadi had them separated and would not permit them visitors. After a time they were brought before him again. He tried three times to win them over to the Mohammedan rite but without success. They were executed by royal decree on 13 March 857 by the bank of the river. At the hour of death the cadi again made an attempt to persuade them to enter his religion, but they refused. Rudericus was executed first, and then the cadi made a final attempt to persuade Salomon to yield to his requests. When Salomon refused, he too was beheaded. Eulogius testifies that when he heard of the martyrdoms he went to the place of execution and approached closer than anyone else. The bodies of the saints, he says, were resplendent in beauty. The Moslems took the stones sprinkled with the blood of the martyrs and threw them into the river to prevent the Christians from having them as relics. Their bodies were tied to large stones and thrown into the river but were recovered by the Christians three weeks later. As

[19] *Apol. mart.*, 26.

the Christians were joyously bringing the body of Rudericus from where it had been discovered on the bank of the river near the village of *Tertios* after Moslems had revealed its whereabouts to a priest, Eulogius says that "because of the failing of the sun a thick darkness fell and blind night changed the whole aspect of the world."[20] The darkness was dispelled, however, by the many torches of the Christians. (No eclipse of the sun is calculated to have occurred in Spain at this time.) The venerable *pontifex*, presumably Bishop Saul, came with a group of clerics and kissed the uncorrupted remains. Rudericus' body was buried in a magnificent ceremony with the whole church lighted up and all the faithful singing hymns and psalms.[21] The Christians continued to search for the body of Salomon despite the stringent punishment decreed by the palace for those who searched for relics. Salomon's body was found near the town of *Nymphanium* and brought to the town of *Colubris,* where it was buried by priests in the Basilica of SS. Cosmas and Damian. Eulogius concludes the *Apologeticus martyrum* with a prayer beseeching the aid of the martyrs for himself.

Throughout his works Eulogius shows great respect and piety towards the martyrs. He was their defender and their adviser. He was particularly attentive to women martyrs, telling their stories at length and bestowing much praise on them for their virtues. He shows a high regard in his works for virginity, which was characteristic of almost all the martyrs. Even in the case of the married couples, Aurelius and Felix and their wives, once they reached the turning point in their lives they decided to live celibately. Eulogius dwells at some length on the asceticism practiced by many of the martyrs. The asceticism, virginity, and

---

[20] *Ibid.,* 33.

[21] All this was done in secret, and so Saul may still have been in hiding. In a Penitential found at the end of the Albar codex the kissing of the dead is forbidden and a penance of one year is given for the act; cf. Pérez de Urbel and Vázquez de Parga, "Un nuevo penitencial español," AHDE, XIV (1942-1943), 31.

chastity of the martyrs are contrasted with the sensuality which seems to have characterized the Moslem culture.

In his works Eulogius is unusually particular about certain places and times. The dates of the martyrs' deaths are almost all given specifically, many to the day of the week. Other dates, however, such as the death of Abd al-Rahman II, are not given. Neither does he take pains to date the council held in Córdoba in 852 beyond an ambiguous reference to the month. Eulogius has a passion for accuracy in mentioning a town or monastery outside Córdoba. He gives the distance and the direction from Córdoba, and any nearby river or mountain which may serve as a landmark. The churches in Córdoba he is particular to name but does not attempt to locate. He is careful to specify on which side of the river events take place and frequently remarks, "across the river." He notes the town of birth or provenance of almost every martyr. His information is based on knowledge derived from frequent travels in the region about Córdoba and should be exact.

In spite of the deliberate attempt Eulogius makes to record data, however, he fails to provide information on many matters of interest to modern historians about which he was well informed. This resulted probably because he was not interested in problems that concern them, but was wrapped up in one aspect of the Christian world and saw no reason to describe the secular world or the Mohammedan world. He was interested in defending the martyrdoms and in recording the deeds of the martyrs in a hagiographical tradition. Even in the Christian world Eulogius names few people other than the martyrs. Martin and Elizabeth, the abbot and abbess of the double monastery of Tabanos outside Córdoba, are named more than once; Albar and Esperaindeo are named, and so is Artemia the mother of Aurea, Adulphus, and John. Felix, the abbot of the monastery of the Holy Savior at *Pinna Mellaria,* is mentioned, as is a priest Paul. No bishop is named. The renegade *exceptor* is identified by his office and as a personality but is not named. Otherwise the *Memoriale* and the *Apologeticus martyrum* are composed of an indistinguishable crowd of parents, kinfolk, fellow monks and Christians, and Moslem unbelievers.

The *Bayan al-mughrib* of Ibn Idhari provides information about the early years of King Mohammed's reign to supplement that in the Christian Latin sources. Mohammed came to the throne on 23 September 852, the day following his father's death. Shortly afterwards Toledo rebelled and imprisoned its governor, refusing to release him until hostages from Toledo held in Córdoba were released. In the summer of 853, after Fandila's martyrdom, a brother of King Mohammed led an expedition which rebuilt the fortifications of Calatrava and repopulated the place with its people, who had fled in fear of the Toledans. In March 854, when there had been no martyrs for six months, Mohammed sent an expedition against Sindola, the chief of Toledo, but it was ambushed and lost its baggage. In June 854 Mohammed in person won a victory over a force of Toledans and troops sent to their aid by Ordoño of Oviedo, in an ambush at Guadalcelete. In the following month Abundius, the lone martyr of 854, died, and about this time Albar seems to have completed the *Indiculus*. In 855, when Mohammed attacked the hinterland of Toledo, there were martyrs at the end of April. In the summer of 856, the last year recorded in the *Memoriale*, Muza ibn Muza, the ruler of Zaragoza, prompted by Mohammed, marched against Barcelona. At the same time Mohammed besieged Toledo, slaughtering all the livestock he came upon. In this year there were martyrs in mid-April, at the end of June, and in mid-July. Before the major victory of Mohammed over Toledo at Talavera in 857 two martyrs died in mid-March. Eulogius says in the *Apologeticus martyrum* that in this year Mohammed at last obtained the freedom of rule enjoyed by his father and could proceed with the persecution of the Christians. In 858, when there were monks from Paris in Córdoba, no martyrs died. In the summer of this year Mohammed marched against Toledo in person with Odilard and Usuard in his train. The forces of Toledo were so depleted that they would not venture beyond the bridge over the Tagus to fight

Mohammed. The Cordobans then mined the bridge in a ruse and destroyed a large part of Toledo's military force as it collapsed. For Toledo this was a major defeat. In 859 Eulogius and Leocritia died in mid-March, and later Toledo sought a truce from Córdoba.[22]

From Ibn Idhari's account one can see what Eulogius meant when he spoke of Mohammed trying to get control of his realm. One can also understand why Eulogius could not occupy the see of Toledo, to which he was elected.[23] Although an interesting schedule can be devised between the martyrdoms and the military campaigns of Mohammed, it would be hazardous to infer a relationship between the two phenomena.

The martyrdoms and the dispute about them continued without any real interruption from 850 to 859. One cannot be sure whether the intervals between martyrs is best explained by a lack of activity on the part of the Christian confessors or by a lack of prosecution on the part of the Moslems. It is almost in the nature of such phenomena to be sporadic. Every three years appeared a lengthy apologia in defense of the martyrs: Book I of the *Memoriale* (and the *Documentum martyriale*) in 851, the *Indiculus* in 854, and the *Apologeticus martyrum* in 857. These works show a constant belief in the genuineness of the martyrdoms and a constant concern over the attrition of the Christians' faith by Moslem ideas. It should be noted that the martyrs were the object of continual devotion by the Christians. Their relics were held in as high regard in 857 (Rudericus), 858 (by the monks from Paris and the monks of *Pinna Mellaria*), and 859 (Eulogius) as they had been in the first days of the persecution. There is no reason to say that either the persecution or the veneration of the martyrs waned during later years.[24]

[22] Ibn Idhari, *Bayan*, II, 152-157.

[23] F. R. Franke, *op.cit.*, 166, believes that it was influential Christians of Córdoba who objected to any collaboration by Eulogius with the defiant Toledans against King Mohammed and not King Mohammed himself who prevented Eulogius from occupying the see.

[24] Cf. Franke, *ibid.*, 142-168, and Lévi-Provençal, *Histoire*, I, 238.

About a year after the martyrdom of Rudericus and Salomon two monks from Paris came to Córdoba and obtained relics of the martyrs George, Aurelius, and Sabigotho. An account of their journey was written by a monk of the same monastery, Aimoin, who lived toward the end of the ninth century. Their journey is also recorded under the year 858 in the *Annales Bertiniani*.[25]

In 858, Aimoin begins, Usuard and Odilard left the monastery of the Holy Cross and St. Vincent (the future St. Germain-des-Près) to obtain the relics of St. Vincent in Valencia, which was in a state of devastation wreaked by the Saracens. En route they learned that the relics were no longer in Valencia but in Zaragoza, where they were venerated as those of St. Marinus and could by no means be obtained. In Barcelona they heard from Sunifridus, the man next to the count in authority, about the slaughter of Christians in Córdoba "under Abd al-Rahman." Sunifridus and the bishop of Barcelona, Ataulfus, advised them strongly against attempting to reach Córdoba, but when the two monks insisted, they gave them the name of their friend Leovigildus in Córdoba with whom they might stay. Leovigildus was probably the same person who composed the *De habitu clericorum* for the clerics of Córdoba. The count of Barcelona, Hunfridus, gave them a letter to the Saracen ruler of Zaragoza, "Abdiluvar" (Muza ibn Muza), requesting him because of their treaty of friendship to give the monks hospitality and help them get to Córdoba. The letter was made known to Abdiluvar through an interpreter. True to the obligations of friendship, Abdiluvar received the monks with kindness but explained that it was beyond his power at the time to get them to Córdoba. It happened, however, that for the first time in eight years, certain peo-

---

[25] Aimoin's account comes from ms Paris BN Lat. 13760 (the same ms which contains the variant text of the passion of George, Aurelius, Felix, Sabigotho, and Liliosa, *Memoriale*, II, x) ; it was first published by Mabillon in *AA SS OSB* (9 vols.; Paris, 1668-1701), *saec. IV (800-900)*, ii; also edited by Flórez, ES, X, Appendix vi; *SS PP Toletanorum*, II, 620-637; PL 115, 939-960. *Annales Bertiniani*, ed. Waitz, MGH, *Scriptores ... in usum scholarum* (Hanover, 1883).

ple of Zaragoza were setting out for Córdoba and Abdiluvar arranged to have the two monks accompany them.[26] They arrived in Córdoba after a long and arduous journey, having left their servants and baggage in Barcelona and Zaragoza. In Córdoba they went to the Church of St. Cyprian "where the bodies of the holy martyrs Adulphus and John were buried." Here they were received by Jerome, a deacon of that church. When the news spread that there were visitors from France the Christians flocked to see them, marvelling at their courage and the protection accorded them by Providence. Leovigildus, surnamed "Abadsolomes" ('Abd as-Salam),[27] to whom they had been recommended by Sunifridus of Barcelona, received them with great kindness. "True to the etymology of his name," he began to make "vigilant" inquiry into the reasons for their coming. They gave him the messages from his friends in Barcelona and, conceiving a great confidence in him, entrusted him with the secret of their coming. He, calling upon the help of Samson, a priest of Córdoba, began to plan how he could help them.

After they had made known their secret to Samson they learned of the martyrs George and Aurelius and wanted to take the relics of both of them if possible. They knew of the text of their passion, "which the well-remembered and worthy priest Eulogius put down in a true account, though he omitted many things, as he himself told our two monks. Afterwards he too as a joyous and perfect soldier sought Christ the King and was granted a glorious martyrdom."[28] It happened that at this very time Samson was appointed abbot of *Pinna Mellaria*, the monastery about five miles outside Córdoba where the saints' relics lay buried. Samson and Leovigildus learned that some of the monks of the monastery would not give up the relics. Pressing their

---

[26] *Translatio*, 6; the beginning of the eight-year period corresponds with the beginning of the martyrdoms in 850.

[27] *Ibid.*, 7; cf. Franke, *op.cit.*, 12. "Abd as-Salam" (Servant of Peace) is one of the many Arabic epithets for "Servant of God."

[28] *Translatio*, 8.

request and insisting that the bodies of the blessed martyrs would be venerated with greater worship in Paris, they secured the consent of all the monks to part with the relics provided that the bishop would give his consent. But the bodies of the saints were to lie buried where they were until the two monks could leave for home.

King Mohammed of Córdoba, before leaving on an expedition against Toledo, ordered as assembly and decreed that everyone, citizens and strangers, with the exception of the guard leave the city (*civitas*). Usuard and Odilard saw a chance to depart and avail themselves of the protection of the king's army against robbers, who, to judge from Aimoin's account, infested the roads of all Spain at this time. They applied to the monks of *Pinna Mellaria* for the promised relics but were refused, the monks taking advantage of the abbot Samson's absence. Usuard and Odilard then sent certain ones of the faithful of Córdoba to Bishop Saul asking him to intervene personally on behalf of the "Gallic monks." Despite the continued unwillingness of the monks of *Pinna Mellaria* to surrender the relics, Saul obtained them for Usuard and Odilard, who attended as the relics were dug up from beneath the altar. When it came to opening the sepulcher all were made to withdraw except the priests designated by the bishop. Receiving the relics from them as, with hymns and litanies, they lifted them from the tombs, the bishop wrapped them in linens and put them into sacks for carrying. The two monks asked the bishop to seal with his ring the relics directed to King Charles [the Bald], lest they be violated by anyone on the journey. As was remembered from the time of the martyrdoms, says Aimoin, the Christians had rescued the complete body of George, but had failed to find the head of Aurelius. On the other hand, the body of his wife Sabigotho (called Nathalia in Aimoin's account) had been separated from the head, which was interred with the body of Aurelius. Thus it happened that the French monks received the body of George, the body of Aurelius without the head, and the head of Sabigotho (Nathalia).[29]

All this was done in secret out of fear of the Moslems, who would not permit the veneration of the martyrs they had slain. From Aimoin's account it is difficult to tell whether Saul was in hiding at this time or not. After fifty-six days in Córdoba, Usuard and Odilard left on the vigil of the Ascension, 11 May 858, travelling with the army of King Mohammed in the care of a number of Christians who were accompanying the king to battle. Many Christians turned out to bid them farewell. Leovigildus, who had been occupied with business pertaining to the king (*regiis occupatus negotiis*) when the army left Córdoba, joined them on the road and continued with them to Toledo. His sister, Babila, had prepared things necessary for the trip of the monks. With the entry of Mohammed's army into the vicinity of Toledo all the highway robbers withdrew into the stronghold of the city, and Usuard and his companion continued on to Alcalá and Zaragoza. They stopped in Zaragoza and thanked Abdiluvar for his kindness, obtaining from him letters to the castle guards of his region so that they might be given special protection and pass unmolested. In Barcelona they surprised Ataulfus and Sunifridus at their safe return and gave them news of Leovigildus. By way of Gerona they went on to Narbonne and Beziers. Here the account ends, and a second and third book of the translation (*Liber I* and *Liber II de miraculis martyrum*) follow. In them Aimoin recounts numerous miracles reported on the journey from Beziers to Paris.

At the end of the third book of the translation Aimoin tells how Charles the Bald rejoiced at hearing the account of the martyrs, presumably a part of Eulogius' *Memoriale,* and sent "Mancio" to Córdoba to inquire about the truth of the matter. From him on his return he learned what had been missing from their deeds and was worthy of being remembered and recorded. This was that their slain bodies

[29] *Ibid.;* Eulogius accounts for the remains of Sabigotho, but a lacuna in the text of the *Memoriale* deletes the resting place of the heads of the martyrs.

had not been touched even by a fly in the three days they had been left out in the plaza for dogs and birds. Mancio also reported the martyrdom of two sisters which he himself had witnessed. Since it is unlikely that Mancio went to Córdoba before 859, the martyrdoms which he witnessed probably took place at about the same time as the martyrdom of Eulogius, 11 March 859, and are not recorded elsewhere. He probably brought back also the news of Eulogius' death. Elsewhere Charles is reported to have had priests of Toledo say before him a Mass according to the Mozarabic liturgy.[30]

It is worth pointing out that Aimoin's account gives no indication at all that there was a group in Córdoba opposed to the martyrs.

In 859, the year following the journey of Usuard and Odilard, Eulogius died as a martyr. From the sentence with which Albar introduces his account of the passion of Eulogius it appears that the persecution had ceased by the time he was writing. "At the time when the savage rule of the Arabs with deceit and imposture brought misery and destruction to all the land of Spain, when King Mohammed with unbelievable rage and unbridled fury determined to root out the race of Christians, many, terrified by fear of the cruel king and hoping to allay his madness, cruelly and iniquitously seized upon various and ingenious occasions to attack Christ's flock."[31] But many too held fast to their faith, he continues. Some, who kept the faith of Christ only in their hearts, by the grace of God revealed what they had kept hidden and, leaping forward to martyrdom, snatched the crown for themselves from the executioners. Among these was the Arab Christopher, whose passion Albar planned to write elsewhere. This would hardly be the Christopher described by Eulogius as a kinsman of his,[32] with no mention of any Arab background. Aurelius and Felix,

---

[30] *Liber II de miraculis*, xxviii. Cf. David, *Etudes*, 252, and Henry Jenner, "Mozarabic Rite," *Catholic Encyclopedia*, X, 611.

[31] *Vita Eulogii*, 12.

[32] *Memoriale*, II, xi.

their wives, and Flora, says Albar, were secret Christians whose vitae were written by Eulogius.

Albar begins the passion of Eulogius with the account of a noble Moslem girl, Leocritia, who had become a Christian in secret under the tutelage of a relative of hers, the nun Litiosa. As she became older she began to practice her faith more openly. Since her parents persecuted her for her Christian practices, she yearned to make a public profession of her faith. Through messengers she made known to Eulogius, who was "very well known for many such deeds," and his sister Anulo that she wished to go to a safer place among the Christians. Eulogius assumed his accustomed role and, being an eager protector of the martyrs, instructed her by the same messengers to leave home. This she did after feigning a loss of interest in the Christian faith, seizing an opportunity to leave home on the pretext of attending the wedding of some of her kin. Eulogius and his sister Anulo entrusted her to friends so that she might practice her religion freely. Leocritia's parents, greatly upset, searched everywhere for her and had many Christians imprisoned and whipped on the order of the governor (*praeses*) in an effort to find their daughter. But Eulogius had her moved about frequently to elude them, refusing to turn the lamb over to the wolves. Leocritia, meanwhile, was practicing austere penances. Eulogius too passed nocturnal vigils in the Basilica of St. Zoilus, praying for the girl.

In the course of time Leocritia, eager to see Anulo, the sister of Eulogius, came to visit her secretly at night. When her guide did not appear until dawn, Leocritia had to stay on in the house to avoid capture. Meanwhile, her whereabouts was betrayed to the governor, who sent soldiers to surround the house. It happened that Eulogius was there, and the soldiers seized him, bringing him and Leocritia before the governor and the cadi. When the cadi, who hoped to have the two scourged to death, furiously demanded of Eulogius why he had detained Leocritia at his house, Eulogius answered him "patiently and with good grace, as he commonly spoke." "Sir," he replied addressing the governor, "the office of preaching is laid upon us, and it is a part of our faith that we should hold out the light of faith to those seeking it of us, and that we should deny it to no one who is hastening to the holy ways of life."[33] Since Leocritia had applied to him, he continued, he had performed his priestly duty, and he would be glad to do the same for the governor if he would ask him. At this, the governor had rods brought out to beat Eulogius to death, but Eulogius called on him to bring out the sword that his soul might speedily be freed, and he proceeded to reproach the prophet Mohammed and his law. For this, he was brought to the palace, even, says Albar, before the king's councillors. One of the councillors whom Eulogius knew attempted to get him to retract what he had said, promising that they would not search for him thereafter. Just because fools and idiots are dying, he told Eulogius, is no reason for one of your wisdom and holiness to follow them. Eulogius answered that if he but knew the beauty of their faith, rather would he leave his worldly honors for it. He continued to speak to them of the Gospel, calmly enduring insults. He was taken to the place of execution and beheaded on Saturday, 11 March. His body was thrown down alongside the river, where a white dove settled upon it, refusing to be driven away. Albar narrates another marvel associated with Eulogius' body. "A native of Ecija, while performing with others his monthly service in the palace and taking his turn with the watch, at night desiring a drink of water arose and went to the projecting water outlet which comes to that place. There he saw above Eulogius' body, which lay lower down, priests glistening white as snow, holding dazzling lamps, and earnestly reciting psalms. Frightened by this vision he went back to his station, fleeing rather than returning. After telling a companion all about it, he decided to go with him again to the place; but this second time he was unable to see it."[34] The Christians obtained the head

[33] *Vita*, 15.

[34] *Ibid*: Aimoin also testifies that Christians had returned to the military forces of the emir by 858.

of Eulogius the next day and his body three days later. He was buried in the Basilica of St. Zoilus, where he had served as a priest. Three days after the death of Eulogius (quarta post eius martyrii die), Leocritia was martyred for remaining firm in her faith. Her body was thrown into the river, where it floated until it was taken by Christians and buried in the Basilica of St. Genesius in the town of *Tertios*.

Albar does not state the year of Eulogius' death, but this can be determined as 859. The last account in the *Apologeticus martyrum* is of martyrs who died in 857, and Usuard and Odilard saw Eulogius in May 858. There exists a notice of the translation of his body in 859, in which year 11 March fell on a Saturday.[35]

At the end of the *Vita Eulogii* Albar addresses a long passage to Eulogius, a saint in heaven. The first of these three paragraphs (18-20) contains a number of statements illustrative of affective love and resembling somewhat the later thought of the famous sufi Hallaj. Eulogius will certainly hear him, says Albar, "if our own merits assist us, if grave sins do not block the way, and if a pure affection asks it." "I am the one who you said was united to you, to whom and of whom you spoke thus, Let there be no other Albar but Eulogius and may the whole love of each of us be placed nowhere but in the inmost heart of the other (nec alibi quam penes intima Alvari totus sit conlocatus amor Eulogii)." "True love faithfully keeps the feeling of love for one who is absent and as much as it can it shows this towards the lover (servat amor verus in absentem fideliter charitatem et quod sibi poterat hoc exhibet in amantem)." Albar's enumeration of the means of improving his life are of interest also for an understanding of the spiritual background of the martyrs. He begs the intercession of Eulogius: "that I may have the gift of frequent tears, that the love of virtues may be fixed in my erring mind, that affective compunction may always be mine, that my feelings of repentance

---

[35] Cf. Aimoin, *Translatio*, 8. Morales dated the translation of Eulogius' relics in 860 rather than in 859; cf. *SS PP Toletanorum*, II, 410, and PL 115, 722.

may be sincere, that I may be happily granted a desirable place, and may the way thereto not be blocked by inconvenient obstacles. May the bonds of all difficulties be loosed, may the masses of all impediments spring aside, and may obstructing hindrances by the unchangeable right hand of the Most High be changed into aids for His servants. May the gates of my heart be opened to receive the kingdom of the Most High God, and may the proud neck be bent and learn to bear the most sweet yoke of Christ. I would like to ask yet more but I fear to be found guilty of presumption."[36] In the remaining two paragraphs Albar asks blessings in return for the honor he has done to the memory and the remains of Eulogius on earth.

In addition to the life and passion of Eulogius there are also minor pieces in his honor. These minor pieces are three poems by Albar (a hymn, an epitaph, and a prayer) and the prose note that his body was translated to the Basilica of St. Zoilus on 1 June 859. In January 884 the relics of Eulogius and Leocritia were translated to the cathedral of Oviedo, where they rest today.[37]

---

[36] *Vita*, 18; cf. A. Vincent, "Soufisme," DTC, XIV, ii, 2444-2459, especially 2451 with regard to the intermittent identification of the lover and the beloved; cf. Massignon, *Essai*, 314, *id.*, *La passion*, II, 915, and Massignon's translation of *Akhbar al-Hallaj*, 103-165, passim. R. A. Nicholson, "Mysticism," *Legacy of Islam* (Oxford, 1931), 210-238, especially 218, and Alfred Guillaume, "Philosophy and Theology," *ibid.*, 261-280 on Spain, are of interest.

[37] ES, X, 457.

Part III

The Christians of Córdoba after the Martyrdoms:
The Sources of Christian Córdoba after the Martyrdoms

CHAPTER XV

THE *APOLOGETICUS* OF THE ABBOT SAMSON

Except for the two sisters whose martyrdom was witnessed by Mancio when he visited Córdoba for Charles the Bald, after the death of Eulogius probably, no martyrs are known to have died after Eulogius and Leocritia.[1] The three years from 859 to 862 are not reported in the history of the persecution in Córdoba. Leovigildus' *De habitu clericorum* may have been written during these years but it reports practically no events. The next work to be discussed, probably the last to come from this period of Cordoban history, is the *Apologeticus* of Samson,[2] written in 864. Samson was the abbot of the Basilica of St. Zoilus in Córdoba, where Eulogius had served as a priest and where he was buried. In 858, according to the account of Aimoin, Samson had been appointed abbot of the monastery of *Pinna Mellaria*, According to his epitaph, he died in 890.[3]

Samson mentions in his work that the Christians of Córdoba venerated the martyrs and he refers to a Christian who was punished for speaking ill of the prophet Mohammed. But the nature of the persecution changed after the death of Eulogius. King Mohammed abandoned the execution of Christians, and life in Córdoba settled down to a semblance of what it had been in times of peace. A more

---

[1] Aimoin's *Translatio, Liber II de miraculis*, xxvii. Usuard mentions three martyrs of unknown date, Secundinus, Gerontius, and Peter, who may have died in the persecution of the ninth century; B. de Gaiffier, "Les notices hispaniques dans le Martyrologe d'Usuard," AB, 55 (1937), 279-281.

[2] The *Apologeticus* occupies the latter half of ms Madrid BN 10018, the first half of which contains the treatise of Beatus and Eterius against Elipandus of Toledo. Flórez edited the text in ES, XI, 325-516, with a study of the life of Samson, 300-324. The work is not in Migne's *Patrologia*.

[3] *Translatio*, 9; cf. ES, XI, 526.

insidious persecution continued, however, as the king sought to destroy the integrity of the Christian clergy and replace them with venal and heterodox men who were subservient to his regime and amenable to the Mohammedan doctrine. The Christian laity and the churches were subjected to increased taxation in an effort to force them into apostasy or ruin.

The *Apologeticus* tells the story of the dispute between Samson and two Christian henchmen of the Mohammedans. This dispute manifested itself on both a theological and a personal level. Samson provides an excellent record of the theological disputation, including texts of his opponents. On the personal, or political, level the dispute resulted in the exile of Samson from Córdoba. Samson, in attacking the doctrine of his enemy, provides much information about education and intellectual life among the Christians of Córdoba. In attacking the evil lives and evil deeds of his enemies, he offers a wealth of data about the personal lives of Christians and their relations with the Moslems. Indeed, by bringing the personalities into the dispute, Samson describes the social scene perhaps better than Eulogius and Albar.

Samson wrote the *Apologeticus* while he was in exile in Martos (*Tucci*),[4] which is southeast of Córdoba near Jaén, whither he had fled to escape the vengeance of Hostegesis, bishop of Malaga, and Servandus, count of Córdoba. Under the aegis of the emir of Córdoba these two men had combined to exploit the Christians in their care and at the same time to propagate heretical beliefs and evil practices. Hostegesis is not encountered elsewhere in the literature of Córdoba, but Servandus is doubtless the same count of Córdoba mentioned by Albar in a letter to Romanus Medicus.[5]

Samson's work provides information pertaining to the organization of the Church in captive Spain which may be added to that found in the Acts of the Council of Córdoba in 839, previously discussed. Most of the information is found

---

[4] The virgin martyr Flora found refuge in Martos in 845 or 846, in the early days of her persecution, *Memoriale*, II, viii, 8.

[5] Letter IX of the Albar correspondence, 6.

in a passage where Samson gives the names of the bishops who, at the persuasion of Bishop Valentius of Córdoba, retracted a condemnation of Samson obtained from them by Bishop Hostegesis of Malaga.[6] Six sees identified in the Acts of the Council of Córdoba in 839 are mentioned by Samson; they are, with their bishops, Ariulfus of Mérida, Beatus of Ecija, Hostegesis of Malaga, Valentius of Córdoba, Reculfus of Cabra, and an anonymous metropolitan of Seville. The sees of Córdoba and Cabra were no longer united as in 839 but each had its own bishop. Ariulfus, the metropolitan of Mérida, the only person mentioned by Samson who attended the council of 839, did not attend the council of 862, which condemned Samson, but sent a letter to Valentius in Samson's favor. It is doubtful that the Leovigildus whom Samson says refuted Hostegesis on his arrival in Córdoba[7] was the bishop of Ecija at the council of 839, especially since in Samson's time the see of Ecija was occupied by another person. The only sees not mentioned by Samson which were mentioned in the Acts of the Council of 839 are Toledo and Guadix. The sees with their bishops mentioned in the *Apologeticus* but not encountered in the council of 839 are Saro of Baeza, John of Baza, Genesius of Urci (Almeira), Teudegutus of Elche, and Miro of Medina Sidonia. Elsewhere Samson calls Martos a see[8] and mentions Granada as having suffered under a Bishop Samuel, uncle of Hostegesis. In all, Samson mentions thirteen sees. The metropolitan of Seville is almost ignored in the *Apologeticus*. He was not one of the bishops whom Valentius persuaded to retract the condemnation of Samson obtained by Hostegesis. The only mention of him is when Samson remarks rather cryptically that Hostegesis and Servandus in collaboration with the king "ordered the metropolitan bishop to come to Córdoba."[9] If Reccafred was metropolitan of Seville in 864, his influence with the Moslem government

---

[6] *Apologeticus*, preface to Bk. II, 8.
[7] *Ibid.*, II, iv.
[8] *Ibid.*, preface to Bk. II, 10.
[9] *Ibid.*, 8.

had changed considerably from what it was in 851-852.

Part of Samson's refutation of his adversaries is a report on their ancestry and on some of their actions not connected with his own trials. Samson relentlessly enumerates the evils ascribed to them. Hostegesis' father, Auvarnus, had become a Moslem in order to avoid punishment for his defrauding of the poor of the Christian community.[10] Step by step he went through the ritual of becoming a Moslem, which included circumcision and, evidently, the assumption of an Arabic name. By apostasy to Islam Auvarnus seems to have gained an immunity from the provisions of the *Forum iudicum*, which was, as far as is known, the law followed by the Christians. Samuel, the uncle of Hostegesis, was deposed from the see of Granada for his evil deeds, whereupon he came to Córdoba and became a Moslem. "Then he did not fear to persecute the Lord Jesus in His members, to commit His priests and ministers to prison, and to force the altars of God to pay taxes."[11] In the list of bishops of Granada in ms Escorial d-I-1 Samuel is named as the successor of Nifridius, who signed the acts of the Council of 839. He may be too the "mad dog persecutor" of the *Indiculus*.[12] Hostegesis himself at the age of nineteen had uncanonically acquired the office of bishop of Malaga through simony. Prompted by greed, he then began to accumulate a fortune through simony and the extortion of money from those under him. "As for the third of the offerings of the Church, which by law the bishops are wont to receive and to spend in the upkeep of the basilicas and the expenditures for the poor, he, like the sacrilegious and tyrannical man he is, does not take what is given him but extorts what is entered in his books, so that now he is not thought to receive the third but rather to exact taxes."[13] With this money Hostegesis

[10] *Ibid.*, 3.

[11] *Ibid.*, 4.

[12] Cf. Antolín, "El códice emilianense," *La ciudad de Dios*, 74, 389; *Indiculus*, 18.

[13] *Apologeticus*, preface to Bk. II, 2; Samson's words indicate that the restoration of churches was no longer prohibited by Mohammed I.

presented himself at the royal court in Córdoba and sought the favor of those in the palace, participating in debaucheries of drunkenness and lust with them and neglecting his religious duties. While Christians were hungry without, says Samson, the gate of Hostegesis was guarded by soldiers. "But why do I go on with so many things, when, relying on the power of the governor (*praesidalis manus*), he had clerics cut open with blows of the rod by the soldiers in the forum to be dragged through the plazas with their heads shaved and stripped nude, at the voice of a herald crying, 'Let them suffer this who do not pay the taxes owed to the bishop.' I am silent about the rest."[14] One of the sins of Hostegesis about which Samson is not silent is that he obtained a census of Christian men in his diocese for religious purposes and then came to Córdoba to turn the list over to the royal government, asking that his flock in Malaga be burdened with a tax beyond reasonable measure (presumably with Hostegesis acting as tax collector). Early and late, says Samson, he frequented the homes of the consuls and eunuchs in Córdoba. One of his most reprehensible deeds was that on 17 December 863 he failed to solemnly celebrate the vesper office in honor of the Blessed Virgin[15] but visited instead the house of "Hescim," one of the lords of the royal palace. Samson depicts this as a great scandal. "Hescim" was probably Haxim, one of the most powerful figures in Córdoba at this time.[16]

Samson then describes Servandus. "The helper and colleague of that most cruel *Hostis Jesu* is known as Servandus, stupid, and impudent, and puffed up, and arrogant, and avaricious, and grasping, and cruel, and stubborn, and

---

[14] *Ibid.*; the punishment meted out to the clerics resembles that suffered by the merchant John in 851. The "praesidalis manus" probably was under the *praeses* mentioned in the *Vita Eulogii*, 13 and 15, but it may have been commanded by the Christian *comes*, Servandus.

[15] In 656 the Tenth Council of Toledo ordered that the feast of the Annunciation be observed on 18 December because" 25 March frequently came in Lent; cf. Jenner, "Mozarabic Rite," *Catholic Encyclopedia*, X, 616.

[16] Cf. index, "Haxim."

haughty, more audacious than his master. Although in a different order [the laity], he slanders the Church of God with the same cruelty. In punishment for the sins of the people he got hold of the office of count of Córdoba, the patrician city. Being endowed with no dignity of birth, graced by no nobility of family, but rather risen from among the slaves of the Church, he married the cousin of *Hostis Jesu* himself."[17] In Córdoba Servandus fostered the persecution of the Christians which Hostegesis was promoting in Malaga, both making use of taxation. Servandus made many Christians resort to apostasy to avoid payment of the public head tax to the Moslem king.[18] In addition to this he exhumed the bodies of martyrs from beneath the altars and showed them to those loyal to the king, in order to stir up the royal wrath against those who had dared to bury the bodies of those he had slain.[19] Servandus made the basilicas of Córdoba pay tribute to the royal treasury, "taking water from those thirsting and pouring it into the abyss of the sea." By placing unworthy priests to serve in the basilicas, he corrupted the office of the clergy, who "became like dumb dogs, not knowing how to bark, i.e., cheering the wolves and barking at their pastors."[20] What the role of Servandus was in appointing priests to basilicas is not clear. His authority, or influence, in such appointments may have resulted from Bishop Saul's hiding, or death.

Elated with his wicked fortune, Servandus took as colleagues Romanus and Sebastian, father and son, both infected with the error of anthropomorphism[21] and accused

[17] *Apologeticus*, preface to Bk. II, 5; ms "*crudelitate.*" Eulogius and Albar also blame evil rule on the sins of the people. The fact that slaves of the Church existed at this time and could achieve their freedom without becoming Moslems does not agree with what Dozy, *Histoire*, ed. Lévi-Provençal, I, 255ff. and 278ff., says of them.

[18] Apostasy to Islam did not always free one of the head tax; v. supra, 48f., 144, and 219f.

[19] Ms "fidelibus regis" and ausi essent."

[20] *Apologeticus*, preface to Bk. II, 5; cf. Is. 56:10.

[21] *Ibid.*, 6. Anthropomorphism would ascribe human characteristics and limitations to God; cf. G. Bareille, "Anthropomorphites," DTC, I, ii, 1370-1372.

of great crimes of immorality. Romanus, who was eighty years old at the time of Samson's *Apologeticus,* was probably the aged Romanus to whom Albar addressed his letter. He may also have been Comes ibn Antonián, the "mad dog persecutor," or the *exceptor.*[22]

Hostegesis and Servandus began their campaign against Samson in 862, shortly after the election of the virtuous Valentius as bishop of Córdoba. They seized on remarks Samson made that God was everywhere through the immensity of His essence and that His eternal substance can be contained by nothing in nature; and they tried to make him admit with them that He resides only on His throne in heaven, looking down on His subjects like a "vinedresser," that He is within everything by subtlety and not by substance, and that He was contained in the cubicle of the heart of the Virgin. "That beast," Hostegesis, says Samson, "filled with the venom of vipers and blinded to the light of knowledge, clenching his fist and pounding it, said to me, 'Either you will say that Christ was thus contained in the heart of the Virgin, or you will be struck with anathema and deprived of your ecclesiastical office.' "[23] When Samson would not consent to his creed, Hostegesis took out a sentence already drawn up against Samson and coerced the bishops present to subscribe to it against their wills. Valentius, also, yielded to Hostegesis, explains Samson, not wishing to disagree openly with those who had just consecrated him bishop. But, following the council, he induced the other bishops one by one to exonerate Samson from the condemnation.

After Samson had been reinstated by the bishops and placed over the Basilica of St. Zoilus "upon the petition of the clerics and the people," he was called on by royal decree in 863 to translate "from Chaldean speech into the Latin language" letters to be sent to the king of the Franks.[24] This

---

[22] Letter IX of the Albar correspondence.

[23] *Apologeticus*, preface to Bk. II, 7. For the council of 862 cf. Hefele, *Histoire des conciles*, trans. H. Leclercq, IV, i, 312.

[24] *Apologeticus*, preface to Bk. II, 9. The *Annales Bertiniani* record an embassy from Mohammed to Charles the Bald in 863 and the return

he had done before, he says. Servandus thereupon in an unsuccessful effort to undo him accused him of having betrayed the king's counsel to his enemies. On another occasion he accused Samson and Bishop Valentius of being the instigators of a Christian who blasphemed the prophet Mohammed. Servandus proposed to the king that he ask them if the man spoke truth or falsehood. If they replied the truth, then they would be liable to punishment; if they said falsehood, then they would be commanded to slay the man. If they should refuse to do this, the king would know that they had sent the man to blaspheme; and then the king would have Servandus slay all three of them. Samson says, "The heart of the king did not permit such bloodthirstiness, and he reduced the insidious plans of the sinful man to absolutely nothing. 'For when he rose up against us: perhaps he had swallowed us up alive. When his spirit was enkindled against us: perhaps as water he had swallowed us up' (Ps. 123:2-4)."[25]

Meeting without success in these ruses, Hostegesis and Servandus tried to depose Valentius "on the counsel of their father the devil and by the authority (*imperium*) of the Ismaelite king, who does not believe Christ to be the Son of the Most High." Having deposed him then, "as they think," with the help of Moslem *saiones*,[26] they uncanonically elevated to his see a Stephen *Flacco*, without election or appointment, and ordained without the presence or the knowledge of the metropolitan. The metropolitan (of Seville) was summoned to Córdoba and, along with Bishops Reculfus

of the embassy to Córdoba in 865; cf. *Annales Bertiniani*, ed. Waitz, MGH, *Scriptores . . . in usum scholarum*, 66 and 80.

[25] *Apologeticus*, preface to Bk. II, 9. In giving Servandus' words Samson provides three titles of address to the Moslem king: *Vestra Celsitudo*, *Vestra Gloria*, and *Vestra Serenitas*.

[26] *Ibid.*, 8. Originally the *saio* was a member of the *comitatus*. Among the Ostrogoths he came to be an executive official of the king, an equivalent to one of the *agentes in rebus*. Among the Visigoths he was a beadle who assisted the judge, holding his office, however, independently. Cf. Karl Zeumer, "Über zwei neuentdeckte westgothische Gesetze," NA, XXIII (1897), 87f. and 102f.

of Cabra and Beatus of Ecija, was compelled by fear to sit with Stephen in the Basilica of St. Acisclus, presumably the cathedral church of Córdoba. Since all Catholics of the church of Córdoba, "who were called by name at the time of the council," refused to attend this service, a number of Jews and Moslem (*Muzlemiti*) *saiones* sat in their places.[27] At this ceremony priests and ministers who held their offices by virtue of "the nefarious enemy" (Servandus, the Moslems, or the devil) also yielded to fear and confirmed the deposition of Valentius, orthodox as he was. Becoming puerile in their old age,[28] says Samson, "there they have trembled for fear where there was no fear" (Ps. 13:5). Servandus also asked the king to surrender to him all the Christians of Córdoba for a hundred thousand solidi, so that he might vent his wrath on them, but Samson does not say that the king accepted his offer.[29]

At this moment Samson fled to Martos, where he saw copies of Hostegesis' credo and the condemnation of himself, which had been sent to the church there. In order to clear himself of the charges made by Hostegesis and Servandus and to let the Christian brethren of Martos determine for themselves who was the enemy of Christ, Samson composed the *Apologeticus*, publishing therein his own beliefs and refuting the actions and beliefs of his enemies.[30] "I thought it better to change my location than my mind, better to leave the amenities of home than the truth of the faith; for either I had to yield to them or it was no longer a question of words but of swords, nor of fighting with legal judgments but with hands, or with the worst accusations, which

---

[27] Samson would seem to commend those Christians who refused to attend the council as being "Catholics." He would not seem to say that all the Christians of Córdoba attended councils nor that all those who were called by name refused to attend.

[28] This expression is used by Claudianus Mamertus, an author quoted several times by Samson. *De statu animae*, 1; *Claudiani Mamerti opera*, ed. August Engelbrecht, Vol. XI of CSEL (Vienna, 1885), 21.

[29] *Apologeticus*, preface to Bk. II, 8; cf. index, "solidus."

[30] *Apologeticus*, preface to Bk. I, 4f.

it does not befit Christians to use. Therefore, am I to be frightened by the shades of lemures and phantoms, and by the dire sounds of owls and birds of the night, that I do not fight against wicked enemies at least with words? I shall rise up, I shall rise up indeed, and drive off the unwelcome crows, and vultures, and hawks, and harmful birds from the gates of Him Who redeemed me, until the fervor of iniquity dies down and souls are burning with the fire of the Holy Spirit, placed on the venerable altar of His cross."[31]

The two councils described by Samson are travesties of the Council of Córdoba of 839 as shown in those Acts, but it is significant that the instruments of oppression were an evil bishop and an evil Christian lay official. The Moslem power appears primarily as the authority behind the tax exactions perpetrated by the two men. Except for his part in the uncanonical deposition of Bishop Valentius, King Mohammed is not accused of active collusion with Hostegesis and Servandus. The extensive and free communication between the different sees of the Church in Spain which was restored after the persecution of 850-859 is noteworthy. Valentius secured the exoneration of Samson by letter from the bishops of Mérida, Baeza, Cabra, and Ecija. The bishops of Baza, Urci, Elche, and Medina Sidonia gave their agreement to Valentius in person. It is also illustrative of this free and wide communication that Samson knew so much about Hostegesis of Malaga and his uncle Samuel of Granada, and that the texts of Hostegesis against Samson should have been transmitted from Córdoba to Martos. The silence about the see of Toledo probably means that the see was vacant, although the metropolitan may have been separated from Córdoba for other reasons. Toledo was enjoying a truce with King Mohammed, while his armies were marching to the north.[32] The fact that Ariulfus of Mérida communicated with Valentius of Córdoba by letter rather than in person was probably due to his advanced age.

Although these details of persons and events are now the

---

[31] *Ibid.*, preface to Bk. II, 10.
[32] Ibn Idhari, *Bayan*, II, 157-160.

most interesting and important part of Samson's work, they were but a rather long side remark which the author placed in the preface to Book II of his work, and they form but a small part of the whole work. The *Apologeticus* is composed of two books. Samson begins with a preface, in which he says that because of the ignorance and audacity of his enemies he, although unworthy, has been brought to compose his work, which will consist of three books.[33] Then follows a prayer in which the author beseeches the Lord to enlighten him and deign to speak through his mouth.[34] He devotes the first chapter of Book I to praise of the faith, which he says is the basis and source of all good.[35] He concludes the chapter with a credo of his own faith. In the following nine chapters of Book I he presents proofs of the divinity of the Father, of the consubstantiality of the Son with the Father, of the procession of the Holy Spirit from the Father and the Son, of the unity of essence of the Trinity, of the created humanity of the Son, of the one person and two natures of the Son, of the incarnation of the Son in the womb of the Virgin, of the infinity of God, and of the ubiquity of God. These nine chapters contain in brief the treatises Of the Triune God and Of the Word Incarnate, according to García-Villada.[36]

Book II of the *Apologeticus* contains many more chapters and is much longer than Book I. In the preface to Book II Samson gives all the details of his dispute with Hostegesis and Servandus. He collects the texts of his dispute in the first five chapters of the book and then proceeds to an elaborate refutation of Hostegesis in the rest of the book. The first chapter, the credo which Samson delivered to the bishops in the council in Córdoba, is a synthesis of the contents of Book I. In support of his credo Samson quotes from Holy Scripture, Ildefonsus, Augustine, Isidore, and Gregory the Great. The next chapter briefly explains that after three

---

[33] *Apologeticus*, preface to Bk. I, 9; ms "et her*e*seorum stultiloquiis."
[34] Ms "Da sensibus audientium *meram* charitatis tui."
[35] *Apologeticus*, I, i, 5; cf. *Memoriale*, I, 17, and *Apol. mart.*, 9.
[36] García-Villada, *Historia eclesiástica*, III, **142.**

days of study the bishops found nothing wrong with the credo but that nevertheless Hostegesis, in the name of the council, dictated a sentence condemning Samson, and five days later sent a copy to the church in Martos. Samson found it in the hands of the brethren there and was persuaded by them to write a reply to it. Chapter iii is the text of this sentence of condemnation, in which Hostegesis criticizes Samson and explains his own beliefs. Hostegesis accused Samson of having introduced unorthodoxy into the Church. First, he says, Samson approved marriages between cousins too freely. Then, he continues, Samson proceeded to attack certain works of the Fathers used for singing in church. Worst of all, he charges, Samson believed that God is diffused everywhere, like earth, water, air, or light, and is in the devil, idols, and vermin in the same way that He is in holy prophets. But Hostegesis, and those who subscribed to his credo, believe that God is in all things *per subtilitatem* and not *per substantiam*. The sentence then exiled Samson, deprived him of his sacerdotal dignity, forever deposed him from every office of the clergy, and excommunicated him from the body of the Church.

In the fourth chapter Samson tells how Leovigildus, "son of Ansefredus," reprehended Hostegesis when he came to Córdoba in 864, for having introduced the heresy that nature and *subtilitas* are two different things in God. The rebuke by Leovigildus caused Hostegesis to write a second revised credo for the people of Martos, in which he falsely claimed to have won the dispute with his opponent, whom he left unnamed. Rebuked by Leovigildus in some things but not in all, Hostegesis, according to Samson, covered his error with silence and accused Samson of teaching that God was in all things *per subtilitatem* and not *per substantiam*. Although Hostegesis disregarded the matter of essence and *subtilitas* and confessed that God is in all things, he still, says Samson, could not avoid the error of his heresy. For later he denied that God is in rational spirits, irrational animals, or insensate creatures. And lest anyone accuse Samson of making up the statements of Hostegesis, he enters them verbatim in the *Apologeticus*.[37] This second credo of Hostegesis, lengthy and filled with quotations from Scripture and SS. Gregory and Jerome, comprises the fifth chapter. In the sixth chapter Samson presents a prayer in which he invokes the Holy Spirit to help him refute the errors.

In the seventh, eighth, and ninth chapters Samson refutes the first credo of Hostegesis, at first for poor Latin and then for the erroneous beliefs. From the tenth chapter to the twenty-seventh Samson answers the beliefs propounded by Hostegesis in the second credo sent to Martos. The last twelve chapters of this section are devoted to a discussion of why God is present even in vermin and in places where sin is committed, which was one of the main points seized upon by Hostegesis for his condemnation of Samson. At the end of the last chapter Samson states that his work has gone on long enough and that he will bring it to an end. It appears that the text as it exists does contain all three books planned by Samson, especially since he has fulfilled what he promised: "to publish my own faith and to resist the vain sayings of the heretics." It may be that Book II should comprise only the preface and the first five chapters of Book II as it is now divided. In this case Book III would begin with the prayer to the Holy Spirit in chapter vi and continue from chapter vii to chapter xxvii of the present Book II, the actual refutation of the "sayings of the heretics." An appendix promised by Samson, which deals with the degrees of kinship, appears to have been transcribed in the *Emilianense* manuscript of the Escorial.[38]

These last twenty-one chapters, along with the ten chapters of Book I form the bulk of the theological treatise of Samson. They are long-drawn-out and tiring for the reader.

[37] Ms "peto lectorem totum *sese* conferre." The dispute witnesses to the vitality of Latin letters in Córdoba.

[38] *Apologeticus*, preface to Bk. I, 9; *ibid.*, II, viii, 2. Antolín, "El códice emilianense," *La ciudad de Dios*, 74 (1907), 644-649, suggests that a *De gradibus consanguinitatis*, which he publishes, is Samson's work.

Samson's argumentation is elaborate and omits no point, however minor, it seems. In this respect his writing is much like the treatises of Albar, especially the second half of the *Indiculus*. It also bears a likeness to the treatise of Beatus and Eterius against Elipandus of Toledo, which occupies the first half of the manuscript in which the *Apologeticus* is found. Samson's argumentation consists of a large number of quotations from Scripture and the Fathers, arranged so as to show the cogency of his own views and the falsity of the views of his opponent. The beliefs of Samson are orthodox, and those of Hostegesis incline to heresy. The root of the dispute is Christological, whether Christ belongs to the Trinity and whether His humanity precluded His divinity. Perhaps the most salient particular of the argument is over the infinity and the ubiquity of God: is He in vermin and places where sin is committed?

An interesting sidelight on the Christians of Córdoba is afforded in the margin of the tenth-century codex which contains Samson's work. The texts of the *Apologeticus* and of the treatise by Beatus and Eterius contain marginal notes in Arabic indicating the content of the Latin text alongside. Simonet, in an appendix at the end of his monumental work, provides the Arabic text and a Spanish translation of the notes to Samson's work.[39] García-Villada interprets these notes, and those like them in other manuscripts from Toledo, Córdoba, and Seville in the tenth and eleventh centuries as evidence that at that time Christian clerics and monks were more accustomed to Arabic than to Latin. Translations of the Bible and a collection of Spanish councils into Arabic he interprets in the same light.[40]

The personality of Samson appears most vividly in those chapters where he makes sport of Hostegesis for his poor Latin and his ignorant beliefs. In addition, these chapters provide an insight into the scholastic milieu of the Christian intelligentsia of Córdoba. They also are some of the most entertaining reading to be found in the Christian literature

[39] Simonet, *Historia*, Appendix viii, 816-819.
[40] García-Villada, *op.cit.*, 172f.

of Spain at this time. The first two chapters of Samson's ridicule of Hostegesis, chapters vii and viii of Book II, are presented here at length, along with the text of Hostegesis, chapter iii, to which they make reference.

CHAPTER III: COPY OF THE PRONOUNCEMENT DICTATED BY *Hostis Jesu* IN THE NAME OF THE COUNCIL.

In the name of the holy and adorable Trinity.[41] As all of us, humble servants of Christ, the least of priests, were seated in the Council of Córdoba, the while ecclesiastical business was being treated in our assembly, we were content with Christian simplicity given us from above; suddenly a certain corrupt plague, Samson by name, jumped up of his own accord and preached many impieties against God and made many irregular statements, so much so that he would seem rather an idolator than a Christian champion; to such an extent that, in the first place, his assertion would give inordinate license to marriages between cousins: and since he was freely dispensing carnal things to carnal men, he went on to other impieties and gathered supporters for himself from the street corner. And going on to other things, he tried to condemn certain works of the Fathers which were used in church for singing; and he fell into such great impiety and perfidy that he believed so insanely about God as to say, what is wicked to say, that the Divinity of the Almighty is diffused as earth, or water, or air, or light is diffused. So that he said that He is in equal essence in the prophet while he is prophesying, as in the devil, who glides through the air, or in an idol which is venerated by infidels, and even to preach that He is in the tiniest worm, which is wicked to say.

2. But we believe Him to be in all things through subtlety, not through substance. And so far has he fallen into other evils that besides the three persons of the Divinity, that is

---

[41] The invocation of the Trinity by Hostegesis shows that he did not deny the three persons in God.

the Father, and the Son, and the Holy Spirit, Who is without doubt one substance, he asserts that there are we know not what other likenesses, not creatures, but creators; so that he even introduces the vanities of the Gentiles with a plurality of Gods. And his vain assertion slipped so from iniquity of mind on the one hand to perfidy of mind on the other, that he seems to break every rule. And we have condemned him, the author with his error, in anticipation of his tricks and words of vanities, so that Christian simplicity, which cannot yield to error and babblings, may cut off so iniquitous an error from its members. And so we have decreed him exile and deprived of his sacerdotal honor; and forever we abjure him from every office of the clergy; and we even separate him very strictly from the body of the whole Church; lest by the pestilent corruption of infection, the infection of one member reach the others, sound and sincere. Wherefore, we have decided that he is to be cut off by canonical cautery, and we void his vain assertions, content with the Apostolic teaching, "A man that is a heretic, after the first and second admonition, avoid" (Tit. 3:10). If anyone associates with him after our wholesome admonitions then, or joins him; if anyone observes the vain and idle statements of his, or listens, or gives assent. . . .

And this page, containing those stupid claims and others like them, fit to be ridiculed by every Christian, is signed after this with the signature of the bishops.

CHAPTER VII: SAMSON QUOTES THE WORDS OF THE FIRST SENTENCE PROCLAIMED IN THE NAME OF THE COUNCIL BY *Hostis Jesu* AND CRITICIZES WHATEVER THERE WAS OBVIOUSLY WRONG.

1. The cruel *Hostis Jesu* then says: "In the name of the holy and adorable Trinity. As all of us humble servants of Christ, the least of priests, were seated in the Council of Córdoba, the while ecclesiastical business was being treated in our assembly, we were content with Christian simplicity given us from above; suddenly a certain corrupt plague,

Samson by name, jumped up of his own accord and preached many impieties against God and made many irregular statements, so much so that he would seem rather an idolator than a Christian champion."[42] These are the words of the first sentence from his impure mouth, proclaimed in the name of the council. Now, if anyone looks there for Latin, it will be difficult for him to find it. If he looks for orthography, he will find there is none. If he examines the sense, he will at once recognize the words of a madman. Who will fail to hold him deserving of ridicule? Who, not to say a grammarian, or a rhetorician, or a dialectician, or a philosopher, or an orthographer, but anyone so to say, trained only in common[43] letters, who will not say that he is to be laughed at by boys, seeing him trusting in his own folly and having a mind inflated four times over with scum (mentem cuaterno fuco inflatam), still ignorant of the sequence of syllables, and not knowing the tenses of the verbs, and daring to dictate in the name of the bishops such offensive words with the puffing mouth of an old woman? For he is shown to be more a barbarian than a speaker of Latin eloquence.[44] "The least of priests," he says, "seated in the Council of Cordoba, the while ecclesiastical business was being treated in our assembly, we were content (*contempti*) with Christian simplicity (*Christiana simplicitas*) given us from above."

2. Come here before me, I beg, all you who know Latin, and keep from laughing if you can, which I cannot; but if you burst out laughing with me, clap your hands, as laugh-

---

[42] "In nomine sanctae et venerandae Trinitatis. Nos omnes pusilli famuli Christi praesidentes in concilio Cordubensi minimi sacerdotes, cum in nostro conventu ecclesiastica discernerentur negotia, et divinitus dispensata contempti essemus simplicitas Christiana, ex improviso quidam corrupta pestis, Samson nomine, sponte prosiliens multas impietates in Deum, multasque sententias contra regulam praedicavit. In tantum ut immo idolatrix, quam Christianus assertor esse videretur."

[43] Ms "dicam *communium* tantummodo." The enumeration of grammar, rhetoric, dialectics, philosophy, and orthography may represent part of the curriculum pursued in Córdoba.

[44] Ms "facundiae"; cf. index, "*Romani.*"

ers usually do. O admirable eloquence! O fearful pomp of words, not to mention other things now! "Priests of Christ," he says, "are *contempti* with *Christiana simplicitas*." He certainly is that doctor, about whom Blessed Ephraem says, "Before he would be subdued for the good of his soul, he wishes to have subjects; and before he knows the sequence of syllables, he begins to philosophize."[45] Why are they to be called priests and not rather, as you are, *flamines?* O most unfortunate of men, if they have despised (*contempti sunt*) Christian simplicity (*Christianam simplicitatem*), not as you said, but as you perhaps meant to say, but could not because of your stupidity! What is *contemnere* with *m*, as you have written, except "to despise"? As in the saying, "Saints have despised the life of the world." And Paul forbids that his disciple be despised, saying, "These things speak and exhort and rebuke with all authority. Let no man despise thee" (Tit. 2:15). And the Lord complains through the prophet, saying, "As a woman that despiseth her lover, so hath the house of Israel despised me" (Jer. 3:20). For, if they despised (*contempserunt*) Christian simplicity, they withdrew from the Lord, and, despising His faith, as did those whom He reproved, they have made their way wicked. Or perhaps it is *contenti*, "content," that you wished to write, as in that sentence of John the Baptist, commanding the soldiers, "Do violence to no man, neither calumniate any man; and be content with your pay" (Lk. 3:14)? Which is to say, "Let the soldier's pay which you receive be sufficient for you."[46] But it is written with *n*, not with *m*, as you tried to write, O unlearned doctor.

3. But if because of the likeness of the letters of the word *contenti*, it seems to you to be the same[47] as *contempti*, you can be deceived by such an example and easily take *oleum* for *odium*, and *ovium* for *ordeum*, because of the beginnings

---

[45] The same quotation from Ephraem was used by Elipandus of Toledo in his Letter against Migetius, 2 (ES, V, 526).

[46] Samson's examples may be innuendo directed against Hostegesis.

[47] Ms "ipsu*d*."

of the words and the endings of the final syllables.[48] Who at all, hearing such unaccustomed changes of the cases, would not immediately, wrinkling his brow, screwing up his nose, and raising his eyebrow, venture to call you an idiot in all justice? For to say "we were content *(contenti essemus)* with Christian simplicity *(simplicitati Christianae)*," you have said, "*contempti simplicitas Christiana*"; and changing to the nominative case in place of the dative, you, who before committed a barbarism in mixing letters, now have committed a solecism[49] in changing the cases. For to make clear what I am saying, the Evangelist did not say with the nominative case, "*contenti estote stipendia vestra*," as you, inventor of a new Latin, say; but he said "*contenti estote stipendiis vestris*," with the dative case.[50]

4. Wherefore, you should be advised of your ignorance, and you ought to hide your inanities under the cloak of silence. Why do you presume to teach when you do not know the errors in prose or poetry?[51] Why do you, removed from your senses, believe your flatterers, or better your deriders, and not rather, submitting yourself to a master, try to learn so that you can then teach? But you go on and say, "*ex improviso quidam corrupta pestis.*" *Quidam* is masculine, and *quaedam* feminine. And *pestis* is of the same gender as is *mulier*, that is, the feminine. Just as we say *haec mulier*, so we say *haec pestis*;[52] and so you should have said *quaedam pestis*, and not *quidam*, as you have said. Then, having said, "*quidam corrupta pestis*," you go on and say, "Samson by name, jumped up of his own accord and preached many impieties against God and made many irregular statements." And then, O you who are subject to

---

[48] Any particular meaning Samson may have intended by his choice of words is not clear.

[49] Cf. *Probi Donati Servii, qui feruntur de Arte Grammatica libri*, ed. H. Keil, Vol. IV of *Grammatici latini* (Leipzig, 1864), 392f.; Isidore, *Etymologiae*, I, xxxii (PL 82, 106).

[50] Actually *stipendiis* is in the ablative case.

[51] "Vitia et schema"; cf. Keil, *op.cit.*, 397.

[52] Rather than a jest at the expense of women, this would seem to be innuendo aimed at Hostegesis.

every error, the whole assembly heard my faith, put together in brief and synthesized in very few words and references;[53] and before that, whoever of the Christians, as well
as of the Jews and Arabs, who wanted to dispute with me,
knew it.[54] And now in the beginning of this little work
which I have put out for apologetic reasons, whoever did
want, does want, or will want to, can now read and will be
able to read whatever irregular statements are introduced
there and whatever impieties against God. Or is it that
what I have said in piety, in justice, in truth, seems to you,
because you are a proven liar, to be impious, that I believe
God cannot be encompassed in the cubicle of the heart, since
I truly confess Him to be in all things and outside of all
things? For if you think this to be impious, you have to rise
up against the pillars of the Catholic Church after the apostles, Augustine I mean, and Fulgentius, and Gregory, and
Isidore, and Eucherius, and almost all the leaders (*praesules*) of the Church, and as a new dogmatist, contradict
their sayings, who proclaim with one mouth that Christ
was from the essence of Divinity, through Which He was
in the heart of the Virgin, vivifying, animating, enlightening, and protecting, and that He is everywhere whole and
without compass.

5. And do not say, with your erroneous imagination, that
I am the author of that truth, for I do not deny that I am
not the author but I am the last follower of those so proclaiming. After this you say, "so much so that he would
seem rather an idolator (*idolatrix*) than a Christian champion (*Christianus assertor*)." Behold, behold, I beg all you
expert men who know scholarly words to consider the sayings of this author of a new language. Where did he learn
those things? Did he nibble them from Tully, or at the font

[53] Cf. *Apologeticus*, II, i.

[54] It is hard to see how Samson disputed with Moslems about the
Christian faith without having to make statements which not many
years earlier had brought martyrdom to a number of Christians. What
he says here indicates that there was a radical change of policy on the
part of the Moslem authorities.

of Cicero?[55] Has he brought this unheard of noun to our
ears following the examples of Cyprian, Jerome, or Augustine? Or what is more likely true, has he dictated these
stupidities from the teaching of his own heart? *"Idolatrix,"*
he says, *"magis quam Christianus assertor."* If the Latin
language, O fool, did not refuse to receive this, if Roman
eloquence would take it, if cultured lips would show how to
say it, anyone could say *idolator* for a man and *idolatrix*
for a woman, and by the same reasoning what you have
said in the masculine gender, *Christianum,* and not *Christianam,* which expresses the feminine sex, *assertorem,* and
not *assertricem;* then under pretext of blasphemy you could
call me *idolator* and not *idolatrix.* But, since almost all the
codices of our authors that refer to pagans call male and
female worshippers of idols *gentiles,* and never call them
idolatores or *idolatrices,* you should note how much it is a
sign of a disturbed mind to say these things which were
neither spoken at any time, nor heard in any place;[56] and
if the niceties of Latin are such as I have taught, you should
have, had you known, distinguished the gender of nouns,
and not, as a common noun, have burdened one person with
different genders.[57] For, if the blind cloud of ignorance,
concealing the gender of nouns, pronouns, and participles,
hides from your eyes the person and tenses of verbs, you
ought to close off the trumpet of your inarticulate voice with
the lock of your teeth, and not put into writing other verbal
baubles for future centuries to laugh at. For believe me,
in time these clouds of ignorance will gradually be dis-
sipated, and then the fame of the grammatical art will be
restored to Spain, and then it will appear to everybody to
what great errors you are subject, who today are thought by

[55] Samson probably knew that Tully and Cicero were one person
but mocks the ignorance of Hostegesis. Albar likewise uses both names
separately in praising the writings of Eulogius, *Repriorasti, mi domine,*
PL 115, 734ff.

[56] Samson appears to be speaking of a Freudian slip of the tongue.
This is the second time he taunts Hostegesis about women; cf. supra,
"quaedam pestis."

[57] Ms "sub genera taxare diversa."

brute men to know letters.[58] Indeed I am afraid that it will be said to me, "He loses oil and money who sends an ox to school." And so, coming back to the matter at hand, let it be enough for me to have said these things to *Hostis* and to have thus far refuted his lack of knowledge, whom I have shown in short quotations to be a barbarian and cut off from Latin eloquence. For I do not want to criticize his crudeness item by item, since it is proven that he writes little or nothing right, depending not on a basis of knowledge, but on fortuitous chance. For he who does not know how to preserve himself from errors will not be able to discover the brilliance of the Roman language. And so with Virgil we should say to him:

Let him who hates not Baevius love your songs Maevius.
And let him also yoke foxes and milk he-goats.[59]

Declining[60] to cut down the rough growth of his lips and the thorns of his speech, I shall gather all the arms of my eloquence against those things which he wickedly thought about God, and wished to say, although he could not, so that his nonsense, turned into chaff, may be driven away by the fan of the cross from the threshing floor of my Lord.

CHAPTER VIII: CONTINUATION OF THE SENTENCE AND WHAT SEEMS TO HIM TO BE AGAINST IT.

1. Therefore, because I see that the forest of vices of this mumbling rather than speaking centaur, whom I have shown in a few words to know nothing indeed, has grown into so many branches and is entangled and interlaced with so many briars that it would be quite idle to attack all the roots of his errors with scholastic hoes, which would be no small

[58] Samson's statement about the faulty status of Latin learning in Córdoba, made in the wake of the persecution, is less pessimistic about the future than Albar's in the *Indiculus* ten years earlier.

[59] Eclogue 3, 90f. This couplet is quoted by Bodo writing to Albar, Letter XIX.

[60] *Recusantes* was probably intended to modify *nos* as the subject of the sentence, but Samson changed to the first person singular.

labor, or with the trident to destroy the weapons of his polished eloquence, which is shown to be choked with so many
barbarisms, solecisms, metaplasms, acyrologies, macrologies,
amphibologies,[61] and all the faults against correct writing
and speaking, that to say the least it offends learned ears
and expresses a sound more bestial than human. And so I
give those things, as they have been stated, to the prudent
to be criticized; so that I may be free to answer those things
which he thinks wrongly about God and to tense all the
nerves of my discourse for the assault on him. Certainly,
where it happens that I cannot repress laughter I shall suffer my pen to carry on very briefly. After this introduction
then, this negation(*Antiphrasius*) of a doctor in the name
of the bishops adds to the laughable sentences in the preceding chapter, and says, "He fell into such great impiety and
perfidy that he believed so insanely[62] about God as to say,
what is wicked to say, that the Divinity of the Almighty
is diffused as earth, or water, or air, or light is diffused. So
that he said that He is in equal essence in the prophet while
he is prophesying, as in the devil, who glides through the
air, or in an idol which is venerated by infidels, and even to
preach that He is in the tiniest worm, which is wicked to
say. But we believe Him to be in all things through subtlety.
not through substance. And so far has he fallen into other
evils that besides the three Persons of the Divinity, that is,
the Father, and the Son, and the Holy Spirit, Who is without doubt one substance, he asserts that there are we know
not what other likenesses, not creatures but creators, so that
he even introduces the vanities of the Gentiles with a plurality of Gods."

2. But, lest anyone think I will overlook those things
about which he has lied, saying that I ordered an inordinate
number of marriages between kinfolk,[63] or that I will hide

---

[61] Samson probably relies here on Isidore of Seville, *Etymologiae*,
I, xxxii-xxxv (PL 82, 106-109), who followed the tradition of Donatus,
Ars grammatica, ed. Keil, *op.cit.*, 392-395; cf. also Fontaine, *Isidore de
Séville*, I, 125-156, especially 127-137.

[62] Ms *"insane,"* as in the text of chap. iii.

[63] Ms "quae *de* coniugia profliganda."

the criticism of the antiphon in astute silence, let him know
that I wish to make answer about the antiphon when I begin to dispute against the creed which he has inserted in his
document, where he himself decided to put the antiphon and
an exposition of it.[64] And those things which I thought about
the degrees of kindred I plan to publish at the end of the
third book.[65] Then, because the traces of his lie cannot escape the prudent and those whose heart the intimate In-
spirer touches, I hope that the mind of my reader will be
stirred up by the spurring of my prayers and by the stimu-
lations of my supplications so that it can with prudence
distinguish truth from falsehood. For who will not find
there lying invention? Who will not note that the tongue of
my accuser is full of iniquity and guile?[66] For he hears me
say that the essence of Divinity is diffused, as earth, or
water, or air, or visible light, and is equal in prophets, in
demons, in idols, and in worms. And no one is ignorant that
earth and water and air are corporeal things. But that demons are spirits and not bodies, both reason instructs and
the evangelical truth teaches, where it mentions that the
Lord drove a legion out of the body of one man. And how
should I be thought to have said that the Divinity, like any
corporeal thing, is in incorporeal and corporeal things, when
I have often said and say now that He is equally present
always through His own incomprehensible nature in angels
and in demons, in the just and in the wicked? For the body
of a prophet is subject to quantity; and mass is expanded
to be large, or contracted to be small. If I have spoken of
God as a corporeal thing, I could not have said that He is
in corporeal and in incorporeal things with equal essence.
For every body because of its corporeal nature can contain
according to its quantity, and diverse bodies are not circum-

[64] Cf. *Apologeticus*, II, v, 2, and II, xii–xv.

[65] No such text is appended to the *Apologeticus*, which ends on the
recto side of a folio with the verso blank. Several folios have been
cut out, apparently for binding purposes, and the last nine folios of
the ms are devoted to a number of questions about Holy Scripture,
attributed to Augustine, Jerome, Isidore, and Ambrose.

[66] "*dolo*" by conjecture.

scribed[67] by one quantity of mass: for mass varies greatly among the members of a huge beast, of men, and of bugs. For if I had said that God is diffused, as that liar imagines, I would not say, as I have said, that He is whole in individual things, and one in every thing. For a corporeal thing diffused in many things cannot be found whole in one; nor can the natures of earth, water, and air penetrate the metal of gold, brass, or iron, marble, or lead, or even the wood of the forest, out of which the effigies of idols are made; so that I should both say that God is diffused like these elements,[68] and assert that He fills, contains, and circumscribes all things! But because He is incorporeal, He is one and the same inseparably in every creature, and whole in whatever part of the creature. For if He were diffused as air, huge beasts would have more of Him than prophets, since they are expanded into a greater mass of body. But I, following the paths of the Fathers, have always believed and do believe that God is whole through His substance in every individual thing created by Him; and I fear not to say that He works diversely in diverse things.

In support of his belief Samson completes this chapter with lengthy quotations from Gregory the Great, Claudianus Mamertus, Augustine, St. Paul (I Cor. 7:7), Eucherius, and Isidore of Seville.[69]

---

[67] Ms "terminantur."

[68] Although here Samson does not include light among the elements which cannot penetrate metals, marble, or wood, he does include it among the corporeal creatures which are contained in space a few lines later. Samson's cosmology appears to be derived from Claudianus Mamertus' *De statu animae*, where light is regarded as the most penetrating of the four elements, fire belonging to light (*ibid.*, I, 7).

[69] Gregory, *Homiliae in Ezechielem*, II, v, 10 (PL 76, 991); *Moralia in Job*, II, xii (PL 75, 565). Claudianus, *De statu animae*, I, 15, 17, 23, 3, 18, and II, 2; *op.cit.*, pp. 59f., 63, 83, 30f., 64f., and 102. Augustine, *City of God*, X, iii, 2 (PL 41, 280); cf. also Letter 187, "De praesentia Dei," 20 (PL 33, 839 and 847). Eucherius, *Instructionum libri II*, I (De Genesi), ed. C. Wotke, Vol. XXXI of CSEL (Vienna, 1894), 67. Isidore, *Sententiarum libri III*, I, ii, 5 (PL 83, 542), and xii, 6 (PL 83, 563).

CHAPTER XVI

THE CHRISTIANS OF CÓRDOBA
IN THE TENTH CENTURY

The *Apologeticus*, written in 864, brings to a close the history of the Christians of Córdoba in the ninth century. Samson died 21 August 890, according to his epitaph, after having donated a bell to a church near Córdoba in 875.[1] Apart from a few other epitaphs and the notice of translation of the relics of Eulogius and Leocritia to Oviedo in 884, previously noted, the Christians in Córdoba are not heard from again until the tenth century in the reign of Abd al-Rahman III (912-961). In 923 a Eugenia was martyred in Córdoba, and in 925 Pelagius, a captive youth from Galicia, died in Córdoba for his faith. Pelagius is one of the few saints to be added to the patron saints of the Christians of the North after the seventh century. His popularity reached even Germany, where the nun Hrotswitha composed his passion in verse. Some years after the death of Pelagius, Argentea, the daughter of Ibn Hafsun of Bobastro according to García-Villada, was martyred with Vulfura, who had come to Córdoba from Gaul to preach the Faith. A Dúnula from Cadiz left Spain on a peregrination to Byzantium and the East, where he died as a martyr in Egypt. In 974 a Dominicus Sarracenus and his companions were martyred in Córdoba.[2]

The account of an exchange of ambassadors between Abd al-Rahman III and Otto I offers an opportunity to view the Christians in Córdoba in the latter half of the tenth cen-

[1] ES, XI, 318ff., and 526.
[2] ES, X, 462-471 and 564-570; ES, XXII, 44f.; ES, XXIII, 106-132 and 231-236. David, *Etudes*, 218-242, especially 220 and 234; *Hrotsvithae opera*, ed. Karl Strecker (Leipzig, 1930), 54-66; García-Villada, *Historia eclesiástica*, III, 165f.; Morales, *Divi Eulogii... opera*, 110-119v; Fidel Fita, "San Dúnula, prócer y martyr mozárabe del siglo X," BRAH, 55 (1909), 433-443.

tury.[3] In 951 Abd al-Rahman sent a Christian bishop as ambassador to Otto with a letter that offended Otto with its insults against Christianity. Otto detained the ambassador for three years and sent the monk John of Gorze (of Vandières) on a return embassy to Córdoba in 953. When John arrived in Córdoba he was kept in lodgings outside the capital while attempts were made to get him to withhold Otto's letter, which was suspected of returning insults against the Mohammedan religion. John was told that if Otto's letter insulted Islam the king would have no choice, being bound by irrevocable ties with the people, but to execute him, even though he was a foreigner.[4] An attempt by a Jew of surpassing craftiness to ascertain the secret of John's mission failed. The French monk was next visited by a Mozarab bishop, also named John, who explained to him that the Mohammedans respected and lived together with good Christians, although they completely abhorred the Jews. The Christians had reached a modus vivendi with the Mohammedans, he said, whereby, as long as the Christian religion was not attacked, they collaborated with the Moslems in other things which did not affect the Faith. He urged the French monk to withhold his letter and not break the peace unnecessarily. John of Gorze replied to the bishop with censure for the lack of firmness in their faith shown by the Christians of Córdoba. He had even heard, he said, that the Mozarabs had accepted circumcision and abstained from certain foods with the Mohammedans. We are forced to do this by necessity, the bishop replied. There is no other way to live with them. Thus we hold on to what has been handed down and observed by our ancestors, far back in antiquity. John of Gorze, however, refused to present himself to Abd al-Rahman without the letter. Both the Jew and the Mozarab bishop had been sent by the king in an attempt to deal with Otto's ambassador unofficially.

---

[3] *Vita Johannis abbatis Gorziensis* by John, the abbot of St. Arnulf, ed. Pertz, MGH, *Scriptores*, IV (Hanover, 1841), 335-377; for John's embassy to Córdoba cf. pars. 115-136, pp. 369ff.

[4] *Ibid.*, par. 119.

John of Gorze was to be detained in his quarters outside Córdoba for three years while he refused to compromise the mission Otto had assigned him. On Sundays and feasts he was permitted to go to a nearby church, named after St. Martin, in the company of twelve guards, "which they call *saiones*."[5] It is of interest that these functionaries from Visigothic days reappear in rather similar offices in the days of Eulogius and Samson and again under the first caliph of Córdoba, Abd al-Rahman III. On one of his trips to church John was given a letter in which the caliph threatened to kill every Christian in Spain if John persisted in delivering Otto's letter. The blood of them all, it was pointed out, would be on John's head. Apparently realizing that the threat was empty, John returned a staunch reply to Abd al-Rahman.

Finally the caliph determined to send an embassy to Otto in an attempt to have his letter retracted. Recemundus, a lay Catholic in charge of the chancery, fluent in Arabic and Latin, volunteered for this mission, the caliph promising to grant him any request as a reward for his service. Recemundus asked for and received the episcopacy of Granada, which had recently become vacant. Before leaving for Otto's court Recemundus conferred with John of Gorze about the customs in the land he was about to visit, in particular about the danger of making any "irrevocable" statements, such as could be made to the caliph of Córdoba. In his stay at Otto's court Recemundus met Liutprand of Cremona. When Recemundus returned to Córdoba with another ambassador and another letter from Otto, and the impediment of Otto's earlier letter was removed, Abd al-Rahman III expressed his respect for the integrity of John of Gorze by receiving that monk in a special audience.

Liutprand's *Antapodosis*,[6] a history of the Europe of his own day and its rulers, was suggested to him by Rece-

[5] *Ibid.*, 124; cf. index, "*saiones*."

[6] The *Antapodosis* has been edited by Joseph Becker, MGH, *Scriptores ... in usum scholarum* (3d ed.; Hanover, 1915), 1-158; for references to Recemundus cf. pp. 1, 3, 73, 104, and 131.

mundus, to whom the work is dedicated. Recemundus later performed an embassy for Abd al-Rahman to Byzantium and Jerusalem. He returned from this mission in 961 and dedicated a *calendarium* to the new caliph, al-Hakam II (961-976). The *calendarium* is primarily devoted to astronomical and agronomical subjects. It contains a list of liturgical feasts celebrated by the Mozarabs, whom Recemundus calls "Latins" or "Christians."[7] In this list Recemundus mentions more churches and monasteries in the environs of Córdoba than did Eulogius in his works a hundred years earlier. He also mentions a monastery on the outskirts of Ecija. A number of the participants in the martyr movement of the ninth century are commemorated by Recemundus: 30 April, Perfectus (18 April according to Eulogius); 7 May, the martyr Esperende (if Esperaindeo, not a martyr according to ninth-century sources); 15 September, Emilia (one of the last martyrs under Abd al-Rahman II); 27 September, Adulphus and John (no date given by Eulogius); 7 November, Albar (not otherwise known as a martyr); and 24 November, *"Innucericie"* (perhaps Flora and Maria, who died on 24 November). Recemundus also commemorates Pelagius on 26 June (martyred in Córdoba in A.D. 925). The *calendarium* was first written in Arabic, and later translated into Latin.

Recemundus must have been a man of unusual ability. The post of the royal chancery could not have been an unimportant one, yet Recemundus preferred the episcopacy of Granada. No doubt the rank of bishop enhanced his prestige

---

[7] The text of the calendarium was edited by Dozy, *Le calendrier de Cordoue de l'année 961; texte arabe et ancienne traduction latine* (Leyden, 1873). The Latin text of the liturgical feasts has been edited by Férotin, *Le liber ordinum* (Paris, 1904), xxxiii-xxxv and 451-495, and recently by Angel C. Vega (and F. J. Simonet) in ES, LVI (Madrid, 1957), 137-159. Recemundus says that feasts were celebrated by "Latins," by "Christians," or else makes no reference at all to those who celebrated the feast. He does not seem to be making any distinction between the celebrations in this regard, but neither does his use of the three methods appear to be without any significance. The variation may derive from the sources Recemundus used to compile his text.

in Otto's court, as it probably did in Byzantium. The situation of a Christian bishop serving as ambassador from the Moslem caliph of Córdoba to the Moslem power in Jerusalem, at a time when Byzantium was threatening the Arab power in the Eastern Mediterranean, is rather intriguing. Recemundus made a favorable impression on Liutprand of Cremona. His suggestion to Liutprand to compose a contemporary history of Europe must have been a more ingenious idea then than it appears now. Moreover, following Recemundus' return from the East and the dedication of his calendar of Christian saints to the Cordoban caliph al-Hakam II, a number of Arabic chronicles appeared in Córdoba. Liutprand's *Antapodosis* (probably written between 958 and 962), the *Muktabis* of Ibn Haiyan, and the *Akhbar madjmua*, two Arabic chronicles from the reign of al-Hakam (961-976), all contain verses inserted in the prose text of the history. During the reign of al-Hakam Córdoba began to enter into friendly relations with the Christian kingdom of Navarre.

In the eyes of the German scholar Gams, Recemundus' *calendarium* shows that the Mozarabs at this time were a living part of the Church, adding new saints and feasts to the liturgical year. They also venerated as genuine saints the Christians who had been martyred by the Mohammedans. Between 864 and 961, when their history is in eclipse, Gams says, the Mozarabs did not decline under oppression but enjoyed a relatively favorable life under Abd al-Rahman III and al-Hakam II. They had at least as many churches and monasteries then, and probably more, he says, than in 864, and they practiced their faith without restriction. Outside Córdoba, Gams continues, the story was probably the same. Bishops were highly regarded and capable, and performed important missions for the government of the caliph.[8]

An inscription in a Bible of Toledo dated 988 enumerates five sees in Mohammedan Spain in such a way as to indicate that the Church there was extensive and flourishing, and

---

[8] Gams, *Kirchengeschichte*, II, ii, 455f.

enjoyed freedom of intercommunication. At least six sees are known to have existed in southern Spain at the end of the tenth century.[9]

García-Villada interprets several references by al-Makkari to Christians in the service of Moslem rulers as indicative of the arabization of the Mozarabs rather than a rise in their fortunes. On the basis of his own palaeographical studies he concludes that in the tenth and eleventh centuries the Visigothic script reached its peak in Toledo, Córdoba, and Seville. Unfortunately, he says, the Mozarabs produced no original work of importance in these years. On the contrary, he points out, they seemed to be losing proficiency in Latin and falling back on Arabic translations. Their religion, however, remained orthodox and made a good impression on the Arabic historian Ibn Hazam, even though they had no apologist of the stature of Esperaindeo or Samson to reply to him.[10]

Much the same situation appears to have prevailed in the tenth century as in the ninth. There were fewer martyrs, and both Moslems and Christians were apparently anxious to preserve the somewhat delicate relations between themselves. One can understand that the Christians of Córdoba at the time of Recemundus were little inclined to put themselves to the trial of a persecution for the sake of a foreign Christian king whose interests may have been entirely political. It is interesting to note with regard to this modus vivendi reached between Christians and Mohammedans in Spain that the German, Boniface Gams, sides with the Christians and singles out the *calendarium* of Recemundus as a sign of the continuing vitality of the Christian church in Spain, whereas his Spanish counterpart, García-Villada, sides with the German John of Gorze and regards the overtures of the Christian bishop John to Otto's ambassador as a sign of debility on the part of the Christians.[11] The

[9] *Ibid.*, 445ff.; cf. ES, X, 286f.; the inscription is published in ES, VII, 93.
[10] García-Villada, *op.cit.*, 167-174.
[11] *Ibid.*, 164.

political loyalty of the Christians in Spain appears to have been fundamentally municipal, a condition which Louis the Pious recognized in 826.

Papal bulls of Gregory IX in 1236 with regard to the reconquest of Córdoba ignore any Christian cult which may have existed there when the city was captured. Gregory praises Ferdinand III for having secured the return of the city and church of Córdoba to the Christian cult and grants him episcopal authority in the appointment of four prebendaries of the church of Córdoba as well as the authority to appoint the rectors of churches in areas reconquered from the Saracens. Gregory authorizes the archbishop of Toledo to appropriate Moslem temples for use as Christian churches. In neither of two accounts by Rodrigo Jiménez de Rada, who played an important role in the reconquest of Andalucía, can one tell whether or not there was a Christian cult in Córdoba at the time of its capture in 1236. F. Pérez notes that fourteen parishes were established there following the reconquest and in 1239 two friaries were founded there. Raymond of Peñafort in a letter to the Master General of the Dominicans in 1246 advocated missions to Moslem Spain and North Africa because there were a number of Christian soldiers and captives there, as well as Christian slaves who did not know Arabic and apostates from Christianity.[12]

By the year 1300, when Bishop Pedro Pascual[13] of Jaén died as a martyr in Granada, Christians in Moslem Spain were not so separate from their brethren in the rest of Spain, France, and Rome as they had been in previous centuries. Pedro Pascual, born in Valencia about 1220, benefited from

[12] Registro Vaticano, no. 18, Gregorii IX Bullar., an. X, 214-216 and 249, pp. 190-191, 318, and 327v. The analysis of Lucien Auvray, *Les registres de Grégoire IX. Recueil des bulles de ce Pape publiées ou analysées d'après les manuscrits originaux du Vatican*, II (Paris, 1907), 473ff., omits details of interest. Rodrigo Jiménez de Rada, *De rebus Hispaniae*, VII, viii, and IX, xvi-xvii (*SS PP Toletanorum*, III, 154 and 205-207). F. Pérez, "Cordoue," DHGE, XIII, 864. José M. Coll, "Escuelas de lenguas orientales en los siglos XIII y XIV (Periodo Raymundiano)," *Analecta sacra Tarraconensia*, XXI (1948), 138.

[13] Cf. "Pedro, 6 de Diciembre," ESPASA, XLII, 1311-1313.

the favor of James I of Aragon. After obtaining his doctorate of theology and being ordained in Paris, where he met Thomas Aquinas and Bonaventure, he went to Rome, where he joined the Order of Our Lady of Mercy in 1250. For a while he taught philosophy in Barcelona and Holy Scripture in Zaragoza. In Zaragoza he tutored Sancho, the son of James I, who became archbishop of Toledo. Pedro Pascual directed the archbishopric for Sancho until the latter's death in 1275. After extensive travels in Spain and Italy he again went to Paris and defended the dogma of the Immaculate Conception, later returning to Spain, where he continued the defense of the dogma (1291-1294). Having been made an abbot in the diocese of Braga, he was named to the see of Jaén in 1296 by Pope Boniface VIII. He retained the income from the abbacy in Braga because the diocese of Jaén, vacant for seven years, was in ruin as a result of Moorish invasions. A year later Pedro Pascual was captured by the Moors of Granada and remained in captivity until he died in Granada a martyr on 6 December 1300.

In the hopes of a rich ransom for him the Moors permitted the aged bishop freedom to move about Granada, write, preach, and dispute with Moslem and Jewish doctors. Twice the bishop used his own ransom money to ransom children and young women whose faith and virtue were endangered in their captivity. The last work he wrote in Granada, against the errors of Islam, so aroused the Moslems that the ruler agreed to execute him. His relics were relinquished gratis to envoys from Baeza and Jaén and were buried in Baeza.

He wrote a number of works, several of which have been lost. Written in Latin and in the dialects of Valencia and Castille, they are mostly of a catechetical or polemical nature and include treatises against the Jews, Moslems, and advocates of divination and horoscopy. The biography of Pedro Pascual by Juan Pardo de Villegas in 1614 is the source of all others. His works have been published by a fellow Mercedarian.[14]

---

[14] *Obras de S Pedro Pascual*, ed. Pedro Armengol Valenzuela (4 vols.; Rome, 1906-1908).

CHAPTER XVII

MOZARAB CULTURE AND SPANISH MOSLEM CULTURE IN THE TRADITION OF THE WEST

Miguel Asín Palacios points out in his monograph on Ibn Masarra (883-931) and his school that the culture of Moslem Spain was based on Islamic culture of the East and had no connection with the culture of Visigothic Spain. Asín notes that although two important Spanish Arabic historians, Said of Toledo and Ibn Hazam of Córdoba, mention Greek, Persian, and Christian writers of the East, they do not know Spanish Latin writers of Visigothic or Roman times. The Arabs did not adopt the Visigothic tradition, according to Asín, because it was too poor to attract even Spanish Christians, not to speak of alien Moslems.[1] Actually, however, the Christians of Córdoba did continue the interest in theology and religious matters, which preoccupied writers of the Visigothic period. Isidore's *Etymologiae* with their encyclopaedic secular erudition, an isolated phenomenon even in Visigothic Spain, may have been neglected by the Mozarabs but they were known to them. Quite naturally the Moslems were not interested in pursuing the study of Catholic theology.

Until the ninth century, says Asín, there was no sign of a philosophical awakening among the Arabs in Spain.[2] During the reigns of Abd al-Rahman I and al-Hakam I there were examples of theological heresy mixed with anti-Arab nationalism on the part of certain Spanish Moslems, which the two rulers moved quickly to crush, although without complete success. As a result of ruthless repression Spain

---

[1] Miguel Asín Palacios, "Ibn Masarra y su escuela, origines de la filosofía hispanomusulmana," *Obras escogidas*, I (Madrid, 1946), 21f. This discourse was read before the Real Academia de Ciencias Morales y Políticas in 1914.

[2] *Ibid.*, 23.

became, in the view of Asín, the most orthodox of Islamic countries. Heresies current in the East were but faint echoes in Córdoba, where orthodox Malekites held control of the intellectual and religious life. In their intolerance against the introduction of new ideas the Malekites were supported by the state. Theirs was the only school of canon law permitted, and they regarded as heresy attempts to analyze their dogma. They believed that if the emirate of Córdoba was to be preserved the most rigid dogmatic unity was necessary. A few ideas did, according to Asín, trickle in with Spanish Moslems returning from studies in the East, or with visiting sages from the East, or were current among the members of secret societies. Asín cites the introduction of the books of Yahiz of Basra, the existence of several independent thinkers of the mu'tazil sect, and the occurrence of heresy as examples of freethinking in the emirate of Córdoba in the ninth century.

Asín's picture of strict censorship on the part of the Malekites agrees with what Ibn Khaldun says of the Spanish Umaiyads. It was only after the fall of the Umaiyads in Spain, says Ibn Khaldun, that Spanish Moslems were permitted to make the pilgrimage to Mecca.[3] But such restrictions do not accord with Ibn Haiyan's description of an intellectual renaissance as a result of the cultural zeal of the emir Abd al-Rahman II (822-852), previously discussed. The mu'tazil sect referred to by Asín was gnostic, and taught that theology is subject to rational investigation. It arose before the fall of the Umaiyads in A.D. 750. Polemical apologetics, philosophical argumentation, and grammatical exegesis were characteristic of its protagonists. It held for strict monotheism and was strongly anti-anthropomorphist in its studies of the nature of God and the nature of the created world.[4] The Moslems of Córdoba, to judge from the

[3] Ibn Khaldun, *The Muqaddimah. An Introduction to History*, trans. Franz Rosenthal (3 vols.; New York, 1958), II, 100.

[4] Alfred Guillaume, "Philosophy and Theology," *Legacy of Islam*, 262ff.; H. S. Nyberg, "al-Mu'tazila," EI, III, 787-793.

Latin sources, influenced Christian thought in Córdoba towards anthropomorphist ideas of God.

Mathematics, astronomy, and medicine, says Asín, were studied privately in Córdoba, but it was not until al-Hakam II in the middle of the tenth century relaxed the restriction on studies in Córdoba that schools in these subjects appeared. The study of physics, metaphysics, or philosophy was even more difficult to pursue. They had to be studied as part of other sciences. The life and surroundings of hermits and ascetics proved to be fruitful for the cultivation of these studies. From the first days of the conquest of Spain, Asín states, ascetics had been held in high regard. Their life was based on the models of Christian monasticism in the East, and they had reproduced closer at hand, he points out, the Christian monasteries of Andalucía. In the eighth century Spanish Mohammedan asceticism was personal and private, he says, but by the ninth century many of these ascetics were experienced and learned cenobites teaching their doctrine to the people who came to listen to them. The ascetic doctrine which they taught was based on the Koran and on Christian asceticism in the East as they came to know it from Mohammedan sources. Asín concludes his picture of intellectual life in Córdoba in the ninth century by bringing out four elements, "the mu'tazil heresy, batini and esoteric doctrines, metaphysical systems of Greek origin, and Islamic asceticism or monasticism," as those which were to be synthesized in the system and person of Ibn Masarra, who was a forerunner of Spanish sufism, or mysticism.[5] Asín thus connects the classical and Christian culture of the East with the twelfth- and thirteenth-century intellectual movements of Western Europe through Spain by Ibn Masarra and the sufis.

The *Batiniyya* sect of Islam, which arose in Iraq in the eighth century, stressed the inward meaning (*batin*) of sacred texts as opposed to the apparent meaning (*zahir*). Their method was symbolical or allegoristic. Their interpretations of sacred texts (*ta'wil*), were imparted to the elite

[5] Asín, *op.cit.*, 35-37.

(*kh*ass), who were initiated into the sect with ceremony. The elite were expected to dissimulate with regard to the beliefs, which were secret, and not reveal them to the ignorant generality (*'amm*). The cosmology of the *Batiniyya* was derived from neo-Platonic sources and justified the religious hierarchy of the sect. The terminology and conceptions of the *Batiniyya* influenced Sufi thought.[6]

The intolerance of certain Cordoban rulers and the Malekite sect, which would deter Moslems from the study of Christian culture, should be included as a reason for the lack of a connection between the culture of Visigothic Spain and that of Moslem Spain. It would seem prudent not to dismiss too readily the importance of Christian writers of Córdoba who flourished about fifty years before Ibn Masarra. Possible relationships between the indigenous Christian culture and Moslem culture in Spain deserve further study. In the middle of the ninth century the Christian literature of Córdoba was devoted almost entirely to the martyrs and to theological disputation. As Asín points out, the theological disputation was dominated by Biblical and Patristic quotation.[7] Most of the Christian theological disputation was concerned with Christological questions about the divinity and humanity of Christ. But much of it was devoted to the same subject matter which was of primary concern to Ibn Masarra, a system of theology and cosmology which came to grips with the problems of anthropomorphism and pantheism. Ibn Masarra appears to have inclined towards a pantheism. The most important theological treatise of the Cordoban Christians, the *Apologeticus* of Samson, was written to refute an errant Christian bishop who frequented the homes of Mohammedan nobles and collaborated with them in trying to introduce a heresy about the nature of God into the church of Córdoba. Even more important with regard to Ibn Masarra and the later sufis is the widespread monastic asceticism attested to in the works of Eulogius and Albar. Although Asín points out that these monasteries were un-

[6] M. G. S. Hodgson, "Batiniyya," EI, I, 1098-1100.
[7] Asín, *op.cit.*, 22.

der the very eyes of the Mohammedans in Córdoba, he does not seem to consider that they had a direct influence on the theological thought and the ascetic practice of the Moslems. Mozarab writings are generally dismissed as an influence on the Arabs in Spain because they were diffuse in thought and labored in style in comparison with the subtle delicacy of mediaeval scholasticism of three or four centuries later. But this inferiority of the Mozarab theological treatises in analytical acumen and lucidity of style, and the apparent isolation of Mozarab source material from Spanish Arabic source material, would not preclude Mozarab culture from having been a factor in the development of Spanish Mohammedan culture. The Christian Latin texts attest to lively theological debate, to schools, and to monastic asceticism. Their monastic asceticism was remarkable for its intensity and the extent of its cultivation. It is idle to claim that Christian doctrine and the Christian way of life had no effect on Mohammedan society when Christians were martyred for preaching their faith and had their monasteries in the hills outside Córdoba torn down. In the *Memoriale sanctorum* there are many examples of the influence exerted by the martyrs and the monasteries upon Mohammedans and upon Christians living as Mohammedans. Most of these examples arise out of mixed marriages, which, after the first group of voluntary martyrs had died for their faith, probably produced most of the martyrs of Córdoba. Inspired by the first martyrs, some Moslems adopted the religion of their Christian spouses, and Christians who had kept their religion secret because one of their parents was a Mohammedan openly declared themselves to be followers of the Christian faith.

The judgment of Asín, which would deem Mozarab culture unimportant and relegate it to obscurity, seems too harsh. The importance of so many Christian Latin works in a period from which there are no Arabic works cannot be overlooked. The works are not brilliant, but they represent a culture which had a good deal of life and which continued relationships with northern Spain, France, Germany, and even Byzantium and Palestine as late as the tenth century. It is difficult to tell whether Mozarab culture gave way more before Arabic Moslem culture or more before the new Latin culture of the Reconquest. It seems to have fared better under the Arabs, however, than did Arabic culture after the Reconquest. García-Villada says that the Arabic culture of Spain disappeared because it did not respond to the desires of the people nor was it important enough to impose itself successfully. Spanish Christians in the north and in the south dissociated themselves from it, he says, and continued the traditional culture of their Visigothic ancestors—Catholic, apostolic, and Roman.[8] Such a judgment would not seem to be so true of Mozarab culture.

[8] García-Villada, *Historia eclesiástica,* III, 28.

CONCLUSION

Many historians have devoted attention to the study of Mozarabic Spain in the ninth century. Almost all authors are critical of the cultural level of the Christians, and a number are even hostile to the Christian martyrs and authors. The pattern of this history outside Spain and to a large extent in Spain has been established by Dozy and his followers. Less accepted have been the more favorable writings of Morales, Flórez, Gams, Simonet, and García-Villada. Actually all the authors have had to seek their information in the rather abundant Christian Latin source material, because the Arabic sources, all of a later date, have little to offer on the period apart from chronicles of battles and collections of anecdotes. They confirm data which the Latin sources give about Moslem rule, but for the most part they ignore the Christian population.

Careful study of the works of the Mozarabs shows that, contrary to the general opinion, their culture formed part of a tradition and was of some significance. Their tradition was extensive and their intellectual life was vigorous, and both were closely associated with the Church. The organization of the Church persisted in Moslem Spain and functioned efficiently in a normal manner.

The Mozarabs continued in the cultural tradition of the Visigoths. Their literature includes numerous works of a wide variety dating from 754 to 864 or later. The earliest work following the invasion of Spain by the Arabs is a rather careful chronicle of Spain beginning with Visigothic rule and extending to the year 754, which contains data about the status of the Christians and the Church during the first years of Arab rule.

In conjunction with the loss of her privileged position after the Arab conquest the Church suffered from an abundance of heresy, which churchmen combatted rather vigorously. Elipandus of Toledo attacked Migetius for heresy and obtained a condemnation of the error in a council held in Betica. Pope Adrian I expressed concern about Egila, a bishop from Gaul sent to Spain for mission work, lest he go astray into errors he encountered in Spain. Adrian's letters indicate that the hierarchy of Spain was well-organized and still functioned as a national group. One of the errors of concern to Adrian was Adoptionism, which, though a heresy, evidenced a vital interest in theology. The fight against Adoptionism began inside Spain as early as 785, when Eterius and Beatus attacked it in a lengthy and cogent treatise against Elipandus. Through a long passage quoted by Albar a treatise against Elipandus by a Basiliscus, probably from the Asturias, also is known. Aided from the outside, Spain freed itself of the heresy. Documents of the Adoptionist controversy attest to the eloquence of Spanish letters and the skill of their dialectic as well as to a measure of strong invective. Elipandus showed an extraordinary jealousy for the authority of the see of Toledo in the face of what he probably regarded as an insurgent primacy in the Asturias and intervention by the Frankish church. Communications existed between Elipandus and a group in Córdoba, apparently in consultation about doctrine. A treatise by Teudula, metropolitan of Seville, also known through Albar, testifies to resistance against Adoptionism in Betica.

The rather mysterious Commentary on the Apocalypse compiled by Beatus of Liébana in the late eighth century came to be one of the most highly prized works of the Middle Ages. One may consider the chronicles of Oviedo written in the late ninth century as a part of Mozarab culture, particularly since one of the chronicles states that the founder of the kingdom of Oviedo sought to establish there the whole order of the Visigoths in church and state, as it had been in Toledo.

In 826 Louis the Pious suggested to the people of Mérida that, because of unjust taxation, they break their allegiance to the king of Córdoba and ally with him and enjoy the right to live under their own law. The Acts of the Council of Córdoba in 839, which recount the condemnation of an heretical group by eight bishops, give evidence of the authority and independence normal in such an ecclesiastical act. They also give information about how the Church was organized in Moslem Spain and how the hierarchy functioned which may be added to information from Samson's *Apologeticus* and lists of bishops from the Chronicle of Albelda and elsewhere. A closer glimpse into the church of Córdoba during the persecution is afforded by an undated treatise of Leovigildus, who shows a meticulous concern for propriety in matters of custom and dress among the clergy.

Besides a large body of verse on nature and religious themes, apparently intended to constitute a basis for the cultivation of Latin poetry in Córdoba, Paul Albar, the dean of Latin letters in Córdoba, contributed a remarkable variety of literature to the intellectual life of the period. Against the apostate Bodo, Albar argued that Christ is the Messias, using standard mediaeval dialectics, i.e., quoting and interpreting Scripture and the Fathers to prove his point. Albar relied upon Jerome, Isidore of Seville, Julian of Toledo, and Josephus for his argumentation. In these letters Albar illustrates a weakness for harsh invective in the tradition of Elipandus of Toledo. This correspondence is an example of disputation between Christians and Jews in Córdoba before the persecution, a phenomenon which Samson notes took place after the persecution also. In correspondence with John of Seville, Albar argued, somewhat surprisingly it would seem in the light of his poetic and lay interests, against the study of secular letters in Christian education, advocating instead the study of Scripture and the Fathers. In the same correspondence he discussed Christological problems (the one divine person and the two natures in Christ), the origin of the soul, and the existence of evil. John replied on all points except the existence of evil. John also transmitted to Albar an important biography of the prophet Mohammed for the collection of the Christian apologists in Córdoba. The Christological matter arose again in correspondence between Albar and Esperaindeo, with reference to Christian unorthodoxy apparently arising from

Moslem attacks on the divinity of Christ. Albar's correspondence with Bishop Saul and Romanus Medicus describes personal matters of a religious and legal nature. The letters offer information about penitential practices, legal proceedings, and the juridicial organization among the Christians of Córdoba. They show too that Latin was used for informal business matters among the Mozarabs as well as in formal treatises. If one could determine the uncertain meaning of several statements in a letter from one anonymous bishop to another, possibly referring to a council held in Córdoba in 852 or after, a more accurate idea could be had about certain irregular matters which seem to have occurred in Córdoba.

Although Albar's *Indiculus* is neither the first nor the most important treatise to defend the martyrs of Córdoba, it is the most concise and contains a unique study of the prophet Mohammed as a type of Antichrist. The Church and the martyrs did not have to rely on the clergy for their defense in the persecution but had a zealous layman, apparently trained in law, to argue on their behalf. At the end of the *Indiculus* Albar makes a well-known criticism of the lack of interest in the Latin culture of the Church shown by the Christian laity, who were more interested in Arabic letters. Albar's *Confessio,* a devotional manual of contrition, indicates the wide scope of his interest and talent and may be of basic importance for the study of spiritual life in Córdoba.

The works of Eulogius are voluminous and monumental. Eulogius himself was an extraordinary man, devoted to sanctity and learning. His journey to Pamplona in 848 or 850 must have been an event of much importance in the Mozarab world of learning. In conscientious fulfillment of his priestly duty he ministered to the Christians in prison, composing the *Documentum martyriale* to instill constancy of faith and fortitude against the trials of their passion in the virgin martyrs Flora and Maria and martyrs who were to follow them. With the same zeal he championed the martyrs throughout the persecution, recording their victories in the *Memoriale sanctorum* and the *Apologeticus martyrum*. Finally, in caring for a young convert to Christianity in the exercise of his priestly duties, he came to lose his own life as a martyr. Eulogius is deserving of respect for his humility and scrupulosity of conscience, which prevented him from offering himself as a martyr, and should not be maligned as one who had not the courage to practice what he preached. Like Albar, Eulogius takes care to show that the Moslems provoked the martyrs to come forth, but his approach in the *Memoriale* and the *Apologeticus martyrum* has a more spiritual basis. He seeks to prove that the martyrs were doing the will of God with pure motives and that the lack of miraculous phenomena did not argue against the genuineness of their sacrifice. Eulogius' thesis, which comprises a comprehensive study of the subject of voluntary martyrdom, is theologically sound. His contribution to the field of hagiography is, of course, extraordinary. His writings show a profound perspective of history and understanding of life. He was wise and prudent, distinguished by piety and humility, and not at all the fanatic some would make him out to be.

Besides an apologetic treatise on martyrdom Eulogius offers a description of the state of the Church during the persecutions of Abd al-Rahman II and Mohammed I. Many details about the daily life of the Christians, the society in which they lived, and their position under the Moslem authorities can be gleaned from his works. He makes it clear that, far from contemning the martyrs, the majority of the Christians took great pains to retrieve their relics and bury them with reverence in various basilicas and monasteries. In this particular Eulogius' testimony is supported by that of Samson and by Aimoin's account of the trip of Usuard and Odilard to Córdoba. The eagerness of the Moslems to destroy the relics offers rather conclusive proof that they were disturbed at the Christians' veneration of them as saints. Many of the martyrs, it must be noted, died not for voluntary confessions of the Christian faith but for abjuring

Islam. Many came to Córdoba from other cities of the realm and some even from the East.

Aimoin's account of the journey of two monks from Paris to Córdoba in 858 introduces testimony about the martyrs of Córdoba by witnesses not participants in the persecution, nor even Mozarabs. According to the two Frankish monks, Bishop Saul, Eulogius, Samson, and Leovigildus were venerable men, and the martyrs were venerated as saints by the Christian population. Aimoin says nothing about criticism of the martyrs in Córdoba. His narrative contains a picture of Christian rule in Barcelona and a glimpse of Christians in Zaragoza. Personal contact such as the monks had with Muza ibn Muza is rarely described in historical accounts of that famous Banus Kasi ruler. The description of hazardous travel conditions between Córdoba and Toledo and between Zaragoza and Barcelona are of interest.

After the death of Eulogius, Albar composed the vita and the passio of the saint. Following the same model which Eulogius had used in the vitae of martyrs in his own works, Albar describes first the exemplary virtues of Eulogius' life and then the holy and brave course of his death.

Except for a few epitaphs and accounts of later martyrs, the literature of the Christians of Córdoba comes to an end in 864 with the *Apologeticus* of Samson, a major theological study which comes to grips with the problems of anthropomorphism and pantheism. Samson provides a lively picture of the life of the Christians in the period following the martyrdoms and testifies to the continuing resistance of the Church against corruption fostered by Moslems and venal Christians. According to the *Apologeticus*, which describes the organization of the Church in Betica better than any other source, the Christians had a goodly number of sees south of the Guadalquivir. Although subject to some coercion, the bishops could act with independence of the pressure exerted on them by Bishop Hostegesis of Malaga, who was supported by the emir. Samson, in confirming the picture of Christian society given by Eulogius and Albar, shows as much skill in the use of invective as Albar and Elipandus.

His sketches of his enemies furnish an abundance of information about the Christians, not only in Córdoba, but in Malaga and, to a certain extent, in Granada and Martos. Samson's remark that he had professed his belief publicly in disputation with Moslems and Jews would seem to indicate that the martyrs won their point on the issue of expressing their faith in public. Like other Mozarab authors, Samson was familiar with many earlier writers.

In the next century the embassy of John of Gorze from Otto I to the caliph of Córdoba occasioned a description of the Christians of the Moslem capital. A Christian layman, Recemundus, was in charge of the royal chancery and bishops performed diplomatic missions for the Moslem ruler. The caliph in turn had the power to secure a vacant see for Recemundus, probably one of the best educated men in the realm. Although Christians collaborated with Moslems in secular matters, relations between the two peoples in matters of religion seem to have been sensitive. The circumspection of Abd al-Rahman III in dealing with John of Gorze, approaching him first through a Jewish agent and then through a bishop, indicates that he was desirous not to execute him. John, although kept in isolation from the population of Córdoba except for visits to church, seems to have understood the delicate position of the caliph, and so was not moved by Abd al-Rahman's threats to slay Christians unless John compromised his mission. Recemundus performed another embassy for Abd al-Rahman to Byzantium and Jerusalem. After this mission he compiled a calendar of Christian saints and dedicated it to Abd al-Rahman's successor, al-Hakam II. It was about this time that the caliphs of Córdoba began to enter into alliances and marriages with the rulers of Navarre.

Although the Mozarabs were successful in living with the Moslems and learning their culture, their own culture, particularly in the ninth century, was centered upon and unified by the Church, which was not only the custodian and purveyor of learning and tradition from the past but also the educator and trainer for immediate tasks confronting the Christians. The Church provided the school, the curriculum, and the master for learning, including apparently the study of law. Intellectual life went on within the sphere of her influence. The monasteries where the Christians pursued spiritual perfection were a part of the ecclesiastical organization of the Mozarab church.

Eighteen sees and more than twenty-two bishops in Moslem Spain are known from the Cordoban sources of the ninth century. Most of the information about the organization of the Church comes from Samson's *Apologeticus* and the Acts of the Council of 839. Many bishops of Toledo, Seville, and Granada are named in ms Escorial d-I-1. Toledo, Seville, and Mérida continued as metropolitan sees. In connection with the councils of 862 and 864 Samson mentions eleven sees (Seville, Mérida, Córdoba, Malaga, Ecija, Cabra, Baeza, Baza, Almeira, Elche, and Medina Sidonia) — and two sees besides (Granada and Martos). The Acts of the Council of 839 list Toledo, Seville, and Mérida, plus five suffragan sees of Seville, one (Guadix) not mentioned by Samson. Eulogius praises the bishops of Zaragoza, Sigüenza, Alcalá, and Toledo, and Aimoin speaks of the same bishop of Zaragoza with favor. Eleven of the eighteen sees were south of the river Guadalquivir, and Córdoba is on the north bank of the river. Samson names eight bishops who rescinded the condemnation of him which Bishop Hostegesis of Malaga had obtained from them, but other bishops may have attended the council of 862 who did not rescind their judgment of Samson. Too little is known about the provinces of Toledo and Mérida in these days to permit a discussion of their suffragan sees. All the councils held in Moslem Spain met, so far as is known, in Córdoba, the capital.

In the councils of 839 and 862 the bishops appear to have acted with independence and authority, intercommunicating freely. The coercion exerted by Hostegesis in 862 came to naught, and his "council" of three bishops in 864 seems to have been without result. According to the letter of the anonymous bishop, every bishop he knew would have put up with infringements of ecclesiastical law rather than let his flock suffer harm. Bishop Saul was a pious and conscientious pastor, and the faults Albar charges him with, if true, were not grievous. Only three of the twenty-two bishops are depicted as being of reprehensible character, Hostegesis of Malaga, Samuel of Granada, and Reccafred of Seville. Although failings and irregularities occurred, they seem to have been neither accepted nor condoned by the Christian community. As a rule, the bishops were able men, solicitous for the salvation of their flocks. There is no reason to criticize them as incompetent, given to simony, or lacking the confidence of their flocks.

The usual way for a bishop to attain a see was by election or appointment, with consecration at the hands of or with the approval of the metropolitan. Although the Moslems exacted payments from some bishops on their elevation, they do not seem to have claimed a right to do so. Neither do they seem to have sought to dictate to the bishops or to countermand their authority. Whatever control they had over the bishops seems to have been achieved by taxation or by means of a Reccafred or a Hostegesis.

All of the councils after that of 839 seem to have had irregularities associated with them. Eulogius says that the council of 852 dissimulated its decision. Albar criticizes vehemently a council that may have been that of 852. The anonymous bishop defends a council against criticism from another metropolitan. Bishop Saul says that the differences between him and his adversaries will have to be settled by a legitimate council. The condemnation of Samson in 862 was rescinded by eight bishops, and the "council" of 864 was a travesty. Laymen attended the council denounced by Albar and the council of 864, and the *exceptor* denounced Eulogius in the council of 852.

The cathedral church of Córdoba seems to have been the Basilica of St. Acisclus. There were at least four other basilicas in Córdoba and a number in towns nearby. In addition, there were other churches in Córdoba, apparently built after the invasion of 711, since King Mohammed ordered them torn down. There were at least eight monasteries in the neighborhood of Córdoba, a few some distance away. Those in charge of basilicas and monasteries appear to have held the title of Abbot. There were besides, subdeacons, deacons, and archdeacons, priests, and archpriests. The title of confessor seems to have been restricted in use, but its specific meaning is not clear. There were monks and nuns in monasteries and evidently nuns too who lived in their homes. It appears that Eulogius also lived at home. Priests and abbots could move from a basilica to a monastery and vice versa, or from a basilica to one of the churches in and around Córdoba, but they do not seem to have moved back and forth between basilicas. Samson was abbot of a monastery in 858 and abbot of a basilica in 862. Clerics mentioned by Eulogius in the *Memoriale* remained in the same basilicas in which they received their training, unless sent to a monastery or a church to minister to the needs of the Christians there. Eulogius himself, though he sought learning in a number of basilica schools, remained a priest of the Basilica of St. Zoilus. The martyrs were buried, if possible, in the basilica or monastery to which they had belonged. There may have been an affiliation between certain basilicas and certain monasteries. Among the laity some appear to have been regarded as elders, or "pillars of the church." Records were kept of the names of the parishioners.

Every basilica seems to have had its own school, headed by a master. Attendance at the schools was not restricted to clerics or to those of the basilica parish. Other laymen than Albar attended basilica schools, and students came to study in them from outside Córdoba. It seems unlikely that women attended the basilica schools, but some of them learned to read Latin and devoted themselves to the study of religious works. They may have studied at home with tutors, or they may have learned from nuns who were not living in monasteries, such as Anulo, the sister of Eulogius, or Litiosa, the relative of Leocritia. Although Holy Scripture and other religious works were studied in the monasteries, there seem to have been no formal schools there. The situation described above, perhaps less developed, evidently prevailed in other cities, to judge from Albar's correspondence with John of Seville, Samson's experience in Martos, and the independence and self-reliance shown by bishops of other sees.

Holy Scripture was the basic text studied in the schools, and all studies appear to have been centered around theology. Law may have been learned by apprenticeship rather than in the basilica schools, but the education of Albar, who seems to have been a lawyer, was practically the same as that of the priest Eulogius. Characteristic of Christian learning in Córdoba is the collection of texts. The trip of Eulogius to the north of Spain, where he found many texts to bring back to Córdoba, presumably was an event of much importance for the Christians of Córdoba. Several Cordoban authors indicate that they were engaged in a systematic collection of a body of theological knowledge, particularly about Christology. To a lesser extent they collected data about the prophet Mohammed to refute. The results of their activity appear in the large body of apologetical literature they wrote. If the Christians of Córdoba did not have a common library, or use various libraries in common, they were generous in exchanging texts.

Evidence seems to indicate that among the Christians of Córdoba there existed a group of scholars, official or unofficial, dedicated to compiling apologetical and polemical material for use against the teachings of the Moslems. Eulogius and Albar refer to themselves as belonging to the *peritissimi,* and Eulogius says that the *peritissimi* agree that they have not in vain collected texts against the Moslems. The whole collection activity of the Christians may have been intended primarily for the use of the *peritissimi.* The biographies of the prophet Mohammed recorded by John of Seville and Eulogius, other excerpts about Mohammed given by Eulogius, the lost work of Esperaindeo against the teachings of Mohammed, the information about the Moslem prophet provided by Albar in the second part of the *Indiculus*, Albar's correspondence with John of Seville, Esperaindeo, and Bodo, Samson's *Apologeticus*—all point to the collection of data about the prophet and his teachings which could be used in debate with the Mohammedans. The treatise of Leovigildus illustrates further the zeal of the Mozarabs in compiling a body of knowledge about their religion, to counter Moslem abuse of the clergy for their distinctive garb. There is ample evidence that disputation was carried on. The major works of Albar, Eulogius, and Samson show skill in debate. Albar's correspondence with John of Seville, besides being a collection of various texts on certain subjects, is an exercise in disputation. Albar conducted a serious disputation with Bodo, and Samson says that he disputed in public with Moslems and Jews.

So much evidence of the collection of texts and a body of knowledge and so much literature devoted to Christological discussion and debate show that the Mozarabs recognized a perilous threat to their faith and were anxious to combat it.

By far the most frequently quoted work in the Christian literature of Córdoba is Holy Scripture, St. Paul in particular. Quotation from other authors, mostly Patristic, occurs for the most part in certain letters of the Albar correspondence and in the *Apologeticus* of Samson. Most of Albar's quotations from sources other than Scripture are found in his letters to John of Seville and Bodo. As a result of the careful work done by Madoz, more is known about the sources of the Albar correspondence than about other Mozarab writings. In an index to this correspondence Madoz lists forty-nine authors representing a hundred works, not counting five councils and twenty-one letters of Jerome, mostly found in the letters written by Albar. Madoz has traced many brief phrases which Albar uses as his own to earlier writers and has pointed out that Albar and John knew many authors second-hand, especially from Jerome and the *Collectio Hispana* of councils.

Apart from Holy Scripture Albar's major source is Jerome. He also quotes from Augustine, Gregory the Great, Eusebius, Cyril of Alexandria (evidently through Dionysius Exiguus), Fulgentius of Ruspe, Rufinus, Apollinaris of Laodicea (as Athanasius), Ambrose, Josephus, Eucherius, Junilius, Claudianus Mamertus, Arnobius the Younger, Hilary of Poitiers, and Vigilius of Tapsus (as Augustine). There is no reason to think that Albar knew Greek writers otherwise than in translation. He knew Origen probably through Rufinus, Aquila and Theodotion probably through Jerome, and he attributes to Jerome a work on ecclesiastical dogma which today is attributed to Gennadius. Among Spanish authors Albar knew Isidore, Julian of Toledo, a pseudo-Ildefonsus, Beatus and Eterius, and, of special importance, three authors not otherwise known, Vincent, Teudula, and Basiliscus. It is important that he seems to have known the *Peregrinatio* of Egeria. Traces of Virgil, Ovid, Martial, the *Disticha Catonis*, Arator, Dracontius, and Sedulius appear in his works. John of Seville introduces a few authors not met in Albar's works: St. Braulio, two pseudo-Augustines, one of whom was quoting the *Corpus Hermeticum*, a pseudo-Ambrose, and a few authors found in *florilegia* or the acts of councils. The biography of the prophet Mohammed is John's most important quotation. Bodo's only quotation, from Virgil, is interesting because it was used later by Samson. Esperaindeo quotes pseudo-Vigilius, the second council of Seville, an unknown poet, and a *quaestio* of unknown origin. The letter of the anonymous bishop quotes an unknown work of Julian of Toledo, Augustine, letters of Popes Anastasius II, Celestine I, and Innocent I, the last found in the *Collectio Hispana*.

In the first part of the *Indiculus luminosus* Albar quotes only Scripture, Gregory the Great, Jerome, Isidore, and Arnobius the Younger. Most of his quotations in this work occur in his discussion of the prophet Mohammed as a type of Antichrist, the second part, which he models after Jerome and Gregory. In this part of the work he also quotes Aquila and Theodotion (through Jerome it seems), and Hilary of Poitiers.

Eulogius rarely quotes anyone but Holy Scripture. He quotes Jerome and Gregory the Great a few times, and brings in Augustine, Sedulius, Cato, Arnobius the Younger, Eusebius of Caesarea, and the vitae of a number of saints. Two lines of poetry from Juvencus and Sedulius are quoted by him. From his trip to the north he brought back works by Augustine, Virgil, Juvenal, Horace, Porphyrius, Aldhelm, and Avienus. Leovigildus in his work on clerical dress makes but one non-Scriptural quotation, from Gregory the Great.

Almost all the quotations of Samson occur in Book II of the *Apologeticus*. Strange to say, Samson almost ignores Jerome, the favorite of Albar, quoting him but twice. Most of his quotations are from Gregory the Great, with a large number from Augustine. He quotes extensively from Isidore, Claudianus Mamertus (whom he refers to as "our"), Julian of Toledo, and Fulgentius. In addition Samson brings in Ildefonsus, Eucherius, Cassian, Hilary, Cyprian, Ephraem of Syria (in Latin), Virgil, Juvencus, Sedulius, and refers to the Council of Ephesus. In a list of the Fathers he enumerates Augustine, Fulgentius, Gregory, Isidore, and Eucherius, but not Jerome. He mentions Jerome, Augustine, and Cyprian along with Cicero as stylists.

An assortment of data is known about the more mechanical aspects of Christian Latin letters in these days. Eulogius says that the Moslems broke into his house when he had the *Memoriale* written on "sheets and scraps." Albar and Saul indicate in letters that a type of shorthand was in use. There are several references to "transcription," as if into a more permanent record. Acts of councils were propagated and notices of anathema were posted in public places. The works of Eulogius, Albar, and Samson were intended for publication and distribution of some kind. Albar indicates that many Christian youths devoted much time to Arabic letters, an activity which would require a fair number of manuscripts. One of the poems attests to at least one beautiful manuscript (a Bible) produced in Córdoba.

The culture of the Christians of Córdoba was based on and

expressed in Latin letters. It appears that the chaotic grammar and orthography encountered in many of the texts may derive in part from later scribes as well as from the authors. Although Samson criticizes Hostegesis for errors of grammar and orthography which characterize much of the Latin writing of the time, his own text contains the same errors. Samson seems to indicate that, besides grammar and orthography, the Christians studied rhetoric, dialectics, philosophy, and "common letters," not to mention theology. Although Albar speaks of philosophers with scorn, Samson mentions them as one of the groups that could not fail to laugh at the words of Hostegesis. Eulogius also speaks of them favorably and includes philosophers (Arabic presumably) among the advisers of the king. Rhetoric is perhaps the most characteristic feature of the Latin writings. With great diligence the Mozarabs sought out the most complicated way of expressing their ideas. Their dialectic is sound and skillful. Abusive invective may have been studied as a rhetorical or dialectical device. As a rule, the authors appear to have first given careful thought to their compositions and then to have constructed a comprehensive and cogent outline. They filled the outline with as many data as they could, and finally perfected their work by seeing how cleverly they could express themselves. Almost all authors show a fondness for parallelism, especially showing contrast. Albar is most proficient in this technique, carrying it out at times to three or four echelons.

The apparent neglect of secular Latin letters by the Christians is offset by their solid accomplishments in ecclesiastical literature. The competition from Arabic letters should also be taken into account. Asín's explication that Malekite intolerance did not permit the Moslems to pursue secular or philosophical studies can be reconciled with Albar's claim that Christian youths were neglecting Latin literature for Arabic rhetoric and the study of Arabic philosophers, although it need not be. In any event, the language which offered preferment in the government of Córdoba was Arabic. Among the Christians therefore the study of Latin lacked a stimulus it enjoyed in the rest of Europe, the advantage it offered for a political career. Being restricted to use in the Church and in the Christian judicial system, and being identified with a subject people, Latin letters among the Mozarabs labored under a serious handicap. Burdened with discriminating taxation and occupied continually with threats against their faith, the Christians could ill afford to subsidize and cultivate a secular literature in Latin.

Knowledge of Arabic was not restricted to the Christian laity. A number of clerics were proficient in the language. Eulogius, Albar, and Samson transliterate Arabic words or phrases, the king called upon Samson for bilingual services, a number of martyrs were fluent in Arabic, and some martyrs had held posts in the government. Bilingual skill seems to have been cultivated by the Christians, the Moslems showing no interest in Latin. In addition to requiring servants with a knowledge of Latin for his relations with the Christian church and law and the Christian population, the Moslem ruler had need of men to compose diplomatic correspondence and to perform embassies to rulers of Latin Europe. The clergy as well as the laity performed these bilingual tasks.

It is unfortunate that more is not known about Christian asceticism and monasticism around Córdoba. Aside from the martyrs their tradition seems to have disappeared. The spiritual fervor nurtured in the monasteries appears to be one of the most important characteristics of Mozarab culture. Eulogius describes the monasteries in a general way and depicts instances of the ascetic way of life, but his picture is incomplete. Al-Makkari does no more than mention the existence of monasteries outside Córdoba in the eleventh century. Characteristic of Mozarab monasticism were the double monasteries, apparently established by families, where the sexes lived in adjoining cloisters. The ascetic discipline practiced after the reception of the sacrament of Penance and the guidance of a *Confessio* may have played important roles in the monastic life of the Mozarabs. Asín denies any influence of Mozarab asceticism and monasticism on Moslem sufism, but it is difficult to ignore the juxtaposition of the two ways of life. It remains to be demonstrated in the sources how much Christian asceticism was conscious of mysticism and how much it knew of the sufis.

The status of Christian women is of particular significance in the history of this period. Some of the most illustrious martyrs were women. The fame of Artemia and Elizabeth as abbesses was widespread. The double monastery of Tabanos appears to have been endowed with money inherited by Elizabeth and Columba. Among the Moslems, it may be noted, the inheritances of widows and orphans were committed to the care of the cadi. When King Mohammed ordered the monastery of Tabanos destroyed, the group of women moved to the premises of a basilica in Córdoba and did not disperse. The spiritual life of women appears to have been practically the same as that of the men, contemplation and the study of Holy Scripture. The fact that some women were educated and knew Latin is of importance. Besides the nuns in the monasteries, there were other nuns in Córdoba who apparently lived pious lives in their homes. The religious zeal of mothers and relatives for the Christian faith appears frequently. The status of Christian wives is considerably different from the polygamy of the Moslems, which the Christians branded as adultery. In society and before the law, Mozarab women continued to hold the respectable positions they held under Visigothic rule.

Mozarabic names are of some interest. They are of Latin, Gothic, Greek, and Hebrew origin, but one cannot conclude to the ancestry of a person from the evidence of his name. Most of the bishops had Visigothic names: Wistremirus, Ariulfus, Leovigildus, Reccafred, Amalsuindus, Nifridius, Wiliesindus, Sisemundus, Reculfus, Saro, Miro, Teudegutus, Ataulfus, and apparently Hostegesis. Saul and Samuel have Hebrew names. Some bishops had Latin names: Quiricus, Beatus, Valentius, Senior, Genesius, and Venerius. The name John should probably be regarded as part of the Latin tradition rather than of the Hebrew. Visigothic or Germanic names were also popular among the Christian population: Albar, Ansefredus, Walabonsus, Athanagildus, Sabinianus, Wistremundus, Sisenandus, Theodemirus, Gumesindus, Fandila, Louis, Witesindus, Argemirus, Rudericus, Hunfridus, Sunifridus, Nunilo, Alodia, Anulo, Niola, Sabigotho, Benildis, Froysinda, and Babila. More Latin names occur: Essperaindeo, Romanus Medicus, Perfectus, Aurelius, Julianus, Felix, Abundius, Amator, Emila, Servandus, Flavius, Petrus, Cercilius, Auvarnus, Servus Dei, Habentius, Paulus, Rogellus, Sanctius Tiberinus, Gratiosus, Flora, Maria, Liliosa, Litiosa, Digna, Columba, Pomposa, and Aurea. Several names are of Greek origin: Eulogius, Anastasius, Isidore, Christopher, Sebastian, Leocritia, George, Stephen, and Jerome. Hebrew names were of lesser popularity: Samson, Isaac, Jeremias, Elias, Joseph, Salomon, and Elizabeth. Most of the Mozarabs are referred to by a single name. When two appellations are used one may be a title (the abbot Samson), or designate the place of one's origin (John of Seville). It is not always clear, however, whether one is dealing with an epithet, a title, or a cognomen (Felix Manichaeus, Julianus Confessor, Paul Albar, Romanus Medicus). Besides being the second appellation of Paul Albar, Albar was the single appellation of the brother of Eulogius. References to Leovigildus, "son of Ansefredus," and Felix, "son of Gratiosus," call to mind the Arabic appellation *ibn*, an epithet common to many languages. Aimoin refers to Leovigildus with the cognomen *Abadsolomes* (*Abd as-Salam*), of Arabic origin.

One of the most important problems of the history of the Cordoban Christians at this time remains to be discussed: Were the Christians slain in the persecution true martyrs? Between them Eulogius and Albar refute almost every argument ever brought against the martyrs, except, of course, recent charges that those involved in the martyr movement were motivated by sociological and psychological forces of which they were not aware. Their basic arguments are that the martyrs were provoked to their professions and spoke on behalf of justice, and they could not take part in scandal to the injury of the Christian faith. Eulogius also argues repeatedly that they were inspired by the Holy Spirit.

More modern critics who are opposed to Christian doctrine or who are committed to a relativistic attitude towards truth will not be moved by the appeal of Eulogius and Albar to justice, but will continue to maintain that the provocation came from the Christians and to doubt the purity and sanity of the martyrs' motives. But they cannot well maintain that the movement was unpopular among the Christians of Córdoba or that the question of the martyrs was finally resolved in a decision unfavorable to the martyrs. The attitude of Moslems and Christians toward the martyrs' relics precludes any doubt of the reverence shown them by the majority of the Christian faithful and by the Christian clergy. Whatever decision was made in ecclesiastical council following the ambiguous and provisional decree of 852 is not known. There is more evidence that the compromise reached in 852 was unpopular with the Christian faithful and clergy, than there is to the contrary. There is also reason to believe that the Moslems were not anxious to resolve the confusion caused by the council of 852.

The fact that in some cases the Moslems offered enticements to Christians to become Moslems and in other cases were willing to overlook apostasy from Islam in return for the repudiation of Christianity shows that they were moved less by meticulous concern for the fulfillment of their own law than by a hostility to the Christian religion. One may question the prudence of the martyrs in acting as they did. Even in their own day many Christians who sympathized with them wished that they would have withdrawn in silence until the Moslems searched them out. Such prudence, however, should be judged in the light of scandal which would have resulted from the silence. Inasmuch as the Moslems baited the first martyr, Perfectus, and taunted the Christians for their silence in the lull after the council of 852, it would seem that they intended to force an issue sooner or later. It would be difficult to present a case that the persecution in Córdoba was not serious enough to justify the acts of the martyrs. The authors of the sources maintain that there was sufficient reason to profess Christianity and denounce Islam openly. The circumstances for some of the martyrdoms are different than they are for others. Each martyr may be judged individually. Whereas some of them could have avoided martyrdom without sin, others had no choice but to act as they did.

St. Thomas says that there are instances where one may undergo martyrdom even if the act is not necessary for one's salvation. These cases are to be understood according to "the preparation of the mind," i.e., that in a particular situation one should react in a particular way. Pope Benedict XIV, in discussing voluntary martyrdom, says that the situation in Córdoba without doubt justified and very probably required that the Christians offer themselves for martyrdom. He notes Eulogius' claim that silence would have exposed the faith to dangers and oppression would have followed if the martyrs had not given testimony of their faith without being called upon to do so by the Mohammedans.[1]

The difficulties of language encountered in many passages of the Latin sources encourage hasty interpretations of the texts and lead to unwarranted conclusions. A more careful investigation of the writings shows that many of the unfavorable ideas about the Mozarabs, expressed by a number of writers before Dozy, cannot be maintained. There is so much evidence, concrete and circumstantial, as to the vitality of Mozarab culture that it is difficult to understand how a contrary idea was ever accepted. The weight of evidence that the martyrs were revered by the Mozarab church and by the Mozarab people is so preponderant that only prejudice it seems will arrive at the opposite conclusion. In the

---

[1] St. Thomas, *Summa theologica*, IIa-IIae, q. cxxiv, 1 and 3; Benedict XIV, *De servorum Dei beatificatione, et beatorum canonizatione*, III, xvi, 10, and xvii, 6. Cf. Paul Allard, "Martyre," *Dictionnaire apologétique de la foi catholique*, III, 331-492, especially 413ff.; R. Hedde, "Martyre," DTC, X, i, 220-254; H. Leclercq, "Martyre," DACL, X, ii, 2359-2512, especially 2381-2384, and *id.*, "Confessor," DACL, III, ii, 2508-2515; J. P. Kirsch, "Martyrer," LTK, VI, 995-998.

light of the evidence presented by Eulogius and Albar it is difficult to take the part of the Moslems against the Christians in the religious persecution. The intellectual and spiritual culture of the Mozarabs was both vigorous and solid. Their society was virtuous and important. And their martyrs were blessed and genuine. Further study of their history and literature should produce a yet more favorable picture of the Mozarabs.

APPENDIX I

1. The text of Leovigildus' *De habitu clericorum* according to ms Heredia-Spínola varies from the text as edited by Serrano in BRAH, 54 (1909), 500-518. Ms reading is given for page—line number of Serrano's text.

500—10, auctoritatem; 14, partibus. 501—13, inlicitam; 22, ornent; 32-33, prudentibus ac idiotis. 502—31, aberent. 503—23, propatendo. 504—2, Id est ob; 8, est ei: obtimam; 11-12, neclexerimus; 23, esse, de se debet incipere et sibi; 30, offerre; 34, viso illum inquid; 36, observasse. 505—17, preposuit; 20, Quam ob rem; 28, fincta. 506—23, subvenerit ei, ne. 507—27, in suo. 508—3, necessitet; 12, stipulabit; 18, iustificemus; 27, in omnibus; 29, manifestum quia; 35-36, predicamtium. 509—5, demtas Jherosolimitarum; 27, a dextris; 30, noscuntur; 32, abiciamus. 510—29, prosam. 511—5, eternam, manifestatus; 13, agebit; 25, totam; 29, conversare fecit; 31, sinistro. 512—5, peccando; 14-15, viduam; 30, eius celatur. 513—2, nossent, equm censerunt; 15, In sinistris; 17, subdiacunorum; 23, percutionis ut utantur, sed psalmogravi; 24, singuillatim; 25, exarcebor; 28, his subdiaconus; 30, tunc levitarum; 31, orarem quam utebatur in. 514—12, eam; 14, festivitatibus; 25, sit et exortari. 515—28, aspectus. 516—2, Hispaniam; 24, aderere cui; 26, dicente; 29-30, autem qui uxorem. 517—1, spiri/talibus; 4, victam; 10, grecisco; 14, minime; 16, Nam; 20, benefacit. His; 25, divisionem; 26, alteram; 35, reppellitur. 518—6, onore, non in; 11, Dei non.

2. Albar's *Confessio* in ES, XI, 62-80, varies from the Albar codex of Córdoba. Ms reads: par. 1: (62) residendo *r*egis; (63) primam dignitate*m*; nemo (*ne* erased) scit; In qu*em* iniquitas; devilium *manus* (not animus); Tu vite via. Par. 2: (64) *ad*que vitiorum; *hac* usque; (65) domin*i*um ejus; no*n* valui; tibique devitam (*soli* written in above); do-

minio conditam; *et* sicut ille; es*u* dimersus; deflend*a* ruin*a* deveni; **(66)** *mici* restitue; mirabili*a* redemisti; iniquitates *me* dimerserunt me *in* inferni; qui *erat* jam diversum; acciperet. *Quoniam* qui a; subjugar*unt* dominio; propri*e* arbitrii subjugab*it*; **(67)** veram *quam* sis; sicut *tu* ipse; **(68)** *o*pponam?; quia ipsu*t* quod; firmissime (credam changed to) *credate* (no *me*) similes; omnes *stos* tibi. Par. 3: f*o*ratum tenet; **(69)** potenter dirip*u*isti; notitia*m* vigeat; unaqu*e*que noxa; clementer imp*e*rtis; *spirituale* fomentum; detru*d*emur *g*ee*n*na; a*b* isto; **(70)** Per qu*a* verba mea pondere *sub* pressa non val*e*t ad te pergere rect*a*; Nam quid est aliu*t*; per *seorum* pede; insonaret infus*a*; me jam m*a*ndatum; ea *e*numerare; levia viden*t*er; quantitate mai*o*rum; oculo*s* mentis; **(71)** jactanti*e* van*e*; *maius* testimonio; miserorum *e*xpolio; ut tu *nosti*; *vee* misero mici; statim van*e*glori*e*; in lud*i*cra; *s*epe proru*ar;* sensu sentir*i*; **(72)** me *egrum* inremediabiliter; quererem qu*em* cust*us* omnium; ips*is* non; **(73)** ipsu*t* ratiocinandi; *ad* te daretur; c*o*nludi*um* hostibus; *ex* seips*um* rationem quam inquir*at*; ag*i*tur nescit. Par. 4: **(74)** obstaculum ipsu*t*; *domi*natione iniquissimi; hoc ipsu*t*; ipsam (no *meam*) iniquitatem; **(75)** adtingere grado*s*; *e*o*s*dem valeam; qui nutante*s*; **(76)** ex aqua*m*; ita *aduc*; se *e*xtimat; **(77)** superbire *conaret* numquam inlicita*m*; assiduitate*m* ejusdem ligatus *an* segnitia; non largire*t*; pia exta*t*; **(78)** judicando condemna*t*; judicando d*e*cernis; **(79)** *quem* iniquitas; tu gresso*s*; respect*a* pietatis; labare (*me* written above) hoc; qua*d*iduanus; ego ment*u*aliter; cauterio *me* mundandum; **(80)** quia no*sti*; vitio me*a* concepta; after "Ecce Domine credi" one-third line blank and marginal note "emendi"; me totum *tivi* comi*si*; saeculorum. *Amen.* Finit.

APPENDIX II

The edition of the Albar correspondence by Madoz varies from the text of the Albar codex of Córdoba. Some variations are not noted below: *sed* is usually *set* in the ms; *cum* is sometimes *quum* in the ms; variations of *n* and *m*, and of *b* and *v*, are not noted unless unusual; *h* appears when unnecessary and is lacking when expected. Variations noted in the critical apparatus of Madoz are not noted here unless the critical apparatus is in error. For a description of the Albar codex cf. Janaro Artiles, "El códice visigótico de Alvaro Cordobés," *Revista de la Biblioteca, Archivo y Museo del Ayuntamiento de Madrid*, IX (1932), 201ff.; Paul Ewald, "Reise nach Spanien im Winter von 1878 auf 1879," NA, VI (1881), 382f.; Sage, *Paul Albar*, 221ff. References below are to paragraph and (page).

Letter I. 1: (89) novit *que* inter, auct*i*ori lumine, (90) in *me* sensus, subti*l*issima. 2: (91) loci consequent*ia*, cum sens*uu*m. 3: ne dice*s*eris. 5: (93) e*x*ul erat, ado*b*tivum. 6: tertio reverente*m*. 7: (94) perdic*t*ionis inmergeris, et Deu*m* similiter, altero*a*doratur. 8: (95) sapientias *ut* naturas, ab alterut*ero*. 10: filium fact*um*. 11: Theo*f*oron. 12: (96) ex semin*i* David, quoniam (not *quam*) et que, Si enim *c*ognovissent. 14: (97) presum*t*orem.

Letter II. 1: (98) dulcedinis *vestre* non accepi ideo et nunc *conatus* sum, o hom*ni*um, radicat*a*m amore, ex*s*cisa geris, tigri*n*umve, (99) nequeat *verbi aliter* respondere, novi spineta contorta? *Ubi est liverale illut ingenium quasi tecum congenitum litterarum?* Exciderunt. 2: (100) rict*u* suo. 3: (101) sola*c*ius si, commune do*m*um Ioannem.

Letter III. Greeting: (102) sug*e*ssio. 1: O magne dom*i*ne (dn*ē*) et sapien*tu*m, *a*fflictio, que*m* non ex. 2: (103) tranquilli *l*itoris, sublimissime dom*i*ne, habebam *ut* suades, antistro*f*am, Tu*m* deinde. 3: (104) *f*ili*p*enses, consequentibus *quum* magna, que retro sunt, *s*toriam Domini. 4: (105) vale amo*s*e, (106) et *virtute* et somnis, ibi qu*e* legimus, (107)

419

ergo *omnibus* potest. 5: sit in perdic*t*ione, (108) semper sofistic*e*, ad*n*otatum est. 6: nostra *quia* dictum, (110) aliquod *ditatis*, (111) secundum *id* quod de eo natus est *id* David *set* secundum, (112) Apollinarist*e*, Domini dic*a*nt et, hi mi*c*i. 7: eius transgre*ss*ione, (113) facies *qua* colonus, Predestinatu*s* enim. 9: (114) tri*tt*ici, Direxi *v*obis.

Letter IV. 1: (115) ne *i*perba*t*onicis. 2: (116) so*ll*ertia indagatione, manent *et* a te, nunc mi*l*ia miliorum, forte expro*br*arem. 3: (117) nostros *per* has, extenuabant ob*l*ecta, nullatenus *ea* omittebant. 4: non semper *imperitus fuit*. *Ecce sinon semper* saltim vel. 5: *per quem* illa omnia. 6: (118) Ai*s* enim, in resurrectione*e*, ei iam *tunc* res, in resurrectione*e*, a doctore ill*o* intellegendum est dictum *est dictum* fuisse, incongruente*s* negotio, me f*ra*t*res* ego, li*t*teralem artem. 7: (119) periti*e* enim, et peri*t*ia non est, in tantum *reicio* et, metaplasmu*s*, consequentibus addid*it*, inquit *interfectos*. Sapienti*a*, (120) seque ignotu*m*, seculari quorum, comprobat*os*. 8: li*t*terarum interdum, con*m*enticia, captive *t*radendum, (121) profertu*m* est, ad fruct*o* sensuum seu sententiarum: *et* sicubi in e*os*dem aliquid, a Goli*a* gladio, professus *es* faciens non ex *vero* Israel*i*tam. 9: (123) ausilia quereret, sunt *hec* et frivola. 10: (125) mali *nec* quod, (126) Ille *enim* Donati, previde*bar* divinis. 11: grammaticam a*ss*eras, editione*m* Symmaci, (127) grammaticam *sid* dicimus. 12: *Quo* vero. 14: (129) d*i*rivare conaris, pro oratoria*s* debes accipere pomp*as*. 15: (130) ob*l*ectum recolimus. 17: nescio quā olimina cupis, benedictione*m* Abrae, aren*a* maris, (131) ad effectos. 18: artis *que* adsecutus. 19: Sanctum (scm) Iheronimum. 20: (132) docet quanta *eloquentia set quanta* evidentia doceat, (133) non *tale est* huius. 21: auctore *homnium* consecrata, per *qua* se rationabiliter, verbis a*p*arent. 22: (134) interna devinc*u*nt, esse eufrasia, *nicil* aliud, dicis *esse* versatos, replica*s* verba, dictum doctore*m* ad, precepta et doctrin*a*, rationem quid*a*m, solet *ei* prepositioni. 23: (135) contra eclesia libris, inquit inep*t*is, divinitus sancit*a* et, explicare *se* non, *A nostri* (ansi) Apostoli. 24: (136) patrum dece*n*dentium, Igitur sententiar, pro unione*m* persone, Christum induamus natu-

ris, quia natur*arum* explicuerit, *divitas* relinquerat. 25:
(137) Dictum *vero* sancti, (138) preclari sententi*a*, non *pro*
persona, pro *per*naturarum, confirmativ*e* respondis. 26:
pacto aus*um* es. 29: (141) Necnon et ill*u*d, tempor*a* secu-
*lar*ia. 30: si eum creatur*a* tantum, (142) nolis proba*r*is.
31: (143) priore epistol*e* dilucide, pro captu viriu*m* mea-
rum. 32: (144) *quia* hec male. 34: (145) adsumentem
*invisi*bilem et, Pro han*c* etiam. 35: (146) utpote *qui* responsum, Prestitit *enim* quod, nec ipsa*m* mors, iun*x*erit.
36: *preglacrimis* potuimus, in trinitate*m* personam, (147)
*quar*nitatem libera. 37: Epheseni con*c*ilii, aucmen*tanto*
confecimus, aliqua minu*a*re, sacrilege ment*i*.

Letter V. 1: (148) ipse comotum, (149) quo pacto *c*ludendi
mihi, crediti o*v*iat parvitas, locis ex*it*at volumtas, de*l*citur
impos, fecunditate*m* eloquentie. 2: (150) karissime adul-
tos, nostrum a*c*cusat, (151) spirital*i* vigore. 4: oculis addi-
t*u*, divinitas ope*r*abatur, (152) ficum inserer*e*, *non contine*ns
pineta, et pul*b*erea, diale*t*ici stricti, causas indaga*r*es sunt,
(153) in terra in*d*idera*n*t, ad *in*licita ausum. 5: modo
mult*um* recesserit, (154) dicta *veris* scripti*s*, ex*s*iccasti,
doctrin*a* sitientes. 6: hec et alia*s*. 7: multos discu*r*sas,
(155) libro*s* quos, de ill*u*d quod, (157) elaborata *id* multis,
P*i*tagoras, (158) nascatur ex anim*e*, ut Turtallianu*s* Apol-
li*a*ris. 8: (159) ex qu*a* caro, ut e*i*s nisi, fieri hōms, ad
pena*s* ventum, prorsus inveni*a*s (or inveni*at*), prius tempor*a*, (160) imo absurdi*d*ate, in *e*legendo, censuit. Sentiat,
cum ita *sit*, (161) anime si, creation*i*s sententia, funda*n*tis-
simam, *Per* quo, idem *sanctus* Agustinus, sanctum presbyter*em*. 9: a *sancto* Iheronimo, Ruspens*e*, (162) qua*t*tuor
opiniones, *pr*espicuo claret, opinion*e* contendit, vigil in*i*enio,
(163) scatu*rr*ientibus, maxime re*t*iceret et meato*s*, perur-
*gue*bat. 10: a Deo (no *primo*) sigillatim, aliqua corpor*e*,
protopla*u*sti, Absurdum enim *et* satis, et *omnis* modis, mun-
datur *qui* immobilem, redemtion*em* illius, (164) alieno *qui*
libera, revelet seren*atim*.

Letter VI. 1: (165) Deo e*g*imus, his *omnibus* presul.
3: (166) a*ff*atus est. 4: (167) super *ea* sunt, Et Esd*r*a,
man*u*m tuarum, tue *ea* que. 6: (169) divers*a* sanxerunt,

a*pp*aruit. 7: regna*b*it in omnibus. 9: (170) reg*a*le culmen, (171) coniu*n*gio, prophet*e* (or prophet*ie*), in infernum era DCC*XL*VII, Era millesima centesima *XL*III anno Arabum CCCCL*XL*VII*I*. 10: dom*i*ni Eulogii.

Letter VII. Title: (172) Speraindeo *Albari* directa. Greeting: Speraindeo *Abbati* Albarus. 1: valid*a* vos. 2: (173) ipsorum nequissi*mum*, veritatis resec*atum*.

Letter VIII. This letter, from the title "Item epistola..." to par. 3 "conscribam. Finit," comes from the Albar codex of Córdoba; from par. 3 "Fides unius..." to the end "atque creavit" it comes from ms 22 of the Cathedral of León, folios 5-8. 1: (174) et mens mea *ex mens mea* extuaret, maris gurgit*us*, (175) *postergum*, intonet clar*ae*. 2: contri*cti*onem, qui*pp*iam, (176) cum Prol*em* eius *orum*que, hoc tractar*i*, qui*pp*iam. 3: (177) quia *ex* hoc, aliud *hoc* expetitis, absque norma*m*, so*ll*ertia. No comparison has been made between the text of Madoz and ms 22 of León.

Letter IX. Greeting: (185) summo dom*i*no meo Romano Albar*o*. 1: Anteriorum *m*eorum serenissime dom*i*ne, a*ff*ectum, digesto*s* et impolito textu confectos, (186) o dom*i*ne. 2: sublimissime dom*i*ne, incunab*u*lis, omnes *advers*antes mihi, a*ff*ectione, (187) fortuit*u* casu. 3: moriturum incur*s*at, acc*a*satoribus. 4: fu*gens*, (188) principem mi*tt*eremus, inpeditus *et* de *quod* fuerat *gestum* non, invasiones *n*olebat, re*nn*ui, pro tant*a que*, et merit*um* multum. 5: (189) serenissime dom*i*ne, ingem*e*sco, quali*tatem* mentis, nostra d*i*sperantes. 6: dom*i*ni Servandi.

Letter X. 1: (191) quove a*c*cerrimo, sublimissime dom*i*ne, sequi*pp*ede, fraternalem au*s*ilium, (192) pre cunct*o*s, per immanitat*e*, iustissima*s* ultionum, quas *per*pere, iusti a*s*sidua, mi dom*i*ne. 2: mi dom*i*ne, severitat*i* iudicii, sanctissime dom*i*ne, obst*i*pui, (193) crudelitatis ed*i*ctu, probatissimas sanctio*r*is, san*c*xit, *pr*espicuaque, (194) privelegia. 3: metropolitan*is* episcopi, A*c* secretis, (195) intra Dei ecclesi*a*, quod nullu*s* de his, divinitatis affec*tum*, (196) usurpatione nomin*e*, hoc egi*o*, facit superbi*a*, Et quia *ut* canonica. 4: (197) denotaremus infami*o*, so*ll*ertia, (198) censure contri-

*b*it, insequuntur *a minus* ordine, *pre*spicitur. 5 : nota*m* redu-
cimus, (199) decret*um* firmissimo man*um*, *quo* metropolitanorum, et caritat*i*, devia nit*et*.

Letter XI. Title: (200) Saulo *a* episcopo. Greeting: meo
Saul*i* episcop*i* Pauli. 1 : miser*ie mee*, mede*ll*am. 2 : (201)
exclusus *mansi remedio et licet reconciliationem aliunde valerem frui* si vellem, sententia*m* formidavi, meamque illi*s*,
operis bon*i*.

Letter XII. Folio 82 begins with the title. Title: (203)
Albaro *directum*. 1 : sed vell*e* ut. 2 : (204) aut im*becill*itas,
(205) occi*s*unt corpus.

Letter XIII. Title: (206) Albari Saul*i a* episcop*i* directa.
2 : (207) non dubitat? (*Pater* not in ms, instead a mono-
gram somewhat similar to a Greek "phi") o quanta. 3 : invectione*m* suam, vestre bea*ti*tudini, (208) suggesser*int*.
Quant*i* a, sine co*ni*bentia. 4 : (209) *postergum*, (210) mi
dom*i*ne.

Letter XIV. 2 : (212) fave *meus*, page*lle*, adspargere fas*c*es,
scientia*m* digerunt *et* Iacob, (213) tenuitatis scientia. 3 :
(214) discordi*a* a, di*ll*uvii, Et *ad* dilluvio, indidere su*mm*am.
4 : (215) mundi *quam* Iacob, (216) ingerere nenia*s*, Iuda
fuisse (*t* erased), Arta*r*xerse, sine altar*i*, Intelligis (erasure)
istos, Post que*m*. 5 : (217) Ioachi*m*, Cui succe*s*it, Antipatris
(one line erased) interfecto, firma*v*itis, (218) Danielo *d*ixit.
6 : (219) trium mens*uum*. 7 : (220) synag*oie*, tam illud
quam, (221) professum propheta*t*um, doctore*s* extat, re*nn*u-
as, vobis co*ni*bentia *profetarum* co*nt*ineat dicta, vel no*b*is vel
vobis, vel *c*amo, post h*a*rum.

Letter XV. None.

Letter XVI. In margin beside title: ista epistola eum
confregit. 1 : (223) synag*oie*, (224) synag*oie*. 2 : (225)
dicas in*l*ectum, facultat*um*, aut *certe* semivivum. 3 : (227)
reperies *qui* abscondita, Ostent*e* mihi, (228) editio Psalmo-
rum. 4 : (231) lingue heb*r*ee, codicum *nos* varietate, urgue-
ris. 5 : quo gre*s*u, expositionem *dime*rans, (232) ceteris re-
probati*s*, munis *aut* dubium, Dies nobie*s*, triginta qu*i*que. 6 :
octingentesima *septuagesima* octava, (233) quadragesimo

sexto (no *anno*). 7: templum *a* Zorobabel, utroque premeret, iuxta *profetam* (prftā), (234) ad ips*o* annorum *pre*venerimus. 9: pauc*i* eligentur, (235) fi*n*gat sponte. 10: ali*g*enigene, scies *quia* poterant, (236) etas pro*f*ectior, non *deneger* ab eo, iam reliquer*i*t, (237) ex*s*cidia, in*im*inet, nativitas vo*b*is. 11: vin*c*xit, (238) cloaca dimers*u*s, infla-tion*em* ventris instripid*u*, Non te put*e*t, Va*l*e tuumque, bre-v*em* responsum, gaudi*o* faciat. The lower half of the folio after the end of the letter is cut out.

Letter XVII. 1: (239) hec verba*m* mea, legem *verissimis.* 2: Fil*ii* hominis, et dic*i*s ad eos.

Letter XVIII. In margin beside title: ista epistola omnes assertiones iniqui dextruxit. 1: (242) Et in tanta*m*, desqui-sitione, freno lingu*a*, *c*amo iustitie. 2: talia proms*isi*se, ut Vi*r*ilius, (243) aliquid reprobatur, *que* sequitur, (244) teruntur ficmenta, (245) faciendi *d*esquirit. 3: labris testi-mon*i*s, (246) et intel*l*ge, non illustra*r*etur, si*c*o mare, (247) damnationem cognit*a.* 4: negar*i* possunt, (248) *que* multa per, impleta *est*, ex israelitica. 5: (249) Intel*l*gis nempe, et brev*i*or imo, Dei cult*u*, (250) preteritum po*s*uit, siccato vellere, et instruc*t*iones, idolatrie consecrat*i.* 7: (251) hu-mane nature. 8: haberi forte (forte*m* perhaps), (252) ab*l*ectionem populi, intel*l*gis quod, contr*i*stabas me, (253) vox addidit, ter sanct*o*s. 9: (254) cognitum reli*n*querunt. 10: (255) tui r*a*ctando, con*i*ciendo, profer ea, fructos ma-los, Ut et *per ferrum et* per indomabilem. 11: (256) mundi-tia, (257) aut *lumen* proprium, su*mm*unt, permane*t* clara, Et *quoniam* ore, pollut*a*mque, blasfemare *est* ausus, (258) meritos, spiritosque, tali contagi*o*ne, sementi furt*u*, terra frut*i*care, quia *a* sator. 12: immundum De*o.* (259) per membr*i*s, cunctis besteis, *que* in Deum, multotie*n*s. 13: (260) Recte *hoc* diceres, nimius incedis, portent*u*osum. 14: obscur*a*t multotie*n*s, (261) vidisses (no *et*) vidisse, etiam ri-tos, delubri*s* defleat, quiddam *v*alba. 16: (263) ad pastorem *et visitatorem* animarum, (264) cur vener*i*as, plures adsu*m*-*m*as. 17: Et *tu* mihi, et manu fort*i* vel, (265) cuius mater-nu*s*, (266) mana*b*it origine, *Quoniam* si perpetue, in ter-ra*e*na. 18: (267) sententia firm*i*s, *Israel* (no *et*) Iuda, profere *s*toriam, usque (no *ad*) consummationem, (268) *que* stulta persua*s*ione, *aligeniginis,* que*que* vox, pia responsione*m*. 19: Sed quantu*s,* (269) in disputatione, te*x*ax nodosus, cate*l*as, (270) evenire pre*dixit quia non suo in tempore sed in dies venturos evangelii testamentum dandum esse* previdit. Audi, *I*saias, adi*p*e pinguium, (271) solem*t*nitates, solem*t*nitates, quasi scintil*l*e, vestra flama, quam aliqu*i*d. 20: Hec ergo *v*enient. 21: (272) *quem* tot, suscipiam ea; *quoniam* gladio, consumm*i*tur restauratur. Conquere*r*is, (273) vestram (no *demonstrat*) perpetuam. 22: post parv*o* sic. 23: (274) mi*tt*e me, nolite intell*i*gere, Intel*l*igis vecordie. 24: (276) animo tracta*s,* pessimo clau*dis.*

Letter XIX. (277) su*pp*restitiosum.

Letter XX. Title: (279) reciproca*c*io. (281) vitandum pronuntia*b*it.

APPENDIX III

LETTER X OF THE ALBAR CORRESPONDENCE AND THE *INDICULUS*

The similarity of words and phrases is supported by a correspondence of ideas in parts of the two works. The similarities do not seem to indicate a single author, because at times the words of one work seem to reply to words in the other. Moreover, one work appears to have been written by a bishop and the other by a layman. Some of the similarities may be accidental or may represent standard expression, but an over-all view of the similarities seems to point to a relationship between the two works. It seems more likely that the passages in the *Indiculus* are modelled after passages in the letter than the other way around. The phrases in the letter, however, may repeat the words of another document, such as a decree, and Albar may be directing his words towards this document rather than towards the bishop's letter.

1. Letter X, 2: Sed quia . . . liberum potuit utcumque . . . respicere lumen. Albar calls his work the *Indiculus luminosus* and in the preface three times refers to the Lord as *lumen*.

2. The bishop's basic charge against his critics is that they are proud, presumptuous, and audacious, in defiance of regular ecclesiastical authority. Albar in the beginning of the *Indiculus* stresses that he is not speaking out of presumption and audacity; that as one of the *peritissimi* he has a responsibility to defend the Church against errors; that his proof for what he says is in Holy Scripture; and that he trusts in the Lord to speak through his mouth.

a) Letter X, 2: non temeritatis ausu; 4: ausu temerario. *Indiculus*, preface: non temeritatis ausum; ut temerarius arguar; 3: non temeritatis ut illi aestimant.

b) Letter X, 2: nec usurpatione instinctu. *Indiculus*, preface: non enim ad haec ex me ipso fidens surrexi sed ex te; ut usurpator condemner.

c) Letter X, 2: insolentie vel levitati adscribitur ... superbie elevare calcaneum. *Indiculus,* preface: non humano tenui confidens arbitrio ... neque iniquo elevatus superbie tipho, aut inflatus invidiae zelo; 1: nec contra communes fidei vincendi livore insurgimus; 2: non superbe sed constanter; 11: Hanc vero superbiam ... (the whole paragraph discusses *superbia*).

3. Letter X, 3: Sed siti sunt nonnulli fervore Domini frigi [di], vane glorie iactantie tumidi, scientia nudi, superbia rigidi, qui dissensionum et simultatum serentes contagia contra caritatis et unanimitatis precepta Dei veneratione mysterii et divina invocatione sacrati, infamare tentant quibusdam levibus opinionibus sacramenta. *Indiculus,* 2: Sed quia siti sunt nonnulli fervore spirituali indigni, amore fidei frigidi, pavore terreno et ictu gladii territi, qui non pressa voce, sed rauca fauce, dissoluto labio, obtorta lingua, martyrium nostro tempore gestum invectione minus idonea detrahunt vel sugillant, et diabolo quantum in eis est palmam victoriae tradere non recusant; vestrum frigidum ... intellectum.

4. Letter X, 2: Quanta vero pro tempore a beatissimis fidei nostre auctoribus, id est apostolis, temperantie lege, et discretionis bono, dispensata extiterint, et acta eorum apertissima luce, prespicuaque referunt claritate: et sanctissimi Iheronimi admirabilis, et cunctis seculis preconabilis viri testantur epistole. *Indiculus,* 16: Sed forsitan aliquis simulationem in causis talibus dispensatorile asserit dignam, et apostolorum auctoritate vel legis hanc frivole intenditur adfirmare. Percurrant breviter ipsas dispensatorias rationes, et aperte inveniet nullus in causis principalibus officiosum mendacium frequentasse.

5. Letter X, 4: cur improvida insequuntur a minus ordine vel aliorum de vita plectantur sententia, omnino non video. *Indiculus,* 19: cur biothenatum praesulem rennuant nescio, dum testes Christi et veritatis ministros damnatione vero asserant et congruo subjacere judicio.

6. Letter X, 2: hereticisque in contentia concordantes, parvisque homunculis inexpertis et insciis complacentes. *Indiculus*, 9: qui eorum erroribus contradicunt hereticos et inscios judicamus; 14: hereticos eos esse publice clamaverunt; 19: Miror tamen aliquos invenire praeparvos, forsan non homines sed vere cum minoratione dicendos homunculos. Cf. also Letter XIII, Albar to Saul, 1 and 2: homunculi.

7. Letter X, 2: ut pene eisdem in aliquid obviare non sit eius cuncta se iudicio et exemplo patrum asserit innodare. *Indiculus*, 4: Esto nunc arbitres justi et non favorabilem ventosam et flavilem sed veram proferte rationis sententiam justitiae vinculis innodatam.

8. Letter X, 2: que vera sunt ... exsequere; tantis se testimoniorum probationis munierunt, tantisque Patrum sententiis; veraciori et probatiori indagatione probata in meliori ductu; cum iuxta canonicas verissimas et universalis seculis probatissimas sanctionis ... probatissimas sanxit decretis; quod veritatis indagine et testimoniorum scientie; 3: (of Isidore) his documentis verificis; 4: canonica institutione formati verissimis constitutionibus adprobare; illas generales sententias verissime competunt. *Indiculus*, 2: Et miror quo ingenii genere poterit veritas nuncupari ubi error adscribitur pro Christo et veritate succumbi; Poterat enim verus Magister si vestrum frigidum algore divino sequeret intellectum dicere: Veritatem supprimite, justitiam occultate, et quae vera sunt, ubi timor vestrum concuserit sensum, corde solummodo retinete, ut vivatis nullo terrente securi.

9. Letter X, 4: Quod si episcoporum superinspectio huiusmodi freno sanctionis constringitur; quo plebium camo ora cludere ratum est, que inlicita et non sibi debita intentare presumens de sacerdotum sibi adrogat excessibus iudicandum? *Indiculus*, 20: ubique absque rationis camo procedens, et habenis laxatis metarum fines magis transiliens quam adimplens.

10. Letter X, 5: Si quis autem ... pravitate cordis et livore mentis ... levia intentare conaverit ... maleloquacium

properatur insania, qui unanimitatis despicientes collegium, per abrupta et devia nitent lapsu casuri precipiti in altum tendere gressum. *Indiculus,* preface: ne qui per devia et abrupta, per inania et caduca, per tumida et stulta, per indecora et elata, per levia et inflata, operibus inserviendo sinistris quotidie ambulo. Cf. too Letter IX, Albar to Romanus Medicus, 3: lapsu precipiti; Letter XI, Albar to Saul, 2: in nullo a veritatis seu possibilitatis regulis deviare, and mentem hactenus per devia oberrantem; *Vita Eulogii,* 5: devio calle, and 20: per prona et abrupta; *Memoriale,* I, 19: per devios calles; *Apologeticus martyrum,* 28: Quomodo declinare in devium.

11. Letter X, 4: Nec ignoro generales ... sententias que ... generalem superborum non consulentium patrie sed scandala et controversias adserentium amputant simultates. Sed his quorum cervices tumor superbie inflat et licentie, studentes quemlibet superbissimum proterve defendere, vel in parte secedentes universitatis derelinquere ausu temerario collegium ... illas generales sententias verissime competunt. *Indiculus,* 1: Nec contra comunes fidei vincendi livore insurgimus, sed e regione Chaldaeorum cornua ventilantes terrestria stillatione veracia conculcamus ... ne ... nos contra Ecclesiam bella clamitet intentasse.... Absit enim ut Catholica et universalis ecclesia contra sua viscera pugnet. Absit iterum ut contra matrem filii arma summant.

APPENDIX IV

Flórez' text of the *Indiculus luminosus* (ES, XI, 219-275) contains a number of variations from the manuscript (the Albar codex of Córdoba). Many of the errata listed below result in no change of the meaning of the text, but they may be of interest in the study of linguistics or Albar's grammar. When Flórez' notations of ms readings are correct, they are not noted here. Many variations have not been noted. They may be summarized as follows: ms usually reads *e* for *ae*; *v* and *b* are interchanged; *b* and *p* are sometimes interchanged; *t* appears frequently for *d* (e.g., *set* for *sed*); *n* appears frequently for *m*; *e* and *i* are frequently interchanged; *h* appears frequently before a vowel when not needed (e.g., *homnium*) and is not used frequently when required (e.g., *ominum*); *c* and *qu* are interchanged; *u* and *o* are interchanged; *f* is used for *ph; volumtas* appears for *voluntas; prespicuus* appears for *perspicuus; mici, nicil, immo,* and *dextruere* are usual spellings.

The title, *Indiculus luminosus* (219), does not appear in the ms. Preface: (219) emanar*i* virtutum, ante conspect*u*, (220) linguas infant*u*m, ut temerarius arguar*, cumule*m* scelera, (221) conter*a*t et prosternat, impios ill*a* qu*a*, Deus regna*t*. eclesie que homnis. Par. 1: *spirituali* vigore, deput*e*tur igni, (222) *still*atione veracia, per qu*a* nos, firma*b*it auctoritas. Par. 2: fervore *spirituali*, hictu gladio, dissolut*a* la*vi*a, gestum invectione, vel sugill*u*nt, Karissimi not Reverendissimi, (223) per tot*o* orb*e*, ob ali*a* caus*a*, (224) ad injust*o* erumpentibus, percussione confodi*u*nt. Par. 3: *lumen* cernentibus, repr*e*ndere, (225) Domini extan*s*, illi *ex*timant, cantico versi, de quo*d* gestum, (226) *storiae* fabulas, pro ver*a* jurament*a*, pe*c*toribus retinentes, inopinat*u* casu, audaci proposit*u*, (227) in ipsu*t* diei, libidin*e*que, per*i*merunt, aelati? for delati. Par. 4: Nonne *pre*spicuum, ob zelo, a cultor*es* Dei, Antichristi discipul*o*s. Par. 5: (228) *i*nmund*e*m ab ips*a*, talium nube*m*,

430

in se sermo, *arta* custodia. Par. 6: per omn*i* regno, per-cus*s*erit, (229) surd*e* aure, persecutione*m* nos, *o*viant per-viantes, cantico inhonest*o*, (230) *vaselice* signum, pro con-vent*um* eclesiae adunand*um*, derisione, contum*i*arum. Par. 7: diximus imple*a*tur, perpetrat*ur*, dignos malediction*i*. Par. 8: (231) Ia*h*el, et dextera, Sancta Sanctorum, pro ae-tern*um* vite stat*um* sine fine futur*um* pugn*a* spiritual*ia*, vel regn*um* terren*um*, precedidend*um*, qui maledicentes, (232) quasi denotans, ipsu*t* predicasse, fuisse*t* delusi. Par. 9: erroribus *eorumque inquinati fulgentes se dicunt esse fetoribus* cum enim, sign*um* crucis, omnia inspiciente, (233) pro vendibilia muner*a*, *pos* tergum, erroribus contradic*it*, pon*e*ntes pe*r*. Par. 10: (234) per quo ministerio, *est* con-tradenda, per omn*i* saeculo, fidei teneren*tur*, Contra qu*ibus*, (235) inrep*r*ensibilis, *qui* circa. Par. 11: *storias* requira-mus, inreligios*i* animi, (236) ha*n*c severitate*m*, a*b* hos au-ctore*s* crudele*s*, quam pius, indisciplinata*m* molledinem, al*i*genarum, (237) Videan*s* nostri, *diurno* sermone, pieta-te*m* horum incongrua*m* set crudelitate*m* ha*n*c sancta*m*. Par. 12: jac*t*ator devilis, (238) conpr*e*nsum. Par. 13: pugne-que *spirituali*, *et* stren*uus*, (239) sequipe*dis*, perfide la-ta*m*, Christian*ismi* ordinis, evigilans ips*o*. Par. 14: *sic* respond*it*, vestr*a* collegio, nemin*i* provocante, (240) pres-viter*es*. Par. 15: quum causa*m*, Et: Os *qui*, abtissi-mu*m* titulu*m*, Et *aut* (for *haud*), fidei veritate*m*, Hec que foris, (241) impet*i*rent, Pen*e*semus, *i*nfidelium corda. Par. 16: Read *dispensatorile*, fribole intendi*tur*, (242) prin-cipale*m* noberant, membri quem, *qui* ex hoc, idola colend*i*. Par. 17: Haec auctoritates, absque detrimenta, aetate*m* nostr*am*, adulescent*ium* arbitrant*ur* *Eleazarus*, presenti tempor*is*, (243) exemplum fortem, simulant*ur* set vere *fru-ere*, factum provabile*m*, qua Deus, simulat*um* fidei Docu-ment*um*. Par. 18: proba*te* nostro, (244) aer*ium* et distur-bationes, *Hen* enim. Par. 19: (245) *et* martirium, subjacer*i*, non *es* mundata. Par. 20: (246) vis*e* inscitie, obitus per qua displicere, artium disciplina*m*, aliquid opinat, invectio *e*ffrenata, (247) sordida turg*it*, fulg*it*, docmate negligent*ur*, dentibus stridente, injung*i*tur, *percipitur* fortia, m*o*etarum *fines.* Par. 21: parvissimo oper*e*, (248) Apocalipsi*n*, aliqu*a* simili, multoti*us* elebatum, a regn*a* cetera, puta*v*it quod poss*e*t, (249) Gr*e*gorum, colla victric*e*, grandia trutina*ns*, aus*o*, storias, ipse unu*s* tempus, mens*uu*m, septuaginta anni*s*. Par. 22: (250) nubem conscend*i*, scientia, un*a* e*a*demque res, figura*m* id ipsut, (251) quae specialiter, perd*i*torum, han*c* sententia*m*, intell*e*get, ha*n*c priorem, un*e* adsignetur, (252) intactu*s* divinus. Par. 23: ex ac *g*erationis, juncta menti (*tus est* has been erased), (253) conjugium qu*em*, qua*m* illi. Par. 24: don*o* jugitur, desider*i*um pingu*i*orem. Par. 25: (254) consurg*i*t, Quod ist*e*, su*p*prestitioso, videar hoc, proprie dic*i*, (255) ipse feri*e*, ipsius dom*ui*, ad ipsu*t* tempus, eis o*s*tenderi*t*, (256) ex*i*git, per *quibus* dirigitur, partem pede. Par. 26: per hoc nom*ine*, (257) scribere *no-vit*, intelligens *prepotionum*. Par. 27: specie*m facie*, (258) princip*iarum* viarum, prior substantia*m*, ex *heticorum*, humec*t*ibus, *exa*crabilis furia, (259) qu*a*m radicitus, signo crucis. Par. 28: preparat*i* magis, *sudibus* nares, (260) *sudibus* forat, potes Leviathan, pro *eum* momentis, interpellant (*si* erased) preces, qua(*s* erased) fabuloso, *per omni* gestu, per cunct*is* moment*is*, famili*ari et* preconavili, (261) perdidit (no *et*) frequenti oration*i*, *quoniam* caduca, fluxa *lavili*, *J*emahascar, a capit*e* perfido, (262) qui *legi mee*, incurrens (no *super*) superbiae, figuretur *in* corpore. Par. 29: injustis compet*entem*, quia *ad* te, animas audi*en*t*um*, (263) pro *eum* eleganti, prevarica*ntum* fit, *pre*spicua, (264) Una un*a* conjungitur, Una alter*e*, viti*e* glutinati, inflatio *pectoris*, per qu*a* se, versutia l*atius*, quasi pal*f*ebras, (265) ignis accens*i*, inania tend*entes*. Par. 30: Per nar*ibus*, eius odorific*us*, fum*ine* nomine, materia*m* abtiori, In *collo* eius, Egestas ver*i*, (266) ma*s*sam, memor*u*mque eius, quia *et* predicantes, mundi car*d*ina, (267) nostro tempor*is*, re-*pre*nsionis, in*l*ectionis decipula, feni moll*ed*inem, non malleu*m* est, reputari, somniar*i*. Par. 31: lutum contem-n*ens*, interfecit *n*os, tempore *a*ccidisse, *P*re*spicua, (268) doctore*m* non, probroso discessu, orator*u*m facundia, in ea, fulg*i*t, non *obiat*, ordinem propria*m*, (269) set *c*um super, (270) *pre*calcantes. Par. 32: intellegentias *fixi*. Par.

33: hec (no *vel*) quasi, (271) Dei Fil*ium*, ab *eos* quos. Par. 34: ju*go* quo, (272) tipum *adventus sui: sic et Antichristus pessimum regem Antiocum qui sanctos persecutus est templumque violavit. Recte tipum* suum, de omne*s* hereti*cos*, Antichristo*s* multi. Par. 35: repriorare, (273) de Apocalyps*in pre*tenui, nostrum *hunc* tempore, reperitur regn*um*, premio emi*mus*, (274) ipsu*t* facinus, caractere*m* crudelissime ferre, convinci*endos*, pro elegantia*m* ... dissertam*, intentus volumina, constri*n*ctaque, *legem* suam, (275) *ut* ipsis, *hinc* expositioni.

A number of quotations used by Albar in the *Indiculus* have been located. They are given below.

Par. 2 (223), *Hoc ... seminarium;* cf. Jerome, *Commentariorum in Evangelium Matthei*, I, x (PL 26, 65B). Par. 2 (224), *Plerumque ... armatus;* cf. Gregory, *Moralia in Job*, XXXI, xxviii (PL 76, 605C). Par. 10 (234f.), *Nec ... corda;* cf. Arnobius Junior, *Commentarii in Psalmos*, xviii (PL 53, 349D). Par. 10 (235), *Muti ... vias;* cf. Jerome, *Commentariorum in Isaias prophetam*, XV, lvi (PL 24, 545C). Par. 11 (237), *Non ... pietas;* cf. Jerome, *Epistola CIX, Ad Riparium presbyterum*, 3 (PL 22, 908) ; Jerome also cites the examples of harshness which Albar treats in detail. Par. 15 (241), *Horiones ... jactantur;* cf. Isidore, *De natura rerum*, xxvi, 9 (PL 83, 999B). Par. 22 (251), *dicente Aquila: Et super ... intelligitur;* cf. Jerome, *Commentariorum in Danielem*, 11:37ff. (PL 25, 571C) ; for Aquila cf. R. Ceillier, *Histoire générale*, II, 142f. Par. 25 (254 and 255), *Et hec ... gratis;* cf. Jerome, *loc. cit.* (PL 25, 572A) ; *Ideo ... dominatum* is not in Jerome; for Theodotion cf. Ceillier, *op. cit.*, 143f. Par. 26 (256), *Nam ... sonat;* cf. Gregory, *Moralia in Job* (PL 76, 644), and Isidore, *Etymologiae*, VIII, xi, 27 (PL 82, 317). Par. 27 (257), *Cartilago ... firmitatem;* cf. Gregory, *op. cit.* (PL 76, 655A and 662A). Par. 27 (258), *Ac si ... extitit* and *Elati ... voluptates;* cf. Gregory, *op. cit.* (PL 76, 664C and 669Df.) : for *Protegunt umbrae ...* (258), cf. (PL 76, 675) ; for *salices infructuosae* and *Multitudinem ... dicavit*

(259), cf. (PL 76, 676A and 677A). Par. 28; for *Per nares* ... *enervat* (259f.), cf. PL 76, 681B; for *Leviathan* ... *hominum* (260), cf. PL 76, 682C and Isidore, *Etymologiae*, VIII, xi, 28 (PL 82, 317); for *qui hamo vere* ... *transfixus est* (260), cf. PL 76, 682C and 683A; for *Nec tantum* ... *tentat* (260), cf. PL 76, 686A; for *Cuius et maxilla* ... (260), cf. PL 76, 686; for *Et bene* ... *pedicam* (261), cf. PL 76, 692A, 692C, and 693A; for *Totiens* ... *denotatur* (261), cf. PL 76, 694B; for *Servato* ... *fortia* and *Intra* ... *subdit* (261), cf. PL 76, 695Df. Par. 29: for *Calliditatem* ... *penetrabit?* (263), cf. PL 76, 702B; for *Subauditur* ... *manifesto*, cf. PL 76, 703A; for *Scuta* ... *fragilia*, cf. PL 76, 705B; for *corpus* ... *transfigi* (264), *obduratae enim sunt et conjunctae*, and *Spondent* ... *nuntiare*, cf. PL 76, 706B, 708B, and 710B. Par. 31 (267), Gregory (PL 76, 736C) also quotes Jn. 16:2. Par. 34 (272), *Sicut igitur* ... *credendus est;* cf. Jerome, *Commentariorum in Danielem*, xi (PL 25, 565-568, especially 566A). Par. 34 (272), *Ego* ... *seducent;* cf. Jerome, *Commentariorum in Evangelium Matthei*, IV, xxiv, 5 (PL 26, 176B). Par. 35 (272), *Antichristos* ... *Antichristus est;* cf. Hilary, *Contra Arianos* (PL 10, 610C).

APPENDIX V

AMBROSIO DE MORALES AND THE EDITION OF EULOGIUS' WORKS

The disappearance of the manuscript of Eulogius' works after the edition of the works in 1574 has made it very difficult to study in detail certain matters which are studied about any text. It is possible that later writers made additions to the text of Eulogius. At the end of Book VIII of the Chronicle Morales lists certain criteria for the acceptance of information about saints—what official writers of the Church have said of martyrs of their time; official condemnations of martyrs by their persecutors; authoritative lives of the saints; liturgical readings; *sanctorales* of old which merit credibility; general agreement and the tradition of a large part of the Church—criteria which may have induced a mediaeval editor to supplement Eulogius' account. Possession of the manuscript would remove the study of such a problem from 1574 to the date of the mansucript.

Moreover, Bishop Ponce de León, the discoverer of the manuscript of Eulogius' works, and Ambrosio de Morales, generally regarded as the editor of the works, in editing the text of Eulogius may have corrected words and phrases which would better not have been corrected. Both Ponce de León and Morales admit that the manuscript was in bad condition and that the Visigothic script was difficult to read. In his scholia to the *Vita Eulogii* and the works of Eulogius, Morales notes a number of corrections of the text made by him. In his treatise on the language of Eulogius he says that he did not change unusual words or the speech of Eulogius, but that he did emend the bad Latin and orthography. The meaning of some passages in parts of the Albar codex and in other Mozarabic texts is so obscure as a result of ellipses and unusually bad Latin that in some cases the text can be deciphered only with the knowledge of a comparable

435

text. Eulogius' works contain a few such passages but fewer than their share it seems. The fact that Morales notes several minor changes made by him and the fact that in the Chronicle he avoids giving a specific meaning to one of the most difficult passages in Eulogius' works, the description of the council of 852 in the *Memoriale* (II, xv, 3) indicate that no major changes were made by him.

A number of scholars in the past and in the present seem to have directed their attention to these matters and, without going so far as to raise questions, have contributed remarks or studies which can be of value. It seems unlikely, however, that anything less than the reappearance of a manuscript of Eulogius' works will definitively settle certain questions about the manuscript and the text.

A critical discussion of Ambrosio de Morales,[1] the editor of Eulogius' works, is of fundamental importance in a study of the manuscript and text of Eulogius' works. Morales was a man of scholarly interests, a professor of rhetoric at the University of Alcalá and a royal chronicler of Philip II. He devoted himself with great industry to the study and the writing of the early history of Spain. Several times Philip II appointed him to make inventories of libraries in search of materials with which to enrich the royal library of San

---

[1] The most recent study of Morales is that by Rafael Ramírez de Arellano, *Ensayo de un catálogo biográfico de escritores de la provincia y diócesis de Córdoba con descripción de sus obras* (2 vols.; Madrid, 1922-1923), I, 349-380. Narciso Alonso Cortés, "Sobre Ocampo y Morales," *Estudios dedicados a Menéndez Pidal*, I (Madrid, 1950), 197-219, discusses royal notices granting the two men the pay of a chronicler and excusing them from attendance at court so that they can do their work. Cf. also Enrique Redel, *Ambrosio de Morales, estudio biográfico* (Córboda, 1909); a pamphlet by Ramon Cobo Sampedro, *Ambrosio de Morales, apuentes biográficos* (Córdoba, 1879); Bartolomé José Gallardo, *Ensayo de una biblioteca española de libros raros y curiosos* (4 vols.; Madrid, 1863-1889), III, 886-888; Nicolas Antonio, *Bibliotheca Hispania nova* (2 vols.; Madrid, 1672), I, 51-53; Henrique Flórez, *Viage de Ambrosio de Morales . . .* (Madrid, 1765), i-xxvi; the biography of Morales by Flórez appears also at the beginning of vol. III of Benito Cano's edition of the Chronicle (8 vols.; Madrid, 1791).

Lorenzo at the Escorial. Through Morales' hands passed much of the extant source material pertaining to early Spanish history. Probably the most important project of his life was the writing of a comprehensive history of Spain in Spanish, the *Corónica general de España*, begun by Florián de Ocampo.[2]

A statement by Morales at the end of the Chronicle that on 21 March 1583 he was seventy years old[3] apparently is a reference to his birthday. The date of his birth could have been either 21 March 1513, or 11 March (the feast of St. Eulogius), due to the Gregorian calendar change which was

[2] Florián de Ocampo, *Los quatro libros primeros de la crónica general de España* (Zamora, 1543); this edition was apparently published without Ocampo's consent; cf. F. Cifuentes, *Noticias historicas* ... (Cano ed. XIV), 121. Ocampo published the Chronicle with a fifth book in 1545 and again in 1553 in Medina del Campo. Morales republished these books and continued the Chronicle, *La corónica general de España que continuava Ambrosio de Morales* ... (3 vols.; Alcalá and Córdoba, 1574-1586). Morales' first volume consists of five books (VI-X) covering the period from 200, B.C., to the kingdom of the Visigoths. His second volume in 1577, also published in Alcalá, consists of two books (XI-XII) bringing the history up to the entry of the Arabs into Spain. The third volume continues the history to the death of Bermudo III in 1037. The Chronicle has been re-edited by Manuel Ortiz de la Vega, *Las glorias nacionales* ... (6 vols.; Madrid and Barcelona, 1852), vols. I and II, and by Benito Cano (8 vols.; Madrid, 1791). Vols. IX and X of Cano's edition (1792) contain Morales' treatises on the Antiquities of Spain and his report on his *viage santo* to the north of Spain (published by Flórez in 1765); vols. XI and XII (1792) contain the continuation of the Chronicle by Prudencio de Sandoval, *Historia de los reyes de Castilla y de León* (Pamplona, 1615); vols. XIII-XV contain F. Cifuentes' edition of *Opusculos castellanos de Ambrosio de Morales...*, *Noticias historicas sacadas del archivo de Uclés...*, and *Ambrosii Morales opuscula historica quorum exemplaria in R. D. Laurentii bibliotheca vulgo del Escorial custodiantur...* (all three vols.; Madrid, 1793).

[3] Cf. Flórez, biography of Morales at the beginning of the *Viage*, par. 3. Morales' statement has not been found in Cano's edition of the Chronicle. In his "Apologia por la legitimad de los privilegios de la santa iglesia de Santiago de Galicia...," dated 5 February 1588, Morales says that he is seventy-four years old; cf. Cifuentes, *Opusculos castellanos*, 432.

introduced in October 1582. Morales' parents were of long established Cordoban families. His father, Dr. Antonio de Morales, belonged to the medical profession and was one of the first catedráticos of philosophy at the University of Alcalá. From the family of his mother, Mencia de Oliva, Morales also derived benefits. Her father, Fernan Pérez de Oliva, held a degree in medicine and wrote a book on geography. Her brother, of the same name as his father, studied in Italy and taught in Paris before he became a catedrático and later Rector of the University of Salamanca. Morales acknowledges a debt to his uncle Fernan Pérez de Oliva for his early education. Pérez de Oliva was appointed by Charles V to tutor Philip II but died before he could assume the duties.[4] In his immediate family Morales' brother, Augustine de Oliva, was a medical doctor, whose son, Gerónimo de Morales, continued in the same profession. Morales' sister, Cecilia, married Luis de Molina, governor of Archidona. From this union was born Luis de Molina, a noted jurist and author, and Antonio de Morales, bishop of Tlaxcala in Mexico, to whom Morales dedicated the last part of the edition of the works of Eulogius in 1574.[5]

---

[4] Ramírez de Arellano, *op.cit.*, I, 477.

[5] Almost all information about Morales' family comes from his own words. His references are brief, except for one to his father in his *Discurso general de las antigüedades de España*, "Los nombres que tuviéron, y agora tienen los lugares" (Cano ed., IX, 29f.), and a number of statements about his uncle Pérez de Oliva in an edition of the latter's work (Cifuentes, *Noticias historicas*, 127-134 and 155-158). Cf. Morales' prologue to Bk. VI of the Chronicle; Chronicle, IX, ix, 2, 4, XIII, vi, 3, and XV, liv, 9. Morales makes several statements about his family in the *Discurso general de las antigüedades*, a long work loosely arranged and difficult to refer to; cf. Cano ed., IX, 7-30, 101, and X, 29, 39, 46; cf. also *Opusculos castellanos*, 432, 466, and *Noticias historicas*, 4, 248. Information about Morales and his father is given by Alvar Gomez de Toledo, *De Francisci Ximenii Cisnerii, Hispaniae cardinalis et archiepiscopi Toletani, vita et rebus gestis. Libri octo* (Alcalá, 1569), Bk. IV (cf. *Hisp. ill.*, I, 1008). Information about Morales' nephew Antonio de Morales, bishop of Tlaxcala, is given by Gil Gonzalez Dávila, *Teatro eclesiástico de la primitiva iglesia de las Indias occidentales, vidas de sus arzobispos, obispos, y cosas memorabiles de sus sedes* (2 vols.; Madrid, 1649-1655), I, 76, 90f., and 115.

Flórez indicates that he is convinced that Morales was the same person who in 1532 entered the monastery of Valparaiso near Córdoba and in 1535 left the monastery after having mutilated himself. Flórez apparently investigated the story in detail, but, although he and most of the biographers of Morales accept the story as true, Nicolas Antonio seems to doubt it. Flórez bases his belief upon a record in the book of registers of the monastery which states that "Ambrosio de St. Paula, or Morales," left the monastery, "was ordained in the world, went to Alcalá de Henares and studied diligently, was chronicler of the Emperor Charles V, our lord, and still lives in Alcalá."[6] Flórez adduces other documents to confirm the identity of Ambrosio de St. Paula with Ambrosio de Morales, but some of these documents appear to have been written as late as 1575, when Morales was a person of note. An account of the mutilation is also found in an anonymous eighteenth-century manuscript of the Biblioteca Provincial of Córdoba called *Casos raros de Córdoba* which is devoted to a series of strange reports.[7] The only source for the story appears to be the report in the book of registers of the monastery of Valparaiso, the account in *Casos raros* being based upon it. There is no evidence in other biographical data about Morales to support the story. Morales most probably was not a chronicler of Charles V, before 1556. It is unlikely that he obtained the title before the death of Florián de Ocampo in the reign of Philip II, probably about 1560. Another reason for doubting the story of the mutilation is the evidence that Morales was a priest. Philip II in appointing Morales procurator in the cause of the canonization of St. Didacus of Alcalá in February 1567 refers to him as a priest of the

[6] Flórez, biography of Morales, par. 11; cf. also Ramírez de Arellano, *op.cit.*, I, 352f. The text of profession in the monastery attributed to Morales has been edited in the *Boletín de la Academia de Córdoba* (1951), no. 65.

[7] *Casos raros ocurridos en la ciudad de Córdoba sacado de un MS que poseia D. Pedro de Salazar y Gongora, obispo que fue de esta ciudad,* dated 1758, Bk. II, par. 21, 123v. A microfilm copy of this unpublished work may be obtained from Servicio Nacional de Microfilm, Madrid.

diocese of Córdoba. Morales himself says that he said several Masses in the prison in Seville where St. Hermenegild had been confined. Recognizing that mutilation would have been a hindrance to ordination, Flórez supposed that Morales obtained a Papal dispensation to leave his monastic vows and be ordained.[8] The supposition is unnecessary, of course, if the account in the book of registers does not pertain to Morales.

In September 1541 Morales began a *Memoria sanctorum*, "qui orti sunt in Hispania, vel alibi nati, eorum corpora in eadem provincia seu regione foeliciter requiescunt, de quibus in divino cultu, aut in ecclesiis Hispaniae recitatur. His accessere et alii qui licet minime recitentur, non minimam tamen populorum devotionem et sanctitatis nomen et opinionem habent." Later Morales added two more books to this work.[9] From 1541 to 1545 Morales is listed as a student at the University of Alcalá.[10] His position at the university thereafter, however, is not clear. Several times he identifies himself as a catedrático of rhetoric there, but the position seems to have been somewhat apart from the norm. Although two entries in university records refer to him as a catedrático, he is not usually accorded either that title or the title of "maestro," as are his fellow professors.[11] In February 1567 Morales, "presbyter Cordubensis diocesis, historicus noster, et in Complutensis academia publicus eloquentiae professor," was ordered by Philip II to collect data for the canonization of James, or Didacus, of St. Nicholas.[12] In October 1570 the chair of rhetoric held by Morales was

[8] Cf. Cifuentes, *Ambrosii Morales opuscula*, 190-205; Chronicle, XI, lxvii, 6; Flórez, biography of Morales, par. 13.

[9] Flórez, biography of Morales, par. 18.

[10] Archivo Historico Nacional in Madrid, Universidad de Alcalá, Pruebas de curso de 1540 a 1545, 476F, 155 and 173v.

[11] *Ibid.*, Matriculas de 1548 a 1573, 431F-435F, passim; cf. the matriculas for the years 1552, 1554, 1555, 1557, 1559-1563, 1566-1569. The entries concerning Morales for 1549 in 431F, 4v and 81v, appear to be irregular.

[12] Ms Madrid BN 5734, 13-25; cf. *Ambrosii Morales opuscula*, 190-205.

awarded to someone else,[13] but Morales continued to use the title of catedrático. In October 1572 Luis Estrada, the abbot of Huerta and the ecclesiastical censor of the edition of Eulogius' works, calls Morales a very erudite man, formerly *magister primarius* of eloquence at the *academia* of Alcalá.[14] During most of his years at the university Morales taught Livy,[15] the main source for a large part of his Chronicle. Several of Morales' students became illustrious in their later life, the most famous perhaps being Don Juan of Austria.

It is not known when Morales became a royal chronicler. The earliest he is identified by the title is in 1567 in the appointment as procurator by Philip II. Flórez' statement that Morales was a royal chronicler of Charles V[16] is based upon the report from the book of registers of the monastery of Valparaiso. Although the title of royal chronicler did not necessarily indicate an official capacity as an historian,[17] in the case of Morales is does seem to have been associated with his work on the Chronicle begun by Ocampo.

The first five books of the Chronicle by Ocampo cover the period from the Deluge to about 200, B.C. Most of the account is based on legend, but Ocampo's description of the geography of Spain deserves attention. During Ocampo's later life illness and preoccupation with other duties prevented him from working on the Chronicle. His statements about work he did on the history of Spain subsequent to 200, B.C., are discounted by Morales and other contemporaries of Ocampo, but Morales also indicates that Ocampo, although he may not have written the history, did considerable research on the later periods.[18]

[13] Archivo Historico Nacional in Madrid, Universidad de Alcalá, Registro de actos y grados, 399F, 145v.

[14] *Divi Eulogii . . . opera* (Alcalá, 1574), ii.

[15] Archivo Historico Nacional in Madrid, Universidad de Alcalá, Libro de la Facultad de artes desde el año de 1563 hasta el de 1642, 430F, 2-48.

[16] Flórez, biography of Morales, par. 22.

[17] Flórez, *ibid.*, refers to Gil González Dávila, *Grandezas de Madrid*, 330.

[18] For a biography of Ocampo cf. Cano's edition of the Chronicle,

In 1555 on the false report of Ocampo's death Philip II in Brussels awarded his office to Dr. Juan Paez de Castro, who immediately sought to have Ocampo's books and papers collected so that his work would not be lost. Paez established himself in Quer (Guadalajara) and worked on the Chronicle until 1569, when he became ill. After the death of Paez in January 1570 Morales made a survey of his books and papers at the command of Philip II. Paez contributed nothing to the text of the Chronicle except a Prologue which is a preliminary treatise on the preparation required for the writing of history and on the heuristic aspect of historical method.[19] Both Ocampo and Paez were ecclesiastics.

Morales became a royal chronicler and began to work on the Chronicle it appears sometime between the actual death of Ocampo (about 1560) and 1567, when he is identified by the title for the first time. In 1564 Morales testifies that he had all of Ocampo's papers and had begun to write the Chronicle. His testimony may not contradict the same claims made by Paez in correspondence with Gerónimo Zurita between 1555 and 1569, but there is no explanation of a division of the work on the Chronicle between Paez and Morales. Morales did not succeed Paez during the latter's lifetime, for it is evident in a letter written from Paez to Zurita in January 1569 that Paez still was responsible for

I, the introduction. Cf. Ocampo's prologue to the Chronicle (Cano ed., I, xii f.) ; Morales' prologue to Bk. VI of the Chronicle (*ibid.*, III, vi ff.) ; his discourse on privilegios before Bk. XIII of the Chronicle (*ibid.*, xviii) ; Chronicle, XV, xvii, 1 (*ibid.*, VIII, 43) ; letter of Ocampo to Dr. Vergara, *Noticias historicas* (*ibid.*, XIV, 120-124) ; letter of Ocampo to Sr. Galarza (*ibid.*, 124-126) ; letter of Morales to Alvar Gomez of Toledo (*ibid.*, 256-258) ; E. Garibay y Zamolla, *Los XL libros del compendio historial . . .*, I, v, 12.

[19] Most of the information about Paez de Castro comes from a number of letters by him to Gerónimo Zurita between 1545 and 1569 ; cf. Diego Josef Dormer and Juan Francisco Andres de Uztarroz, *Progressos de la historia en el reyno de Aragon* (Zaragoza, 1680), passim, especially 458-493. The Prologue has been published by E. Esteban, "De las cosas necessarias para escribir historia," *La ciudad de Dios*, 28 (1892), 601-610, and 29 (1892), 27-37, with introductory notes; the first part of the Prologue offers biographical data about Paez.

the Chronicle, and Philip's commission to Morales in 1570 to inventory Paez's books and papers states that Paez was working on the Chronicle.[20] The fact that Paez contributed no text to the Chronicle may be explained by his devotion to the thorough collection and study of sources, including works in Greek and Arabic. Morales probably benefited more than he states from the research of Ocampo and Paez. Besides Ocampo and Paez, other contemporaries of Morales were of assistance to him—Ponce de León, Alvar Gomez of Toledo, and Andreas Resende for examples. The reigns of Charles V and Philip II witnessed a phenomenal amount of historical scholarship in Spain.

Morales had broad interests. He travelled extensively within Spain. He was a student of epigraphy, numismatics, place names, privilegios (which entailed rudimentary palaeography and diplomatics), and hagiography. In his account of the martyrs of Córdoba he regularly notes saints who are mentioned in the martyrologies of Usuard, Adon, "Equilinus," and the Roman martyrology. Morales' interest in so many subjects enabled him to utilize a great deal of source material in his study of Spanish history. The broad scope of his writings is evident in his treatises on various subjects included in the edition of Eulogius' works, the Chronicle, and the three volumes of miscellany edited by Cifuentes. His life of the Countess Matilda of Canossa, the unfinished work on the conquest of the Holy Land, and his description of the battle of Lepanto may be mentioned. A number of short works, comments, notes, and reports by Morales appear in several manuscripts of the Escorial and the Biblioteca Nacional of Madrid. Gonzalo Argote de Molina in his *Nobleza del Andaluzia* in 1588 says that he used a *Libro de privilegios, letreros y sepulchros* collected by Morales and an *Annotaciones al Conde don Pedro* by Morales. Morales wrote Latin poetry, including a hymn of about eight hundred lines in honor of St. Hermenegild. He was interested in the cultivation of Spanish as a literary medium and wrote

---

[20] Morales' letter to Alvar Gomez of Toledo, *Noticias historicas*, 257; Dormer, *Progressos*, 78 and 484-489.

a number of essays on moral topics. Late in his life he published a revised edition of a devotional treatise, the *Arte para servir a Dios,* which had been written originally by the Franciscan Fr. Alonso of Madrid. In 1585 Morales published the works of his deceased uncle, Fernan Pérez de Oliva, together with a few of his own works.[21]

It seems that Morales knew some Greek and Arabic, but his proficiency in these languages is open to question. Among the works he published in his later life is a translation of the Greek Table of Cebes from his early life, but it has been argued that he worked from a Latin copy rather than the Greek original. He examined Greek and Arabic manuscripts belonging to Paez de Castro, who knew these languages, and it appears that Argote de Molina received Arabic works from Morales.[22]

The account of Morales' *Viage santo* was published by Flórez in 1765. In March 1572 Morales presented to the censors for approval his first part of the Chronicle, together with a work on the martyrdom of St. Hermenegild and presumably the edition of the works of Eulogius, and planned to make a pilgrimage to Santiago de Campostella. On 8 May 1572 the king commissioned him to survey the Asturias, León, and Galicia for manuscripts and the relics of saints to be brought to the Escorial. One of the tasks assigned Morales it seems was to verify that the relics of Eulogius and Leocritia were in Ovideo.[23] When Morales returned from the journey is not known. He reported to his superior for the trip, Dr. Martin Velasco, at the end of February 1573 and in November 1573 submitted a written report, the *Viage santo,* to Antonio Gracian. A note by Flórez to the text of the *Viage* says that Morales was on his trip in November

[21] Cf. ms Madrid BN 472; Ambrosio de Morales, *Las obras del maestro Fernan Pérez de Oliva . . . con otras cosas que van añadidas . . .* (Córdoba, 1586).

[22] Pablo Lozano y Casela, *Paráfrasis árabe de la tabla de Cebes, traducida en castellano é illustrada con notas* (Madrid, 1793), xi; Guillermo Antolín, *Catálogo de los códices latinos de la real biblioteca del Escorial* (5 vols.; Madrid, 1910-1923), I, xxi.

[23] *Viage santo,* 83f. (Cano ed., X, 107f.).

1572, but no source for the information is given.[24] There was a good deal of opposition in Spain to Philip's plan to collect important relics and manuscripts in the Escorial as a monument to his father. Many cathedrals and monasteries were naturally reluctant to part with their treasures. Diego Hurtado de Mendoza, bishop of Burgos, expressed disapproval of the way books were being collected. In 1571 Gerónimo Zurita gave most of his library to a group of ecclesiastics in Zaragoza before he died.[25] The libraries of Paez de Castro and Ponce de León were not the only ones Philip transferred to the Escorial.

On 21 September 1591 Morales died in Córdoba. His remains were translated to Madrid in 1844 for the proposed Pantheon, but were returned to Córdoba when the project was abandoned.[26] He has been highly regarded as a historian since he began to work on the Chronicle. Rather extensive biographical studies have been made of him, but several important aspects of his work have yet to be treated. The list of his works is not complete. What would seem to be an authoritative list of them, "Original letters of Ambrosio de Morales in which he gives an account of the state of printing of his works," is unfortunately missing from the manuscript which is supposed to contain it.[27] Morales' dependence on his contemporaries and predecessors has not been studied, and a critical evaluation of his contribution to Spanish historiography is lacking. The amount of source material which he introduced into the study of Spanish history should be surveyed. In the tradition of chronicles of Spanish history which begins before Isidore of Seville and continues with the Chronicle of 754, the chronicles of Oviedo and León, with Lucas of Tuy, Rodrigo Jiménez de Rada, Rodrigo Sánchez de Arévalo,[28] and others after him in the

[24] *Viage*, 1st para. (Cano ed., X, 7).

[25] Antolín, *op.cit.*, I, xxxvii and xlvi.

[26] Flórez, biography of Morales, pars. 50-52; Ramírez de Arellano, *op.cit.*, 363.

[27] Ms Madrid BN 892, 87-94.

[28] *Roderici Santii episcopi Palentini Historiae Hispaniae* (Rome, 1470), in *Hisp. ill.*, I, 121-246; Richard H. Trame, *Rodrigo Sánchez de*

fifteenth and sixteenth centuries, the position of Morales needs to be determined.

Morales' life and work are difficult to investigate. Most of the information about him comes from his own pen and in many instances was written long after events occurred. He edited much of his early work later in life and published or transcribed it into manuscripts. Sometimes he introduces Spanish versions of his earlier Latin work without giving notice to the reader. Besides introducing work of his early life in his later work, Morales also introduces inconspicuous interpolations into later editions of his early writings. In more than one instance the investigation of details about Morales comes to an end with missing folios or records.

A study of events surrounding the publication of Eulogius' works by Morales in 1574 reveals problems of somewhat mysterious import concerning the disappearance of the manuscript from which the edition was made and concerning the amount of credit to be given to Ponce de León, bishop of Placencia, for the editing of the text of Eulogius' works. Ponce de León[29] was a native of Córdoba, born in 1499. He received his early education under his paternal uncle, who was *primicerius* and canon of the church of Córdoba. At the University of Salamanca Ponce de León distinguished himself in the study of canon law and the Fathers. Elected to the Supreme Council of the Inquisition by Charles V in 1546, he later became bishop of Ciudad Rodrigo. He took part in the Council of Trent and became bishop of Placencia in 1560 under Philip II. Towards the end of his life he was appointed Inquisitor General of Spain. He died 19 January 1573. He was devoted to scholarly interests, especially the ecclesiastical history of Spain, and he accumulated a large personal library.

Arévalo, 1404-1470. Spanish Diplomat and Champion of the Papacy (Washington, 1958), especially 191f. Sánchez de Arévalo may be more important in Spanish historiography than appears.

[29] Much information about Ponce de León comes from Morales' letter to the bishop at the front of the edition of Eulogius' works, iv ff., and from the bishop's letter to the city of Córdoba, *ibid.*, 107f.; cf. ESPASA, 46, 247.

After his death Morales inventoried his books and papers before they were delivered to the Escorial in November 1573. Many of these books perished in a fire at the Escorial in 1671.[30]

Eulogius' works are not mentioned in a list of works once thought to have been in Oviedo in 882,[31] and for this reason probably Ponce de León concluded that the manuscript was brought to Oviedo in 884 with the relics of Eulogius. The first mention of the unique manuscript of Eulogius' works is that it was one of a number of books loaned by the church of Oviedo on 10 September 1557 to Ponce de León when he was bishop of Ciudad Rodrigo. This statement, which says that the books were not returned, appears in ms Madrid BN 13121, from the eighteenth century. The statement is not dated, but it was composed before 1572 because Morales mentions it in a report sent to Philip II in May of that year.[32] After the edition of Eulogius' works in 1574 the manuscript of his works completely disappeared. In Book XV of the Chronicle, which was published in 1586 but which have been written any time after 1574, Morales says that he returned the manuscript to Oviedo.[33] Luis de Carvallo, archivist of the cathedral of Oviedo, states about 1600 that the manuscript was in Oviedo.[34] Flórez in 1753 says that he was as-

[30] Cf. ms Escorial &-II-15, 238. A catalogue of mss of the Escorial from the sixteenth century before the fire of 1671 is published by Antolín, *op.cit.*, V, 331-487; cf. also Antolín, "La libreria de D. Pedro Ponce de León, obispo de Plasencia." *Revista de archivos, bibliotecas y museos*, XX (1909), 383.

[31] Cf. Antolín, *Catálogo*, III, 485-486. Agustín Millares Carlo, *Los códices visigóticos de la catedral toledana* (Madrid, 1935), 50ff., and A. C. Vega, "El 'Liber de haeresibus' de San Isidro de Sevilla y el 'Códice Ovetense,' " *La ciudad de Dios*, 171 (1958), 269f., think that the list comes from Toledo, perhaps from Seville originally. M. Manitius, *Geschichte der lateinischen Literatur des Mittelalters*, I, 421, notes that most of the works which Eulogius brought back from his journey to the north of Spain in 848 or 850 appear in this list.

[32] Ms Madrid BN 13121, 130f.; *Noticias históricas* (Cano ed. XIV), 98.

[33] Chronicle, XV, xv, 1 (Cano ed., VIII, 39f.).

[34] Luis Alfonso de Carvallo, *Antigüedades y cosas memorables del principado de Asturias* (Madrid, 1695), 240.

sured in Oviedo that the manuscript was not then extant.[35] There is no trace of the manuscript among the personal books and manuscripts of Morales, which he gave away during his lifetime to his friend, Gonzalo Argote de Molina of Seville. When Argote de Molina died his library was scattered.[36] With the king interested in the library of the Escorial the manuscript might have been made part of that collection, but there is no record of it there. A. S. Ruiz suggests that ms Escorial R-II-18 is the manuscript which contained Eulogius' works, Antolín having previously noted that the first part of this manuscript may have been written by Eulogius of Córdoba.[37] In view of the edition of Eulogius' works Morales apparently did not feel a need to describe the manuscript as carefully as he did a number of other manuscripts, such as the Azagra codex.[38] In two notes in ms Madrid BN 5734 Morales mentions the manuscript of Eulogius' works, saying in one place that he then had the manuscript and had worked on it for a long time and in the other place that the church of Spain would have a precious treasure and a rich jewel in the works of Eulogius when they were published.[39] Writing in the Chronicle in 1586 Morales seems to rely on the words of Ponce de León

---

[35] ES, X, 450f.

[36] Morales' will, published by Ramírez de Arellano, *op.cit.*, I, 380, mentions no books. Gonzalo Argote de Molina, *Nobleza de Andaluzia* (Seville, 1588), al lector and 18v, says that he had all Morales' books from him during his lifetime. Antonio Palma Chaguaceda, *El historiador Gonzalo Argote de Molina, estudio biográfico, bibliográfico, y critico* (Madrid, 1949), 52, quotes Diego Ortiz de Zuñiga, *Annales eclesiásticos y seculares de la muy noble y muy leal ciudad de Sevilla, metrópoli de la Andalucía* (Madrid, 1677), from the pages where he discusses Argote's mss (62-78) to the effect that many of Argote's valuable books and mss were lost through neglect and were scattered after his death. Cf. also Celestino López Martínez, *Algunos documentos para la biografía de Argote de Molina* (Seville, 1921), 80-83.

[37] A. S. Ruiz, *Obras completas de San Eulogio* (Madrid, 1959), lvii; Antolín, *Catálogo*, III, 481-487.

[38] Morales' note to the reader before the *Vita Eulogii*.

[39] Ms Madrid BN 5734, 320v and 322v.

in 1572 for what he has to say of the manuscript.[40]

Information about Ponce de León and Morales with respect to the edition of Eulogius' works comes from several notices at the front of the edition of the works in 1574 and from four letters in the edition, two by the bishop and two by Morales. The earliest notice is the ecclesiastical approval for the edition granted by Luis Estrada, abbot of Huerta, on 18 October 1572. Estrada gives credit for the appearance of the works first to Eulogius, then to Ponce de León, and thirdly to Morales. He says that the works were found and emended (ab innumeris mendis tineisque vindicata) by Ponce de León and annotated by Morales. The brief approval by the civil censor, Gerónimo Zurita, dated 1 February 1573, applies only to Morales' treatise on the Antiquities of Córdoba and says nothing about Eulogius' works. The pronouncement of Philip II on 13 July 1573 granting Morales the rights to the edition contains little information about the work done by Ponce de León and Morales. According to the king, an application by Morales on behalf of Ponce de León was presented to the council, along with the works of Eulogius, with a request for a license to print the works. The request was approved by the censors. After the death of Ponce de León, the pronouncement continues, there was no provision for the work or the printing of the work in his will, and the heirs would not continue the printing at the expense of the estate. Thereupon Morales, one of the heirs, secured from the other heirs the right to print the works of Eulogius. The edition was inspected again by the council and approved. In a notice to the reader Morales speaks of the responsibilities for the editing of the works, inherited from Ponce de León, as if they were an additional burden

---

[40] Chronicle, XV, xv, 1. Morales' statement that the ms was taken to Oviedo with the relics of Eulogius was made by Ponce de León in 1572 in a letter to Philip II. Cf. Ponce de León in his letter to the city of Córdoba, "Tanta erat vetustas et priscorum characterem atque membranae et ipsius etiam compaginationibus manifesta differentia" and Morales, Chronicle, XV, xv, 1, "Y el libro es tan antiguo en la forma de la letra gótica y en la manera de pergamino y encuadernación, que se puede muy bien creer estaba y escrito entonces."

for him. He claims credit for all the work done in the preparation of the works for the press, except the discovery of the manuscript, but says that he is unwilling to detract from the memory and fame of Ponce de León and so leaves intact the prefaces to the edition as they were before the death of the bishop.

There are two letters by Ponce de León in the edition. In one the bishop dedicates the edition to Philip II, and in the other he commends the veneration of the martyrs to the people of Córdoba. In most of the letter to Philip II, at the beginning of the edition, he praises the king for his zealous promotion of the publication of historical sources and tells how his own efforts in the study of hagiography have been rewarded by discovery of the works of Eulogius, which have added to the history of Spanish saints the accounts of almost fifty martyrs known otherwise by name only. At the end of this letter Ponce de León describes the codex of Eulogius' works. It was of parchment, very old, apparently contemporary with Eulogius, and in Visigothic script. It was brought to Ovideo from Córdoba, he believes, with the relics of Eulogius not long after his martyrdom. Ponce de León says that Morales clarified many passages in the works of Eulogius with explanatory notes. Morales also, says the bishop, contributed to the edition a number of accounts of Cordoban martyrs who died after Eulogius.

The bishop's letter to the church and the city of Córdoba recounts how he devoted himself for many years to the search for manuscripts pertaining to the ecclesiastical history of Spain. In this search he discovered many things previously unknown about the ecclesiastical councils of Spain. One of the greatest treasures he discovered was the manuscript of Eulogius' works, which he vaguely remembered having heard of before. Moved by patriotic feelings for his native city of Córdoba, he decided to publish the work, but found that the script and the age of the book, which were assets as far as authenticity was concerned, were a source of great difficulty for him and his helpers in the transcription of the codex. He would have continued the emendation and annotation of the text himself had not his episcopal duties prevented him and had not Ambrosio de Morales, a fellow Cordoban, offered to do that part of the work for him. Morales spared no effort in making the works of Eulogius more correct, richer, and clearer. Thus, Eulogius, Ponce de León, and Morales, all Cordobans, contributed to the edition. It is now for the priests and people of Córdoba to revere the martyrs, he concludes. This letter to the people of Córdoba appears at the end of Eulogius' works in the edition of 1574. Neither it nor the letter to Philip II is dated.

Both letters of Morales in the edition seem to be letters of dedication. In the first, to Ponce de León, he speaks as if he were dedicating to him the edition of the works of Eulogius. In the second he dedicates the last part of the book to his nephew, the bishop of Tlaxcala. Morales' letter to Ponce de León, at the beginning of the edition, is the only one of the four letters which is dated. More than half of this letter is devoted to a eulogistic account of the bishop's life. After a word on the importance of the discovery of Eulogius' works, Morales tells how Ponce de León appointed him to supervise the emendation, annotation, and at last the editing of the works. Such a task was doubly pleasing to Morales since it redounded to the glory of both Eulogius and Córdoba. Glory also accrued to the see of Toledo, to which Eulogius was elected as the successor of Wistremirus. Morales consecrates the edition to God, dedicates it to Eulogius and the martyrs, offers it for the glory of Córdoba, and finally refers it to Ponce de León. The letter is dated in Alcalá, in the month of November, 1572.

For three reasons it appears that this letter may actually have been written after the death of Ponce de León, which occurred 19 January 1573. The lengthy, somewhat detailed biography and eulogy of the bishop seems more appropriate for a deceased person than for a living one. Also, since Morales did not report to his superior for the *viage santo* until the end of February 1573, he may not have returned from the trip as early as November 1572. It seems unlikely that the bishop would have dedicated the edition to the king and Morales would have dedicated it to the bishop at the same time in the lifetime of Ponce de León.

Morales had written to his nephew, Antonio de Morales, the bishop of Tlaxcala, previously and advised him of the imminent edition of the works of Eulogius. His nephew in reply requested a copy of the edition. Now, says Morales, not only does he send a copy, but he dedicates the last part of the edition, which is all his own work, to his nephew. All my own work too, he says, was the work on the edition of Eulogius' writings, except for the discovery of the manuscript. So much more of the care, and work, and expense of completing the edition has fallen to me since the death of Bishop Ponce de León. I know that you will be glad to hear that I am occupied with such a blessed work, just as we are all happy to hear of your elevation to the episcopacy and just as we rejoice at the appointment of your brother, Luis de Molina, as councillor of the royal Senate. Morales' letter to the bishop of Tlaxcala is followed by the accounts of Cordoban martyrs after the time of Eulogius mentioned by Ponce de León in his letter to Philip II.

Study of the prefatory material in the edition of Eulogius' works shows that Morales sought credit for more of the work done on the edition than Estrada or Ponce de León granted him, credit which has since been given to him. It would be of interest to know whether Ponce de León or Morales established the text of Eulogius' works. At the end of Book I of the *Memoriale sanctorum* in connection with a poem in honor of the birth of Ferdinand, the son of Philip II, Morales notes that he had proceeded that far by 4 December 1571.[41] Five months later, in May 1572, he prepared to leave on his journey to the North. The discrepancies in statements about the work done on the text of Eulogius' writings seem to derive from arguments about the expense of printing the works. They are not connected with the disappearance of the manuscript of the works. In fact, the authenticity of the text is supported by the report that the edition

41 *Divi Eulogii ... opera*, 32v.

was presented to the censors on two separate occasions, once on behalf of Ponce de León and once by Morales. Morales introduces into his scholia information learned on his trip to the north of Spain and he seems to have modified slightly some of the prefatory material, but it is unlikely that he altered the text of Eulogius' writings after the death of Ponce de León. After study of the problems surrounding the edition of Eulogius' works it appears that Ponce de León, the discoverer of the manuscript, may be a more important figure in the historiography of Spain in the sixteenth century than is recognized.

SELECT BIBLIOGRAPHY

ABBREVIATIONS

AASS   Acta sanctorum
AB   *Analecta Bollandiana*
AHDE   *Anuario de historia del derecho español*
Auct. antiq.   *Auctores antiquissimi* (in MGH)
BN   Biblioteca Nacional, Bibliothèque Nationale
BRAH   *Boletín de la Real Academia de la Historia*, Madrid
CHE   *Cuadernos de historia de España*, Buenos Aires
CSEL   Corpus scriptorum ecclesiasticorum latinorum
DACL   *Dictionnaire d'archéologie chrétienne et de liturgie*
DHGE   *Dictionnaire d'histoire et de géographie ecclésiastiques*
DTC   *Dictionnaire de théologie catholique*
EI   *Encyclopaedia of Islam*
ES   *España sagrada*
ESPASA   *Enciclopedia universal ilustrada europeo-americana*
Hisp. ill.   Andreas Schott, *Hispaniae illustratae seu rerum urbiumque
          Hispaniae, Lusitaniae, Aethiopiae et Indiae scriptores varii*
          (4 vols.; Frankfurt, 1603-1608).
LTK   *Lexikon für Theologie und Kirche*
MGH   Monumenta Germaniae historica
NA   *Neues Archiv der Gesellschaft für ältere deutsche Geschichts-
          kunde*
Pauly-Wissowa   *Real-encyclopädie der classischen Altertumswissen-
          schaft*
PL   J.-P. Migne, Patrologiae cursus completus, series latina.
RE   *Realencyklopädie für protestantische Theologie und Kirche*
SS PP Toletanorum   Francisco Cardinal Lorenzana y Butron, *SS PP
          Toletanorum quotquot extant opera* (3 vols.;
          Madrid, 1782-1793).
TLL   *Thesaurus linguae latinae*

SOURCES

Abd al-Rahman II, Letter to Emperor Theophilus of Byzantium in
     839. Ed. and trans. Lévi-Provençal, *Byzantion*, 12 (1937),
     17-24.
Acts and Correspondence of the Council of Frankfurt in 794. Ed.
     Werminghoff, MGH, *Concilia*, II, *Concilia aevi carolini*, I,
     111-171.
Acts of the Asturian kings. Ed. Barrau-Dihigo, *Revue hispanique*,
     46 (1919), 1-191.

Acts of the Council of Córdoba in 839. Ed. Flórez, ES, 15, 8 unnumbered pages.

Adrian I, Pope, Letters. Edd. Flórez, ES, 5, Appendix X; Gundlach, MGH, *Epistolarum* t. III, *Epistolae merowingici et karolini aevi*, I, 636-648; Cenni (in PL 98, 333-346 and 373-386).

Aimoin, *De translatione SS martyrum Georgii monachi, Aurelii, et Nathaliae ex urbe Corduba Parisios.* Edd, Mabillon, *AASS OSB, saec. IV (800-900)*, ii (Venice, 1738, V, 46-61); Flórez, ES, 10, Appendix X; Lorenzana, *SS PP Toletanorum*, II, 621-637; PL 115, 939-960.

Akhbar Madjmua. Ed. and trans. Lafuente y Alcántara, *Ajbar machmua....* Vol. I of *Colección de obras arábigas....* Madrid, 1867.

Albar, Paul, *Confessio.* Ed. Flórez, ES, 11, 62-80; PL 121, 397-412.

——, Correspondence. Edd. Flórez, ES, 11, 81-218; PL 121, 411-514; Lorenzana, *SS PP Toletanorum*, II, 637-642; PL 115, 959-966; Madoz, *Epistolario de Alvaro de Córdoba*, Madrid, 1947.

——, *Indiculus.* Ed. Flórez, ES, 11, 219-275; PL 121, 513-556.

——, Poems. Edd. Flórez, ES, 11, 275-290 and 560-563; Lorenzana, *SS PP Toletanorum*, II, 408-411; PL 115, 720-724; PL 121, 555-566; Traube, MGH, *Poetae latini aevi carolini*, III, i, 126-142.

——, *Vita Eulogii.* Edd. Flórez, ES, 10, Appendix VI; and in all editions of Eulogius' works except that of de la Bigne. Trans. Morales, *Corónica*, XIV, xxvii; Sage, *Paul Albar*, 190-214; Ruiz, *Obras completas*, 1-41.

Al-Khushani, History of the Cadis of Córdoba. Ed. and trans. Ribera, *Historia de los jueces de Córdoba por Aljoxani.* Madrid, 1914.

Al-Makkari, The History of the Mohammedan Dynasties in Spain. Trans. Pascual de Gayangos. 2 vols. London, 1890-1893.

Annales Bertiniani. Ed. Waitz, MGH, *Scriptores...in usum scholarum*, Hanover, 1883.

Ascaricus and Tusaredus, Letters. Ed. Heine (in PL 99, 1231-1240).

Beatus of Liébana, Commentary on the Apocalypse. Edd. Flórez, *Sancti Beati presbyteri Hispani Liebanensis in Apocalypsin... commentaria...*, Madrid, 1770; Sanders, *Beati in Apocalypsin libri duodecim*, Vol. VII of *Papers and Monographs of the American Academy in Rome*, Rome, 1930.

Beatus and Eterius, Letter to Elipandus. Ed. Galland (in PL 96, 893-1030).

Charters and Diplomas of Charlemagne, Louis the Pious, and Charles the Bald (812-854). Ed. Claude Devic, Joseph Vaissete, *et al.*, *Histoire générale de Languedoc avec des notes et les pièces justificatives*, II, 73-295. Toulouse, 1875.

Chronicle of Albelda. Edd. Flórez, ES, 13, Appendix VI; PL 129, 1123-1146; Gómez-Moreno, BRAH, 100 (1932), 600-609.

Chronicle of Alfonso III. Edd. Flórez, ES, 13, Appendix VII; PL 129, 1111-1124; García-Villada, *Crónica de Alfonso III*, Madrid, 1918.

Chronicle of Roda. Edd. Barrau-Dihigo, *Revue hispanique*, 33 (1910), 235-264; García-Villada, *Crónica de Alfonso III*, Madrid, 1918, 99-131; Gómez-Moreno, BRAH, 100 (1932), 609-621.

Chronicle of 741. Edd. Flórez, ES, 6, Appendix X; Mommsen, MGH, *Auct. antiq.*, XI, *Chronica minora*, II, 333-359.

Chronicle of 754. Edd. Flórez, ES, 8, Appendix II; PL 96, 1253-1280; Tailhan, *Anonyme de Cordoue*, Paris, 1885; Mommsen, MGH, *Auct. antiq.*, XI, *Chronica minora*, II, 333-369.

Chronicle, Prophetic. Ed. Gómez-Moreno, BRAH, 100 (1932), 622-628.

Chronicon Moissiacense. Ed. Pertz, MGH, *Scriptores*, I, 282-313, and II, 257-259; PL 98, 1411-1434.

Cixila, *Vita Ildefonsi*. Edd. Flórez, ES, 5, Appendix VIII; Lorenzana, *SS PP Toletanorum*, I, 96-99.

Collectio Hispana. Ed. Arévalo (in PL 84, 23-848).

Cyprian, Poems. Edd. Flórez, ES, 11, 524-527; PL 121, 567-568; Traube, MGH, *Poetae latini aevi carolini*, III, i, 144-146.

Defensoris *Liber scintillarum*. Ed. Rochais. Vol. 117 of *Corpus Christianorum, series latina*, 1-234. Turnhout, 1957.

Eldefonsus, *Revelatio*. Ed. Mabillon (in PL 106, 883-890).

Elipandus, Letters. Edd. Flórez, ES, 5, Appendix X; PL 96, 859-882; Menéndez Pelayo, *Historia de los heterodoxos españoles*, VII (vol. 41 of *Edición Nacional*), 161-174.

Eterius. Cf. Beatus.

Eulogius, Opera (*Memoriale sanctorum, Documentum martyriale, Apologeticus martyrum*). Edd. Morales, *Divi Eulogii ... opera*, Alcalá, 1574; Schott, *Hisp. ill.*, IV, 213-372; de la Bigne, *Bibliotheca veterum patrum;* Lorenzana, *SS PP Toletanorum*, II, 394-561; PL 115, 705-870. Ed. and trans. Ruiz, *Obras completas de San Eulogio*. Córdoba, 1959.

————, Letters and Correspondence with Albar. Edd. Flórez, ES, 11, 290-299; and in all editions of Eulogius' works; PL 115, 731-736, 819-820, and 841-852.

Evantius, Letter. Ed. Sáenz de Aguirre (in PL 88, 719-722).

Fath-l-Andalus. Ed. and trans. Joaquín de González, *Fatho-l-Andaluci, Historia de la conquista de España*. Algiers, 1889.

Felix of Córdoba and Peter, Letters. Ed. Morin, *Revue bénédictine*, 15 (1898), 289-295.

Fragmentum chronici Fontanellensis. Ed. Pertz, MGH, *Scriptores*, II, 301-304.

Gregory IX, Pope, Bulls. Registro Vaticano, 18. Ed. Lucien Auvray, *Les registres de Grégoire IX*, II. Paris, 1907.

Hrotswitha, *Passio sancti Pelagii pretiosissimi martiris qui nostris temporibus in Corduba martirio est coronatus*. Edd. Schurzfleisch (in PL 137, 1093-1102); Winterfeld, MGH, *Scriptores . . . in usum scholarum, Hrotsvithae opera*, 52-62; Strecker, *Hrotsvithae opera*, Leipzig, 1930, 54-66.

Ibn al-Kutiya, History of the Conquest of Spain. Ed. and trans. Ribera, *Historia de la conquista de España por Abenalcotía. . . .* Vol. II of *Colección de obras arábigas. . . .* Madrid, 1926.

Ibn Haiyan, *Al-Muktabis*. Ed. Antuña, *Ibn Haiyan. Al-Muktabis, tome troisième. . . .* Paris, 1937. Trans. Guarieb, CHE, 13-32 (1950-1960), passim.

Ibn Idhari, *Al-Bayan al-mughrib*. Edd. Dozy, 2 vols., Leyden, 1848-1851; Colin and Lévi-Provençal, 2 vols., Leyden, 1948-1951. Trans. Fernández y González, *Historia de al-Andalus por Aben-Adhari de Marruecos*, Granada, 1860; Fagnan. *Histoire de l'Afrique et de l'Espagne intitulée al-Bayano-l-Mogrib*, 2 vols., Algiers, 1901-1904.

Indicium penitentie. Ed. Pérez de Urbel and Vázquez de Parga, AHDE, 14 (1942-1943), 5-32.

Indiculum de adventum Enoc et Elie adque Antichristi libris duobus, id est Daniellis et Abocalissen Ioannis a beato Iheronimo expositum. Ed. Vega, *La ciudad de Dios*, 171 (1958), 262-268.

Interrogatio. Ed. Jean Leclercq, *Hispania sacra*, 2 (1949), 327-338.

Inventarium librorum anno 882. Ed. Antolín, *Catálogo*, III, 485-486.

Jiménez de Rada, Rodrigo, *De rebus Hispaniae*. Ed. Lorenzana, SS PP *Toletanorum*, III, 5-208.

———, *Historia Arabum*. Ed. Lorenzana, SS PP *Toletanorum*, III, 242-283.

———, *Appendix prima, series regum Hispaniae*. Ed. Lorenzana, SS PP *Toletanorum*, III, 284-324.

John, abbot of St. Arnulf, *Vita Johannis abbatis Gorziensis*. Ed. Pertz, MGH, *Scriptores*, IV, 337-377.

Jonas of Orleans, *De cultu imaginum*. Ed. from *Bibliotheca veterum patrum, saec. ix* (in PL 106, 305-388).

Leovigildus, *De habitu clericorum*. Ed. Serrano, BRAH, 54 (1909), 496-517.

Lists of bishops. *Incipiunt nomina defunctorum episcoporum Spalensis sedis vel Toletane atque Eliberritane sedis;* ed. Antolín, *La ciudad de Dios*, 74 (1907), 388-389. Edd. Flórez, ES, 4, Tr. 3, par. 346, 349, 355; Simonet, *Historia*, 808-812; Leclercq, *Hispania sacra*, 2 (1949), 93.

Louis the Pious, Letter to the people of Mérida. Ed. Hampe, MGH, *Epistolarum t. V*, i, 115-116.

Mozarabic liturgy. Ed. Lorenzana (in PL 85 and 86). Marius Férotin, *Le Liber ordinum en usage dans l'Eglise wisigothique et mozarabe d'Espagne du cinquième siècle.* Vol. V of *Monumenta ecclesiae liturgica.* Paris, 1904. Marius Férotin, *Le Liber mozarabicus sacramentorum et les manuscrits mozarabes.* Vol. VI of *Monumenta ecclesiae liturgica.* Paris, 1912.

Peter. Cf. Felix.

Rasis, Chronicle. Ed. Pascual de Gayangos, "Memoria sobre la autenticidad de la Crónica denominada del moro Rasis," Vol. VIII of *Memorias de la Real Academia de la Historia,* in 100 pages numbered separately. Madrid, 1852.

Recemundus, *Calendarium.* Ed. Dozy, *Le calendrier de Cordoue de l'année 961; texte arabe et ancienne traduction latine.* Leyden, 1873. Edd. Latin text: Libri, *Histoire des sciences mathématiques en Italie,* I, 461; Férotin, *Le Liber ordinum,* 451-495; Simonet and Vega, ES, 56, 137-159.

Samson, *Apologeticus.* Ed. Flórez, ES, 11, 325-516.

———, Poems. Edd. Flórez, ES, 11, 527-528; Traube, MGH, *Poetae latini aevi carolini,* III, i, 146-147.

Translatio sanctarum virginum et martyrum Christi Nunilonis et Alodiae. Ed Pellizer de Salas (in AASS, October IX, 645-646).

Treaty of Abdelaziz and Theodemirus. Ed. Casiri, *Bibliotheca,* II, 106; Codera and Ribera, *Bibliotheca,* III, 258-259; Simonet, *Historia,* 797-798. Trans. Casiri, *Bibliotheca,* II, 105-106; Simonet, *Historia,* 798; García-Villada, *Historia,* III, 30-31; Lévi-Provençal, *Histoire,* I, 32-33; Gaspar Remiro, *Historia de Murcia musulmana* (Zaragoza, 1905), 13-15.

Tusaredus. Cf. Ascaricus.

Usuard, *Martyrologium.* Ed. Du Sollier, Antwerp, 1714; AASS, June VI and VII; PL 123, 452-992, and PL 124, 1-860.

Sources for Appendix V, "Ambrosio de Morales and the Edition of Eulogius' Works," are not given here. Authors referred to occasionally may be traced through the index; see al-Nuguairi, Ambrose, Amulo of Lyons, *Annales regii,* Apringius, Arnobius the Younger, Augustine, Claudianus Mamertus, Cumian, Dhuoda, *Disticha Catonis,* Donatus, Egbert of York, Eucherius, Eugene of Toledo, Gregory the Great, Pope Gregory III, Hincmar of Reims, Husayn ibn Mansur Hallaj, Ibn 'Abdun, Ibn Abi Riqa, Ibn Khaldun, Ildefonsus, Isidore, Jerome, Julian of Toledo, Junilius Afer, Koran, Liutprand of Cremona, Lupus of Ferrières, Paschasius Radbertus, Pedro Pascual, Porphyrius, Rodrigo Sánchez de Arévalo, Theophanes, Thomas Aquinas.

SECONDARY WORKS

Aigrain, René. "L'Espagne chrétienne," *Grégoire le Grand, les états barbares et la conquête arabe (590-757).* Vol. V of *Histoire de l'église.* Edd. Fliche and Martin. Paris, 1938.

Amann, Emile. "L'Adoptionisme espagnol de VIIIe siècle," *Revue des sciences religieuses,* 16 (1936), 281-317.

——. *L'époque carolingienne.* Vol. VI of *Histoire de l'église.* Edd. Fliche and Martin. Paris, 1937.

——. "L'expansion chrétienne en occident," *L'église au pouvoir des laiques, 888-1057.* Vol. VII of *Histoire de l'église.* Edd. Fliche and Martin. Paris, 1940.

Allard, Paul. "Martyre," *Dictionnaire apologétique de la foi catholique,* III, 331-492.

Amador de los Rios, José. *Historia crítica de la literatura española.* 7 vols. Madrid, 1861-1865.

Antolín, Guillermo. *Catálogo de los códices latinos de la Real Biblioteca del Escorial.* 5 vols. Madrid, 1910-1923.

——. "*De habitu clericorum* (siglo IX)," BRAH, 55 (1909), 102-120.

——. "El códice emilianense de la Biblioteca de el Escorial," *La ciudad de Dios,* 72-74 (1907), passim.

——. "La librería de D. Pedro Ponce de León, obispo de Plasencia." *Revista de archivos, bibliotecas y museos,* 20 (1909), 371-400.

Antonio, Nicolas. *Bibliotheca Hispana sive Hispanorum qui usquam unquamve sive latini sive alia quavis lingua scripto aliquid consignaverunt notitia....* 2 vols. Madrid, 1672. The 2d edition of this work comprises *Bibliotheca hispana vetus...,* 2 vols., Madrid, 1788, for authors up to A.D. 1500, and *Bibliotheca hispana nova...,* 2 vols., Madrid, 1788, for authors from 1500 to 1684.

Antuña, Melchor M. "Abenhayán de Córdoba y su obra historica," *La ciudad de Dios,* 139-140 (1924-1925), passim.

——. *Ibn Haiyan. Al-Muktabis, tome troisième: Chronique du regne du calife umaiyad Abd Allah à Cordoue.* Paris, 1937.

——. "Ibn Hayyan de Córdoba y su historia de la España musulmana," CHE, 4 (1946), 5-72 (published posthumously).

Argote de Molina, Gonzalo. *Nobleza del Andaluzia.* Seville, 1588.

Artiles, Jenaro. "El códice visigótico de Alvaro Cordobés," *Revista de la biblioteca, archivo y museo del Ayuntamiento de Madrid,* 9 (1932), 201-219.

Asín Palacios, Miguel. "Ibn Masarra y su escuela. Orígines de la filosofía hispanomusulmana," *Obras escogidas,* I, 1-216. Madrid, 1946.

Auzias, Léonce. *L'Aquitaine carolingienne (778-987).* Toulouse and Paris, 1937.

Ballesteros y Beretta, Antonio. *Historia de España y su influencia en la historia universal.* 12 vols. Barcelona and Madrid, 1922-1953.

Barrau-Dihigo, Louis. "Etude sur les actes des rois asturiens (718-910)," *Revue hispanique,* 46 (1919), 1-191.

———. "Recherches sur l'histoire politique du royaume asturien (718-910),"*Revue hispanique,* 52 (1921), 1-360.

———. "Une rédaction inédite du pseudo-Sébastien de Salamanque," *Revue hispanique,* 23 (1910), 235-264.

Baudissin, Wolf Wilhelm Graf von. "Alvar von Corduba," RE, I, 426-428.

———. "Eulogius," RE, V, 594-597.

———. *Eulogius und Alvar. Ein Abschnitt spanischer Kirchengeschichte aus der Zeit der Maurenherrschaft.* Leipzig, 1872.

Beer, Rudolf. *Handschriftenschätze Spaniens. Bericht über eine im Auftrage der kaiserlichen Akademie der Wissenschaften in den Jahren 1886-1888 durchgeführte Forschungsreise.* Vienna, 1894.

Benedict XIV, Pope. *De servorum Dei beatificatione et beatorum canonizatione.* Vols. I-VII of *Opera omnia.* 22 vols. Prato, 1839-1847

Beuter, Pero Anton. *Primera parte de la corónica general de toda España.* Valencia, 1546.

Bishko, Charles Julian. "Gallegan Pactual Monasticism in the Repopulation of Castile," *Estudios dedicados a Menéndez Pidal,* II, 513-531. Madrid, 1951.

———. "Salvus of Albelda and Frontier Monasticism in Tenth-Century Navarre," *Speculum,* 23 (1948), 559-590.

———. "The Date and Nature of the Spanish *Consensoria Monachorum,*" *American Journal of Philology,* 69 (1948), 377-395.

Cabaniss, Allen. "Bodo-Eleazar: A Famous Jewish Convert," *The Jewish Quarterly Review,* 43 (1952-1953), 313-328.

Cabrol, Fernand. "Mozarabe (La liturgie)," DACL, XII, i, 390-491.

———. "Mozarabe (Messe)," DTC, X, ii, 2518-2543.

de las Cagigas, Isidro. *Los mozárabes.* 2 vols. Madrid, 1947-1948.

Casiri, Miguel. *Bibliotheca arabico-hispana Escurialensis sive librorum omnium mss quos arabice ab auctoribus magnam partem arabo-hispanis compositos bibliotheca coenobii Escurialensis complectitur recensio et explanatio.* 2 vols. Madrid, 1760-1770.

Ceillier, Remy. *Histoire générale des auteurs sacrés et ecclésiastiques....* New ed. 14 vols. in 15. Paris, 1858-1863.

Cirot, Georges. *De codicibus aliquot ad historiam Hispaniae antiquae pertinentibus olimque ab Ambrosio de Morales adhibitis disserit....* Bordeaux, 1924.

Clark, Charles Upton. *Collectanea hispanica.* Paris, 1920.

Cobo Sampedro, Ramon. *Ambrosio de Morales. Apuntes biográficos.* Córdoba, 1879.

Codera, Francisco. "Manuscrito de Aben Hayán en la biblioteca de los herederos de Çidi Hammouda en Constantine," BRAH, 13 (1888), 53-61.

Coll, José Maria. "Escuelas de lenguas orientales en los siglos XIII y XIV (Periodo Raymundiano)," *Analecta sacra Tarraconensia,* XXI, i (1948), 115-138.

David, Pierre. *Etudes historiques sur la Galice et le Portugal de VIe au XIIe siécle.* Lisbon and Paris, 1947.

Diaz y Diaz, M. C. *Index scriptorum latinorum medii aevi hispanorum.* Madrid, 1959.

Dormer, Diego Josef, and Andres de Uztarroz, Juan Francisco. *Progressos de la historia en el reyno de Aragon.* Zaragoza, 1680.

Dozy, R. P. A. *Histoire des musulmans d'Espagne jusqu'à la conquête de l'Andalousie par les Almoravides.* New ed. by Lévi-Provençal. 3 vols. Leyden, 1932.

———. *Spanish Islam: A History of the Moslems in Spain.* Translated by Francis Stokes. New York, 1913.

———. *Recherches sur l'histoire et la littérature de l'Espagne pendant le moyen âge.* 3d ed. 2 vols. Leyden, 1881.

Dubler, César E. "Sobre la crónica arábigo-bizantina de 741 y la influencia bizantina en la peninsula ibérica," *Al-Andalus,* 11 (1946), 283-349.

DuCange, Charles DuFresne, sieur. *Glossarium mediae et infimae latinitatis.* New ed. 10 vols. Paris, 1937-1938.

Ferrua, Antonio. "Ascarico," *Enciclopedia cattolica,* II, 82.

Fita, Fidel. "San Dúnula, prócer y mártir mozárabe del siglo X," BRAH, 55 (1909), 433-443.

Flórez, Henrique, et al. *España sagrada. Teatro geográfico-histórico de la iglesia de España.* Various eds. 57 vols. Madrid, 1747-.

Fontaine, Jacques. *Isidore de Séville et la culture classique dans l'Espagne wisigothique.* 2 vols. Paris, 1959.

Franke, Franz Richard. "Die freiwilligen Märtyrer von Cordova und das Verhältnis der Mozaraber zum Islam (nach den Schriften des Speraindeo, Eulogius und Alvar)," *Gesammelte Aufsätze zur Kulturgeschichte Spaniens,* XIII, 1-170. Münster Westfalen, 1958.

de Gaiffier, Baudouin. "La lecture des actes des martyrs dans la prière liturgique en Occident," AB, 72 (1954), 134-166.

———. "Les notices hispaniques dans le Martyrologe d'Usuard," AB, 55 (1937), 268-283.

———. "Les notices hispaniques du Martyrologe romain," AB, 58 (1940), 79-89.

———. "Un calendrier franco-hispanique de la fin du XIIe siècle," AB, 69 (1951), 282-323.

Gallardo, Bartolomé José. *Ensayo de una biblioteca española de libros raros y curiosos.* 4 vols. Madrid, 1863-1889.

da Gama Barros, Henrique. *Historia da administração publica em Portugal nos seculos XII a XV*. 2d ed. by Torquato de Sousa Soares. 11 vols. Lisbon, 1945-1954.

Gams, Pius Bonifacius. *Die Kirchengeschichte von Spanien*. 3 vols. in 5. Regensburg, 1862-1879.

García Gallo, Alfonso. *Curso de historia del derecho español*. Vol. I: *Introducción e historia de las bases de formación del derecho, de las fuentes y del derecho publico*. 5th ed. Madrid, 1950.

García Gómez, Emilio. "A proposito de Ibn Hayyan," *Al-Andalus*, 11 (1946), 395-423.

García-Villada, Zacarías. *Crónica de Alfonso III*. Madrid, 1918.

————. *Bibliotheca patrum latinorum Hispaniensis*. Vol. II. Vienna, 1915. (Published in *Sitzungsberichte der philosophisch-historischen Klasse der kaiserlichen Akademie der Wissenschaften*. Vol. 169. Vienna, 1913.)

————. "El códice de Roda recuperado," *Revista de filología española*, 15 (1928), 113-130.

————. *Historia eclesiástica de España*. 3 vols. in 5. Madrid 1929-1936.

————. "Notas sobre la 'Crónica de Alfonso III,'" *Revista de filología española*, 8 (1921), 252-270.

————. *Organización y fisionomía de la iglesia española desde la caida del imperio visigótico en 711 hasta la toma de Toledo en 1085*. Madrid, 1935.

Garibay y Zamolla, Esteban de. *Los XL libros del compendio historial de las chronicas y universal historia de todos los reynos de España*. 3 vols. Antwerp, 1571.

Godefroy, L. "Mensonge," DTC, X, i, 555-569.

Gómez Bravo, Juan. *Catálogo de los obispos de Córdova. Primera parte en que se trata de los obispos desde el principio de la iglesia christiana hasta el año de 1236 en que fué conquistada Córdova de los Sarracenos por San Fernando*. Córdoba, 1739.

Gómez-Moreno, Manuel. "Las primeras crónicas de la Reconquista: el ciclo de Alfonso III," BRAH, 100 (1932), 562-628.

————. Book Review of García-Villada's *Crónica de Alfonso III*, BRAH, 73 (1918), 54-58.

González Dávila, Gil. *Historia de las antigüedades de la ciudad de Salamanca: vidas de sus obispos y cosas sucedidas en su tiempo*. Salamanca, 1606.

Goussen, Heinrich. *Die christlich-arabische Literatur der Mozaraber*. Vol. IV of *Beiträge zur christlich-arabischen Literaturgeschichte*. Leipzig, 1909.

Grillmeier, Alois. "Adoptionismus," LTK, I, 153-155.

Guasch, Luigi. "Mozarabica liturgia," *Enciclopedia cattolica*, VIII, 1496-1503.

Guillaume, Alfred. "Philosophy and Theology," *The Legacy of Islam*, 239-283. Oxford, 1931.

Hedde, R. "Martyre," DTC, X, i, 220-254.

Hefele, Joseph. *Histoire de conciles d'après les documents originaux.* Trans. H. Leclercq. 8 vols. in 16. Paris, 1907-1921.

Ibañez de Segovia, Gaspar. *Examen chronológico del año en que entraron los moros en España.* Madrid, 1687.

———. *Obras chronológicas.* Valencia, 1744.

Jenner, Henry. "Mozarabic Rite," *Catholic Encyclopedia*, X, 611-623.

Juynboll, T. W. "Kadi," EI, II, 606-607.

Kirsch, J. P. "Martyrer," LTK, VI, 995-998.

Kubitschek, W. "Aera," Pauly-Wissowa, I, i, 606-666.

Lambert, Aimé. "Ascaric," DHGE, IV, 881-884.

———. "Assamah ben Malik," DHGE, IV, 1081-1083.

———. "Astorga," DHGE, IV, 1199-1226.

———. "Athanaild," DHGE, IV, 1304-1305.

———. "Aurariola," DHGE, V, 694.

———. "Balech ben Baxir el Coxairi," DHGE, VI, 379.

———. "Basiliscus," DHGE, VI, 1240.

Lambert, Elie. "Le voyage de Saint Euloge dans les Pyrénées en 848," *Estudios dedicados a Menéndez Pidal*, IV, 557-567. Madrid, 1953.

Lambot, Cyrille. "L'homelie du pseudo-Jérome sur l'assomption et l'évangile de la nativité de Marie d'après une lettre inédite d'Hincmar," *Revue bénédictine*, 46 (1934), 265-282.

Leclercq, Henri. "Acrostiche," DACL, I, i, 356-372.

———. "Confessor," DACL, III, ii, 2508-2515.

———. *Les martyrs; recueil de pièces authentiques sur les martyrs depuis les origines du christianisme jusqu'au XXe siècle.* 15 vols. Paris, 1902-1924.

———. *L'Espagne chrétienne.* Paris, 1906.

———. "Martyre," DACL, X, ii, 2359-2512.

———. "Messe," DACL, XI, i, 513-774.

———. "Romani, Romania, Romanus," DACL, XIV, ii, 2507-2514.

Leclercq, Jean. "Textes et manuscrits de quelques bibliothèques d'Espagne," *Hispania sacra*, 2 (1949), 91-118.

———. "Un tratado sobre los nombres divinos en un manuscrito de Córdoba," *Hispania sacra*, 2 (1949), 327-338.

León Tello, Pilar. "Inventario de códices y fondos documentales fotocopiados," Servicio Nacional de Microfilm. Boletín num. 2 (año 1954). Madrid, 1954.

Lévi-Provençal, Evariste. "Abd al-Rahman I, II, III," EI, I, 81-84.

———. "Aljamía," EI, I, 404-405.

———. *L'Espagne musulmane au Xème siècle. Institutions et vie sociale.* Paris, 1932.

————. *Histoire de l'Espagne musulmane.* 3 vols. Paris and Leyden, 1950-1952.

————. "Mozarabs," EI, III, 611-612.

————."Umaiyads," EI, IV, 1004-1012.

————. "Un échange d'ambassades entre Cordoue et Byzance au IXe siècle," *Byzantion,* 12 (1937), 1-24.

Lichtenstädter, Ilse. "Musta'rib(a)," EI, III, 771.

Loewe, Gustav, and Hartel, Wilhelm von. *Bibliotheca patrum latinorum Hispaniensis.* Vol. I. Vienna, 1887. (Published in *Sitzungsberichte der philosophisch-historischen Klasse der kaiserlichen Akademie der Wissenschaften.* Vols. 111-113. Vienna, 1885-1886.)

Lopez de Baena, Joseph. *Vida y glorioso martyrio del esclarecido doctor y martyr San Eulogio electo arzobispo de Toledo y natural de la ciudad de Córdoba.* Córdoba, 1748.

Madoz, José. *Epistolario de Alvaro de Córdoba.* Madrid, 1947.

————. "La literatura en la epoca mozárabe," *Historia general de las literaturas hispanicas,* I, 259-274. Ed. G. Diaz-Plaja. 5 vols. Barcelona, 1949-1958.

Manitius, Max. *Geschichte der lateinischen Literatur des Mittelalters.* 3 vols. Munich, 1911-1931.

Mariana, Juan de. *Historiae de rebus Hispaniae libri XXV.* Toledo, 1592-1595.

Marineus Siculus, Lucius. *Opus de rebus Hispaniae memorabilibus....* Alcalá, 1533.

Masdeu, Juan Francisco de. *Historia crítica de España y de la cultura española.* 20 vols. Madrid, 1783-1805.

Massignon, Louis. *Akhbar al-Hallaj. Recueil d'oraisons et d'exhortations du martyr mystique de l'Islam, Husayn ibn Mansur Hallaj....* 3d ed. Paris, 1957.

————. *Essai sur les origines du lexique technique de la mystique musulmane.* Paris, 1954.

————. *La passion d'al-Hasayn-ibn-Mansour al-Hallaj, martyr mystique de l'Islam exécuté à Bagdad le 26 mars 922.* 2 vols. Paris, 1922.

————. "Tasawwuf," EI, IV, 681-685.

Medina, Pedro de. *Libro de grandezas y cosas memorables de España.* Seville, 1549.

Menéndez Pelayo, Marcellino. *Historia de los heterodoxos españoles.* 8 vols. Vols. 35-42 of *Edición nacional.* Santander, 1946-1948.

Menéndez Pidal, Ramón. *Historia de España.* 6 vols. Madrid, 1947-1956.

————. *Orígines del español, estado lingüístico de la península ibérica hasta el siglo XI.* Vol. III of *Obras completas.* 3d ed. Madrid, 1950.

Meyer, Wilhelm. *Gesammelte Abhandlungen zur mittellateinischen Rythmik.* 2 vols. Berlin, 1905.

Millares Carlo, Agustin. *Los códices visigóticos de la catedral toledana.* Madrid, 1935.

Mommsen, Theodore. "Additamenta IV, V," "Additamentum VI," MGH, *Auct. antiq.*, XI. *Chronica minora*, II, 323-333 and 370-375.

———. "Aera," NA, 18 (1893), 271-273.

Morales, Ambrosio de. *La corónica general de España que continuava Ambrosio de Morales, natural de Cordova, coronista del Rey Catholico nuestro señor Don Philipe segundo deste nombre, y cathedratico de Rhetorica en la Universidad de Alcalá de Henares....* 3 vols. Alcalá and Córdoba, 1574-1586.

———. *Divi Eulogii Cordubensis martyris doctoris et electi archiepiscopi Toletani opera. Studio et diligentia illustrissimi ac reverendissimi domini Petri Poncii Leonis a Corduba episcopi Placentini summique fidei christianae per regna et ditiones Philippi II. regis catholici inquisitoris reperta. Eiusdem sanctissimi martyris vita per Alvarum Cordubensem scripta. Cum aliis nonnullis sanctorum martyrum Cordubensium monumentis. Omnia Ambrosii Morales Cordubensis regii historicii scholiis illustrata eiusque cura et diligentia excussa. Operum catalogus sequitur post praefationes.* Alcalá, 1574.

———. *Opusculos castellanos de Ambrosio de Morales, cuyos originales se conservan inéditos en la real biblioteca del monasterio del Escorial, ahora por la primera vez impresos, ordenados, y anotados con varias noticias históricas.* Ed. Francisco Cifuentes. Madrid, 1793.

———. *Noticias históricas sacadas del archivo de Uclés de sus sepulcros y calendar y del testamento del Infante Don Enrique, con un crónicon hasta ahora no publicado.* Ed. Francisco Cifuentes. Madrid, 1793.

———. *Ambrosii Morales opuscula historica quorum exemplaria in R. D. Laurentii Bibliotheca vulgo del Escorial custodiuntur: nunc primum in lucem edita atque exacta diversorum codicum recensione recognita et adjectis quibusdam notulis illustrata.* Ed. Francisco Cifuentes. Madrid, 1793.

———. *Viaje de Ambrosio de Morales por orden del Rey D. Philipe II. a los reynos de León, y Galicia, y principado de Asturias. Para reconocer las reliquias de santos, sepulcros reales, y libros manuscritos de las cathedrales y monasterios.* Ed. Henrique Flórez. Madrid, 1765.

———. *Las obras del maestro Fernán Pérez de Oliva... con otras cosas que van añadidas....* Córdoba, 1586.

Morin, Germain. "Un évêque de Cordoue inconnu et deux opuscules inédits de l'an 764," *Revue bénédictine*, 15 (1898), 289-295.

Mullins, Sister Patrick Jerome. *The Spiritual Life according to Saint Isidore of Seville.* Washington, 1940.

Muñoz y Romero, Tomás. *Colección de fueros municipales y cartas pueblas de los reinos de Castilla, León, Corona de Aragon y Navarra.* Madrid, 1847.

Navascués, Joaquín Maria de. *La Era "...AS."* Madrid, 1951.

Neuss, Wilhelm. *Die Apokalypse des hl. Johannes in der altspanischen und altchristlichen Bible-Illustration (Das Problem der Beatus-Handschriften).* 2 vols. Münster Westfalen, 1931.

Nicholson, R. A. "Mysticism," *The Legacy of Islam,* 210-238. Oxford, 1931.

Norberg, Dag. *Syntaktische Forschungen auf dem Gebiete des Spätlateins und des frühen Mittellateins.* Leipzig, 1943.

Nyberg, H. S. "al-Mu'tazila," EI, III, 787-793.

Ocampo, Florián de. *Los cinco libros primeros de la crónica general de España.* Medina del Campo. 1545.

Orlandis, José. "Los monasterios familiares en España durante la alta edad media," AHDE, 26 (1956), 5-46.

Ortiz de la Vega, Manuel. *Las glorias nacionales, grande historia universal de todos los reinos, provincias, islas, y colonias de la monarquia española....* 6 vols. Madrid and Barcelona, 1852.

Paez de Castro, Juan. "De las cosas necessarias para escribir historia," *La ciudad de Dios,* 28-29 (1892), 601-610 and 27-37.

Pérez, F. "Cordoue," DHGE, XIII, 837-871.

Pérez, de Urbel, Justo. *Los monjes españoles en la edad media.* 2 vols. Madrid, 1933-1934.

———. *San Eulogio de Córdoba.* Madrid, 1928. 2d ed. Madrid, 1942.

———. *A Saint under Moslem Rule.* Adapted and translated by a Benedictine of Stanbrook Abbey. Milwaukee, 1937.

———. and Vázquez de Parga, Luis. "Un nuevo penitencial español," AHDE, 14 (1942-1943), 5-32.

Polheim, Karl. *Die lateinische Reimprosa.* Berlin, 1925.

Quilliet, H. "Adoptionisme au VIIIe siècle," DTC, I, i, 403-413.

Ramírez de Arellano, Rafael. *Ensayo de un catálogo biográfico de escritores de la provincia y diocesis de Córdoba con descripción de sus obras.* 2 vols. Madrid, 1922-1923.

Redel, Enrique. *Ambrosio de Morales. Estudio biográfico.* Córdoba, 1909.

Rivera, Juan Francisco. *Elipando de Toledo. Nueva aportación a los estudios mozárabes.* Toledo, 1940.

———. "La controversia adopcionista del siglo VIII y la ortodoxia de la liturgia mozárabe," *Ephemerides liturgicae,* 47 (1933), 506-536.

———. "San Ildefonso de Toledo, autor de un sermón de filiación dudosa," *Revista española de teología,* 6 (1946), 573-588.

Roa, Martin de. *De Cordubae in Hispania Baetica principatu, et de auctoritate et antiquitate sanctorum martyrum Cordubensium, ac de Cordubensi Breviario.* (Translation: *Antiguo principado de Cordova en España ulterior, o Andaluz.* Córdoba, 1636.)
————. *Flos sanctorum. Fiestas i santos naturales de la ciudad de Cordova. Algunos de Sevilla, Toledo, Granada, Xerez, Ecija, Guadix, i otras ciudades i lugares de Andaluzia, Castilla, i Portugal.*... Seville, 1615.

Rosseeuw St.-Hilaire, E. *Histoire d'Espagne depuis les premiers temps historiques jusqu'à la mort de Ferdinand VII.* 14 vols. Paris, 1844-1879.

Ruiz, Agustin S. *Obras completas de San Eulogio. Edición bilingüe.* Córdoba, 1959.

Sage, Carleton M. *Paul Albar of Córdoba: Studies on His Life and Writings.* Washington, 1943.

Sánchez Alonso, Benito. *Fuentes de la historia española e hispano-americana.* 3d ed. 3 vols. Madrid, 1952.
————. *Historia de la historiografía española.* 2d ed. 2 vols. Madrid, 1944-1947.
————. "Mayerne Turquet y los historiadores españoles del siglo XVI," *Estudios dedicados a Menéndez Pidal,* I, 589-599. Madrid, 1950.

Sánchez de Feria y Morales, Bartolomé. *Palestra sagrada, o Memorial de santos de Córdoba, con notas y reflexiones críticas sobre los principales sucesos de sus historias.* 4 vols. Córdoba, 1772.

Schmitz, M. [A. Huici-Miranda]. "Baldj b. Bishr," EI, I, 990-991.

Séjourné, Paul. *Le dernier père de l'église. Saint Isidore de Séville.* Paris, 1929.

Serrano, Luciano. "*De habitu clericorum,* obra inédita del presbítero cordobés Leovigildo (siglo IX), publicada según un manuscrito visigoda, único que se conserva," BRAH, 54 (1909), 496-517.

Simonet, Francisco Javier. *Historia de los mozárabes de España, deducida de los mejores y más auténticos testimonios de los escritores cristianos y árabes.* Vol. XIII of *Memorias de la Real Academia de la Historia.* Madrid, 1903.

Stickler, A. M. "Hispana collectio," LTK, V, 390.

Tarapha, Franciscus. *De origine ac rebus gestis regum Hispaniae liber.* Antwerp, 1553.

Tailhan, Jules. *Anonyme de Cordoue. Chronique rimée des derniers rois de Tolède et de la conquête de l'Espagne par les arabes.* Paris, 1885.
————. "La ruine de l'Espagne gothique," *Revue des questions historiques,* 31 (1882), 341-408.
————. "Les espagnols et les wisigoths avant l'invasion arabe," *Revue des questions historiques,* 30 (1881), 5-46.

Traube, Ludwig. "Pauli Albari carmina," MGH, *Poetae latini aevi carolini*, III, i, 122-126.

Turquet de Mayerne, Louis. *Histoire générale d'Espagne.* 2d ed. Paris, 1608. (English translation by Edward Grimeson. London, 1612.)

Vaseus, Joannes. *Rerum Hispanicarum chronicon.* Salamanca, 1552. (In *Hisp. ill.* I, 572-727.)

Vega, Angel C. "El 'Liber de haeresibus' de San Isidro de Sevilla y el 'Códice Ovetense,'" *La ciudad de Dios*, 171 (1958), 239-270.

Vila, Salvador. "El nombramiento de los walies de al-Andalus," *Al-Andalus*, 4 (1936), 215-220.

Villanueva, Jaime. *Viaje literario a las iglesias de España.* 22 vols. Madrid, 1803-1852.

Vincent, A. "Soufisme," DTC, XIV, ii, 2444-2459.

Vives, José. *Inscripciones cristianas de la España romana y visigoda.* Barcelona, 1942.

――. "Über Ursprung und Verbreitung der spanischen Ära," *Historisches Jahrbuch*, 58 (1938), 97-108.

Zeumer, Karl. "Über zwei neuentdeckte westgothische Gesetze," NA, 23 (1897), 75-112.

Ziegler, Aloysius K. *Church and State in Visigothic Spain.* Washington, 1930.

Other works may be traced through the index or bibliographical footnotes. A number of secondary works are discussed in the Introduction.

INDEX